Mastering Active Server Pages 3

Mastering Active Server Pages 3

Mastering™ Active Server Pages 3

A. Russell Jones

BPB PUBLICATIONS

B-14, CONNAUGHT PLACE, NEW DELHI-110001

FIRST INDIAN EDITION 2000

Distributors:

MICRO BOOK CENTRE
2, City Centre, CG Road,
Near Swastic Char Rasta,
AHMEDABAD-380009 Phone: 6421611

COMPUTER BOOK CENTRE
12, Shrungar Shopping Centre, M.G. Road,
BANGALORE-560001 Phone: 5587923, 558464

MICRO BOOKS
Shanti Niketan Building, 8, Camac Street,
CALCUTTA-700017 Phone: 2826518, 2826519

BUSINESS PROMOTION BUREAU
8/1, Ritchie Street, Mount Road,
CHENNAI-600002 Phone: 834796, 8550491

DECCAN AGENCIES
4-3-329, Bank Street,
HYDERABAD-400001 Phone: 4756400, 4756967

MICRO MEDIA
Shop No. 5, Mahendra Chambers, 150 D.N.
Road,
Next to Capital Cinema V.T. (C.S.T.) Station,
MUMBAI-400001 Ph.: 2078296, 2078297, 2002732

BPB PUBLICATIONS
B-14, Connaught Place, **NEW DELHI-110001**
Phone: 3325760, 3723393, 3737742

INFO TECH
G-2, Sidhartha Building, 96 Nehru Place,
NEW DELHI-110019
Phone: 6438245, 6415092, 6234208

INFO TECH
Shop No. 2, F-38, South Extension Part-1
NEW DELHI-110049
Phone: 4691288, 4641941

INFO TECH
B-11, Vardhman Plaza, Sector-16,
Electronics Nagar, **NOIDA-201301**
Phone: 914-512329, 515917, 515918

BPB BOOK CENTRE
376, Old Lajpat Rai Market,
DELHI-110006 PHONE: 2961747

Original ISBN 0-7821-2619-7

Printed in India by arrangement with
SYBEX Inc., USA.

ISBN 81-7656-259-9

Published by Manish Jain for BPB Publications, B-14, Connaught Place
New Delhi-110 001 and Printed by him at Pressworks, Delhi.

*I dedicate this book to my wife, Janet,
for her patience and support during my near
absence over the past year, and to my children:
Meredith (7) for her valentines and notes,
and Barry (4) for his unselfish gift of a toy
motorcycle. In innumerable ways, all three
helped to make this book a reality.*

ACKNOWLEDGMENTS

I would like to thank Microsoft and the ASP team for creating a product as flexible and useful as ASP. Thanks to Chuck Campbell at WebSoft Publishing for introducing me to Web development many years ago. Thanks to Bob Yeager and Margo Pearson at InterCom for their encouragement, and to Robin Mitts at Shell for her patience. Thanks to Jeff Hadfield for his hard work on the foreword. Thanks to the editorial team at Sybex, in particular, Denise Santoro Lincoln, Colleen Strand, Galen Miller, and Greg Guntle. Once again their guidance, humor, and expertise have greatly improved the product, the process, and the author.

Finally, I would like to thank you for buying this book. I hope you find it useful, that you learn a lot, and that you have as much fun reading it as I had writing it.

A. Russell Jones

FOREWORD

Before you can master ASP, you've got to resign yourself to some cold facts. Active Server Pages are more than the recipients of an unfortunately confusing acronym —a new crop of businesses called ASPs (Application Service Providers) provide offsite resources for Web hosting, enterprise application hosting, and more (What's worse, ASPs often allow you to run ASP.)—ASP is an underlying technology instead of a product.

Because ASP is a Microsoft technology, it's automatically maligned as well. And it's difficult for Microsoft to defend itself; since ASP is a technology, not a specific product, you'll never see Microsoft running ads telling you ASP is cool. You might hear fine things about FrontPage, InterDev, or Visual Basic WebClasses. You might even hear about ASP integration in the next version of Visual Studio. But Microsoft doesn't have a history of telling a solid, technology-focused story (XML being the only notable exception).

The good news, for you, is the author of this book. Russell Jones is a contributor to *Visual Basic Programmer's Journal* valued by our readers because he can make mildly confusing or brutally complex concepts as straightforward as, say, a scene in *Gone With the Wind* (to choose an example from Chapter 1). He's a seasoned programmer who knows how to *solve* business problems with technology—not just discuss them academically. He's flat-out fun to read. And he's easily impressed by prolific flattery.

There's more good news for you: ASP's a technology with more than just a past and present (like, say, something in maintenance mode like FoxPro). It's got a future as well. At this writing, Microsoft has just recently divulged bits of its next generation of development tools, and key features depend on ASP. These key features provide the foundation for Microsoft's plans to be as significant in the Web space as it has been on the desktop.

What are the features? In general terms, Microsoft will be making Visual Studio's tools as viable on the server as they have been on the desktop. Of course, you can program IIS now—using ASP—and that's what Dr. Jones will tell you about in this book. But the concepts, objects, and actions you'll learn here will serve you well as development moves clearly to the server.

Microsoft is still not scoring major points in the public relations battle, although tons of sites are run on Windows and specifically on Windows servers. But if you know Windows and you know ASP (again, this book), you're going to be well-positioned to take advantage of Microsoft's all-out effort to reclaim their rightful place in the Web server universe.

Look, here's the bottom line: Read this book. Learn its concepts. Try them today. Well-implemented ASP will give your sites flexibility and power. And Dr. Jones will teach you what you need for the future of your Web development, your business, and the Web.

Jeff Hadfield

Publisher, *Visual Basic Programmer's Journal*
and *Visual C++ Developers Journal*

www.vbpj.com and www.vcdj.com

CONTENTS AT A GLANCE

TABLE OF CONTENTS

PART V   ACCESSING DATABASES WITH ASP AND ADO

INTRODUCTION

This book is a guide written specifically for people who want to learn how to use ASP to build dynamic, interactive Web sites and applications. Microsoft's Active Server Pages (ASP) technology has revolutionized Web-building because it blends several very different types of code into a seamless whole. ASP itself is not a language, it's more of a melting pot. Take a healthy helping of HTML; sprinkle liberally with built-in Web capabilities; add a dash of scripting technology; season with tried-and-true ActiveX components or Java applets; and you have an ASP-based Web site.

What Should You Know Already?

You have to know how to read. Seriously, you need to have a project in mind. Sure, I'll provide plenty of examples and small projects for you to work on, but I've found that to really learn a computer language, or in the case of ASP, several languages, it helps to have a project that *you* want to work on. Alternately, a mean boss and a tight deadline often work wonders. Actually, I'm not sure what you need to know, but I am sure of the things you do not have to know:

- You don't have to be an HTML guru—in fact, you don't have to know HTML at all (although that would help).

- You don't have to know Visual Basic, VBA, VBScript, Java, JavaScript, Perl or any other programming language (although any of these would help).

- You don't have to know anything about Web servers or databases (although such knowledge may prove useful).

- Finally, you don't need to know anything about ASP—you'll learn more than you probably wanted to know by the end of this book.

What kind of project should you choose? Try not to select something that's critical for your job—you don't need the pressure when you're trying to learn a new language. Instead, find a Web application that you admire and try to duplicate it. Use the clean-room approach, where you don't copy the site and extend it; you re-create it as if it were your own idea. Alternatively, if you already have a Web application in mind, you're well on your way to becoming an ASP programmer.

What Have I Assumed about You?

If you buy this book and read it, we're likely to spend a substantial amount of time together. Therefore, you might want to know up front who I think you are. Every author writes to an imaginary audience; and mine has some specific characteristics. If any of these are not true, you may want to reconsider buying this book. I have assumed that:

- You want to learn how to build dynamic Web sites or applications with ASP or you want to improve your current abilities to do so.

- You enjoy experimenting with and understanding technology, not just copying code from a CD.

- You want to know what the possibilities of ASP are, not just the built-in capabilities.

- You are willing to spend a significant amount of time learning the technology.

I don't expect you to read every word in this book (all at once). I do expect you to progress through the book in the order in which chapters appear. I expect you to begin later chapters having already mastered the material in the preceding chapters. This book is not a reference book and I won't promise that any individual chapter will stand alone. This book will not be as useful to those who skip around as to those who read it sequentially.

What's in This Book?

This book contains a comprehensive discussion of ASP technology and a cursory glance at several related technologies. You'll get an introduction to HTML and Cascading Style Sheets (CSS)—but this book is not an HTML or CSS primer or reference. You'll get an in-depth explanation of the ASP object model, along with discussions of the best ways to use the ASP objects and ASP itself. You'll see an intensive discussion of Microsoft's VBScript scripting language, and a less intensive, but still useful introduction to JScript, Microsoft's JavaScript variant. You'll see how to use scripting languages to read and write data from/to files and databases, how to set up Web sites, and how to extend ASP using Common Object Model (COM) objects.

Why Am I Writing This Book?

Usually, books only publish short dry tidbits about an author's professional qualifications. I've decided to include a little more to give you a better idea about who I am and why I'm writing this book.

My Background

My background is in music, computer-based training (CBT), interactive video training (IVT), and most recently, web-based training (WBT), database applications, and general-purpose human resources (HR) Web-based applications. I've been involved with computers since 1979, when I was an undergraduate piano student at the University of Tennessee, and I discovered Dr. Donald Pederson's music theory computer lab full of brand-new Apple II microcomputers with 8K of main memory. Back then small was not only beautiful—it was imperative! My first program of substance taught people how to recognize and write chords—one facet of a class that fellow musicians call ear-training.

That work sparked a fascination with computers that continues to this day. After completing a master's degree in music theory, I attended the University of Illinois to work on a doctorate in secondary education. The university was the site of the first important computer teaching system, called PLATO. As a research assistant, I worked with Dr. Esther Steinberg, author of *Teaching Computers to Teach*, investigating the relative importance of various interface features for beginning vs. expert computer users.

My Work

I began working for InterCom Training, Inc. shortly before completing my Ph.D (my employers were kind enough to give me a leave of absence to complete it in 1990). At InterCom I worked as a programmer, instructional designer, and project and team leader for over 11 years. I've been working with ASP technology since version 1.0. I began creating interactive Web sites with Visual Basic in 1995. When Microsoft announced ASP in late 1996, I saw the technology as a quantum leap in productivity over other Web technologies available at that time. The Web was obviously going to change the way businesses thought about data and applications. Although many businesses already had—or were in the process of acquiring—a Web presence, the idea of *interactive* Web sites was just beginning to reach the corporate consciousness.

Since then I've created several dozen Web applications of varying sizes, from small, slightly interactive Web sites to corporate database search engines, data-intensive mainframe simulations, and globally available HR applications.

I recently joined VF Services, an apparel company that numbers Lee Jeans, Healthtex, Wrangler, and Russell Athletic among its many brands, where I'm working on large-scale imaging databases, systems design, and technical education.

My Writing Experience

For the past year, I've written the Interactive Developer column in the *Visual Basic Programmer's Journal* every other month. Articles don't really prepare one for writing a book other than providing some organizational skills and linguistic practice. In fact, the two aren't much alike at all. Despite their comparatively Lilliputian dimensions, articles are probably more difficult than books. Articles force you to be concise—which is anathema to technical book authors, whose primary task is to be complete.

Fortunately for you, this is my second book. I recently finished a book for Sybex called the *Visual Basic Programmer's Guide to ASP and IIS Applications*. Despite the title, that book has very little directly to do with ASP—it's primarily a guide to writing Web applications with Visual Basic (VB) WebClass technology. I learned a great deal from writing it, and you get the benefit of that experience in this book.

My Teaching Experience

I have had the good fortune to be a teacher several times and in several different areas. I've taught piano, music theory, ear-training, computer programming, and reading. I've also taught (or helped teach) how to handle venomous snakes, how to use mainframes, how to run oil refinery equipment, how to build transformers, and how to plan your career. But I don't always enjoy teaching as much as I enjoy learning. Therefore, I try to keep this in mind whenever I'm teaching—it's not just the information that's important. In fact, the information usually must become automatic before it's truly useful. It's what you can do with the information that's important. For me, the best part of learning is that sudden realization that you've just expanded your ability to connect patterns of knowledge.

The best part of any artistic endeavor is what my wife Janet and I call being in "the zone," that state of being in which you perform a creative process while metaphorically looking over your own shoulder. You can reach the zone while teaching because teaching is an art. You can reach it while learning, when a process suddenly becomes automatic or an idea becomes clear; and you can most certainly reach it by programming, because programming is as artistic as painting or music. I've reached it in this book, several times. I hope you will too.

What Will You Learn?

By the end of the book, you will have had a thorough grounding in ASP technology, and you should be ready to tackle any project from simple Web sites to complete Web applications. To be proficient in ASP, you need to learn more than a little VBScript. ASP, by itself, is merely a method for making decisions: what HTML to return, what object to launch, which browser is the client running, and so forth; therefore, a great deal of this book discusses technologies necessary, but peripheral, to ASP.

You'll learn how the Internet works and how it should influence the way you think about your Web sites and applications. You'll learn the basics of HTML. You will, of course, learn ASP scripting—primarily VBScript, ASP's default scripting language, but also a little about JScript. You'll learn how to use ASP to work with files, databases, and external COM objects. You'll also learn a little about how to extend ASP's capabilities by creating your own COM objects with Visual Basic. Finally, you'll begin to explore a technology that's changing the way Web applications work—XML.

You'll practice a lot. As a former professional musician I believe fervently in the power of practice. I realize that not everyone wants to write out code, but I can also tell you that writing code is the best way to learn it. For those who refuse such practice, I have (reluctantly) provided a CD to accompany this book. You will find all of the named listings and the completed projects on the CD. I hope you find the code on the CD helpful *after* you finish the book—or at least, after you complete each individual chapter.

Practically every chapter contains code—usually quite a lot of code. I hope you type most of it. I happen to believe that there's a direct correspondence between the amount of code you physically type and your facility with the art of programming. You cannot become an expert programmer unless you type a great deal of code. I doubt seriously that you can become an expert designer either unless you type a great deal of code.

Most programming books fall into one of three categories: those that contain no large projects and are primarily reference works; those that contain one or two large projects that you extend as you work your way through the book; and those which use small projects to illustrate specific language features. (For all of you programming book aficionados in the audience, there's a fourth type—those which metaphorically peer over the authors' shoulders as they illuminate the dark inner workings of some arcane programming mystery.)

This book is the small project type. I've read a great many programming books and I've never once found a large-project type where the project interested me enough to bother actually building it. Many of the chapters contain small projects.

From these, you should be able to extrapolate the applications that *you* want to build. In some cases, you'll be able to modify the code directly for your own applications; in others, you should be able to build on the ideas these projects contain. I've tried to write them so you don't always have to run the projects to learn their major features. I hope you find them useful.

What Do You Need?

You'll need several programs to work your way through the projects in this book. You probably already have most of them.

You Need a Web Server   You'll need to have either Internet Information Server (IIS) or Personal Web Server (PWS) with the ASP extensions installed. For much of the first part of this book, you could also use a Unix server running Chili!Soft ASP. (A trial version of Chili!Soft ASP is included on the CD-ROM.)

You Need a Browser   I personally recommend Internet Explorer (IE) 5—the examples in this book were developed using IE 5—but any browser, including Netscape browsers will serve. ASP is a server-side technology that can provide content to any browser client. Note that some of the examples in this book will not run with Netscape browsers because they don't support nearly as much of the World Wide Web Consortium's (W3C) Document Object Model (DOM) specification as IE. Some of the examples won't run with versions of IE earlier than version 4.*x*. If you're using a version 3.*x* browser or earlier, you should upgrade to get the most out of this book.

You Need an Editor   I recommend the editor that comes with Microsoft InterDev because it color-codes HTML and script, but others are, if not equally capable, certainly perfectly adequate. You can write any pure ASP example or project in this book with nothing but Windows NotePad—which should immediately tell you something about ASP—it isn't dependent on any specific development environment. You can do everything you need with any text editor.

You Need Visual Basic   For Chapter 26, *Build Your Own Components*, you'll need Microsoft Visual Basic (VB) 5 with service pack 2 (sp2) or VB 6 to actually build the components. If you don't have VB or don't plan to build the VB examples, don't worry, I'll provide pre-compiled components and you can run them on your own server.

What's on the CD?

The CD contains all of the code examples from the book, plus compiled components, databases, and SQL code. While pre-written code can get you running quickly, it's not the best way to learn to write ASP code; the best way is to write it yourself. Sure, it's tedious to copy code, but the physical act of writing code teaches you a great deal more than passively copying it does. Enough lecturing.

The code consists of a single site called MasteringASP. To use the code, you'll need to set up a virtual directory on your server called MasteringASP. First, copy the MasteringASP directory and all subdirectories to your server, then follow the directions in Chapter 2, *Introduction to IIS* to set up the site. The code for each chapter is in a separate subdirectory named Chapter1, Chapter2, etc. For some of the chapters, you'll need to set additional permissions for your Web server's account so you can create and write to files. Whenever you need additional permissions, they're explicitly stated in the book.

In addition to IIS administration, you should obtain sufficient permissions to be able to administer Microsoft Transaction Server (MTS), renamed to COM+ in Windows 2000. You'll need those additional permissions to create and install Common Object Model (COM) components in the later chapters.

The CD also contains Chili!Soft ASP Developer Edition, a cross-platform version of ASP that runs on NT and now Linux systems. For more details on Chili!Soft ASP, see the white paper from Chili!Soft included on the CD.

PART I

Basic Active Server Pages

PART I

Basic Active Server Pages

CHAPTER

ONE

Behind the Scenes— How Active Server Pages Work

Active Server Pages (ASP) technology is actually a very simple idea. Wouldn't Web sites be powerful tools if you could mix HTML and code? And they are, as you will see. ASP lets you use the power of a Web server to process user requests and provide dynamic, individualized, content based on logic, file, and database data, and also process the user's individualized data. In other words, ASP lets multiple users simultaneously run a program on your Web server. Essentially you have the power of a mainframe computer, coupled with the graphics-processing ability of a local workstation, all wrapped up in a cross-platform viewer—the browser—and packaged in a world-standard communications mechanism—the Web. This book shows you how to tap into that power to deliver flexible, individualized applications.

In essence, a Web application consists of a series of short conversations between a Web server and a browser. Remember in *Gone With the Wind* when Scarlett O'Hara was surrounded by a group of young men at the Twelve Oaks barbeque, all trying to engage Scarlett in conversation. The eager young men initiated the conversation and Scarlett responded to them. The user/server relationship operates much the same way. Each user (browser) initiates requests from the server, and the server, much like Scarlett, responds quickly to each request. Each user, while engaging your Web page, feels as though they have your full attention. Your goal in a Web application is to be Scarlett. You want to capture everyone's attention and respond to each individual while showing preference to none.

ASP lets you treat users as unique entities, even though all of them are running the same program on the same machine—your Web server. Obviously, running a complex program for multiple users on one computer takes a lot of resources. Fortunately, Microsoft makes sure those resources are at your disposal. ASP provides:

- A way to save individualized data for each user

- Access to the file system

- Access to databases

- A means to launch and control any component Object Model (COM) component

In short, ASP allows you to build multiuser applications, which means you can leverage ASP to provide application scalability. If you plan your ASP applications carefully, they can scale from a single-server application that can handle 30-100 simultaneous users and a few thousand hits per day to multi-server (Web farm) applications handling thousands of simultaneous users and millions of requests per day.

ASP isn't a single technology. Using ASP effectively requires that you learn a collection of tools, languages, techniques, and technologies. These didn't spring into being suddenly; each is a topic in its own right, with an evolutionary history that began before ASP. Before we jump into ASP technology, a little history lesson.

Introduction to ASP

The best way to introduce ASP is to give a little background on the technologies that existed before ASP, why new capabilities were needed, and how ASP meets those needs.

Beyond HTML

HyperText Markup Language (HTML) is a tagged text file format used to format Web content for display—usually in a browser. HTML is a very simple language with only a few commands. That's part of the reason HTML instantly became popular. Until HTML, the only way for a non-programmer to display text and graphics easily was to use a What-You-See-Is-What-You-Get (WYSIWYG) word processor. Unfortunately, everybody had to have the same operating system, the same word processor, and sometimes even the same version of the word processor to view your documents. HTML changed all that, and changed the world as well. Today, even though HTML is considerably more complex than it was originally, a few hours of instruction still suffices to train people well enough so they can create fairly complicated pages.

You'll see much more detailed information about HTML in Chapter 4, *HTML Basics*, but as an example of how straightforward HTML is, here are a few examples:

```
<p>This is a paragraph</p>
<b>This text is bold</b>
<ol>
    <li>This is an ordered list</li>
    <li>This is an ordered list</li>
    <li>This is an ordered list</li>
    <li>This is an ordered list</li>
</ol>
```

The angle brackets (<>) separate content from layout. The text between the angle brackets is layout, or markup. Markup controls how the browser displays the content, which is all of the text not between angle brackets.

HTML's simplicity was one important factor in its rapid adoption; another equally important factor is its ability to navigate easily between files. By pointing and clicking with a mouse, a user can move between files without knowing where those files are located. Such navigation is called hypertext, a concept invented by Ted Nelson over 30 years before HTML brought hypertext navigation to the world.

Despite, or perhaps because of its simplicity, HTML rapidly became the display language of choice for the World Wide Web (WWW). Paeans were written describing how the Web would become the new panacea for delivering timely information to millions of eager readers all over the world. But that scenario wasn't quite right. Sure, people formatted millions of pages of text and graphics and placed them on the Web, but those eager readers immediately started complaining that the information wasn't specific enough for them. They wanted personalized pages that acted like their favorite Windows programs, sites that remembered their personal preferences, communications, interactivity—in short, they wanted applications, not just information.

Enter CGI

HTML needed some help. As a simple layout language, HTML is without peer, but as an application engine, it leaves a great deal to be desired. Help quickly appeared in the form of Common Gateway Interface (CGI) applications. A CGI application runs entirely on the server. When a browser contacts the server and makes a file request, the CGI application returns HTML just as if it were an HTML file. The difference is that the CGI program can process information sent by the browser and return HTML that differs in response to varying conditions. CGI programs can send one type of information to one user, and another type of information to another user, or send different files based on the type and version of browser the user is running.

Although you can write CGI programs in almost any language, most early CGI programmers used Perl, a language with powerful text-processing capabilities. Because Perl is a scripting language, many CGI programs are called CGI scripts. A scripting language is a relatively small, usually interpreted (not compiled) language. Web site designers immediately began using pre-written CGI scripts to perform simple calculations, such as counting the number of users who visited their pages. Other CGI programs backed the Web search engines, indexing content and storing the indexes in powerful databases.

These CGI programs used HTML forms to accept search requests from users, search the databases, and provide customized responses. CGI programs were the forerunners of the new, active Web. Simple, stored pages sufficed for information display, but people now used Web applications to find those pages. Web site programmers began to use CGI programs to provide dynamic content rather than static HTML.

Unfortunately, CGI programs had several shortcomings. The Web is a world of small transactions. Each transaction consists of a single request or a series of short requests by the browser. When you request a page, the Web server supplies the page, then forgets about you. For busy sites, such requests may happen at the rate of 100 requests per second or more. The first generation of CGI programs consisted of executables that had to be loaded into memory for each request. The CGI program would then process the request and terminate. All of this loading and unloading used up time and resources on the server. It obviously takes considerably more memory and Central Processing Unit (CPU) time to load a program and execute it than it does to simply return the contents of an HTML file. Web server designers began to look for a more efficient method to deliver dynamic content.

ISAPI and NSAPI

For post-CGI programming, the leading vendors of Web server software decided to provide hooks into the Web server itself. The concept they standardized on is called Internet Server Application Programming Interface (ISAPI), or on Netscape servers, Netscape Server Application Programming Interface (NSAPI). Using these hooks, programmers working in C and other general-purpose programming languages could write applications to process requests and return dynamic content like CGI programs. Unlike CGI programs, these new ISAPI programs remained loaded in memory in the server's address space. Thus ISAPI programs could perform the same tasks as CGI programs, but without the overhead of loading and terminating the program for each request.

Microsoft introduced two different kinds of ISAPI programs: filters, which intercept Web requests before the server sees them, and applications, which process Web requests. Officially, ASP is an ISAPI application. Don't confuse the term application with the applications you build with ASP. In this book, I'll refer to the ASP application as the ASP engine. The ISAPI ASP application is a single Dynamic Link Library (DLL) (asp.dll) that parses files and executes the code they contain.

Benefits of ASP

There are many benefits to ASP and they will be discussed throughout this chapter. However, the following are a couple of general reasons why ASP is the choice for so many.

ASP is Language-Independent

The ASP engine does not depend on a single language. In fact, the ASP engine doesn't actually execute the code you write. Instead, ASP is a language-independent scripting host. The ASP engine works with any scripting language that is compatible with the Microsoft Scripting Host requirements. It can even work with code written in multiple scripting languages on the same page.

The ASP engine differentiates scripting code from HTML, then asks the appropriate scripting engine(s) to execute it. Most of the code in this book is VBScript, the default ASP scripting language, but you'll also see a significant amount of JavaScript, and some PerlScript.

ASP is for Non-Programmers

One of the holy grails of computing is to find a language that ordinary people (read non-programmers) can use to perform programmer-type tasks. It's based on the idea that programmers will create reusable, general-purpose entities (the blocks) and anybody with a few hours to spare can then hook them together to create complex programs. Don't worry. Simplicity in programming is a moving target.

In the earliest days of computing, programmers used machine language, flipping switches to manipulate bits and bytes. Assembly language changed all that—assembler was the glue that let non-programmers manipulate the bits and bytes easily. As assembler grew increasingly complex, languages like Fortran and C became the glue that connected assembly-language modules. Back in the pre-Windows, Disk Operating System (DOS) days, a simple scripting language used in batch files was supposed to be the glue. You could hook simple batch files together to automate other programs and perform complex tasks. However, the original batch language grew until only programmers could use it. Just a few years ago, Visual Basic was the glue language; now Visual Basic is the language that creates the building blocks. Today the glue language is ASP—and it's true that ASP, as it exists today, is better suited for glue-like tasks than it is for mainstream processing, but that may change.

Nevertheless, you should understand that ASP is not a low-level programming language. It's not a database language either, although you can access databases from it. If you're thinking about using ASP as a front-end for your data warehouse/ data-scrubbing functions, think again. ASP is not a component-building language. If you're planning to learn ASP to create the next great word processor or spreadsheet, plan harder. ASP is not a mathematical modeling language, it's not a graphics manipulation language, and it's not a Graphical User Interface (GUI) builder.

ASP's strength lies in providing simple decision-making capability to what would otherwise be static HTML pages, and in coordinating and monitoring back-end components to return quick HTML responses to disparate clients. In other words, ASP is the glue.

But it's not yet simple glue. Although you may not need to be a programmer to build simple ASP pages, you need to become a programmer to build ASP applications. Becoming a programmer is more of a state of mind, of talent, and of practice, than a matter of education. In other words, given talent and time to practice, you can learn to be a programmer.

As with all arts, there's a healthy dose of technical craftsmanship involved with ASP applications programming, and that's what you will get from this book. Your aim should be to make the underlying code generation so automatic that you can focus on the larger problems. If you want to be successful with ASP, write lots of small programs, work on them until they're elegant, then combine them into larger, more complex programs as you become comfortable with the basics. Along the way, you'll find that ASP is not, in itself, a complete programming solution. You'll find other areas, equally as interesting as ASP, that will help you build useful and aesthetic Web applications.

Other Methods for Delivering Dynamic Content

ASP is not the only method for delivering dynamic content—it's just one of the newest. Other methods preceded ASP (and yet other methods will follow). In the mid-90's the hot Web technology was CGI programs, which let Web servers do something besides serve up static HTML pages.

What is a CGI Program?

CGI programs are small executables that the server executes in response to a request from a browser. The CGI program processes the request in code and returns HTML to the browser. The difference between a CGI program and a static Web page is that the HTML returned to the browser can be different based on who's making the request, where they are, what time it is—almost anything you can think of. Fortunately, Microsoft recognized that CGI programs aren't the most efficient way to process requests for active content. The reason they're inefficient is that the server must load the CGI program for each request.

The underlying explanation has its roots deep in HyperText Transfer Protocol (HTTP). An HTTP request is a short transaction between a client and a server. Neither the server nor the client remembers each other once the transaction is complete.

Imagine two people wandering through a party. Every time they pass each other they introduce themselves, have a short conversation, then drift apart, but never remember meeting each other. Alternately, consider the movie *Groundhog Day*, in which one day continuously repeats itself. The people in the film do the same things and say the same things each day. The only one who realizes that they're living the same day repeatedly is the leading character, played by Bill Murray. Web requests are like that, except there's no Bill Murray character to notice.

Because both the server and client treat each HTTP transaction as a brand-new entity, they must go through an elaborate series of handshakes for each request. Worse, because the server forgets the client after each transaction, it also destroys any CGI program that it invoked to process the request. The server must then reload the CGI program for the next request. Loading executable programs often takes longer than executing the program. For a Web site, loading programs is a non-productive activity; the point is to use the server as efficiently as possible.

What Is ISAPI?

To help eliminate the overhead associated with CGI applications, Microsoft introduced the Internet Server Application Programming Interface (ISAPI). It takes just as long to load an ISAPI application as a CGI program, but the server doesn't destroy ISAPI applications at the end of each request. Instead, they stay loaded, either as long as the server is running or for a pre-determined length of time. There are two types of ISAPI programs, ISAPI applications and ISAPI filters.

ISAPI Applications

ISAPI applications run *after* the Web server has seen the request. ISAPI applications let you add functionality to a Web server while still taking advantage of all the other features the server offers. The ASP engine is an ISAPI application. Internet Information Server (IIS) passes requests for ASP files to the ASP engine, which processes the request to provide dynamic content.

ISAPI Filters

ISAPI filters run *before* the Web server has seen the request. ISAPI filters let you monitor or intercept requests for special processing. For example, a program to categorize requests and allot server bandwidth based on the requesting user's IP address would be a good candidate for an ISAPI filter. The program would intercept the requests and filter them before they reached the Web server. Alternatively, a filter could function like a firewall, to block requests from non-trusted sources.

What are the Advantages of ASP over HTML?

HTML is a simple and flexible formatting and layout language, but it has no programming constructs. If you need to display static text and images, HTML is perfect. If you need to display content that changes often, or if you need to display content tailored for individuals, HTML is sadly lacking. The problem is that HTML lacks any decision-making capability.

For example, suppose you want to display the nationwide voting results based on voter interviews. You set up the infrastructure to place the results in a database. Your HTML front-end displays a map of the United States. When a client selects one or more of the states, you want to display a table showing a breakdown, by county, of the anticipated voting results for that state.

If you were creating the site weeks after the election when all the results had been tallied, HTML would serve perfectly. But to display the live data implies that the results may change hour-to-hour or minute-by-minute. Even a small army of HTML coders would have a hard time keeping up with the election results. To display live data, you need a programming language, and HTML is not a programming language.

ASP scripting provides the functionality you would need to read the database, obtain the up-to-the-minute results for that state, group them by county, and create a custom HTML response based on the fresh data.

Content that changes with each request is called *dynamic content*. Sites that provide only static content can quickly become boring. Dynamic sites dominate the Web today. Sites that provide dynamic content, especially those in which the user interacts with the content rather than simply pointing and clicking to change pages, are called Web applications.

What Is ASP's Competition?

The Web is the new paradigm for delivering applications because it is globally accessible; allows for centralized administration; immediate, single-point upgrades; and delivers an application to multiple clients on several operating systems using the same code base. Everybody's working in this new paradigm. Therefore, ASP has plenty of competition. Of course, it depends how you define competition. The various vendors are busily differentiating their products by positioning them as something more than Web development environments.

Also, ASP is a difficult product to categorize; it isn't a development environment per se (you can develop ASP pages with any text editor); and it isn't a language (you can develop ASP pages using any of several scripting languages). Similarly, you can use ASP to build simple Web sites or complex applications.

ASP's major competitors in the application arena are Application Server vendors, Sun's JavaServer Pages, Java itself, C++ ISAPI applications, and Visual Basic. Microsoft's preferred tool for building ASP sites is Visual InterDev. Its major competitors in the site-building arena are FrontPage, HomeSite, DreamWeaver, and a host of shareware and freeware site builders/HTML editors.

Application Server Vendors

ASP's high-end competitors started out as Web application development environments. Some of them have since metamorphosed into Application Server vendors. This simply means they're bundling their application development environments as enterprise-level software—usually with hardware and service contracts. Cold Fusion, Bluestone, and NetDynamics are three competitors in this category. All three provide HTML tag extensions and custom commands that let you easily access databases, format pages, and deliver customized content. All are powerful (and relatively expensive) solutions.

The main advantage of Application Servers is that they make it less difficult to build complex pages that scale easily. Their main disadvantages are that they require custom server installations, they often charge by the number of clients, and may obscure the low-level details—some even hide the code—which makes it difficult to make changes to differentiate your site from others built with the same packages.

JavaServer Pages

Sun recently introduced JavaServer Pages (JSP) which I believe will, in the long run, become ASP's principal competition. JSPs run on several different Web servers already, including Apache (Unix), NetScape, and IIS servers. ASP can also run on Unix via ChiliSoft's Chili!ASP product, but at the loss of some functionality.

Java

Sun originally touted Java as the universal client-side language for the Web, but it soon became apparent that its performance wasn't going to be sufficient for that purpose. Recently though, Java has found a new home on the server. Java is similar to C++, but has some features, such as automatic memory management, that make it a better rapid development environment. In addition, Java development environments have improved considerably in the past few years—several are now equally as full-featured as Microsoft's Visual Studio suite.

Java itself is an excellent language that, like Microsoft's Visual Basic, can be either interpreted or compiled. When compiled into native code, Java is nearly as fast as compiled C code.

A large number of C and C++ developers found it easy to move to Java because of the similarity in the syntax of the two languages. The development of Enterprise Java Beans (similar to Microsoft's COM technology) coupled with Java's ability to run on several different operating systems may make Java the language of choice for developing business connectivity Web applications.

VB IIS Applications

Microsoft itself competes with ASP technology on both the low and high end of the scale. On the high end, Visual Basic 6 added a class module called WebClasses. WebClasses build on ASP technology, but let you compile your code into ActiveX DLLs.

Theoretically, compiled code should make applications run faster. In practice, the speed of your application depends on many variables, most of which are unrelated to whether your code is compiled or interpreted. The main advantage of compiled applications is that when you sell code, the clients can't see the code; they can use the application, but can't modify it. The main disadvantage is that you must register the compiled ActiveX DLLs on the server, which means you can't modify the code as easily after deploying the application.

Others (e.g., C++)

You can write Web applications with almost any language, but many development shops select C++ because it has the best low-level access to Windows, it's extremely fast, and C++ code is even somewhat portable to other operating systems. Although C++ isn't strictly an ASP competitor, I've included it here because it's an excellent choice for commercial application development. If you're planning to use ASP to develop commercial applications, you should be aware that your competition might be using faster technology.

How ASP Compares with its Competition

ASP has several major advantages over most other Web application development languages or environments, especially for intranet development.

ASP code resides in text files   Text files are easy to modify, even after deployment. It's a tremendous advantage to be able to fix a problem remotely using a text editor. Web applications that depend on compiled code or registered ActiveX objects are much more difficult to maintain and upgrade. Beyond that, I can assure you that you'll be able to edit the code you write today with a text editor tomorrow—there are no Integrated Development Environment (IDE) version dependencies with text files. That's not the case with most other code development environments because they constantly improve, and frequently change. They're usually (but not always) backwardly compatible with their own earlier versions, but they're rarely editable with another environment's editors. With ASP files, anyone can edit the code with a text editor.

ASP code times out   IIS stops executing ASP pages after 90 seconds by default. You can (and normally should) adjust this to a shorter value. Therefore, if you accidentally write an endless loop, or allow someone to request a million records, you won't tie up the server beyond the timeout interval. Many Internet Service Providers (ISPs) who won't usually host compiled applications will host ASP applications—partly because the scripts time out.

ASP code is server-safe   ASP code runs in a limited space—for example, you can't natively read or write binary files with ASP. It's very difficult, if not impossible, to completely crash an IIS server with native ASP script. That's another reason many ISPs will host ASP applications when they refuse to host Web applications developed with other technologies.

ASP code doesn't require registration   The IIS install program installs the ASP runtime DLLs, scripting DLLs, Microsoft ActiveX Data Objects (ADO) DLLs, and the Microsoft Scripting Runtime DLL—and that's the only code you need to run ASP applications. Most other development tools require additional server-side installs and registry operations. Some require you to install special server applications. This may not seem like much trouble on a development server, but it causes problems in production, especially when you just want to correct a misspelling or make a minor change.

ASP applications are usually small   Because all the DLLs are already installed on the server, you need only deliver the code files, images, and support files to make an ASP application run—and those files are usually small and highly compressible. Note that this becomes less and less true as you add compiled ActiveX components to your application.

You can upgrade ASP applications without stopping IIS   Although it may not sound like it, this is a major advantage. It's no advantage at all when your application is the only one running on the server, but when there are dozens of applications running on the same server (typical of larger businesses), no one wants to stop or shut down the server to make changes in your application. You must usually schedule such changes, often well in advance. The problem is that no one can predict what the effect of stopping the server will have on all the applications running on that server. Put yourself in a user's position. You wouldn't want to have your application suddenly stop responding and possibly lose data just so someone else could upgrade an application.

How to Use ASP

Now that you know more about ASP's capabilities, how should you approach using it to build your applications? The way to use ASP depends on the size of your application, the number of clients you expect to have, the capacity of your server(s), whether your application is for an intranet or the Internet, and the time and resources you have available for development. The most scalable sites use ASP's scripting capabilities as a front-end to Microsoft Transaction Server (MTS) components that do all the database access and most of the business logic processing. But you don't have to use ASP that way. At the cost of some speed and a lot of scalability, ASP is perfectly capable of handling quite a few users without help from external COM objects or MTS.

I recommend that you use ASP alone for learning. As your scripting and database capabilities grow, you can begin to build and use COM objects. When your scalability requirements outgrow ASP's intrinsic capabilities, you can begin to use MTS.

Simple Text Processing

Use ASP script for simple text processing. This is ASP's strong point, as it usually involves a series of simple decisions about how to format responses. Avoid using ASP script for complex string manipulations, especially in loops, because it's too slow.

Complex Decision-Making

Use ASP for complex decision-making. Computers are extremely fast at making simple decisions, and ASP scripts, although they're not the fastest languages around, are more than adequate for making such decisions. When you combine decision-making with text processing, you have the building blocks to create personalized, interactive applications.

Intermediary Between Browser and COM Components

As your decision-making and data processing requirements grow, you can purchase or build COM components. As you increase your use of server-based COM components, ASP becomes the intermediary between the browser and these back-end components. As I said earlier—ASP is glue.

How *Not* to Use ASP

Just as ASP has its strong points, it also has its weak points, which are:

- ASP is an interpreted, not a compiled language, therefore it's inherently slower than other, compiled solutions.

- ASP doesn't have strong variable typing—all variables are Variants. Variants are convenient, but are also larger and slower than typed variables.

- ASP must insert `include` files each time they're used.

- ASP treats all `object` variables as late-bound objects. It must request information about the object for each property or method access, which slows down the response.

In contrast, compiled languages usually have strong variable typing, which means the programmer must specify the type and range of content each variable will have. That means more work for the programmer, but less work for the program, because it eliminates decisions. Similarly, `include` files in compiled programs are included only once, at compile time, and object references can be early-bound, which means the compiler checks property and method names and parameters at compile time, not at runtime.

As Business Logic

ASP isn't at its best when implementing business rules for two reasons. First, because such rules often involve many object property or database accesses. Languages like VB or C++ use *early binding* to access `object` variables. That means that the compiler knows the set of properties, methods, arguments, and return values exposed by an object at compile time. In contrast, ASP must ask the object for a list of its properties and methods at runtime—and it must do this for each property or method access. That type of object access is called *late binding*. Late-binding, as you can imagine, is several times slower than early binding. Late binding isn't usually a problem unless you need to access an object many times, such as in a loop, or in implementing complex business rules.

Second, and probably more important, the ideal program model places business rules into objects to create a clean separation between the rule implementation and the interface. Placing business rule code in ASP pages along with formatting and interface code violates that separation, not least because the code may be repeated in many places. If you need to change a rule that has been isolated in a single object, you can replace that object with minimal effect on the rest of the application code. If the business rule code is intermixed with interface and formatting code, it can be much more difficult to change. Note that separating business rules also allows you to test those rules separately from the program, and to reuse the same rule code in other applications.

As Database Access Logic

ASP isn't meant to be a data-access component. Just like business rules, and for the same reasons, ASP works better when you use it to format the results returned by data-access objects than when you use ASP script to communicate directly with the database. As long as you're making read-only queries, there's little difference between using data-access objects and ADO code in ASP pages. But when your applications need to update a database in complex ways, you're much better off isolating the data-access code in an external object.

As a Primary Means of Complex Data Processing

ASP can perform complex decisions, but you shouldn't ask or expect it to perform well for data-intensive operations. Remember, ASP doesn't have typed variables, can't perform early binding, and is an interpreted language. For data-intensive operations you want as much speed as possible. Often, you'll want to offload processing from your Web server to another server, and that's possible only if you place the code into external COM objects.

What You Can Do with ASP

ASP lets you perform several operations that are difficult or impossible with straight HTML. I'll list most of them in this book, but you should understand that just because you *can* do something with ASP doesn't mean you *should* perform that operation with ASP. The goal of all Web sites and applications is to respond to the client as quickly as possible, making the site an interactive experience rather than an exercise in patience.

Make If...Then Decisions

Most programming is about making simple decisions. For example, when a user selects an item from a drop-down list, your application will do one thing or another depending on which item is selected. That implies that your application can make a decision. In pseudocode:

```
If user clicked TX then
    'Save user's selection in a variable
```

```
        Session("LastUserSelection") = "TX"
        Show list of state parks in Texas
    ElseIf user clicked TN then
        ' Save user's selection in a variable
        Session("LastUserSelection") = "TN"
        Show list of state parks in Tennessee
    End If
```

The code shows that you're going to make a decision based on which state abbreviation a user selected from a list of states. You want to save the user's selection for future use, and then display a new list of state parks for the selected state.

Similarly, when the user returns to the list after looking at the state park list, you'll probably want to leave the list in the same state it was in when the user left it—with either TX or TN selected. The following pseudocode loop checks the value of the Session("LastUserSelection") variable saved in the previous code listing:

```
For Each State In StateList
    If Session("LastUserSelection") = State then
        ' Display the item as selected
    Else
        ' Display the item unselected
    End If
Next
```

Most programming consists of a series of such decisions. Note that the first decision—that of displaying a list of state parks based on a selection—is semi-possible with HTML. For example, you could present a list of state abbreviations formatted as hypertext links, each of which redirected the user to the appropriate state park page; but the second decision—that of reselecting the user's last choice—is not possible with HTML because there's no way to remember which link the user chose last.

Process Information from Clients

HTML has the capability to create interactive forms—no doubt you've seen many of them. A form is a place for the user to enter or select data. HTML also has the capability to send or *submit* that data to the server for processing. However, HTML does not have the ability to process the submitted data. To process data you must have a programming language and HTML is a layout language.

ASP provides several native objects that let you access data sent by clients. You'll explore these objects in detail in Part II of this book. You can store data, make decisions, alter the data, send it back to the client—basically, you can do whatever you want. The ASP objects make it easy to process client data.

Access Databases and Files

ASP by itself has no database connectivity or file-reading abilities; however, you can use the ADO objects installed with ASP to access databases and the Microsoft Scripting Runtime FileSystemObject and TextStream objects (also installed with ASP) to read and write text files. HTML has no access to external data other than through hyperlinks. You can link two documents together with an <a> anchor tag containing a Uniform Resource Language (URL) to display data, but you can't read or write files.

Format Responses

With ASP you can respond differently to different clients. That means you can take the results of a database query or data from a file, format it on the fly, and return the results to a client. For example, you can hide or show data based on a client's permission level. In a student report card application, for example, you would want to let teachers and school administrators view and change data for their own students—but you wouldn't want to let students change the data! Similarly, you would want students to see only their own report cards, not those of other students.

With ASP you can use the same data set for all users, but format the responses based on identity. You can also easily change the look and feel of the response, change colors and controls, adjust to multiple screen resolutions, and more. by running condition-specific code on the server. HTML is static—a page is a page is a page. You can't show only part of a page, you can't show different pages based on identity, and you can't change page results for a single user without changing them for all users.

Launch and Communicate with COM Objects

With ASP you aren't limited to the capabilities of scripting languages, nor to the properties and methods of the intrinsic ASP objects. ASP can launch Component Object Model (COM) objects. A COM object may contain almost any kind of functionality, but all COM objects have one thing in common—they can communicate with one another. ASP ships with several COM objects, including `Scripting .Dictionary`, `Scripting.FileSystem`, `MSWC.BrowserType`, and `TextStream`. You can purchase, download, or create your own COM objects with Visual Basic, C++, or any of several other languages. You can even create COM objects with a text editor with VBScript or Jscript, using a technology known originally as Remote Scripting, and now included as part of the Windows Scripting Host. Initially, you could use these text file-based COM objects to run code on the server from a browser, thus the term remote scripting.

Regardless of the language used to create your COM objects, you can launch and control them from an ASP page. COM objects you can use with ASP pages have several names. You'll see them advertised and described as MTS components, ActiveX controls, ActiveX Documents, and Active Template Library (ATL) objects. But they're all exactly the same thing—COM objects. Some COM objects run on the server and some run (on IE) on the client. You can easily extend the functionality of your applications through COM components in exactly the same way other developers extend their Windows applications. There are many commercial, free, and shareware COM components available on the Web, at Microsoft's site, and from third-party vendors.

Control Transactions

You can use ASP to create mission-critical transactional applications. A *transaction* is any set of tasks that must either all complete successfully or all fail completely. The classic example is a financial transaction. When you pay by check or credit card, the bank must remove the money from your account and credit the merchant's account. If either part fails, you want both parts to fail. Forcing failure is a difficult process, because it means you have to undo the parts of the transaction that have already completed.

Fortunately, there's software available to help you monitor and control transactions. IIS 4 ships with a transaction monitor called Microsoft Transaction Server (MTS), which manages the process for you. In Windows 2000 (which includes IIS 5) MTS is part of a group of services called COM+, but from a programmer's point of view, both versions manage transactions the same way. All you need to do is group the operations into a transaction. If the transaction fails, MTS can automatically roll back the parts of the transaction that have already been completed.

Applications that use transactions typically must monitor the transaction to determine its status, and not all transactions complete instantaneously. Some transactions take minutes or days to complete. In addition, transactions may not all occur on machines or in code under your control. In the financial transaction, for example, the merchant's account may not be (and probably isn't) with the same bank as your account. Transactions that occur on more than one system are called *distributed transactions*. MTS manages transactions on disk, using a program called the Microsoft Distributed Transaction Coordinator (MS DTC). MTS prepares each part of the transaction. When all the parts have signaled their readiness, MTS issues a commit command. As each part of the transaction completes, it notifies MTS, which logs a completion message. MTS notifies the transaction owner (in this case, your ASP page) about the state of the transaction and the outcome.

In Windows 2000, MTS has become part of COM+, and COM objects running in MTS are now called COM+ applications. That's confusing terminology, but it's part of Microsoft's strategy to eliminate monolithic applications. Instead of creating large applications, you should begin to think about and design your applications as a set of reusable, small, and lightweight components.

How Web Requests Work

Whenever a user enters a URL into a browser's address field, clicks a link, or submits a form, the browser packages up information about itself, the URL, and (in some cases) the user, and sends that information to the server as a Web request. The ASP engine consists of a collection of objects that contain information about the request, the scripting technology used to make decisions about how to handle the request (the code), and the Web server itself. Before you can understand much about what the ASP engine can do, you need to know what happens before the user's request reaches the code in your ASP page.

A Web request requires two components: a Web server and a client. The client is usually a browser, but could be another type of program, such as a spider (a program that walks Web links gathering information) or an agent (a program tasked with finding specific information, often using search engines). In this book, you'll focus entirely on browser clients. The server and the browser are usually on two separate computers, but that's not a requirement. You can use a browser to request pages from a Web server running on the same computer—in fact, that's probably the setup you'll use to run most of the examples in this book. The point is that whether the Web server and the browser are on the same computer, or whether they're on opposite sides of the world, the request works almost exactly the same way.

Both the server and the client must use a defined protocol to communicate with each other. A protocol is simply an agreed-upon method for initiating a communications session, passing information back and forth, and terminating the session. There are several protocols used for Web communications; the most common are HyperText Transfer Protocol (HTTP) and File Transfer Protocol (FTP). Regardless of the protocol used, Web requests are carried over an underlying network protocol called Transmission Control Protocol/Internet Protocol (TCP/IP), which is a global communications standard that determines the rules two computers follow when they exchange information.

The server computer runs an endless loop to check for communication initialization. The client sends an initialization to begin a session. The initialization is a defined series of bytes. The byte content isn't important, the only important thing is that both computers recognize the byte series as an initialization. When the server receives the initialization request, it acknowledges the transmission by returning another series of bytes to the client. The conversation between the two computers continues in this back-and-forth manner. If computers spoke in words, you can imagine the conversation being conducted as follows:

Client	Hello?
Server	Hello. I speak English.
Client	I speak English too.
Server	What do you want?
Client	I want the file /mySite/myFiles/file1.htm
Server	That file has moved to /mySite/oldFiles/file1.htm
Client	Sorry. Goodbye.
Server	Goodbye.
Client	Hello?
Server	Hello. I speak English.
Client	I speak English too.
Server	What do you want?
Client	I want the file /mySite/oldFiles/file1.htm
Server	Here's some information about that file.
Client	Thanks, please send the data.
Server	Starting data transmission
Client	I got packet 1. Send packet 2.
Server	Sending packet 2
Etc.	
Server	All packets sent.
Client	All packets received in good condition. Goodbye.
Server	Goodbye.

TCP/IP is only one of many computer communication protocols, but due to the popularity of the Internet, it has become ubiquitous. You won't need to know much more than that about TCP/IP to use it—the underlying protocol is almost entirely transparent. You do, however, need to know how one machine finds another machine to initiate a communications session.

How a Client Requests Content

When you type a request into the browser address bar or click a hyperlink, the browser packages the request and sends it to a *naming server*. The naming server maintains a database of names, each of which is associated with an IP address. Computers don't understand words very well, so the naming server translates the requested address into a number. The text name you see in the link or the address bar is actually a human-friendly version of an IP address. The IP address is a set of four numbers between 0 and 255, separated by periods. For example: 204.225.113.34.

Each IP address uniquely identifies a single computer. If the first naming server doesn't have the requested address in its database, it forwards the request to a naming server further up the hierarchy. Eventually, if no naming server can translate the requested name to an IP address, the request reaches one of the powerful naming servers that maintain master lists of all publicly registered IP addresses. If no naming server can translate the address, the failed response travels back through the naming server hierarchy until it reaches your browser. At that point, you'll see an error message.

If the naming server can find the request, it caches the request so it won't have to contact higher-level naming servers for the next request to the same server. The naming server returns the IP address to the browser, which uses the IP address to contact the Web server associated with the address. Many Web pages contain references to other files that the Web server must provide for the page to be complete; however, the browser can request only one file at a time. For example, images referenced in a Web page require a separate request for each image.

Thus, the process of displaying a Web page is usually a series of short conversations between the browser and the server. Typically, the browser receives the main page, searches it for other required file references, and then begins to display the main page while requesting the referenced files. That's why you often see image placeholders when a page is loading. The main page contains the references to other URLs that contain the images, but not the images themselves.

What the Server Does with the Request

From the Web server's point of view, each conversation is a brand new contact. By default, a Web server services requests on a first-come, first-served basis. Web servers don't remember any specific browser from one request to another (actually, the latest version of the HTTP protocol, HTTP 1.1, does have the ability to maintain a connection over multiple requests, which speeds up your Web access considerably).

Parts of a URL

The line that you type into the browser address field is a Uniform Resource Locator (URL). The server breaks the requested URL into its component parts. Forward slashes, colons, periods, question marks, and ampersands, called delimiters, make it easy to separate the parts. Each part has a specific function. Here's a sample URL request (the URL doesn't really exist):

```
http://www.someSite.com/VisualBasic/default.htm?Page=1&Para=2
```

Table 1.1 shows the name and function of each part.

TABLE 1.1: URL Parts and Description

URL Item	Function	Description
http	Protocol	Tells the server which protocol it should use to respond to the request.
www.someSite.com	Domain name	This part of the URL translates to the IP address. The domain name consists of several parts separated by periods: the host name—www; the enterprise domain name—someSite; and the top-level Internet domain name—com. There are several other top-level Internet domain names, including org (organization), gov (government), and net (network).
VisualBasic	Virtual directory	The server translates this name into a physical path on a hard drive.
default.htm	Filename	The server will return the contents of the file. If the file were an executable file (such as an ASP file) rather than an HTML file, the server would execute the program contained in the file and return the results rather than returning the file contents.
? (question mark)	Separator	The question mark separates the file request from additional parameters sent with the request. The example URL contains two parameters, Page=1 and Para=2.
Page	Parameter name	Programs you write, such as ASP pages, can read the parameters and use them to supply information.
= (equals sign)		The equals sign separates a parameter name from the parameter value.
1	Parameter value	The parameter named Page has a value of 1. Note that all parameter values are sent as string data. Your programs are free to interpret the values as numbers, but you will have to cast or change them to numeric form.
& (ampersand)	Separator	The ampersand separates parameter=value pairs.
Para=2		Second parameter and value.

Server Translates the Path

You don't make Web requests with real or physical paths, instead, you request pages using a virtual path. After parsing the URL, the server translates the virtual path to a physical path name. For example, the virtual directory in the URL `http://myServer/myPath/myFile.asp` is myPath. The myPath virtual directory maps to a local directory like `c:\inetpub\wwwroot\VB\myFile.asp`, or to a network Universal Naming Convention (UNC) name like `\\someServer\somePath\VB\myFile.asp`.

Server Checks for the Resource

The server checks for the requested file. If it doesn't exist, the server returns an error message—usually `HTTP 404 - File Not Found`. You've probably seen this error message while browsing the Web; if not, you're luckier than I am.

Server Checks Permissions

After locating the resource, the server checks to see if the requesting account has sufficient permission to access the resource. For example, if the requesting account is the anonymous account, and the user has requested a file for which that account has no read permission, the server returns an error message, usually `HTTP 403 - Access Denied`. The actual error text depends on the exact error generated. There are several sub-levels for 403 error messages. You can find a complete list of error messages in the IIS Default Web Site Property dialog (refer to Chapter 2, *Introduction to IIS*). The contents of most error messages are customizable. By default the server reads error message text from the HTML files in your `$windows$\help\common\` directory, where `$windows$` is the name of your NT directory, usually named WINNT.

How the Server Responds

Graphics files, Word documents, HTML files, ASP files, Executable files, CGI scripts—how does the server know how to process the requested file? Actually, servers differentiate file types in several different ways.

Internet Information Server (IIS) differentiates file types based on file extensions (such as ASP, HTM, EXE, etc.) just like Windows Explorer. When you double-click on a file or icon in Windows Explorer, it looks up the file extension in the registry, a special database that holds system and application information. The registry contains one entry for each registered file extension. Each extension has an associated file type entry. Each file type entry, in turn, has an associated executable file or file handler. The server strips the file extension from the filename, looks up the associated program, and then launches that program to return the file. IIS follows the same series of steps to determine how to respond to requests.

Most Web servers also use file extensions to determine how to process a file request, but they don't use registry associations. Instead, they use an independent list of file extension-to-program associations. The entries in these lists are called MIME types, which stands for Multipurpose Internet Mail Extensions, because email programs need to know the type of content included with messages. Each MIME type, just like the registry associations, is associated with a specific action or program. The Web server searches the list for an entry that matches the file extension of the requested file.

Most servers handle unmatched file extensions by offering to download the file to your computer. Some servers also provide a default action if you request a URL that doesn't contain a filename. In this case, most servers try to return one of a list of default filenames—usually a file called `default.htm` or `index.htm`. You may be able to configure the default filename(s) for your server, either globally for all virtual directories on that server, or for each individual virtual directory on that server.

The server can begin streaming the response back to the client as it generates the response, or it can buffer the entire response and send it all at once when the response is complete. There are two parts to the response: the response header and the response body. The response header contains information about the type of response. Among other things, the response header can contain a response code, the MIME type of the response, the date and time after which the response is no longer valid, a redirection URL, and any `cookie` values the server wants to store on the client. Cookies are text strings that the browser saves in memory or on the client computer's hard drive. The cookie may last for the duration of the browser session, until a specified expiration date, or permanently. The browser sends cookies associated with a site back to the server for each subsequent request for that site.

What the Client Does with the Response

The client, usually a browser, needs to know the type of content with which the server has responded. The client reads the MIME type header to determine the content type. For most requests, the MIME type header is either `text/html` or an image type such as `image/gif`, but it might also be a word-processing file, a video or audio file, an animation, or any other type of file. Browsers, like servers, use registry values and MIME type lists to determine how to display the file. For standard HTML and image files, browsers use a built-in display engine. For other file types, browsers call upon the services of helper applications or plug-ins that can display the information. The browser assigns all or part of its window area as a canvas onto which the helper program or plug-in paints its content.

When the response body consists of HTML, the browser parses the file to separate markup from content. It then uses the markup to determine how to lay out the content on-screen. Modern HTML files may contain several different types of content in addition to markup, text, and images; browsers handle each one differently. Among the additional content types are:

Cascading Style Sheets (CSS)   CSS style sheets contain information about how to format the content. Modern browsers use CSS styles to assign fonts, colors, borders, visibility, positioning, and other formatting information to elements on the page.

Script   All modern browsers can execute JavaScript, although they don't always execute it the same way. The term JavaScript applies specifically to script written in Netscape's JavaScript scripting language, but two close variants, Microsoft's Jscript and the ECMA-262 specification (ECMAScript), have essentially the same syntax and support an almost identical command set. In addition to JScript, Internet Explorer supports VBScript, which is a subset of Visual Basic for Applications (which, in turn, is a subset of Microsoft's Visual Basic language).

NOTE   The complete ECMA-262 specification can be found at http://www.ecma.ch/stand/ecma-262.htm.

ActiveX components or Java Applets   These small programs execute on the client rather than the server. ActiveX components only run in Internet Explorer on Windows platforms, (roughly 60% of the total market when this book was written) whereas Java applets run on almost all browsers and almost all platforms.

XML   Extensible Markup Language (XML) is similar to HTML—both consist of tags and content. That's not surprising, because both are derived from Standard Generalized Markup Language (SGML). HTML tags describe how to display the content, and to a limited degree, the function of the content. XML tags describe what the content is. In other words, HTML is primarily a formatting and display language, whereas XML is a content-description language. The two languages complement each other well. XML was first used in IE 4 as channels. With IE 5, Microsoft has extended the browser's understanding of and facility with XML so that today you can use it to provide data islands in HTML files. You can also deliver a combination of XML and Extensible Stylesheet Language (XSL) (a rules language written in XML that's similar in purpose to CSS) to generate the HTML code on the client. The XML/XSL combination lets you offload processing from the server, thus improving your site's scalability.

How ASP Requests Differ from HTM Requests

Until a request for an ASP file reaches the server, it is identical to an HTM request. The naming server finds the host server in the same way and the browser makes exactly the same request as it does for an HTM file. At that point, however, the server routes the request to the ASP engine rather than the default IIS response engine. The ASP engine reads the requested file, either from disk or from the IIS file cache, then parses the file.

The ASP engine then takes three actions, in this order, which you will find is important when you begin coding later in this book:

1. The ASP engine inserts any `include` files. `Include` files are separate files that IIS can place into a requested file. After the insertion, IIS processes the file exactly as if the inserted file were part of the originally requested file. The insertion of `include` files occurs before the ASP engine processes any code.

2. The ASP engine begins to interpret the code. It interprets code in sequence, except for code sections marked as Functions or Subs. Refer to the *Methods, Functions, Routines, and Subroutines* sidebar for an explanation of the terminology used in this book.

3. The ASP engine returns the response. You can control whether the engine begins to return the response immediately (unbuffered response) or whether it stores the response string until the response is complete (buffered response) via IIS settings.

Bear in mind that the browser knows nothing about what technology is running on the server. To the browser, all responses are simply a string of characters or numbers. The MIME type of the response determines how the browser treats the response.

Methods, Functions, Routines, and Subroutines

In VBScript you can write inline code, which is code that executes in the physical order in which the code appears in the file. You can also write code methods, which are blocks of code you can call by name. A method usually (but not always) consists of reusable code—the kind of thing you might want to do over and over again. In VBScript there are two kinds of methods: Subs, also called subroutines, which perform a unit of work but do not return

Continued on next page

a result, and Functions, which are exactly the same as subroutines except they do return a result. Subs and functions are often interchangeable. It's a matter of much debate and programming style whether you need to return a result.

For example, a good candidate for a subroutine is the process of appending text to a file. To append text to a file, you need to open the file, append the text, and close the file. It's easy to write that as inline code, but you will probably need to write almost exactly the same routine over and over again as you build applications. Therefore, you can move the code to a subroutine instead. You might call the routine appendToFile. You pass the subroutine the name of the file and the text to append, and the subroutine opens the file and appends the text. For example:

```
Sub appendToFile(aFilename, someText)
    ' open the file aFilename
    ' append the text
    ' close the file
End Sub
```

By wrapping the inline code in a subroutine you've made it reusable, because the same code will now work with any file and any text. You can make it a subroutine rather than a function because you don't need to return any result.

In contrast, a good candidate for a function is the process of adding an arbitrary set of numbers together. You might call the function addNumbers. You pass the addNumbers function a Variant array of numbers. The function adds the numbers and returns the result. For example:

```
Function addNumbers(vNumberArray)
    Dim i
    Dim result
    For i = 0 to ubound(vNumberArray)
    For i = 0 result = result + vNumberArray(i)
    Next
    addNumbers = result
End Function
```

Both functions and subroutines are known generically as methods. You may also see me use the word routines, which means exactly the same thing. Methods typically refer to code packaged in objects, whereas routines typically refer to code packaged in code modules, but you'll find them used more or less interchangeably in this book and in the industry.

What is the *ASP.DLL*?

The ASP Dynamic Link Library (DLL) is the code behind the ASP engine. There are at least three versions of the ASP.DLL; version 3 ships with Windows 2000. Although I have no doubt that internally the DLL has changed significantly since version 1, unlike most Microsoft technology, the public interface has remained almost exactly the same. That's because ASP (and I'll repeat this several times) is not a language—it's a scripting host. Therefore, it doesn't need to change unless the basic requirements of a scripting host change.

What is Script?

I've mentioned script several times, but what is script? Unfortunately, I don't have a very clear answer for you because the answer depends on whom you ask. To Microsoft, script is any ActiveX programming language that exposes an interface compatible with the Windows Scripting Host. The two most common scripting languages for Microsoft applications are VBScript and JScript or JavaScript, although there are other compatible scripting languages—PerlScript for example. To Netscape, script means JavaScript. To Sun Microsystems, script means JavaScript that runs on the server as JavaServer Pages (JSPs), a recent ASP knock-off.

To almost everyone, script means a small, relatively limited interpreted language. You need to know what interpreted code is to understand the previous sentence. Computers don't understand code as you write it. Instead, other programs translate the code you write into machine instructions. There are two ways to make the translation. You can translate the code at runtime, which means the computer reads a line or block of code from your code file, makes the translation, and then executes the code. That process is called interpreting the code, and it's done by a program called an interpreter.

Alternatively, you can translate the code and store the resulting machine code in a file. When you execute the file, the computer reads the machine instructions directly. That kind of translation is not performed at runtime; a program called a compiler translates the code before the computer begins to execute it. The compiler and the interpreter do much the same thing, but the compiler is more efficient because it isn't under any time constraints. It compiles the code offline. The interpreter is less efficient, because it has to translate the code to machine instructions and run it almost instantaneously.

Script languages are small only in comparison with full-featured languages. VBScript is a subset of the Visual Basic language. In contrast, JavaScript is not a subset of Java, although the two languages share much of the same syntax. Netscape invented JavaScript because they needed a safe way to run code inside a browser. JScript and JavaScript are not quite identical, but they will evolve to become identical over time, due to the ECMA standards.

Almost all browsers can execute JavaScript. IE is the only browser that can execute VBScript. So why is the main language in this book VBScript? There are several reasons. First, ASP is a server-side technology. All the ASP code you will ever use runs on the server, not the browser. The language you use on the server doesn't affect the browser one way or the other. Second, VBScript is the default language that Microsoft chose to deliver with Active Server Pages. That means that most of the example code that comes with ASP is in VBScript; the examples you'll see in most other sources are in VBScript; and there's much more information available for VBScript-based ASP pages than for JScript or any other scripting language.

Nevertheless, you are perfectly free to use other ActiveX-compatible scripting languages—and you may want to consider doing so if you're familiar with Java, C, or Perl, or if your applications will demand much client-side scripting. Yes, that's right, script code can run either on the server or the client. This is probably the most confusing point for beginning ASP programmers. Just remember this, if it's ASP code, it will run on the server before the response has been completed. If it's client-side code, it will run on the client only after the browser has begun to receive the response.

> **NOTE** JScript and JavaScript are not the same thing. Although they have an almost identical feature set, they are completely independent, created and marketed by Microsoft and Netscape, respectively. I'm going to use the term JScript for server-side ASP script and JavaScript for client-side script in this book even though you may actually be using JScript on the client (you are using JScript if you're working with IE browsers).

If the majority of your target audience uses Netscape browsers, if you're creating applications for the public that will run on the Internet, or if you think your application's user base is broader than Windows, you should use JavaScript for all your client-side script.

How Does the Server Separate Script from Content?

When the ASP engine parses the file, it separates server-side script from content in two ways. As the programmer, you must separate your script from content with a delimiter, which is an arbitrary character or sequence of characters that separates values. Delimited text files often have only a single delimiter—the comma or tab character. ASP script has two delimiters, one to mark the beginning of a code block and another to mark the end of the code block. The ASP code start delimiter is a left angle-bracket and a percent sign, and the end delimiter is the percent sign followed by a right angle-bracket; for example <% your code here %>.

You may also separate code from script using a more traditional, HTML-like syntax. Using this method, the code begins with a `<script>` tag and ends with a `</script>` tag. To use this syntax with ASP script, write the script as follows:

```
<script language="JScript" RunAt="Server">
' your code here
</script>
```

Note the text `RunAt="Server"` in the `<script>` tag. If you don't include that text (called an attribute) the server will ignore the script, but the browser will try to execute the script on the client side. In other words, `<script>` tags by default, delimit client-side script. To force the ASP engine to process scripts as server-side code, you must add the `RunAt="Server"` attribute.

My advice is not to use the `<script RunAt="Server">` syntax—it's too easy to confuse the syntax and cause unnecessary errors. Use the bracket-percent delimiters instead. In some editors, like HomeSite, FrontPage, and Visual InterDev, the editor will change the text color for script between the bracket-percent delimiters, which can help you differentiate script from HTML.

How/When Does the Server Process Script?

When the server invokes the ASP scripting engine, it first parses the file and inserts any `include` files. It then collects the script portion by finding all the script delimiters. The ASP engine treats all non-script content as strings that it writes verbatim back to the client. Next, the scripting engine creates variables and external components invoked by the script. Finally, it begins interpreting the script, executing each command and sending results to the client (or buffering the results, depending on server settings).

At the completion of script processing, the scripting engine destroys variables and external components created for the script. If the results were buffered, the server returns the contents of the buffer to the client.

How Does the Browser Act with ASP Sites?

This is important because it is one of the most common misconceptions of beginning ASP programmers: The browser has no concept of ASP sites, HTML sites, or any other kind of site. The browser is completely, utterly, and totally ignorant of the way a server processes its requests. To a browser, there's no difference between an ASP page and an HTM file. Browsers don't request specific kinds of content, they just request that the conversation with the server follows one of the standard communications protocols.

Now that you know about ASP in general and how Web requests work, you can move forward by learning to create your own sites on IIS. In the next chapter, you'll create a site called MasteringASP that you'll be able to use for the rest of this book.

CHAPTER

T W O

Introduction to IIS

■ **Valuable Features of IIS**

■ **Introduction to the MMC**

■ **Creating a Virtual Directory**

■ **Stopping and Starting the Server**

■ **Other Entries in the MMC**

Internet Information Server (IIS) is important because it currently owns (depending on who you believe) about 40 percent of the total Web server market. That percentage rises considerably, to somewhere between 60 and 80 percent, if you ask companies what Web server they use for their intranets. As an ASP developer, that means your applications can potentially run, without modification, on well over half of all the Web servers in the world.

In addition, IIS is an extremely fast Web server. *InfoWeek* recently published the results of two tests that show IIS on NT is as much as $2\frac{1}{2}$ times faster as competing servers on other operating systems.

But there are still other reasons why IIS is important, particularly for developers already familiar with Microsoft products. First, IIS runs as a Microsoft Transaction Server (MTS) component (or COM+ application in Windows 2000). That means that it can pool (share) database connections and launch, control, and participate in transactions. All of these features (including ASP itself) are standard with IIS 5. Second, IIS is programmable. Given sufficient permissions, you can access, control, and modify IIS and its Web sites with COM-compliant languages— including ASP script. Finally, you can extend and customize IIS via Internet Server Application Programming Interface (ISAPI). And, of course, IIS is free with the NT 4.0 Option Pack or with Windows 2000. Two somewhat less-capable versions, Peer Web Services (for NT 4 Workstation) and Personal Web Server (for Windows 95/98), both called PWS, also include ASP—and both are free.

Both IIS and PWS include a File Transfer Protocol (FTP) server that lets you upload and download files. IIS also includes a Network News Transfer Protocol (NNTP) server capable of serving newsgroups. The Windows 2000 version of IIS ships with a Simple Mail Transport Protocol (SMTP) server for sending email. It has the Web Distributed Authoring and Versioning (WebDAV) extensions that let authenticated users create folders and edit files directly on the server. From a user's perspective, these Internet Folders look and act almost exactly the same as local folders and files. Because Windows 2000 and IIS 5 are relatively new, many of you may still be using the previous version of NT and IIS. For that reason, I've included information about both NT 4/IIS 4 and Windows 2000/IIS 5. Fortunately, there aren't many changes. If you're familiar with Web administration for IIS 4, you'll feel right at home with IIS 5. If you don't have Windows 2000/IIS 5 yet, you'll be glad to know that almost everything you learn about NT 4/IIS 4 will remain applicable when you do upgrade.

Valuable Features of IIS

IIS provides integrated security and access to a wide range of content, works seamlessly with COM components, and has a graphical interface—the Microsoft Management Console (MMC)—that you can use to create and manage your ASP applications. Before you can create an ASP application, you must work with IIS to give the code and resources for your application a place to live. In this section, you'll create a virtual directory called MasteringASP, tell IIS that it's an application, not a static site, and set a few properties. Although I know you're eager to dive into ASP code, I strongly suggest you read this section first and follow the procedure to set up the MasteringASP application. I don't expect you to absorb all of this information on first reading, but you should leave this section with a strong sense of the range of services that IIS provides.

IIS Provides Integrated Security

On the Internet, most sites allow anybody to connect to the site. The exceptions are commercial sites where you pay a one-time or monthly fee to access the site. Sites that restrict access are called secured sites. Secured sites use either integrated security or login and password security.

IIS supports both of those methods. IIS integrates with Windows NT/2000 security, so if you're building intranet applications where everyone has an NT account and uses IE, you can use Windows' built-in security rather than requiring logins and passwords. IE (but not Netscape) will authenticate with the application transparently—without requiring an additional login and password.

IIS lets you set up security restrictions on a site-by-site basis. Because IIS integrates with MTS, you can also use MTS role-based security to limit access to COM components used by your application. An MTS role is much like an NT group; both consist of a named list of users. The difference is that all users in a role have exactly the same permission level. That means you can set up a few roles that allow or restrict access to any number of COM components. IIS 4 itself and all its applications are COM components that run under MTS, which means you can use MTS roles to restrict access to your entire application.

IIS Provides Access to Content

All Web servers can deliver HTML files, but they differ widely in how they treat other types of content. Most servers let you add and modify Multi-purpose Internet Mail Extensions (MIME) types, but IIS integrates directly into the Windows registry. That means IIS natively understands how to treat most common Windows file formats, such as text (TXT) files, application initialization (INI) files, executable (EXE) files, Microsoft Word (DOC) documents, PowerPoint (PPT) presentations, Excel (XLS) spreadsheets, and many others.

IIS Provides an Interface for COM

You can control many parts of IIS using COM. IIS exposes many of the server's configuration settings via the IIS Admin objects. These objects are accessible from ASP and other languages. That means you can adjust server configuration and create virtual directories and Webs programmatically. IIS 4 and higher store settings and Web information in a special database called the *metabase*. You can even define your own Web extensions in the metabase to customize IIS at a very low level.

Programmatic control of the Web server is extremely important for Integrated Development Environments (IDEs) such as Visual Studio, and for HTML and site management applications like FrontPage, HomeSite, and DreamWeaver, but IIS also provides another easy-to-use management interface called the MMC, for use outside of an IDE or programming language.

IIS exposes a COM interface through a set of objects called the IIS Admin objects. You can use these objects with ASP or any COM-compliant language to alter the metabase programmatically. For example, you can use the IIS Admin objects to create new sites and virtual directories or alter the properties of existing sites and virtual directories.

Introduction to the MMC

The Microsoft Management Console (MMC) is a program that lets you control most aspects of a Windows 2000 computer from a single common interface. The MMC works through snap-ins, which are the programs that do the actual work. The MMC isn't solely an IIS management tool; instead, it's a management environment that hosts snap-in management applications. In NT 4, IIS and MTS snap-ins shared the MMC. In Windows 2000, you can use the MMC to perform almost all administrative tasks. I'm introducing the MMC before you begin ASP programming because you need to be able to create and destroy Web sites as you learn, and because this book doesn't require that you use an IDE. IDEs perform site creation and destruction for you, but often don't provide any other control over the Web server. You need to learn how to manually create, manage, and destroy sites so you can deploy your ASP applications to other servers.

You can also extend (or co-opt) the MMC by writing your own snap-ins, thus integrating your application directly into the administrative interface to the computer.

To launch the MMC:

In NT 4   Click Start ➤ Programs ➤ Windows NT 4.0 Option Pack ➤ Microsoft Internet Information Server ➤ Internet Service Manager (see Figure 2.1).

FIGURE 2.1:

How to launch the MMC in NT 4

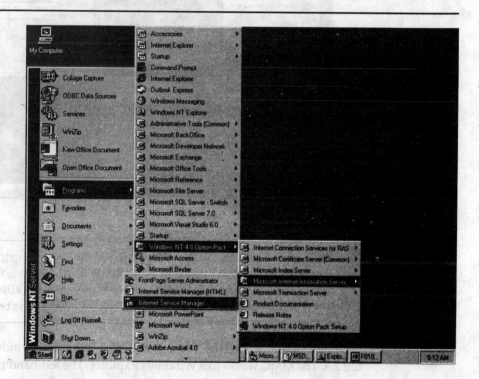

In Windows 2000   Click Start ➤ Programs ➤ Administrative Tools ➤ Internet Services Manager (see Figure 2.2).

There are multiple ways of reaching the Internet Information Services applet. In Windows 2000, you can reach the IIS applet through Start ➤ Settings ➤ Control Panel ➤ Administrative Tools ➤ Internet Services Manager.

Your view of the MMC (the items in the outline list in the left-hand panel) differs depending on which way you launch the MMC and the set of items you have installed on your server. No matter which way you reach it, the functionality of the applet is identical.

You can also extend (or co-opt) the MMC by writing your own snap-ins, thus the inte...

FIGURE 2.2:

How to launch the MMC in Windows 2000

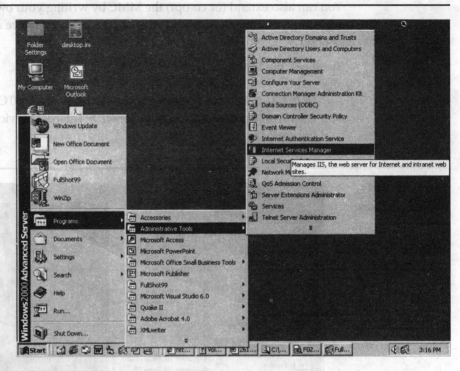

TIP

Because you'll probably use the MMC often, you can create a shortcut to it. Create the shortcut icon on an Active Desktop toolbar or on your desktop for easy access. Set the shortcut target to `C:\WINNT\system32\mmc.exe C:\WINNT\System32\inetsrv\iis.msc`, and set the Start in property to `C:\WINNT\System32\inetsrv`.

When you first launch the MMC, you'll see a two-paned window similar to Figure 2.3. The MMC works like Windows Explorer. The left-hand pane contains an expandable hierarchical outline list of items or entries. Entries higher in the hierarchy are parent items; items below parent items in the hierarchy are child items. Parent items may be open, or expanded (you can see the child items in the list), or closed (the child items are invisible). To expand the list of child items for a closed parent item, either double-click on the text of the parent item or click the plus (+) sign next to the parent item.

When you click an item in the left-hand pane, its child items appear in the right-hand pane. When you expand an item, its child items appear in the left-hand pane under the selected item.

FIGURE 2.3:

Internet Information Server applet in MMC (IIS 4)

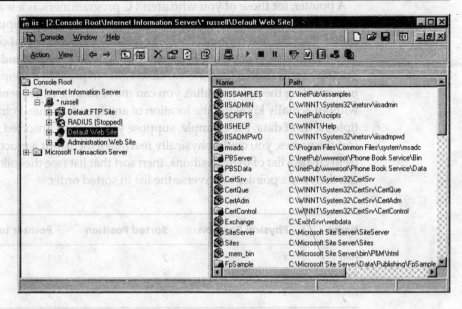

Each time you close the MMC you have an option to save the current view. Also, because the MMC is a management application host, you may have different snap-ins installed and a different view than shown in Figure 2.3.

To administer IIS, regardless of your initial view, find the IIS item in the left-hand pane and expand it. Depending on your network setup, you may see a list of computers running IIS on your network. Find the computer you want to administer and expand that item. (Figure 2.3 shows the item for the computer Russell expanded, in Windows NT.)

You'll see a list of IIS-related applications. Note that IIS is a collection of servers, not a single server; it contains both an FTP and HTTP server by default, but may also contain additional servers, depending on which parts of BackOffice you have installed. The default HTTP server root directory is called the Default Web Site. Find that item and click on it.

When you click on the Default Web Site you'll see a list of items in the right-hand pane. These are the child items for the Default Web Site. When you expand the Default Web Site item, that list becomes visible in the left-hand pane. Use the outline list to drill down to the item you need to work with.

Each child item in the Default Web Site has an icon. The icons that look like folders with a blue globe in the lower right-hand corner are virtual directories. A virtual directory is a pointer to a physical directory.

A pointer, for those of you who aren't C programmers, is a way of inserting a layer of indirection between one thing and another. You manipulate the pointer rather than the real content. Pointers are an extremely useful concept. You can accomplish almost anything in programming with a layer of indirection. The term pointer comes from using one variable value to point to a memory location. By incrementing the pointer value, you can move through a sequential array of values without actually knowing the location of any specific value. Pointers provide multiple views of data. For example, suppose you have an unsorted list of names. To sort the names, you could physically rearrange them, but a much faster way would be to create a list of their positions, then sort that list (see the following table). You can then use a pointer to traverse the list in sorted order.

Name	Physical Position	Sorted Position	Pointer to Sorted Position
Fred	1	2	1
Bob	2	1	2
John	3	3	3

Virtual directories work the same way—they point to a physical directory. For example, suppose you put some content in the directory C:\myContent\HTMLFiles. You'd like to publish that content via your Web server, but you want to call the site CurrentSales. Rather than renaming the directory, you create a virtual directory, call it CurrentSales, then point it to the physical directory containing the files. A virtual directory is just a name associated with a physical directory.

You may have multiple virtual directories that all point to the same physical directory, but each virtual directory points to only one physical directory.

Other items in the list have an icon that looks like documents in an open box. These items are IIS applications. An IIS application is also a virtual directory. Marking a directory as an IIS application implies that the content for that virtual directory is dynamic content—that is, content generated at runtime.

Find the application titled IISHELP and click on it. This is the virtual directory that contains the help files for IIS and several associated technologies. In the right-hand pane, you'll see a list similar to Figure 2.4 if you're running NT 4.

In IIS 4, you'll see two types of icons. The folders with the blue globe icon in the lower right-hand corner are virtual directories. The plain folder icons are simply subdirectories. This view shows that you can nest virtual directories—one virtual directory can contain another, lower-level, virtual directory. Remember that the contents of a virtual directory are identical to that of its associated physical directory. Also, you can designate any physical directory as a virtual directory, so the idea of nesting virtual directories shouldn't surprise you. Although the nested virtual directories don't exist in IIS 5 under the IISHelp folder, you can nest virtual directories in IIS 5 in exactly the same way.

FIGURE 2.4:

IISHELP application virtual directory contents (IIS 4)

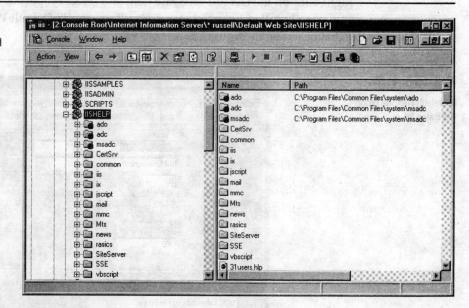

IIS Root Web Options

The Default Web Site (also called the Root Web) is the highest-level directory for your server. When you create a new site, it runs in the process address space of the Root Web by default. That means if you create an application in the Root Web address space and that application crashes, you'll probably crash the entire Web server. Don't do that. Seriously, this is the first important programming point you need to understand to create Web applications: You have to learn to share; your application is probably not the only application on the server.

With IIS 3, errant applications crashed the server regularly. However, since version 4, you can configure your application to run in a separate process. Selecting the latter option protects the server from your application. Unfortunately, running in a separate process also somewhat degrades performance. I suggest you develop and deliver betas and early versions in a separate process. After your application is thoroughly tested, you can move it into the server's process address space.

NOTE The important thing to remember is that new applications and virtual directories inherit the Default Web Site configuration. Therefore, you should be aware of the standard configuration and the options for changing the settings.

Right-click on the Default Web Site item and select Properties from the pop-up menu, usually called a context menu. You'll see the IIS Default Web Site Properties dialog shown in Figure 2.5.

FIGURE 2.5:

IIS Default Web Site Properties dialog (IIS 4)

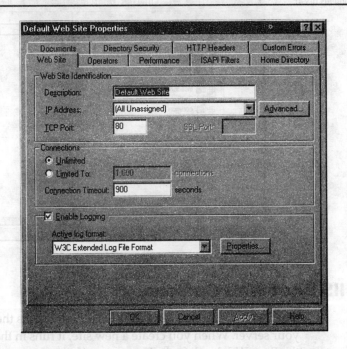

From the Default Web Site Properties dialog, you can configure the basic properties of your IIS HTTP server, including access and security restrictions. I'm not going to explain every feature of IIS here, but it's worth your time to take a look at the most commonly used features. I will discuss each of these common features in the following sections.

Directory Security Tab

Click the Directory Security tab on the IIS Default Web Site Properties dialog. From this tab, you control the base access permissions for this site (see Figure 2.6).

Click the Edit button in the first section of the dialog, Anonymous Access and Authentication Control. You'll see the Authentication Methods dialog in Figure 2.7.

FIGURE 2.6:

Default Web Site Properties,
Directory Security tab (IIS 4)

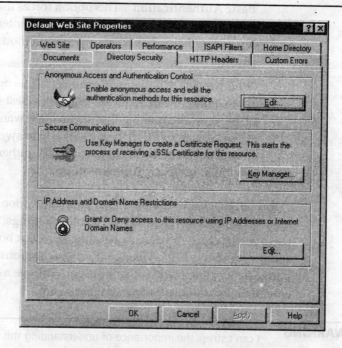

FIGURE 2.7:

Authentication Methods dialog (IIS 4)

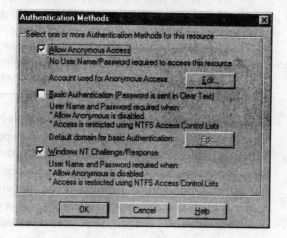

In the IIS 4 dialog, there are three checkboxes:

Allow Anonymous Access   When this option is checked, users can view
content in your site without any authentication. Normally, you would use
this option for sites on the Internet, or for sites where you don't mind if
anyone views the content.

Basic Authentication   This option forces users to sign on with their user ID and password before they can view content in the site. Note the warning on the dialog box. Don't use this method of authentication where security is critical.

Windows NT Challenge/Response   This option uses Windows NT security to authenticate requests. This is the best setting for intranet sites where all the users are running IE and you don't want to allow anonymous requests. It's only useful with IE because IE can answer the challenge, whereas other browsers cannot. If you want to use NT authentication with non-IE browsers, you must use Basic Authentication.

You can check any combination of authentication options, but checking Anonymous Access effectively disables the other settings. If you want to authenticate users with a mix of browsers including IE, check both the Basic Authentication and the Windows NT Challenge/Response options. IE users will authenticate transparently. Users with other browsers will see a dialog box where they must enter their network username and password.

WARNING   I can't stress the importance of understanding this security model too highly—I guarantee that it will cause headaches for you when you begin deploying applications. When your site allows Anonymous Access, you must understand that the rights individuals have when they connect to your site are Guest account rights to the local NT computer and network. Typically, Guest account access rights are insufficient for some operations—for example, writing files on the server. Operations that may work wonderfully for you during development can fail immediately in production based on account permission settings.

Network authentication through Windows NT Challenge/Response provides the highest level of security, but isn't always possible, because it only works with IE. Basic Authentication is better than no authentication, but sends usernames and passwords over the network in plain text form. This leaves your network open to attack by unscrupulous people who use network sniffer software to steal security information. Anonymous Access allows everyone access to the site via a Guest account, called, by default, IUSR_MACHINENAME.

Click the Edit button next to the Allow Anonymous Access checkbox. You'll see a small dialog box through which you may reassign the anonymous user account to a different account (see Figure 2.8).

FIGURE 2.8:

IIS Anonymous User Account
dialog (IIS 4)

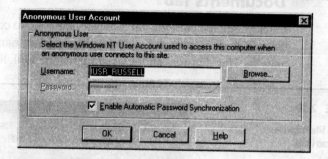

To change the account, type the name of the account you want to use, enter the
password for that account, check the Enable Automatic Password Synchroniza-
tion option, and then click the OK button. IIS will ask you to verify the password.
Enter it again and click the OK button. The checkbox option keeps the password
used by IIS and the anonymous account password in sync. If you don't check this
option and you change the password for the anonymous account, IIS will fail
when it tries to map the anonymous user to this account because it won't have
the correct password.

You can set a different anonymous user account for each site in IIS 4 and higher. If
you're security conscious (and you should be), I advise you to do this for each site
you create. That way, any additional permissions you grant to anonymous users for
one site are isolated to that site; you won't have security breaches due to extraneous
permission levels assigned due to requirements for a different site. For example,
you might set up a network account that has write access to a directory so users can
upload files to your site.

TIP

You should change the default IIS account IUSR_MACHINENAME to a network
account that you can control for each Web site you create.

Alternatively, you could edit the IUSR_MACHINENAME account rights for the specific
files and permissions you need to have for your site. For example, if you want to log
errors to a file or upload files to a directory, you could grant the IUSR_MACHINENAME
account read/write access to that file or directory. Note that when you do this, all
users of any anonymous site on your server where the IUSR_MACHINENAME is the
default account acquire permission to write to the files and directories. You may
never see a security breach because of such permission assignments, but it's better
to anticipate security problems than to repair them after they occur.

Finally, you may want to uncheck the Allow Anonymous option for intranet
sites, because you can then track usage by the real username of the person accessing the site. Each person then has the same rights as they normally have for the network and you ensure that only authenticated network users connect to your site.

Documents Tab

Click on the Documents tab. This tab lets you to control whether your site has a default document, and if so, what the name or names of the default document(s) may be. The controls on the Documents tab look like Figure 2.9.

FIGURE 2.9:

Default Web Site Properties, Documents tab (IIS 4)

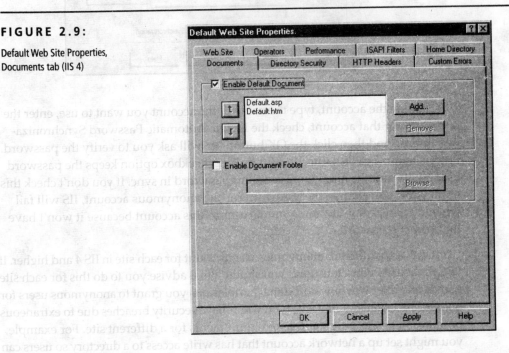

A default document is a document that appears if a user doesn't specify a document. For example, the URL http://www.microsoft.com/ is a valid URL, but doesn't specify a document. For such requests, you can set IIS to search for a default document. IIS searches the directory for any file in the default document list and returns the first match, if one exists; otherwise, it returns an error message.

Typically, you should name your default documents default.(ext), but you may call them whatever you like. For example, on many UNIX sites the default document is named index.htm. When you create a site, IIS turns this option on and creates two default document names: default.htm and default.asp. To specify more than one default document name, separate the names with semicolons. If you don't want to display a default document, you should either turn this option off, or avoid the default.htm and default.asp filenames.

Home Directory Tab

Click the Home Directory tab. The controls on the tab look like Figure 2.10.

FIGURE 2.10:

Default Web Site Properties,
Home Directory tab (IIS 4)

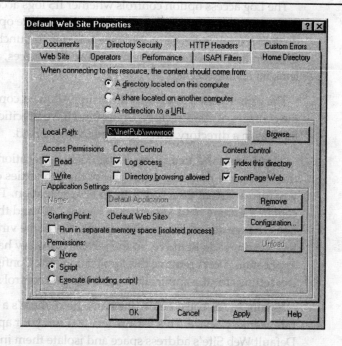

You control the location of content files using the Home Directory tab. The top three option buttons, under the title When Connecting to this Resource, the Content Should Come From: control the source directory or computer for site content. The default setting is A Directory Located on this Computer. Clicking either of the other options changes the tab's controls and content. Store your content locally unless you have a specific need to keep your content on a different computer, because it's faster to retrieve local content than network content.

By default, the root Web directory is \inetpub\wwwroot, which stands for Internet Publications\World Wide Web Root Directory—your HTTP server—but you can change it to any valid directory or network share. You can even redirect the request to a completely different server. To change the root Web directory, enter the full drive and pathname or network share.

The checkboxes below the Local Path field control permissions for file, logging, FTP, indexing, and (in IIS 4) FrontPage Web operations. If you don't have the Microsoft FrontPage extensions installed on your server, you may not see the FrontPage Web option. If you don't have the Microsoft Index Server installed, you may not see the Index this directory option. The Read and Log access options are checked by default. If you uncheck the Read access option, users will not be able to access HTM files in the site. You should not normally check the Write option because it lets people post files to your server. You should never check the Write option if you also select the Execute option (at the bottom of the dialog), because people can then post and run malicious executable programs on your server.

The Log access option controls whether IIS logs access to the site. You don't have to log access, but I strongly advise you to leave the option checked (although you do gain a small increase in response speed if you uncheck the option). Access logging can help you track usage on files and resources, as well as help you find problems when they occur.

The option called Directory Browsing Allowed controls whether people can list the contents of the directory. Unless you have specific reasons to let people browse the files in a directory, leave this option unchecked.

Now look at the area of the dialog titled Application Settings. You'll probably use this area more than any other part of the Properties dialog because this is where you turn a virtual directory into an IIS application. The Application Settings area contains a name field (disabled in Figure 2.10) and three buttons. The button captions change depending on the current state of the virtual directory. In this case, the top button reads Remove, so the virtual directory has already been set as an IIS application. Don't remove this application. The Configuration button lets you control settings for the application—just like you control settings for the Web site itself.

Finally, in IIS 4, just below the name field, there's a checkbox titled Run in Separate Memory Space. This feature lets you run your applications outside the Default Web Site's address space and isolate them in their own memory area. You'll find this is an important feature for development. If you check this box for applications you create, you can shut down your application independently of other applications running on the same server. You'll learn more about why this is important later. For now, you should remember that IIS lets your applications run in either the root Web address space or in their own memory space. Your applications run more quickly in the root Web address space, but in their own memory space they're isolated from problems that may occur with other applications.

Look back at the top of the dialog. If you click the option titled A Redirection to a URL, the dialog changes to look like Figure 2.11.

To redirect the request, specify the URL for the redirection target in the Redirect to field. You must enter the full URL. For example, `http://servername/path/` if the target is on another computer. To specify more about what happens to the request during the redirection, you may also check one or more of the options below the Redirect To Field.

Checking the Exact URL Entered Above option always redirects to the destination URL, regardless of the specific file requested by the client. Checking the A Directory Below This One option lets you redirect to a child directory. If you use this option, you can specify only the child virtual directory, without the full HTTP URL, for example, `/mySubDirectory`. Checking the A Permanent Redirection For this Resource option sends a message to the client that the site has moved permanently.

FIGURE 2.11:

Default Web Site Properties,
Home Directory tab, Redirect
to: option (IIS 4)

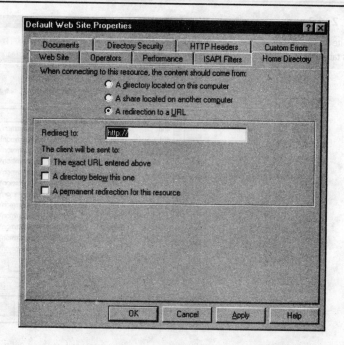

In addition, you can specify which portions, if any, of the original request to supply to the redirect URL using redirect variables and wildcards. You won't need to redirect your site to work with the HTML and ASP examples in this book. If you do need to know more, click the Help button on the dialog for a complete explanation of the redirect variables and wildcards you can use.

Custom Errors Tab

When you click on the Custom Errors tab, you see a list of error values with the associated messages, or the filename that contains the error text (see Figure 2.12).

The Custom Errors tab lets you send custom error messages in place of the IIS default error messages. For example, you may never want to return a 403;11 Password Changed error message; instead, you might want to return an Access Denied error message. You can override a default error message by creating a custom error message.

To create a custom error message, select the error item, then click the Edit Properties button. Alternatively, just double-click the error message you want to change. You'll see the dialog box in Figure 2.13.

There are three types of error message options—Default, File, and URL, although the URL type is not always available.

FIGURE 2.12:

Default Web Site Properties,
Custom Errors tab (NT 4)

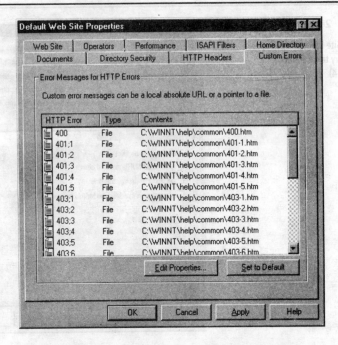

FIGURE 2.13:

Custom Errors, Error Mapping
Properties dialog (IIS 4)

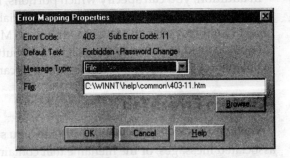

The default messages are hard-coded and you cannot change them. Select the Default type to cancel a custom error message. The File message type obtains the error message text from a file. The URL message type obtains the error message text from a URL. Select the Message type. If you selected the File or URL type, enter or select the appropriate path and filename or URL.

If you no longer need the custom message, you can restore the default IIS error message by selecting an error, then clicking the Set to Default button on the Custom Errors tab (see Figure 2.12).

HTTP Headers tab

By clicking the HTTP Headers tab, you are able to perform several tasks that you may need (see Figure 2.14). From the HTTP Headers tab you can:

- Set content expiration (the length of time a browser can use cached content before it returns to the server to request an updated version)

- Set the rating for your site, based on the Recreational Software Advisory Council (RSAC) rating

- Add or change MIME types

- Supply custom header information

FIGURE 2.14:

Default Web Site Properties, HTTP Headers tab (IIS 4)

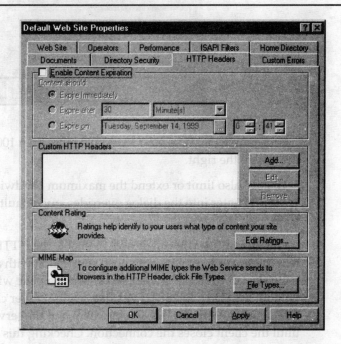

For ASP sites, you should check the Enable Content Expiration option and specify that the content should expire immediately. Don't change the option in the Default Web Site Properties dialog—change it on a site-by-site basis.

Performance Tab

From the Performance tab you can improve the Web server's response time by moving the slider to the expected number of hits per day (see Figure 2.15).

FIGURE 2.15:

Default Web Site Properties, Performance tab (IIS 4)

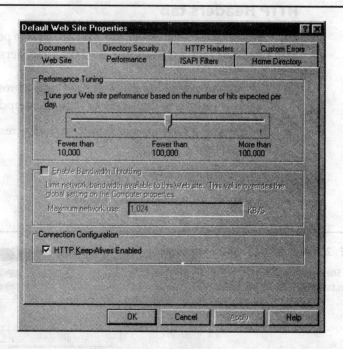

For example, if you expect to receive more than 100,000 hits, move the slider all the way to the right.

You can also limit or extend the maximum bandwidth the site can use. The value you enter into the dialog overrides any default value set at the computer level.

Finally, in IIS 4, you can disable or enable the HTTP Keep-Alives flag, which tells the server to maintain an open connection with a client to service multiple requests. For example, if your server sends a page with 10 graphic references without the HTTP Keep-Alives flag set, the server closes the connection after each request. With the flag set, the client and the server maintain a connection until the client closes the connection. Checking this option will improve the response time to complete an entire page request, graphics, and all. The HTTP Keep-Alives option is enabled by default.

Other Default Web Site Tabs

There are three other tabs on the Default Web Site Properties dialog that I have not covered: the Web Site, Operators, and ISAPI Filters tabs. I've never had to change any of these properties—the defaults have worked fine for me. If you need to change them, consult the documentation.

The Web Site tab controls the name, IP address, and TCP port number of the Default Web Site. You can also set the maximum number of simultaneous connections and the connection timeout value, enable or disable logging, or change the name and location of the log file. It's worth exploring the log options just to see what you can choose to log, as opposed to the items IIS logs by default.

The Operators tab lets you add accounts (grant Operator privileges) to the list of users who can administer the Web server. The accounts you add have full control over all aspects of the Web server if they are members of a Windows NT Administrators group; non-administrators may perform only a subset of the available administration functions.

The ISAPI Filters tab lets you add or change the order in which ISAPI filters are loaded. ISAPI filters, as you may recall from Chapter 1, run before the Web server has seen the request. The order in which filters are loaded is important if any of the filters change the request.

Virtual Directory Properties

Each virtual directory inherits the properties of its parent, but you may also override some of those properties using the Properties dialog for each virtual directory. Find the IISHELP item again and right-click on it in the left-hand pane of the MMC, then select Properties from the context menu. You'll see a dialog window similar to Figure 2.16.

FIGURE 2.16:

IISHELP Properties
dialog (IIS 4)

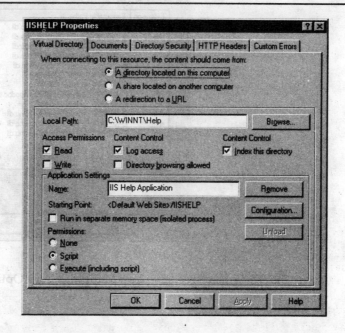

At this point, the dialog contents should look quite familiar. Only five of the tabs from the Default Web Site are available at the virtual directory level. The Virtual Directory tab contains the same items as the Home Directory tab for the Default Web Site. The contents of the other four tabs—Documents, Directory Security, HTTP Headers, and Custom Errors—are also same as those for the Default Web Site. Changing a setting at the virtual directory level overrides the setting that the virtual directory inherited from its parent. Conversely, when you change a setting at a higher level, IIS warns you if any child directories have settings that differ from the parent. You can elect to override the custom child settings at that point.

IIS Applications and Properties

As you saw earlier, there are two different types of virtual directories—Web sites and Web applications. You set properties for the root Web from the Home Directory tab and other virtual directories from the Virtual Directory tab. Open the MMC, find the IISHELP application under the Default Web Site, and select Properties from the context menu. Click the Configuration button. You'll see the Application Configuration dialog (see Figure 2.17).

FIGURE 2.17:

Virtual Directory, Application Configuration dialog (IIS 4)

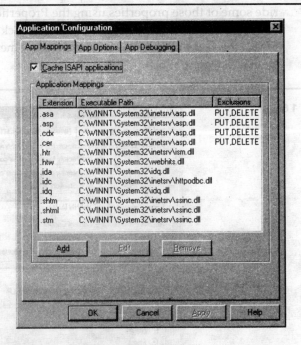

The dialog has three tabs: App Mappings, App Options, and App Debugging.

App Mappings Tab

The App Mappings tab (shown in Figure 2.17) lets you associate extensions with specific executables. The extensions you'll work with in this book, ASA and ASP, should already be mapped to the file `asp.dll`. You shouldn't need to change any of the application mappings.

At the top of the App Mappings tab, you'll see a checkbox captioned Cache ISAPI Applications. Caching the application keeps the files in memory. Because ASP applications are ISAPI applications, you can improve the response time for your applications by checking this option.

If you do need to add an application mapping, use the Add button. To change an existing mapping, select the item you want to change, then click the Edit button. To delete an existing mapping, select the item you want to delete, then click the Remove button.

App Options Tab

Click the App Options tab (see Figure 2.18).

FIGURE 2.18:

Application Configuration, App Options tab (IIS 4)

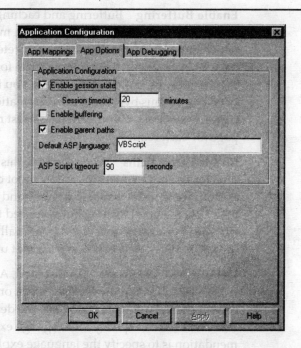

The App Options tab controls several important options for ASP applications:

Enable Session State This option enables or disables Session state. Briefly, enabling Session state lets your ASP application store information for a specific user in memory on the server. Normally, you would enable this option; however, ASP applications scale much better if you disable Session state. The subject of state maintenance is both important and complex. You'll see a great deal more about it in this book. For now, just remember that you can turn off Session state using the App Options tab.

Session Timeout   The Session timeout value controls how long the server maintains information about a specific user after that user has stopped interacting with your application. The server has no way of knowing that a user isn't going to return to your application. For example, if a person visits your site, views a few pages, then walks away from the computer, you don't want to maintain any in-memory information about that user forever. The Session timeout lets you release that information from memory after a configurable length of time. By default, the Session timeout is 20 minutes. Depending on your application's needs, you may want to adjust that value up or down. Maintaining Session information too long wastes server resources; setting the value too small risks alienating your users who expect the application to behave much like a desktop application, which doesn't have a timeout value.

Enable Buffering   Buffering and caching are the same thing. Enabling Buffering lets the server cache pages in memory. ASP pages use script, which must be interpreted. The interpreter reads the code in your ASP page and compiles it to an intermediate form, called p-code, before executing the code. By buffering the pages, you tell the server to cache the compiled pages, thus bypassing the compilation step and speeding up your pages. In contrast, unbuffered sites must reload, parse, and compile each page for each request.

Enable Parent Paths   When checked, this option lets you refer to pages in directories above your application's root directory using the dot-dot (. .) syntax. The dot-dot syntax is a shorthand way to reference a parent directory. This is a good feature, but you need to be aware that it is also a security risk, because people could potentially run applications in a parent directory. When unchecked, you cannot use the (. .) syntax.

Default ASP Language   As installed, ASP's default scripting language is VBScript. If you typically use JScript or another scripting language, you can set the default here. If you use the default language for your pages, you don't have to specify the language explicitly in each page. My recommendation is to specify the language explicitly in each page. That way, your scripts won't break if some other administrator changes the default language setting, or if you move your application to another server, where the default language setting may be different from yours.

TIP

Don't rely on the default language setting—specify the script language explicitly in each file. That way, your scripts won't break if another Server Administrator changes the default language, or if you move your application to another server, where the default language setting may be different from yours.

ASP Script Timeout   This setting controls how long scripts run before the ASP engine stops executing them. By default, the ASP engine will run scripts for 90 seconds. There are some good reasons to set the default to a smaller value—especially during development. For example, one common mistake programmers make when writing a loop is forgetting to increment the loop value. Consequently, the loop continues to run forever—and steals all the CPU cycles in the process. Another common mistake is to write a loop to wait for an event, such as a message from a database connection that an operation has completed. But sometimes, the event never occurs, leaving your program stuck in another endless loop. The ASP engine protects your server from such mistakes by stopping execution after a defined period of time. You don't have to worry about those instances when the script needs to run longer than the default value—you can adjust the timeout setting with script for any individual page. I've found that a reasonable value is 15 seconds. Almost all your pages will complete their processing within the 15-second limit. For those that can't, increase the value for those pages only.

App Debugging Tab

The App Debugging tab lets you enable or disable debugging for your site, and also lets you override the error messages sent when errors occur (see Figure 2.19).

There are two debugging flag checkboxes at the top of the dialog. The first one, Enable ASP Server-side Script Debugging, controls whether the ASP engine enables the Microsoft script debugger when running ASP scripts. With the debugger enabled, you can set breakpoints, watch variable values, and step through code at runtime in the Visual Studio IDE. The debugger can be useful to help you find problems in your code, but it's a far cry from the debugger in Visual Basic. Given the rudimentary debugger, other debugging techniques can be just as effective with ASP in its current implementation.

The second debugging flag, Enable ASP Client-side Script Debugging, is an anticipatory option—anticipatory because it doesn't work yet. Microsoft has reserved the checkbox for a future version.

If you enable the server-side debug option, be sure to turn it off before deploying your site because it slows down server response time.

FIGURE 2.19:

Application Configuration,
App Debugging tab (IIS 4)

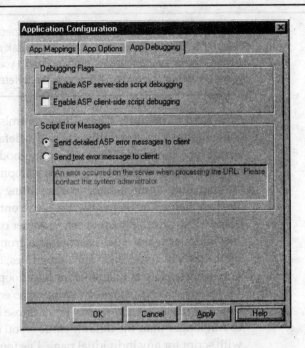

The second part of the dialog, Script Error Messages, lets you override error messages that would normally appear on the client's browser. This option can be critical when you don't want clients to see information about your site. For example, suppose your script tries to open a file and the operation fails. During development, you should write a detailed error message that states where the error occurred, what the error is, and which file failed to open properly. To send the detailed error message, select the Send Detailed ASP Error Messages to Client option. After deployment, however, you may not want clients to know the directory where the file resides, the name of the file, or even which operation may have failed. To hide the message, click the Send Text Error Message to Client option and type the text of your custom message into the text field.

IUSR_MACHINENAME, IWAM_MACHINENAME

By default, the IIS installation creates two Guest accounts during installation: IUSR_MACHINENAME and IWAM_MACHINENAME, where MACHINENAME is the name of your server. IIS uses the IUSR_MACHINENAME account for sites that run in the root Web address space, and uses the IWAM_MACHINENAME account for sites that run in their own address space. Don't worry about the address space differences for now; just remember that neither account has sufficient rights to perform every operation you need.

When you have Anonymous Access in effect and a user connects to your site, IIS impersonates the IUSR_MACHINENAME account on behalf of that user for the duration of the connection. That means that every user who connects to your site inherits the permissions set for the IUSR_MACHINENAME account. There are some other problems with impersonation that I'll cover in the chapter on external ActiveX DLLs, but for now, just remember that the connecting users are not authenticated as the IUSR_MACHINENAME account—they haven't logged on and entered a password—IIS simply impersonates the account.

Because the IUSR_MACHINENAME account is a Guest account, it has Read permissions for local and network directories. For ASP sites, the IUSR_MACHINENAME account will typically also have script execute rights (you assign those via the Properties dialog using the Home Directory or Virtual Directory tab), but will not have Create, Write, or Delete permissions.

To complicate matters, IIS impersonates a different account for virtual directories that run in a separate address space. For those connections, IIS uses the IWAM_MACHINENAME account. IWAM_MACHINENAME is also a member of the Guest group, but it is a member of the MTS Impersonators group. Members of the MTS Impersonators group have rights to launch Distributed Common Object Model (DCOM) applications under MTS, whereas the Guest group does not. Other than that, there is no difference between the two accounts. Neither account has sufficient rights to modify files, which can be a problem.

For example, you may need to log error messages or store user information in a file—but neither the IUSR_MACHINENAME nor the IWAM_MACHINENAME account has permission to create a file or write to an existing file.

None of these difficulties causes problems as long as you're aware of how IIS treats anonymous Web requests. You can easily use NT's New Technology File System (NTFS) permissions to assign Change (Read, Write, Delete, and eXecute) rights for the required directories and files. The problem usually arises when developers move their site from development to production.

One final note: Virtual directories inherit the properties of their parent directory, so when you create a new site IIS assigns the IUSR_MACHINENAME account as the anonymous user account by default (assuming you haven't modified the anonymous account for the root Web). Remember that you can change the account used for anonymous connections on a site-by-site basis, and you should. If you don't change the account, its permissions tend to grow over time, as you give Write or Change permissions to more directories and files. This opens your site to security breaches. Instead, create an account specifically for your application. Give the account only the permissions it needs to run your application. Keep a log of the permissions you grant to the account. That way, when you need to move your application to a new server, you can recreate the account and assign the same permission level on the new server. Assigning specific accounts for each application limits your security risks and ensures that your application will continue to work as expected.

Creating a Virtual Directory

This is an interactive section and you should perform the actions described on your IIS server, if you have one. If you don't, I'll summarize the actions you should take at the end of the chapter and you can use it for a reference.

Before we begin, several tools can create Web sites for you; FrontPage and Visual InterDev spring to mind immediately. There's nothing wrong with using the capabilities of these tools as long as you follow the steps listed at the end of this chapter, skipping those steps that the tools accomplish for you, before you try to deploy your application.

What is a Virtual Directory?

I've explained this briefly already, but it deserves a section of its own. A virtual directory is a pointer to a real or physical directory. For example, the virtual directory /VB may physically reside at C:\inetpub\wwwroot\Visual Basic. A virtual directory is nothing more than a shorthand name for a physical directory. When a user requests a URL, the server looks up the virtual directory name and translates it to a physical directory before accessing the resource. Therefore, any directory may be a virtual directory.

You usually access directories below your virtual directory by their real names. Using the previous example, you might have a directory called C:\inetpub\wwwroot\Visual Basic\images\icons\people. Connections that request files from that directory would use the /VB virtual directory name, but would use the real path of the subdirectories: http://myServer/VB/images/icons/people/filename.gif. For simplicity, there's nothing to stop you (and in fact, some good reasons to encourage you) to create virtual directories for subdirectories as well. First, there's no point in typing lots of extra characters in your URLs, unless you like to type. If you were to create a virtual directory called PeopleIcons, you could write the same URL request as http://myServer/PeopleIcons/filename.gif. Second, you have now severed the link between the physical representation of the directory structure and the URL. You can now take the directory C:\inetpub\wwwroot\Visual Basic\images\icons\people and move it anywhere you like without changing a single line of code. The only thing you'll need to change is the source directory for the virtual directory name—in other words, you change the pointer to point to a new location. If, instead, you had to move the directory and you didn't have a virtual name, you'd need to search every file in your application that might request an image from the icons\people directory and modify the code appropriately.

Finally, creating virtual directories hides the physical implementation of your site from the users. You may use a standard directory hierarchy for the site, or you may move any part of the site to any directory on your server.

IIS Application Options

There are two types of IIS applications. One type runs in the address space of the Default Web Site. That means the application shares memory with IIS. The other type runs in a separate address space, which means the application gets its own memory area and the application does not share memory with IIS.

Applications that run in the Default Web Site address space run slightly faster than those that run in an isolated process.

During development and beta testing, I urge you to run your applications in an isolated process. Running your application in an isolated process keeps you from having to stop and start the server if problems occur. It also makes the process of developing ActiveX objects for use with your application much easier.

You can switch an application from an isolated process to the Default Web Site process and back by checking or unchecking the Run in separate memory space (isolated process) option on the Virtual Directory tab of the virtual directory Properties dialog for your application. Under the hood, when you create an isolated process, IIS creates a new MTS/COM+ application. The result is that you can shut down an application running in an isolated process without affecting any other applications running on the same server. If, instead, you run your application in the Default Web Site address space, problems with your application potentially affect all other applications running on the same server. That's why it's so important for you to develop and test in an isolated process, when such problems are most likely to occur.

You should run your applications for one or two months in an isolated process, even on production servers, when your application shares the server with established applications. The bulk of application changes occur within the first few months of rollout; therefore, it's highly likely you will need to modify the application even after it moves to a production server. If you're using COM components, you will need to shut the process down to upgrade the components. If you're running in an isolated process, shutting the application down won't affect other applications on the server. The only exception to this is if your application suffers because of the speed differential between isolated process applications and those that run in the server's address space. In those cases, you'll just have to bite the bullet and shut down the server long enough to upgrade the components.

Setting NTFS Permissions

Windows NT 4 can use two types of disk formats, the New Technology File System (NTFS) and the File Allocation Table (FAT) system. Windows 2000 can use three: NTFS, FAT, and FAT32. NTFS provides security down to the individual file level, whereas FAT provides no file security. NTFS stores data more efficiently than FAT. Windows 2000 also directly supports file compression and encryption for

NTFS-formatted volumes. FAT32 works like FAT, but stores data on the disk more efficiently and recognizes larger disk sizes. Most NT/2000 servers use NTFS. You *must* use NTFS for servers that function as domain controllers and for computers running Active Directory.

Windows NT/2000 uses an Access Control List (ACL) to determine whether an account has permission to perform an action. If your application allows anonymous access and the application needs to write files, you will need to give the `IUSR_MACHINENAME` or `IWAM_MACHINENAME` account permission to write to the files. If the files already exist, you can grant write permission for those files only; if your application also needs to create or destroy files, you must grant write and delete permission for the directory where the files will be created.

Use Windows Explorer to set the ACL permissions for files and directories. Open Windows Explorer and navigate to the directory in which you wish to grant permissions. The `IUSR_MACHINENAME` account already has read access to most local files. I'm going to grant additional permissions for a file named `c:\MasteringASP\MasteringASP.log`.

The way you set file permissions in Windows 2000 has changed somewhat. I'll explain the process in NT 4, then briefly show you the process for Windows 2000.

Setting NTFS Permissions in NT 4

To grant permission for a single file, navigate to the file and right-click on the filename (see Figure 2.20).

FIGURE 2.20:

NTFS file context menu

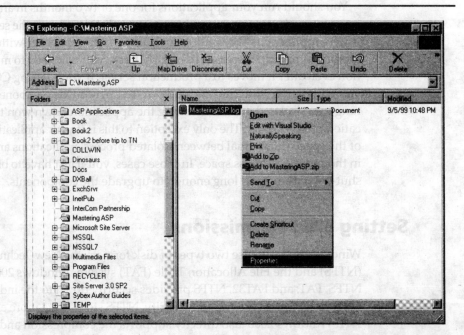

Next, select Properties from the context menu, then click the Security tab on the resulting dialog. You'll see the dialog in Figure 2.21.

FIGURE 2.21:

MasteringASP.log Properties, Security tab (NT 4)

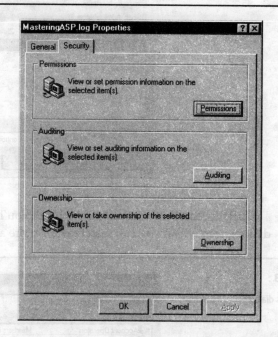

There are three buttons on the Properties dialog: Permissions, Auditing, and Ownership. The Permissions button lets you set access permissions for the file. The Auditing button lets you turn auditing on and off and select the type of auditing you wish the computer to perform. The Ownership button lets you assign ownership rights to the file. The owner of a file may always change ACL permissions for that file.

I'll explain the Auditing features later; for now, click the Permissions button. You'll see the dialog in Figure 2.22.

From the File Permissions dialog, you can add or change permissions for local or network accounts. Note that the Administrators group and the System account already have Full Permissions to the file—that means they can perform any operation on the file, including deleting the file or assigning permissions. The Everyone group has Change rights (RWXD) to the file, but don't be fooled—counter-intuitively, members of the Guest group are not members of the Everyone group. To grant write permission to the IUSR_MACHINENAME and IWAM_MACHINENAME accounts, you'll need to add the accounts to the ACL shown in the account list.

FIGURE 2.22:

File Permissions dialog

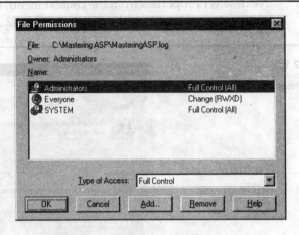

Click the Add button to add an account. You'll see the Add Users and Groups dialog, from which you can select one or more accounts (see Figure 2.23).

FIGURE 2.23:

Add Users and Groups dialog

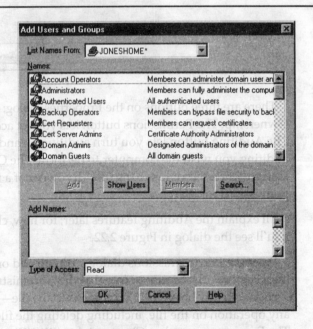

Select the domain for the account(s) you want to add. In this case, you want to add a local account, so select the local domain (the computer name) from the List Names From combo box. By default, the Add Users and Groups dialog lists group accounts, not user accounts. Click the Show Users button to list the user accounts. Scroll through the accounts until you find the IUSR_MACHINENAME account. Click on the account to select it, then click the Add button. The account you selected will appear in the Add Names list at the bottom of the dialog. Add the `IWAM_MACHINE-NAME` account as well.

Just below the Add Names list is a combo box entitled Type of Access. Click the combo box and select Change from the drop-down list. At this point, the dialog should look like Figure 2.24 (the names will be the names from your computer).

FIGURE 2.24:

Add Users and Groups dialog (after adding accounts)

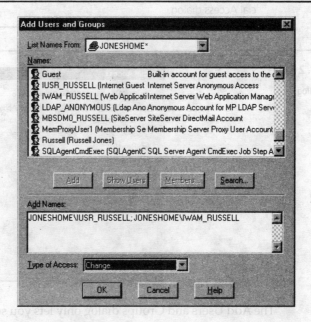

Click OK to save the changes. If your changes were saved properly, the two added accounts will be visible in the File Permissions dialog (see Figure 2.25).

FIGURE 2.25:

File Permissions dialog (after adding accounts)

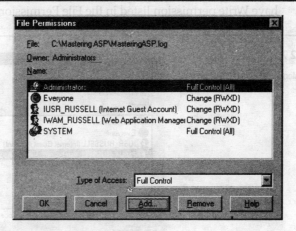

One more step. The two accounts now have Change rights—but you don't want them to be able to read, delete, or execute the file. You'll want to change the permissions to write-only. To do that, double-click on the IUSR_MACHINENAME entry in the list. The Special Access dialog appears (see Figure 2.26).

> **TIP**
>
> You must double-click on an entry in the File Permissions dialog to reach the Special Access dialog.

FIGURE 2.26:

Special Access dialog

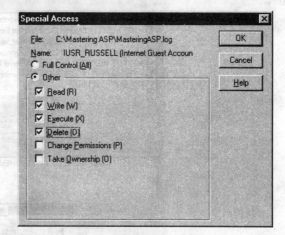

The Add Users and Groups dialog only lets you set file permissions to No Access, Read, Change, or Full Control, but the Special Access dialog lets you grant any individual permission or combination of permissions to a group or user account. Uncheck everything but the Write checkbox, then click OK. Repeat the same steps for the IWAM_MACHINENAME account. The end result should be that the two accounts have Write permission listed in the File Permissions dialog (see Figure 2.27).

FIGURE 2.27:

File Permissions dialog (actions complete)

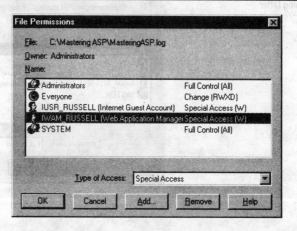

Click OK to close the File Permissions dialog, and OK to close the Mastering ASP.log Properties dialog.

Now that you understand the MMC, virtual directories, NT security, and can change NTFS permissions, you're ready to create your own virtual directory that will serve as the root directory for projects in the rest of this book.

Setting NTFS Permissions in Windows 2000

In Windows 2000, the dialogs for setting file permissions are somewhat different. Although the result is the same, the process is simpler and takes fewer dialogs than in NT 4. When you right-click on a file and select Properties from the context menu, you see the dialog in Figure 2.28.

FIGURE 2.28:

MasteringASP.log Properties dialog (W2K)

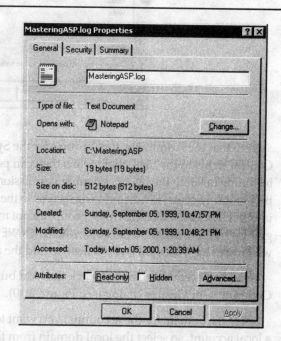

To set file security properties, click the Security tab (see Figure 2.29).

If any groups, users, or computers already have any access rights to the file, they appear in the top panel of the dialog. From this dialog, you can add or change permissions for local or network accounts. To change access rights for an existing account, select the appropriate entry in the top panel. The bottom panel changes to reflect the permissions assigned to the entry selected in the top panel. Check or uncheck the desired permissions in the bottom panel.

FIGURE 2.29:

MasteringASP.log Properties,
Security tab (W2K)

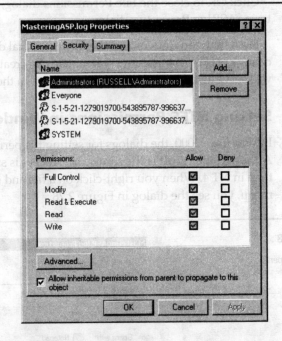

Note that the Administrators group and the System account already have Full Control rights to the file—that means they can perform any operation on the file, including deleting the file or assigning permissions. The Everyone group has Modify, Read & Execute, Read, and Write access to the file, but don't be fooled—counterintuitively, members of the Guest group are not members of the Everyone group. To grant write permission to the IUSR_MACHINENAME and IWAM_MACHINENAME accounts, which are Guest accounts, you'll need to add the accounts explicitly.

To add an account to the list, click the Add button. You'll see the Select Users, Computers, or Groups dialog (see Figure 2.30).

Select the domain for the account(s) you want to add. In this case, you want to add a local account, so select the local domain from the Look In drop-down list. Scroll through the accounts until you find the IUSR_MACHINENAME account. Remember that MACHINENAME refers to the name of your server. Click on the account to select it, then click the Add button. The account you selected will appear in the Add Names list at the bottom of the dialog. Add the IWAM_MACHINENAME account as well. After you select both accounts, the dialog will look similar to Figure 2.31.

When you are finished selecting accounts, click the OK button to continue. You'll return to the previous dialog. Any new accounts now appear in the top panel (see Figure 2.32).

FIGURE 2.30:

Select Users, Computers, or
Groups dialog (W2K)

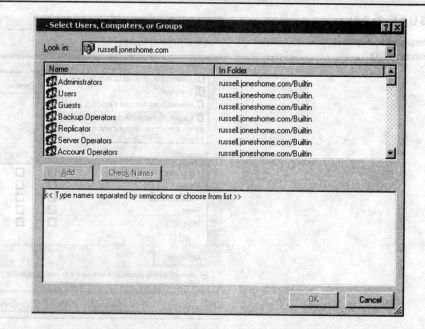

FIGURE 2.31:

Select Users, Computers, or
Groups dialog (W2K)

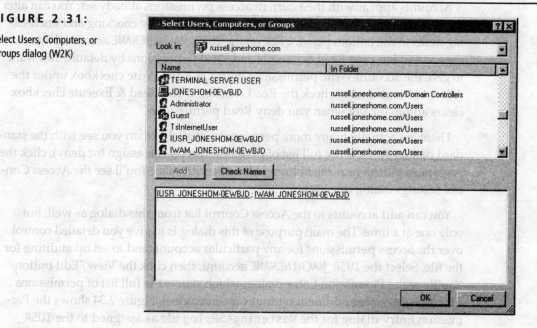

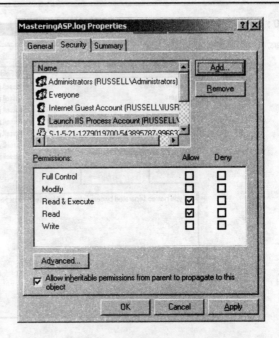

Accounts appear with their current access permissions already set. You can alter the access permissions as needed for the new accounts by checking and unchecking items in the bottom panel. Click on the IUSR_MACHINENAME account. Note that the account has only Read & Execute and Read permissions by default. You want to give the account Write permissions only. Click the Write checkbox under the Allow column, and uncheck the Read checkbox. The Read & Execute checkbox clears automatically when you deny Read permissions.

There are actually many more permissions available than you see with the standard dialog. To view the full list of permissions you can assign (or deny), click the Advanced button near the bottom of the Securities tab. You'll see the Access Control Settings dialog (see Figure 2.33).

You can add accounts to the Access Control list from this dialog as well, but only one at a time. The main purpose of this dialog is to give you detailed control over the access permissions for any particular account, and to set up auditing for the file. Select the IUSR_MACHINENAME account, then click the View/Edit button. You'll see the Permission Entry dialog, which shows the full list of permissions for a file (there are additional settings for directories). Figure 2.34 shows the Permission Entry dialog for the MasteringASP.log file as assigned to the IUSR_MACHINENAME account.

FIGURE 2.33:

Access Control Settings dialog (W2K)

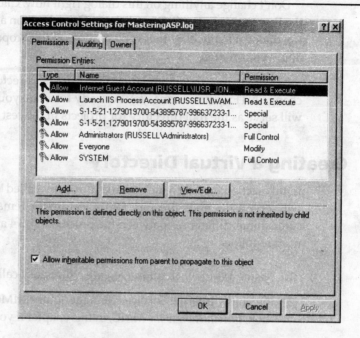

FIGURE 2.34:

Permission Entry dialog for the MasteringASP.log file and the IUSR_MACHINENAME account

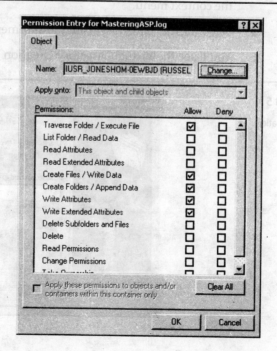

Don't change anything on this dialog right now. Click the Cancel button to close the Permission Entry dialog. Click the Cancel button again to close the Access Control dialog. Finally, click the Apply button on the Properties (Security tab) dialog to apply your changes.

Now that you understand the MMC, virtual directories, NT security, and can change NTFS permissions, you're ready to create your own virtual directory that will serve as the root directory for projects in the rest of this book.

Creating a Virtual Directory

In this section, you'll create a virtual directory called MasteringASP. This directory will serve as the root directory for projects in the remainder of this book. There are some minor differences between the process in IIS 4 and IIS 5. I'll list the steps you need to follow:

1. Using Windows Explorer, create a directory called MasteringASP.

2. Open the Internet Services Manager in the MMC (follow the steps in the section, *Introduction to the MMC*, in this chapter if you don't know how to do this).

3. Find the Default Web Site and select it, then right-click on it. Select New from the context menu.

4. Select Virtual Directory from the sub-menu.

5. You'll see the Virtual Directory Creation Wizard (see Figure 2.35).

FIGURE 2.35:

Virtual Directory Creation Wizard (IIS 4)

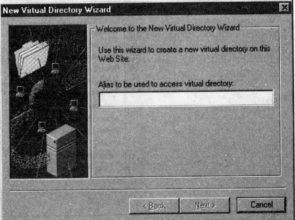

6. In IIS 4, enter the name `MasteringASP` into the Alias field. This is the name that people will use to access the virtual directory. Click the Next button to continue. In IIS 5, the process is the same, except that you must click the Next button from the first wizard screen to see the Virtual Directory Alias dialog. Enter the name `MasteringASP` into the Alias field, then click the Next button to continue.

7. Enter the physical path of the directory you created in Step 1, then click the Next button.

NOTE   At this point, if you haven't created the directory, or if you mistyped the directory path, the wizard will display an error. You can still recover. Switch to Windows Explorer and create the directory, or correct your typing and try again.

---

8. In IIS 4, accept the defaults (Allow Read Access and Allow Script Access) from the wizard and click the Finish button. In IIS 5, accept the defaults (the Read and Run Scripts checkboxes are checked), then click the Next button.

9. In IIS 4, the wizard closes immediately. In IIS 5, you see a completion screen first and you must click the Finish button to continue. The wizard will close and you should see your new virtual directory highlighted in the left-hand pane of the MMC.

10. Right-click on your new virtual directory and select Properties.

11. In IIS 4, check the Run in Separate Memory Space option. In IIS 5, change the Application Protection drop-down setting to High (isolated).

12. Click OK (or Apply in IIS 5) to save your changes.

You now have a virtual directory marked as an IIS application that runs in its own memory space. I'm going to discuss just a little more about IIS and the MMC, and you'll be ready to begin writing HTML and ASP files. You now have a virtual directory in which to put the files you create in the rest of this book, secure that your knowledge of the infrastructure is sufficient to solve any problems that may occur.

Stopping and Starting the Server

At some point in your ASP work, you'll need to stop and start IIS. Stopping and starting the server is, by itself, a trivial operation. I've included this section because you need to know why and under what conditions you must start and stop the server, and what impact your actions will have on other applications running on the same server.

You stop any of the servers listed in the MMC in the same way. To stop a server, click on the server you want to stop, then click the square Stop icon on the toolbar. Alternatively, select the server, then right click and select Stop from the context menu.

Sometimes it's more convenient to stop a server from the services applet. To reach the services applet:

- In NT 4, click Start ≻ Settings ≻ Control Panel and double-click on the Services icon.

- In Windows 2000, click Start ≻ Programs ≻ Administrative Tools ≻ Services.

You'll see a list of services. Find the service you want to stop. For example, the HTTP server (your Default Web Site) is called the World Wide Web Publishing Service, and your FTP server is called the FTP Publishing Service. In NT 4, select the service and then click the Stop button. In Windows 2000, select the service and then click the square Stop icon on the toolbar, or right-click the service and select Stop from the context menu.

In a production environment, you may need to minimize server downtime. You can write a batch file to start the server service, replace one or more DLLs, and restart the service. For example, the following batch file stops the World Wide Web service, un-registers a DLL, replaces the DLL, registers it, then restarts the service:

```
net stop w3svc
regsvr32 "c:\Components\Chapter19\ClassRecords.dll" /u
copy "c:\temp\ClassRecords.dll", "c:\Components\Chapter19\Class-
Records.dll"
regsvr32 "c:\Components\Chapter19\ClassRecords.dll"
net start w3svc
```

Why Start and Stop the Server?

ASP is an ISAPI application. That means that IIS loads the ASP DLL the first time a user requests a file with an ASP extension (ASP files are associated with the ASP DLL). Remember, one of the advantages of ISAPI over CGI applications is that once loaded, an ISAPI DLL stays loaded. IIS, like most other programs, loads DLLs into its own address space. Therefore, to unload the DLL you have to unload the program. Unlike most programs, you don't really want to stop your server permanently, therefore, you start and stop the server—called "cycling" the server or sometimes "bouncing" the server to release any in-memory DLLs.

You need to cycle the server whenever you must delete, update, or replace a loaded DLL used by the server, because the server will have a lock on the file. You can't delete or replace a locked file. The only way to release the lock is to stop IIS. Fortunately, you can minimize the impact by running your applications in an isolated process.

After stopping the server, you can replace COM component DLLs. If you find that the DLLs are still in use, you may need to stop and start the IIS Admin service to release the lock on the file. If you're running components in MTS/COM+, you should shut down the package before replacing the DLL.

What Happens When you Stop the Server?

When you stop the server, not only is the server unavailable for requests, but any cached information is lost. That's not a problem during development when your application resides on a development server, because no critical applications should reside on a development server. It's even less of a problem if you develop applications on your own computer (highly recommended), because the only person affected is you.

It is a problem if you must develop on a production server—one that is in use for other business purposes. You will need to balance your need to stop the server against the error messages and possible loss of data for other people using other applications on that server. That's why it's not a good idea to develop on a production server.

Unloading IIS Applications

You can avoid cycling the server (usually) if you set the option to run your applications in their own memory space (in an isolated process). Setting that option lets you unload the application by clicking the Unload button on the Virtual Directory tab of the Properties dialog for your virtual directory.

If your application runs in the Default Web Site address space, you must stop and restart IIS to unload your application. If your application runs in the pooled application space (under IIS 5), unloading your application will stop all the pooled applications.

Other Entries in the MMC

So far, I've discussed only the HTTP (Default Web Site) IIS server. IIS contains an FTP server, and (depending on the installed options) perhaps SMTP and NNTP servers as well. I'm not going to go into any depth on these servers. Most of the information you've seen so far applies equally well to the FTP server, so I'll be brief.

Creating New HTTP Sites

So far, you've seen the Default Web Site and you've created a new virtual directory under the Default Web Site. IIS has the capability to serve more than one site. If you click New from the Default Web Site context menu, you can create either a new Site or a new Virtual Directory. Each site must have its own IP address, so if you're going to create a new site, you must know the IP address you want to assign to the new site. You also have the option to assign the TCP port (default for HTTP servers is port 80) if you have special needs for that site. Other than that, creating a new site is much like creating a new virtual directory.

The Default FTP Site

The File Transfer Protocol (FTP) copies files from one location to another. Using FTP, you can view and select files on another computer and copy them to your computer. If you have sufficient permissions, you can also upload files from your computer to an FTP server. IIS has an FTP server, as well as an HTTP server.

Just like the IIS HTTP server has a Default Web Site, the FTP server has a Default FTP Site. The site should be listed just above the Default Web Site entry in the MMC. You can create new FTP sites and virtual directories using the same steps you use to create new HTTP sites and directories (see Figure 2.36).

FIGURE 2.36:

Default FTP Site Properties
dialog box

Adding FTP Content

To add content to an FTP site, copy the files to the physical directory. The new files appear in FTP directory listings.

FTP Site Properties

IIS Default FTP Site and virtual directory properties are similar to the HTTP properties. There are fewer tabs and they have different titles, but you've seen enough of the contents in the preceding discussion of the HTTP dialogs that I'm confident you will have no problems working with them.

I'm not going to explain the dialogs in detail because FTP site operations are outside the scope of an ASP book. ASP uses the HTTP server exclusively, although you can manipulate the metabase from ASP to create new FTP sites or alter the properties of existing sites.

The IIS Administration Site

Managing IIS from a Browser

IIS provides local browser-based administration. If you don't want to open the MMC, you can use a browser to manage IIS. To reach the IIS administration site, open a browser on the server and navigate to `http://localhost/IISADMIN/`. You must log on as an administrator on the server to use IIS browser-based administration.

Other than the fact that the screens and dialogs look different in the browser than in the MMC, there's little difference in functionality between MMC-based IIS administration and browser-based IIS administration.

IIS Browser-Based Management Limitations

You can use the MMC to manage IIS on remote computers if you have administrator rights on the remote computer. You cannot use a browser to administer IIS on remote computers, except through a Secure Sockets Layer (SSL) connection. You cannot use remote browser-based administration at all unless you alter the default IP connection settings for the IISADMIN virtual directory.

In this chapter, you've seen how to create a virtual directory and set its properties. In the next chapter, you'll see how HTML acts as a world standard layout engine, and makes it extremely easy to deliver text and graphic content to people anywhere in the world.

CHAPTER

THREE

ASP Requirements

- ■ The Need for ASP

- ■ Scripting Capabilities

- ■ Recognizing Individuals

- ■ Database Access

- ■ State Maintenance

- ■ ASP Extensibility

This chapter contains the overall plan for the remainder of this book. Using ASP requires that you become familiar with several different technologies. In Chapter 2, *Introduction to IIS*, you saw that you needed to learn a considerable amount about Web server administration so you can create, control, and transfer your ASP applications. In this chapter, you'll see how ASP clusters several other technologies together to create a complete environment for creating and delivering Web-based applications.

The Need for ASP

In the beginning, there was HTML. HTML admirably serves the purpose of displaying information—as long as you aren't too picky about exactly how that information looks, where content appears on the screen, don't need to update the content too often, and don't need users to interact with that data. In other words, there are several aspects of information display that HTML doesn't serve well, or at all.

Nonetheless, there's a tremendous advantage in being able to use browsers and HTML as a common file format and in being able to use TCP/IP and the Web as common networking standards. Individuals and businesses both benefit from increased access to information regardless of its location, common navigational mechanisms, and reduced costs. HTML plays an important role in information display.

ASP is an attempt to merge the advantages of HTML with the need to provide up-to-date, individualized information, and to make users active participants in the Web rather than passive viewers. ASP takes the Web, which is a relatively passive medium, like TV, and provides the capability to make it an active medium, like other computer applications.

At the same time, ASP gives developers a way to deliver such applications in a centralized manner. Rather than installing a program on each user's machine, ASP lets people run programs on a remote server. Because the code resides in a single place, the application developers can update the program for all users very easily.

Browsers can all render HTML, but they don't all render HTML equally. The result is that HTML developers often need to create several versions of pages—essentially parallel Web sites—to account for the differences in the way browsers interpret HTML. Because HTML is a static language, even small differences between browsers may require developers to create and maintain several versions of a page.

HTML is a simple layout language, one which is easily changed, but one which doesn't lend itself well to content that changes often. Displaying a list of links to articles presents different challenges than displaying a list of current stock prices, and both are different than providing transactional forms for e-commerce purposes.

As businesses began to take advantage of the Web, the need for a way to display rapidly changing content grew exponentially, and is still growing and changing from month to month.

Finally, there's a huge difference between providing content to users and obtaining information from users. HTML lets users send data to the server using forms. Programmers wrote special programs, called CGI programs, to process the data from those forms, but CGI programs were inefficient, and difficult to write, debug, and maintain. There was a need for an easy-to-use method of processing form data.

ASP addresses all of these concerns, and that's one of the reasons why the topic is so large. HTML authors can use ASP as a decision-maker. Rather than having to write and maintain several complete versions of pages for different browsers, they can keep the content in a single file and change only those parts of the output that are browser-dependent. ASP even helps them know which type of browser a person is using, through the Browser Capabilities component.

Content that changes rapidly often resides in databases. Through ActiveX Data Objects (ADO) ASP can connect to databases and format database data into HTML. This gives businesses the best of both worlds—they can take advantage of the Web and HTML to deliver rapidly changing content anywhere in the world. This ability is forcing fundamental changes in the way people think about work, travel, shopping, and communications.

Finally ASP, unlike many other computer technologies, provides solutions to many different problems; therefore, it attracts people with widely varying skills. Advertising and marketing personnel see ASP as a way to increase interest in products, because it can activate sites to make them more exciting. HTML developers see ASP as a way to better deliver content to disparate browsers. Database developers see ASP as a way to deliver data to a common platform, reducing the development time for creating reports and forms. Systems personnel see ASP as a way to centralize applications and reduce the number of support and maintenance calls.

Because of the differing goals and backgrounds of the people attracted to ASP, any book that purports to teach ASP must take into account the differing skills that people bring to the table. Therefore, in this book, because it's called *Mastering ASP*, I've chosen to include information about all aspects of ASP, from HTML, to scripting, to database access, to creating and extending ASP via custom ActiveX components.

If you already know some of this material, you may be able to skip through those sections. For example, HTML authors may skip the introduction to HTML. VB programmers may be able to skip the VBScript chapter. Be tolerant if you are already an expert at one or more of these technologies because it's highly likely that others aren't.

Scripting Capabilities

ASP is a response to a need to display and process rapidly changing and personalized information. It uses HTML as its display mechanism primarily because a large number of people already have a browser that can render HTML efficiently. The concept of a central server processing data for display by remote computers is not new, but ASP's role in providing these services for Web servers and Web browsers is relatively new. As a server-side technology, ASP addresses the area of information display by replacing static files with decision-making capabilities.

For example, if you want to display one type of information for clients using Netscape browsers, and a different type for clients using IE, you may either maintain two separate files or deliver the content dynamically. To make such decisions in ASP, you use server-side script, which is code that runs on the server. A pseudo-code version of the decision looks like this:

```
' show animated text
IF browser type is IE
THEN use dynamic HTML to animate text
ELSE use an animated graphic file
```

Why are decisions such as this important? Why not use the animated GIF file (the lowest common denominator) for clients using both types of browsers? The answer is that downloading an animated graphic file takes more time than providing the same type of experience using dynamic HTML. In addition, animated graphics are much less flexible. For example, changing the text displayed during an animation requires re-creating the entire animation file. It's much easier and faster to change the text in code than to re-create an entire animation.

If the only advantage scripting conferred were the ability to minimize the differences between browsers, a technology like ASP would be just useful, not imperative; but an even more important consideration is that people want information tailored to their needs. People want Web sites to remember their preferences, show them pertinent information, provide easy ways to navigate, be attractive and dynamic; in short, they want personalized applications. ASP provides personalization by letting you tailor content to individuals rather than the public at large.

To do that, ASP must provide a way for the server to recognize an individual, differentiate that individual from all others accessing the server, and respond with content specifically designed for that individual. In this, ASP comes close. It lets you recognize an individual browser, but not an individual user; in other words, if people share computers you can only recognize an individual by securing your site and requiring users to enter an ID and password. So that you can recognize and supply individualized content, ASP has several built-in objects that let you:

- Obtain information from a browser (the Request object)

- Respond to that specific browser (the Response object)
- Associate a specific request with a specific browser (the Session object)
- Store and retrieve information global to an application (the Application object)
- Obtain information about the hosting server (the Server object)
- Integrate ASP with other objects (the ObjectContext object)
- Manage errors and error-reporting (the ASPError object)

These objects are called the ASP intrinsic objects because they're built in. By themselves, however, the intrinsic objects are only one part of the power of ASP. To use them effectively, you need to be able to make decisions, repeat actions, and store information—and to do that, you need a programming language.

One of the best decisions Microsoft made with ASP was to separate the intrinsic ASP objects from any specific scripting language. Instead, ASP contains a scripting host, which means you can use any scripting language. Another good decision was to make VBScript, a subset of the most popular programming language in history, ASP's default language. This decision leveraged the enormous investment that Microsoft and its customers have made in both Visual Basic (VB) and its Office cousin, Visual Basic for Applications (VBA), ensuring that anyone who could write code for Word, Excel, or Access, as well as the entire VB programming community, would be able to use ASP very quickly.

The intrinsic ASP objects coupled with the power of scripting languages is a powerful tool, but is still missing several requirements—specifically, personalization capabilities, database access, and state maintenance. In the next sections, I'll show you how Microsoft extended ASP to provide those capabilities.

Recognizing Individuals

Web servers typically provide content to any browser that requests it, without knowing who the person requesting the content is; in other words, most Web requests occur anonymously. If you want to provide personalized content, you must have a way to differentiate one browser from another.

ASP accomplishes this through the Session object and a concept called cookies. I'll discuss cookies in-depth later, but in essence, a cookie is an item of information that the Web server instructs the browser to store. The browser then sends the cookie back to the Web server with each subsequent request to the same server.

For each request, ASP creates a Session object. The Session object checks to see if the request contains a specific cookie called the ASPSessionID cookie. If the request contains the cookie, ASP tries to match that cookie with a Session object from an earlier request; if not, ASP creates a unique `ASPSessionID` and instructs the browser to save it as a cookie and send it with each subsequent request.

Using the `ASPSessionID` cookie as a unique key, ASP can associate any number of additional items of information with that particular browser. Note that this personalization scheme doesn't require that the server know any more about the person requesting the information than any other anonymous request—ASP doesn't know how many times that particular browser has visited the site, who the user is, or any other information about that user other than the default information sent by the browser with every Web request. In other words, ASP doesn't intrude on people's privacy any more than any other site that requires cookies.

You, as the application developer, can impose additional restrictions such as login/password requirements to help identify individuals and provide personalization services. The `ASPSessionID` is the underlying method that makes personalization work.

Again, just as with HTML, ASP capitalizes on the cookie capabilities that browsers already have. Almost all browsers can accept cookies. The only thing ASP does is to guarantee that the cookie it sends each browser is unique, ensuring that it can later associate that cookie with additional information.

Database Access

As I mentioned, HTML has no facilities for displaying rapidly changing information. One of the most common ways to store such information is in databases, and ASP provides an excellent method for connecting to databases and retrieving or updating their information. That method is known as ActiveX Data Objects (ADO). ADO is a high-level method for accessing information in a wide range of data stores, from corporate-level SQL databases such as SQL Server or Oracle, to workgroup and personal databases such as Microsoft Access and Excel. ADO works through a provider, which is a driver that translates the high-level ADO commands to the lower-level commands that each database or program understands.

The advantage of this method is that, as a developer, you only need to learn a single set of data access commands; as long as the data store you want to use has an ADO provider, you access all data storage devices in almost exactly the same way.

Rather than individual data items, databases tend to work on entire sets of data records. Each record may contain multiple items of information, called fields. It's best to think of the data in terms of a table or grid, where the rows are the records and the columns are the fields. For example, a spreadsheet is a grid. The rows are numbered and the columns are lettered. For example:

	A	B
1	100	200
2	300	400

You can identify any value in the grid by combining the row number and the column letter. In the preceding grid, for example, 1A specifies the value 100, while 2B specifies the value 400.

ADO works through queries and commands. A query requests information from the database, while a command instructs the database to carry out a specific action, such as updating a row (record) or column (field). The result of a query is a list of one or more records, called a record set.

As you can imagine, when you combine decision-making capability (scripting) with HTML and database access, displaying record set information becomes a fairly simple process of formatting the record set data into an HTML table, or combining the values with other HTML markup to create lists, personalized messages, shopping carts—the possibilities are endless.

Between HTML, scripting, personalization, and database access, you now have almost all of the requirements for creating powerful centralized applications. There's only one thing missing—the ability to remember where a person is in your application and what that person is doing. Remembering that information is called state maintenance, because you are keeping track (maintaining) the person's current state within your application.

State Maintenance

State maintenance is the process of keeping track of a user's progress through your site or application. ASP uses the ASPSessionID cookie to map individual browsers to data associated with an individual session. In addition to keeping track of which browser is requesting a page, ASP can associate other information with that browser. To appreciate this, you have to realize that Web servers don't normally save any information between requests—each request is treated as a brand new request. However, now that ASP extends the Web server to differentiate between the same page request by one browser and another browser, you'll find that you quickly want the Web server to remember what a person has already requested.

For example, if you create a page that asks users to enter their name, those users have a right to expect that you will remember that name in future pages, at minimum for the entire session. You can store the name in a Session object variable. Now you can retrieve the name on any subsequent page request and feel confident that you won't accidentally display the wrong name to the wrong user.

Saving personal information isn't the only type of state maintenance. Consider an auction site. You want to display the latest bid for every item currently at auction. That information changes constantly, as people submit, change, or retract bids. As a user, if you make a bid, you most certainly want the view of that item to change, not only for you, but also for everyone looking at the site. In other words, the auction site needs to maintain state on every item in the auction. In this example, the auction site designers probably maintain state in a database and use ADO to retrieve the latest bid information for each item. But they might easily choose to store the items themselves, which change less often than the bids, in the Application object.

The Application object can store information like the Session object. When you store data in the Session object, the data is available only to that session. In contrast, data stored in the Application object is available to any page in the application; in other words, the information is global to the application.

The combination of the Request object, which contains information sent by the browser; the Response object, which lets you send data back to the browser; the Application object; the Session object; and access to databases, almost completes the requirements for a system able to provide personalized pages even when the information to be displayed changes rapidly. The only remaining requirements for ASP to be the equal of a local executable application are access to other components and the host computer's file system. As you probably expect by now, ASP provides those capabilities as well.

ASP Extensibility

The Server object gives your ASP application access to the power of the host computer. Using the methods and properties of the Server object, your application can create and access external COM components. Used in conjunction with the ASP ObjectContext object, you can give these external components the ability to use other ASP objects (like the Session, Application, Server, Request, and Response objects) in the same way you use them from ASP script. That means you can extend ASP to accomplish any task you can perform with a standard executable.

Because you can extend ASP through external components, Microsoft provides a set of components with ASP that extends its capabilities. The Microsoft Scripting

Runtime provides access to the file system; the Browser Capabilities component provides a method to differentiate between browsers; ADO provides access to databases—and the list goes on. In addition, there are numerous third-party, commercial, shareware, and freeware components that extend ASP so you can send email, manage online chat and discussions, read and analyze the Web server logs, and perform many other tasks. In short, ASP provides all of the tools to create centralized multiuser applications.

ASP code executes on the server, which is why you can use ASP to deliver content to a wide variety of browsers—even those running on non-Windows platforms. You don't have to limit your applications to server-side script, you can extend your applications' capabilities with client-side script as well. Note that using client-side capabilities isn't strictly an extension of ASP, but you can design your applications so the client-side code runs in concert with your server-side code, effectively extending the capabilities of your application. You can even use ASP code to write client-side code. That's exciting, using code to write other code!

Most browsers can run Java applets and JavaScript; some can also use ActiveX controls (COM objects) and VBScript. You can take advantage of these browser capabilities to provide an interactive experience for your users that's much different than browsing static Web pages.

To sum up: ASP is a collection of technologies that includes HTML, the ASP intrinsic objects, scripting languages, file access, database access, and control of external COM components. The remainder of this book explores this collection of technologies in detail.

CHAPTER
FOUR

HTML Basics

This chapter contains a brief tour to teach you the basics of HyperText Markup Language (HTML) structure and editing. If you already know HTML, you can probably skip this chapter and move directly to Chapter 5, *The Response Object*. If you're not already comfortable with HTML, read this chapter and practice creating HTML files using the included files as a starting point. You will need to feel comfortable with HTML before you begin scripting. HTML is a simple idea that, like many simple ideas, you can leverage, combine, and extend to build very complex structures.

What Is HTML?

HTML is a layout language. It contains commands that, like a word processor, tell the computer—in a very loose sense—what the content of the document is. For example, using HTML you can tell the computer that the document contains a paragraph, a bulleted list, a table, or an image. The HTML rendering engine is responsible for actually displaying the text and images on the screen. The difference between HTML and word processors is that word processors work with proprietary formats. Because they're proprietary, one word processor can't directly read another word processor's file format—they usually need a special program, called an import/export filter, to translate one file format to another.

In contrast, HTML is an open, worldwide standard. If you create a file using the commands available in version 3.2 or earlier, it will display on almost any browser running on almost any computer with any operating system—anywhere in the world.

HTML is a small subset of a much more full-featured markup language called Standard Generalized Markup Language (SGML). SGML has been under development for about 15 years and contains a great many desirable features that HTML lacks, but it is also very complex to implement. That complexity makes it both difficult to create and difficult to display properly.

HTML was developed as a small subset of SGML to provide a lightweight standard for displaying text and images over a slow dial-up connection—the World Wide Web, best known as the Web. Originally, HTML had very few features—it has grown considerably in the past few years. Nevertheless, you can learn the core command set for HTML in just a few hours.

HTML contains only two kinds of information—*markup*, which consists of all the text contained between angle brackets (<>), and *content*, which is all the text *not* contained between angle brackets. The difference is that the browser doesn't display markup; instead, markup contains the information that tells the browser

how to display the content. For example, the HTML `<html><head><title>`
`</title><body></body></head></html>` is a perfectly valid HTML file. You can
save that set of commands as a file, navigate to it in your browser, and display the
file without errors—but you won't see anything, because the file doesn't contain
any content. All the text in the file is markup.

In contrast, a file with this content: `This is a file with no markup` contains
no markup. Although most browsers will display the contents of a file with no
markup, it is not a valid HTML file.

The individual parts of the markup between the brackets are tags, sometimes
called commands. There are two types of tags—start tags and end tags, and they
appear in pairs (although they may be widely separated in the file). The single
difference is that the end tag begins with a forward slash; e.g., `</html>`.

What Does HTML Do?

HTML lets you create structured documents. The heading commands separate
and categorize sections of your documents. HTML also has rudimentary commands to format and display text, display images, accept input from users, and
send information to a server for back-end processing. In addition, it lets you create special areas of text or images that, when clicked, jump, or *hyperlink* from one
HTML file to another, thus creating an interlinked series of pages.

The series of pages you create via hyperlinks is a program; however, it isn't a
program like the ones you'll learn to create in this book because a series of pages
has no intelligence and makes no decisions. All the functionality resides in the tag
set selected by the HTML author (note that people who write HTML are called
authors, not programmers). A series of pages linked in this manner is called a site,
or Web site.

Despite the lack of decision-making capability, a Web site serves two extremely
useful purposes:

1. It provides a way for non-programmers to create attractive sites full of useful
information. (Of course, it also provides a way for people to create unattrac-
tive sites full of useless information, but I won't pursue that.)

2. In conjunction with the Internet, it makes that information globally available.

Why HTML Is Important

Until HTML, it wasn't so easy to create screens full of information that anyone
could read. First, there was no easy way to display anything without either writing a program or using a presentation program like PowerPoint. The problem

with using a particular program was that the output was only available to people using the same operating system and the same program—usually only to those with the same version of the program.

HTML is important because it provided millions of people with access to information online that they could not or would not have seen any other way. HTML is the first easy method for non-programmers to display text and images on-screen without limiting the audience to those who own or have access to the same program (or a viewer) that the author used to create the content. In a sense, browsers are universal content viewers and HTML is the universal file format. In fact, HTML and plain text are the only universal file formats, although I have high hopes for XML.

The Limitations of HTML

Despite its popularity, availability, and the fact that it is a universal file format, HTML has some serious limitations as a way to create structured documents, as a layout language, and as a file format. First, plain HTML has no way to specify the exact position of content on a page, either horizontally, vertically, or along the z-axis, which controls the layers in which objects appear. Second, HTML, as I've said already, is not a programming language; it has no decision-making capabilities. Third, HTML is a fixed language. This is both good and bad. It's good because most browsers can display most HTML. But it's also bad because the limited command set encourages—no, forces—companies to build proprietary extensions to perform more advanced functions.

Many of the useful concepts available in HTML today, such as forms, tables, script, frames, and Cascading Style Sheets (CSS) began as proprietary extensions, but were later adopted and standardized by the World Wide Web Consortium (W3C). They have now become part of the HTML command set.

Syntax—Tags and Attributes

A valid HTML file has only a few requirements. Look at the following example:

```
<html>
<head>
<title>Hello World</title>
</head>
<body>Hello World
</body>
</html>
```

The example contains both tags and content. A tag is text enclosed in angle brackets (<>). If you look at the file in a browser, you'll see that it looks similar to Figure 4.1.

FIGURE 4.1:

Hello World file
(`HelloWorld.htm`)

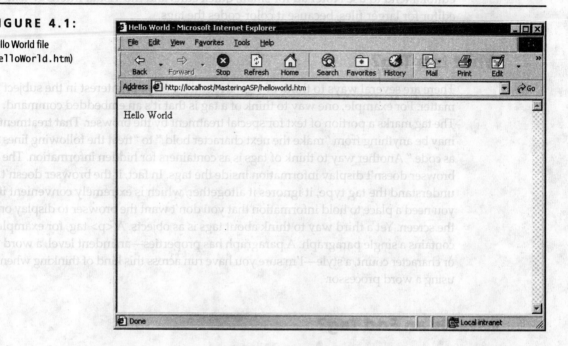

The `HelloWorld.htm` file is a short, but complete, HTML file. All HTML files begin with an `<html>` tag and end with a `</html>` tag (read end html or close html). Between those two tags there are other tags as well as content, so `<html>` tags can contain other tags. Tags that contain other tags are called, appropriately enough, containing tags, or in Microsoft's documentation, block elements. I'll use the term block elements in this book to mean a tag that can contain other tags. Note that the `<head>` ...`</head>` tag is also a block element; among other things, it can contain the `<title>` ...`</title>` tag.

HTML tags have two parts—a start tag and an end tag. Although not all browsers require you to write the end tag in all cases, you should immediately get into the habit of doing so. As you move into XML (and you probably will want to move into XML at some point) the end tags are required in all cases.

NOTE

At this point, I'm going to stop writing both the start and end tags in the text every time I refer to a tag. For example, rather than writing `<head></head>` every time I need to refer to that tag, I'll just write `<head>`. You can infer that the end-head tag is present.

HTML files are text files. They contain only two kinds of content—commands, also called tags or markup, and content. You can edit an HTML file with any text editor. I tend to use NotePad for small, quick edits and the Visual InterDev text editor for larger files, because it color-codes the tags.

What Is a Tag?

There are several ways to think of tags, depending on your interest in the subject matter. For example, one way to think of a tag is that it's an embedded command. The tag marks a portion of text for special treatment by the browser. That treatment may be anything from "make the next character bold," to "treat the following lines as code." Another way to think of tags is as containers for hidden information. The browser doesn't display information inside the tags. In fact, if the browser doesn't understand the tag type, it ignores it altogether, which is extremely convenient if you need a place to hold information that you don't want the browser to display on the screen. Yet a third way to think about tags is as objects. A <p> tag, for example, contains a single paragraph. A paragraph has properties—an indent level, a word or character count, a style—I'm sure you have run across this kind of thinking when using a word processor.

What Is an End Tag?

The end tag is there to mark the end of the portion of the document influenced by the start tag. Computers aren't very smart—once you turn on bold text, it's on until you explicitly turn it off. Just a warning—most browsers will allow you to skip some of the most common end tags, but take my advice and don't skip them. In the future, you're likely to want to convert some of those documents to XML—and in XML, end tags are required.

Why Does HTML Look Like <this>?

The bracketed commands used in HTML have a long history. HTML inherited its syntax from SGML, but that's not the only use for bracketed commands. I first saw them in XyWrite, a word processor that was most popular with journalists precisely because it used HTML-like embedded commands. The reason it was so popular is bound up in bits and bytes, but it's an interesting story, so bear with me.

Each character you type on a computer is associated with a specific number. There are several different sets of these numbers for different computer systems, but the most common—even today, is called American Standard Code for Information Interchange (ASCII). For example, the ASCII value of an uppercase A is 64, a space is 3?, and a zero is 48. The computer doesn't represent numbers as you do—

it performs binary arithmetic. For historical reasons, most modern microcomputers work with bits in multiples of 8. Each set of 8 bits is called a byte—and a byte can hold 256 unique values—enough for the alphabet, the numbers and punctuation, some control characters, some accented characters, and a few lines suitable for drawing simple images.

All the standard characters have a value below 128. Most file types, including word processors of that time, used the upper range of characters as embedded commands. For example, a file format might use 157 as a marker for the beginning of a paragraph and 158 as the marker for the end of the paragraph. The reason they did this is because it made the files much smaller if they could limit the commands to one or two characters. You have to remember that at that time, memory was expensive and in limited supply. In contrast, the smallest possible XyWrite command was three characters long—many people thought that was a waste of space.

Back to the story…. Reporters were among the first people to use electronic computer communications to send files over the telephone system. Early versions of communications programs could use only seven of the bits for content—the last bit was a stop bit. As it turned out, they couldn't use programs that needed the upper range of characters because they would lose the formatting if they transmitted the file electronically. So XyWrite made its mark by being the first word processor to use bracketed commands.

OK, enough stories. The real reason HTML uses the bracketed commands is much less interesting—the bracketed commands are easy for people to read and write and it's relatively easy for a program to parse—which means to separate into its component parts.

Attribute Syntax

Tags contain one main command, but an unlimited number of associated values, called attributes. Each attribute has a name and a value. You must separate the attribute from the command or any preceding attribute value by white space. White space includes spaces, tabs, and carriage return/line feed characters. The browser ignores this white space (except when it doesn't exist). White space—to a browser, is another form of command typically called a delimiter. A delimiter is any character or sequence of characters that separate one item from another. Using white space as a delimiter is completely natural—that's what people use between words.

Different types of delimiters mean different things. For example, in addition to using white space between words, we also use periods between sentences. In HTML, angle brackets separate tags, white space separates attributes, and an equals sign separates the name of an attribute from its value. Similarly, HTML uses quotes to delimit the value because an attribute value might contain any of the other delimiters: white space, equals signs, or angle brackets.

Here are some examples:

```
<font face="Arial" size=12>
```

The `<font>` tag has two attributes—`face` and `size`, each of which has a value. Not all values are that simple. Consider this tag:

```
<input type="hidden" name="txtPara" value="He was a
codeslinger, lean and nervous, with quick hands that
could type or shoot with equal accuracy.">
```

Once again, not all browsers require the quotes around every attribute value; but to repeat, even though they aren't required, you should school yourself to enter them every time. I can assure you that failing to enter the quotes around attribute values will cause problems for you at some point in your ASP programming career. Here are two versions of an HTML tag, one with and one without quotes:

```
<input type="text" value="This is my value.">
<input type=text value=This is my value>
```

If you load both of these lines into a browser you won't see anything because they're tags, not content. But if you wrap them in a `<form>` tag, they'll show up as text input controls—single-line text boxes for those of you familiar with VB. The first version will contain the text `This is my value.` But the second version will contain only the word `This`. That's because without the quotes, the browser has to fall back on the next delimiter to mark the end of the attribute value. In this case, the next delimiter is a space. The browser then ignores the next three words in the sentence because they aren't recognizable keywords and they aren't properly formed attributes—they don't have an equals sign or a value.

You may use either single- or double-quotes to delimit the attribute value; in other words, both of these are equally valid:

```
<script language='VBScript'>
<script language="VBScript">
```

You can embed quotes in a value in two ways:

1. Switch the outer enclosing quotes to the opposite type; e.g., `value="Mary's socks"`, or `value='The word is "important"'`

2. Enter each inner quote twice; e.g., `'value=Bill''s cat'`

More HTML Syntax

Attribute values have the most involved syntax. The other syntax rules for HTML are straightforward:

- White space is optional. Unless you specifically include tags to force the browser to include the white space, the browser will ignore it. The sentences "Welcome to Active Server Pages!" and "Welcome   to   Active Server   Pages!" both print exactly the same way on-screen when rendered by a browser.

- Case is irrelevant. HTML parsers ignore case, so you can write tags in either uppercase <FONT> or lowercase <font>. Having said that, you should try to be consistent (yes, case is relevant in XML). Choose either uppercase or lowercase for tags and use them consistently.

- The order of tags is important. An enclosing tag must completely enclose any inner tags. For example, <font size=12><b>This is bold</font></b> is an invalid HTML syntax because you must close the <b> bold tag before the <font> tag. The proper way to write the tags is <font size=12><b>This is bold</b></font>.

These simple rules will help you write perfect HTML every time:

- Write the ending tag when you write the beginning tag. For example, don't write <HTML> then expect to remember to type the end </HTML> tag later. Write them both at the same time, then insert the content between the tags.

- Write tags in lowercase—they're easier to type.

- Use templates. Templates are pre-written files into which you place content. Templates save a lot of time because they already contain the required tags.

- Indent enclosed tags. Set the tab or indent levels in your editor to a small value—I find three spaces works well; that's enough to make the indents visible, but not so much that longer lines scroll off the page.

- Use comments liberally. A comment, in HTML, is text enclosed in a tag that begins with a left angle bracket, an exclamation point and two dashes, and ends with two dashes and a right angle bracket: <!--This is a comment-->. Comments help you understand the content and layout of a file. They can also help separate sections visually. Browsers don't render comments, so you can use them whenever you like.

Creating a Simple Page

You should usually start a new file with an HTML template. The most basic HTML template contains only the required tags. You fill in the content as needed. Type the following listing into your HTML editor, then save it as `template.html`.

```
<html>
<head>
<title><!-- Title --></title>
</head>
<body>
<!-- Your content here -->
</body>
</html>
```

You'll use that file a great deal. If you're using a dedicated HTML editor, it probably loaded a similar file as soon as you selected New from the File menu.

Add a title between the title tags. Replace the comment `<!-- Title -->` with the title `HTML Is Easy`. Move past the first `<body>` tag and add your content in place of the comment `<!-- Your content here -->`. The completed file will look similar to Listing 4.1.

LISTING 4.1   HTML Is Easy (ch4i1.htm)

```
<html>
<head>
<title>HTML Is Easy</title>
</head>
<body>
<h1 align="center">HTML Is Easy</h1>
<p>Although HTML has about 100 different tags, you'll
quickly find that you use only a few of them. The most
useful tags are the paragraph tag--the tag that encloses
this paragraph; the <b>bold</b> tag, the <i>italics</i> tag
(most commonly seen in Microsoft products as the <strong>
strong</strong> tag; the heading tags; the
<font face="Courier" size=4>font</font> tags, also used to
produce <font color="red">colored </font><font color="blue">
text</font>; and the most useful of all--the table tags, used
to produce formatted tables, both with and without borders.</p>
<!--<p> </p>-->
<table align="center" border="1" width="50%">
<thead>
  <tr>
      <th align="center">Product</th>
      <th align="center">Price</th>
```

```
        </tr>
        <tr>
            <td align="left">Cap</td>
            <td align="right">$14.50</td>
        </tr>
        <tr>
            <td align="left">Boots</td>
            <td align="right">$49.99</td>
        </tr>
    </table>
    </body>
</html>
```

After you have entered the listing, save it as a file, then view it in your browser. To do that, type file://<drive><path><filename> where drive is the drive letter where you saved the file, path is the directory or hierarchy of directories, and filename is the actual name of the file. In your browser, the page should look similar to Figure 4.2.

FIGURE 4.2:

HTML Is Easy (ch4i1.htm)

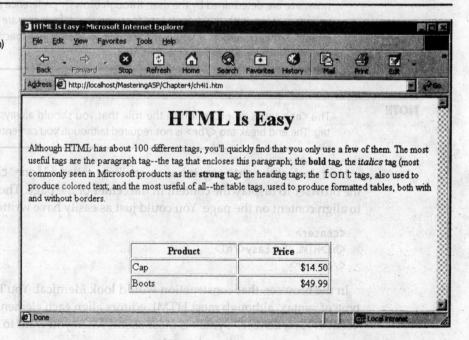

When you view Listing 4.1 in a browser, you will notice several features. The title appears in the title bar of the browser window, not in the body of the document. That's because the title isn't properly part of the document at all—it's part of the header; that's why the <title> tag is inside the <head> tag.

If you entered the text exactly as it's written, you will notice that the line breaks in the listing and the line breaks in the browser are different. Each line you entered (although you can't see it) ends with two characters, called a return and a line feed (ASCII characters 13 and 10). The browser treats these as white space and ignores them. If you aren't willing to let the browser break lines for you, you'll need to explicitly break the lines yourself, using a <br> break tag.

Another interesting feature is that the line breaks are relative to the area of the screen into which the browser renders content, called the client area of the window. Resize your browser window and watch what happens to the text. As you change the width of the browser window, the browser re-renders the text, changing the line breaks so the text still fits inside the window—the text listing just gets longer.

> **NOTE**
>
> In what font did your browser render the paragraph text—a serif font like Times New Roman, or a sans serif font like Arial? What's the point size? As an HTML page designer, you should bear in mind that the default font face and the default point size are determined by the user, through browser preference settings, not by your document. Both the default font face and the default size are user-selectable in both Netscape and IE. If you want the text to appear in a specific face or size, you must include the appropriate font tags.

> **NOTE**
>
> The <br> tag is an exception to the rule that you should always enter the end tag. The end break tag </br> is not required (although you can enter it if you like).

Next, look at the <h1> tag. It has an attribute called `align="center"` that forces the browser to display the content in the center of the page. There's another way to align content on the page. You could just as easily have written this:

```
<center>
<h1>HTML Is Easy</h1>
</center>
```

In the browser, that construction would look identical. You'll still see that type of syntax, although most HTML editors align each element separately. The `<center>...</center>` syntax is most useful when you want to force the alignment of many consecutive elements.

The <p> paragraph tag encloses the entire paragraph. You could change the paragraph alignment by adding an alignment tag. Try that. Add an `align="right"` attribute to the <p> tag, then refresh the browser page.

TIP

You should refresh the browser after making any changes to an HTML file. I've seen numerous instances where people complain that their code changes aren't displaying properly, when the real problem is that they forgot to refresh the browser. Refreshing the browser forces it to re-parse and re-display the page, thus incorporating any changes you've made since the last time the browser displayed the page.

Note that the <b> bold tag and the <strong> tag do exactly the same thing—they both produce bold text. The difference is that the <b> tag explicitly makes text bold, while the actual displayed result of a <strong> tag is not specified by HTML—that's up to the creators of the rendering engine. In practice, all the popular rendering engines make the text bold.

You'll find a similar situation exists with the <i> tag. An <i> tag explicitly means italicize the text, but many HTML editors use the <em> emphasis tag instead. Again, the displayed result of an <em> tag isn't specified by HTML—the rendering engine is free to emphasize the text in any fitting manner. In practice, all the popular rendering engines italicize the text.

You can use color names (e.g., red or blue) and most modern browsers will display the text in the intended color. Both IE and Netscape understand color names (although they understand different sets of color names). I'll show you a browser-independent way to specify colors in the *Fonts and Colors* section in this chapter.

You can change the font using the <font> tag. Note that the command that changes the font is the face attribute. Most people misuse the word font when they actually mean font face. Also, the size attribute—specified as 5 in Listing 4.1, doesn't mean the point size, as is typical with word processors, it means the relative size of the text compared to the default size selected by the user. The standard text size is 3, so the word font shows up in a larger point size than the surrounding text.

At the end of the paragraph, there's a second, very short paragraph that contains only a single line: . That stands for non-breaking space. The starting ampersand and the ending semicolon are required. There are a number of these commands, one for each non-alphanumeric character. You can use them to insert characters that the browser won't normally print, such as the left angle bracket (<) and right angle bracket (&gt), which stand for less than and greater than, respectively. The non-breaking space forces the browser to render the paragraph. Browsers ignore empty paragraph tags because they contain no content. A normal space won't work because it's white space, which browsers also ignore. The non-breaking space is an invisible character.

The <table> tag contains three attributes, an align="center" attribute, which forces the browser to align the table in the center of the screen; a border="1" attribute, which causes the browser to place a visible, one-pixel wide border around each table cell; and a `width=50%` attribute, which causes the browser to render the table in half of the available horizontal screen space (if possible). Again, resize your browser. Notice that the table width changes as the width of the window changes. Make the browser window so narrow that the table won't fit. You may need to scroll down to view the table as the browser window gets narrower. What happens? At some point, the table will no longer fit in half of the screen space. At that point, the browser gives up and simply renders the table in the center of whatever space is available. When that space becomes too small, the browser begins to clip the right edge of the table.

The table itself contains two separate sections: a `<thead>` section containing `<th>` tags comprises the head section of the table. `thead` stands for table head. The `<th>` tags contain the column headers. You don't have to have a `<thead>` section, but if you use one in combination with the `<th>` tags, the browser automatically makes the column headers bold. The `<tbody>` section of the table contains the data. The `<tr>` table row tags delimit the rows, while the `<td>` table data tags delimit the individual cells in each column. The closing tags are required for all table-related tags, except the `<th>` column header tags, for which closing tags are optional.

Now that you've seen a complete HTML file, I'm going to spend a short amount of time explaining the use of each common HTML element more completely.

Formatting Text

HTML makes formatting text extremely easy—as long as you aren't too picky about how that text looks, where the lines break, or exactly where the text is relative to other elements of the page. You control the appearance of text by the use of heading styles, fonts and colors, paragraphs, and lists.

List Styles

You've already seen how to use font and paragraph tags. HTML also contains tags to format bulleted and numbered lists. A bulleted list is an unordered list, one where the physical order of the items is unimportant. Therefore, in HTML, use a `<ul>` unordered list tag to create a bulleted list. You place a `<li>` list item tag around each item in the list:

```
<ul>Things To Do
    <li>Go to the grocery store</li>
    <li>Pick up the dog from the vet</li>
    <li>Shop for a new computer</li>
</ul>
```

You create a numbered list when the order of the items in the list is significant. In HTML, use a `<ol>` ordered list tag. You still use `<li>` tags for the list items, just as in an unordered list:

```
<ol><b>Things to do--in order</b>
    <li>Go to the grocery store</li>
    <li>Pick up the dog from the vet</li>
    <li>Shop for a new computer</li>
</ol>
```

Figure 4.3 shows how these two list types appear in the browser, with headings to help you differentiate the two types.

FIGURE 4.3:

List styles (ch4i2.htm)

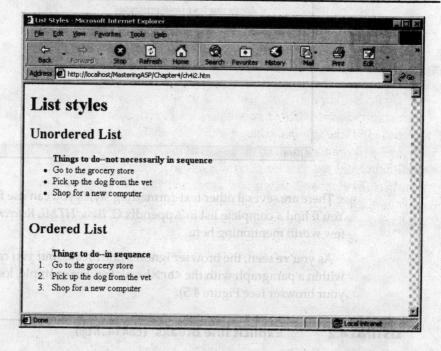

You can nest lists one inside another. The browser indents subordinate lists one level beyond the containing list tag indent level (see Figure 4.4).

```
<ol><b>Things to do--in order</b>
    <li>Go to the grocery store</li>
    <li>Pick up the dog from the vet</li>
    <ul><b>Remember these items</b>
        <li>Buy a new dog-tag</li>
        <li>Ask for new flea powder prescription</li>
    </ul>
    <li>Shop for a new computer</li>
</ol>
```

FIGURE 4.4:

Nested lists (ch4i3.htm)

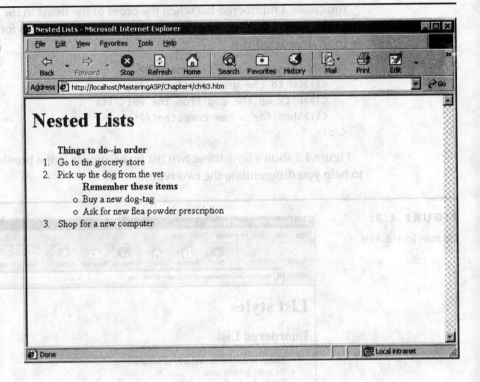

There are several other text-formatting styles you can use for special purposes. You'll find a complete list in Appendix C, *Basic HTML Reference*. But there are a few worth mentioning here.

As you've seen, the browser ignores line breaks, but you can force a line break within a paragraph with the <br> break tag. For example, look at Listing 4.2 in your browser (see Figure 4.5).

LISTING 4.2   **Explicit line breaks** (ch4i4.htm)

```
<html>
<head>
<title>Explicit Line Breaks</title>
</head>
<body>
<h1>Explicit Line Breaks</h1>
<p>This paragraph doesn't contain any line breaks.
The browser inserts the line breaks when it renders the
file on-screen. The browser will readjust the line breaks
if you resize the browser window.</p>
<p>This paragraph <i>does</i> contain line breaks.<br>
The browser breaks the lines at the &lt;br&gt; tags.<br>
```

```
when it renders the file on-screen.
The browser will <i>not</i> readjust the line breaks<br>
if you resize the browser window.</p>
</body>
</html>
</body>
</html>
```

FIGURE 4.5:

Explicit line breaks
(ch4i4.htm)

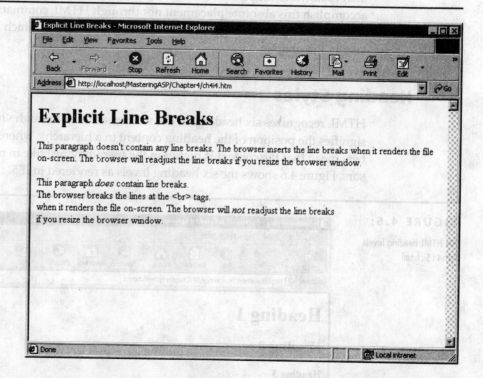

The first paragraph doesn't contain any line breaks. The second paragraph contains a line break at the end of each line. The first paragraph resizes if you shrink the browser window. The second paragraph resizes the lines as well, but always keeps the explicit line breaks intact.

I'll end this formatting section with two short notes. First, many excellent HTML editors perform a great deal of the tedious, low-level formatting for you, and I've seen many sites which use their advanced formatting features to great effect. However, until you're completely comfortable with basic HTML, my advice is that you avoid these advanced editors. The problem is that they do so much for you. The idea in this book is for you to understand HTML and ASP to the point where you are comfortable writing them with nothing more than a simple text editor. Therefore, I advise you to use a simple text editor until you're absolutely sure you can edit any HTML that the advanced editors may insert.

Second, it's tempting to try to defeat the browser's default rendering of text, but you should avoid that temptation until you have mastered the default renderings. I can assure you that you can create very attractive and functional pages with nothing more than the default HTML commands. Again, the more advanced HTML editors may actually inhibit your learning. You can specify the placement of text and images down to the pixel level in these editors. You need to keep in mind that they accomplish this absolute placement not through HTML commands, but instead with Cascading Style Sheets or embedded styles—both of which I'll cover briefly later in this chapter.

Heading Styles

HTML recognizes six heading levels, written as <h1> through <h6>. The number signifies the position of the heading content in a hierarchy, where the smaller numbers mean that the content is higher in the hierarchy, just like in most word processors. Figure 4.6 shows the six heading levels as rendered in IE5.

FIGURE 4.6:

Six HTML heading levels
(ch4i5.htm)

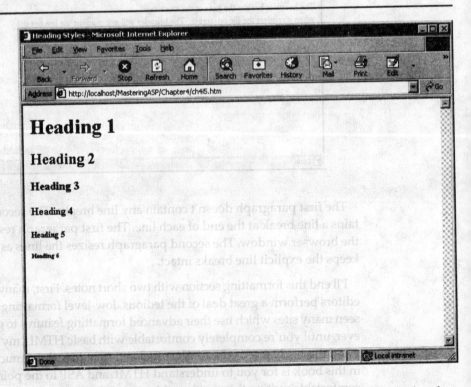

Again, the formatting of the displayed heading is browser-specific. The heading levels will not appear identical in different browsers.

HTML is supposed to be a way of creating structured documents. You organize the document by heading levels, like an outline. The top level <h1> might be the document title. Essentially, all other portions of the document would be subordinate to the <h1> level. You would then apply the <h2> style to each major subordinate level, and <h3> to each subheading inside the <h2> level. For example, this chapter structured in HTML would look like this:

```
<h1>Chapter 4: HTML Basics</h1>
    <h2>HTML is just Markup and Content</h2>
        <h3>What HTML Does</h3>
        <h3>Why HTML Is Important</h3>
        <h3>HTML's Limitations</h3>
    <h2>Syntax--Tags and Attributes</h2>
        <h3>What Is a Tag?</h3>
        <h3>What Is an End Tag?</h3>
        etc...
```

Note that this is a relatively weak scheme for creating structured documents because the heading levels aren't block elements—there's no way in HTML to specify that the content for the subordinate tags belongs to the previous, higher-level tag. That means that you can't, for example, select an <h2> tag and get all the <h3> tags and text associated with that <h2> tag. Instead, the association scheme is by position. The internal HTML parser rule is that all text following a heading level belongs to that heading level until it reaches the next heading level. Also note that the browser doesn't format the content following a given heading level any differently than the text for a higher level. The only visual clue to the heading level is the format for the header itself; the renderer doesn't provide a visual clue, like indentation, to help you differentiate content in the various levels.

Fonts and Colors

You've already seen a brief example of how to use the <font> tag. In this section you'll explore it in more depth. Font tags by themselves are useless; they need one or more attributes to accomplish a change in the visual representation of the text enclosed by the tag (called the tag text). Font tags can take the following attributes:

Face   Changes the tag text font typeface to the specified face. If that face is not available on the client computer, the browser uses the default browser font. You can increase the likelihood that the browser will select a similar font by listing more than one face in the <font> tag. For example, the tag <font face="GreenMonster, Arial, Times New Roman"> specifies that your preferred font faces, in order, are GreenMonster (which, as far as I know, doesn't exist), Arial, and Times New Roman. The browser will first try to use GreenMonster. When that fails, it will use Arial, which should normally work on Windows platforms.

Size   Changes the tag text font size to the specified size. The size is a number. You can append letters to define how the browser should interpret that number. By default, the browser interprets the font size number relative to the default text size (3).

Color   Specifies the color for the tag text. IE and Netscape both understand a set of named colors. Unfortunately, they understand different sets. But all browsers understand a color representation called RGB (Red, Green, Blue). The RGB color values consist of three hex byte values, concatenated together to form a 6-character string. Typically, you append a number sign (#) in front of the string. For example, the color #000000 signifies black. Even though the spaces don't appear, think of the string as if it were written #00 00 00. The first two zeroes are the red component; in this case, no red. The second two zeroes are the green component and the third set of zeroes are the blue component. Since the value of each color component in this example is 0, the value defines the color black. Each component can have 256 values—from 0 to 255. Unfortunately, you have to write them as hexadecimal values, not the more familiar decimals. Refer to *The Hexadecimal System and RGB Color Values* sidebar for more information about how to translate the values from decimal to hexadecimal.

TIP

You don't really need to learn the hexadecimal system to write RGB color values (although it helps). One of the easiest ways to translate between decimal and hex comes with every Windows computer—the Calculator accessory. Click the View menu in the calculator, then click Scientific. The calculator will change its appearance. Click the Dec (decimal) button, then enter a number and click the Hex button to translate from decimal to hex. Conversely, click the Hex button and enter a hex value, then click the Dec button to translate from hex to decimal.

The Hexadecimal System and RGB Color Values

Humans tend to work with decimal (base 10) systems, probably because we have ten fingers. But computers commonly work with several different bases: base 2 (binary), base 8 (octal), and base 16 (hexadecimal). Hexadecimal is usually called hex for short in programming terminology. The reason hex is convenient is that a two-digit hex number can represent all the numbers from 0 to 255, which equates to the number of values one byte (8 bits) of information can hold. Another way to think of a byte is 2^8 power. Remember, each bit can hold only a 0 (zero) or a 1, so a computer's native arithmetic base is base 2.

Continued on next page

Each byte holds two nibbles. A nibble is four bits and can hold 16 unique values—from 0 to 15. Nibbles translate very easily to hexadecimal because each hex number can represent a single nibble. Just like the decimal system has 10 digits, the hex system has 16. The standard digits 0 to 9 represent the first ten values, and we use letters from A to F to represent the remaining six values. Just as in the decimal system where each column is a multiple of ten, the columns in the hex system are multiples of 16. So the number 10 is A and the number 15 is F. After 15, you need to start a 16's column, so the value 16 can be represented as 10—meaning one sixteen and no ones.

Examples:

DECIMAL	HEX	DECIMAL	HEX
0-9	0-9	15	F
10	A	16	10
11	B	32	20
12	C	64	40
13	D	81	51
14	E	255	FF

Each RGB color value is one byte with a decimal value from 0 to 255; thus, you can represent each value with two hex digits, from 00 to FF. To translate between the two systems, use modulo arithmetic. Divide the decimal value you need by 16 to find the value for the first digit and use the remainder for the value of the second digit. For example, the hex representation of 17 is 11 (17 / 16 = 1, with a remainder of 1). The hex representation of 200 is C8 (200 / 16 = 12, with a remainder of 8).

To translate the other direction, simply multiply the leftmost digit by 16 and add the decimal value of the digit in the rightmost column. For example, B9 = ((11 * 16) + 9) = 185.

Paragraph Tags, Div Tags, and Spans

Paragraph <p> tags are block elements that surround paragraph text. They can contain child tags, such as text or image formatting commands. A paragraph tag can contain a table. You can force the browser to render a paragraph aligned left (default), right, or centered by adding an alignment attribute; for example <p align="center">.

Divs, often called layers, are a way to divide your document into separate sections. You can think of a <div> tag as an artificial separation between areas of the document, just like heading levels. The primary difference is that <div> tags are block elements. You can retrieve all the text and HTML associated with a <div> tag by asking the <div> tag for its contents. By default, a <div> tag acts like a paragraph tag and accepts the same attributes. For example, you can right-align the contents of a <div> tag by adding an align="right" attribute to the tag. The W3C added the <div> tag to make up for the weak implementation of heading levels. Divs were originally implemented as <layer> tags in Netscape, where their main purpose was to help control where elements appear along the z-axis.

Spans have no default formatting. Their main purpose is to allow you to add specific formatting or actions, via style sheets or script, to sections of text smaller than a paragraph or a div. You can see the difference in Listing 4.3.

LISTING 4.3   **Div and Span Experiments (ch4i6.htm)**

```
<html>
<head>
<title>Div and Span Experiments</title>
</head>
<body>
<span>This is a span.</span>
<span>So is this.</span>

<p> </p>

<div>
    <span>This is a span.</span>
</div>
<span>So is this.</span>
</body>
</html>
```

The file contains two copies of the sentences This is a span, and So is this. each surrounded by a <span> tag. The only difference is that the first span (the indented line) in the second copy is part of a <div> tag. If you view the code in Listing 4.3 in your browser, it should look similar to Figure 4.7.

You'll see more about <span> and <div> tags when you work with individual elements on the page through the Document Object Model (DOM). In this book, which concentrates on server-side programming, <div> and <span> tags are relatively unimportant. I've included them here because most modern HTML editors, such as FrontPage and DreamWeaver, use <div> and <span> tags extensively to isolate document elements in block tags over which you have z-axis control. You're likely to see a lot of them if you use an HTML editor.

FIGURE 4.7:

Div and Span experiments
(ch4i6.htm)

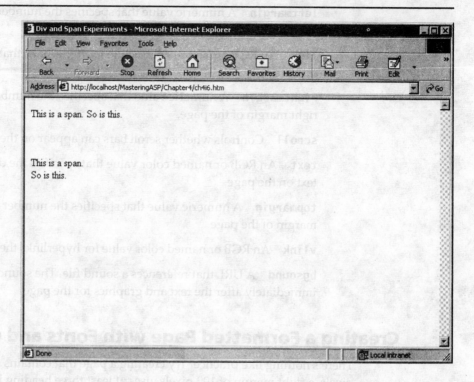

The *<body>* Tag

The <body> tag accepts several attributes that can help improve the overall look
of your pages by giving you control over the page background color and margins,
and even add background images to your pages. To add a background color, use
a bgcolor attribute. For example, the following <body> tag changes the background color of the page to hot pink:

```
<body bgcolor="#FC00B3">
```

Here's a list of <body> tag attributes and their values:

alink   An RGB or named color value for selected hyperlinks. A hyperlink is selected/activated when a user moves the focus or the mouse to
the link.

background   A URL that references an image.

bgcolor   An RGB or named color value that specifies the background
color for the page.

bottommargin   A numeric value that specifies the number of pixels in the
bottom margin of the page.

leftmargin A numeric value that specifies the number of pixels in the left margin of the page.

link An RGB or named color value for hyperlinks that have not been activated.

rightmargin A numeric value that specifies the number of pixels in the right margin of the page.

scroll Controls whether scroll bars can appear on the page.

text An RGB or named color value that specifies the default color for text on the page.

topmargin A numeric value that specifies the number of pixels in the top margin of the page.

vlink An RGB or named color value for hyperlinks the user has visited.

bgsound A URL that references a sound file. The sound file downloads immediately after the text and graphics for the page.

Creating a Formatted Page with Fonts and Colors

There's nothing like practice. Try creating a page that contains a left margin of 100 pixels, a right margin of 100 pixels, uses at least three heading levels, a list, and assorted font color and formatting commands. Listing 4.4 contains a sample document for reference purposes.

LISTING 4.4   Sample Formatted HTML Page (ch4i7.htm)

```
<html>
<head>
<title>Introduction to the DOM</title>
</head>
<body bgcolor="#ffffc0" leftmargin="100"
    rightmargin="100">
<font size=3>
<h1 align="center">Introduction to the Document
Object Model (DOM)</h1>
<h2>Differing Implementations in Netscape and IE

<p><font size=2 face="Verdana">
The World Wide Web Consortium (W3C) released a
specification for treating the various elements that
can appear on an HTML page as <i>objects</i>. The
```

purpose of the DOM is so you can programmatically access the various elements on the page.</font></p>

<p><font size=2 face="Verdana">
Unfortunately, the two most popular browsers have differing implementations of the DOM object model. Microsoft's Internet Explorer (IE) browser has the most complete implementation. Since version 3, both Netscape and IE have exposed form and input elements to scripting languages. Starting with version 4, IE now exposes almost every tag, or element, to programmatic control. To do this, Microsoft added some new attributes to every tag, the most important of which is an ID that uniquely identifies that element on the page. In contrast, Netscape's (version 4) implementation is rather limited.
</font></p>

<h2>DOM Objects</h2>
<p><font size=2 face="Verdana">
Before you can understand DOM objects specifically, you need to understand objects in general. An object is the computer analogue of a "real" object.
</font></p>

<h3>Object Properties and Methods</h3>
<p><font size=2 face="Verdana">A ball makes a good example. A ball has physical properties--it is (usually) round, it has a color, it has a bounce factor, and to some degree, shares all these characteristics with every other ball. You can represent these properties as characteristics common to all balls--and you can also represent these properties in program variables.</font></p>

<p><font size=2 face="Verdana">A ball can also act, or be the subject of action. For example, you can roll a ball, throw a ball, or bounce a ball. These actions are called "methods." All objects have properties and/or methods. The properties are the intrinsic or acquired characteristis of the object, while methods are actions. In practice, there is some conceptual overlap between the two. For example, a ball's color is clearly a property, but the ball's velocity could be implemented as a method as well as a property, e.g. "The ball's velocity is 0." (property) or "Change the ball's velocity to 100.", which is the equivalent of throwing the ball (property <i>or</i> method?).</font></p>

```
<p><font size=2 face="Times New Roman">
The following lists show some of the properties and methods
of a ball object.</font></p>
<h3>Ball Properties</h3>
<font color="#0000ff">
    <ul>
        <li>Shape</li>
        <li>Color</li>
        <li>Diameter (side-to-side)</li>
        <li>Diameter (front-to-back)</li>
        <li>Diameter (top-to-bottom)</li>
        <li>Composition</li>
        <li>Bounce factor</li>
        <li>Surface Texture</li>
        <li>Position</li>
        <li>Velocity</li>
        <li>Direction</li>
        <li>Acceleration</li>
    </ul>
</font>

<h3>Ball Methods</h3>
<font color="#0000ff">
    <ul>
        <li>Roll</li>
        <li>Bounce</li>
        <li>Collide</li>
        <li>Move</li>
    </ul>
</font></h2>
</font>
</body>
</html>
```

The page is too long to show in a single image, but it's on the CD. To view the file in your browser, navigate to the **Chapter 4** directory and double-click on the ch4i7.htm file.

Including Images on Your Web Site

It's hard to imagine a Web site without images. It's also hard to imagine a much easier way to get images onto a page than HTML. With very little effort you can intermix images and text, and even wrap text around the images. All your image work begins with the <img> tag.

The Image Tag

To place an image on a page, use an `<img>` image tag with a `src=URL` attribute that specifies which file you want to send. Interestingly, the server doesn't send the image file data with the rest of the page; instead, the browser parses the HTML and text in the page, then begins requesting associated content from the server, such as images. That's why you often see a page load, then see the images begin to appear a few seconds later.

Sometimes the images don't appear in your browser window in sequence. The browser requests the images sequentially, but the server may not respond to the requests in the same sequence. That's something to keep in mind as you design your pages.

There are a few optional attributes for the `<img>` tag. The `width="number"` and `height="number"` attributes specify the width and height of the image, respectively. Both the `width` and `height` attributes are optional. If you don't include the attributes, the browser will show the image at its original size.

Optional tags are just that—optional. You can include them if you want to or leave them off; but like most choices, there are consequences for either action you take. Because the default action of the browser is to show your images at the original size, leaving the `width` and `height` attributes off would seem to be a good choice most of the time—and it is, for small images. However, when you include the `width` and `height` attributes, the browser can reserve the screen area for the image before returning to the server to ask for the image file data. When you don't include the `width` and `height` attributes, the browser places a missing image icon in place of the image. Here's the problem. If the browser knows how big the image is going to be, it can complete the calculations for the layout of the remainder of the page. If the browser doesn't know how big the image is going to be, it has to delay the final layout until after it has retrieved the images from the server. It may even have to move text and images that have already been rendered. The end result is that your pages load more slowly when you don't include the optional `width` and `height` tags.

Most images placed in HTML pages are either Graphics Interchange Format (GIF) files or Joint Photographic Experts Group (JPEG) files, which are smaller than other image file formats because they're highly compressed. There's no technical impediment to using other file formats—although the client browsers may not be able to display them without special viewers. Netscape can natively display both GIF and JPEG files. IE adds Windows bitmap (BMP) files to that list. IE can use plug-ins or ActiveX extensions that provide viewers for other file formats, but Netscape can natively use only plug-ins. There is a third-party plug-in that lets Netscape browsers use ActiveX controls. For example, Macromedia's Flash format requires users to download the Flash Viewer before viewing Flash content.

Unlike a standard executable program, missing resources don't bother a browser much—it simply ignores any resources that may be missing. If the resource would normally be visible, the browser may display the missing-image icon in its place.

In addition to the `src`, `width`, and `height` attributes, you can specify how you want to align your image relative to the containing tag. For example, the containing tag for most images would be the `<body>` tag, so if you left-align an image in the `<body>` tag, the image will appear aligned to the left edge of the page. If you were to place that same left-aligned `<img>` tag inside a table cell, the image would appear aligned to the left edge of the table cell, not the left edge of the page.

In addition to the `right` and `left` values you might expect, the `align` attribute may also take some less common values. Table 4.1 shows the result of certain alignment keywords.

TABLE 4.1:   Table Alignment Attributes

Alignment Attribute	Result
ABSBOTTOM	Aligns the image at the lowest possible point relative to the text. The ABSBOTTOM is the bottom of the longest descender of the text.
ABSMIDDLE	Aligns the image in the absolute center of the text.
BASELINE	Aligns the image with the baseline of the text.
BOTTOM	Aligns the image at the bottom of the containing tag.
LEFT	Aligns the image at the left edge of the containing tag.
MIDDLE	Aligns the image in the horizontal center of the containing tag.
RIGHT	Aligns the image at the right edge of the containing tag.
TEXTTOP	Aligns the image with the top edge of the text.
TOP	Aligns the image at the top edge of the containing tag.
BORDER	An integer width that determines the width of the border. The default width is 1. A value of 0 means no border.
HSPACE	An integer value that determines the spacing between the left and right edges of the image and any surrounding items.
ISMAP	This attribute has no value, but when it is present, the image is treated as a server-side image map. An image map is one or more images that function like anchor tags—they hyperlink to an anchor tag in the current document, another document, or another URL. Server-side image maps are rarely used with modern browsers. When the user clicks an image defined as a server-side image map, the browser sends the mouse coordinates of the click event to the server. You have to process the click using ASP or a CGI script to initiate an action.
USEMAP	This attribute takes the name of a `<map>` tag as a value. It specifies that the browser should use the touch areas defined in the `<map>` tag to determine whether the user clicked in a hyperlinked area of the image. The `<map>` tag defines a client-side image map.
VSPACE	An integer value that determines the spacing between the top and bottom edges of the image and any surrounding items.

Placing Images on a Page

By default, the browser places the image on the page in the position where it is parsed. However, some actions change the default position. For example, if the first tag on the page is an `<img>` tag, the image will appear at the top left corner of the client area of the browser window. The client area is the portion of the window where content appears. It excludes the border, status bar, and any toolbars. Any text following the image would appear starting at the right bottom edge of the image, because placing the image on the page first moves the baseline to the bottom of the image (see Figure 4.8).

FIGURE 4.8:

Default image alignment
(`ch4i8.htm`)

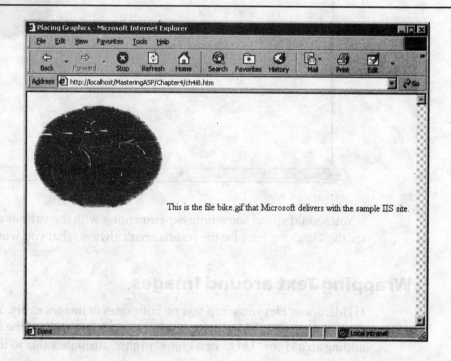

If you were to alter the `<img>` tag by adding an alignment attribute, the rendered position of the image would change. For example, `<img src="someURL/topImg .gif" align="right">` will align the image at the top right corner of the client area. You might expect that adding text in the file after the image would wrap the text so it would begin on the first line following the image, and below the bottom edge of the image. But that's not how the browser renders the file. Changing the alignment renders the image on the right, as expected, but the browser begins plotting text at the top left corner of the client area (see Figure 4.9).

Just for interest, if you were to go back and explicitly add an `align="left"` attribute to the tag in the file displayed in Figure 4.8 (`ch4i8.htm`), the text will plot at the top right corner of the image rather than the bottom right corner.

FIGURE 4.9:

Right-aligned image
(ch4i9.htm)

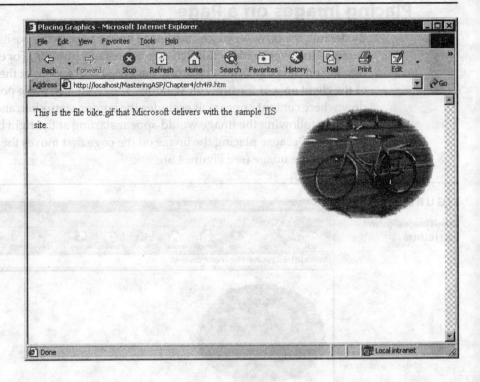

You should spend some time experimenting with the various attribute settings for the <img> tag because the results aren't always what you would expect.

Wrapping Text around Images

HTML doesn't let you wrap text on both sides of images easily. You can wrap text around three sides of an image aligned to the left or right of the containing tag by adding an align="left" or align="right" attribute value to the <img> tag.

If you want to insert an image in a text line—for example, an icon or small image—you can place the image by centering it in the text line (see Figure 4.10).

Background Images

Both IE and Netscape support background images. You specify the background image as an attribute to the <body> tag. For example:

```
<body background="http://myserver/mysite/someimage.gif">
```

The image appears on the page as a background image, which means that any other content appears on top of the image—in other words, the z-order of the image is 0. As an example, I've plotted a list on top of an image in Figure 4.11.

FIGURE 4.10:

Inline images (ch4i10.htm)

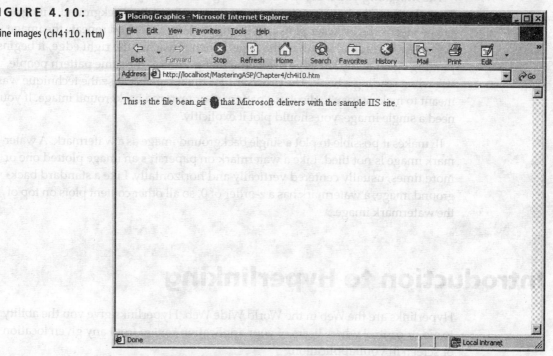

FIGURE 4.11:

Background image

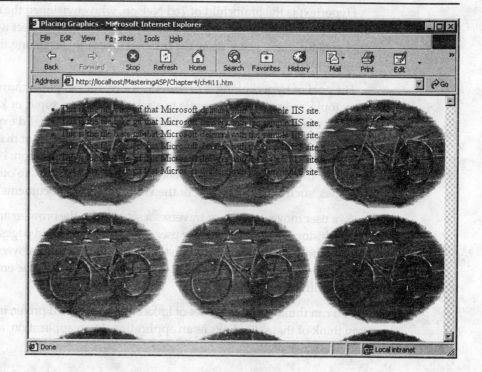

The first thing you'll see about this image is that it's plotted multiple times. That's because the browser tiles the image across the entire background. Tiling an image means the browser plots it at the upper left corner and repeats the image across the horizontal width of the page. When it reaches the right edge, it begins plotting again at the left edge below the first graphic—the same pattern people use when reading a book. The browser tiles the image because the technique was meant to make it easy to display a patterned or textured background image. If you need a single image, you should plot it explicitly.

IE makes it possible to plot a single background image as a watermark. A watermark image is not tiled. Like a watermark on paper, it's an image plotted one or more times, usually centered vertically and horizontally. Like a standard background image, a watermark has a z-order of 0, so all other content plots on top of the watermark image.

Introduction to Hyperlinking

Hyperlinks are the Web in the World Wide Web. Hyperlinks give you the ability to aid or control where users of your application can go from any given location or screen in your application.

Hypertext is the brainchild of Ted Nelson, who envisioned the entire set of human knowledge as hyperlinked content. His Xanadu project worked toward that goal for many years. Now the Internet is rapidly achieving that goal, albeit in an unstructured manner.

The goal of hyperlinking is to provide a way for people to move from one position, topic, or knowledge granule to a related position, topic, or knowledge granule. For example, if this document were in electronic form, I'd expect a hyperlink from every instance of a term related to ASP to a definition of that term and from every HTML tag to a definition of that tag. From the definition, I'd expect a link to one or more examples, to any related terms, and perhaps to other related technologies, such as SGML, XML, or the W3C standards documents.

As a user moves among, or traverses a set of links, the browser application maintains a history list that enables the user to traverse the visited pages in reverse order. Modern browsers maintain your history list—often for several weeks. They also let you jump many steps backward at one time by formatting the entire history as a series of links!

You can think of the entire set of links as a Web, but I'd prefer, in this book, that you think of that set of links as an application. In an application, as opposed to a

Web site, you have specific goals in mind—you want to guide the user from one logical point to another. In contrast, in a Web site or on the Internet, the user may simply be browsing without any specific goal in mind. Therefore, in an application, links serve both as information connectors and as application action initiators. For example, a button on a form is a link, but its function is to initiate an action in the application. A navigation button is a link, but it doesn't necessarily link to related information—it may link to a menu, or it may exit the application altogether.

The Anchor Tag

In HTML, the primary means of linking one location to another is the anchor, or <a> tag. It's a very simple scheme that uses URLs to move between locations. You specify the URL as an href attribute value. For example:

```
<a href="http://myserver/mysite/mypage.htm">
Go To My Page
</a>
```

The browser formats the text following the anchor tag as the link, so in the previous example, the only visible portion of the link is the phrase Go To My Page. The browser continues to format text following the <a> tag as link text until it encounters the closing </a> anchor tag. Everything between the start and end of the anchor tag, including spaces (an exception to the rule that browsers ignore white space), is the link text.

There are two types of anchor tags—links and bookmarks. Their functions are completely different.

Links are anchor tags that act as the trigger for a hyperlink—when you click on the link, it begins or triggers the linking action. Bookmarks are anchor tags that act as the destination for a link—you can jump to a bookmark, but bookmarks aren't visible and you can't click on them. The browser formats anchor tags that contain links as underlined, colored text—blue by default. Browsers generally plot links in a different color after the user has visited the link target.

To create a bookmark you must give the anchor tag a name attribute. For example:

```
<a name="Bookmark1">
```

You can jump to a bookmark in the same document or in a different document. Basically, a bookmark is a way to jump to a place in a document other than the top of the document, which is the default link target. To jump to a different position in the same document, you would write a link tag like this:

```
<a href="#Bookmark1">
```

Note the pound (#) sign in front of the `href` attribute value. The pound sign informs the browser that the link target is a bookmark rather than a document. You can also link to bookmarks in other documents by appending the pound sign and the bookmark name to the end of the URL. For example:

```
<a href="http://myserver/mysite/mypage.htm#Bookmark1">
```

You'll see many pages set up with a set of links at the top of the page that jump to bookmarks further down in the page. Typically, you'll also find that each bookmarked section has a link back to a bookmark at the top of the menu, so that after reading a section, you can jump back to the menu to select a different section. There are some good reasons to set documents up like this rather than as a set of linked pages. A single, long document with a menu is less work to create and requires only a single trip to the server. A single, long document is also easy to print. On the other hand, it's often more difficult to read long documents because you have to scroll through them.

Listing 4.5 contains an example of a document with a menu and internal bookmarks for each section. The spacing (`<p> </p>`) paragraphs are just to put enough white space on the page to force the page to scroll—you wouldn't need them in a normal document. In the browser, the menu page looks like Figure 4.12.

FIGURE 4.12:

A menu page with several sections (`ch4i12.htm`)

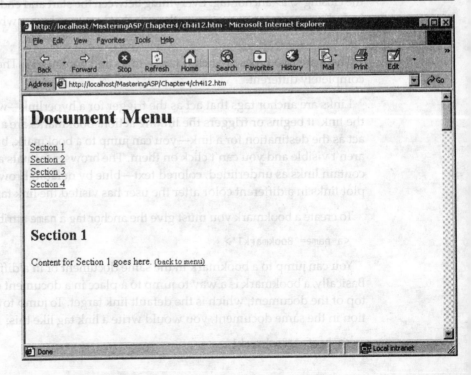

LISTING 4.5   **A Menu Page with Several Sections** (ch4il2.htm)

```
<html>
<head>
<title></title>
</head>
<body>
<a name="Menu">
<h1>Document Menu</h1></a>
<a href="#Bookmark1">Section 1</a><br>
<a href="#Bookmark2">Section 2</a><br>
<a href="#Bookmark3">Section 3</a><br>
<a href="#Bookmark4">Section 4</a><br>
<p> </p>
<a name="Bookmark1">
<h2>Section 1</h2></a>
Content for Section 1 goes here.
<a href="#Menu"><font size="2" color="red">(back to menu)</font></a><br>
<p> </p>
<p> </p>
<p> </p>
<p> </p>
<p> </p>
<p> </p>
<p> </p>
<p> </p>
<p> </p>
<p> </p>

<a name="Bookmark2">
<h2>Section 2</h2></a>
Content for Section 2 goes here.
<a href="#Menu"><font size="2" color="red">(back to menu)</font></a><br>
<p> </p>
<p> </p>
<p> </p>
<p> </p>
<p> </p>
<p> </p>
<p> </p>
<p> </p>
<p> </p>
<p> </p>
<p> </p>
```

```
<p> </p>
<p> </p>
<p> </p>
<p> </p>
<p> </p>
<a name="Bookmark3">
<h2>Section 3</h2></a>
Content for Section 3 goes here.
<a href="#Menu"><font size="2" color="red">(back to menu)</font></a><br>
<p> </p>
<p> </p>
<p> </p>
<p> </p>
<p> </p>
<p> </p>
<p> </p>
<p> </p>
<p> </p>
<p> </p>
<p> </p>
<p> </p>
<p> </p>
<p> </p>
<p> </p>
<p> </p>
<p> </p>
<p> </p>
<a name="Bookmark4">
<h2>Section 4</h2></a>
Content for Section 4 goes here.
<a href="#Menu"><font size="2" color="red">(back to menu)</font></a><br>
<p> </p>
<p> </p>
<p> </p>
<p> </p>
<p> </p>
<p> </p>
<p> </p>
<p> </p>
<p> </p>
<p> </p>
<p> </p>
<p> </p>
<p> </p>
```

```
<p> </p>
<p> </p>
<p> </p>
<p> </p>
<p> </p>
<p> </p>
<p> </p>
</body>
</html>
```

So that you can see a different style, Listing 4.6 contains a multiple-choice question formatted as a set of short linked pages.

NOTE
The lines that begin with asterisks are *not* part of the listing—they serve to separate and explain the HTML in each file.

LISTING 4.6   **A Set of Linked Pages (ch4i13a.htm-ch4i13e.htm)**

```
*************************************************************
* This file (ch4i13a) contains the multiple-choice         *
* question. Each distractor is a link to another page      *
* that contains the feedback for that distractor.          *
*************************************************************
<html>
<head>
<title></title>
</head>
<body>

<p>Which of the following is <em>not</em> a valid anchor
tag type?</p>
<ol>
   <li><a href="ch4i13b.htm">A link to another document.</a>
   <li><a href="ch4i13c.htm">A link to a specific position in
   a document.</a>
   <li><a href="ch4i13d.htm">A link to a previous
   document.</a>
   <li><a href="ch4i13e.htm">A link to the Back button on the
   browser.</a>          </li></ol>
<p>Click on your answer.</p>

</body>
</html>
```

```
************************************************************
* This file (ch4i13b) contains the feedback for the       *
* first (incorrect) distractor.                           *
************************************************************
<html>
<head>
<title></title>
</head>
<body>

<p>Incorrect.</p>
<p>You selected: "1. A link to another document." That is a valid tag
type.
Click <a href="ch4i13a.htm">continue</a> to try again.</p>

</body>
</html>
************************************************************
* This file (ch4i13c) contains the feedback for the       *
* second (incorrect) distractor.                          *
************************************************************
<html>
<head>
<title></title>
</head>
<body>

<p>Incorrect.</p>
<p>You selected: "2. A link to a specific position in a document." That
is a valid tag type.
Click <a href="ch4i13a.htm">continue</a> to try again.</p>

</body>
</html>
************************************************************
* This file (ch4i13d) contains the feedback for the       *
* third (incorrect) distractor.                           *
************************************************************
<html>
<head>
<title></title>
</head>
<body>

<p>Incorrect.</p>
<p>You selected: "3. A link to a previous document." That is a valid
tag type.
```

```
Click <a href="ch4i13a.htm">continue</a> to try again.</p>

</body>
</html>
************************************************************
* This file (ch4i13e) contains the feedback for the       *
* fourth (correct) distractor.                            *
************************************************************
<html>
<head>
<title></title>
</head>
<body>

<p>Correct.</p>
<p>You selected: "4. A link to the Back button on the browser." That is
not a valid tag type.
</body>
</html>
```

If you look at this set of pages in a browser, you'll see the question first (see Figure 4.13).

FIGURE 4.13:

Multiple-choice question
screen (ch4i13a.htm)

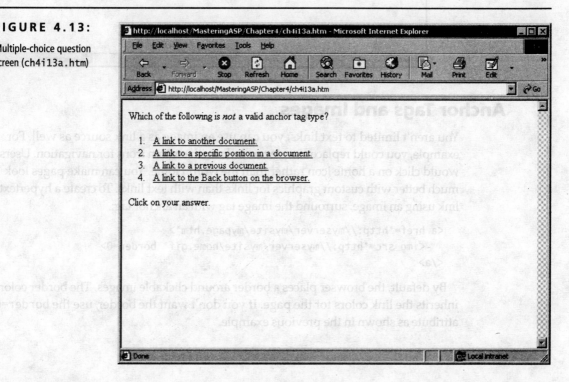

As you click on each distractor, you'll see pages similar to Figure 4.14. I won't show them all because you can get the files from the CD and view them in your browser. Figure 4.14 shows what happens if you select the first distractor.

FIGURE 4.14:

Feedback for multiple-choice question

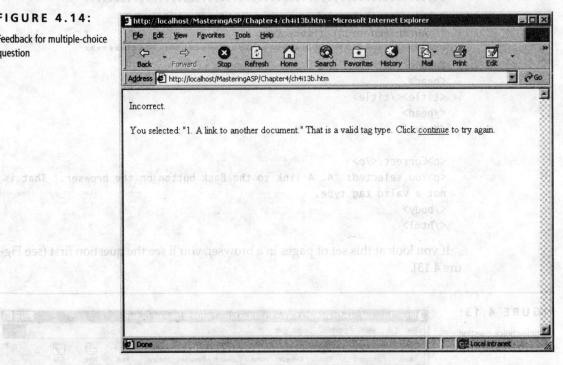

Anchor Tags and Images

You aren't limited to text links; you can use an image as a link source as well. For example, you could replace simple text links with custom icons for navigation. Users would click on a home icon rather than the word Home. You can make pages look much better with custom graphics for links than with text links. To create a hypertext link using an image, surround the image tag with an anchor tag:

```
<a href="http://myserver/mysite/mypage.htm">
   <img src="http://myserver/mysite/home.gif" border=0>
</a>
```

By default, the browser places a border around clickable images. The border color inherits the link colors for the page. If you don't want the border, use the `border=0` attribute as shown in the previous example.

Formatting Tables

Tables consist of rows and columns. Because the browser ignores white space, which includes tabs, you usually use tables in HTML to display any items that you must separate with white space. Note that this does not necessarily apply to browsers that are version 4 and higher—you can use absolute positioning to force items to display at specific pixel locations. Nevertheless, even with modern browsers, tables are useful for more than displaying columnar data.

The `<table>` tag contains several other tags that serve to delimit the columns and rows. Tables may have three sections—a header, a body, and a footer. The header and footer rows are fixed rows—they're not supposed to scroll (although they do in most browsers). The header and footer are optional; you don't have to include them to have a valid table. If you do include either a header or footer, then you also need to include the body section. Tables may also have a `<caption>` tag. The browser formats the caption above the first row. Border settings for the table don't apply to the caption.

In addition, tables in IE can contain `<colgroup>` and `<col>` tags that can help simplify table formatting. The `<colgroup>` tag defines a set of columns, while the `<col>` tag defines an individual column within the column group.

Table, Table Row, Table Data Tags

Tables begin with a `<table>` tag. You delimit each row with a `<tr>` table row tag and each column with a `<td>` table data tag. The following HTML describes a simple two-row, two-column table:

```
<table>
   <tr>
      <td>
         Row 1, Col 1
      </td>
      <td>
         Row 1, Col 2
      </td>
   </tr>
   <tr>
      <td>
         Row 2, Col 1
      </td>
      <td>
         Row 2, Col 2
      </td>
   </tr>
</table>
```

> **WARNING**   Be very careful to close all the table tags. Some browsers, such as IE, will close the tags for you and the table will display properly; but others will not, and the table will not display at all or will display incorrectly. Microsoft's documentation states that the end tags are optional for most table elements, but the end tags are optional only if the rendering engine is IE.

As you can see from the previous listing, a table can contain an arbitrary number of rows, and each row may contain an arbitrary number of columns.

If you place the previous code listing in a standard HTML template wrapper and view it in a browser, it's not particularly appealing—it looks like two tabbed columns (see Figure 4.15).

FIGURE 4.15:

Simple HTML table
(ch4i14.htm)

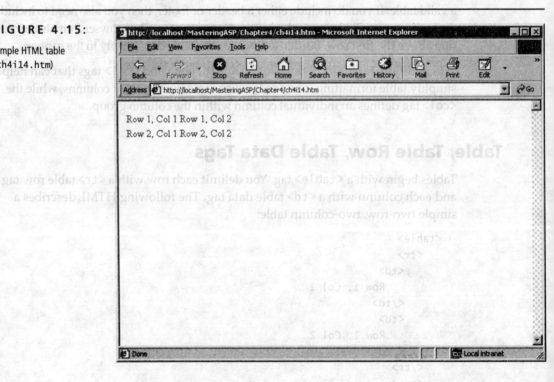

Fortunately, you can add attributes to the `<table>` tag to control its placement and improve its appearance. Attribute values for the `<table>` tag apply to all the columns and cells of the table unless you override them with attribute values for individual columns, rows, or cells. The following list contains the most common attribute values; you can find the rest in Appendix C, *Basic HTML Reference*:

align   The `align` attribute can take one of three values: `left`, `right`, or `center`. It controls the horizontal placement of the table on the page.

background The background attribute, like the background attribute for the <body> tag, accepts a URL that references an image file. The browser displays the image with a z-order of 0, so all the table data plots on top of the background image.

bgcolor The bgcolor attribute takes an HTML color value that controls the background color of the entire table. You can override the bgcolor value for any individual row or cell.

border The border attribute takes an integer value that controls the width of the border around the table and around each individual cell. The default value is 0—no border.

cellpadding The cellpadding attribute takes an integer value that controls the spacing between the contents of a cell and its border.

cellspacing The cellspacing attribute takes an integer value that controls the spacing between cells.

cols The cols attribute specifies the number of columns in a table. When used, it can significantly increase the speed at which the browser can render a table. Without this attribute, the browser must parse the entire table to determine the maximum number of columns in a row, whereas if you use the cols attribute, the browser can begin rendering rows immediately.

height The height attribute takes an integer value that informs the browser of the final height of the area required to render the table. Like the cols attribute, including the height attribute can significantly increase the speed at which the browser can render a table. You may specify the height in pixels or as a percentage of the height of the visible client area.

width The width attribute takes an integer value that informs the browser of the final width of the area required to render the table. Like the cols and height attributes, including the width attribute can significantly increase the speed at which the browser can render a table. You may specify the width in pixels or as a percentage of the width of the visible client area.

If you take the table from the example at the beginning of this section, align it in the center of the page, specify the width and height, apply a caption, add a border and pad the cells, the first two lines of the listing would look like this:

```
<table border="1" align="center" cellpadding="3" cellspacing="2"
width="60%" height="80%">
<caption>Simple Table With Formatting</caption>
```

If you look at the altered table in a browser, it looks like Figure 4.16.

FIGURE 4.16:

Simple table with borders
(ch4i15.htm)

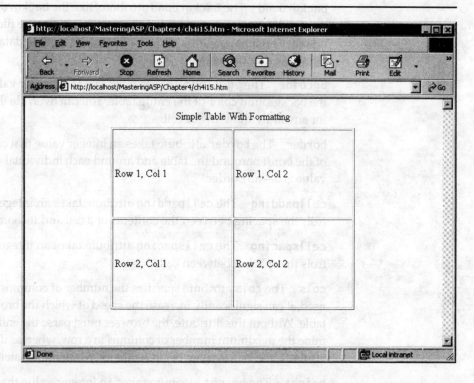

As you can see from the example, `<tr>` tags specify the table rows. You can use the `align` and `bgcolor` attributes with the `<tr>` tag. The `<tr>` tag can also take an `valign` attribute that controls the vertical alignment of the cell contents in that row. The possible values are `baseline`, `bottom`, `center`, and `top`.

The `<td>` tag accepts `align`, `background`, `bgcolor`, and `valign` attributes. In addition, the `<td>` tag can take `colspan` and `rowspan` attributes. The values for `colspan` and `rowspan` are integers. They specify the number of columns and rows over which the cell extends. You need these attributes when you have a table in which rows contain differing numbers of columns. For example, if you wanted to add a third row to the table in Figure 4.16 that contained only one column and was twice the height of the other rows, you could specify the row as follows:

```
<tr>
    <td colspan="2" rowspan="2" align="center" valign="center">This is a
    double-width, double-height cell with centered contents.</td>
</tr>
```

After adding the new row, the table looks like Figure 4.17.

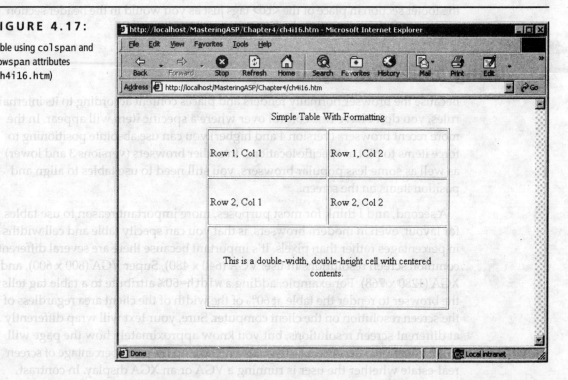

Table Header and Footer Tags

You can separate a table into three main functional parts—a header section, one or more body sections, and a footer section. The primary purpose of the header and footer sections is to duplicate the header and footer on each page when the user prints multipage tables. For tables without borders, you can separate sections in the body of the table with horizontal lines by placing the content into multiple body sections. You may have only one header and one footer section in a table.

To define the header section, use a <thead> tag. You may have multiple rows within the header section. You can also automatically format the header cells with bold text by using <th> table header tags in the header section rather than <td> table data tags.

You may have multiple <tbody> table body tags in a table. Each <tbody> tag defines one section of the table body. By default, a table has a table body section even if you don't define one explicitly. The browser separates multiple table body sections with horizontal lines.

You define the footer section with the <tfoot> table footer tag. The footer section may contain multiple rows. There's no corresponding <tf> tag for footer sections to parallel the <th> tag for the header section. However, you may use <th> tags in the footer section in place of the `<td>` tags just as you would in the header section to format the footer row(s) in bold text.

Using Tables for Layout

Because the browser normally renders and places content according to its internal rules, you don't have fine control over where a specific item will appear. In the more recent browsers (version 4 and higher) you can use absolute positioning to force items to plot at specific locations. In earlier browsers (versions 3 and lower) as well as some less popular browsers, you still need to use tables to align and position items on the screen.

A second, and I think for most purposes, more important reason to use tables for layout, even in modern browsers, is that you can specify table and cell widths in percentages rather than pixels. It's important because there are several different common screen resolutions in use: VGA (640 x 480), Super VGA (800 x 600), and XGA (1280 x 768). For example, adding a `width=60%` attribute to a table tag tells the browser to render the table at 60% of the width of the client area regardless of the screen resolution on the client computer. Sure, your text will wrap differently at different screen resolutions, but you know approximately how the page will look to different users because the table will take up the same percentage of screen real-estate whether the user is running a VGA or an XGA display. In contrast, using pixel-based positioning sets the position of items without regard to the width and height of the screen.

Here's an example. Suppose I wanted to add custom numbered images instead of the numbers for the distractors in the multiple-choice question example (Listing 4.6), but I still wanted people to be able to click on the text of each distractor to answer the question. I could use two links rather than a single, all-text link. The first anchor tag would surround the custom image for each distractor. The second anchor tag would surround the text of the distractor. Both links would navigate to the same page. I would change the first page as follows:

```
<html>
<head>
<title></title>
</head>
<body>
    <p>Which of the following is <EM>not</EM> a valid anchor
    tag type?</p>
    <a href="ch4i13b.htm"><IMG SRC="images/1.gif" border="0"></a>
    <a href="ch4i13b.htm">A link to another document.</a><br>
    <a href="ch4i13c.htm"><IMG SRC="images/2.gif" border="0"></a>
```

```
<a href="ch4i13c.htm">A link to a specific position in
    a document.</a><br>
<a href="ch4i13d.htm"><IMG SRC="images/3.gif" border="0"></a>
<a href="ch4i13d.htm">A link to a previous document.</a><br>
<a href="ch4i13e.htm"><IMG SRC="images/4.gif" border="0"></a>
<a href="ch4i13e.htm">A link to the Back button on the
    browser.</a><br>

<p>Click on your answer.</p>

</body>
</html>
```

Using Image Maps

An image map is similar to an image link except that you can define one or more clickable areas on the image. The clickable areas map to a bookmark or URL. For example, a map of the United States might show the outlines of each state—and each state would be a link to a different location. To create the complete image map with individual state images, you would need to create each image, then place the images on the page using absolute positioning, so the images would align properly with each other. Alternatively (and much more simply) you could use a single image and define the clickable areas for the states along the state boundary lines.

There are two kinds of image maps—server-side maps and client-side maps. Server-side image maps tell the browser that when a user clicks on the image, the browser should send the coordinates of the clicked point to the server. A program (such as an ASP page) on the server must determine whether the coordinates are in a valid clickable area and, if so, hyperlink to the appropriate page. Server-side image maps were the only type of image maps available until version 3x browsers appeared. Server-side image maps are still useful when you want to partition an image into many rectangular areas with script, or when your clients may be using older browsers. However, each click by the user forces the browser to send information to the server for processing, so server-side image maps are normally an inefficient use of resources.

NOTE   You won't work with server-side image maps in this section, only client-side image maps.

Client-side image maps define the clickable areas of the image and the URL associated with each area in client-side HTML. The client shoulders the burden of processing user mouse clicks, thus avoiding the round trip to the server generated by server-side image maps.

How Image Maps Work

To a computer, a screen is like a table, with a single pixel in each cell. Each pixel has a column number and a row number. The first pixel is in the upper left corner of the screen in column 0, row 0. Usually, you specify pixels with two integer values separated by a comma, for example 0, 0, or 100, 100. Another way of thinking about the computer screen, for those of you who remember plotting graphs in math class, is as an X-Y grid. The column number of each pixel (the first number) is the x-axis value, and the row number (the second number) is the y-axis value. Any points you plot appear in quadrant 4—the area below the x-axis and to the right of the y-axis.

You use the same method to refer to pixels within an image rendered on a screen, except that the pixel locations are defined as offsets from the top left corner of the image, not the top left corner of the screen. So if you have a square image, 100 pixels on a side, and you plot that image at location 100, 100 on the computer screen, the actual top left corner pixel of the image is 100, 100, but you would refer to pixels within the image as if that same pixel's location were 0, 0—the first row and first column of the image itself.

You can define any rectangle using the top left corner and the bottom right corner of the rectangle. I'll separate the individual pixel definitions with semicolons for clarity. For example, the rectangle covered by that image is 100, 100; 199, 199. From those two pixels, you can infer that the corners of the rectangle are top left 100, 100, top right 199, 100, bottom right 199, 199 and bottom left 100, 199.

If you were to divide that 100-pixel square image into four areas, you would define them as rectangles—in this case, squares—each 50 pixels per side. The points you would use are offsets from the top left corner of the image. So, moving clockwise starting at the top left corner, the first rectangle would be 0, 0; 49, 49; the second, 51, 0; 100, 49; the third, 51, 49; 99, 99; and the last, 0, 50; 49, 99.

You aren't limited to rectangles. You can also define circular areas and polygons. As you can imagine, figuring out the actual pixel values for rounded shapes or irregular polygons is rather difficult. Fortunately, you rarely have to calculate the values yourself. There are several image map editors available that let you trace or draw the borders of the mapped areas visually.

Creating Client-Side Image Maps

You create a client-side image map with the `<map>` tag. For example, Listing 4.7 shows the HTML to create the client-side image map described in the previous section—a square image divided into four equal-sized smaller squares, each of which is a hyperlink to a different document or bookmark.

The <map> tag is a named block element that contains a set of <area> tags, each of which defines a clickable area of the image. The <map> tag itself does not have to be in the same file as the <img> tag that uses the map coordinates. Using the United States map example, you could define the <map> tag containing the clickable areas for the states in one file, then reference that file from multiple pages, each of which might contain the same image map. That way, if you wanted to change one of the clickable areas, you would only have to change the file containing the image map definition.

The <area> tag defines the target URL for the link and the coordinates for the clickable region(s) of the image. You may create multiple <area> tags for a given image. Each <area> tag must have a shape attribute and a coords attribute containing the appropriate coordinates as a comma-delimited string. The shape attribute has three possible values:

- circ or circle
- poly or polygon
- rect or rectangle

When the shape attribute value is circ or circle, the coords attribute requires three values: the x and y coordinates of the center point, and the radius. When the shape attribute value is poly or polygon, the coords attribute value is a list of x and y coordinates that define the polygon. When the shape attribute is rect or rectangle, the coords attribute value contains the x and y coordinates of the upper left and bottom right corners of the rectangle.

LISTING 4.7   Client-Side Image Map Example (ch4i19a.htm)

```html
<html>
<head>
<title>Client-Side Image Map</title>
</head>
<body>
<map name="fourSquares">
    <area shape=rect coords="0, 0, 49, 49"
        href="ch4i19b.htm#upperLeft" border="0">
    <area shape=rect coords="51, 0, 100, 49"
        href="ch4i19b.htm#upperRight" border="0">
    <area shape=rect coords="51, 49, 99, 99"
        href="ch4i19b.htm#lowerRight" border="0">
    <area shape=rect coords="0, 50, 49, 99"
        href="ch4i19b.htm#lowerLeft" border="0">
```

```
</map>
<IMG SRC="images/bluesquare.gif" usemap="#fourSquares" border=0>
</body>
</html>
```

Tools for Creating Image Maps

There are several commercial-quality tools for creating image maps. All of them work similarly. You load an image into a map editor, then draw a rectangle, circle, or polygon over the image hotspots. The image map editing software outputs the HTML for the image map, sometimes just the map definition, but more often, the link tags and the map definition.

Even if you only need to create simple rectangular hotspots on your images, image map tools can save you a significant amount of time.

Here are three popular resources; others are probably equally capable. Note that none of these solutions is free and I don't recommend one over another.

- Microsoft FrontPage 98 or FrontPage 2000
- MapEdit (shareware)
- JImageMap (Java solution)

You can download MapEdit and JImageMap from many shareware sites on the Internet.

Understanding Frames

To understand frames, you need to go back in time to the beginning of Windows itself. A window is an area of memory that contains a bitmap—a rectangular area of pixels. Each program owns one or more windows, and each window is either a top-level window or a child window. All windows are children of the desktop window—which you can think of as the screen itself.

For example, open up any program in Windows and look at the screen. You'll see a title bar, a window frame, and a client area. You may see additional items, such as a toolbar with buttons and other controls, and a status bar. Each of these items is a separate window. Each has specific properties, such as height and width, and a background color. Now think about your screen if you open up multiple windows. If you think of the programs you open as items in a stack, one window is always on top. The z-order value controls the position of each window in that stack. The window on top (the active window) has a z-order of 0. All other windows appear behind the active window and have higher z-order values. Unless you maximize all the windows, each window probably appears in a slightly different position on screen, meaning that each window has its own rectangle.

The programs' main windows are top-level windows. Each item, such as a toolbar button, is a child window. The child windows, although they are complete windows in their own right, appear and disappear with their parent window. If you minimize the program window, all the child windows disappear from the screen as well.

In the browser, you define child windows using a concept called *frames*. Frames are a sub-area of the main window, but you treat each frame as if it were a completely separate browser. Each frame can navigate independently to a page. To the computer, each frame is a child window with most of the capabilities of a stand-alone browser, except that each frame is subservient to the top-level browser window. Frames must plot in the top-level browser window's screen area, and they minimize when you minimize the top-level window. You can think of frames as an easy way to divide the browser window into separate windows of varying sizes.

Frames can't exist by themselves—you must define them using a concept called a *frameset*. A frameset must be defined in its own page—you can't define a frameset and put content (other than a <noframes> tag) within a single HTML file; however, you may define more than one frameset in a single page. A frameset isn't visible—it's a containing tag for frames. A frameset contains one or more frames or framesets. The frames themselves are usually visible, although there are some good uses for invisible frames. You use the <frameset> tag to define a frameset and the <frame> tag to define a frame. For example, to create a frameset that divides the browser client area into two equal-size frames, you would write a <frameset> tag, as follows:

```
<frameset rows="50%, *">
    <frame name="topFrame" src="top_1.htm">
    <frame name="bottomFrame" src="bottom_1.htm">
</frameset>
```

For browsers that don't support frames (rare these days) you can add a <noframes> tag.

```
<frameset rows="50%, *">
    <frame name="topFrame" src="top_1.htm">
    <frame name="bottomFrame" src="bottom_1.htm">
    <NOFRAMES>You need a frames-enabled browser to view
        this site!</NOFRAMES>
</frameset>
```

Browsers that support frames ignore the <noframes> tag. Other browsers will display the text of the <noframes> tag because it's the only HTML content in the file that does not appear between tags—remember, browsers ignore tags they don't support.

You define the size of the frames in pixels or in percentages. Note that you can use an asterisk in place of a value to define the last frame as "all the rest of the available area." In other words, I could have defined the frames as rows="50%, 50%" and the results would be identical. The asterisk notation is particularly useful when you are defining frames in pixels. Often, you don't know the width of the browser screen, so it's difficult to define the last frame exactly. For example, suppose I want to divide the screen vertically into two frames. The left-hand frame will contain a list of links, and I want it to be 200 pixels wide. I want to display content in the right-hand frame—but I don't know whether the remaining available area is 440 pixels wide (VGA), 600 pixels wide (Super VGA), or 1080 pixels wide (XGA). Therefore, I could define the frameset using the asterisk, as follows:

```
<frameset cols="200, *">
    <frame name="leftFrame" src="left_1.htm">
    <frame name="rightFrame" src="right_1.htm">
</frameset>
```

You can't use both the rows and cols attributes within the same frameset, but you can nest framesets to accomplish the same result. For example, the following code defines a frameset with the screen divided vertically into two equal-sized frames. The frameset contains a second frameset that further divides the right-hand frame horizontally into two equal-sized frames (see Listing 4.8).

LISTING 4.8   **Nested Framesets (ch4i18a.htm – ch4i18d.htm)**

```
***********************************************************
* This file (ch4i18a) contains the frameset definitions  *
***********************************************************
<html>
<head><title>Nested Framesets</title></head>
<frameset cols="50%, *">
    <frame name="leftFrame" src="ch4i18b.htm">
    <frameset rows="50%, *">
        <frame name="rightTopFrame" src="ch4i18c.htm">
        <frame name="rightBottomFrame" src="ch4i18d.htm">
    </frameset>
</frameset><noframes>You need a frames-enabled browser to
            view this page.</noframes>
</frameset>
</html>
```

```
*************************************************************
* This file (ch4i18b.htm) shows up in the left-hand        *
* frame. The other files (ch4i18c and ch4i18d) are         *
* identical except for the title and text                  *
*************************************************************
<html>
<head><title>ch4i18b.htm</title></head>
<body>
     This is ch4i18b.htm
</body>
</html>
```

In the browser, Listing 4.8 looks like Figure 4.18.

FIGURE 4.18:

Nested framesets
(ch4i18a.htm –
ch4i18d.htm)

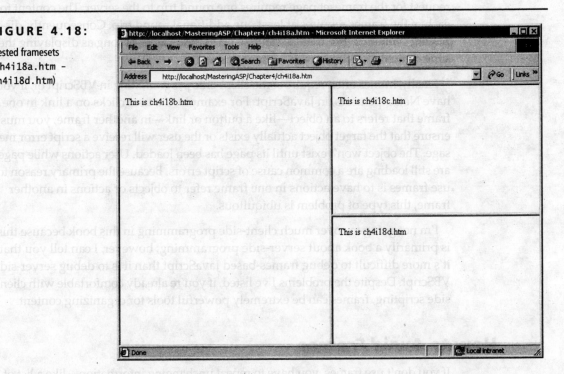

Advantages/Disadvantages of Frames

The primary advantages of frames are that they display content independently and can separate content visually. You can define a link in one frame which displays content or triggers an action in another frame without redrawing the entire screen.

Another less important advantage of frames is that you can create resizable frames. A user can drag the frame border(s) to increase or decrease the viewing area covered by the frame. This feature can be useful. The easiest way to see it in action (if you're using IE) is to click the Search button on your browser's toolbar, and perform a search. You can drag the right-hand border of the Search frame to change the relative sizes of the search and content windows.

The primary disadvantage of frames is that they are more difficult to create and control. To create the two-frame screen from the previous listing you must create three pages: one that contains the frameset definition and one page for each of the frames.

Another disadvantage of frames is that they take longer to display. The browser's request for the frameset page requires one round trip to the server. The content for each of the frames requires at least one additional round trip. Consequently, displaying content in two frames can take up to three times as long as displaying the same content in a single page without frames.

Finally, frames often require some client-side programming in VBScript or, if you have Netscape users, in JavaScript. For example, if a user clicks on a link in one frame that refers to an object—like a button or link—in another frame, you must ensure that the target object actually exists or the user will receive a script error message. The object won't exist until its page has been loaded. User actions while pages are still loading are a common cause of script errors. Because the primary reason to use frames is to have actions in one frame refer to objects or actions in another frame, this type of problem is ubiquitous.

I'm not going to cover much client-side programming in this book because this is primarily a book about server-side programming; however, I can tell you that it's more difficult to debug frames-based JavaScript than it is to debug server-side VBScript. Despite the problems I've listed, if you're already comfortable with client-side scripting, frames can be extremely powerful tools for organizing content.

How to Avoid Frames

If you don't use frames, you have to repeat unchanging information—like a list of navigational links—on each page. Most servers have a mechanism for doing that; in IIS, you can use include files to place the content on each page. An include file is exactly what it sounds like—it's a reference to another file that the server includes with the response. The server replaces the include directive with the contents of the include file. For example, if you wanted to place a copyright notice at the bottom of every page, you could create an include file that contained the HTML for the copyright notice. You would place an include directive referencing your footer file on each content page. The server would include the HTML for the footer in the response. To the browser, the response appears just as if you had explicitly written the HTML for the footer into each page. In other words, the browser doesn't care (and doesn't know) whether the response contains HTML from one file or one hundred different files as long as the response contains valid HTML.

In concert with `include` files, you can use tables to arrange elements in specific areas on the screen. Before absolute positioning of on-screen elements became possible in browsers, tables were the most common way to arrange content.

Controlling Element Position

There are two methods for positioning content on the screen. The first method uses absolute positioning with Cascading Style Sheet (CSS) styles, and is by far the easiest method. The second method uses a mixture of tables and transparent images. I haven't introduced you to CSS yet, so you may want to skip to the following section before reading this one; but I promise that this is simple enough that you won't need much CSS knowledge to use the technique. I'll address each method individually.

> **WARNING** The absolute positioning technique works only with browsers that can use CSS styles.

Controlling Element Position with CSS Styles

First, a warning: absolute positioning works only in version 4 and higher browsers, and unfortunately, the syntax and approach for Netscape and IE browsers are slightly different. IE treats each element on the screen—every paragraph, button, font tag—every HTML tag, as an object. Therefore, each tag that you've seen so far can take several other attributes in addition to the ones I've listed. One such attribute is a `style` attribute. There are multiple values for styles. In this section, you're concerned only with the `position:absolute` value.

To position an object in IE, you add the `style` attribute, set the position to `absolute`, and specify the pixel location where you want the top left corner of the object to appear. For example, to display an image at point 50, 50, write the image tag as follows:

```
<img src="image/bike.gif" style="position:absolute; left:50; top:50">
```

This type of style usage is called an inline style because you specify it inside the tag. The value of the `style` attribute, like all attribute values, is a string.

Within the string you can specify multiple `style` settings. You separate the settings from each other with semicolons and you separate the setting values from the setting names with colons. In this example, the words `Hello World` plot at point 100, 100.

```
<div style="position:absolute; left:100 top:100">Hello World</div>
```

Controlling the Z-Order Position

Using styles, you can also control the z-order position of an element. All visible elements in a browser have a z-order value. Elements with higher values appear above elements with lower values. In standard HTML, the position of an element in the HTML stream determines its z-order position. In other words, elements toward the end of the HTML stream will appear above elements earlier in the stream. CSS supports a `z-index` attribute that controls the relative z-order position of each element. For example, to plot the text `Hello World` on top of the bike image element, you can write a page like Listing 4.9.

LISTING 4.9   **Controlling the Z-Order Position (ch4i20.htm)**

```
<HTML>
<HEAD>
<TITLE></TITLE>
</HEAD>
<BODY>
<div style="position:absolute; left:100; top:100; z-index:0">
   <img src="images/bike.gif" border=1>
</div>
<div style="position:absolute; left:100; top:100; z-index:1">
   <b><font size="5" color="blue">Hello World</font></b>
</div>
</BODY>
</HTML>
```

The `z-index` value of 1 forces the browser to plot the text on top of the image, which has a `z-index` value of 0. Now, you may not be impressed, but I sure was when I saw this for the first time, because until that point, you had to use table cell background images to plot text on top of an image.

CSS styles support relative positioning as well, in which the browser determines an element's position relative to the position of its parent. You can express both absolute and relative positions in either pixels or percentages, using either positive or negative values. I'm a big fan of using percentages to specify positions whenever possible. If you use percentages, you isolate your page elements from dependence on the client's screen resolution. Also, the positions of display elements remain constant relative to the screen even when the browser changes size.

For example, in Listing 4.10, the `<span>` tag containing the text I'm Here! plots above and to the left of its parent `<div>` tag.

LISTING 4.10   Absolute and Relative Positioning (ch4i21.htm)

```
<html>
<head>
<title></title>
</head>
<body>
<div style="position:absolute; left:100; top:100; z-index:0">
    <img src="images/bike.gif" border="1" WIDTH="227" HEIGHT="179">
</div>
<div style="position:absolute; left:100; top:100; z-index:1">
    <b><font size="5" color="blue">Hello World</font></b>
    <span style="position:relative; left:-100%; top:-100%;
    z-index:2"><b><font size="5" color="red">I'm Here!</font></b></span>
</div>
</body>
</html>
```

Figure 4.19 shows how the previous listing plots in a browser.

FIGURE 4.19:

Absolute and relative positioning (ch4i21.htm)

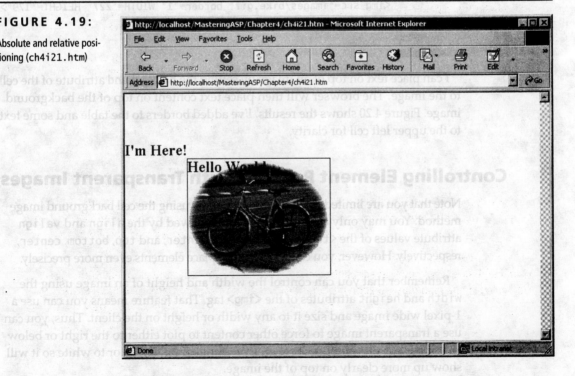

Controlling Element Position with Tables

You can accomplish similar results by using tables, although it's much more time-consuming and not as accurate. By varying the width and height of the table cells, you can place elements more or less where you want them to appear on the screen. For example, to place a graphic at the point 100, 100, you can create a table with two columns, no border, and four cells. By assigning the top left cell a width and height of 99, you can be sure the bottom right cell area will start at 100, 100.

```
<table cols="2">
    <tr>
        <td width="99" height="99">
             
        </td>
        <td>
             
        </td>
    </tr>
    <tr>
        <td width="99" height="99">
             
        </td>
        <td>
            <img src="images/bike.gif" border="1" WIDTH="227" HEIGHT="179">
        </td>
    </tr>
</table>
```

I can place text on top of an image by setting the background attribute of the cell to the image. The browser will then place text content on top of the background image. Figure 4.20 shows the results. I've added borders to the table and some text to the upper left cell for clarity.

Controlling Element Position with Transparent Images

Note that you are limited in the placement of text using the cell background image method. You may only assign the positions allowed by the align and valign attribute values of the <td> tag: left, right, center; and top, bottom, center, respectively. However, you can use a trick to place elements even more precisely.

Remember that you can control the width and height of an image using the width and height attributes of the <img> tag. That feature means you can use a 1-pixel wide image and size it to any width or height on the client. Thus, you can use a transparent image to force other content to plot either to the right or below it. Listing 4.11 shows the technique. I've changed the text color to white so it will show up more clearly on top of the image.

FIGURE 4.20:

Controlling element position
with tables (ch4i22.htm)

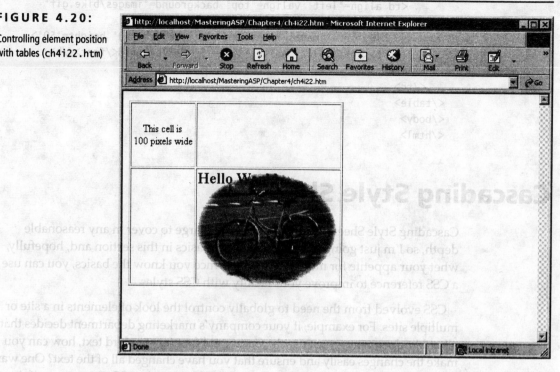

LISTING 4.11   **Controlling Element Position with Transparent Images (ch4i23.htm)**

```html
<html>
<head>
<title></title>
</head>
<body>
<table border="1" cols="2">
   <tr>
      <td align="center" valign="center" width="99" height="99">
         This cell is <br>100 pixels wide
      </td>
      <td>
          
      </td>
   </tr>
   <tr>
      <td width="99" height="99">
          
      </td>
```

```
        <td align="left" valign="top" background="images/bike.gif"
           WIDTH="227" HEIGHT="179">
           <img src="images/transparent.gif" width="50" height="50">
           <b><font color="white" size="5">Hello World</font></b>
        </td>
      </tr>
    </table>
  </body>
</html>
```

Cascading Style Sheets

Cascading Style Sheets (CSS) is a subject too large to cover in any reasonable depth, so I'm just going to briefly cover the basics in this section and, hopefully, whet your appetite for more knowledge. Once you know the basics, you can use a CSS reference to improve your facility with CSS styles.

CSS evolved from the need to globally control the look of elements in a site or multiple sites. For example, if your company's marketing department decides that all public documents must use the Garamond font for standard text, how can you make the changes easily and ensure that you have changed all of the text? One way is to search every document for text content, then apply a `<font>` tag specifying the Garamond font for each occurrence—but that's terribly time-consuming and error-prone. It would be better if there were a way to specify how an element appears once; changes to the specification would then cascade down to each occurrence.

What Cascading Style Sheets Do

CSS technology allows you to make global changes such as those described in the previous paragraph much more easily. A CSS defines attributes for element types. The style sheet definitions appear inside a `<style>` tag—usually placed in the `<head>` section of the document. This type of style definition is an embedded style sheet because it's embedded into the document. The power of CSS styles is the following:

- You can define styles that apply to all instances of an element type.

- Child elements inherit the style assigned to their parent.

- You can override the inherited style using other style sheets or inline styles

- You can reference style sheets—the style definitions don't have to exist in each document.

For example, you can alter the font for all text in a document by defining a CSS style for the <body> tag:

```
<style type="text/CSS">
        body {font: 12pt Garamond;}
</style>
```

The style contains one *selector*: body, and one *rule*: {font: 12pt Garamond;}. The rule specifies that text in the selector will appear in 12-point Garamond. A document that contains this rule will render all text in the Garamond font.

Controlling Appearance with Styles

To see CSS in action, type or copy the code from Listing 4.12 into a file, save it, then open the file in your browser. Note that the text appears in your browser's default font—you'll change that in a minute.

LISTING 4.12   **Cascading Style Sheet Example** (ch4i24.htm)

```
<html>
<head>
<title>Cascading Style Sheet Example</title>
<!--<style type="text/css">
        body {font: 14pt Garamond;}
</style>-->
</head>
<body>
<h1>Cascading Style Sheet Example</h1>
<h2>Look at the face and size of the following text</h2>
<p>This is a simple HTML file. In the head section of
this file, there's a Cascading Style Sheet. When the
&lt;style&gt; tag is commented out, the text in the
document appears in your browser's default font. When you
uncomment the &lt;style&gt; tag, the text appears in
14-point Garamond (if you have the Garamond font
installed on your computer).</p>
</body>
</html>
```

Now, reopen the file and remove the comment tag around the <style> tag. Save the file and refresh your browser. You should see the screen change. Figures 4.21 and 4.22 show the difference between the file with no style sheet and the file viewed with the style sheet in effect. Both files use the code from Listing 4.12, but I uncommented the <style> tag to create Figure 4.22.

FIGURE 4.21:

Text without style sheet
applied (ch4i24.htm)

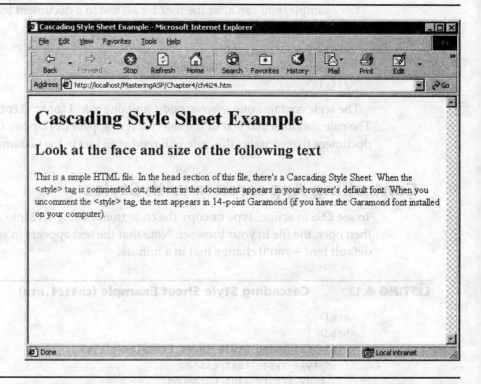

FIGURE 4.22:

Text with style sheet applied
(ch4i24.htm)

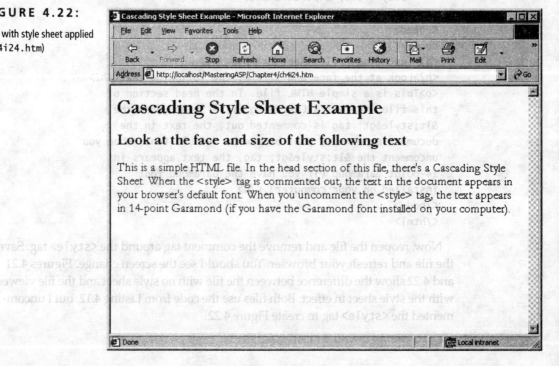

Types of CSS Styles

There are four types of CSS styles. You've seen two of them already—inline styles and embedded styles.

Inline styles   Attributes of an element. You enter them using a `style=` `"style definition"` attribute and value inside an element's tag.

Embedded styles   Style tags embedded in the `<head>` section of a document.

Linked styles   References to external style sheets. You enter them using a `<link>` tag in the `<head>` section of a document. The document containing the style sheet definition usually has a `.css` extension.

Imported styles   External style sheets imported into an embedded or linked `<style>` tag. You import a style sheet using the `@import: url(someURL.` `css)` command syntax. The browser imports and processes imported style sheets rules before it processes rules that appear explicitly within the `<style>` tag.

The browser processes style rules in the order in which they appear, and rules that appear later take precedence over rules that appear earlier. Similarly, rules that apply specifically to an element take precedence over generic, inherited rules.

Overriding CSS Styles

It's nice to be able to define styles that apply globally to element types, but what about those instances when you don't want a global style to apply to a specific element? You can have multiple rules that apply to an element. Specific style rules override general style rules. For example, if you wanted the body text to appear in Garamond, but not the heading text, you could add a second rule to your `<style>` tag:

```
<style type="text/css">
    body {font: 14pt Garamond;}
    h1 {font: 24pt Arial;}
    h2 {font: 18pt Arial;}
</style>
```

You can always override styles defined in a `<style>` tag with inline style attributes. For example, suppose the following `<h1>` tag appeared in the same document as the `<style>` tag above:

```
<h1 style="font: 10pt Arial">
```

The heading would appear in 10-point Arial because inline styles take precedence over more generic style rules.

Referencing External Style Sheets

You don't have to include the style sheet with each page; you can save the style sheet in a separate page and reference it from each file. Style sheets in other files are called *linked* or *external* style sheets. For example, the following `<link>` tag tells the browser to retrieve the style sheet definition from the file specified by the `href` attribute. You place the `<link>` tag in the head section of the document.

```
<link rel="stylesheet" type="text/css" href="mystyles.css">
```

Another way to reference external style rules is to import them into an existing `<style>` tag. For example, suppose the following style rules exist in a document called `siteRules.css`.

```
<style type="text/css">
    body {font: 14pt Garamond;}
    h1 {font: 24pt Arial;}
    h2 {font: 18pt Arial;}
</style>
```

In your document, you can import the rules in the `siteRuless.css` file using an `@import` command inside the `<style>` tag:

```
<style type="text/css">
    @import: url(siteRules.css);
    li {font: 10pt Times New Roman;}
</style>
```

The effect of the preceding `<style>` tag is the same as if you had written:

```
<style type="text/css">
    body {font: 14pt Garamond;}
    h1 {font: 24pt Arial;}
    h2 {font: 18pt Arial;}
    li {font: 10pt Times New Roman;}
</style>
```

Using Classes in Style Sheets

In addition to defining styles for standard HTML elements, you can define your own styles by creating a selector name. Styles with selector names that you create are called classes because you use them to subclass an element. The advantage of creating class styles is that you can apply them to any element using the `<class>` attribute. For example, if you create a style that turns the text red, you can easily apply it to any element in your document:

```
<style type="text/css">
    .redText {color:red;}
</style>
```

```
<p class="redText">
    This paragraph appears in red
</p>
<p>
    This paragraph appears in the default color
</p>
```

Control Hyperlink Appearance

In most static Web sites, the links change color when you click on them to show that you have visited that link destination. That behavior is not so desirable in applications, where a person may click on the same link many times to accomplish a task. You can use CSS styles to control how your links behave. Links have three pseudo-classes called :link, :visited and :active. The :link pseudo-class controls how the link appears normally, when it's neither active (the user has clicked the mouse button on the link) nor visited (the user has navigated to the link target). To keep visited links from changing color, set the same style for both the :link and :visited pseudo-classes:

```
<style type="text/css">
    a:link {color:blue}
    a:visited {color:blue}
</style>
```

Final Words about CSS Styles

You can do a great deal more with CSS styles than just change fonts; however, you won't need advanced training in style sheets to work with the ASP examples and projects in this book. Nevertheless, I urge you to begin learning and applying CSS styles now. As you build larger sites, CSS styles become increasingly important for controlling and modifying the look and feel of your pages.

In this chapter, you've seen how to use HTML as a display engine for content. So far, all of the content has been static content—text included in the HTML file itself. In the next several chapters you'll see how ASP lets you create pages dynamically.

PART II

Intrinsic ASP Objects

PART II

Intrinsic ASP Objects

C H A P T E R

F I V E

The Response Object

- ■ Introduction to ASP Objects

- ■ What is a Response?

- ■ Sending Text with the Response Object

- ■ Sending Text with Embedded Quotes

- ■ Using Variables

- ■ Mixing HTML and Response Code

- ■ The Response.Cookies Collection

- ■ The Response.AddHeader Method

- ■ Additional Response Properties/Methods

ASP exposes seven objects that you can use to send HTML and data to the browser, retrieve information from the browser, communicate with the server, cache data for individuals and your application, and handle errors. You don't need to have any programming background to use these objects—in fact, you don't even need to know what an object is to use ASP. Nevertheless, a little background can't hurt.

Introduction to ASP Objects

An object is nothing more than a set of properties and methods all wrapped up together with some property values. A property is a value that belongs to the object. For example, `breed` is a property of a horse object; the `numberOfWheels` is a property of a vehicle object, etc. To programmers using an object, a property looks like a value. Sometimes you can get the value and set the value—the property is read/write. Sometimes you can only get the value—the property is read-only. In unusual cases, you can set the value, but not get it—the property is write-only.

Another way to think about properties is that they describe the state of an object. For example, a door object may have an `Open` property. The property may take only two values—`True` or `False`—either the door is open or it's closed. You might not agree to that and say that a door may be partially open, and you would be correct. You might create your door object with a range of `Open` property values from 0 to 100. A value of 0 means the door is closed, a value of 50 means it's half-way open, and a value of 100 means the door is fully open. In either case, the value of the `Open` property describes the state of the door.

In addition to properties, objects also have methods. A method differs from a property because a method does something, whereas a property is something. Consider a dog object. A dog object has a color, a breed, a height—these are properties. A dog object can run, jump, bark, roll over—these are methods. Typically, methods cause the object to do something—often based on its state. In other words, the methods of an object and the state of the object interact with each other and are often mutually dependent on each other.

To use most objects from a programming language, you must first create an instance of the object you want to use. An object instance is a single copy of an object. You create an instance of an object by creating an object variable, then assigning a new copy of an object to the variable. The process of creating an object instance is called instantiation. You instantiate an object when you create an instance of that object.

You don't have to instantiate ASP objects. The seven objects that ASP exposes are called intrinsic objects because you don't have to create them—they're always available for you to use on any ASP page. The objects are:

Response Object   Used to send information to the client

Request Object   Used to retrieve information included with the request from the client

Server Object   Used to communicate with the server

Application Object   Used to store (cache) information about your application

Session Object   Used to cache information about a specific browser instance (which usually, but not always, corresponds to a single user)

ObjectContext Object   Used to initiate and control transactions and create new objects through Microsoft Transaction Server (MTS)

ASPError Object   Used to obtain information about errors that occur while the ASP engine processes a script

These seven objects are at the heart of ASP programming. You will become intimately familiar with some of the properties and methods of ASP objects because you will use them constantly. While you need not memorize every single property and method, you should at least be aware of all the possibilities. In the rest of this part of the book, you'll explore each of these objects in detail.

What Is a Response?

When a browser requests data from the server, the server responds, either with a redirect message, the requested data, or an error. The response has two main parts. The response header contains directives and/or information about the impending content, such as the type of content, the expiration date, cookies, etc. The response body contains the data.

For HTML requests, the response data comes directly from the Web server, which reads and returns the contents of an HTML page. For ASP pages, the response data comes from the ASP object called the Response object.

Sending Text with the Response Object

The process the Web server uses to return a response to the browser is complex, but returning a response using the Response object couldn't be easier. You return a response by using the `Write` method of the Response object:

```
<%
Response.Write "The Response.Write method is great!"
%>
```

Note the bracket-percent (<%) delimiters around the code. The delimiters, as you may recall, separate script from content in an ASP page. The entire ASP file looks like Listing 5.1.

LISTING 5.1   The `Response.Write` Method (ch5i1.asp)

```
<%@ Language=VBScript %>
<html>
<head>
</head>
<body>
<%
Response.Write "The Response.Write method is great!"
%>
</body>
</html>
```

Two features differentiate this file from a standard HTML file. First, the top line in the file, `<%@ Language=VBScript %>`, tells the ASP engine that the default scripting language used for the page is VBScript (the @ sign is required and denotes a script directive, as opposed to script code). Second, the `Response.Write` line contains the content. The content isn't in HTML; you now control the content with script. You can change the script to return any response you want.

You try it. Create a text file and insert the contents of Listing 5.1. Create a subdirectory called `Chapter5` as a subdirectory of the physical directory for the `MasteringASP` virtual directory you created in Chapter 2. If you're not sure where to create the subdirectory, open the Microsoft Management Console (MMC), and look on the Virtual Directory tab of the `MasteringASP` virtual directory for the physical path. Create the `Chapter5` subdirectory in that path. Save the file as `ch5i1.asp` in the new `Chapter5` subdirectory.

NOTE

In the rest of this book, I'm going to assume that you have created the `Mas-teringASP` virtual directory, that you have marked it as an IIS application, and that it runs in an isolated process, with Script access rights. If you haven't created the virtual directory, create it now, then save Listing 5.1.

Test the `ch5i1.asp` file by navigating to it in your browser. You can use the URL:

```
http://yourServer/MasteringASP/Chapter5/ch5i1.asp
```

Replace yourServer in the URL with the name of your server. If you don't know what your server's name is (usually it's the same as the name of your computer), you can use the generic server name `localhost` if you're using a local Web server (one running on your computer). For example:

```
http://localhost/MasteringASP/Chapter5/ch5i1.asp
```

You should see the text `The Response.Write Method is great!` in your browser. If you see an error message instead, make sure your Web server is running; ASP is installed on your server; you have set up the `MasteringASP` virtual directory as described in this section; and you created the `Chapter5` subdirectory. Check to make sure the file is there and that you typed the correct URL into the browser.

NOTE

For best results, I recommend you follow the directory structure used on the CD and put the listing files for each chapter into a separate directory. The full virtual path for Listing 5.1 is `http://localhost/MasteringASP/Chapter5/ch5i1.asp`.

Sending Text with Embedded Quotes

The `Write` method accepts a text string. You must surround the text you pass to the `Write` method with double-quotes. Suppose the text string you want to write already contains double-quotes? How do you write the string then? Change the text of the `Response.Write` line to:

```
Response.Write "The "Response.Write" method is great!"
```

Save the file and run it again by refreshing your browser. You should see the following error message (the path and line number in line 3 of the error message may differ on your computer—that doesn't matter):

```
Microsoft VBScript compilation error '800a0401'
Expected end of statement
```

```
/MasteringASP/Chapter5/ch5i1.asp, line 7
Response.Write "The "Response.Write" method is great!"
------------^
```

There are some minor differences between the error messages you receive when running ASP with IIS 4 and ASP under IIS 5. For example, under IIS 5 in Windows 2000, the error message is:

```
Microsoft VBScript compilation (0x800A0401)
/MasteringASP/Chapter5/ch5i1.asp, line 7, column 22
Response.Write " The "Response.Write" method is great!"
------------^.
```

Note the added column number in the more recent version. In both versions, the caret (^) in the last line of the error message points to the position in the line where the error occurred (more accurately, the beginning of the point where the ASP engine could no longer process the file). The error text `Expected end of statement` means that the VBScript parser interpreted the double-quote before the word `Response` as the closing quote in the line. In other words, the syntax is incorrect. Syntax errors are the most common errors in programming ASP—and the easiest to correct.

You must use the correct syntax to send embedded quotes. You can use any of several methods to send strings containing embedded double-quotes. Each is useful in different situations.

Using Double-Quotes

The first method is to double the quotes. Change the text line as follows, then run the file again:

```
Response.Write "The ""Response.Write"" method is great!"
```

This time the text will appear in your browser properly. Try one more change. Suppose the quoted text appears at the end of the line.

```
Response.Write "The Response.Write method is ""great!""
```

When you run that, you get an error as well. The reason is there's no closing quote. Add a third double-quote to the end of the line and the `Write` method will work properly.

```
Response.Write "The Response.Write method is ""great!"""
```

The parser isn't very smart—it just counts quotes. You must have an even number of quotes for the text to print properly. Knowing that simple rule can help you debug such errors quickly.

Using the *Chr()* Function

You may remember from Part I that the computer represents every text character as a number. You can take advantage of a simple VBScript function that returns a character based on the number of that character, the Chr() function. You may also remember that functions return values. In this case, you provide the ASCII value of the character you want to use as an argument, and the Chr() function returns the character as its return value. For example, the code below prints the same text on the screen as the previous example:

```
Response.Write "The Response.Write method is "
Response.Write Chr(34)
Response.Write "great!"
Response.Write Chr(34)
```

Of course, that looks like a lot of code to write just to avoid a couple of double-quotes. You can compress that code into one line using concatenation. Concatenation is the process of combining text strings. In VBScript, you use the ampersand (&) character to combine two strings:

```
Response.Write "The Response.Write method is " & _
    Chr(34) & "great!" & Chr(34)
```

NOTE   In a code editor, the previous example would all be on one line. In this book, because the code has to fit within the width of the page, I've broken the code lines by using the VBScript line continuation character, the underscore (_), to break long code lines into several shorter lines. You do not need to enter the underscore in your own code unless you want to continue code lines on the next line. If you do, note that you must precede the underscore with a space and that the underscore must be the last character in the continued line. In this book, you'll see several types of code: HTML, VBScript, JScript, SQL, and XML/XSL code. Of these, only VBScript requires a line continuation character.

Using HTML Escape Syntax

Another way to print strings with embedded quotes is to take advantage of HTML escape syntax. In HTML, you send special characters such as a right-bracket or greater-than (>) symbol by using HTML escape syntax. For example, > for (>) and < for (<). A double-quote is " as shown here:

```
Response.Write "The Response.Write method is & _
    "&quot;great!&quot;"
```

Note that this works only when the output medium is HTML. If you're using VBScript to write text to a program that doesn't understand HTML, you can't use this method.

Using Variables

You don't have to send static text to the `Response.Write` method. You can place text you want to send in a variable and pass the variable as the argument to the method. To declare a variable, use the `Dim` statement. In VBScript, the keyword `Dim` stands for Dimension. You should dimension variables before you use them, although you're not required to do so in VBScript. Listing 5.2 contains an example showing how to create a variable and use it with the `Response.Write` method.

LISTING 5.2   **Using Variables with the `Response.Write` Method (`ch5i2.asp`)**

```
<%@ Language=VBScript %>
<%
Dim myString
myStrng = "This text is stored in a variable."
Response.Write myString
%>
```

Before you run the code in Listing 5.2, look at the line that assigns the text string to the `myString` variable. I deliberately misspelled the variable in the listing. Copy or enter the code into the `ch5i2.asp` file and save it to your `Chapter5` directory. View the file in your browser using the URL:

```
http://localhost/MasteringASP/Chapter5/ch5i1.asp
```

NOTE   At this point, I'm going to stop reminding you of the URLs required to test these files. All the code in this book uses the `MasteringASP` virtual directory except where specifically noted. The ASP files are in a subdirectory named by chapter. Image files, when needed, are in an images subdirectory.

You won't see an error message—but you won't see any output either. This bug is a feature in VB and VBScript (that Microsoft should probably remove) called automatic variable declaration. Microsoft's interpreter tries to treat every word in your code that is not a keyword, a function name, or an object, as a variable. If you haven't declared the variable explicitly, VBScript helpfully declares it for you, without asking.

You can turn off this feature and I strongly recommend that you do. To turn off automatic variable declarations, put the line `<% Option Explicit %>` at the top of every file, just under the `<%@ Language=VBScript %>` directive. For example:

```
<%@ Language=VBScript %>
<% option explicit %>
```

The `Option Explicit` line tells VBScript to raise a syntax error if it encounters variables that you have not dimensioned. If you don't include this line, VBScript tries to interpret every unrecognized word as a variable. That's convenient, but as you've seen, it leads to subtle, hard-to-find errors.

After adding the `<% Option Explicit %>` directive to your page, if you forget to dimension a variable, the ASP engine displays an error stating that the variable is undefined. For example:

```
Error Type:
Microsoft VBScript runtime (0x800A01F4)
Variable is undefined: 'myStrng'
/MasteringASP/Chapter5/testVarType.asp, line 4
```

Mixing HTML and Response Code

Some ASP pages, like the ones you've seen so far, contain only script, but most ASP pages contain a mixture of HTML and script. For example:

```
<%@ Language=VBScript %>
<% option explicit %>
<%
Dim LastName
Dim FirstName
LastName="Jones"
FirstName="Russell"
%>
<html><head><title>Mixing Script and HTML</title></head>
<body>
My name is <%=FirstName%> <%=LastName%>.
</body>
</html>
```

The equals sign in the code `<%=FirstName%>` is a shorthand way to code `Response .Write`. It's equivalent to `<%Response.Write Firstname%>`. If you think about this for a minute, you can see that the process of returning HTML to the browser works like this. The ASP engine:

1. Dimensions and sets the values of the variables `LastName` and `FirstName`.

2. Finds the end-of-script delimiter.

3. Begins sending HTML.

4. Encounters the start-of-script delimiter and reads the script up to the next end-of-script delimiter.

5. Evaluates the value of the variable `FirstName`, retrieves the string returned from the `Response.Write` method, and sends the string to the browser. It repeats that process for the `<%=LastName%>` code.

6. Finishes sending the HTML.

7. Destroys the variables and frees their memory.

You can intermix script and HTML freely in this manner as long as you remember the script delimiters.

NOTE   Although you can intermix script and HTML using the script delimiters, the ASP engine runs more efficiently if you minimize the number of script delimiters in your code. In other words, it's faster to write HTML with script than it is to frequently switch between HTML and script mode.

Writing HTML with Script

Of course, you don't have to separate your HTML from your script code—you can write HTML with script. Remember that the output from an ASP page isn't script text and HTML text—it's just a string of characters or bytes. The browser carries the burden of separating the data stream from the server into its component parts. Listing 5.3 shows how you can write a table using script.

LISTING 5.3   **Writing HTML with Script (ch5i3.asp)**

```
<%@ Language=VBScript %>
<% option explicit %>
<html>
<head>
<title>Writing HTML with Script</title>
</head>
<body>
<%
dim table
dim tableEnd
dim tr
dim trEnd
dim ltd
```

```
dim rtd
dim tdEnd
table="<table align='center' width='60%' bgcolor='#FFEE00' border='1'>"
tableEnd="</table>"
tr="<tr>"
trEnd="</tr>"
ltd="<td>"
rtd="<td>"
tdEnd="</td>"
With Response
    .Write table
    .Write tr
    .Write ltd & "<b>Response Feature</b>" & tdEnd
    .Write rtd & "<b>Mastered</b>" & tdEnd
    .Write trEnd
    .Write tr
    .Write ltd & "Write text" & tdEnd
    .Write rtd & "<img src='images/redcheck.gif'>" & tdEnd
    .Write trEnd
    .Write tr
    .Write ltd & "Write text using the Chr() function" & tdEnd
    .Write rtd & "<img src='images/redcheck.gif'>" & tdEnd
    .Write trEnd
    .Write tr
    .Write ltd & "Write text with variables" & tdEnd
    .Write rtd & "<img src='images/redcheck.gif'>" & tdEnd
    .Write trEnd
    .Write tr
    .Write ltd & "Write HTML with script" & tdEnd
    .Write rtd & "<img src='images/redcheck.gif'>" & tdEnd
    .Write trEnd
    .Write tr
    .Write ltd & "Write script with script" & tdEnd
    .Write rtd & "In progress" & tdEnd
    .Write trEnd
    .Write tableEnd
end with
%>
</body>
</html>
```

There are a couple of interesting features in the previous listing. The first one you should notice is that VBScript supports a notation called With...End With. The With statement lets you set a default object. You can then write numerous references to that object without repeating the object name each time. You supply the name of the object immediately following the `With` statement. When you're finished using the object, you use the `End With` statement. A group of program statements that belong together comprises a block, or code block. You should indent the lines between the beginning and the end of the code block because indentation makes the code much easier to read.

It's convenient not to have to type the word `Response` repeatedly, but that's not the main reason to use a `With...End With` block. The real reason is that it speeds up your code. ASP script languages use late-binding. Every time you reference an object in script, the script engine must query the object for its methods and parameters. Using the `With...End With` block lets the engine cache the object methods so it doesn't have to make the query every time. I use the `Response.Write` method nearly 30 times in the script, so using the `With...End With` notation saves a little time. Time and memory are the most precious resources on your server. Any time you can save a little without much effort, do so.

Another feature you should notice is that you can use a single-quote in HTML anywhere you can use a double-quote. For example, you would normally write the `<table>` tag as follows:

```
<table width="60%" bgcolor="#FFEE00" border="1">
```

In the following example, however, I've substituted single-quotes for the double-quotes within the `<table>` tag:

```
table="<table width='60%' bgcolor='#FFEE00' border='1'>"
```

Using single-quotes for attribute values makes it much easier to write HTML with script because you don't have to worry about doubling the quotes or using the `Chr()` function. Figure 5.1 shows how the table looks in the browser.

Finally, you may think this is a trivial example because I've just substituted variables for the `<table>` tags, but writing HTML with script is a powerful feature—as powerful as CSS styles. Here's why. Suppose I need to center the rightmost column and increase its width, and align the leftmost column at the top of each cell. To center a column, I would normally need to add an `align="center"` attribute to each `<td>` tag in each row. Using script, I can redefine the `ltd` (left column) and `rtd` (right column) variables to change all the columns simultaneously. Figure 5.2 shows the result of that change using the following code:

```
ltd="<td width='70%' valign='top'>"
rtd="<td width='30%' align='center'>"
```

In this book, you'll see even more powerful ways to write HTML with script.

FIGURE 5.1:

Writing HTML with script
(ch5i3.asp)

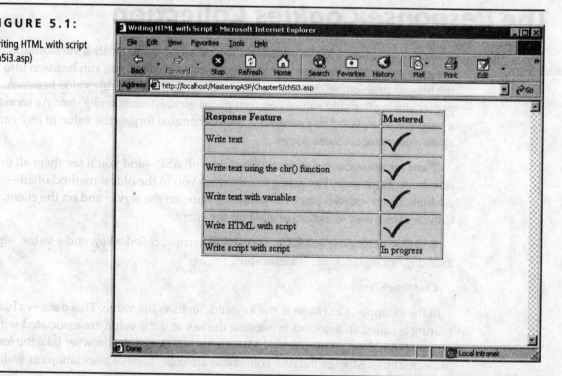

FIGURE 5.2:

Writing HTML with script
(ch5i3a.asp)

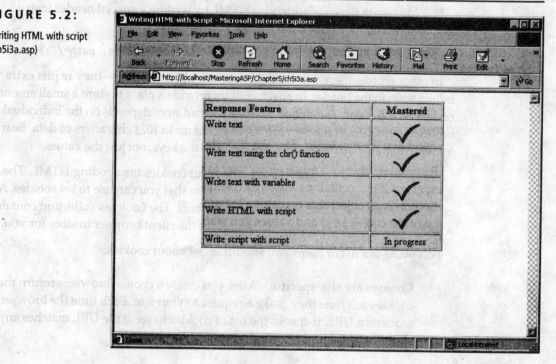

The *Response.Cookies* Collection

You can't program without variables. You've seen how to create a variable and assign a string to it. As soon as you begin using variables, you run head-on into the biggest problem with Web applications—keeping a variable value between pages. Storing variable values between pages is called *maintaining state*. As soon as a page has completed its processing, the ASP engine forgets the value of any variables you create on those pages.

There are several ways to maintain state with ASP—and you'll see them all in this book. Right now, I'm going to introduce you to the oldest method of all—cookies. There are two places to maintain state: on the server and on the client. Cookies are a way to maintain state on the client.

A cookie, in its simplest form, consists of a name, called a key, and a value, separated by an equals sign. For example:

```
LastName=Jones
```

In the example, `LastName` is the key and `Jones` is the value. This `name=value` pairing is called an association because the key and the value are associated with one another. Most values passed between the server and the browser take the form of associations. Most of the ASP collections are collections of associations as well.

You can create a cookie with pure HTML by writing a special header instruction containing the value of the cookie. For example:

```
<meta http-equiv="set-cookie" content="LastName=Jones; path=/";>
```

In other words, there's nothing mysterious about cookies—they're just extra information in the header. In effect, cookies provide a place to store a small amount of data on the client. The size of the data you can store depends on the individual browser; however, all modern browsers accept up to 1024 characters of data. Bear in mind that the maximum data size includes the keys, not just the values.

Fortunately, there's a much easier way to set cookies than coding HTML. The Response Object contains a `Cookies` collection that you can use to set cookies. A collection is an object that contains a list of items. The `Cookies` collection contains a list of the cookie keys and values you want the client browser to store for you.

Following is a list of items you should know about cookies:

Cookies are site-specific   After you create a cookie, browsers return the cookie each time they make a request to your site. Each time the browser requests a URL, it checks the list of cookies to see if the URL matches any stored cookie. If the browser finds a match, it sends all the stored cookie values for that site.

Cookies are secure   The browser sends cookies only when they match a specific domain and server—no other site can read cookies you have set for your site. The `path` parameter (refer to the previous example) lets you set cookies that apply only to a specific path within your site. The browser only sends the cookies if the requested URL matches the domain, server, and path.

Expiration Date/Time   You can set an expiration date and time after which the cookie expires and is no longer valid. If you set the expiration date, the browser writes the cookie to disk. If you don't set the expiration date, the browser maintains the cookie in memory only—the cookie expires when you close the browser. Note that cookies written to disk apply to every open instance of the browser, because all instances of the browser have access to the cookies on disk. In-memory cookies apply only to a single instance of the browser—the browser doesn't share in-memory cookies among different instances.

Secure Cookies   Browsers and servers that communicate normally send data as plain text—that includes cookies. Developers often use cookies to store sensitive information, such as usernames and passwords. With little effort, unscrupulous people can read the cookie values. You can specify that a cookie may be sent only over a secure connection (for example, via HTTPS). The browser will not send a secured cookie over an unsecured connection. Cookies sent via a secure connection are encrypted and cannot (easily) be read by hackers.

To set a cookie, you must provide both a key and a value. For example, to set a cookie with the key ModelName and the value PathFinder, you would write:

```
Response.Cookies("ModelName") = "PathFinder"
```

You can create cookies with more than one value. Each of the multiple values is a sub-value. The terminology here is somewhat murky, because Microsoft's documentation also refers to cookies with multiple values as cookies with Dictionaries. That's useful only if you know what a Dictionary object is. I think it's easier, especially at this stage, for you to think about cookies with one value and cookies with multiple values, although you may not think so after you read the next paragraph.

When you create cookies with multiple values, each sub-value is associated with a sub-key. One way to think about these sub-keys and sub-values is as a tree structure. The top-level key has a single value, which itself may be comprised of multiple pairs of keys and values. Each value may contain multiple pairs of keys and values. In other words, you can have multi-level cookies. Here's an example of a cookie with sub-values:

```
Response.Cookies("Employees")("President") = _
    "Bob Herschfield"
Response.Cookies("Employees")("VPSales") = _
    "Xiang Do"
Response.Cookies("Employees")("VPMarketing") = _
    "Bob Herrera"
Response.Cookies("Employees")("VPResearch") = _
    "Cynthia Fleming"
```

One reason to create cookies with sub-values is to help limit the size of the data the browser sends with each request. There's no point in sending extra names if you can associate multiple values with a single name. Because the browser sends all the cookie values associated with your site every time, you can see that saving a few bytes can add up quickly.

For example, suppose (to make the math easy) you store 1 kilobyte (KB), which is 1024 bytes, of information in cookies for each visitor to your site. Assume the average visitor views 10 pages. That means you generate 11 KB of network traffic for each visitor in addition to the page content for your site. If you have 100 simultaneous users, that's over a megabyte (MB) of extra information flowing back and forth over the network every 10 pages—and that's if you don't change the cookie. If you change the cookie values, the server must re-send them, generating twice the network traffic.

Today, a few extra MB of network traffic isn't usually a problem—especially on an intranet. However, when you consider that most people still access the Internet through 56 kilobit (Kb) or slower connections, you can see why you might want to limit the amount of information.

The most important reason to limit cookie size is that your server must parse the cookie values out of the raw HTTP data stream from the browser for each request. Parsing is a relatively fast operation, but server response time is critical. Don't tie it up needlessly.

The Response object takes care of sending the cookie to the browser, and the browser takes care of storing it and returning it to the server for subsequent requests to your site. All you need to do is set the cookie value(s) in the Response .Cookies collection.

To clear or delete a cookie, set its value to an empty string:

```
Response.Cookies("someKey") = ""
```

You'll see more about cookies in Chapter 6, *The Request Object*, in the section on the Request.Cookies collection.

The *Response.AddHeader* Method

The server and browser send cookies in the header section of an HTML document. You can't see them on the browser, even if you use the View Source feature that most browsers have, because the browser removes the header directives from the page before it renders the page.

Just as the Response object has a `Cookies` collection to help you send cookies, it has a `Response.AddHeader` method you can use to send more generalized header information. For example, one common use of headers is to send a message to the browser, informing it that a resource is no longer available at the requested location, but that the resource can be found at a new location. You can specify the length of time the browser should wait before requesting or redirecting to the new location.

Just a reminder: The `Response.AddHeader` method does nothing that you can't do with pure HTML. To add a redirect header in HTML, you can use a `<meta>` tag. For example:

```
<META HTTP-EQUIV="REFRESH" CONTENT="3">The refresh directive causes the
browser to request the page after a specified interval—in this example,
every three seconds. By adding a URL value, you can tell the browser to
request a different page. Specifying a refresh with a different page
constitutes a redirection.<META HTTP-EQUIV="REFRESH" CONTENT="5;
URL=http://www.microsoft.com/">
```

Note that in the previous example there are two separate header values, the refresh time and the redirection URL, separated with a semicolon. You can add the header with the `Response.AddHeader` method even more easily. For example:

```
<% Response.AddHeader "Refresh","2;URL=http://www.microsoft.com/"%>
```

Semicolons separate multiple values in the `Response.AddHeader` method just as in HTML. You can see redirection in action by creating an ASP page containing the script and HTML in Listing 5.4. The listing contains two pages, the page containing the script and the redirection target page.

LISTING 5.4   **Redirection with `Response.AddHeader` (ch5i4.asp)**

```
<%@ Language=VBScript %>
<% option explicit %>
<% Response.Buffer = True %>
<% Response.AddHeader "Refresh","5;URL=ch5i4a.asp"%>
<!-
The following meta tag contains the equivalent HTML redirect header
<meta http-equiv="refresh" content="5; url=http:ch5i4a.asp>
->
<html>
<head>
```

```
<title>Response AddHeader Redirection Example</title>
<script language="JavaScript">
window.setTimeout("timer()",1000,"JavaScript")
function timer() {
    var s = document.all.item("jumpTime").innerText;
    /* alert(s); */
    var time = parseInt(s);
    time = time - 1;
    document.all.item("jumpTime").innerText = time;
    if (time > 0) {
        window.setTimeout("timer()",1000,"JavaScript");
    }
}
</script>
<!-
```

Here's the same script in VBScript

```
<script language="VBScript">
call window.setTimeout("timer",1000,"VBScript")
Function timer()
    dim  time
    time =    document.all("jumpTime").innertext
    time = time -1
    document.all("jumpTime").innerText = time
    If time > 0 Then
        call window.setTimeout("timer",1000,"VBScript")
    End If
End Function
</script>->
</HEAD>
<BODY>
The resource you have requested has moved. The new location is:
<a href="http://localhost/
MasteringASP/Chapter5/ch5i4a.asp">ch5i4a.asp</a>.
<p>
If your browser supports redirection, it will
jump to the new location in <span id="jumpTime">5</span> seconds.

</BODY>
</HTML>
**********************************************************************
*
* The following HTML page is the redirection target (ch5i4a.asp)
**********************************************************************
*

<%@ language=VBScript %>
<% option explicit %>
```

```
<HTML>
<HEAD>
<META NAME="GENERATOR" Content="Microsoft Visual Studio 6.0">
</HEAD>
<BODY>

<P>You have been redirected to this page.</P>

</BODY>
</HTML>
```

You'll notice that the listing contains client-side script, because I wanted you to be able to see the browser count down to the redirection time. The counting and the redirection actually have nothing to do with one another. The browser redirects because of the header directive, not because of the timer or the script. I've included both JScript and VBScript versions, but I commented out the VBScript version on the CD.

You should also notice one other feature. The third line of the listing contains <% Response.Buffer = True %>. You must include that line if you want to redirect within your script after the server has sent any HTML. The server typically sends headers first, then begins sending the HTML. After the server has sent the headers, it cannot change them—they're already on the client computer. Therefore, if you anticipate changing header information during script processing, you must buffer the output—store all the output in memory before beginning the process of sending it to the browser. The buffered response includes both the headers and the HTML. So if you buffer the response, you can change your mind at any point and send a redirect header to the browser.

The *Response.Redirect* Method

The Response.AddHeader method is useful for redirection when you know in advance that you need to redirect and you have the exact location of the redirection URL, however, you need another method to redirect dynamically—when you don't know the exact URL.

For example, redirection is particularly useful when you're making decisions based on a user's actions. Suppose you had a list box containing product names. Based on the user's selection, you want to make a database connection and obtain the most recent information about that product to construct an HTML page about that product for the user. You've associated each product with a specific ASP page on the server. Until the user selects a product, you have no way of knowing which page to run. In pseudocode, the logic looks like this:

```
If the user selected Books
   show the Book main page
```

```
ElseIf the user selected Housewares
    show Housewares main page
ElseIf the user selected Electronics
    show the Electronics main page
End If
```

You accomplish the redirection itself with the `Response.Redirect` method, which takes one argument. For example, to redirect a user to Microsoft's home page, you would write:

```
Response.Redirect "http://www.microsoft.com/"
```

The `Response.Redirect` command takes effect immediately. The server does not process code that appears after the `Response.Redirect` command and does not send any HTML already in the buffer.

If you forget to include the `<% Response.Buffer = True %>` command at the top of the page, the server will raise an error when it tries to execute the `Response.Redirect` command. For example:

```
Response object error 'ASP 0156 : 80004005'

Header Error

/MasteringASP/Chapter5/ch5i4.asp, line 41
The HTTP headers are already written to the client browser. Any HTTP
header modifications must be made before writing page content.
```

> **NOTE** Forgetting to buffer the response is probably one of the most common mistakes beginning ASP programmers make. Fortunately, Microsoft has changed the default buffer setting in IIS 5 to **True**, which means you don't have to turn buffering on to redirect unless you have turned off buffering for the site using the Internet Service Manager.

Forcing ASP Pages to Refresh

ASP pages are, by nature, dynamic. In contrast, HTML pages are static. A great deal of work in the Web arena has gone into improving the response time for HTML pages. One of the best ways to improve response time is to move the page source closer to the requesting browser. To help do that, most browsers cache pages on your hard drive. The first time you load a page it may take a long time, because the browser must retrieve the page content from a remote server, but after the first request the browser caches the page. Subsequent requests for the same page load from the cache, so the page displays very quickly.

Similarly, many proxy servers also cache pages. When a browser makes a request through a proxy server, the proxy checks to see if it has a copy of the page. If so, it returns the page to the browser, avoiding a long round trip to the remote server.

Page caching works beautifully for static HTML pages, but doesn't work well at all for ASP pages. ASP pages often change because the back-end content has changed or the content changes in response to user input. If the browser displays a cached page, the page may be out of date, or may not respond properly to user input. The ASP server-side code does not run because the proxy intercepts the request before it reaches your server. The Response object has several properties that can help solve this problem.

The *Response.Expires* and *Response.ExpiresAbsolute* Properties

These relatively simple properties add response headers to the page. You use them to force the browser to request a new copy of your page rather than loading it from the browser's cache.

The Response.Expires property sets the length of time, in minutes, until the page content is no longer valid. After the specified number of minutes, the page expires. Until the page expires, the browser can display a cached copy of the page and does not have to re-request the page from the server. After the page expires, the browser must return to the server to display the page. For example, Response.Expires = 10 tells the browser that the content of the page is valid for up to 10 minutes.

The Response.ExpiresAbsolute property is exactly like the Expires property, except that you specify the date and time when the page expires rather than the number of minutes. For example, Response.ExpiresAbsolute = #January 10, 2005# specifies that the browser can load the page from its cache until 01/10/2005. The pound (#) sign specifies that the string contains a date value.

The good news is that these properties are simple to use. The bad news is that they don't work all the time. When they don't work, your ASP application may not work either. The problem doesn't lie with the commands themselves—they do add the proper header values to the response; it's that not all browsers act the way you might expect. Netscape browsers are particularly guilty of this improper behavior.

The *Response.CacheControl* Property

Page-caching problems are not always the browser's fault. Proxy servers cache pages too. Therefore, even if you include an expiration time or date on your pages and the browser honors the expiration, the proxy server may intercept the browser's request and return a cached page. Proxy servers don't always honor the expiration date either. To force the proxy to request a fresh copy of the page, you can use the `Response.CacheControl` property.

The `Response.CacheControl` property adds a response header that tells the proxy server not to cache the page. The property can take one of two string values: `Public` or `Private`. The default value is `Private`. Set the value to `Private` if you do not want proxy servers to cache the page and `Public` if you do want the proxy to cache the page. For example, you might want the proxy to cache pages that consist entirely of HTML code—even when the pages have an ASP extension. Most proxy servers will not cache pages if the `CacheControl` value is set to `Private`.

Unfortunately, not all proxy servers honor the `CacheControl` header either. ASP programmers have evolved a sure-fire method to force ASP page requests to refresh from the application server rather than from the cache. That method involves changing the URL in some unimportant way for each request. For example, you can append a date/time value to the end of each URL. Using this method, a simple anchor tag might look something like this:

```
<a href="somePage.asp?UniqueURL=09/09/1999 2:54:52 AM">
    Click for somePage
</a>
```

Because the time changes constantly, the browser and the proxy see the URL as unique. Therefore, they request the page from the server rather than from a cache. One solution is to write a routine that can automatically append date values to your URLs.

The *Response.AppendToLog* Method

Even in the modern programming world, some things never change. One of those things is the need to write status or error information to a file. For security reasons, you don't normally want to give anonymous users the ability to write files to your server. If you can't write files, where can you store the information?

One place you can write the information is in the Web server log. By default, IIS keeps a log of every request to the Web server. The `Response.AppendToLog` method lets you write messages to that log. It couldn't be simpler. All you do is provide the method with the character string you want to write to the Application log. For example:

```
Response.AppendToLog "Greetings from the Mastering " & _
    "ASP crowd."
```

Those of you who have written log code for other languages probably immediately notice that there's no time stamp on the message. That's because the IIS logging service does that for you automatically. If you haven't ever looked at the IIS log, you should do so. First, create a page to log a message (see Listing 5.5).

LISTING 5.5   IIS Log Message Example (ch5i5.asp)

```
<%@ Language=VBScript %>
<% option explicit %>
<% Response.AppendToLog "Greetings from the Mastering " & _
    "ASP crowd." %>
<html>
<head>
</head>
<body>
<p>Message written to the IIS Log</p>
</body>
</html>
```

Load the page into your browser. When you load the page, the script writes the log message. Here's how you can find it. In the Internet Services Manager application, right-click on the Default Web Site entry, then select Properties. At the bottom of the Default Web Site Properties dialog, make sure that the Enable Logging checkbox is checked. If it's not, check it and run the IIS Log Message example in Listing 5.5 again. Click the Properties button and note the path shown in the "Log file directory" field. By default, the path is **%SystemRoot%\System32\LogFiles**. The **%SystemRoot%** notation refers to your WinNT directory. IIS starts a new log file periodically based on the settings in this dialog (see Figure 5.3).

FIGURE 5.3:

Extended Logging Properties dialog, General Properties tab

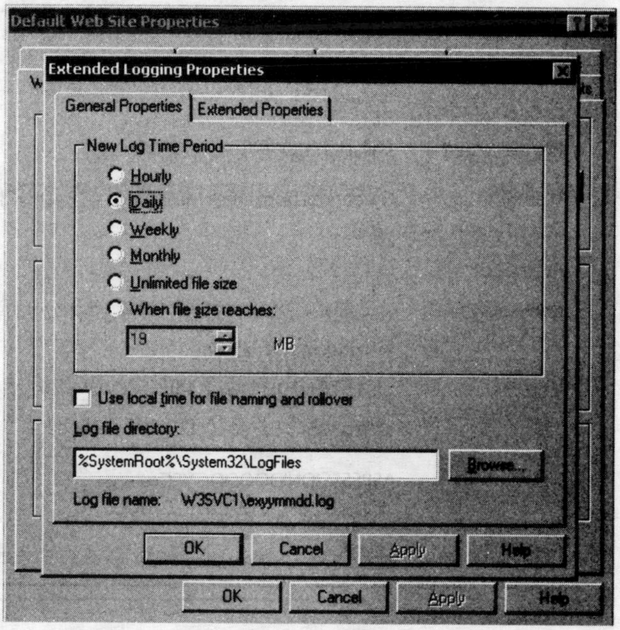

IIS names files according to the format string `exyymmdd.log`. Using Windows Explorer, navigate to the log file path and find today's file. Double-click on the file to open it in Notepad. Your message will be at or near the end of the file.

In addition to the time and date, the IIS log shows you:

- the client IP address and username (if available)
- the `request` method (GET or POST)
- the name of the requested file
- the return status from the server
- the number of bytes sent
- the client browser type string
- any cookies
- the Referer (the name of the file that linked to the requested file, if available).

For example, using the `Response.AppendToLog` method generated the following entry on my computer. Your log file may have different fields because you can control which fields appear in the log with IIS 5.

Field	Value
Time/Date	1999-10-06 04:19:37
Client IP	169.254.25.129
Request Method	GET
File requested	/MasteringASP/Chapter5/ch5i5.asp
Message	Greetings+from+the+Mastering+ASP+crowd.
Server Status	200
Bytes Sent	271
Browser Type	Mozilla/4.0+(compatible;+MSIE+5.01; +Windows+NT+5.0)
Cookies	ASPCLIENTDEBUG=1;+SITESERVER=ID= 79eb3d5438d3eb10cf23d6f3cff266e2;+ ASPSESSIONIDQQQQGYFC= ICLLKDGBFCMMHNPEGCFIJOLC
Referer	*Blank*

The only field you can control directly with the `Response.AppendToLog` method is the Message field.

Additional Response Properties/Methods

The Response object has several other properties and methods besides those you've seen, but most of them are much simpler. Table 5.1 contains a complete list of the methods and properties. You'll see some of these methods in the examples in this book after you've worked with a little more code and with HTML forms.

T A B L E 5 . 1 : Response Properties, Methods, and Collections

Property/Method	Description
AddHeader Method	Adds a header value to the returned page.
AppendToLog Method	Appends a string to the Message field of the IIS log.
BinaryWrite Method	Used to write non-textual data to the browser. You can use this method to send image, audio, or other binary to the browser. You'll see more about the BinaryWrite method in Chapter 6, The Request object.
Buffer Property	Buffers the character stream sent to the browser until page processing completes. You must turn buffering on to issue any commands that write header values, such as Response.Redirect. Accepts values of either True or False.
CacheControl Property	Controls whether proxy servers should cache the page. For pages that may change from request to request, you should set this property to the string value Private. For pages that don't change, you should set the CacheControl property to the string value Public.
Charset Property	Controls the character set the browser uses to render the page. The default is ISO=LATIN-1. For example, to change the character set to ISO-LATIN-7, use <% Response.Charset= "ISO-LATIN-7" %>.
Clear Method	Clears the contents of the server response buffer. If you are in the middle of processing a page and some condition causes you to want to restart the page, you can clear the buffer (assuming you're buffering the response) by issuing the Response.Clear command.
ContentType Property	Sets a header value that specifies what type of content the page contains. The default value is text/html. You may need to change this, particularly if you use the Response.BinaryWrite method to send binary data.
Cookies Collection	You use this collection to write both per-session and persistent cookies to the client browser.
End Method	Ends the response. This command takes effect immediately. The server will not process any code or HTML that follows the Response.End command.
Expires Property	Sets the time interval, in minutes, before the page expires. Until the specified interval elapses, the browser may re-display the page from cache. After the specified period, the browser must return to the server to re-display the page.

Continued on next page

TABLE 5.1 CONTINUED: Response Properties, Methods, and Collections

Property/Method	Description
ExpiresAbsolute Property	Sets an exact time when the page expires. Before the specified time, the browser may re-display the page from cache. After the specified time, the browser must return to the server to re-display the page.
Flush Method	Sends any buffered content to the browser. You might want to do this for long pages. Note that the Response.Flush method raises an error if you have not set the Response.Buffer to True.
IsClientConnected Property	Before you get excited about this method, it doesn't do what you might think. There's no way to find out whether a specific client is using your application except when a TCP/IP connection is actually in effect. The IsClientConnected property is useful only for determining whether you should continue to process a script. For example, if a page takes a long time to respond, you can use this property to check whether the client is still connected. If not, there's no point in continuing to process the script. Note that the IsClientConnected property does not tell you which client is connected.
Pics Property	Adds an HTTP header value containing a Platform for Internet Content Selection (PICS) label. The PICS label contains a rating for the page. Using this system, parents can determine the levels of content their children can see. For more information, refer to the PICS specification on the W3C Web site: http://www.w3.org.
Redirect Method	Sends a header to the browser telling it to request a new page. You specify the URL for the page along with any QueryString variables and values.
Status Property	Sets the value of the status line returned by the server. You may have seen this error before—404 Not Found. You set the Status property to return a specific number and explanation to the browser. The HTTP specification defines the set of valid status values and their meanings.
Write Method	Writes text and HTML content to the browser.

In this chapter, you've seen how to use the Response object to send HTML to the browser. In the next chapter, you'll see how to use the Request object to receive information from the browser.

CHAPTER

SIX

The Request Object

- **Obtaining Information from the Browser**

- **The *Request.ServerVariables* Collection**

- **The *Request.Cookies* Collection**

- **The *Request.QueryString* Collection**

- **Introduction to HTML Forms**

- **The *Request.Form* Collection**

- **Other Request Object Properties/Methods**

Just as the Response object is your link to send content to the browser, the Request object is your link to receive content from the browser. The Request object consists of several collections that encapsulate the information sent by the browser for each request.

Obtaining Information from the Browser

The Request object contains information that the browser sends to the server. Remember that both the server and the browser treat every request as a brand new communication. Therefore, for every request, the browser must include all the information required for communication—its IP address, the type of information requested, all form content, QueryString variables, browser type information, etc.

You use the Request object to read that information. The ASP engine packages it all up nicely for you. Just like the Response object shields you from having to write HTML headers or communicate directly with the server, the Request object shields you from having to parse out the information sent by the browser.

The Request object contains five different collections of information:

    ClientCertificates   Contains security information

    Cookies   Contains cookie values sent by the browser

    Form   Contains information the user enters into input controls and information your application has stored in form variables

    QueryString   Contains information sent with the URL

    ServerVariables   Contains information that the server automatically parses for every request

You'll do almost all your work with these collections. I listed them in alphabetical order, but that's not how I intend to present them. My purpose is to get you up-and-running as fast as possible. If you follow the order in this book, you'll be able to create pages very quickly.

As you saw in the previous chapter, a collection object contains a list of items. The items may or may not be in order, and may or may not be related to one another.

ASP collections are all essentially identical in that they consist of a list of names, called keys, associated with values. Each key is associated with a single Variant value (note that the value may be another list). For example, an ASP collection might look like this:

```
LastName="Doe"
FirstName="John"
Age=33
```

This collection has three keys (LastName, FirstName, and Age) and three values ("Doe", "John", and 33).

ASP collections all share three properties and methods:

- **Count** The number of items in the collection. The first item (unlike an array) has an index of 1, not 0. To retrieve the count, use the syntax variable = CollectionName.Count.

- **Item** This method lets you retrieve an item by name or index number. To retrieve an item, use the syntax variable = CollectionName.Item("Key-Name") or variable = CollectionName.Item(index).

- **Key** This method lets you retrieve a key value by index. In practice, you'll rarely use this method. Use the syntax variable = CollectionName.Key.

In addition, you can access the items in an array using the For Each...Next syntax. The For Each...Next is a block construct that iterates, or progresses sequentially through the collection, letting you operate on each item in turn. Iteration is often called enumeration. With the ASP collections, the For Each...Next iteration returns the key, not the value.

All ASP collections (and most other VB and VBScript collection objects) have a default property, the Item property. In contrast to the Count or Key properties, you don't have to supply the Item keyword to access the property. For example:

```
<%
' You must supply the Count keyword to access the count
Response.Write Request.CollectionName.Count
' But you don't have to supply the Item keyword
' to access an item
Response.Write Request.CollectionName(KeyName)
%>
```

In the next sections, you'll see each of the major ASP collections in detail.

The *Request.ServerVariables* Collection

The Request.ServerVariables collection contains standard information automatically sent by the browser for every request. The easiest way to study the ServerVariables collection is to make a request to an ASP page, then print all the keys and values in the collection back to the browser. Listing 6.1 contains a routine that works for all collections that contain single values for each key (assuming you change the collection name in the code). As written, it does not work for collections that contain child collections or arrays as values. I'll show you how to write a more generalized routine in Part III, when you learn about subroutines and functions.

LISTING 6.1   Request.ServerVariables List (ch6i1.asp)

```
<%@Language="VBScript"%>
<% option explicit %>
<html>
<head>
<title>Request ServerVariables List</title>
</head>
<body>
<h2>Request ServerVariables List</h2>
<%
Dim V ' for Variant
For Each V in Request.ServerVariables
    Response.Write V & "=" & Request.ServerVariables(V)
Next
%>
</body>
</html>
```

Table 6.1 shows the list of ServerVariable keys and values. I'd show it to you in the browser, but the list is too long to fit in one or even two screen prints.

NOTE   The list of server variables depends partly on your version of IIS, and partly on where your browser was *prior* to the page that contains the script, so your list may be slightly different than this one.

TABLE 6.1: Request.ServerVariables List

Key Name	Value
ALL_HTTP	HTTP_ACCEPT:*/* HTTP_ACCEPT_LANGUAGE:en-us HTTP_CONNECTION:Keep-Alive HTTP_HOST:localhost HTTP_USER_AGENT:Mozilla/4.0 (compatible; MSIE 5.0; Windows NT; DigExt) HTTP_COOKIE:ASPSESSIONIDGQGQQQCH=BAHFCBOCAHNCJDHBBGFBGHKC HTTP_ACCEPT_ENCODING:gzip, deflate
ALL_RAW	Accept: */* Accept-Language: en-us Connection: Keep-Alive Host: localhost User-Agent: Mozilla/4.0 (compatible; MSIE 5.0; Windows NT; DigExt) Cookie: ASPSESSIONIDGQGQQQCH=BAHFCBOCAHNCJDHBBGFBGHKC Accept-Encoding: gzip, deflate
APPL_MD_PATH	/LM/W3SVC/1/Root/MasteringASP2
APPL_PHYSICAL_PATH	C:\INetPub\WWWRoot\MasteringASP2
AUTH_PASSWORD	
AUTH_TYPE	
AUTH_USER	
CERT_COOKIE	
CERT_FLAGS	
CERT_ISSUER	
CERT_KEYSIZE	
CERT_SECRETKEYSIZE	
CERT_SERIALNUMBER	
CERT_SERVER_ISSUER	
CERT_SERVER_SUBJECT	
CERT_SUBJECT	
CONTENT_LENGTH	0
CONTENT_TYPE	
GATEWAY_INTERFACE	CGI/1.1
HTTPS	Off
HTTPS_KEYSIZE	
HTTPS_SECRETKEYSIZE	
HTTPS_SERVER_ISSUER	
HTTPS_SERVER_SUBJECT	
INSTANCE_ID	1
INSTANCE_META_PATH	/LM/W3SVC/1
LOCAL_ADDR	127.0.0.1
LOGON_USER	
PATH_INFO	/MasteringASP2/chapter6/ch6i1.asp
PATH_TRANSLATED	C:\INetPub\WWWRoot\MasteringASP2\chapter6\ch6i1.asp
QUERY_STRING	
REMOTE_ADDR	127.0.0.1

Continued on next page

TABLE 6.1 CONTINUED: Request.ServerVariables List

Key Name	Value
REMOTE_HOST	127.0.0.1
REMOTE_USER	
REQUEST_METHOD	GET
SCRIPT_NAME	/MasteringASP2/chapter6/ch6i1.asp
SERVER_NAME	Localhost
SERVER_PORT	80
SERVER_PORT_SECURE	0
SERVER_PROTOCOL	HTTP/1.1
SERVER_SOFTWARE	Microsoft-IIS/4.0
URL	/MasteringASP2/chapter6/ch6i1.asp
HTTP_ACCEPT	*/*
HTTP_ACCEPT_LANGUAGE	En-us
HTTP_CONNECTION	Keep-Alive
HTTP_HOST	localhost
HTTP_USER_AGENT	Mozilla/4.0 (compatible; MSIE 5.0; Windows NT; DigExt)
HTTP_COOKIE	ASPSESSIONIDGQGQQQCH=BAHFCBOCAHNCJDHBBGFBGHKC
HTTP_ACCEPT_ENCODING	gzip, deflate

This is a very useful routine and you should keep it handy. I typically keep these generalized types of routines in include files, so I can find them easily. Over time, many of the Request.ServerVariable collection key names become familiar, but no one is likely to remember them all. It's faster to run the routine than spend time hunting for the proper key name in the online help files.

TIP You will find that you rarely need most of these values. I've listed the ones I use most often. Depending on your application's requirements and security specifications, you may use others just as often.

APPL_PHYSICAL_PATH The physical path of your application. Does not include the name of the requested file. This value is useful because you should never hard-code a path in your application, if possible.

LOCAL_ADDR The IP address of the server hosting your application.

LOGON_USER The network username of the browser requesting this resource (applicable only if the IIS Allow Anonymous security option is turned off.

PATH_INFO   The full physical path to the requested file. This value is useful if you redirect, but still need to know the name of the originally requested file.

SERVER_NAME   The name of the server as requested by the user. Note that all servers support the name shown in this example, localhost.

SERVER_PORT   The IP port number—usually 80 for HTTP servers.

HTTP_USER_AGENT   The make and version of the requesting browser.

One final note about the Request.ServerVariables collection: it's slow. Unlike most of the ASP collections, the server does not automatically parse the items in the ServerVariables collection for each request. Instead, the server initializes all the values the first time you request an item from the collection on an ASP page. Subsequent queries to the collection during the same page execution are as fast as retrieving values from any other collection. If possible, you should avoid using the ServerVariables collection on every request. You'll see that most of the dynamic data—cookies, QueryString data, and form data—reside in other ASP collections, so you won't often need to check the ServerVariables collection for those values.

For most applications, the best way to use the ServerVariables collection is to make a single request to initialize the collection when the application or session starts. You then cache the data so you can use it later without having to reinitialize the collection.

The *Request.Cookies* Collection

If you look at the Value column in Table 6.1, you'll see that one of the keys is HTTP_COOKIE. The values in the HTTP_COOKIE key are repeated in the ALL_HTTP and ALL_RAW values. Of course, the browser doesn't really send the information three times—the Request.ServerVariables collection provides several views of the information, each presented in a different way. For example, in all these views the cookie values exist in a single string, separated with semicolons and other delimiters.

You can read the cookies from the Request.ServerVariables collection, but it's much more convenient to read them from yet another view of the browser information called the Request.Cookies collection.

The Request.Cookies collection and the Response.Cookies collection are complementary, but don't contain the same information. You can't query the Response.Cookies collection for its contents, but you can add or modify cookies using the collection methods. Conversely, you can't alter the `request.Cookies` collection, but you can query it for its contents. In other words, the `Response.Cookies` collection is write-only, whereas the `Request.Cookies` collection is read-only.

If you set a `Response.Cookie`, it will appear in the next request from the client browser. If you clear a cookie, it will not appear in the `Request.Cookies` collection in the next request from that browser, and if you alter a cookie, its value changes in the `Request.Cookies` collection in the next request from that browser.

To read a cookie, you use a syntax that should, by now, start looking familiar—with the `Item` property. Again, the `Item` method is the default property, so you don't have to write the `Item` keyword:

```
MyVar = Request.Cookies("someKey")
```

You can iterate through the cookies keys with the `For Each...Next` syntax:

```
Dim V
For Each V in Request.Cookies
    Response.Write V & "=" & Request.Cookies.Item(V)
Next
```

Unfortunately, the previous example works only with single-value cookies because as you will recall from Chapter 5, in the section on the `Response.Cookies` collection, cookie values may contain sub-values.

You retrieve a sub-value by specifying the name of the appropriate sub-key. For example:

```
Response.Write Request.Cookies("Employees")("President")
```

If you request the value of a cookie and that cookie has multiple values, the ASP engine returns a single string containing all the sub-keys and sub-values separated by ampersands. You can determine whether a cookie has sub-keys through the `HasKeys` property. The `HasKeys` property returns the Boolean value `True` if the cookie has sub-keys. The following example creates two cookies. The first cookie has only a single value, but the second cookie has two values.

```
Response.Cookies("OneValue") = "One Value"
Response.Cookies("TwoValues")("FirstValue") = "First Value"
Response.Cookies("TwoValues")("SecondValue") = _
    "Second Value"
```

Assume that you're now looking at code in a subsequent ASP page—after the browser stored the cookies set in the previous example. Listing 6.2 shows the different results you can get by querying the `Request.Cookies` collection.

LISTING 6.2   **Ways to Query the** Request.Cookies **Collection (ch6i2.asp)**

```asp
<%@ Language=VBScript %>
<% option explicit %>
<%
Dim V
Dim Vsub
Response.Cookies("OneValue") = "One Value"
Response.Cookies("TwoValues")("FirstValue") = "First Value"
Response.Cookies("TwoValues")("SecondValue") = _
    "Second Value"
%>
<html>
<head>
</head>
<body>
<%
Response.Write "Request.Cookies(""OneValue"")=" & _
    Request.Cookies("OneValue") & "<br>"
' writes "One Value"

Response.Write "Request.Cookies(""OneValue"").HasKeys=" & _
    Request.Cookies("OneValue").HasKeys & "<br>"
' writes "False"

Response.Write "Request.Cookies(""TwoValues"").HasKeys=" & _
    Request.Cookies("TwoValues").HasKeys & "<br>"
' writes "True"

Response.Write "Request.Cookies(""TwoValues"")=" _
    & Request.Cookies("TwoValues") & "<br>"
' writes "FirstValue=First+Value;SecondValue=Second+Value"

Response.Write " Request.Cookies(""TwoValues"")(1)=" & _
    Request.Cookies("TwoValues")(1) & "<br>"
' writes "Second Value"

Response.Write " Request.Cookies(""TwoValues"")(""SecondValue"")=" _
    & Request.Cookies("TwoValues")("SecondValue") & "<br>"
' writes "Second Value"

Response.Write Request.Cookies(1)(2) & "<br>"
' writes "First Value"
```

```
For Each V In Request.Cookies
    If Request.Cookies(V).hasKeys Then
        Response.Write V  & "<br>"
        For Each VSub in Request.Cookies(V)
            Response.Write "      " & _
            VSub & "=" & Request.Cookies(V)(VSub) & "<br>"
        Next
    Else
        Response.Write V & "=" & Request.Cookies(V) & "<br>"
    End If
next
%>
</body>
</html>
```

As you can see, there are several ways to access the cookies—by index number, key, and sub-key. You should also notice that the cookies don't always reappear where you might think. When I created the two-value cookie, I added the `FirstValue= "First Value"` association before the second value. However, as you can see by the last line in the example, the value at index (1)(2) is `"First Value"`. What this tells you is that you should access cookies by name rather than index unless you're absolutely certain what the results will be.

The last part of Listing 6.2 shows you how to iterate through a collection that contains cookies with multiple sub-keys and values:

```
<%
Dim V
Dim Vsub
For Each V In Request.Cookies
    If Request.Cookies(V).hasKeys Then
        Response.Write V & "=" & Request.Cookies(V) & "<br>"
        For Each VSub in Request.Cookies(V)
            Response.Write "      " & _
            VSub & "=" & Request.Cookies(V)(VSub) & "<br>"
        Next
    Else
        Response.Write V & "=" & Request.Cookies(V) & "<br>"
    End If
next
%>
```

Cookies are particularly useful when you don't want to store data on the server, or when you can't store data on the server. You should be aware that any data you store on the client may be lost or deleted if the user changes machines, formats a drive, or simply deletes the contents of the cookies directory.

The *Request.QueryString* Collection

Another way to pass data between the client and the server is through the Query-String collection. QueryString data is passed in the URL along with the request. You may remember back in Chapter 1 in the section *Parts of a URL* that requests may contain parameters. The parameters are the items in the QueryString collection. For example, the URL shown below has two parameters:

```
http://myServer/myApp/search.asp?1=George&2=Washington
```

You can find the parameters in the ServerVariables collection in the QUERY_STRING item, but there they appear in raw, unparsed form. For the previous URL, the value of the Request.ServerVariables("QUERY_STRING") variable would be 1=George&2=Washington. That's not too bad, but consider this URL:

```
http://myServer/myApp/search.asp?search+type=whole+word+only&search+
location=index&search+titles=True&1=Washington&2=George+&amp;+Martha
```

Sure, you could write code to parse the URL, but you probably have better things to program. It's much more convenient to let the ASP engine parse the QueryString for you. QueryString parameters, like most Web values, are an association consisting of a name and a value, in the form name=value. In the QueryString collection, the names become the keys.

Like the other ASP collections, you can retrieve the count of items in the collection, retrieve any individual item, or iterate through all the items. For example:

```
Dim queryCount
Dim V
' retrieve the count
QueryCount = Request.QueryString.Count

' retrieve the first item in the collection
V = Request.QueryString(1)

' retrieve the item with the key "searchTitles"
V = Request.QueryString("searchTitles")

' iterate through all values
For each V in Request.QueryString
    Response.Write V & "=" & Request.QueryString(V)
Next
```

In your ASP applications, you'll either construct URLs with parameters in advance, before you send a page to the browser, or your users will construct them by selecting or clicking objects on the page. Listing 6.3 contains the code to create a single page with several links. When you click on one of the links, the page displays the parsed `QueryString` collection for the URL contained in the selected link.

LISTING 6.3   Retrieving `QueryString` Data (ch6i3.asp)

```
<%@ Language=VBScript %>
<% option explicit %>
<html>
<head>
</head>
<body>
<h2>Values Appear Here</h2>
<%
dim V
if Request.QueryString("ShowQueryString") = "True" then
   for each V in Request.QueryString
      Response.Write V & "=" & Request.QueryString(V) & "<br>"
   next
end if
%>
<hr>
<h2>Click on one of the links</h2>
<a
href="ch6i3.asp?ShowQueryString=True&FirstName=Russell&LastName=Jones">
   Russell Jones
</a><br>
<a href="ch6i3.asp?ShowQueryString=True&Employees=5&1=Bob+Franklin&2=
George+Lukas&3=Sarah+M+Myers&4=Jocelyn+Templeton&5=Brenda+Lewis">
   Show Employees
</a><br>
<a href="ch6i3.asp?ShowQueryString=False&Values=0">
   This link won't show any values
</a>
</body>
</html>
```

In the browser, if you click on the middle link (Show Employees), the screen looks like Figure 6.1.

FIGURE 6.1:

Retrieving QueryString data (ch6i3.asp)

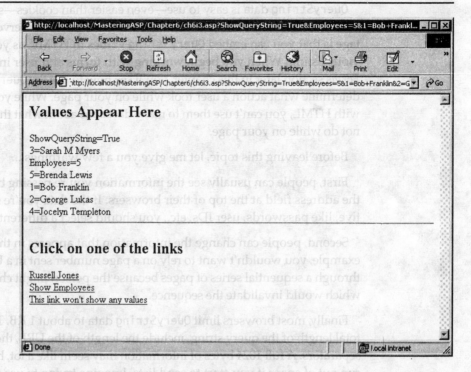

Take a closer look at the link constructions in Listing 6.3 and the example at the beginning of this section. You will notice that the links in Listing 6.3 don't have any spaces, and that I've replaced the ampersand (&) sign in the links at the beginning of the section with the HTML-encoded symbol &. That's because you can't send characters with an ASCII value below 33 as regular characters. You must encode them instead. As you might expect, ASP provides an object that can encode the data for you. I'll show you how to do that in Chapter 7, *The Application and Server Objects*. The important things to know right now are the following:

- You separate the query string from the URL with a question mark.
- You separate names (key) from values with an equals sign.
- You separate key-value pairs from each other with ampersands.
- URL data cannot contain spaces—you must replace spaces with plus signs.
- The Request object decodes the data for you.

That's right, you didn't have to decode the data to display it in Listing 6.3—the Request object handled that transparently. In the next chapter you'll see how ASP can encode the data for you, too.

QueryString data is easy to use—even easier than cookies—so it's extremely convenient when you need to send a few data values to the server. Another advantage is that you can embed QueryString values in HTML, as you saw in the previous listing. When you begin working with forms and user input in the *HTML Forms* section later in this chapter, you'll see how to use the QueryString values to determine what action a user took while on your page. While you can set cookies with HTML, you can't use them to make decisions about what the user did or did not do while on your page.

Before leaving this topic, let me give you a few warnings....

First, people can usually see the information you're passing back and forth in the address field at the top of their browsers. If the data you're sending is sensitive, like passwords, user IDs, etc., you should select a different method.

Second, people can change the information that appears in the address line. For example, you wouldn't want to rely on a page number sent in a URL to track a user through a sequential series of pages because the person might change the number, which would invalidate the sequence.

Finally, most browsers limit QueryString data to about 1 KB. To calculate the total length of the query string, include the length of the URL, the keys, and all the separators. A full 1024 bytes of information may seem like a lot, but you can quickly run out of space if you start to send lists. Imagine trying to use the employee list example in Listing 6.3 in a 300-person company and you'll understand how the limitation on QueryString data can affect your application. Don't use QueryString data where the potential for the data to grow too large might suddenly affect your application. For example, don't use it to pass long, free-form text strings.

Introduction to HTML Forms

You use HTML forms to activate your page. Before version 4.*x* browsers, an HTML page without a form was a static image. People could read information from your page, look at graphics, and hyperlink from one page to another in your site or other sites, but they could not interact with the page. The only way to put input controls—such as buttons, text boxes, and list boxes—on your page was to use a form. In IE 3 you could place a button on the page without a form, but not in Netscape 3.

In this section, you'll see how to construct a form and how to submit or post a form. Submitting a form sends the data entered or selected by the user to the server. You'll also see how to read the submitted data on the server so you can use it to customize your application's response.

Forms are block tags that can contain input controls and HTML. A <form> tag can contain four optional parameters:

name   A name for the form. You should always name your forms so you can manipulate the input controls in the form and the form itself with client-side code.

action   The URL where you want the browser to send the data.

method   You can send or post data to the server using either of two methods. The post method sends the data in single lines. The get method concatenates the form data into a single line and appends the resulting string to the URL, like a query string. Use the post method unless you have a good reason not to.

target   The name of the frame where you want the response to appear. If the frame doesn't already exist, the browser opens a new window and assigns the value of the target attribute as its name. You don't need this attribute unless you're using frames.

Here's an example <form> tag:

```
<form name="frmTest" action="test.asp" method="post">
```

When the user submits the form named frmTest, it will send the data using the post method to the page named test.asp in the directory where the current page originated.

If you neglect to enter them, HTML supplies default values for the action and method attributes If you omit the action attribute, the form posts data to the current page. If you don't specify a method, the form sends data using the get method.

WARNING   Forgetting to specify the post method is a common error. Always specify the post method. The get method will not work with the techniques described in this section.

This is a difficult topic to teach because it's a chicken-and-egg problem. Which should I discuss first—forms themselves or the process of reading form data? If I discuss forms first, you won't know how to work with the Request.Form collection to view the data. On the other hand, without discussing forms, it's difficult to show you what the Request.Form collection does. I'm going to show you the Request.Form methods first because the Request.Form collection has exactly the same methods and properties as the other Request collections you've seen so far. Then I'll discuss forms. After that, I'll tie it all together. Feel free to reverse the order of the topics if you prefer.

The *Request.Form* Collection

When a browser submits form data using the post method, the ASP engine parses the raw HTTP form data and stores it in the Request.Form collection. The form collection, like other ASP collections, stores data by key. If a key has more than one value, the values are stored in indexed form. The Request.Form collection has a default Item method. You don't have to include the Item keyword to retrieve a value from the collection. For example, to retrieve the value of the item with the ProductID key, you would write

```
productID=Request.Form.Item("ProductID")
```

Taking advantage of the default Item method, you could write

```
productID=Request.Form("ProductID")
```

The keys are not case-sensitive. You might just as easily write

```
productID=Request.Form("productid")
```

You can retrieve the number of items associated with a form using the Count method:

```
itemCount=Request.Form.Count
```

If the form contained more than one control with the name productID you can retrieve the values using an index number. For example:

```
productID1=Request.Form("productID")(1)
productID2=Request.Form("productID")(2)
```

Indexed values start with 1. You can retrieve the number of values associated with a key using the Count method:

```
productCount=Request.Form("productID").count
```

If you request the value of a key with multiple values, the Item method returns a comma-delimited list:

```
productID=Request.Form("productID")
Response.Write productID
```

If the productID key had two values, 10225 and 34199, the output from the previous example would be 10225,34199.

Like other ASP collections, you can retrieve a key by index. For example, to determine the value of the first key in the collection, you could write

```
Response.Write Request.Form.Key(1)
```

You can iterate through all the Request.Form keys using the For...Next method:

```
Dim i
```

```
For i = 1 to Request.Form.count
    Response.Write Request.Form.Key(i) & "<br>"
next
```

Note that the position of the key-item associations may not and probably does not correspond to the corresponding position of the values in the form.

Submitting a Form

The easiest way to submit a form is to have a submit button on the form. When you have a submit button on a form, the browser automatically sends the data when the user clicks the button. Listing 6.4 contains an example of a simple form.

LISTING 6.4   **Simple Form Example (ch6i4.asp)**

```
<%@ Language=VBScript %>
<%
Response.Write "Test=" & Request.Form("test")
%>
<html>
<head>
</head>
<body>
<form name="junk" method="post" action="ch6i4.asp">
    <input type="submit" name="test" value="Test">
</form>
<p> </p>
</body>
</html>
```

Listing 6.4 is an example of a form that submits data to itself. Look at the `<input>` tag contained in the `<form>` tag. The form contains one user-input element. In this case, the element type is a submit button (`type=submit`) named `test`. The submit button has a `value="Test"` attribute. The `Test` value functions as both the button caption and the data returned to the server when the browser submits the form.

When you click the test button, the browser submits all the data associated with the elements in the form to the server. In this case, the `action="ch6i4.asp"` attribute causes the form to submit the data to the same file that contains the form itself. You could optionally omit the `action` attribute in this case, because a form submits to the page that contains the form by default. The first time you view the file, the code writes the output `"Test= "` but no value, because you haven't submitted the form yet. After you click the test button, however, the code also writes the value of the form variable associated with the `test` key—Test=Test.

Figure 6.2 shows the output from Listing 6.4 after submitting the form.

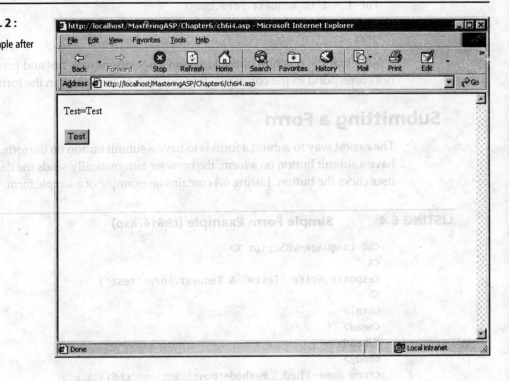

Input Element Types

Forms can contain several types of input elements. Another name for input elements is controls, probably because Windows uses that term for input elements (buttons, text fields, lists, etc.), and on Windows platforms at least, the HTML input elements look and act similar to Windows controls. I'll use both terms in this book. For some input elements, the closing tag is not required—for others it is.

In a browser, as in Windows, each button and each field type is appropriate for a specific type of user input. You should select the appropriate input types when building forms because the input types have become so familiar that the type alone acts as a cue, which helps the user interact quickly and accurately with the form.

I've grouped all the input element types into three areas: Buttons, Text Input, and Select Lists.

Buttons

Submit button   Submits the contents of a form to the server. For example:

```
<input type="submit" name="Submit" value="Submit">
```

Reset button   Resets a form to its original state before the user altered any of the values or form input elements. Form reset buttons were once common, but are becoming rare as input elements become more sophisticated. For example:

```
<input type="reset" name="Reset" value="Reset">
```

General-purpose buttons   You control the result via client-side script. In the following example, clicking the cancel button fires a script containing a routine called doCancel().

```
<input type="button" name="Cancel" value="Cancel" onClick="doCancel()">
```

For submit, reset, and general purpose buttons, the data from the value attribute does double-duty as both a caption and the value returned to the server when the user submits the form.

Checkboxes   Use checkboxes to let a user select more than one item from a group. Note that the text (caption) associated with the checkbox appears between the <input></input> tags, and that the ending tag is required. For example:

```
<input type="checkbox" name="chkFullScreen">
   Show Full Screen</input>
```

The checkbox control doesn't use a value attribute: The checkbox returns the keyword on when the user has checked the box and returns nothing if the box is not checked. This was a poor choice on the part of the designers. It would have been much better if they had let the control take a value attribute for a checked value and a value attribute for an unchecked state, such as checkedValue="someValue" uncheckedValue="someOtherValue". At the very least, the control should return either True or False, but it doesn't. You're stuck with on or nothing. You can check for the return value using an If...then test in script. For example:

```
chk1 = (Request.Form("chk1") = "on")
```

If the user checked the control, the script engine will evaluate the expression Request.Form("chk1") = "on" and return a Boolean True value. If the user did not check the control, the result of the expression will be a Boolean False.

You control the initial state of the checkbox with the checked attribute. The checked attribute has no associated value. For example, the following checkbox will appear checked:

```
<input type="checkbox" name="chkFullScreen" value="FullScreen" _
   checked>
   Show Full Screen"</input>
```

Radio buttons   Use radio buttons to let a user select only one option from a group. When a user clicks one of the buttons, any other radio button in the same group that is already selected turns off, and the selected button turns on. The result is that the user can select only one item. You group radio buttons together by creating multiple buttons with the same name. Don't use a single radio button on a form because once it's selected, you cannot turn the selection off. Note that like the checkbox input type, the text (caption) associated with the radio button appears between the <input></input> tags. For example:

```
<input type="radio" name="optPermissionLevel"
    value="Guest">Grant Guest Permission</input>
<input type="radio" name="optPermissionLevel"
    value="User">Grant User Permission</input>
<input type="radio" name="optPermissionLevel"
    value="Administrator">Grant Administrator Permission</input>
```

You control the initial state of a radio button with the checked attribute. The checked attribute has no associated value. For example, in the following radio button group, the Grant User Permission checkbox appears selected:

```
<input type="radio" name="optPermissionLevel"
    value="Guest">Grant Guest Permission</input>
<input type="radio" name="optPermissionLevel"
    value="User" checked>Grant User Permission</input>
<input type="radio" name="optPermissionLevel"
    value="Administrator">Grant Administrator Permission</input>
```

Radio buttons, unlike checkboxes, do have a return value. If you don't enter an explicit value, the control returns the caption.

Image controls   You can use images to replace submit buttons using the image input type. The main reason people want to do this is because images look much better than gray buttons. For example:

```
<input type="image" src="bluecheck.gif">
```

Note that because the image replaces a submit button, the browser submits the form immediately if the user clicks the image. For both submit buttons and image controls, you can intercept the form submission in client-side script. You'll see how to do that later in this book.

Text Input

Single-line text input (text type)   Use single-line text controls to capture short one-line text elements like names, filenames, zip codes, telephone numbers, etc. You set the initial content with the value attribute. For

example, the following input appears blank initially (it has a null-string
("") value):

```
<input type="text" name="txtLastName" value="">
```

You can limit the number of characters a person can type into a text control
with the maxlength attribute. For example, the following text input will
allow a user to type no more than 20 characters:

```
<input type="text" name="txtLastName" value="Doe" maxlength=20>
```

After a user alters the contents of a text control, the value attribute contains the altered text.

Password input   The password input is identical to the single-line text
input, except that it only shows asterisks when a user enters content into
the element. Despite the fact that you can only see asterisks, the element's
content is not encrypted. You can read the content with both client-side
and server-side script.

Multi-line text input   Use multi-line text (textarea) input elements to let
the user type one or more paragraphs of information. The textarea element
differs from the previous input elements in that it does not use an <input>
tag. Instead, you use a <textarea> tag. The ending tag is required. For
example:

```
<textarea name="txtAnswer">
  This is the initial content for the
textarea input element</textarea>
```

By default, textarea elements are two lines high and about 20 characters
wide, but you can control the width and height of the element using the
cols and rows attributes. You specify the number of columns and rows in
characters. The following example creates a textarea 50 characters wide
and 5 lines high:

```
<textarea name="txtAnswer" cols="50" rows="5">
  This is the initial content for the
textarea input element</textarea>
```

The textarea element always has a scroll bar on its right-hand edge. The
scroll bar is disabled when all the content fits into the visible area, and automatically enables when the number of content rows exceeds the number of
visible rows in the element.

Selection and Pick (select) Lists

There are two styles of lists—drop-down and fixed. I've treated them separately,
but they're actually the same control—a select control. You create a select list

with a `<select>` tag, not an `<input>` tag. The closing `</select>` tag is required. The `<select>` tag is a `block` element that contains `<option>` tags. Each `<option>` tag defines one item or option in the list. To add items to the list, you create a series of `<option>` tags. The `</option>` end tag is not required, but you should include it anyway. Use the `selected` attribute (no value required) to initialize the selection for the list. For example:

```
<select name="list1">
    <option selected value="1">Item 1</option>
    <option value="2">Item 2</option>
    <option value="3">Item 3</option>
</select>
```

You may add a `value` attribute to each option. If the `value` attribute exists, the browser returns the value when the user submits the form; otherwise, it returns the text of the option.

Drop-down lists   Use drop-down lists where the user needs to select one item from a short list.

Fixed lists   Use a fixed list where the list is long, or where the user may need to select more than one item from the list. By default, lists have the drop-down style. You create a fixed list by including a `size` attribute for the `<select>` tag. For example, to change the previous example into a fixed list, add the `size=3` attribute:

```
<select name="list1" size=3>
```

By default, lists allow the user to select only a single item. You can enable multiple selections by including the `multiple` attribute (no value required) with the `<select>` tag. For example:

```
<select multiple name="list1" size="3">
```

One common problem with lists is that the browser renders them just as wide as their widest item, which often looks strange when the list contains a series of short items. In modern browsers you can set the width of a `select` list using the `style` attribute. For example:

```
<select multiple name="list1" size="3" style="width: 100">
```

In earlier browsers, you can adjust the width (not entirely satisfactorily) by adding a number of no-break spaces (` `) to one of the items. For example, the following list will appear wider than the one-character width of the widest item:

```
<select multiple name="list1" size="3">
    <option selected value="1">1   </option>
    <option value="2">2</option>
```

```
     <option value="3">3</option>
   </select>
```

Getting the list width to appear correctly using this method is a matter of trial and error. If all your browser clients are version 4 or higher, I recommend you use the `style` attribute to set the width of your `select` lists.

Hidden Form Values

Sometimes you need a place to store values, but you don't want them to appear on the page. You can use the `input` element type `hidden` to store invisible values. Keep in mind that the values aren't truly invisible—users can view the values by selecting Show Source from the browser's menu—so don't store values in `hidden` `input` elements that you don't want the user to know. You create a `hidden` `input` element by setting the `type` attribute value to `hidden`. For example:

```
   <input type="hidden" value="myHiddenValue">
```

The browser sends the values of `hidden` `input` elements just like it sends `text` `control` values. `Hidden` `form` values can be very useful, and you'll see them in future examples in this book.

Working with Forms

Because input controls are your primary means to interact with and get information from your users, you'll work with forms constantly in the rest of this book. Therefore, you should spend some time exploring how to create and alter the various types of `input` tags. I'll give you a big head start by creating a common form, then discussing how you might change it to make it more attractive or improve its functionality.

Listing 6.5 contains the HTML for a common type of input form that captures demographic information about visitors to your site. Like the example in the previous listing (Listing 6.4), the form posts the information back to the same page, which conveniently keeps both the code to process the form and the form itself in a single file. Create or copy this file from the CD and place it in the `MasteringASP` virtual directory that you created in Part I.

LISTING 6.5   **User Demographic Information Form (ch6i5.asp)**

```
<html>
<head>
<title>User Demographic Information Form</title>
</head>
<body>
```

```
<%
dim firstname
dim lastname
dim address1
dim address2
dim city
dim state
dim zip
firstname = Request.Form("firstname")
lastname  = Request.Form("lastname")
address1 = Request.Form("address1")
address2 = Request.Form("address2")
city = Request.Form("city")
state = Request.Form("state")
zip = Request.Form("zip")
Response.write Request.ServerVariables("REQUEST_METHOD") _
    & "<br>"
if Request.ServerVariables("REQUEST_METHOD") = "POST" then
Response.Write "FirstName=" & firstName  & "<br>"
Response.Write "LastName=" & lastname & "<br>"
Response.Write "Address1=" & address1 & "<br>"
Response.Write "Address2=" & address2 & "<br>"
Response.Write "City=" & city & "<br>"
Response.Write "State=" & state & "<br>"
Response.Write "Zip=" & zip
end if
%>
<hr>
<p>This is an HTML form. It should look familiar. It contains several
text boxes and two buttons. All the values are required.
Fill out the form and click the Submit button. To reset the form to
the initial values, click the Reset button.</p>
<p><b>Enter your information, then click Submit</b></p>
<p>
<form name="frmUserInfo" action="ch6i5.asp" method="post">
<table border="1" cellPadding="1" cellSpacing="1" width="75%">
  <tr>
    <td width="30%"><B>First Name</b> </td>
    <td colspan="2"><b><inputname="FirstName"></b></td>
  </tr>
  <tr>
    <td><b>Last Name</b> </td>
    <td colspan="2"><input name="LastName"></td>
  </tr>
  <tr>
    <td><b>Address1</b></td>
```

```
        <td colspan=2><input name="address1"></td>
    </tr>
    <tr>
      <td><b>Address2</b></td>
      <td colspan=2><input name="address2"></td></tr>
    <tr>
      <td><b>City</b></td>
      <td colspan=2><input name="city"></td></tr>
    <tr>
      <td><b>State</b></td>
      <td colspan=2>
        <select name="State">
          <option selected value=AL>AL
          </option><option value=AK>AK</option>
          <option value=AR>AR</option><option value=AZ>AZ</option>
          <option value=CA>CA</option><option value=CT>CT</option>
          <option value=DE>DE</option><option value=FL>FL</option>
          <option value=GA>GA</option><option value=HI>HI</option>
          <option value=IA>IA</option><option value=ID>ID</option>
          <option value=IL>IL</option><option value=IN>IN</option>
          <option value=KS>KS</option><option value=KY>KY</option>
          <option value=LA>LA</option><option value=MA>MA</option>
          <option value=MD>MD</option><option value=ME>ME</option>
          <option value=MI>MI</option><option value=MN>MN</option>
          <option value=MO>MO</option><option value=MS>MS</option>
          <option value=MT>MT</option><option value=NE>NE</option>
          <option value=NH>NH</option><option value=NC>NC</option>
          <option value=ND>ND</option><option value=NJ>NJ</option>
          <option value=NM>NM</option><option value=NV>NV</option>
          <option value=NY>NY</option><option value=OH>OH</option>
          <option value=OK>OK</option><option value=OR>OR</option>
          <option value=PA>PA</option><option value=PR>PR</option>
          <option value=RI>RI</option><option value=SC>SC</option>
          <option value=SD>SD</option><option value=TN>TN</option>
          <option value=TX>TX</option><option value=UT>UT</option>
          <option value=VT>VT</option><option value=VA>VA</option>
          <option value=WA>WA</option><option value=WI>WI</option>
          <option value=WV>WV</option><option value=WY>WY</option>
        </select>
      </td>
    </tr>
    <tr>
      <td><b>Zip</b></td>
      <td colspan=2><input name="zip"></td>
    </tr>
```

```
<tr>
  <td align=center> </td>
  <td align=center width=110><input name="Submit"
    type=submit value=" Submit "></td>
  <td align=center width=100><input name="Reset" type=reset
    value="  Reset  "></td>
</tr>
</table>
</form>
</p>
</body>
</html>
```

This form contains examples of most of the input control types. The only ones missing are general-purpose buttons and image controls. Take a close look at the HTML in the example. Some of the attribute values don't have double-quotes around them. The quotes aren't required for values that don't contain spaces, and some HTML editors don't put them in. I've let it slide here, but you should use the quotes because if you include them all the time, you can avoid hard-to-debug problems for multi-word values. In addition, you'll need the quotes in the future for your HTML to become valid XML.

Look at the button captions. In modern browsers you can use CSS styles to set the button width, but for earlier browsers you must adjust the width using extra spaces in the caption if you don't like the default button width.

The first thing you'll need to do when dealing with posted form data is to capture the values on the server. My advice is to create variables on the server that exactly match the names of the elements in the form, using the form in Listing 6.5. For example:

```
<%
dim firstname
dim lastname
dim address1
dim address2
dim city
dim state
dim zip
firstname = Request.Form("firstname")
lastname  = Request.Form("lastname")
address1 = Request.Form("address1")
address2 = Request.Form("address2")
city = Request.Form("city")
state = Request.Form("state")
zip = Request.Form("zip")
%>
```

The names of the variables on the server match the names of the controls in the form. Making the names match is half the battle. Much of Web programming consists of moving data values from one form and machine to another. Later in this book you'll extract values from database tables and put them into Recordset objects. You'll transfer the values from the recordset to the HTML page and from the HTML page to client-side script, into form variables, and back to the server. It quickly becomes difficult to debug the process if the names don't match.

The main reason to transfer the Request.Form values into variable values is because it's much faster to access local variable values than values stored in an object, or worse, in an object collection. That's because late-bound scripting languages must query the object for its methods and properties each time you reference the object in script. The rule of thumb is to create a local variable if you're going to access an object property more than once on a page.

TIP   Create a local variable if you need to access an object property more than once on a page.

For any form the user fills out, you're highly likely to need the value more than once. First, you'll need to validate the contents. Second, if the contents aren't valid, you need to re-display the form with an error message asking the user to re-enter the missing or invalid data. Finally, you're likely to want to do something with the values, like store them in a database or file, or use them to generate another page—otherwise, you wouldn't have had the user fill out the form in the first place! In fact, you should make it a general rule to follow this process for handling form data on the server:

1. Store the form data in local variables.

2. Validate the required values.

3. Re-display the form with appropriate messages until all required values are valid.

4. Store the values for future reference.

Typically, beginning programmers try to skip steps 1 and 2—to their eventual regret—because it's a programming fact that human beings are often unable to enter data correctly. Therefore, if you ask people to fill out a form, you can guarantee that some will make mistakes. If you don't correct their mistakes, errors will occur.

Now that you have the values in local variables, it's relatively easy to validate the values. I'll discuss data validation in more detail later, after you've learned more about VBScript and JavaScript. Assume for the moment that people will either fail to fill out required fields, or will enter the wrong data type into the field. For example, a user might mistakenly type a number into the LastName field. Names don't contain numbers, (well OK, there are names like John Jacob Astor IV that contain Roman numerals) so if you find Arabic numerals in a name, you can normally consider it to be invalid data. This type of error is a data entry error. Similarly, a person might fail to enter an email address when the form clearly states that an email address is required. This type of error is an error of omission.

You should catch and correct errors of omission and invalid data types before you try to process the form data in any way. To correct the errors, you must re-display the form and ask the user to correct the errors. When you re-display the form, you'd better show it with the values the user entered still there, or they'll be angry when they have to re-enter all the data.

There are two ways to re-display a form—the old way and the right way. The old way is to return a server message that states the error and asks users to click the Back button on their browser to return to the form. Don't use that strategy. Re-create the form on the server with the error message and the form data on the same page.

To re-create the form with the user's data, you need to set the value of each control to the value entered by the user. For checkbox and radio button controls, include the checked attribute for the elements that correspond to the user's selection. For text and textarea controls, set the value property to the value you stored in your local variable. For select lists, include the selected attribute for the options that correspond to the user's selection.

At this point, you should see the form validation and re-display process in action. Listing 6.6 contains the form along with the code to check values and re-display the form when the user submits invalid data. You don't have to study or understand the validation code at this point—I'll cover that in Chapter 9, *Introduction to VBScript* and Chapter 10, *Introduction to JScript*. You should though, take a brief look at the amount of code it takes to validate values. A human can look at the form and immediately see that the values are invalid, but you need to tell the computer how to look at the form values. Even with all the validation code in this form, the user can still enter invalid values. For example, the form will accept a zip code of 00000 or a zip code of −000000000000 without complaint, even though neither of those values are valid zip codes.

LISTING 6.6   **Form Validation and Re-display Process (ch6i6.asp)**

```
<%@ Language=VBScript %>
<% option explicit %>
<html>
<head>
```

```
<title>User Demographic Information Form</title>
</head>
<body>
<%
dim firstname
dim lastname
dim address1
dim address2
dim city
dim state
dim zip
dim chk16
dim getNews
dim newsletter
dim notes
dim i
dim errorMsg
errorMsg=vbnullstring

if Request.ServerVariables("REQUEST_METHOD") = "POST" then
    firstname = Request.Form("firstname")
    lastname  = Request.Form("lastname")
    address1 = Request.Form("address1")
    address2 = Request.Form("address2")
    city = Request.Form("city")
    state = Request.Form("state")
    zip = Request.Form("zip")
    getNews=Request.Form("getNews") = "on"
    newsletter=Request.Form("newsletter")
    notes=Request.Form("notes")
    firstname = trim(firstname)
    lastname = trim(lastname)
    address1 = trim(address1)
    address2 = trim(address2)
    city = trim(city)
    state = trim(state)
    zip = trim(zip)
    if len(lastName) = 0 then
        errorMsg = "You must enter your last name."
    else
        for i = 1 to len(lastName)
            if instr(1, "abcdefghijklmnopqrstuvwxyz'", _
            mid(lastName,i,1), vbTextCompare) = 0 then
                errorMsg="The last name you entered is " & _
                "invalid. Please re-enter your last name."
                exit for
```

```
                  end if
            next
      end if
      if len(errorMsg) = 0 then
            if len(firstName) = 0 then
                  errorMsg="You must enter your first name."
            else
                  for i = 1 to len(firstName)
                        if instr(1, "abcdefghijklmnopqrstuvwxyz '", _
                              mid(firstName,i,1), vbTextCompare) = 0 then
                              errorMsg="The first name you entered " _
                                    & "is invalid. Please re-enter your " _
                                    & "first name."
                              exit for
                        end if
                  next
            end if
      end if
      if len(errorMsg) = 0 then
            if len(address1) = 0 then
                  errorMsg="You must enter your address."
            else
                  ' can't check addresses for validity easily
            end if
      end if
      ' don't check address2 because it may not be required.
      if len(errorMsg) = 0 then
            if len(city) = 0 then
                  errorMsg="You must enter the city in which you live."
            else
                  for i = 1 to len(city)
                        if instr(1, "abcdefghijklmnopqrstuvwxyz '", _
                              mid(city,i,1), vbTextCompare) = 0 then
                              errorMsg="The city you entered is invalid. Please " _
                                    & "re-enter the name of the city in which you live."
                              exit for
                        end if
                  next
            end if
      end if
      if len(errorMsg) = 0 then
            if len(zip) = 0 then
                  errorMsg="You must enter your zip code."
            elseif len(zip) < 5 then
                  errorMsg="The zip code you entered is invalid. Please " _
                        & "re-enter the zip code."
```

```
        elseif len(zip) > 5 and instr(zip,"-") = 0 then
            errorMsg="The zip code you entered is invalid. Please " _
                & "re-enter the zip code."
        elseif len(zip) > 12 then
            errorMsg="The zip code you entered is invalid. Please " _
                & "re-enter the zip code."
        else
            for i = 1 to len(zip)
                if instr(1, "0123456789-",mid(zip,i,1), _
                    vbBinaryCompare) = 0 then
                    errorMsg="The zip code you entered is invalid. " _
                        & "Please re-enter the zip code."
                    exit for
                end if
            next
        end if
    end if
    if len(errorMsg) = 0 then
        if len(getNews) > 0 then
            select case newsletter
            case "Daily", "Weekly", "Monthly"
                ' OK
            case else
                errorMsg="Select how often you wish to receive our " _
                    & "newsletter via email."
            end select
        end if
    end if
    if len(errorMsg) = 0 then
        ' no validation errors occurred
        Response.Write "FirstName=" & firstName  & "<br>"
        Response.Write "LastName=" & lastname & "<br>"
        Response.Write "Address1=" & address1 & "<br>"
        Response.Write "Address2=" & address2 & "<br>"
        Response.Write "City=" & city & "<br>"
        Response.Write "State=" & state & "<br>"
        Response.Write "Zip=" & zip & "<br>"
        Response.Write "Receive Newsletter=" & getNews & "<br>"
        Response.Write "Newsletter Schedule=" & newsletter & "<br>"
        Response.Write "Notes=" & notes
        Response.End
    end if
end if
%>
<hr>
<p>This is an HTML form. It should look familiar. It contains several
text boxes and two buttons. All the values are required.
```

Fill out the form and click the Submit button. To reset the form to
the initial values, click the Reset button.</p>
<p><b>Enter your information, then click Submit</b></p>
<p>
<form name="frmUserInfo" action="ch6i6.asp" method="post">
<%
if len(errorMsg) > 0 then
    ' show the appropriate error message if a validation error occurred.
    Response.Write "<p><font color='red'>" & errorMsg & "</font></p>"
end if
%>
<table border="1" cellPadding="1" cellSpacing="1" width="75%">
  <tr>
    <td width="30%"><b>First
      Name</b> </td>
    <td colspan="2"><b><input type="text" name="FirstName"
      value="<%=firstname%>"></b></td>
  </tr>
  <tr>
    <td><b>Last Name</b> </td>
    <td colspan="2"><input type="text" name="LastName"
      value="<%=lastname%>"></td>
  </tr>
  <tr>
    <td><b>Address1</b></td>
    <td colspan=2><input type="text" name="address1"
      value="<%=address1%>"></td>
  </tr>
  <tr>
    <td><b>Address2</b></td>
    <td colspan=2><input type="text" name="address2"
      value="<%=address2%>"></td></tr>
  <tr>
    <td><b>City</b></td>
    <td colspan=2><input type="text" name="city"
      value="<%=city%>"></td></tr>
  <tr>
    <td><b>State</b></td>
    <td colspan=2>
      <select name="State" width="165">
        <option value=AL>AL</option><option value=AK>AK</option>
        <option value=AR>AR</option><option value=AZ>AZ</option>
        <option value=CA>CA</option><option value=CT>CT</option>
        <option value=DE>DE</option><option value=FL>FL</option>
        <option value=GA>GA</option><option value=HI>HI</option>
        <option value=IA>IA</option><option value=ID>ID</option>

```
                    <option value=IL>IL</option><option value=IN>IN</option>
                    <option value=KS>KS</option><option value=KY>KY</option>
                    <option value=LA>LA</option><option value=MA>MA</option>
                    <option value=MD>MD</option><option value=ME>ME</option>
                    <option value=MI>MI</option><option value=MN>MN</option>
                    <option value=MO>MO</option><option value=MS>MS</option>
                    <option value=MT>MT</option><option value=NE>NE</option>
                    <option value=NH>NH</option><option value=NC>NC</option>
                    <option value=ND>ND</option><option value=NJ>NJ</option>
                    <option value=NM>NM</option><option value=NV>NV</option>
                    <option value=NY>NY</option><option value=OH>OH</option>
                    <option value=OK>OK</option><option value=OR>OR</option>
                    <option value=PA>PA</option><option value=PR>PR</option>
                    <option value=RI>RI</option><option value=SC>SC</option>
                    <option value=SD>SD</option><option value=TN>TN</option>
                    <option value=TX>TX</option><option value=UT>UT</option>
                    <option value=VT>VT</option><option value=VA>VA</option>
                    <option value=WA>WA</option><option value=WI>WI</option>
                    <option value=WV>WV</option><option value=WY>WY</option>
                </select>
            </td>
        </tr>
        <tr>
            <td><b>Zip</b></td>
            <td colspan=2><input type="text" name="zip"
                value="<%=zip%>"></td>
        </tr>
        <tr>
            <td><b>Receive Newsletter?</b></td>
            <td colspan=2>
                    <input type="checkbox" name="getNews" <%if getNews then
Response.write "checked"%>>I would like to receive your newsletter via
email.</input>
            </td>
        </tr>
        <tr>
            <td><b>Newsletter Schedule</b></td>
            <td colspan=2>
              <input type="radio" name="newsletter" value="Daily"
                <%if newsletter="Daily" then Response.write
                "checked"%>>Daily</input><br>
              <input type="radio" name="newsletter" value="Weekly"
                <%if newsletter="Weekly" then Response.write
                "checked"%>>Weekly</input><br>
              <input type="radio" name="newsletter" value="Monthly"
                <%if newsletter="Monthly" then Response.write
```

```
              "checked"%>>Monthly</input>
          </td>
        </tr>
        <tr>
          <td><b>Notes</b></td>
          <td colspan=2>
            <textarea name="notes">Enter any additional notes
        here.</textarea>
          </td>
        </tr>
        <tr>
          <td align=center> </td>
          <td align=center width=110><input name="Submit" type=submit
              value=" Submit "></td>
          <td align=center width=100><input name="Reset" type=reset
              value=" Reset "></td>
        </tr>
      </table>
    </form>
  </p>
</body>
</html>
```

In a browser, the blank form looks like Figure 6.3.

After the user has filled in some information and submitted the form, any errors will appear at the top of the form. For example, in Figure 6.4, the user omitted the zip code.

FIGURE 6.4:

User demographic informa-
tion form—error message
(ch6i6.asp)

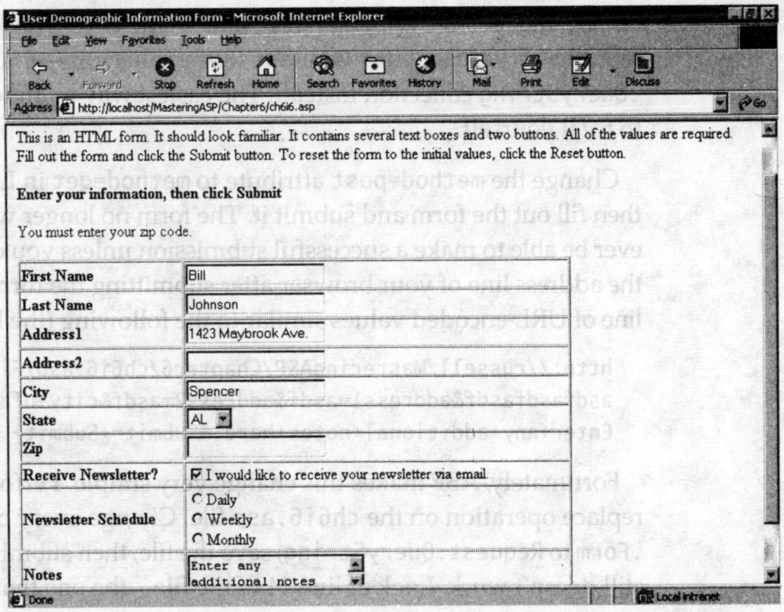

If no errors occur, the form displays the values and stops processing the page so the form doesn't re-display (see Figure 6.5).

FIGURE 6.5:

User demographic informa-
tion form—successful sub-
mission (ch6i6.asp)

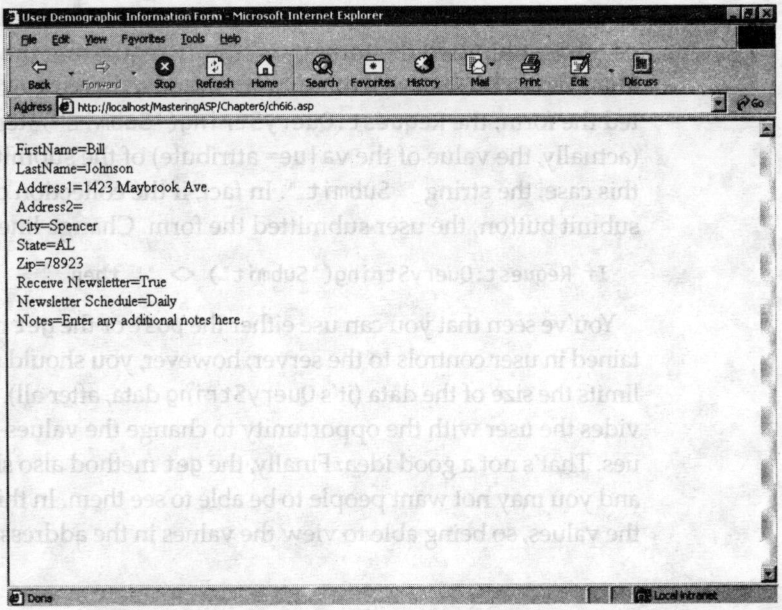

Post vs. *Get* Method

You normally post form data using the *post method*, but there's another method called `get` that you can use to send data to the server. When you use the *get method*, the browser appends form data to the URL. That means you can't retrieve it on the server using the `Request.Form` collection—you must use the `Request.QueryString` collection instead. The easiest way to understand the difference is to try it yourself.

Change the `method=post` attribute to `method=get` in Listing 6.6, save the file, then fill out the form and submit it. The form no longer works properly. You won't ever be able to make a successful submission unless you change the code. Look at the address line of your browser after submitting the form. You should see a long line of URL-encoded values similar to the following (the line breaks are mine):

```
http://russell/MasteringASP/Chapter6/ch6i6.asp?FirstName=asdf&LastName=
asdfasdfasdf&address1=asdf&address2=asdf&city=dfa&State=AL&zip=&notes=
Enter+any+additional+notes+here.&Submit=+Submit+
```

Fortunately, ASP makes this change very simple. Perform a global search-and-replace operation on the `ch6i6.asp` file. Change every occurrence of `Request.Form` to `Request.QueryString`, save the file, then submit the form again. Oops—still doesn't work. Look at line 24 of the file—the one that reads:

```
If Request.ServerVariables("REQUEST_METHOD") = "POST" then
```

That line is the culprit. It's testing for the `post` method. If the form is posted, the page validates the input; if the method used to request the page is `get`, the test bypasses all the validation checks. You just changed the form to the `get` method, so the test always fails. You'll have to use a different method to check whether the user has submitted the form or is simply requesting the form for the first time. You can use the value of the submit button to make the check. If the user submitted the form, the `Request.QueryString("Submit")` item will contain the value (actually, the value of the `value=` attribute) of the submit button on the form—in this case, the string " Submit ". In fact, if the collection contains any value for the submit button, the user submitted the form. Change line 24 to:

```
If Request.QueryString("Submit") <> "" then
```

You've seen that you can use either the `post` or the `get` method to send data contained in user controls to the server; however, you should use `post`. The `get` method limits the size of the data (it's `QueryString` data, after all). The `get` method also provides the user with the opportunity to change the values—possibly to invalid values. That's not a good idea. Finally, the `get` method also shows the variable names, and you may not want people to be able to see them. In this case, the user entered all the values, so being able to view the values in the address line is immaterial.

One final note. You've also seen two methods to determine whether a user submitted a form. One method is to test the value of the `Request.ServerVariables` (`"REQUEST_METHOD"`) variable. I used that method in Listings 6.5 and 6.6. The second method is to test the value of a known form variable—like the submit button value. If the value is absent, the user didn't submit the form. Use the second method. The first method forces the server to initialize the entire `ServerVariables` collection values, so it's both inefficient and slow.

TIP

Don't use the `Request.ServerVariables("REQUEST_METHOD")` value to test for form submission; test the value of a known form variable instead. Using the `REQUEST_METHOD` value forces the server to initialize the entire `Request.Server-Variables` collection, so it's both inefficient and slow.

Don't Take Collection Shortcuts

The ASP engine tries to be helpful—sometimes too helpful. For example, you can write `Request("someValue")` without explicitly naming one of the collections. When you do that, the Request object searches the collections in turn and returns the first value in any collection that matches the key.

You can see how easily that can lead to problems. For example, suppose I have a cookie named `UserID` and the user has just posted a form that contains a field also named `UserID`. I might normally retrieve the cookie using the syntax `Request-("UserID")`. For most pages, that would work just fine. Using that syntax though, the Request object returns the value of the first key called `UserID`. When there are multiple values, which one will it find, the value in the `Cookies` collection or the one in the `Form` collection? I'll let you discover the collection search order on your own, but I'll also warn you not to depend on it. Microsoft may change the collection search order at any time.

Speed is another consideration. If you don't specifically include the collection name, the Request object searches all the collections until it finds a matching key. You can significantly improve your response time by specifying which collection contains the key.

WARNING

Even though it's not required, always specify the Request collection name. In other words, write `Request.ServerVariables("name")` rather than `Request("name")` even though—most of the time—the result is identical.

Other Request Object Properties/Methods

This is a wrap-up section. You've seen most of the properties and methods of the Request object, and you'll see the rest later, but for completeness, I'll list and briefly explain the few properties and methods that remain.

The `Request.TotalBytes` property tells you the total size of all bytes sent by the browser with the request. It's relatively useless except when you use it in concert with the `Request.BinaryRead` method.

The `Request.BinaryRead` method lets you read the raw binary form data sent by the browser. Of course, you can read text information with it as well, but the `Request.Form` collection you've already seen makes it much easier to do that. If you want to experiment with the `BinaryRead` method, you should be aware that after you've used the `BinaryRead` method, you may no longer use or refer to the `Request.Form` collection. If you do, the ASP engine raises an error. Note that "refer to" includes indirect, as well as direct references. For example, you can write `Request("someValue")` without explicitly naming one of the collections. When you do that, the Request object searches the collections in turn and returns the first value in any collection that matches the key.

The `Request.ClientCertificate` collection contains security certificates (unique binary values) that the browser sends when it requests information from a secure site via the HTTPS protocol. Not all browsers support security certificates. The server uses security certificates to identify a specific user. The `Request.Client-Certificate` collection is always empty when the browser requests information via the standard HTTP protocol. To obtain security certificate values, you must set up a secure site on your server via IIS. You'll see more about the `Request.Client-Certificate` collection and secure sites in Chapter 23, *Controlling Access and Monitoring*.

CHAPTER

SEVEN

The Application and Server Objects

- Web Sites are Multiuser Programs

- Introduction to Threads—How IIS Handles Simultaneous Requests

- Application Variables—Sharing Data Between ASP Instances

- Application Lock/Unlock Methods

- How to Use Application Variables

- Mini-Project: Exploring Application Variables

- The Server Object

- When NOT to use Application Variables

I've grouped the Application and Server objects together because they both provide your application with global data—information that applies to all users of your application. The Server object lets you control and query IIS programmatically, giving you access to Web services that you would otherwise need to code for every application.

The Application object is a collection object similar to the ASP collections you've already seen. It stores data in key-value association pairs. You can retrieve individual values or iterate through all the items in the collection. The main difference between the Application object and other ASP collections is that there's only one Application object for all users of your application. All the other collections are user-specific—the ASP engine creates them for a single transaction or session.

Because all ASP sessions in an application share the Application object, you must understand the potential problems that can occur with shared data in a multiuser environment.

Web Sites Are Multiuser Programs

Your task in building Web applications is to force a single computer—your Web server—to perform the processing work for a large group of users. You probably have a computer on your desktop that's nearly as powerful as your server (in fact, it might be your server). When you're the only person using a computer, the computer spends most of its time waiting on you.

That's easy to say—maybe this anecdote will help you understand just how fast computers are. At one point in my life, I helped connect a computer to a 55-key electronic piano keyboard. Pressing a key on the keyboard closes two electrical circuits—one at the top of the keystroke and one at the bottom. The computer checked keys in a loop; it started at one end of the keyboard (key 0) and incremented a counter until it got to the last key (key 54). By checking each key in turn, the computer could detect when you pressed one or more keys. I wanted to measure how evenly people could repeat notes. I wrote a small program to watch what the computer was doing. I found that if I repeated a single note on the keyboard—as fast as I could press and release the key—the computer searched the entire keyboard an average of 36 times between each keystroke. In other words, from my perspective, I was rapidly repeating a note. From the computer's perspective, every once in a while, the slow human would press a note. The computer spent most of its time waiting on me to press the next key. That was with a 1 Mhz Apple computer. Imagine how much faster a modern processor is!

Rather obviously, one person and one computer don't make a highly efficient person-to-machine ratio. Computers measure time and work in cycles. A modern processor cycles 600 million times each second or faster. It doesn't matter to the computer whether each cycle is a work cycle—one in which it performs a task— or a no operation (NOP) cycle, one in which it waits for the next task. Web servers let multiple people share an application running on a single computer or group of computers.

Introduction to Threads—How IIS Handles Simultaneous Requests

Web servers must handle simultaneous requests from multiple users. Sometimes, usage is low. For example, you might be the only person connected to the application. At other times the computer may receive several requests per second. Ideally, you want the users waiting on the results to feel that the server has handled their request in a timely fashion.

To keep track of requests, the Web server puts them in a queue. A queue is a list in which you add items at one end and remove them at the other—like a production line. The queue holds requests or tasks that are waiting to be processed.

IIS queues tasks, but it doesn't start one task, work on that task until it's complete, then begin the next one; it works on several tasks at once. Of course, a computer can't work on multiple tasks simultaneously—there's only one processor after all. Instead, it uses time slices. A time slice is a very short amount of time— typically measured in millionths or billionths of a second. IIS loads the state of one task, works on it for a time slice, then saves the state of that task, switches to the next task and works on it for a time slice. All this happens very rapidly—so rapidly that, to a human, the computer appears to be doing several things simultaneously. The process is called *task switching*.

The number of simultaneous tasks that the computer works on depends on the number of threads you have assigned to IIS. A thread is a single task. A program might use one thread for its entire life, or it might spawn multiple threads so it appears to be doing several things at once. For example, using Windows Explorer, you can start copying a large set of files and still browse other directories on your computer. Although it's not exactly true, for purposes of this discussion, you can think of a thread, a task, a program, and a request, as the same thing. The more active threads, the more tasks the computer performs simultaneously.

Unfortunately nothing is free. There's a penalty for creating more threads. The computer must save and restore the state of each task as it switches from one task to the next. The overhead of saving and restoring task states takes a larger percentage of processing power as the number of threads grows. Also, there's a finite amount of time. Every thread you create forces the computer to share the available time among more tasks, which means that each active task takes longer to complete.

IIS balances the need to process each request quickly with the need to process multiple requests. If it used only one thread, a long request—like formatting data from a large database table—would force all other requests to wait until the active request was complete. If it uses too many threads, it wastes processor cycles on task switching overhead, and the response time for all requests—even short ones—becomes too slow.

Because processing time is precious, you can limit the number of threads each program can create. The ASP engine, by default, starts with three initial threads, but can spawn more depending on the number of pending requests in the queue. IIS has a default pool of eight threads for all Web services. It assigns threads to the various services (HTTP, FTP, Admin service, etc.) as needed. You can increase the number of threads allocated to both ASP and the IIS thread pool. For example, if you have a very fast processor, you might be able to double the number of threads without significantly affecting the users' perception of response time.

The reason I've taken you through this discussion is that you need to understand that while only one thread is active at any given microsecond, several tasks may be active during the course of a single request. Each may be trying to access or change data that your request depends on.

For example, suppose you have one page in your application. That page opens a file that contains a single number. Your script reads the value of the number, increments it (adds one to the value), then writes the value back to the file and closes the file. With one user and one thread, there's no problem. With 10 users and 1 thread, there's no problem. IIS queues the requests, and each request opens the file, increments the value, and closes the file. However, as soon as you allow more than one user and more than one thread, you have the potential for collisions. With multiple threads, IIS task-switches among several requests simultaneously. One thread may open the file and read the value, but another thread then acquires the processor. That thread also opens the file and reads the value. When IIS activates the first thread again, it increments the value and writes the value back to the file. But the second thread does the same thing—overwriting the counter value not with the next incremental number, but with the same number.

As long as each thread accesses unshared resources, multi-threading works beautifully, but you can see that you must handle shared resources carefully. ASP lets you work with shared resources through the Application object.

Application Variables—Sharing Data between ASP Instances

In a standard Windows application, you can store variable values that all modules in the program can access or change—global values. The Application object gives you a place to store global values for Web applications. As you've seen, you must consider threading issues when dealing with shared resources. The Application object provides methods for ensuring that only one thread can access a resource at a time. It's up to you to use those methods responsibly.

The Application object consists of a list of named values held in a collection called Contents. You can add a value to the collection with the default Value property:

```
Application.Value("Name") = "John"
```

Because the Value property is the default, you don't have to use it explicitly. This works just as well:

```
Application("Name") = "John"
```

You retrieve a value either from the Contents collection, by key:

```
Response.Write Application.Contents("Name")
' displays "John"
```

or with the Value property:

```
Response.Write Application.Value("Name")
' also displays "John"
```

You can also access values with an index rather than a string key:

```
Response.Write Application.Contents(1)
' displays "John"
Response.Write Application.Value(1)
' also displays "John"
```

You can remove the value of an item from the Application object by setting the item associated with a key to a null string or to the special Empty value:

```
Application.Contents("Name")= ""
Application.Contents("Name")= Empty
```

If you're using VBScript, you should generally use the built-in null string constant rather than writing a null string constant. For example:

```
Application.Contents("Name")= vbNullString
```

In early ASP versions you cannot remove a key from the Application object's Contents collection. The MSDN documentation for the Application object that accompanies Visual Studio 6 contains two errors. First, it states that you can remove an individual item using the Remove method of the Contents collection. Second, it states that you can remove all the items (clear the collection) using the RemoveAll method. Neither method exists.

The Contents collection implements a Count property that tells you the number of items in the collection:

```
AppCount=Application.Contents.Count
```

You can use the Count property to iterate through each item in the collection. The following example sets up several Application object items, each has an integer value. The loop block increments each value by 1:

```
Dim i
Application("Item1") = 1
Application("Item2") = 2
Application("Item3") = 3
For i = 1 to Application.Contents.Count
    Application.Contents(i) = Application.Contents(i)  + 1
Next
Response.Write Application("Item1") & "<br>" ' writes 2
Response.Write Application("Item2") & "<br>" ' writes 3
Response.Write Application("Item3") ' writes 4
```

Application Lock/Unlock Methods

There's only one Application object per IIS application, shared among many users. Any session can access values in the Application object, but you need to ensure that only one session has permission to change the values at any given time. To do that, you lock the Application object before adding or changing a value, and unlock it when you have finished your modifications. For example:

```
Application.Lock
Application("myKey") = myValue
Application.Unlock
```

If you forget to lock the Application object, multiple scripts may try to change the Application object values all at the same time, causing errors. If you forget to unlock the Application object, it unlocks automatically when the ASP page completes. Don't rely on that default behavior. Unlock the object as soon as you have completed your modifications.

WARNING   Unlock the Application object as soon as you have completed your modifications.

If a script tries to access the Application object while it's locked by another process, the script waits (blocks) until the Application object becomes available. If the script cannot access the object after a timeout period, the ASP engine raises an error.

TIP   You don't have to lock the Application object to retrieve values, just to add or change them.

How to Use Application Variables

You should use the Application object sparingly. Every time a script references the Application object, it must check to make sure the object isn't locked, search the collection for the named or indexed key, and retrieve the value. If another process is using the Application object, the script blocks until the Application object is free.

That's a relatively slow process at the best of times, but it's much slower if many sessions are all trying to access the Application object at the same time.

You can store both-threaded objects in the Application object, but not apartment-threaded objects, such as those you create with Visual Basic. For example, you can create an instance of the AdRotator object that Microsoft delivers with IIS and ASP and store the object in the Application object. Subsequent scripts can reference that object by key.

Despite the fact that you can store objects in the Application object, my advice is, unless you absolutely have to, don't store objects in the Application object. To understand why, you need to know more about Microsoft Transaction Server (MTS) and COM+ applications, but briefly; there's no great benefit to storing an object at the Application level unless that object takes a long time to initialize. Even then, there are other ways to cache data.

TIP   Unless you absolutely have to, don't store objects in the Application object.

Having said that, I'll soften it a little. For small sites, it's probably OK to store objects, because the chance of contention is small.

You should always make a local copy of a variable if you're going to use the value more than once. The overhead involved in making a local copy is much lower than multiple Application object accesses. For example:

```
' Do this:
Dim myVar
myVar = Application("myKey")
```

```
if myVar = "Bob" then
    ' do something
elseif myVar = "Joe" then
    ' do something else
end if
```

```
' Don't do this
if Application("myKey") = "Bob" then
    ' do something
elseif Application("myKey") = "Joe" then
    ' do something else
end if
```

You can store arrays of values in an Application variable. For example, you might create an array of network usernames for the people who are currently accessing your Web application (requires IE 4 or higher and an IIS security setting of NT Challenge/Response).

You store an array just like any other variable. For example:

```
Dim arrNames
arrNames = Array("Bob", "Joe", "Fred", "Felicia", "Boris")
Application("arrNames") = arrNames
```

You can also retrieve an array just like any other variable:

```
arrNames = Application("arrNames")
```

But you can't update an array in the same way you might update a single-value variable. Instead, you must store the array in a local variable, alter the array values, then store the array back into the Application object. For example:

```
<%
Dim arrNames
arrNames = Array("Bob", "Joe", "Fred", "Felicia", "Boris")
Application.Lock
Application("arrNames") = arrNames
Application.UnLock
```

```
' later in the script or in another script...
' change Fred to Freddie (arrays are 0 based by default)
```

```
' retrieve the array into a local variable
arrNames = Application("arrNames")
' make the update
arrNames(2) = "Freddie"
' store the array back into the Application object
Application.Lock
```

```
Application("arrNames") = arrNames
Application.Unlock
```

You should follow the lock, update, and unlock pattern for every change you make to an Application variable.

Mini-Project: Exploring Application Variables

You've seen that the Application object holds global data—values available to all pages of an ASP application. Here's a practical example. One warning: This example is not practical for a large and busy site.

You're going to build three ASP pages in your MasteringASP virtual directory. On each page, you want to show the total number of hits that page has received during the lifetime of the application.

> **NOTE**　　An ASP application begins the first time a user accesses any page in the application, and ends when the last session ends or times out.

Name the three pages ch7i1a.asp, ch7i1b.asp, and ch7i1c.asp. Each page should contain almost exactly the same code:

```
<%@ Language=VBScript %>
<% option explicit %>
<% Response.AddHeader "Refresh","0"%>
Dim pageCount
Application.Lock
Application("pagename") = Application("pagename") + 1
pageCount = Application("pagename")
Application.Unlock
"This page has been visited " & pageCount & " times."
```

Replace the word pagename in each page with the actual name of the page. For example, Listing 7.1 shows the full listing for the ch7i1a.asp file—I'm not going to show the full listing for the other two files (ch7i1b.asp and ch7i1c.asp), but you can find them on the CD.

LISTING 7.1　　　　**AppCounter Application (ch7i1a.asp)**

```
<%@ Language=VBScript %>
<% option explicit %>
```

```
<% Response.AddHeader "Refresh","0"%>
<html>
<head>
</head>
<body>
<%
Dim pageCount
Application.Lock
Application("ch7i1a") = Application("ch7i1a") + 1
pageCount = Application("ch7i1a")
Application.Unlock
Response.Write "This page has been visited " & pageCount & " times."
%>
</body>
</html>
```

You'll probably remember that the line <% Response.AddHeader "Refresh" ,"0"%> tells the browser to request a refreshed copy of the page once every N seconds. In this case N=0, so the browser displays the page and immediately requests an updated copy, causing the corresponding Application variable to update as fast as the cycle can repeat.

Open three copies of your browser. Resize them so they all fit on the screen (see Figure 7.1).

FIGURE 7.1:

Exploring Application variables

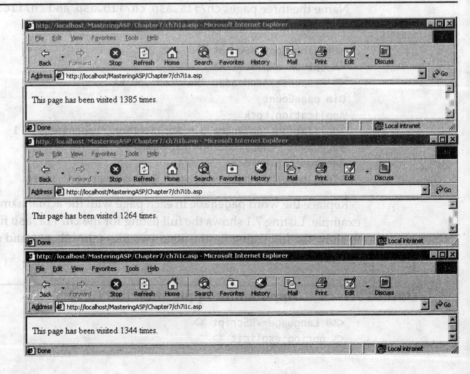

You should see the numbers change rapidly as each browser refreshes its page. Each page rapidly requests an updated page from the server, forcing the code to fire and update the Application variable for that page. Try opening more browsers. Do you ever see a collision (an error message)?

The Server Object

The ASP Server object gives you high-level access to the server itself. Using its properties and methods, you can create objects, execute code in other ASP files, translate virtual paths to physical paths, and perform server-side redirects. Here's where ASP begins to become truly interesting and powerful.

The *Server.ScriptTimeOut* Property

One of the reasons that Internet Service Providers (ISPs) allow ASP scripts to run on their servers is that the scripts can't run forever. By default, scripts time out after 90 seconds. The ASP engine controls how long a script can run. For example, suppose you accidentally wrote a script containing an endless loop, as in Listing 7.2.

LISTING 7.2   Endless Loop Script Example (ch7i2.asp)

```
<%@ Language=VBScript %>
<% option explicit %>
<%
dim i
dim j
i = 10
j = 9
Do While i > j
    i = i + 1
    Response.Write i
Loop
%>
```

The script in Listing 7.2 contains a loop that cannot end. The test at the beginning of the loop checks to see if the value of the variable i is less than the value of the variable j. If not, the loop increments the value of i, then checks again. The problem is that i will never be less than j. The initial value of i is higher than the initial value of j, and i always increases. Therefore, the loop is an endless loop, and the script will run until the timeout period expires. At that point, the server raises an error (see Figure 7.2).

FIGURE 7.2:

Script timed out default error message (ch7i2.asp)

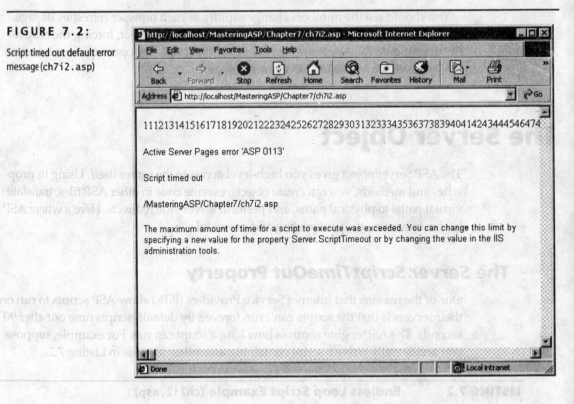

By default, the ASP engine will stop a script after 90 seconds (you may remember from Chapter 2 that you can set the timeout value using the IIS Properties dialog). Ninety seconds is more than adequate for most scripts—in fact, I usually set the value to 20 seconds; but for very busy sites, you may need to adjust the default value. You can set the default timeout period for your application from the Microsoft Management Console (MMC) using the virtual directory properties dialog (refer to Chapter 2, *Introduction to IIS*).

Using the `Server.ScriptTimeout` property, you can set a longer or shorter value for an individual page. The property takes an integer value—the number of seconds until the script times out. For example, if you ran the code in Listing 7.2, you may have noticed that your server was sluggish while the script was executing because the loop used almost all the server's processing power.

TIP This tip applies to the server computer only. If you want to see how much processing power the script uses, right-click on your task bar and select Task Manager from the context menu. Click the Performance tab. The dialog shows you the percentage of the total processing power available that is currently in use on your computer. Normally, the value is low—less than 3 percent; but while the script is executing, you'll see the percentage rise to 100 percent and remain there until the script times out.

Add the following line to the script below the line `<% option explicit %>`:

```
<% Server.ScriptTimeout=10 %>
```

Save the file and refresh your browser to run the script again. This time the server processes the script for only 10 seconds before it times out.

The best way to protect your server is to set a relatively short default ASP Script-Timeout value via the MMC. You can then change that value using the `Server`.`ScriptTimeout` property when you think a page might take longer to execute than the default timeout period. For example, a reasonable default timeout value is 20 seconds. If your pages take more than 20 seconds to execute, many people won't wait for them anyway. An exception might be a large or complex report. The database query alone might take longer than 20 seconds. In such special cases, you can warn the user that the page might take a long time to load, increase the `Server`.`ScriptTimeout` value, and then deliver the page.

If your site is very busy, you may find that 20 seconds is too short. In that case, you can use the MMC to increase the server timeout value, although you (and your viewers) would probably be better served by optimizing your pages.

You should try to keep your scripts as short as possible except in special instances. Users have no way of knowing what the server is doing—they're watching the hourglass cursor on their browsers—so you should try to make the server respond with something as quickly as possible.

The *Server.HTMLEncode* Method

Throughout this book, you've seen odd symbols such as ` ` for a non-breaking space, `&gt;` for a greater-than (>) sign, and `&lt;` for a less-than (<) sign. These are HTML-encoded characters called *escape sequences*. You must use these symbols when you want to display non-alphanumeric information accurately in a browser. A few of the most common escape sequences quickly become familiar, but what about the symbols for characters you use less often, such as #, (), or ^? Do you really want to look them all up in a reference table or memorize them?

The `Server`.`HTMLEncode` method can solve this problem. The method takes one argument—the string you want to encode. For example, suppose you want to display the text `If x < y then String1=String1 & "<"` in a browser. The encoded HTML is `If x &lt; y then String1=String1 &amp; &quot;&lt;&quot;`. That's awkward to write and remember. Using the `Server`.`HTMLEncode` method, you would write:

```
<% Response.Write Server.HTMLEncode _
   ("If x < y then String1=String1 & ""<""")%>
```

Remember that the <%= symbol is shorthand for `Response.Write`, so an even shorter method is:

```
<%=Server.HTMLEncode("If x < y then String1=String1 & ""<""")%>
```

The *Server.URLEncode* Method

You may remember from Chapter 6 that `QueryString` data (data included in a URL) is also encoded. Unfortunately, you don't encode URL data using the same escape sequences as HTML. In the section *The Request.QueryString Collection*, I promised that ASP could help you encode URL data. For example, the following URL contains several parameters:

```
http://myServer/myApp/search.asp?search+type=whole+word+only&search+
location=index&search+titles=True&1=Washington&2=George+&amp;+Martha
```

Like the `Server.HTMLEncode` method, the `Server.URLEncode` method takes a single string argument. You can pass the arguments in the URL to the `Server.URLEncode` method as a normal text string. The method returns the URL-encoded string. For example, suppose you had a link that, when clicked, would request this URL:

```
<a href="http://myServer/myApp/search.asp?search+type=whole+word+only&
search+location=index&search+titles=True&1=Washington&2=George+&amp;+
Martha">Search for George and Martha Washington</a>
```

An easier way to write the URL is:

```
<a href="http://myServer/myApp/search.asp?<%=Server.URLEncode("search
type=whole word only&search location=index&search titles=True &1=Wash-
ington&2=George & Martha")">Search for George and Martha Washington</a>
```

If you were to click on that URL, you would see this in the browser address field:

```
http://myServer/myApp/search.asp?search+type%3Dwhole+word+only%26
search+location%3Dindex%26search+titles%3DTrue+%261%3DWashington%262
%3DGeorge+%26+Martha
```

NOTE   The `ch7EncodeMethods.asp` file contains the code examples for this section and the previous section, but the links are bad links—they don't go anywhere.

For those of you who are interested, URL-encoded data is simply a substitution of an escape character—in this case, the percent sign—concatenated with the ASCII value of the replaced character shown in hexadecimal notation. For example, the ampersand in the URL in the phrase George & Martha has an ASCII value of 38. The hexadecimal equivalent of 38 is 26 (two sixteens and six ones).

NOTE

For a more complete explanation of the hexadecimal notation system, refer to the sidebar *The Hexadecimal System and RGB Color Values* in Chapter 4, *HTML Basics*.

When to Use the *HTMLEncode* and *URLEncode* Methods

Use the HTMLEncode method when you need to show symbols that browsers use for other purposes. For example, you can't display a word inside angle brackets in a browser without adding additional HTML tags like <code> or substituting the < or > HTML encoding for the brackets. Use the Server.HTMLEncode method to display the string instead:

```
Server.HTMLEncode("<code>")
```

Use the URLEncode method whenever you want to write QueryString data to a browser. For example, you should use the method on most anchor tag HREF parameter values unless you're sure the value contains only characters, numbers, and standard QueryString symbols like the question mark, ampersand, or plus sign. Always encode the string if it contains spaces.

The *Server.CreateObject* Method

One of the most powerful aspects of ASP is that it's extensible. Through the Server .CreateObject method, you can launch and use almost any COM object. For example, Microsoft delivers ASP with several different COM objects that you can use in your applications, but you can also create your own objects with VB, or even (through remote scripting) with VBScript or JScript. The syntax of the Server .CreateObject method is:

```
Server.CreateObject(<ProjectName>.<ClassName>)
```

Replace the <ProjectName>.<ClassName> parameters with the corresponding project and class name of the object you want to create.

To show you how easy this can be, Listing 7.3 contains a simple object written as a remote scripting component. You don't need to worry about the code right now—just how you use it from an ASP script.

LISTING 7.3   DateFunctions.WeekdayName **Component** (DateFunctions.wsc)

```xml
<?xml version="1.0"?>
<component>

<?component error="true" debug="true"?>

<registration
    description="DateFunctions"
    progid="DateFunctions.WeekDayName"
    version="1.00"
    classid="{af9e4dc0-489a-11d3-b0f0-204c4f4f5020}"
>
</registration>

<implements type="Automation" id="Automation">
    <method name="getWeekDayName">
        <PARAMETER name="aDate"/>
    </method>
</implements>
<script language="VBScript">
<![CDATA[

function getWeekDayName(aDate)
    getWeekDayName = WeekdayName(Weekday(Date))
end function

]]>
</script>

</component>
```

The component returns the day of the week (Sunday, Monday, etc.) for any date you pass it. Remote scripting components are COM components, so you must register them before you can use them from an ASP script. To register the DateFunctions .WeekDayName component, right-click on the file and select Register. In response, you should see a message box similar to Figure 7.3.

FIGURE 7.3:

Successful scripting component registration message

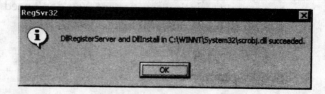

Next, you need to create an ASP page in which to use the `WeekDayName` object. Use the code in Listing 7.4.

LISTING 7.4   Server.CreateObject Example (ch7i4.asp)

```
<%@ Language=VBScript %>
<html>
<head>
</head>
<body>
<%
dim DayNamer
set DayNamer = Server.CreateObject("DateFunctions.WeekDayName.1.00")
Response.write "<p>In the year 2000, Christmas is on " & _
    DayNamer.getWeekDayName(#12/25/2000#) & "</p>"
%>
</body>
</html>
```

The code in Listing 7.4 creates an instance of the object `WeekDayName` and asks it for the name of the day on which Christmas falls in the year 2000. In the browser, the code prints:

```
In the year 2000, Christmas is on Monday
```

You'll see and use the `Server.CreateObject` method extensively in this book. One note: If you're not sure of the project name or class name of an object you want to use, you can search for it in the Windows Registry.

WARNING   Editing the registry can cause your computer to fail. Edit the registry with extreme caution. Make sure you have a backup copy before you edit the registry.

To search for a class in the Windows Registry, click Start, Run, then type `regedit`. You'll see the Registry editor window, as shown in Figure 7.4.

The Registry is a hierarchical list of keys and values. Click the plus sign next to the HKEY_CLASSES_ROOT key to expand it. You'll see a list of file extensions. Use the scroll bar to scroll down past the file extensions. Immediately following the last file extension, you'll see a list of `project.class` items, arranged alphabetically. All classes properly registered on your computer are in the list.

FIGURE 7.4:

Windows Registry Editor application (`regedit.exe`)

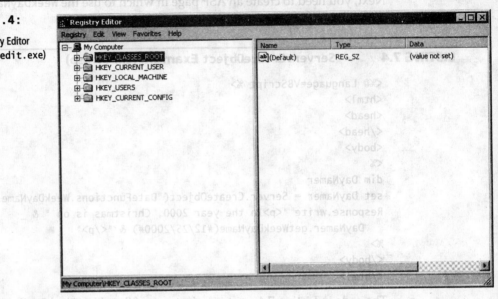

The *Server.Execute* Method and the *Include* Directive

Not all code is in COM objects. Sometimes it's more convenient (or necessary, because of your permissions on the server) to keep your code in ASP files. In previous versions of ASP, you could use a server-side `include` directive to include the contents of a file. The file could contain code routines. For example, suppose you wanted to place a footer containing the current date on every page. You could copy the HTML code to create the footer to every page, but that would be hard to modify—what if the footer requirements change? Instead, you could create a page that writes the footer, then reference that code from other pages.

By placing the code in a separate file, you can now modify it in one place, but still use it from any other page. There are two ways to accomplish this: the `include` directive and the `Server.Execute` method.

The code for the footer file might look like Listing 7.5.

LISTING 7.5   **Footer Code Page (`writeFooter.asp`)**

```
<table align="center" style="position:relative; top: 250" width="95%">
    <tr>
        <td>
MyCompany Inc.
        </td>
```

```
      <td align="right">
          <%=Now()%>
      </td>
   </tr>
</table>
```

Listing 7.5 writes a table 350 pixels below the previously plotted item, which effectively puts it at the bottom of the screen. It writes the company name on the left side of the page and the current date on the right side (see Figure 7.5).

FIGURE 7.5:

Main page with footer

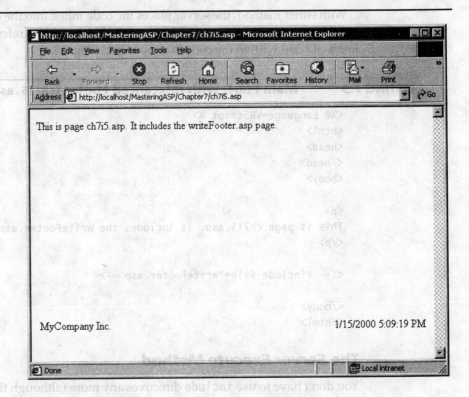

The *include* directive

You format an `include` directive as an HTML comment containing the appropriate commands. The syntax is:

```
<!-- #include PathType = FileName -->
```

The `PathType` value can be either `FILE` or `VIRTUAL`. Use `FILE` with an absolute path to the file. For example, if I save the `writeFooter.asp` file in the same directory as my main file, I could include it using an `include` directive, as follows:

```
<!-- #include FILE = "writeFooter.asp" -->
```

If my main file were in a directory called c:\myProgram and I were to put the include files in a specific includes subdirectory (c:\myProgram\includes), the include directive would look like this:

```
<!-- #include FILE = "includes\writeFooter.asp" -->
```

Alternatively, I could place my include files in a specific virtual directory and reference them using a VIRTUAL path:

```
<!-- #include VIRTUAL = "/includes/writeFooter.asp" -->
```

With either method, the server places the code inline into the current file, replacing the include line with the contents of the file. I can now reference the function just as if I had written the code as shown in Listing 7.5.

LISTING 7.5   **Main Page, with referenced Footer (ch7i5.asp)**

```
<%@ Language=VBScript %>
<html>
<head>
</head>
<body>

<p>
This is page ch7i5.asp. It includes the writeFooter.asp page.
</p>

<!-- #include file="writeFooter.asp"-->

</body>
</html>
```

The *Server.Execute* Method

You don't have to use include directives any more (although they still work). Now you can use the Server.Execute method instead. The Server.Execute method is more flexible and handles transactions better than was possible with include directives. To execute a file, simply pass the filename to the Server.Execute method:

```
Server.Execute "someFile.asp"
```

The code in the target file has full access to all the intrinsic ASP objects, as well as any other objects you instantiated on the main page. For example, you can replace the include directive in Listing 7.5 with a call to Server.Execute:

```
Server.Execute "writeFooter.asp"
```

A transaction is a unit of work that must either complete without errors or fail completely. Although you haven't seen any information about transactions yet, you should know that the Execute method treats transactions in an intuitive manner—the transaction crosses all files executed during the transaction, which includes files you call with the Server.Execute method. In other words, if you begin a transaction, then execute another file, the executed file is treated as part of the transaction. You'll see more about transactions in Chapter 20, *Controlling Transactions in ASP*.

The *Server.Transfer* Method

In Chapter 5, you saw how to use the Response.Redirect method to force the browser to request a different file from the server. In previous ASP versions, this was the only way to transfer execution from one file to another on the server. The problem with the Response.Redirect method is that the redirect message must travel from the server to the browser, then to the server again. That's highly inefficient. In addition, as an ASP programmer, you had to store any form or URL data sent with the initial request so the values would be available to the redirected target script.

Fortunately, Microsoft has added the Server.Transfer method to the current version of ASP. The Server.Transfer method performs a server-side redirect. That means that the redirect occurs entirely on the server. The browser requests a file, the server redirects the request to another file, and the browser receives the results. Because the browser is no longer involved in the redirect, the Server.Transfer method also maintains the contents of form and Querystring data, so they are available in the redirected script. Using the Server.Transfer method is much more efficient. You should preferentially use Server.Transfer over Response.Redirect with modern ASP scripts.

For example, suppose a restaurant displays a list box containing the days of the week. You want to display the menu for the day that the user selects in an <iframe>. The inline frame is in every way a complete browser window except that it doesn't display any toolbars or the status bar. The advantage of using an inline frame is that you can position the frame very easily on the screen without using a frameset page. Like all frames, you can change the content in one frame without affecting content already displayed in another frame.

WARNING   The <iframe> or inline frame tag, is specific to IE, and does not work in Netscape.

Listing 7.6 contains the code for the main page. I haven't spent much time formatting the page because I want you to be able to see how it works without cluttering up the HTML with formatting commands.

LISTING 7.6   **The Peasant Restaurant Menu Selection Page (ch7i6.asp)**

```
<%@ Language=VBScript %>
<html>
<head>
</head>
<body>
<H1>The Peasant Restaurant Site </H1>

<form name="frmWeekDay" action="ch7i6a.asp" method="post">
<h3>Select a day to see the menu </h3>
<table align="left" width="60%">
    <tr>
        <td>
            <select name="WeekDay">
                <option value="Sunday" selected>Sunday</option>
                <option value="Monday">Monday</option>
                <option value="Tuesday">Tuesday</option>
                <option value="Wednesday">Wednesday</option>
                <option value="Thursday">Thursday</option>
                <option value="Friday">Friday</option>
                <option value="Saturday">Saturday</option>
            </select> <input type="submit" value="Submit">
        </td>
    </tr>
</table>
</form>
</body>
</html>
```

Listing 7.6 contains the main page of the application. The `<form>` tag's `action`
parameter shows you that the browser will submit the form to the `ch7i6a.asp`
file. On submission, the user's selection will be in the `Request.Form("WeekDay")`
variable, because `"WeekDay"` is the name of the `<select>` tag. The `ch7i6a.asp` file
retrieves the user's selection and performs a server-side redirect to either the Sunday menu page (`SundayMenu.asp`) or the normal menu page (`NormalMenu.asp`)
depending on the user's selection (see Listing 7.7).

LISTING 7.7   **The Peasant Restaurant Redirection Page (ch7i6a.asp)**

```
<%@ Language=VBScript %>
<% option explicit %>
<%
dim selectedDay
```

```
if not isEmpty(Request.Form("WeekDay")) then
    selectedDay = Request.Form("WeekDay")
    if selectedDay = "Sunday" then
        Server.Transfer("SundayMenu.asp")
    else
        Server.Transfer("NormalMenu.asp")
    end if
else
    Server.Transfer "ch7i6.asp"
end if
%>
```

The script first checks to see if the expected form data exists:

```
if not isEmpty(Request.Form("WeekDay"))
```

If the user submitted the form properly, the `Request.Form("WeekDay")` value will not be empty. If the value is empty (for example, if a person types the address of the file into a browser), the script performs a `Server.Transfer` back to the weekday selection list page. This is a good example of defensive coding. The value should not be empty, and will not be empty normally, but you should never write an `if` statement without an accompanying `else` unless you're absolutely certain that the `else` condition can never happen. In this case, it can—you can test it for yourself. Type the URL `http://MasteringASP/Chapter7/ch7i6a.asp` into your browser and press the Enter key. The script will immediately redirect you back to the menu selection page because the `Request.Form("WeekDay")` variable is empty.

Notice that although the user is free to select any day of the week, they can see only two menu pages—`SundayMenu.asp` and `NormalMenu.asp`. Listing 7.8 contains both files.

| **LISTING 7.8** | **The Peasant Restaurant Menu Pages (SundayMenu.asp, NormalMenu.asp)** |

```
'****************************************************************
'SundayMenu.asp
'****************************************************************
<%@ Language=VBScript %>
<%option explicit%>
<html>
<head>
</head>
<body>
<h1>The Peasant Restaurant Site</h1>
<h2>Menu for Sunday</h2>
<a href="ch7i6.asp">
```

```
<font color="red" size="2">(back to list)</font></a>
<h3>Main Course</h3>
<p>Pot Roast with Gravy (all you can eat)</p>
<h3>Vegetables (select two)</h3>
<p>
    Braised Potatoes<br>
    Baby Carrots in Hollandaise Sauce<br>
    Steamed Broccoli<br>
    Cauliflower<br>
</p>
<h3>Dessert (select one)</h3>
<p>
    Apple Pie a la mode<br>
    Chocolate tart<br>
    Rice pudding<br>
</p>
</body>
</html>
'************************************************************
'NormalMenu.asp
'************************************************************
<%@ Language=VBScript %>
<%option explicit%>
<html>
<head>
</head>
<body>
<h1>The Peasant Restaurant Site</h1>
<h2>Menu for <%=Request.Form("WeekDay")%></h2>
<a href="ch7i6.asp">
<font color="red" size="2">(back to list)</font></a>
<h3>Main Course</h3>
<p>Gruel</p>
<h3>Vegetables (select one)</h3>
<p>
    One Raw Onion<br>
    One Raw Potato<br>
</p>
<h3>Dessert (NA)</h3>
<p>
    Only on Sunday<br>
</p>
</body>
</html>
```

The *Server.MapPath* Method

It's always best to avoid writing absolute paths into your source code whenever possible. For example, on your development server, you might want to open a file in the current directory. You developed the application and have control of the server, so you know the file's exact location. You could easily write code to open the file using an absolute path, such as `C:\MasteringASP\Chapter7\someFile.txt`.

Now consider what might happen when you deploy the application. What if the server manager has decreed that the `C:` drive on your target server may not contain application code. All of the paths in your application are suddenly wrong. You should never rely on resource names. Always put them in an easily updated file. That way, when the resource names or locations change, as they inevitably do, you can solve the problem easily by changing only one file.

That advice may be useful, but it doesn't always meet your needs. To open a file, you have to have a physical path, not a relative path. The `Server.MapPath` method can provide that path for you. The `Server.MapPath` method accepts one argument—a virtual or relative path—and returns the corresponding physical path, assuming it exists. Using this method, you can often avoid all physical file references completely. For example, suppose I need to know the physical path to the `root` directory of my application. Assume that the virtual directory name is `MasteringASP`. The following code will supply the physical path:

```
<%
Dim physicalAppPath
physicalAppPath = Server.MapPath("/MasteringASP")
Response.Write "The physical path is: " & physicalAppPath
%>
```

Figure 7.6 shows the result of executing the previous example.

Unfortunately, that code doesn't really release you from your dependence on names. Your code still depends on the virtual directory name `MasteringASP`. Instead, it's usually better to depend on the relative position of files to one another. For example, suppose your server administrator changes the name of the virtual directory hosting your application. Don't laugh—it happened to me once when a company changed names. The virtual directory name was changed as well. Fortunately, my application didn't reference any virtual directory names.

FIGURE 7.6:

Result of Server.MapPath method

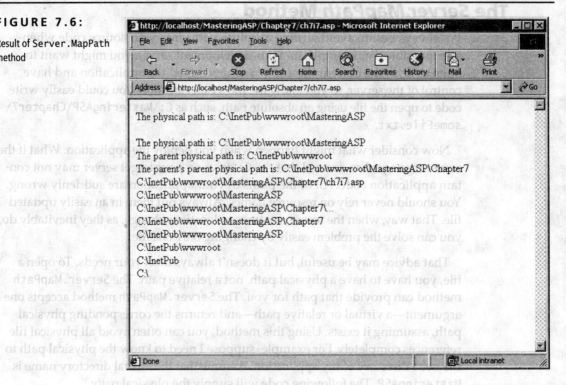

Rather than use virtual directory names, you can rely on the relative position of any given file to the application root. By using dot-relative path syntax, you can reference a directory above the current directory. You've probably seen dot-relative syntax if you've ever used DOS to list the contents of a directory. A single dot means the current directory. Two consecutive dots mean the parent directory. For example, assume the code below resides in a file in a subdirectory below the application root. The script displays the physical path of the application root using dot-relative notation.

```
<%
Dim physicalAppPath
physicalAppPath =
Server.MapPath("..")
Response.Write "The physical path is: " & physicalAppPath
%>
```

You can turn off ASP's ability to access parent paths with the dot-relative notation by using the ASPEnableParentPath property. You can set this property using the MMC in the Application Configuration dialog, App Options tab. Check the Enable Parent Paths checkbox to allow scripts to use dot-relative notation. The

ASPEnableParentPath property is set to true by default, but it's a security risk because scripts using it can access directories higher than the virtual directory level. Using this technique, you can reference any directory up to and including the root directory of the drive. For example, this script shows you the entire path hierarchy from the executing file to the root of the drive:

```
<%
dim s
dim aPath
aPath = "."
s = Server.MapPath(Request.ServerVariables("URL"))
do
    response.write s & "<br>"
    if right(s,1) <> "\" then
        if len(aPath) > 2 then
            aPath = aPath & "/.."
        else
            aPath = aPath & "."
        end if
        s = Server.MapPath(aPath)
    else
        exit do
    end if
loop
%>
```

NOTE   The ch7i7.asp file on the CD contains all the code in this section.

The Server.MapPath method just performs a translation—it does not check to see if the physical path result is a valid path. For example, you can get the physical path for a non-existent directory:

```
Response.Write Server.MapPath("/MasteringASP/DoesNotExist")
```

The method dutifully responds with the path c:\InetPub\wwwroot\Mastering-ASP\DoesNotExist even though the directory does not exist.

If the path you want to map starts with a slash, the server attempts to map the corresponding virtual directory. If the path parameter does not start with a slash, the server attempts to map the path relative to the current directory.

The *Server.GetLastError* Method

ASP scripts raise three different types of errors:

- Pre-processing errors

- Script compiling errors

- Runtime errors

Pre-processing errors occur when the ASP pre-processor, which inserts the contents of `include` files, is unable to find an `include` file reference. Script compiling errors occur when the script compiler finds an unrecognized token or missing, required keyword. You should catch pre-processing and script compilation errors during development and testing. Runtime errors can crop up any time due to a variety of factors, including logic errors, and missing, locked, or altered resources. Most of these errors fall within an error range that IIS recognizes as a 500;100 custom error.

When the ASP engine raises a 500;100 error, IIS creates an `ASPErrorObject` and fills it with information about the error. It then transparently issues a `Server.Transfer` command to a default URL, `/iishelp/common/500-100.asp`, to display the error information.

For example, Figure 7.7 shows part of the default error page generated by trying to compile the following script, in which the variable i is undefined.

```
<%
for i= 1 to 10
    sum=sum+1
next
%>
```

The default page is fine during development, but may not meet your needs in production. For example, you might not want to display the path to your ASP files or the code that failed in a production application. You can easily substitute your own custom help file to replace the default page. To substitute a custom error page, open the MMC, select the Default Web Site entry, right-click on your application's virtual directory name, select Properties, then select the Custom Errors tab (see Figure 7.8).

FIGURE 7.7:

Default error page

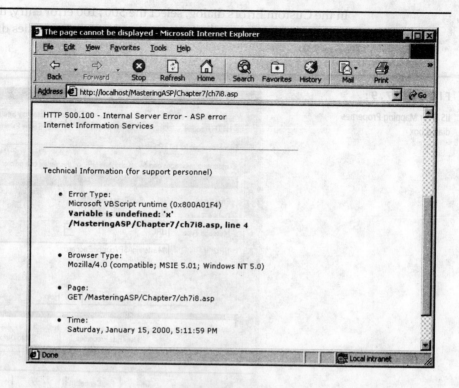

FIGURE 7.8:

IIS virtual directory properties, Custom Errors tab

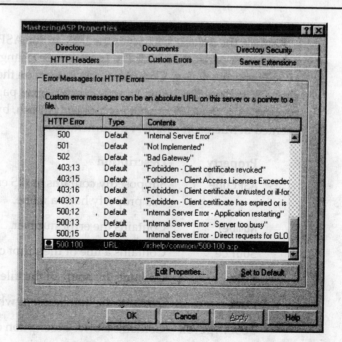

In the Custom Errors dialog, select the 500;100 error entry, then click the Edit Properties button. You will see the Error Mapping Properties dialog shown in Figure 7.9.

FIGURE 7.9:

IIS Error Mapping Properties dialog box

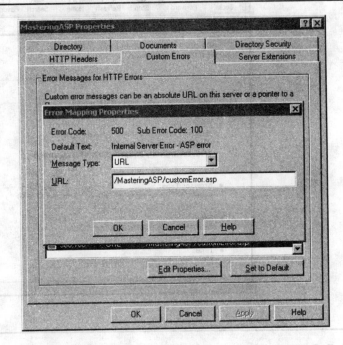

Replace the default URL with the URL of the ASP page you want to display when errors occur, then click OK to save your changes and close the Error Mapping Properties dialog. Click the Apply button on the Custom Errors dialog, then click OK to close the dialog. In your custom error page, you can display any of the properties of the ASPErrorObject object (which, by the way, are poorly documented in Microsoft's MSDN documentation):

Property	Description
ASPCode	Supposedly contains an IIS error code—I have yet to see this property have a value.
Number	Contains the error number.
Source	Contains a line of the script code where the error occurred.
File	Contains the name of the file where the error occurred.
Line	Contains the line number where the error occurred.
Description	Contains a brief description of the error.

The IIS documentation states that all ASP runtime errors raise a `500;100` error. That doesn't seem to be true. The server performs a `Server.Transfer` for script pre-processing errors and code compilation errors only. Some runtime errors seem to generate the error as well, but the runtime error example in the documentation—a `division by 0` error—does not make it to the `Server.Transfer` method. Instead, it displays a simple default error message.

Listing 7.9 shows the code for an error display page. The file is in the root directory of the `MasteringASP` application on the CD, not in the `Chapter7` subdirectory. You can modify this code to meet your needs.

LISTING 7.9   Substitute `500;100` Error Display Page (`customError.asp`)

```
<%@ Language=VBScript %>
<html>
<head>
</head>
<body bgColor=whitesmoke>
<p>
<%
dim ASPErr
Set ASPErr = Server.GetLastError
%>
</p>
<h1 align=center style="COLOR: orangered">Sorry...</h1>
<h2 align=center>An Error Occurred While Processing Your Request</h2>
<h4 align=center>Please write down the following information,
then call the Help Desk</h4>
<table align="center" border=5 bgColor="#b0c4de" cellpadding=3>
   <tr>
      <td>IIS Error Code</td>
      <td width="50%">
         <b>
         <%
         if ASPErr.ASPCode = "" then
            Response.write " "
         else
            Response.write ASPErr.ASPCode
         end if
```

```
                                %>
                            </td>
                        </tr>
                        <tr>
                            <td>ASP Error Number</td>
                            <td width="50%">
                                <b><%=ASPErr.Number%></b>
                            </td>
                        </tr>
                        <tr>
                            <td>Error Source</td>
                            <td width="50%">
                                <b><%=ASPErr.Source%></b>
                            </td>
                        </tr>
                        <tr>
                            <td>Error occurred in</td>
                            <td width="50%">
                                <b><%=ASPErr.File%></b>
                            </td>
                        </tr>
                        <tr>
                            <td>Line number</td>
                            <td width="50%">
                                <b><%=ASPErr.Line%></b>
                            </td>
                        </tr>
                        <tr>
                            <td>Description</td>
                            <td width="50%">
                                <b><%=ASPErr.Description%></b>
                            </td>
                        </tr>
                    </table>

                </body>
                </html>
```

In a browser, the same script error shown earlier in Figure 7.7 now looks like Figure 7.10.

Objects

FIGURE 7.10:

Substitute 500;100 error display page

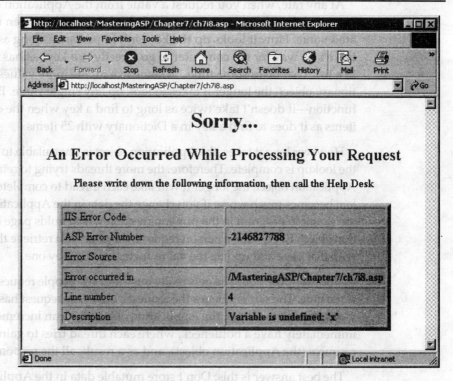

When NOT to use Application Variables

If you can store global data in the Application object, why not store all your data there? The answer requires that you go back and think through how the Application data must be stored and how your application accesses and stores the data.

Microsoft states that the Application object is a Dictionary. That may be true, but it isn't the same Dictionary object they provide in the Scripting DLL for you to use (you'll see more about that Dictionary object in Chapter 11, *The Scripting Dictionary Object*). A Dictionary object is a type of collection—one in which retrieving a value by key is much faster than retrieving a value by index number. You've already seen two other Dictionary-like objects—the Request object and the Response object. All these objects store data with key-value associations. Dictionary object keys—the names you associate with values—are strings. The values are Variants, which means they can hold any type of value: number, string, array, or object. In other words, a Dictionary object holds a collection of keyed values.

At any rate, when you request a value from the Application dictionary using a key, some internal code must run that looks up the key, then returns the associated value. How it looks up the key isn't important as long as you realize that there's no way for the computer to go directly to a key—it has to look up the key in a list. That takes some time. To some extent, the more values you store in a Dictionary object, the longer it takes to look up any single value. But it's not a linear function—it doesn't take twice as long to find a key when the dictionary stores 50 items as it does to find a key in a Dictionary with 25 items.

However long it takes, the Application object is unavailable to other threads until the lookup is complete. Therefore, the more threads trying to retrieve data from the Application object, the longer it will take each thread to complete its task. The problem becomes much worse if you change the data in the Application object. Consider the example program in the previous section which holds page hits in the Application object. Every time a person requests the page, you retrieve the value associated with that page and update the value, incrementing it by one.

Now, suppose your site gets really busy and 100 people request your page at the same time. The server queues the requests, but every request has to wait for the previous request to unlock the Application object so it can increment the value. You immediately have a bottleneck, where each thread tries to gain access to a scarce resource (the Application object), and as a result, all the responses become slow.

The best answer is this: Don't store mutable data in the Application object. I realize that's not a completely satisfactory answer; sometimes you have limited choices. The next best answer is this: Update the Application object as infrequently as possible. Using the previous example, if you just want to know roughly how many page hits have occurred on each page, you might keep that data for each session. When the session ends or times out, you could update the Application object totals for that session. Because sessions are much less likely to end simultaneously than requests are likely to occur simultaneously, that would keep the Application object free to deliver fairly up-to-date totals without the bottleneck.

You can see from the project in the previous section example that the Application object can lock, update, and unlock very rapidly. Just because you can do something, however, doesn't mean you should do it. If you build an application in which every page accesses Application data, you may have problems scaling your application. ASP provides a better option for data that you need on every page—the Session object.

C H A P T E R

E I G H T

8

The Session Object

- ■ What is a Session?

- ■ The *global.asa* File

- ■ Exploring Sessions and the *global.asa* File

- ■ Web Sites vs. Standard Windows Programs

- ■ Associating Data with Individuals

- ■ *Session* Variables

You'll probably spend more time thinking about the Session object than any other intrinsic ASP object. That's because the Session object is your easiest route to individualizing HTML pages and creating dynamic sites, and after all, that's the reason you're using ASP in the first place.

You use the Session object to store values associated with a single browser. The Session object itself is exactly like the Application object you explored in the previous chapter, except that a single session has exclusive use of one Session object. You don't need to lock and unlock the Session object the way you do the Application object, because there's no contention. Unfortunately—partly because of the terminology involved—beginning ASP programmers are often confused about sessions, Session objects, when sessions start, when they end, and why any of this matters.

What Is a Session?

I've used the word *session* throughout this book to mean the interval a single user spends interacting with your application during a contiguous length of time. In an ASP application, a session has a more specific meaning. A session begins when a browser instance requests a page in your application, and ends when you abandon the session via code, when the session times out, or—if the browser refuses the session cookie—immediately.

An ASP session is specific to a given cookie. That can be confusing because a cookie and a single browser are not the same thing. Bear in mind that the ASP engine identifies sessions by looking for the existence of an ASPSESSIONID cookie. You may have more than one browser window open and attached to the same session if both browsers have the same cookie.

ASP's reliance on cookies can cause problems because some people set their browsers to refuse cookies. There are ways to use ASP without cookies, but for this chapter, assume that all browsers accept cookies.

> **NOTE**   There are ways to use ASP without cookies, but for this chapter, assume that all browsers accept cookies.

When Does a Session Begin?

An ASP session begins at a browser's first request for any ASP page in a directory marked as an IIS application. The requested page doesn't have to be a specific page—it can be any file with an ASP extension in the application's virtual directory or from any subdirectory of that directory. The server immediately redirects the user to a file called `global.asa`. You'll see more about that file in the next section. The server generates a cookie header, then runs the code (if any) in the `Session_OnStart` event in the `global.asa` file.

The cookie generated by the server is the `SessionID` cookie. The cookie's key is `ASPSESSIONID` in IIS 3x and `ASPSESSIONIDXXXXXXXX` in IIS 4 and 5. The cookie's value is an encrypted pseudo-random series of letters and numbers. A typical `SessionID` cookie looks like:

```
ASPSESSIONIDQQQQGYFC=ICLLKDGBFCMMHNPEGCFIJOLC
```

Why Is the *SessionID* Cookie Important?

HTTP transactions are stateless; therefore, the server gives the browser a unique token in response to its first request so the browser can identify itself to the server for subsequent requests.

Imagine that you have an inexhaustible list of ID cards. Each card has two matching numbers—one on each half. You're standing at the entrance to a large meeting hall. Every time people approach you, you ask for their ID card. If they don't have a card, you select a new card and give them half. You ask them to write their name on the other half and you keep that half. If they do have a card, you find your matching half so you can greet them by name.

That's what the server does with `SessionID` cookies. It gives each browser a `SessionID` cookie, and keeps the matching `SessionID` value. Any information you want to store about that browser gets stored with the server's copy of the `SessionID`. The next time the browser requests a page, the server can find the information associated with that `SessionID`.

Each cookie is guaranteed to be unique during (but not across) the instance of the IIS program—in other words, as long as IIS is up and running, it will continue to generate unique `SessionID` values.

If the browser accepts the cookie, it will return the cookie on all subsequent requests to that site. The ASP engine keeps a list of the cookies. When the browser sends the `ASPSESSIONID` cookie, the ASP engine matches the cookie value with a server-side list. If it finds a match, then ASP can match an existing Session object with the browser by looking through the list of Session keys.

That's why the `SessionID` cookie is important—with it, the server can recognize the browser and can store and retrieve associated values. Without it, the browser is unknown, cannot be recognized as a repeat visitor, and therefore the server cannot retrieve associated values for that browser.

When Does a Session End?

There are five ways to end a session:

1. The server abandons a session after a defined interval with no activity. You can define the length of interval with the `Session.Timeout` property.

2. You can end a session in code, by issuing a `Session.Abandon` command.

3. You can shut down IIS. This, of course, stops the application and ends all sessions.

4. You can modify the `global.asa` file. If you modify the file and save the changes, the next request by any browser to your application forces IIS to stop the application, ending all sessions.

5. The browser can refuse the `SessionID` cookie. Note that this is the only control the browser has over the session—it can't stop the server from beginning a new session; it can just refuse to let the session continue longer than a single request. You should be aware that the server does start a session even for browsers that refuse the cookie. Remember that the server has no way of knowing in advance which browsers will refuse a cookie and which browsers will not.

The *global.asa* File

Earlier in this chapter, I mentioned a file called `global.asa`. If you have a file titled `global.asa` in the `root` directory of your ASP application, the ASP engine will run the code in the file in the following instances:

*   The application starts (`Application_OnStart` event)
*   A session starts (`Session_OnStart` event)
*   A session ends (`Session_OnEnd` event)
*   The application ends (`Application_OnEnd` event)

You can add code for any or all of these four event procedures. You don't have to write code for any of them, and you don't have to write code for the `OnEnd` event procedures just because you wrote code for the `On_Start` procedures.

All of the script in the file must be enclosed in `<script language="script-LanguageName"></script>` tags. If you place any script in the file outside of the tags, ASP raises an error. You can do two other things in the `global.asa` file—

define static objects using <object></object> tags, at either the Application or the Session level, and define Type Library references. A type library is a file containing a list of properties and methods. ASP (and other COM-pliant applications) use the type library to discover the list of method and property names and parameter types to which an object will respond. VB and Visual InterDev use the information to display the Intellisense drop-down, code-completion lists as you write code.

The ASP engine performs application and session initialization in a specific order:

1. The first person to request a file from your application causes ASP to find the global.asa file in the application's root directory. The server performs the same steps whether or not the global.asa file exists.

2. Immediately after it creates the Application object, ASP calls the Application_ OnStart event (if it exists).

3. When the Application_OnStart event completes, the ASP engine creates a new SessionID, writes the SessionID cookie header, then creates a new Session object and starts the Session.Timeout timer.

4. Immediately after it creates the new Session object, ASP calls the Session_ OnStart event (if it exists).

5. When the session times out or you issue a Session.Abandon command, the ASP engine calls the Session_OnEnd event procedure (if it exists), then destroys the Session object.

6. After the ASP engine destroys the last Session object, it calls the Application_ OnEnd event procedure (if it exists).

You can use the global.asa file to initialize global variables, and gather meta information about your application. You don't have to initialize global variables in the global.asa file—you can just as easily initialize them on the first application page. I've found that the global.asa file is most useful for three things:

- Storing string references that might change
- Cleaning up when a session ends
- Ensuring that all users are out of your site

For example, database connection strings are often out of your control. A server administrator may change the name or location of the database at any time. If you hard-code the connection strings into your application, you may have to change many files to make your application work again. You're much better off storing the connection string(s) in the `global.asa` file, where you can change them relatively easily.

You can use the `Session_OnStart` event to keep track of how many active sessions you have on the server at any given time. For example, you can increment a counter or add the new `SessionID` to an array stored in an Application object whenever the `Session_OnStart` event occurs. Similarly, you can decrement the counter or remove the `SessionID` from the array whenever the `Session_OnEnd` event occurs. For secured sites or sites with passwords where you can associate a `SessionID` with a specific user, you can use the stored `SessionID` to perform interesting tasks, like sending a message to a specific user or group whenever they log on to your application. You can also use the information for administrative queries, like, "Is John Jones connected to a session right now?"

The *Session.TimeOut* Property

When ASP creates a `SessionID`, it also creates a timer and associates it with that `SessionID`. The timer begins at the value of the `Session.Timeout` setting (default is 20 minutes in IIS 4, 10 minutes in IIS 5) and counts down to 0. When the timer reaches 0, ASP ends the session, abandoning all stored information associated with that `SessionID`.

The ASP engine resets the timer to the maximum value every time it receives a page request from the browser associated with the `SessionID`. Therefore, as long as the browser continues to request pages, the session remains active. When the browser stops requesting pages, the timer never gets reset, and eventually reaches 0, which ends the session.

The purpose of the `Session.Timeout` value is to protect the server from storing data associated with a browser forever. Ideally, the server would somehow know when the user has quit the application, but due to the stateless nature of HTTP, that doesn't happen. Instead, to the server, the browser just doesn't return. After a while, there's no point in maintaining that user's data in memory on the server any longer.

The combination of the `Session.Timeout` value and the browser's `SessionID` cookie leads to a problem. What happens when a person doesn't request a new page for more than the default `Session.Timeout` but the browser still has a `SessionID` cookie? The answer is that the `SessionID` cookie value presented by the browser is no longer valid. Any data associated with that `SessionID` is gone. As it happens, ASP lets the browser keep the same cookie value, but associates that cookie with a new Session object on the server.

The *Session.Abandon* Method

You can (and should) give users partial control over when their session in your application ends by giving them the option to exit the program. Usually, you would do this via a Quit or Exit button. When the user clicks the button, you call the Session.Abandon method. The Session.Abandon method is a deferred (delayed) command—it doesn't take effect until after the ASP engine finishes processing the current page.

After the current page has completed, the ASP engine calls the Session_OnEnd method. From that point on, the events occur in the normal end-of-session order, just as if the session had timed out. Therefore, you can write end-of-session code in the Session_OnEnd method, and it works the same way regardless of whether you explicitly end the session via the Session.Abandon method or whether the session times out.

Exploring Sessions and the *global.asa* File

Open (or create) a global.asa file in the root directory of your MasteringASP Web site, and place the code in Listing 8.1 in the file. Because you can have only one global.asa file in an application, I've included several copies of the global.asa file on the CD, named as shown in the associated listing. You can rename them as needed. For example, the global.asa file for the following listing is global_asa_ch8i1.asa.

LISTING 8.1   Global.asa Session Counter Example (global_asa_ch8i1.asa)

```
<SCRIPT LANGUAGE=VBScript RUNAT=Server>
Sub Session_OnStart
    if isEmpty(Application("counter")) then
        Application("counter")=0
    end if
End sub


Sub Session_OnEnd
    Application("counter") = Application("counter") + 1
End Sub
</SCRIPT>
```

The Session_Onstart script in Listing 8.1 checks to see if an Application variable called counter exists. If so, it does nothing; otherwise, it initializes the variable to 0. In the Session_OnEnd event, the script increments the Application("counter") variable. Essentially, this script keeps track of the number of sessions created in your application from the time the application begins until it ends.

To display the values, create a new directory called Chapter8 in your MasteringASP Web site, and save the code in Listing 8.2 as ch8i1.asp.

LISTING 8.2   Session Counter Example (ch8i1.asp)

```
<%@ Language=VBScript %>
<% Response.Expires = -1%>
<html>
<head>
</head>
<body>
<h1>Session.Abandon Example</h1>
<p>
<%
Response.write "Your SessionID is: " & Session.SessionID & "<br>"
Response.write "Application(counter) = " & Application("counter")
Session.Abandon
%>
</p>
<p>Your session has been abandoned. Make a note of your SessionID, then
refresh your browser. Each time you refresh this page, you should get a
new SessionID.
</body>
</html>
```

Note that the SessionID doesn't change when you refresh the page. But you know that the session has been abandoned, because the only way the Application ("counter") variable can increment is when the ASP engine calls the Session_OnEnd event procedure. The SessionID doesn't change because the ASP engine recognizes that you have a valid but unused ASPSESSIONID cookie when you refresh the page, so it doesn't issue a new cookie.

The Session.Abandon code doesn't stop page execution. You can see the HTML that's below the Session.Abandon statement. People often confuse the workings of the Response.End command and the Session.Abandon command. They don't work the same way at all. The Response.End command stops page execution immediately. Ending the Response does not affect the session, whereas the Session .Abandon statement lets the page finish processing, and then calls the Session_OnEnd event procedure.

Note the SessionID, then close your browser. Now open a new copy of your browser and navigate to the page you just created. You should see a new SessionID. The SessionID cookie is an in-memory or transient cookie. When you closed your browser, the cookie disappeared. This time when you navigate to the page, there's no existing `SessionID` cookie; the ASP engine must issue a new one.

Size the browser so it takes up only a quarter of your screen. Open and size three more browsers so you have one browser in each quadrant of the screen. You should have four different `SessionID` values showing in the browser windows (see Figure 8.1).

FIGURE 8.1:

Session counter example
(ch8i1.asp)

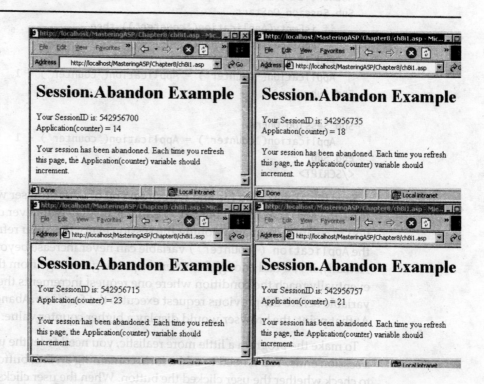

Refresh each browser several times. As you move from browser to browser, watch the `Application("counter")` value. All the clients share the value of Application-level variables. Now open the `global.asa` file in your editor and make a change; for example, add a space to the end of the file. Save the `global.asa` file. Refresh one of the browsers. What happened to the `Application("counter")` value? What you just saw is a useful trick. ASP doesn't give you a way to shut down or reinitialize your application from code directly—there's no `Application .Abandon` method—but any saved change to the `global.asa` file causes ASP to reinitialize the application.

Suppose that instead of counting the total number of sessions created (or rather, abandoned) for your application, you want to track the number of active sessions. You can use the same `Application` variable, but instead of incrementing it during the `Session_OnEnd` event, you want to increment the variable when ASP creates a new session, and decrement the variable when a session ends. Leave all four browsers running. Alter your `global.asa` file to match Listing 8.3.

LISTING 8.3   Global.asa Session Tracker Example (global_asa_ch8i2.asa)

```
<SCRIPT LANGUAGE=VBScript RUNAT=Server>
Sub Session_OnStart
    if isEmpty(Application("counter")) then
        Application("counter")=0
    end if
    Application("counter") = Application("counter") + 1
End sub

Sub Session_OnEnd
    Application("counter") = Application("counter") - 1
End Sub
</SCRIPT>
```

Save the `global.asa` file and refresh several of your browser windows. This time, the `Application("counter")` variable display will never change. Because you're creating, then abandoning the session every time you refresh the page, the `Application ("counter")` variable can never increase beyond a value of 1. Actually, if you had enough browsers requesting the page from the server, you'd eventually reach the condition where one request increments the `Application` variable before the previous request executes the `Session.Abandon` command. At that point, the browser would display a higher counter value.

To make the program a little more realistic, you need to let the user control when a session ends. You'll need to add a form containing an Exit button and the code to check whether the user clicked the button. When the user clicks the button, you abandon the session (see Listing 8.4).

LISTING 8.4   Active Session Counter Example (ch8i2.asp)

```
<%@ Language=VBScript %>
<% Response.Expires = -1%>
<%
dim exitApp
exitApp = (Request.Form("Submit") = "Exit")
%>
<html>
<head>
</head>
<body>
<h1>Session.Abandon Example</h1>
```

```
<p>
<%
Response.write "Your SessionID is: " & Session.SessionID & "<br>"
Response.write "Application(counter) = " & Application("counter")
   & "<br>"
Response.write "Click the button to end your session.<br>"
%>

<input type="Submit" name="Submit" value="Exit">
</form>
<%
if exitApp then
Session.Abandon
%>
</p>
<p>Your session has been abandoned. If you refresh this page, the
Application(counter) variable should increment.
<%
end if
%>
</body>
</html>
```

This time, as you navigate each of your four browsers to the ch8i2.asp file, you should see the Application("counter") value increment. Click the Exit button in one of the browsers to abandon that session, then refresh a different browser. The counter should decrement because the application now has one less active session.

Close one of the browsers and refresh the others. The counter value doesn't change. That's because closing the browser doesn't send a message to the server—your application has no way to know when a user will not return. That's why the Session.Timeout value is important. If the session didn't time out, you'd have to retain the user's information forever.

If you leave the browsers on your screen and wait for a little over 10 minutes, you'd see that all of the sessions had timed out. In other words, the first browser you refresh after 10 minutes would show the counter value as 1.

Web Sites vs. Standard Windows Programs

Now that you've seen how ASP applications work, let's look at how they differ from standard Windows applications. Standard Windows applications often store information between sessions, and ASP applications are no exception; but a user can quit a standard Windows application by closing the window or shutting down

Windows. At that point, the application can still interact with the user—for example, by refusing to close until the user elects to save or abandon changes to the application's data or state.

In contrast, if a user closes an application running in a browser, the session on the server runs until it times out. You can't keep a person from closing the browser, and you can't send a message that the browser is closing, but you can still write well-behaved applications that keep the user's data and/or settings intact between sessions. You can also give the user the opportunity to close the session by putting an Exit button, menu item, or link on the page.

The whole purpose of the Session object is to associate data with individuals, but it's important that you realize there's no perfect way to do that. Sessions don't associate data with individuals—they associate data with a browser instance. If a person opens more than one browser and navigates to your application, the server will store multiple copies of that person's data, one copy for each browser. Most ASP examples (including the ones in the remainder of this book) discuss Session data as if it belonged to a person rather than to a browser. I think that's fine as long as you realize that the server has no way to associate data with a person—it's the browser instance that's important.

Building Web applications means you have to change your focus from programming for one individual to programming for groups. For example, it may be perfectly natural and highly efficient to initialize a Windows application with large amounts of data when the application starts. You can do that in a Windows application because the user has exclusive use of the CPU and memory. Programming a Web application in the same way will quickly overburden your server. Basically, you should remember that you're trying to run the application for multiple users simultaneously, often using a computer that's not much more powerful than your desktop machine. Therefore, you need to plan your application differently. Try to conceive of it as a series of small transactions. For each transaction, you load only the data required for that transaction. When the transaction completes, you clear the data from memory, leaving only enough to load data for the next transaction.

Associating Data with Individuals

You've seen how the ASP engine initializes and destroys sessions. During the time a session is active, you can use the Session object to store data pertinent to that session. The ASP engine takes care of the association for you, but it's your job to remember that the Session object uses resources on your server. That means you need to consider the relationship between the convenience of keeping user data in memory, the number of potential simultaneous users on your site, and the capacity of your server.

The problem of associating data with individuals is the largest and most intractable problem in Web applications, so I'll discuss it at length in Chapter 22, *State Maintenance in ASP Applications*.

Session Variables

Each browser instance gets its own copy of the Session object. The Session object itself contains a collection of key-value pairs just like the other ASP collections. You supply the key, and the Session object stores or retrieves the associated value. Like the Application object, the collection keys are strings and the collection values are Variants, which means you can store any type of data, including objects.

Adding *Session* Variables

To add a Session variable, you simply assign a value to a new key. For example:

```
Session("newKey") = someValue
```

Note that the terminology "new key" really does mean a new key, not an existing key. That's because assigning a value to an existing key replaces the existing value. The Session object does not raise an error or warning if you replace the value:

```
Session("name") = "John"
Session("name") = "Bill"
Response.Write Session("name") ' writes Bill
```

You cannot store a Response or Request object in a Session variable, but you can store other objects. For example, one object you'll see later in this book is a Dictionary object. A Dictionary object is itself a collection of key-value pairs, much like the other ASP collections you've seen. To create an object, use the Server.Create-Object method discussed in Chapter 7, *The Application and Server Objects*.

```
Dim d
Set d = Server.CreateObject("Scripting.Dictionary")
d.Add "name1", "John"
d.Add "name2", "Bill"
set Session("names") = d
```

The previous example creates a new Dictionary object, adds two items, and stores the entire Dictionary in a Session variable called names. Note that there's a difference between storing a scalar value, such as a string in a VBScript variable, and storing an object reference. To store an object reference, you must use the Set keyword.

```
' Store a scalar value
Session("myValue") = 1000
' Store an object
Set Session("myValue") = someObject
```

You retrieve values from the Session object by key:

```
MyValue = Session("myValue")
Set someObject = Session("someObject")
```

Clearing *Session* Variables

You can clear a Session variable by setting it to a null string (" ") or by setting it to the VBScript Empty value. For example:

```
Session("myValue") = ""
Session("myValue") = Empty
```

In VBScript, you normally destroy object variables by setting them to the Nothing keyword:

```
Set Session("myObject") = Nothing
```

Be careful not to confuse the Nothing value with the Empty value—they are not equivalent:

```
Set Session("myObject") = Nothing
Response.Write isEmpty(Session("myObject")) & "<br>" ' writes False
Response.Write isObject(Session("myObject")) & "<br>" ' writes True
```

The previous example shows that Nothing is not equal to Empty, and paradoxically that Nothing is an object in VBScript. That's important. I've seen numerous examples where programmers set object variables to Nothing, then later test the variable value using the isObject() function—which states that the variable is still an object. In contrast, the following example sets the variable to Empty, and the results are what you would expect:

```
Session("myObject") = Empty
Response.Write isEmpty(Session("myObject")) & "<br>" ' writes True
Response.Write isObject(Session("myObject")) & "<br>" ' writes False
```

Finally, Empty is not the same as a null string:

```
Session("myObject") = ""
Response.Write isEmpty(Session("myObject")) & "<br>" ' writes False
Response.Write isObject(Session("myObject")) & "<br>" ' writes False
```

Determining Whether a *Session* Variable Exists

Based on the previous section, you should now be able to tell whether a Session variable exists. The variable exists if a test for Empty returns False. For example:

```
If Not isEmpty(Session("myVar")) then
    Response.write "Not empty."
```

Just because a variable is not Empty does not mean it has a usable value. The value of the variable could be Nothing. Two ways to test the type of value in a variable are the TypeName(variable) function and the VarType(variable) function. These two functions are closely related. The TypeName function returns a string containing the name of the type of variable, while the VarType function returns an integer value that VBScript uses internally to differentiate the type of value held in a Variant variable.

```
Session("1") = "John"
Session("2") = 100
Session("3") = Array("x","y")
Set Session("4") = Server.CreateObject("Scripting.Dictionary")
Response.write Typename(Session("1")) & "<br>" ' writes "String"
Response.write VarType(Session("1")) & "<br>" ' writes 8
Response.write Typename(Session("2")) & "<br>" ' writes "Integer"
Response.write VarType(Session("2")) & "<br>"  ' writes 2
Response.write Typename(Session("3")) & "<br>" ' writes "Variant()"
Response.write VarType(Session("3")) & "<br>"  ' writes 8204
Response.write Typename(Session("4")) & "<br>" ' writes "Dictionary"
Response.write VarType(Session("4")) & "<br>" ' writes 9
```

You'll find that both the TypeName and VarType functions can be useful. For example, the code in Listing 8.5 shows how to iterate through all of the variables in the Session object (except those you create using the <object> tag) with the Session.Contents method. You can use the TypeName and VarType functions to improve the routine.

LISTING 8.5   **Iterating Through** Session **Values with** Session.Contents

```
<%@ Language=VBScript %>
<% option explicit %>
<%
dim V
Session("1") = "John"
Session("2") = 100
Session("3") = Array("x","y")
Set Session("4") = Server.CreateObject("Scripting.Dictionary")
```

```
    for each V in Session.Contents
        if isObject(Session(V)) then
        Response.write V & ", " & "Object: " & Typename(Session(V)) & "<br>"
        elseif (varType(Session(V)) and vbArray) = vbArray then
            Response.write  V & ", " & Typename(Session(V)) & "<br>"
        else
            Response.write  V & ", " & Session(V) & "<br>"
        end if
    next
    %>
```

You have now been introduced to most of the intrinsic ASP objects. To take full advantage of them, you need to write code. In ASP, you have several language choices. In the next two chapters, you'll see how to use the two most popular scripting languages—VB Script and JScript.

PART III

Writing Server-Side Code

PART III

Writing
Server-Side Code

CHAPTER
NINE

Introduction to VBScript

- **Scripting Languages vs. Other Computer Languages**

- **ASP Scripting Options**

- **Getting Started with VBScript**

- **Project: Use VBScript to Control Responses**

- **Project: Build a Date-Formatting Routine**

Scripting Languages vs. Other Computer Languages

Scripting languages are interpreted languages. The server must parse, compile, and execute the script on-demand. In contrast, languages like C++ are compiled languages. You use a program called a compiler to perform the first two steps—parsing and compiling the code—before executing the code. Compilers store a machine-language translation of the code. Interpreted languages are easier to use, while compiled languages are faster and more efficient.

ASP script languages have only one variable type—the Variant variable. A Variant is a relatively large (16-byte) variable that can hold any type of value—Integer, Long, String, Array, Object—any type. Variants are large because they need to be able to contain all other variables, as well as a value describing the type of value they contain. In the previous chapter, you used the VarType function to determine the type of value held in Session variables. Session variables are Variants. The VarType function returns the Variant type value byte.

While scripting languages are easier to use than compiled languages, they also have a large overhead. Because of the extra load on the server required to parse and compile scripting languages, code you write in ASP will not scale as well as code you write in compiled languages. Also, ASP scripts must run on the server. In contrast, compiled code can run on other servers and return the values to an ASP script.

In short, try to think of your ASP scripts as presentation code only. Use script to format responses and make calls to compiled code for efficiency. Use compiled components for database connectivity and to process business logic.

ASP Scripting Options

So far you've seen only VBScript examples in this book; but ASP isn't limited to VBScript. You can currently use any of several scripting languages. Any scripting language that conforms to the Microsoft Scripting Host requirements will work.

VBScript

VBScript is a subset of the Visual Basic for Applications (VBA) language used in the Microsoft Office suite and in many other commercially-available applications, which in turn is a subset of Microsoft's Visual Basic language. All of these languages share an (almost) identical set of keywords, properties, and functions. The biggest difference between them, besides the lack of a few methods in VBScript, is that you can compile VB, but you can't compile VBScript.

VBScript is the default ASP scripting language. Most of the example code available in this book and in other resources is VBScript code.

JScript

JScript is Microsoft's ECMAScript-compatible version of JavaScript. Unlike the relationship between VBScript and VB, JavaScript is *not* a subset of Sun's Java language. The two languages share some common syntax, but Netscape developed JavaScript, not Sun. JScript is a powerful scripting language. Developers commonly use JScript to write client-side scripts because it's the common standard for browser scripting, and not all browsers can run VBScript.

You don't have to limit yourself to JScript on the client; you can use it on the server as well. ASP ships with JScript. To use JScript on the server, you can change the default ASP language to JScript by using the Internet Service Manager application. You can also change the language on a page-by-page basis in your ASP scripts by changing the language tag at the top of each ASP page to the following:

```
<@Language="JScript">
```

PerlScript

Perl is a powerful text-processing language used extensively in Common Gateway Interface (CGI) scripting, before ASP and other choices were available. PerlScript is a subset of Perl that retains most of Perl's functionality. Microsoft does not ship PerlScript with ASP, but you can download it from the Internet. There are both free and commercial versions of PerlScript available.

Others

Any scripting language that conforms to the Microsoft Scripting Host requirements will work. When ASP first appeared, there were many references to a Rexx scripting language. That seems to have disappeared, but it might be underground. I've also seen hints of a PythonScript scripting language. My recommendation is, stick to VBScript or possibly JScript on the server. Most of the comments in ASP newsgroups about scripting languages other than VBScript tend to center around poor support and buggy implementations. If you're more comfortable with Python or Perl than with VBScript or JScript, consider using CGI rather than ASP.

Getting Started with VBScript

The VBScript language provides built-in functions and methods for most common programming tasks. Version 5 added powerful search capabilities and support for creating your own classes and objects.

Keywords

Scripting is a combination of keywords, built-in functions, calls to custom routines, and object methods. Keywords are words that the parser recognizes—they're part of the language. You can't create variables with the same name as a keyword, so it's good to list them up-front, so you can avoid problems.

Table 9.1 lists the VBScript keywords in alphabetical order and a brief description of where/how you use them.

TABLE 9.1: VBScript Keywords

Keyword	Type	Description
Abs	Function	Returns the absolute value of a number.
Addition (+)	Operator	Used to add values.
And	Operator	Used to perform Boolean comparisons and operations.
Array	Function	Creates a Variant array.
Asc	Function	Returns the ASCII value of a character.
Assignment (=)	Operator	Assigns one value to another. In VBScript, you also use the = operator to test for equivalence.
Atn	Function	Returns the arctangent of a number.
Call	Statement	Calls a subroutine or function.
CBool	Function	Returns a Variant of subtype Boolean (either True or False).
CByte	Function	Returns a Variant of subtype Byte (single-byte integer).
CCur	Function	Returns a Variant of subtype Currency (8 bytes).
CDate	Function	Returns a Variant of subtype Date (8 bytes).
CDbl	Function	Returns a Variant of subtype Double (8 bytes).
Chr	Function	Returns the character representation of an ASCII integer value.
Cint	Function	Returns a Variant of subtype Integer (2 bytes).
Clear	Method	Clears the Err object.
CLng	Function	Returns a Variant of subtype Long (4 bytes).
Class	Object	The object returned when you create a class definition using the Class statement.
Class	Statement	Creates a class. You provide the class name, properties and methods.
Concatenation (&)	Operator	Concatenates strings. You can also use the Addition (+) operator to add strings, but it's not a good idea to do so.

Continued on next page

TABLE 9.1 CONTINUED: VBScript Keywords

Keyword	Type	Description
Const	Statement	Creates a constant.
Cos	Function	Returns the cosine of an angle.
CreateObject	Function	Creates an **object** variable.
CSng	Function	Returns a **Variant** of subtype **Single** (8 bytes).
CStr	Function	Returns a **Variant** of subtype **String**.
Date	Function	Returns a **Variant** of subtype **Date**.
DateAdd	Function	Returns a date or time offset by month, week, day, year, minute, second, or hour.
DateDiff	Function	Returns the difference in months, weeks, days, years, minutes, seconds, or hours between two dates or times.
DatePart	Function	Returns the part of a date or time representing the day, weekday, month, quarter, year, minute, second, or hour.
DateSerial	Function	Returns a date offset by the specified number of days, months, and years.
DateValue	Function	Returns a **Variant** of subtype **Date** corresponding to a string date parameter—turns strings into dates. **CDate** does this as well.
Day	Function	Returns the day of the month.
Description	Property	Returns the description of an error stored in the Err object.
Dictionary	Object	A collection object that holds key-value pairs.
Dim	Statement	Declares a variable.
Division (/)	Operator	Divides one number by another.
Do...Loop	Statement	Surrounds code to be repeated in a loop.
Empty	Value	The value of an uninitialized **Variant**.
Eqv	Operator	Identical to Boolean **And**.
Erase	Statement	Clears an array.
Err	Object	Contains error information.
Eval	Function	Evaluates script passed to the function as an expression. You may evaluate only one expression at a time. Refer to the **Execute** statement for a way to execute multiple lines of code.
Execute	Method	Executes a regular expression search for the specified **string** argument.
Execute	Statement	Executes one or more lines of code passed to the statement as a string. You may separate statements with colons or with carriage return/linefeed characters. Script executed in this manner can access global variables, but may only be executed within the context of the currently executing procedure.
ExecuteGlobal	Statement	Executes one or more lines of code passed to the statement as a string. You may separate statements with colons or with carriage return/linefeed characters. Script executed in this manner runs in the global context, can access global variables, and may be called from anywhere else in the script.
Exit	Statement	Exits a subroutine, function, or repeated code block.

Continued on next page

TABLE 9.1 CONTINUED: VBScript Keywords

Keyword	Type	Description
Exp	Function	Returns the natural base of logarithms (e) raised to an exponential power.
Exponentiation (^)	Operator	Raises a value to an exponential power.
False	Value	Boolean logical `False` value of 0.
FileSystemObject	Object	Object that performs disk file operations.
Filter	Function	Returns a subset of a string array based on conditions passed as a parameter.
FirstIndex	Property	Returns the character offset of the first character of a Match object returned from a regular expression search. Translated, that means that the search string was found in the target string, and it appears at the index position pointed to by the `FirstIndex` property. Unlike most other VB collections and the `Instr` function, the character offset of the first character in the searched string is 0, not 1.
Fix	Function	Returns a number truncated to an `integer` value.
For...Next	Statement	Surrounds code to be repeated in a loop a fixed number of times.
For Each...Next	Statement	Surrounds code to be repeated for the number of items in a collection object or array.
FormatCurrency	Function	Formats currency values according to specific criteria.
FormatDateTime	Function	Formats dates and times according to specific criteria.
FormatNumber	Function	Formats numbers according to a specific format string.
FormatPercent	Function	Formats numbers or numeric expressions as percentages.
Function	Statement	Defines the beginning of a function.
GetLocale	Function	Returns the LocaleID of the computer on which the script is running.
GetObject	Function	Returns an object reference for an object loaded from a file. You provide the filename, and optionally, a ProgID. A ProgID consists of a `ProjectName.ClassName` construction, like `Excel.Worksheet`, or `Word.Application`.
GetRef	Function	Returns a function pointer that you can bind to a DHTML event.
Global	Property	Determines whether a regular expression search should match all occurrences or only the first occurrence.
Hex	Function	Returns a numeric value as a hexadecimal string.
HelpContext	Property	Sets or returns a `HelpContextID` value representing the ID of a topic in a help file.
HelpFile	Property	Sets or returns the name of the help file associated with an object.
Hour	Function	Returns the hour from a specified time expression.
If...Then...Else	Statement	Surrounds code you want to execute only if a specified condition is `True`. If the condition is not `True`, you want to execute the code surrounded by the `Else` condition.
IgnoreCase	Property	Determines whether or not a regular expression search is case-sensitive.
Imp	Operator	Used to perform a logical implication on two numbers. I've never found a good reason to use this operator, although there may be one.

Continued on next page

TABLE 9.1 CONTINUED: VBScript Keywords

Keyword	Type	Description
Initialize	Event	Occurs when a VBScript Class object is instantiated.
InputBox	Function	Asks a user for input. Doesn't work for server-side script.
InStr	Function	Returns the index of the first character of a matching sub-string within a string.
InStrRev	Function	Returns the index of the last character of a matching sub-string within a string.
Int	Function	Casts a variable value to an **Integer** value. Use this to change a string to an **Integer** or to truncate real values.
Integer Division (\)	Operator	Divides two numbers and casts the result to an **Integer** (no decimal points).
Is	Operator	Tests for object equivalence. Returns **True** if two object pointers both point to the same object.
IsArray	Function	Returns **True** if the argument is a **Variant** of subtype **Array**. Equivalent to the expression varType(someVar) And vbArray = vbArray).
IsDate	Function	Returns **True** if the argument is a **Variant** of subtype **Date** or can be converted to a **Date** subtype.
IsEmpty	Function	Returns **True** if the argument is a **Variant** with the value **Empty**.
IsNull	Function	Returns **True** if the argument is a **Variant** with the value **Null**.
IsNumeric	Function	Returns **True** if the argument is a number or can be converted to a number.
IsObject	Function	Returns **True** if the argument is a **Variant** of subtype **Object**.
Join	Function	Accepts an array of strings and returns a string separated by the specified delimiter. **Join** is the opposite of **Split**.
LBound	Function	Returns the lower-bound of the array argument.
LCase	Function	Returns a string with all of the characters changed to lowercase.
Left	Function	Returns a string consisting of the beginning of a string through the specified index.
Len	Function	Returns the length of the **string** argument.
Length	Property	Returns the length of a Match object found in a regular expression search.
LoadPicture	Function	Returns a picture object. The command loads an image file from disk. This function works on the server, but doesn't seem to recognize any known properties or methods.
Log	Function	Returns the natural logarithm of a number.
LTrim	Function	Returns a string with all white space (tabs, spaces, carriage returns) trimmed from the left side (front) of the string.
Match	Object	Object returned as the result of a match during a regular expression search.
Matches	Collection	Collection of Match objects resulting from a successful regular expression search.
Mid	Function	Returns a sub-string of a string starting with a specified index and a specified number of characters in length.

Continued on next page

TABLE 9.1 CONTINUED: VBScript Keywords

Keyword	Type	Description
Minute	Function	Returns the minute of the hour as an integer from 0 to 59.
Mod	Operator	Performs modulo arithmetic.
Month	Function	Returns the month of the year as a number from 1 to 12.
MonthName	Function	Returns the name of the month number passed as an argument.
MsgBox	Function	Displays a Windows message box containing the specified message, title, and icon or buttons. Returns a constant designating the button the user clicked. This is useful for client-side script. On the server, VBScript writes MsgBox messages to the NT Application log.
Multiplication (*)	Operator	Multiplies two numbers.
Negation and Subtraction (-)	Operator	Returns a number multiplied by –1, or the difference of two numbers, depending on context. When used between two numeric values with a trailing space, VBScript interprets the minus symbol as a minus sign. When used in front of a numeric value with no trailing spaces, VBScript interprets the minus symbol as the negation operator.
Not	Operator	Used to negate an expression.
Now	Function	Returns the current date and time.
Nothing	Value	The value of an uninitialized object variable.
Null	Value	A value meaning no value, not zero, not a null string, not Empty, and not Nothing.
Number	Property	The error number property of an Err object.
Oct	Function	Returns a numeric value as an octal string.
On Error	Statement	Used to control what happens after an error occurs at runtime.
Option Explicit	Statement	Used to force variable declaration. When Option Explicit is in effect, VBScript raises a compile error when it encounters unrecognized symbols. Without Option Explicit in effect (the default), VBScript creates a new variable when it encounters an unrecognized symbol.
Or	Operator	Used to compare two expressions using Boolean Or logic.
Pattern	Property	Used to set or return the pattern string for a regular expression search.
Private	Statement	Used to create a private (script-level) variable, subroutine, or function.
PropertyGet	Statement	The procedure code to return a property value for a Class object.
PropertyLet	Statement	The procedure code to set a property value for a Class object.
PropertySet	Statement	The procedure code to set an object property value for a Class object.
Public	Statement	Used to create a public variable, subroutine, or function.
Raise	Method	Used to raise an error. The result of raising an error depends on whether On Error Resume Next is in effect and on the current error-processing state.
Randomize	Statement	Used to seed the random number generator.
ReDim	Statement	Used to change the dimensions of an array. You can use this to change the last dimension of a multi-dimensional array only.
RegExp	Object	A regular expression object. Used to perform complex pattern-based searches in a target string.

Continued on next page

TABLE 9.1 CONTINUED: VBScript Keywords

Keyword	Type	Description
Rem	Statement	Used to create a comment. Mostly obsolete. Use a single-quote instead.
Replace	Function	Replaces one or more occurrences of a specified sub-string within a string with a different sub-string. The replacement sub-string need not be the same length as the original sub-string.
Replace	Method	Replaces one or more occurrences of a specified sub-string within a string with a different sub-string in a regular expression search. The replacement sub-string need not be the same length as the original sub-string.
RGB	Function	Changes a set of three individual color values into a single Long color value in RGB format.
Right	Function	Returns the specified number of characters from the right-hand side (end) of a string.
Rnd	Function	Returns a random number between 0 and 1.
Round	Function	Rounds floating-point numbers to a specified number of decimal places.
RTrim	Function	Removes white space (tabs, spaces and carriage returns) from the right-hand side of a string.
ScriptEngine	Function	Returns a string containing the name of the currently executing script engine.
ScriptEngineBuildVersion	Function	Returns the build version number of the currently executing script engine.
ScriptEngineMajorVersion	Function	Returns the major version number of the currently executing script engine.
ScriptEngineMinorVersion	Function	Returns the minor version number of the currently executing script engine.
Second	Function	Returns the second of the minute of the specified Time value.
Select Case	Statement	Block statement that executes code conditionally upon evaluating an expression against several possible cases.
Set	Statement	Sets an object variable reference.
SetLocale	Function	Sets the LocaleID for the script context. You use this to output dates, times, and currency values in the format for the assigned LocaleID.
Sgn	Function	Returns the sign of a number.
Sin	Function	Returns the sine of an angle.
Source	Property	Returns the source where an error occurred. In server-side VBScript, the source always contains the page name where the error occurred.
Space	Function	Returns a string filled with spaces a specified number of characters in length.
Split	Function	Splits a string into an array of sub-strings according to a defined delimiter. Split is the opposite of Join.

Continued on next page

TABLE 9.1 CONTINUED: VBScript Keywords

Keyword	Type	Description
Sqr	Function	Returns the square root of a number.
StrComp	Function	Compares two strings. Returns –1 if the first string is less than the second string, 0 if the strings are equal, and 1 if the first string is greater than the second string. You select whether the comparison is case-sensitive.
String	Function	Returns a string filled with a character repeated a number of times.
StrReverse	Function	Returns a string in which the characters have been reversed.
Sub	Statement	Defines the beginning of a subroutine.
Subtraction (-) and Negation	Operator	Returns the difference of two numbers or a number multiplied by –1, depending on context. When used between two numeric values with a trailing space, VBScript interprets the minus symbol as a minus sign. When used in front of a numeric value with no trailing spaces, VBScript interprets the minus symbol as the negation operator.
Tan	Function	Returns the tangent of an angle.
Terminate	Event	Occurs just before a VBScript Class is destroyed. You use this to clean up by destroying object references and variables.
Test	Method	Executes a regular expression search.
Time	Function	Returns the current time, accurate to 1 second.
Timer	Function	Returns the number of seconds since 12:00 midnight.
TimeSerial	Function	Returns a time offset by the specified number of hours, minutes, and seconds.
TimeValue	Function	Returns the time from the argument. If the argument contains both date and time information, the `TimeValue` function returns the time only.
Trim	Function	Removes white space from both the left- and right-hand sides of a string, and returns the string.
True	Value	Boolean True. In VBScript, `True` is equal to –1.
TypeName	Function	Returns the VBScript internal type name of a `scalar` variable or object.
UBound	Function	Returns the upper-bound of an array.
UCase	Function	Returns a string with all the characters changed to uppercase.
Value	Property	Returns the text of a Match object resulting from a successful regular expression search.
VarType	Function	Returns a constant or (for arrays) combination of constants that represent the VBScript internal type of a variable.
Weekday	Function	Accepts a `Date` argument and returns a number from 1 to 7 representing the day of the week corresponding to the day portion of the argument.

Continued on next page

TABLE 9.1 CONTINUED: VBScript Keywords

Keyword	Type	Description
WeekdayName	Function	Accepts a `Date` argument and returns the string for the day of the week corresponding to the day portion of the argument.
While...Wend	Statement	Conditional loop block. The loop executes until the condition following `While` evaluates to `True`.
With...End With	Statement	Holds a local reference to an object while you perform multiple operations on that object. Using `With...End With` speeds up your code and improves readability.
Xor	Operator	Performs a Boolean Exclusive `Or` operation.
Year	Function	Accepts a date and returns an integer corresponding to the year portion of the argument.

Variables

VBScript has only one type of variable—the `Variant` type, but it can hold any of three kinds of values: scalar values, arrays, and object pointers. VBScript, by default, assumes that any symbol that is not a keyword is a variable. That can cause serious problems in your application if you accidentally mistype a variable name. VBScript accepts the mistyped variable without complaint, but interprets it as a new variable. For example, if you type `Email` when you meant to type `E-mail`, VBScript will create two completely different variables. To keep this from happening to you, include the `Option Explicit` command at the top of every ASP file, then use `Dim` statements to declare your variable names. When `Option Explicit` is in effect, VBScript raises a compile error when it encounters an unrecognized symbol. If you use `Option Explicit` faithfully, you will catch all of your mistyped variable names in testing during the design phase of your project rather than in production.

Scalar variables are simple variables like strings and numbers. The `variant` subtypes for scalar variables are `Boolean`, `Integer`, `Long`, `Single`, `Double`, `Date`, `Currency`, and `String`. To create a scalar variable, you define the variable using the `Dim` statement, then you can assign values to the variable. For example:

```
Dim x
x = 100
Response.Write x
```

Arrays are variants that hold lists of scalar or object pointer values. An `array` variable doesn't really hold a list of values—it holds a pointer to the first position of the collection in memory. If you think about it, you can see that the memory positions must be contiguous—when you create an array, the computer sets aside enough memory to hold the entire array. VBScript supports dynamic arrays, which means you can resize an array after it's created. Although when you do this, the computer creates another memory space that's large enough to hold the new array size, then copies the original array values into the new memory location. Therefore, resizing an array is extremely slow in comparison with creating an array of the maximum size to begin with.

You create an array in one of two ways: either dimension the array when you declare the variable, or dimension a variable, then create an array using the `Array()` function:

```
Dim iArr(25) ' create a 26 item array
```

Alternatively:

```
Dim iArr
iArr = Array()
Redim iArr(23)
```

You use an index to access the values in an array. For example:

```
iArr(0) = 0
iArr(1) = 2
iArr(2) = 4
```

By default, VBScript creates arrays the first index is 0, so a statement like `Dim x(10)` creates an 11-item array. Zero-based indexing is often confusing for beginning programmers, who are used to counting items starting with 1. VBScript lets you dimension arrays starting with any integer value—even negative values. For example, you can create a 10-item array with the following statement:

```
Dim x(1 to 10)
```

Now you have a 10-item array in which the lowest index is 1 and the highest index is 10.

The range of valid array index values is the array bounds. You can find the lower-bound with the `LBound(arrayVariable)` function and the upper-bound with the `UBound(arrayVariable)` function. For example:

```
Dim x(1 to 10)
Response.Write "Lower bound=" & LBound(x) & "<br>"
Response.Write "Upper bound=" & UBound(x) & "<br>"
```

I can assure you that you'll have fewer problems with your code if you always use zero-based arrays. The reason doesn't have anything to do with the way the code works; it's for consistency. If you always use zero-based arrays, then the number of items in your array is always one more than the upper-bound of the array. In any case, even if you decide not to standardize on zero-based arrays, you can find out the number of items in the array with this formula:

```
TotalItems = (ubound(anArray) - lbound(anArray) + 1)
```

The third type of value you can hold in a `Variant` is an object pointer. When you create an object with the `Server.CreateObject` function, VBScript sets aside an area of memory to hold the object's data. The `Server.CreateObject` function returns a pointer to that position in memory. Your `object` variable holds that pointer in much the same way a `Variant` array holds a pointer to the first item in an array. So that VBScript can tell the difference between an object pointer and a value, you must use the `Set` keyword to create object variables. For example:

```
Dim objDictionary
Set objDictionary = Server.CreateObject("Scripting.Dictionary")
```

You can determine whether a variable holds an object, as you've seen, with the `isObject()` method. After you create an `object` variable, you call its methods and properties using dot notation, which you've seen throughout this book with the intrinsic ASP objects. For example:

```
objDictionary.Add someKey, someValue
```

ASP destroys all locally-defined variables when the page ends. Nonetheless, when you're done with an `object` variable, it's good programming practice to set it to the value `Nothing`:

```
Set objDictionary = Nothing
```

Setting the variable to `Nothing` frees up the memory used by the object, making it available for another process to use.

Subroutines and Functions

VBScript gives you the ability to place code into named code blocks, generically called routines or methods. Some languages have only one type of routine—the function. VBScript has two: subroutines and functions. Subroutines are routines that do not return values. They are equivalent to `void` functions in other languages. Functions do return values. In many cases, you could write a routine either as a function or as a subroutine. For example:

```
Sub addStrings(string1, string2, stringTarget) ' concatenate strings
    stringTarget = string1 & string2
End Sub
```

The subroutine `addStrings` concatenates the argument `string1` with the argument `string2` and places the result in the argument variable `stringTarget`. It might be more useful to write the routine as a function. For example:

```
Function addStrings(string1, string2)
    addStrings = String1 & string2
End Function
```

The `addStrings()` function (note the use of parentheses to differentiate subroutines from functions) also adds the strings, but it returns the result. Most languages use an explicit `return` statement to return values. VBScript creates a variable that uses the name of the function itself, so you return the value by assigning the result of the function to the name of the function.

You call subroutines and functions differently. To call the `addStrings` subroutine, use either of these:

```
addStrings string1, string2, stringResult
Call addStrings(string1, string2, stringResult)
```

To call a function, you should assign the function result to a variable. For example:

```
NewString = addStrings(s1, s2)
```

Note that in neither case do the names of the arguments in the call have to match the names of the arguments in the function or subroutine. The types don't have to match either, but you should make every effort to ensure they do, because VBScript will change the variable types as needed to try to make the call work. If the types don't match, you may not get the expected result. For example:

```
Function addStrings(string1, string2)
    addStrings = String1 + string2
End Function

' call the addStrings function
Dim s
s = addStrings(1,2) ' returns 3
s = addStrings("1", "2") ' returns "12"
```

The two examples are not the same—the first example isn't sending strings—it's sending numbers. The `addStrings` function will happily add the numbers, possibly leading to an error in your program.

Variable typing problems are ubiquitous in VBScript because it has no typed variables. Therefore, as you write functions—especially if you write functions for others to use—you should check the input types. Use the casting operators (`CInt`, `CBool`, etc.) to change types where appropriate, and raise errors where casting might be inappropriate. For example:

```
Function addStrings(string1, string2)
    If varType(string1) <> vbString Then
        string1 = cStr(string1)
    End If
    If varType(string2) <> vbString Then
        string2 = cStr(string2)
```

```
      End If
      addStrings = String1 + string2
   End Function

   ' call the addStrings function
   Dim s
   s = addStrings(1,2) ' returns 12 as expected
   s = addStrings("1", "2") ' returns "12" - no change
```

The previous example checks the type of both input arguments and casts them to strings if they're not already strings. Sure, checking input argument types takes a small amount of time, but a small loss in speed is often better than errors.

VBScript lets you create recursive routines. A recursive routine is one that calls itself repeatedly until some condition becomes True. For example, Listing 9.1 changes all or part of a string array to uppercase. You supply the string array variable and the starting and ending index of the items to change to uppercase.

LISTING 9.1   Recursive Routine Example (ch9i1.asp)

```
<%@ Language=VBScript %>
<% option explicit %>
<%
Sub ucaseArray(sArr, istart, iend)
   If istart <= iend Then
      sArr(istart) = ucase(sArr(istart))
      istart = istart + 1
      Call ucaseArray(sArr, istart, iend)
   End If
End Sub
Dim i
Dim istart
Dim iend
Dim sArr
sArr = Array("one", "two", "three")
Response.Write "The original array is:<br>"
For i = lbound(sArr) to ubound(sArr)
   Response.Write sArr(i) & "<br>"
Next
Response.Write "<p>"
Response.Write "Change all of the items to upper case<br>"
Call ucaseArray(sArr, lbound(sArr), ubound(sArr))
For i = lbound(sArr) to ubound(sArr)
   Response.Write sArr(i) & "<br>"
Next
```

```
Response.Write "<p>"
Response.Write "Change only the item at position 1 to upper case<br>"
sArr = Array("one", "two", "three")
Call ucaseArray(sArr, 1, 1)
For i = lbound(sArr) to ubound(sArr)
    Response.Write sArr(i) & "<br>"
Next
%>
```

Figure 9.1 shows the output of the previous example.

FIGURE 9.1:

Recursive routine example

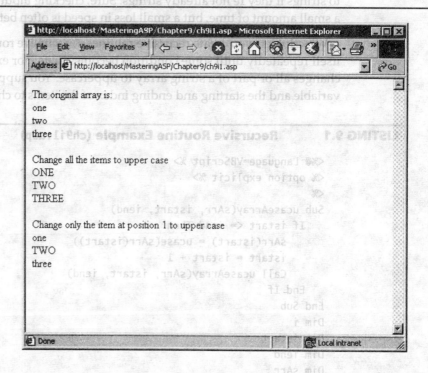

Built-In Functions and Methods

I've already listed all of the built-in functions, but you probably need to see some of them in action, particularly the date and time functions, and the error-handling methods.

The simplest of these is the Now() function. Now returns the current date and time in a Date variable. For example:

```
Response.Write Now() ' writes the current date and time
```

A closely related function, Date(), returns just the date without the time portion.

When you need to calculate a date offset from a known date, such as "two weeks from today," use the DateAdd function. You provide the starting date, the interval, and the size of the offset. For example:

```
' Two weeks from today
Response.Write DateAdd("ww", 2, Now())
```

You specify the offset interval as a string. The valid offset values are:

Offset Interval Value	Meaning
s	Second
n	Minute
h	Hour
d	Day
w	Weekday
ww	Week of year
y	Day of year
m	Month
q	Quarter
yyyy	Year

To calculate a date earlier than a known date, use a negative offset size. For example, the following code fragment shows how to calculate a date exactly one year ago:

```
Response.Write DateAdd("yyyy", Now(), -1)
```

A related function, DateDiff, calculates the interval between two known dates. For example, to find the number of days since January 1, 1900, you would use:

```
Response.Write DateDiff("d", #1/1/1900#, Now())
Response.Write DateDiff("d", "1/1/1900", Now())
```

NOTE   You can specify a date literal (a constant) by surrounding it with number signs. You can freely intermix Date variables, date literals, and date strings in the date and time functions—VBScript performs any necessary conversion for you transparently.

The DateDiff function always subtracts the first date from the second date; therefore, if you reverse the order of the two dates, the function returns a negative number. For example:

```
Response.Write DateDiff("d", Now(), #1/1/1900#)
```

VBScript did not inherit the ubiquitous Format function from Visual Basic. VB programmers use the Format function to format numbers and strings. Instead, VBScript has several separate built-in functions to format numbers and dates.

The FormatDateTime function formats dates in the most common formats. You provide the date and a formatting constant as arguments. For example:

```
Response.Write FormatDateTime(Now, vbGeneralDate)
```

The built-in formats leave a little to be desired—there are only five of them. The table below shows the constants and a sample result for the date January 20, 1999.

Constant	Result
vbGeneralDate	01/20/1999 04:22:13 PM
vbLongDate	Wednesday, January 20, 1999
vbShortDate	01/20/99
vbLongTime	04:22:13 PM
vbShortTime	04:22

It helps at this point to know a little about how VBScript stores dates and times internally. A VBScript DateTime (subtype Date) variable is a Double—8-byte value. The integer portion represents the date and the fractional portion represents the time. Therefore, you can truncate a DateTime to get a date. In addition, if you add or subtract whole numbers from a DateTime value, you change days. For example, if you add 1 to the current date:

```
Response.Write Now() + 1
```

VBScript returns a date one day later at the same time. Similarly, you can write:

```
Response.Write FormatDateTime(CLng(Now()), vbShortDate)
```

Note that you must format the result of the conversion to a Long by using the FormatDateTime function to force VBScript to interpret the value as a Date. Alternatively, you could convert the result of the Long conversion to a date by using the CDate function:

```
Response.Write CDate(CLng(Now()) + 1)
```

Formatting numbers is very similar to formatting dates and times in VBScript. The FormatNumber, FormatPercent, and FormatCurrency functions provide you with the most common formats. All of them work similarly. You must provide the value or expression to format. Optionally, you can provide the number of digits you want to display after the decimal point, whether to use parentheses around negative values, and whether to place commas (or another character, depending on your computer's regional settings) between groups of numbers (as in 1,000,000). The syntax is:

```
FormatCurrency(Expression, DecimalPlaces, _ AddLeadingDigit, Nega-
tiveNumbersInParentheses, _
    AddSeparators)
```

The last three optional arguments all take one of the values from a group of intrinsic constants called TriState constants.

Constant	Value	Description
TristateTrue	-1	True
TristateFalse	0	False
TristateUseDefault	-2	Use the setting from the computer's regional settings.

For example, to format the value 1009.7386 as currency, rounded to the nearest penny, you could write:

```
Dim s
s = FormatCurrency(1009.7386, 2, True, True, True)
Response.Write s
' writes $1,009.74
```

The same call applied to the value -.0246 yields ($0.02). The result is in parentheses because the result is a negative number and the function call set the argument NegativeNumbersInParentheses to True.

Logical Structures

Every modern language has several logical structures. Logical structures let you execute code conditionally. A completed structure forms a code block.

If...Then

There are actually several variations on the If...Then structure, but all of them have the same basic syntax—a conditional test, followed by Then, and the code to execute when the condition is true. The final statement in the code block must be `End If`. For example:

```
Dim i
i = 1
If i = 1 Then
    ' do something
End If
```

A slightly more complex variation adds one or more `ElseIf` tests:

```
Dim i
i = 2
If i = 1 Then
    ' do something
ElseIf i = 2 Then
    ' do something else
End If
```

In some cases, you want to execute some code when all of the `If` and `ElseIf` conditions fail. You use an `Else` condition to do that. For example:

```
Dim i
i = 2
If i = 1 Then
    ' do something
ElseIf i = 2 Then
    ' do something else
Else ' no condition is true
    ' code to execute when all conditions fail
End If
```

In general, it's a good idea to include an `Else` whenever you write an `If`. You'll soon see that, as a human being, you're highly unlikely to consider all of the possible conditions when you first write the routine. The `Else` condition handles those that you miss. For example, suppose you're writing an e-commerce application. The customer will submit a form containing a product type. You want to test the customer's choice against an internal list of product types, taking specific action for each type. If no type matches, you want to raise an error. For example:

```
If productType = "Clothing" Then
    ' do something
ElseIf productType = "Books" Then
    ' do something else
' place other productType conditions here
' after the last condition write the Else condition
Else
    ' no valid product type
    Err.Raise INVALID_PRODUCT, "thisFile.asp", "Invalid Product Type."
End If
```

The Else condition catches product types that don't match any item in the list. In the example, the code raises an error, but you might just as easily decide to set the productType variable to a default value. For example, UnknownProduct, if no known products match.

Select Case

Structures like the product type example in the previous section work just fine as If...ElseIf..Else...End If blocks, but VBScript has another conditional block that takes less code. The Select Case...Case...End Select statement selects a matching case from among many possible cases. For example, you could rewrite the product type example as a Case structure:

```
Select Case productType
Case "Clothing"
    ' do something
Case "Books"
    ' do something else
' place other case conditions here
' after the last condition write the Else condition
Case Else
    ' no valid product type
    Err.Raise INVALID_PRODUCT, "thisFile.asp", "Invalid Product Type."
End If
```

When each condition has only one possible value, the Select Case statement doesn't improve your code much. The real power of Select Case occurs when you need any of several possible values to execute a single statement. For example, suppose that instead of the string Clothing, your application also had to recognize a list of alternate terms such as Clothes, Apparel, Millinery, Lingerie, etc. Written as an If statement, multiple conditions rapidly become awkward and hard to read. For example:

```
If productType = "Clothing" or productType = "Clothes" _
    or productType = "Apparel" or productType = "Millinery" or _
    productType = "Lingerie" or productType = "Hosiery" _
    or productType = "Outer Wear" Then
    ' do something
End If
```

In contrast, as a Select Case statement, the statement is easy to read. For example:

```
Select Case productType
Case "Clothing", "Clothes", "Apparel", "Millinery", "Lingerie", _
    "Hosiery", "Outer Wear"
```

```
            ' do something
      Case Else
            ' perform default action
      End If
```

Boolean Logic

You probably use Boolean logic every day. For example, when you make a decision to buy one item OR another item, but not both, you are using Boolean logic. All Boolean logic has a single output value—either True or False. There are four main Boolean operations. Three of these (AND, OR, and XOR) are binary operators—they require two *operands*—one on either side of the operator. Each operand may be a single value or expression. The NOT operator negates a value and is a unary operator—it requires only one operand. Boolean operations assume that each operand has the value True (non-zero) or False (zero). To the computer, that means you can use any type of numeric value or expression as an operand, because all numeric expressions evaluate to either zero or non-zero. Table 9.2 lists each operation along with a brief description of the results.

TABLE 9.2: Boolean Operands

Operation	Result
AND	True if both operands are True.
OR	True if either operand is True or if both operands are True.
XOR	True if either operand is True, but not if both operands are True.
NOT	True if the operand is False and False if the operand is True.

Strictly speaking, the logic is slightly more complicated than that, because one or both operands could be Null. Logical operations work with Null values. Because a Null value is not a numeric expression, it doesn't evaluate to either True or False; therefore, Null values generally cause Boolean expressions to evaluate to Null. There are only two exceptions:

- For an AND operation, the expression evaluates to False if the first operand is False. That's because the AND operation looks no further than the first value if it is False. There's no point in looking at the second value.

- For an OR operation, the expression evaluates to True if the first operand is True. That's because the OR operation doesn't look at the second value if the first one evaluates to True.

Your best bet is to avoid nulls altogether. You won't generally need to worry about Null values until you retrieve data from a database.

Looping

Very often, you need to perform an operation or series of operations many times. If you've read through the earlier sections of this book, you've already seen several examples of looping using For Each...Next over the intrinsic ASP collection objects. The For Each...Next syntax iterates over each object in a collection. For Each...Next requires a collection object that supports iteration.

When you aren't dealing with objects or when your objective isn't to operate on a collection, you can use one of VBScript's other loop structures. Sometimes you need to loop a pre-determined number of times. For these loop structures, use a For...Next structure. Sometimes, you need to loop while a condition is True, or until a condition is True. For these loops, use a While...Wend or a Do...While...Loop structure.

For...Next

When you need to loop a pre-determined number of times, use a For...Next loop structure. The structure uses a loop control variable to control the number of loops through the code. You provide the loop control variable, the starting value, the ending value, and optionally, an increment or step. You place the code you want to repeat between the For and the Next statements. The syntax is:

```
For <control variable> = <start value> to <end value> Step <increment>
   ' do something
Next <counter>
```

Traditionally, programmers use the variable i (meaning integer) for a control loop variable. For clarity, you can include the control loop variable after the Next statement. The default step value is 1; you do not have to provide a step for loop control variables that should increment by 1. For example, the following For...Next loop executes three times:

```
<%
Dim i
Dim counter
counter = 0
For i = 1 to 3
  counter = counter + 1
Next
Response.Write counter ' writes 3
%>
```

At the end of each loop through the code, VBScript increments the loop control variable and compares it to the ending value. The loop ends when the loop control variable equals the ending value. At the end of the loop in the previous example, the value of the variable counter is 3. The value of the loop control variable itself is, according to the documentation, undefined; therefore, you should not rely on the value of the counter after the loop has completed.

You can change the increment by adding the optional Step value. You must provide a Step value if you want to step backward. For example, the following loop steps backward from 3 to 1:

```
<%
Dim i
Dim counter
counter = 4
For i = 3 to 1 step -1
    counter = counter - 1
Next
Response.Write counter ' writes 1
%>
```

You can exit a For...Next loop early by using the Exit For command. For example, the following loop exits when the value of counter is 1 less than the value of the loop control variable:

```
<%
Dim i
Dim counter
counter = 0
For i = 4 to 1 step -1
    counter = counter + 1
    If counter = i - 1 Then
        Exit For
    End If
Next
Response.Write counter ' writes 2
%>
```

The Step value can be anything you want. For example, to print the even numbers from 0 to 100, you provide a Step value of 2:

```
<%
Dim i
For i = 0 to 100 step 2
    Response.Write i & "<br>"
Next
%>
```

For...Next loops help keep you from coding endless loops, but you must still be careful with them. For example, the following code runs until the Server .ScriptTimeout value stops the file from executing:

```
<%
Dim i
```

```
counter = 0
For i = 2 to 1 step -1
   i = i + 1
Next
%>
```

The previous example loops forever because the test comparing the loop control variable to the ending value always fails. Although the `Server.ScriptTimeout` provides a safety net, endless loops use nearly all of a server's processing power while executing. Avoid coding loops carelessly—endless loops potentially interfere not only with your own application, but also with other applications running on the server.

You can nest loops to any depth you desire, but you cannot cross-nest them. Again, by tradition, programmers use the variable names j and k for nested control loop variables. Of course, you're free to use any valid variable name. The following loop shows how you can nest `For...Next` structures:

```
<%
Dim i
Dim j
For i = 1 to 100
   For j = 1 to 100
      Response.Write i & ", " & j & "<br>"
   Next
Next
%>
```

In the previous example, the `Response.Write` statement in the inner (nested) loop executes 10,000 (100 * 100) times.

While...Wend Loop

A `While...Wend` loop executes until the conditional statement following the `While` becomes `True`. The syntax is:

```
While <condition>
   ' do something
Wend
```

You can see that a `For...Next` loop is actually a `While...Wend` loop in disguise, because the `For...Next` loop has an implicit condition—it tests the control loop variable for equality with the ending value. For example, the following two loops produce identical results:

```
<%
Dim i
```

```
For i = 1 to 3
    Response.Write i & "<br>"
Next

i = 0
While i <= 3
    i = i + 1
    Response.Write i & "<br>"
Wend
%>
```

Both loops execute until the variable i equals 3. While all For...Next loops are While loops, the reverse is not true. For example, you cannot write the following loop as a For...Next loop:

```
<%
Dim s
s = "a"
While s <> "abcdefghijklmnop"
    s = s & Chr(Asc(Right(s,1)) + 1)
    Response.Write s & "<br>"
Wend
%>
```

While...Wend loops are essentially obsolete. They were included in VBScript primarily for compatibility with VB. A newer and more versatile version is the Do...While loop.

Do...While Loop

The Do...While loop, like While...Wend is a conditional loop, but you can place the condition test at either the start or end of the loop structure. This provides you with the ability to force a loop to execute at least once. The syntax is:

```
Do While <condition>
    ' do something
Loop
```

or

```
Do
    ' do something
Loop While <condition>
```

In addition, the While condition statement is optional. You can write an unconditional loop using the syntax:

```
Do
    ' do something
Loop
```

The last version is useful for programs where you want to loop forever, but isn't particularly useful on the server, where the `Server.ScriptTimeout` value limits the execution time of the script. However, it is useful when you don't need or want a conditional test at the beginning or end of the loop. For example, if you want to perform a conditional test in the middle of the loop code, the `Do...Loop` structure is completely appropriate.

The `Do...While (condition)` version may not execute even once because the conditional test at the start of the loop may not evaluate to `True`. In contrast, the `Do...Loop While (condition)` version places the conditional test at the end of the loop, so the loop must execute at least once.

String-Handling

Visual Basic has always had decent string-handling ability. VBScript not only inherited all of Visual Basic's functionality, but also added some extra features. You've already seen how to concatenate strings, but you haven't seen many of the other string operations. VBScript can extract and find sub-strings, compare strings, and split delimited strings into string arrays or create string arrays from delimited strings—all with built-in commands.

Just one mild warning: Strings, to a computer, are arrays of characters. Despite the apparent ease with which you can manipulate strings, you are actually copying contiguous blocks of memory from one place to another. Minimizing the number and size of these operations will make your programs run faster.

Left, Mid, Right, Instr, InstrRev, Split, Join

The three functions `Left`, `Right`, and `Mid` return the leftmost characters, the rightmost characters, or a section from the middle of the string, respectively. For the `Left` and `Right` functions, you specify the number of characters to return. For the `Mid` function, you specify the starting position and optionally, a length. If you don't specify a length, the `Mid` function returns the portion of the string from the specified starting position to the end of the string. Examples:

```
Left("Charlie", 3) ' returns "Cha"
Left("Bill", 22) ' returns "Bill"
Right("Charlie", 3) ' returns "lie"
Right("Bill", 22) ' returns "Bill"
Mid("Charlie", 3, 3) ' returns "arl"
Mid("Charlie", 3) ' returns "arlie"
Mid("Charlie", 3, 24) ' returns "arlie"
```

The examples show that you can easily extract a portion of a string. They should also show you what happens with each of these functions when you request more characters from a string than can be returned. In each case shown above, VBScript returns the number of characters possible, not the number of characters requested;

and it does not raise an error when you request more than the number of possible characters.

The `Instr` and `InstrRev` functions locate the position of sub-strings within strings. Both functions return the index of the starting position of the sub-string within the main string. For example, the string `"intentions"` contains the sub-string `"ten"` starting at position 3:

```
Response.Write instr("intentions", "ten") ' writes 3
Response.Write instrRev("intentions", "ten") ' writes 3
```

Both functions optionally accept a starting position and a `compare` flag that determines whether VBScript performs a case-sensitive or case-insensitive search for the sub-string. Unfortunately, the position of the arguments differs between the two functions. The `Instr` function expects the `start` argument *before* the main string, whereas the `InstrRev` function expects the start argument *after* the search string. Both functions expect the last argument to be one of the `CompareMode` constants.

There are two `CompareMode` constants, `VbBinaryCompare`, which has a value of 0 and `vbTextCompare`, which has a value of 1. Use `VbBinaryCompare` to perform case-sensitive comparisons and `vbTextCompare` to perform case-insensitive comparisons.

Here's a full version of each of the functions:

```
Response.Write instr(1,"event", "vent", vbBinaryCompare)
' writes 2
Response.Write instr(1,"event", "Vent", vbBinaryCompare)
' writes 0
Response.Write instr(1,"event", "Vent", vbTextCompare)
' writes 2
Response.Write instrRev("event", "vent",5,vbBinaryCompare)
' writes 2
Response.Write instrRev("event", "Vent",5, vbBinaryCompare)
' writes 0
Response.Write instrRev("event", "Vent",5, vbTextCompare)
' writes 2
```

Note that although the `InstrRev` function searches backward from the end of the main string, `Response` returns the index position of the sub-string, if found, calculated as an offset from the beginning of the main string. Also, note that the `start` argument for the `InstrRev` function is also an offset from the beginning of the string. In other words, if you want `InstrRev` to search the entire string, you must pass the length of the string in the `start` argument.

Boolean Operations

Most programmers eventually run into situations where they must use Boolean logic. Boolean operations and computers were made for each other because there are only two possible values for the result of a Boolean operation between two bits: 1 and 0.

The computer stores values as binary numbers. A binary number is a series of bits. Moving to the left, each bit can take only one of two values—0 or 1. When set (non-zero), each bit has a value of 2^n, where n is the position starting with 0. The right-most bit in an 8-bit number, when set, is 2^0, or 1. The next bit is 2^1, or 2. Each bit doubles the value of the bit to its right. Therefore, the value 12, to a computer, is 00001100 (no ones, no twos, one four, and one eight).

VBScript supports four Boolean operations: AND, OR, NOT, and XOR. You use the AND operator to see if the bit pattern in two values is the same. Whenever both values contain a 1 in the same position, the result also has a 1 in that position.

If you AND that value with the number 16 (00010000) you get 00000000, because neither pattern contains a 1 bit in the same column as the other. For example:

```
00001100
00010000
_____
00000000
```

An OR operation compares two bit patterns and produces a 1 if either or both bits in a column are 1. For example, the expression 13 OR 17 produces the number 29:

```
00001101
00010001
_____
00011101
```

An XOR operation is the opposite of an OR. It produces a 1 if only one, but not both, of the bits in a column is a 1. For example:

```
00001101
00010001
_____
00011100
```

Finally, the NOT operator reverses the value of its operand. The expression: NOT 01010101 produces 10101010.

Regular Expressions

VBScript version 5 inherited powerful regular expression matching capabilities. I say inherited, because the code to perform regular expression searches was apparently ported more-or-less directly from JScript regular expression searches without regard to anything remotely VB-like. This port serves to keep the two scripting languages roughly in sync, but at the cost (for VBScript programmers) of dealing with zero-based string indexes, which is totally opposed to the general spirit and usual practice of VBScript and VB. In addition, the pattern matching characters (and the documentation) were created for Java/JavaScript/C programmers and not VBScript/VB programmers. Despite this gripe, regular expression searches are extremely powerful and can do much more than the simple `instr()` function.

A regular expression consists of text you want to search for combined with special characters or commands that describe how you want to search. To initialize a regular expression search, you create a RegExp object and set its `Pattern` property. For example:

```
// explicit RegExp creation
rgxp = new RegExp
rgxp.Pattern = "boy"
```

You can perform global (find all matches) searches using the `Global` property and case-insensitive searches with the `IgnoreCase` property. Both properties take Boolean `True`/`False` values. For example:

```
// case-insensitive search
rgxp.IgnoreCase = True
```

```
// global search
rgxp.Global = True
```

After creating a RegExp object and setting its properties, you perform the search with either the `Test` or the `Execute` method. The difference lies in whether you only need to test whether the pattern exists in the target string or whether you want to know where and how often the pattern appears. The result of the `Test` method is `True` if the pattern appears in the target string; otherwise, the method returns `False`.

For example, the following code searches for the word "boy" in the string "Every good boy does fine."

```
Dim s
Dim rgxp
s = "Every good boy does fine."
Set rgxp = New RegExp
rgxp.Pattern = "boy"
Response.Write rgxp.Test(s) & "<br>"
' writes True
```

In contrast, the `Execute` method returns a `Matches` collection. Each Match object in the `Matches` collection represents a single match and has properties for the matched string, the index of the start of the matched string in the target string, and the length of the match. For example:

```
Dim s
Dim rgxp
s = "Peter Piper picked a peck of pickled peppers."
Set rgxp = New RegExp
rgxp.Pattern = "p"
rgxp.IgnoreCase = False
rgxp.Global = True
Set matches = rgxp.Execute(s)
Response.Write "Testing for the pattern " & Chr(34) & _
    rgxp.Pattern & Chr(34) & " in the string " & _
    Chr(34) & s & Chr(34) & "<br><br>"
For Each aMatch In matches
Response.Write "Found a match at position " & _
aMatch.FirstIndex & ". Matched string=" & Chr(34) _
& aMatch.Value & Chr(34) & ". " & aMatch.Length _
& " character(s) were matched." & "<br>"
Next
```

The preceding example finds each lowercase p and returns a collection of Match objects. The output looks like this:

```
Testing for the pattern "p" in the string "Peter Piper picked a peck of
pickled peppers."

Found a match at position 8. Matched string="p". 1 character(s) were
matched.
Found a match at position 12. Matched string="p". 1 character(s) were
matched.
Found a match at position 21. Matched string="p". 1 character(s) were
matched.
Found a match at position 29. Matched string="p". 1 character(s) were
matched.
Found a match at position 37. Matched string="p". 1 character(s) were
matched.
Found a match at position 39. Matched string="p". 1 character(s) were
matched.
Found a match at position 40. Matched string="p". 1 character(s) were
matched.
```

The output shows the Match object's FirstIndex, Value, and Length properties.

The power of regular expression searching lies in its ability to match patterns using special characters and character sequences. Table 9.2 lists the special characters and sequences you may use in a regular expression.

TABLE 9.3: VBScript Regular Expression Pattern Special Characters and Sequences

Character	Description
\	Specifies that the next character is either a special character or a literal (an exact special character match). A literal character preceded by the backslash is called an *escaped* character. Some characters must be escaped because they have other meanings in regular expression syntax. The characters you must escape are: • () - left and right parentheses • [- left bracket •] - right bracket • \ - backslash • * - asterisk • . - period • $ - dollar sign The special characters \b, \B, \d, \D, \f, \n, \r, \s, \S, \t, \v, \w, and \W appear individually in this table.
^	Limits matches to the beginning of a line or string.
$	Limits matches to the end of a line or string.
*	Matches the character preceding the asterisk zero or more times. For example, bo* matches both **bed** and **book**.
+	Matches the character preceding the plus sign one or more times. bo+ matches **book**, but not **bed**.
?	Matches the character preceding the question mark zero or one time. For example, be? matches **best** and **bit**, but not **been**.
.	Matches any single character except a newline (vbCrLf) character.
(pattern)	Enclose a pattern in parentheses to find matched patterns. You can retrieve the matched patterns from the **Matches** collection using the **Item** property and an **index** from 0...N. Use \(and \) to match parentheses.
a|b	Matches either a or b.
{n}	Matches exactly n times, where n is an integer greater than or equal to 1. For example, m{2} matches **immediate** but not **magic**.
{n,}	Matches at least n times, where n is an integer greater than or equal to 1. For example, e{2} matches **seer** but not **her**.
{nMin, nMax}	Matches between nMin and nMax times, inclusive, where both nMin and nMax are integers greater than or equal to 1.
[abc]	Matches any of the characters enclosed in the brackets. [mno] matches the **n** in **bin** or the **m** in **Mom**.
[^abc]	Matches any character *not* enclosed in the brackets. [^mno] matches the **b** and **i** in **bin**, and the **M** in **Mom**.
[a-z]	Matches any one of a range of characters. For example, [a-z] matches any lowercase alphabetic character in the range a through z.
[^d-g]	Matches any one of the characters *not* in the range. For example, [d-g] matches any character not in the range d through g.
\b	Matches a word boundary, such as a space, tab, or punctuation. For example, p\b matches the **p** in the word **help** in the phrase **please help me** and in the phrase **please help**. Place the /b before the pattern to find matches at the beginning of words or at the end of the pattern to find matches at the end of words.

Continued on next page

TABLE 9.3 CONTINUED: VBScript Regular Expression Pattern Special Characters and Sequences

Character	Description
\B	Matches text *not* on a word boundary. For example, \Bp matches the p in the word **help** in the phrase **please help me**, but not the p in the word **please** in that same phrase. That's because the p in **please** lies at the start of a word.
\d	Matches any digit character. Equivalent to [0-9].
\D	Matches any non-digit character. Equivalent to [^0-9].
\f	Matches a formfeed character.
\n	Matches a newline (vbCrLf) character.
\r	Matches a carriage return character.
\s	Matches any white space including space, tab, formfeed, etc. Equivalent to [\f\n\r\t\v].
\S	Matches any nonwhite space character. Equivalent to [^\f\n\r\t\v].
\t	Matches a tab character.
\v	Matches a vertical tab character.
\w	Matches any alphanumeric character, including the underscore. Equivalent to [A-Za-z0-9_].
\W	Matches any non-alphanumeric character. Equivalent to [^A-Za-z0-9_].
\num	Matches **num**, where **num** is a positive integer. \1 matches the first **Item** in the **Matches** collection.
\o	Matches o, where o is an octal value. Octal values must be 1, 2, or 3 digits long. For example, \11 and \011 both match a tab character. Octal values that exceed 256 are treated as if they were two patterns. For example, the pattern \0011 is the equivalent of the patterns \001 & 1. This pattern type lets you use ASCII codes in regular expressions.
\xn	Matches n, where n is a hexadecimal (hex) value. Hex values must be exactly two digits long. For example, \x41 matches the character A. Hex values that exceed two characters are treated as if they were two patterns. For example, the pattern \x041 is the equivalent of the patterns \x04 & 1. This pattern type lets you use ASCII codes in regular expressions.

VBScript Classes

Classes are another feature new to VBScript version 5. Unlike the regular expression syntax, VBScript classes fit the pattern of the language well. A class consists of properties and code that work together as a unit. Most classes contain properties, which are values you can set and retrieve, and methods, which are callable functions or subroutines. Classes may contain both hidden (private) and visible (public) properties and methods.

Unlike most other objects in VBScript, you can't create a Class object directly. Instead, you provide the code for the class, and VBScript returns a reference to the

Class object. You'll find that classes can be extremely useful in both client- and server-side code when you want to:

- Package functionality
- Hide method implementations
- Reuse code
- Simplify your code

You can create classes at both design and runtime. To create a class at design time, you write a `class` script. The `class` script defines the `class` properties and methods. To create a class at runtime, you concatenate the code that defines the class in a string, then issue either an `Execute` or `ExecuteGlobal` statement. Subsequently, you can create a new class instance—more commonly known as an object—and use the properties and methods of that object. Objects instantiated from `Class` code act the same whether you created the class at runtime or design time.

Here's an example. Suppose you want to create a `User` class that exposes first and last name properties and a list of telephone numbers. You would like to create an instance of the `User` class whenever a page starts and save the User information in a `Session` variable each time the page ends. You need to be able to add telephone numbers and display the User information.

To do that, you need to create a `User` class. For example, you might define a `User` class as follows:

WARNING   There are some VBScript code features in the following code that you haven't seen yet. This is not a simple example, but I included it because it illustrates the power of VBScript classes in an ASP page. If you don't understand all of the code right now, you may wish to return to this section later.

```
Class User
    Private mLastName
    Private mFirstName
    Private dTelephones
    Private Sub Class_Initialize()
        Set dTelephones = _
            Server.CreateObject("Scripting.Dictionary")
    End Sub

    Private Sub Class_terminate()
        Set dTelephones = Nothing
    End Sub
```

```
Public Property Let LastName(s)
    mLastName = s
End Property

Public Property Get LastName()
    LastName = mLastName
End Property

Public Property Let FirstName(s)
    mFirstName = s
End Property

Public Property Get FirstName()
    FirstName = mFirstName
End Property

Public Sub addTelephone(atype, anumber)
    If dTelephones.Exists(atype) Then
        Response.Write "This person already has " & _
        "a phone of type " & atype & "<br>"
        Response.end
    Else
        dTelephones.Add atype, anumber
        Response.Write "Added telephone " & atype & ", " _
        & anumber & "<br>"
    End If
End Sub

Public Property Get PhoneInfo()
    Dim V
    Dim s
    For Each V In dTelephones.keys
        s = s & V & "=" & dTelephones(V) & "<br>"
    Next
    PhoneInfo = s
End Property

Public Property Get PhoneCount()
    PhoneCount = dTelephones.Count
End Property
End Class
```

Starting at the top of the class definition, you first see three private variables: mLastName, mFirstName, (the m in the variable names stands for member as in member variable) and dTelephones. The class uses the first two to hold the last and first names. The dTelephones variable will become a Dictionary object where the keys are telephone types like home, work, etc. and the values are the phone numbers.

Next, you see a `Private` subroutine called `Class_Initialize`. This subroutine and the corresponding Class_Terminate subroutine are event procedures, and are optional. They're called event procedures because VBScript raises a `Class_ Initialize` event, which executes the code in the Class_Initialize method (if it exists) when you instantiate an object from a class. Similarly, just before VBScript destroys an object, it raises a `Class_Terminate` event, which executes the `Class_ Terminate` method for the class (if it exists). You can use these event procedures to initialize and destroy (terminate) objects and property values. I've used them to create and destroy the Dictionary object to hold the telephone types and numbers.

The next four `Public` properties let you assign and retrieve the names. A `Property Let` method assigns a value to a property. A `Property Get` method retrieves the value. The names of `Public` properties and `Private` variables do not have to match.

The `Public` method `addTelephone` adds a telephone to the `dTelephones` Dictionary. I should warn you that the class has minimal error-checking. It won't let you add two Home phones, but there's no check for valid telephone numbers or types—feel free to add whatever you like.

The `PhoneInfo` property returns a string consisting of some number of `tele- phoneType=telephoneNumber` items, and the `PhoneCount` property returns the number of `telephone type=number` items defined for this User.

To create a new User object, use the VBScript `New` keyword. For example:

```
Dim aUser
Set aUser = new User
```

The variable `aUser` now holds a reference to an object—a new instance of the User class. You may now set the object's properties. For example:

```
aUser.LastName = "Jones"
aUser.FirstName = "Russell"
Response.Write aUser.LastName & "<br>"' writes "Jones"
Response.Write aUser.FirstName & "<br>"
  ' writes "Russell"
aUser.AddTelephone "Home", "555-1212"
Response.Write aUser.PhoneCount & "<br>"' writes 1
Response.Write aUser.PhoneInfo ' writes "Home=555-1212"
```

All this is interesting, but not particularly useful, because it takes more code than simply storing the values in `Session` variables and retrieving them for each page. But the next example should show you a sample of the power of objects.

You can take advantage of the `Class_Initialize` and `Class_Terminate` methods to automatically save and retrieve User objects to a `Session` variable. You need a name for the Session variable—I've opted to save the User object in a Session variable keyed to the Session.SessionID property, as follows:

```
dim aSessionID
aSessionID = cstr(Session.SessionID)
```

Here are the altered event procedures:

```
Private Sub Class_Initialize()
    Response.Write "User initialize<br>"
    Dim arr
    Dim i
    Dim aTelephone
    Set dTelephones = _
        Server.CreateObject("Scripting.Dictionary")
    If Not IsEmpty(Session(aSessionID)) Then
        arr = Session(aSessionID)
        mLastName = arr(0)
        mFirstName = arr(1)
        For i = 2 To UBound(arr) Step 2
            dTelephones.Add arr(i), arr(i + 1)
        Next
    Else
        ' first initialization
        mLastName = ""
        mFirstName = ""
        Set dTelephones = _
            Server.CreateObject("Scripting.Dictionary")
    End If
End Sub

Private Sub Class_terminate()
    Response.Write "User terminate<br>"
    ' write class info to a Session variable
    Dim arr
    Dim i
    Dim j
    Dim V
    arr = Array()
    ReDim arr(1)
    arr(0) = mLastName
    arr(1) = mFirstName
    i = UBound(arr)
    For Each V In dTelephones.Keys
        i = i + 1
        ReDim Preserve arr(i)
        arr(i) = V
```

```
          i = i + 1
      ReDim Preserve arr(i)
      arr(i) = dTelephones(V)
   Next
   Session(aSessionID) = arr
   Set dTelephones = Nothing
End Sub
```

These two routines automatically store (persist) the User object to an array stored in a Session variable associated with the current SessionID. In the Class_Terminate event, the class stores the first and last names in the first two array positions, then sequentially fills the array with telephone types and numbers. Finally, it stores the completed array in the Session variable.

When the class re-instantiates on subsequent requests, it performs the operations in reverse. The class retrieves the array from the Session variable, sets the first and last name Private property variables, then loops through the array adding items (telephone type and telephone number) to the Dictionary.

I've added Response.Write statements so you can see when the Class_Initialize and Class_Terminate events occur relative to other code in the page.

You must initialize the object the first time the page runs. You can determine whether the page has been run for the current session by testing the value of the Session(SessionID) variable—if it's empty, it's the first request for the page. Listing 9.2 contains the complete page script.

Listing 9.2   **VBScript Class Example**

```
<%@ Language=VBScript %>
<% option explicit %>
<html>
<head>
</head>
<body>
<%
Dim aSessionID
aSessionID = CStr(Session.SessionID)

Class User
   Private m_ID
   Private mLastName
   Private mFirstName
   Private dTelephones
   Private Sub Class_Initialize()
      Response.Write "User initialize<br>"
```

```vbscript
        Dim arr
        Dim i
        Dim aTelephone
        Set dTelephones = _
           Server.CreateObject("Scripting.Dictionary")
        m_ID = aSessionID
        If Not IsEmpty(Session(aSessionID)) Then
           arr = Session(aSessionID)
           mLastName = arr(0)
           mFirstName = arr(1)
           For i = 2 To UBound(arr) Step 2
              dTelephones.Add arr(i), arr(i + 1)
           Next
        Else
           ' first initialization
           mLastName = ""
           mFirstName = ""
           Set dTelephones = _
              Server.CreateObject("Scripting.Dictionary")
        End If
End Sub

Private Sub Class_terminate()
   Response.Write "User terminate<br>"
      ' write class info to a Session variable
      Dim arr
      Dim i
      Dim j
      Dim V
      arr = Array()
      ReDim arr(1)
      arr(0) = mLastName
      arr(1) = mFirstName
      i = UBound(arr)
      For Each V In dTelephones.keys
         i = i + 1
         ReDim Preserve arr(i)
         arr(i) = V
         i = i + 1
         ReDim Preserve arr(i)
         arr(i) = dTelephones(V)
      Next
      Session(aSessionID) = arr
      Set dTelephones = Nothing
End Sub
```

```
            Public Property Let LastName(s)
               mLastName = s
            End Property

            Public Property Get LastName()
               LastName = mLastName
            End Property

            Public Property Let FirstName(s)
               mFirstName = s
            End Property

            Public Property Get FirstName()
               FirstName = mFirstName
            End Property

            Public Sub addTelephone(atype, anumber)
               If dTelephones.Exists(atype) Then
                  Response.Write "This person already has " & _
                     "a phone of type " & atype & "<br>"
                  Response.end
               Else
                  dTelephones.Add atype, anumber
                  Response.Write "Added telephone " & atype & ", " _
                     & anumber & "<br>"
               End If
            End Sub
            Public Property Get PhoneInfo()
               Dim V
               Dim s
               For Each V In dTelephones.keys
                  s = s & V & "=" & dTelephones(V) & "<br>"
               Next
               PhoneInfo = s
            End Property
            Public Property Get PhoneCount()
               PhoneCount = dTelephones.Count
            End Property
         end class
         Dim aUser
         Dim i
         If IsEmpty(Session(aSessionID)) Then
            Response.Write "Initializing new user" & "<br>"
            Set aUser = New User
            aUser.LastName = "Russell"
            aUser.FirstName = "Jones"
```

```
            Call aUser.addTelephone("Home", "111-111-1111")
        Else
            Response.Write "Found User:<br>"
            Set aUser = New User
        End If
        'Response.Write "SessionID = " & aSessionID & "<br>"
        If Request.Form("Add") = "Add" Then
            aUser.addTelephone CStr(Request.Form.Item("PhoneType")),
        CStr(Request.Form.Item("PhoneNumber"))
        End If
        With aUser
            Response.Write "<b>User Info:</b><br>"
            Response.Write "LastName=" & .LastName & "<br>"
            Response.Write "FirstName=" & .FirstName & "<br>"
            Response.Write "PhoneCount=" & .PhoneCount & "<Br>"
            Response.Write "<b>Phones:</b><br>" & .PhoneInfo
        End With
        %>
        <form name="frmTel" method="post" action="">
        <table width="60%" align="center" border="1">
            <tr>
                <td colspan="2">
                    Add a phone number:
                </td>
            </tr>
            <tr>
                <td>
                    <b>Type:</b>
                </td>
                <td>
                    <input type="text" name="PhoneType">
                </td>
            </tr>
            <tr>
                <td>
                    <b>Number:</b>
                </td>
                <td>
                    <input type="text" name="PhoneNumber">
                </td>
            </tr>
            <tr>
                <td colspan="2" align="center">
                    <input name="Add" type="submit" value="Add">
                </td>
            </tr>
```

```
</table>
<br>
</form>
</body>
</html>
```

Try adding several telephone numbers. You should see them appear in the printed list at the top of the screen.

I could give the User class to another programmer as an include file. That's the package functionality aspect of object-oriented programming. That programmer could be trained to create and use User objects very quickly—that's the code reuse aspect.

It's important to understand that I implemented the list of telephone numbers as a Dictionary. If I later change my mind and simply keep them in an array for performance reasons, from the other programmer's viewpoint, the code wouldn't have changed; the PhoneCount and AddTelephone methods would act exactly the same and the store-and-retrieve scheme would still work properly. In other words, I've hidden the method implementation.

Finally, it's much easier for a programmer to use well named objects with methods and properties than to use function calls.

Because VBScript can run on both the client and the server, you can create objects in client-side script as well. Classes are obviously not necessary—there are thousands of sites that work perfectly well without classes and objects. Nevertheless, you'll find that creating classes and using objects soon becomes an integral part of your programming toolkit.

Project: Use VBScript to Control Responses

In this mini-project, you'll write an ASP page that submits information to itself with a form. The problem is to respond with a message, the content of which depends on whether the person submitting the form filled it out completely.

Build a form that requests a person's last name, first name, address, and telephone number. Add a button to submit the form. On the server, when the user submits the form, return a message if any of the following conditions exist:

- The user submitted an incomplete form. For example, if the user neglected to enter a Last Name, you might reply with the message "Your Last Name is required. Please enter a last name."

- The length of either the Last Name or the First Name field is less than two characters or longer than 20 characters.

- The telephone number is incorrect. Assume that all telephone numbers have an area code and a seven-digit number, with or without an extension. You may accept any format for the telephone number. You may accept any length for the address as long as it is not a null string.

- The form contains invalid characters in any field. For example, name fields may contain only alphabetic characters, no numbers and no spaces (yes, I know that in real life, some names contain spaces). The telephone number may contain only numbers, spaces, parentheses, dashes, and the character x or the string ext—case is irrelevant.

If the user filled the form out completely and all entries are valid, return a "Thanks For Your Information" message.

I suggest you try to build the project first, then compare your results with the ch9i2.asp file in the Chapter9 directory on the CD. Hints: See the Len function and take advantage of loops and the built-in VBScript function instr to look for invalid characters. Don't expect your code to be identical to mine; there are literally thousands of possible variations—all of which will produce roughly the same results.

Project: Build a Date-Formatting Routine

This project requires you to create a function that formats dates according to a format string you provide. For example, you might call the function as follows:

```
Dim sMyDate
SMyDate = getFormattedDate(Now(), "mm/yy")
```

The function should return a string formatted according to the second argument. For example, if the date were 02/06/2000, the function should return the string "02/00". The function should recognize any combination of format strings according to the following table:

Format String	Description
d	Formats the day portion of the date with no leading 0 for single-digit days.
dd	Formats the day portion of the date with leading zeros for single-digit days.

m	Formats the month portion of the date with no leading 0 for single-digit months.
mm	Formats the month portion of the date with leading zeros for single-digit months.
mmm	Formats the month portion of the date as an uppercase, three-character month abbreviation, for example, JAN or FEB.
yy	Formats the year portion of the date as a two-digit year, with no century.
yyyy	Formats the year portion of the date as a four-digit year, including the century.

The function should raise an error if the format string contains any invalid characters or internal spaces, but it should work properly if the format string contains leading or trailing spaces. Case is irrelevant.

You should not use the built-in `FormatDateTime` function to build this routine. As a hint, try reviewing the `Split` function and the `Month`, `Day`, and `Year` functions. Try using the `Instr` function combined with a loop to check for invalid format characters.

I suggest you try to build the project first, then compare your results with the `ch9i3.asp` file in the `Chapter9` directory on the CD. Don't expect your code to be identical to mine; there are literally thousands of possible variations—all of which will produce roughly the same results.

CHAPTER

TEN

10

Introduction to JScript

I'll start this chapter with both a confession and a warning. I don't use JScript on the server—I use VBScript. My recommendation to you is that you not use JScript on the server either, unless you already know it from client-side scripting and you just need to get started quickly. The reason has nothing to do with JScript's intrinsic worth as a language, it's because Microsoft provides far more support and examples for VBScript than for JScript as a server-side language.

With that said, JScript works for most of ASP's functionality extremely well. If you plan to use JScript all the time, you should change the default language setting for your site to JScript. Be aware that this does not mean you should write pages that omit the language declaration—they will work on your server, but probably will not work on other servers where the server administrator has not changed the default language setting.

JScript vs. VBScript

JScript is, in some ways, more powerful than VBScript, although VBScript version 5 has almost closed the gap. JScript is case-sensitive, where VBScript is not. JScript is considerably more object oriented than VBScript. JScript is a standard because it conforms to the ECMAScript requirements, but Microsoft has added many proprietary extensions so at JScript can interact with COM objects easily.

JScript is a larger and more complex language than VBScript. It has a more stringent syntax, but less stringent code formatting requirements. For example, white space is irrelevant in JScript. You don't need a line-continuation character, you simply finish the command on the next line. That's because JScript requires a line-termination character (the semicolon). Until version 5, JScript had no error-handling capability, which means you had to perform more data and parameter checking to avoid errors. In contrast, VBScript has had an `On Error Resume Next` command since its inception. You can use the JScript `eval` function to execute code dynamically—in other words, you can execute code by writing more code. VBScript has no such capability.

JScript is much more aware of HTML than VBScript (which is essentially oblivious to HTML) and has numerous formatting and parsing methods for creating and analyzing HTML tags. This reflects its heritage as a client-side language, but it makes it easier to use than VBScript for writing HTML with script.

JScript is case-sensitive—which is a major shift for VB programmers, but natural and familiar to C and Java programmers. The convention for creating function names, method names, and properties is that they should start with a lowercase letter. Object names begin with a capital letter. You should concatenate multi-word names and capitalize the first letter of all words except the first; for example, get-Object, or toString. Unfortunately, the language doesn't always follow these conventions. The result is that you must memorize the capitalization requirements for the built-in names to be productive. I'm not a fan of case sensitivity in programming languages for exactly that reason. The problem gets worse when two different programmers write similar methods—but with differing case in the names. For example, one programmer's object may expose an isString property, while an equivalent function in a different programmer's object may expose an isstring property.

Even in JScript's keywords there are numerous examples of inconsistent case. For example, the multi-word keyword fontsize is all lowercase, whereas the function getDay follows the normal convention, and the function GetObject begins with a capital letter. The JScript keywords are listed in Table 10.1.

TABLE 10.1: JScript Keywords

Keyword	Type	Description
$1 through $9	Keyword	Contains values from the result of the RegExp function.
abs	Method	Returns the absolute value of a numeric expression.
acos	Method	Returns the arc cosine of a numeric expression.
ActiveXObject	Object	Creates and returns references to ActiveX (COM) objects. You provide the class identifier of the object you want to create. For example, var myOjb = new ActiveXObject ("Scripting .Dictionary").
Addition (+)	Operator	Adds values. In JScript, use the addition operator for addition and for string concatenation.
anchor	Method	Surrounds the text of a String object with an <a> anchor tag.
arguments	Property	Contains an array of the arguments passed to the currently executing function.
Array	Object	Contains arrays of any data type. JScript can also handle COM (VBScript-type) arrays via special language extensions.
asin	Function	Returns the arcsine of a numeric expression.
Assignment (=)	Operator	Assigns a value to the variable on the left side of the equals sign.
atan	Function	Returns the arctangent of a numeric expression.
atan2	Function	Returns the angle (in radians) from the x-axis to a specified point (x, y).
atEnd	Method	Returns True if an Iterator object has reached the end of its associated collection.
big	Method	Surrounds the text of a String object with <big> tags.
Bitwise AND (&)	Operator	Performs a Boolean AND operation on two values.

Continued on next page

TABLE 10.1 CONTINUED: JScript Keywords

Keyword	Type	Description
Bitwise Left Shift (<<)	Operator	Shifts the bits of a value one position to the left.
Bitwise NOT (~)	Operator	Negates a value by flipping all the bits from 1 to 0 or from 0 to 1.
Bitwise OR (|)	Operator	Compares two bit patterns and produces a 1 if either or both bits in a column are 1.
Bitwise Right Shift (>>)	Operator	Shifts the bits of a value one position to the right.
Bitwise XOR (^)	Operator	Compares two bit patterns and produces a 1 if only one of the bits, but not both, in a column is a 1.
blink	Method	Surrounds the text of a String object with <blink> tags.
bold	Method	Surrounds the text of a String object with <b> tags.
Boolean	Object	Creates a Boolean value.
break	Statement	Used to end processing in a loop or code block. Processing starts at the code line following the code block.
caller	Property	Provides a reference to the function that called the current function. In other words, the caller property gives you access to the item immediately preceding the current item on the call stack.
ceil	Method	Returns the smallest integer value greater than the value of the argument passed to the method.
charAt	Method	Returns the character at a specified offset within a string.
charCodeAt	Method	Returns the character code for the character at a specified offset within a string.
Comma (,)	Operator	Causes multiple expressions to be evaluated in sequence, as if they were a single expression. It returns the value of the right-most expression in the list.
Comment (//) Single-line version	Statement	Used to place a comment on a single line. You may place the slashes anywhere in the line. The compiler ignores any text on that line following the slashes. For multi-line comments use the /*...*/ syntax.
Comment (/*...*/) Multi-line version	Statement	Used to surround comment lines. The compiler ignores all text between the starting /* characters and the ending */ characters.
Comparison	Operators	Less than (<), Greater than (>), Less than or equal to (<=), Greater than or equal to (>=), Equal (==), Not equal (!=), Identity equality— same object (===), Identity inequality (!==).
compile	Method	Compiles a regular expression. Used to improve the speed of loops and repeated code.
Compound Assignment	Operators	Addition (+=), Bitwise AND (&=), Bitwise OR (|=), Bitwise XOR (^=), Division (/=), Left Shift (<<=), Modulus (%=), Multiplication (*=), Right Shift (>>=), Subtraction (-=), Unsigned Right Shift (>>>=).
concat (Array)	Method	Concatenates two arrays.
concat (String)	Method	Concatenates two strings.
Conditional Compilation	Language Extension	Use in situations where non-Microsoft browsers or servers may not be able to compile the code. You begin conditional compilation using the @cc_on statement, or the @if or @set statements.

Continued on next page

TABLE 10.1 CONTINUED: JScript Keywords

Keyword	Type	Description
Conditional Compilation Variables	Language Extension	These are built-in variables that are either **True** or evaluate to NaN. **@_win32**—true if running on a Win32 system. **@_win16**—true if running on a Win16 system. **@_mac**—true if running on a Apple Macintosh system. **@_alpha**—true if running on a DEC Alpha processor. **@_x86**—true if running on an Intel processor. **@_mc680x0**—true if running on a Motorola 680x0 processor. **@_PowerPC**—true if running on a Motorola PowerPC processor. **@_jscript**—Always true. **@_jscript_build**—Contains the build number of the JScript scripting engine. **@_jscript_version**—Contains the JScript version number in **major.minor** format.
Conditional (trinary) (?:)	Operator	Used to execute one of two statements based on an expression. If the expression evaluates to **True**, JScript executes the first statement. If the expression evaluates to **False**, JScript executes the second statement. The syntax is **expression ? statement1 : statement2**.
constructor	Property	The name for a function that constructs an object.
continue	Statement	JScript does not process code following a **continue** statement in a loop. Instead, it begins processing again at the top of the loop.
cos	Method	Returns the cosine of a numeric expression.
Date	Object	JScript object for manipulating date and time values.
Decrement (–)	Operator	Decrements a value by **1**.
delete	Operator	Deletes a property or an array element.
description	Property	Holds a description of a runtime error.
Dictionary	Object	Object that holds key-value pairs. You can look up a value if you know the key name. The Dictionary object also supports iteration over either the keys or the values.
dimensions	Method	Returns the number of dimensions in a **VBArray** array.
Division (/)	Operator	Divides two numbers.
do...while	Statement	Loop structure that always executes at least once.
E	Property	Returns Euler's constant, the base of natural logarithms, approximately **2.718**.
Enumerator	Object	Object for enumerating or iterating over collections.
Equality (==)	Operator	Tests for equality between two values or expressions.
Error	Object	Object to hold runtime error information. This object is essentially the equivalent of the VBScript Error object, but has only **number** and **description** properties.
escape	Method	HTTP-encodes strings.

Continued on next page

TABLE 10.1 CONTINUED: JScript Keywords

Keyword	Type	Description
eval	Method	Evaluates JScript code. Use this to execute code strings you build at runtime.
exec	Method	Searches a string for a regular expression.
exp	Method	Returns e to the power you supply as an argument to the method.
FileSystemObject	Object	Object used to manipulate the file system.
fixed	Method	Surrounds the text of a String object with `<tt>` teletype tags. The browser renders this text in a fixed-width font such as Courier.
floor	Method	Returns the largest integer value less than the value of the argument passed to the method.
fontcolor	Method	Surrounds the text of a String object with `<font>` tags where the starting tag includes a color attribute.
fontsize	Method	Surrounds the text of a String object with `<font>` tags where the starting tag includes a size attribute.
for	Statement	Used at the start of a **for** loop structure. The syntax is: `for (value; test; increment)` `statement or block` Equivalent to VBScript's **For...Next** statement block.
for...in	Statement	Executes a statement or block for each item in a collection or array. Equivalent to VBScript's **For Each...Next** statement block.
fromCharCode	Method	Creates a string from a list of Unicode values.
Function	Object	Creates a new function.
function	Statement	Declares a new function.
getDate	Method	Returns the integer (1–31) value for the current day of the month stored in a Date object.
getDay	Method	Returns the integer (0–6) value for the current day of the week stored in a Date object.
getFullYear	Method	Returns the year as a four-character integer, (for example, 2001) for the date stored in a Date object.
getHours	Method	Returns the hour of the date stored in a Date object.
getItem	Method	Returns the item at a specified position in a VBArray.
getMilliseconds	Method	Returns the milliseconds past the current second for the time stored in a Date object.
getMinutes	Method	Returns the number of minutes past the hour for the time stored in a Date object.
getMonth	Method	Returns the month as an integer (1–12) for the current month stored in a Date object.
GetObject	Function	Returns a reference to a COM or OLE object stored in a file.
getSeconds	Method	Returns the number of seconds past the minute for the time stored in a Date object.
getTime	Method	Returns the time stored in a Date object.
getTimezoneOffset	Method	Returns the difference (in minutes) between the local time on the computer and Universal Coordinated Time (UTC).

Continued on next page

TABLE 10.1 CONTINUED: JScript Keywords

Keyword	Type	Description
getUTCDate, getUTCDay, getUTCFullYear, getUTCHours, getUTCMilliseconds, getUTCMinutes, getUTCMonth, getUTCSeconds	Method	These methods are identical to the getDate, getDay, etc. methods except that they perform all calculations using Universal Coordinated Time (UTC) rather than the date and time on the local computer. Note that because the computer must calculate UTC dates and times as an offset of the local computer's date/time means your date/time operations are still only as accurate as the local computer's time.
getVarDate	Method	Returns a JScript date from the date stored in a Date object in COM VT_DATE format. You only need to use this method if you're working with date or time arguments received from a VBScript or ActiveX control function or object.
getYear	Method	Returns the two-digit year from the date stored in a Date object.
Global	Object	A JScript object that holds functions that are globally available.
Greater than (>)	Operator	Compares the relative size of two numeric values or expressions. Returns True if the value of the expression on the left side of the operator is larger than the value of the expression on the right side.
Greater than or equal to (>=)	Operator	Compares the relative size of two values or expressions. Returns True if the value of the expression on the left side of the operator is larger than or equal to the value of the expression on the right side.
Identity (===)	Operator	Compares two object variable references and returns True if both variables refer to the same object.
@if	Statement	Conditional if structure. Used to conditionally compile code where the host-scripting environment may not be able to interpret the code correctly.
if...else	Statement	Code block. Performs a Boolean test on an expression and executes the code within the block if the expression evaluates to True.
Increment (++)	Operator	Increments a value by 1.
index	Property	For a RegExp object, returns the index of the first successful search for a regular expression.
indexOf	Method	Returns the starting position of the first matching sub-string within a String object.
Inequality (!=)	Operator	Compares two values or expressions. The operation evaluates to True if the value on the left side of the operator is not equal to the value on the right side.
Infinity	Property	Number object property that contains an initial value of POSITIVE_INFINITY.
input	Property	For a RegExp object, the input property returns the string that was searched.
instanceOf	Method	Returns True if the object is an instance of the specified class argument.
isFinite	Method	Returns True if the argument supplied is a finite number.

Continued on next page

TABLE 10.1 CONTINUED: JScript Keywords

Keyword	Type	Description
isNaN	Method	Returns **True** if the argument supplied is NaN (Not a Number).
italics	Method	Surrounds the text of a String object with <i> italics tags.
item	Method	Property of an Enumerator object. Returns the current item in an enumerated collection.
join	Method	Returns a string consisting of all the elements in a string array joined into a single string with an optional separator character between the values.
Labeled	Statement	A unique identifier that marks a position or label in code. To create a label, append a colon (:) to the end of the label text. For example, myLabel:. The code line following the label is called a labeled statement. If you include a label after a continue statement in a loop, execution continues at the code line following the label.
lastIndex	Property	Property of a RegExp object that returns the index of the last matching sub-string within a string.
lastIndexOf	Method	Returns the starting position of the last matching sub-string within a String object.
lbound	Method	Returns the lower-bound of a VBArray.
length (Array)	Property	Returns the size of an array or collection.
length (Function)	Property	Contains the number of arguments defined for a function.
length (String)	Property	Returns the length of the text for the String object.
Less than (<)	Operator	Compares the relative size of two numeric values or expressions. Returns **True** if the value of the expression on the left side of the operator is smaller than the value of the expression on the right side.
Less than or equal to (<=)	Operator	Compares the relative size of two values or expressions. Returns **True** if the value of the expression on the left side of the operator is less than or equal to the value of the expression on the right side.
link	Method	Surrounds the text of a String object with an <a> anchor tag containing an **HREF** attribute.
LN2	Property	Returns the natural logarithm of 2.
LN10	Property	Returns the natural logarithm of 10.
log	Method	Returns the natural logarithm of a numeric value or expression.
LOG2E	Property	Returns the base 2 logarithm of E (Euler's constant).
LOG10E	Property	Returns the base 10 logarithm of E (Euler's constant).
Logical AND (&&)	Operator	Performs a Boolean **AND** operation.
Logical NOT (!)	Operator	Performs a Boolean **NOT** operation.
Logical OR (||)	Operator	Performs a Boolean **OR** operation.
match	Method	Performs a search for a sub-string using a RegExp object.
Math	Object	A JScript intrinsic object used to perform math operations and retrieve constants.
max	Method	Returns the larger of two arguments.

Continued on next page

TABLE 10.1 CONTINUED: JScript Keywords

Keyword	Type	Description
MAX_VALUE	Property	The largest number you can use in JScript, approximately 1.79E+308.
min	Method	Returns the smaller of two arguments.
MIN_VALUE	Property	The smallest number you can use in JScript, approximately 2.22E-308.
Modulus (%)	Operator	Performs modulo arithmetic.
moveFirst	Method	Resets the current item of an Enumerator object to the first item of its associated collection.
moveNext	Method	Moves the current item of an Enumerator object to the next item of its associated collection.
Multiplication (*)	Operator	Multiplies numeric values.
NaN (Global)	Property	Contains the global initial constant for **NaN** (Not a Number).
NaN (Number)	Property	**NaN** is a special value meaning Not a Number.
NEGATIVE_INFINITY	Property	A value that represents negative infinity.
new	Operator	Creates a new **object** variable.
Nonidentity (!==)	Operator	Returns **True** if the operand on the left side of the operator does not refer to the same object as the operand on the right side.
Number	Object	Used to hold numeric values and constants.
number	Property	Contains a numeric value for a runtime error.
Object	Object	Parent object for all **object** variables.
parse	Method	Parses the text of a String object. Returns the elapsed number of milliseconds between a string or Date and the constant date **January 1, 1970**.
parseFloat	Method	Parses the text of a String object and returns a floating-point value if the String contains a text representation of a number.
parseInt	Method	Parses the text of a String object and returns an integer value if the String contains a text representation of a number.
PI	Property	Returns the value of **pi** (approximately 3.14159).
POSITIVE_INFINITY	Property	Returns a value representing positive infinity.
pow	Method	Returns the value of a numeric expression to the power of an argument you supply to the function.
prototype	Property	Returns a reference to a **prototype** object. New instances of that object type inherit the behavior of the prototype.
random	Method	Returns a pseudo-random number between 0 and 1.
RegExp	Object	Contains the results of a regular expression search.
Regular Expression	Object	Contains the patterns for a regular expression search.
replace	Method	Replaces sub-strings found by a regular expression search with other sub-strings.
return	Statement	Exits a function and (optionally) returns a value.
reverse	Method	Reverses the order of elements in an array.
round	Method	Returns a number rounded to the nearest integer value.

Continued on next page

TABLE 10.1 CONTINUED: JScript Keywords

Keyword	Type	Description
ScriptEngine	Function	Returns a string containing the name of the scripting language in use.
ScriptEngineBuildVersion	Function	Returns a string containing the build version of the scripting language in use.
ScriptEngineMajorVersion	Function	Returns a string containing the major version number of the scripting language in use.
ScriptEngineMinorVersion	Function	Returns a string containing the minor version number of the scripting language in use.
search	Method	Searches a string for matches to a regular expression.
@set	Statement	Conditional variable creation statement.
setDate	Method	Sets the date value of a Date object.
setFullYear	Method	Sets the year of the date value of a Date object.
setHours	Method	Sets the current hour of a time value contained in a Date object.
setMilliseconds	Method	Sets the number of milliseconds past the second for the time value contained in a Date object.
setMinutes	Method	Sets the minutes past the hour for the time value contained in a Date object.
setMonth	Method	Sets the current month of the date value contained in a Date object.
setSeconds	Method	Sets the number of seconds past the minute for the time value contained in a Date object.
setTime	Method	Sets the time value of a Date object.
setUTCDate, setUTCFullYear, setUTCHours, setUTCMilliseconds, setUTCMinutes, setUTCMonth, setUTCSeconds	Methods	These methods are identical to the setDate, setFullYear, etc. methods except that they perform all calculations using Universal Coordinated Time (UTC) rather than the date and time on the local computer. Note that because the computer must calculate UTC dates and times as an offset of the local computer's date/time means your date/time operations are still only as accurate as the local computer's time.
setYear Method	Method	Sets the year of the date value contained in a Date object.
sin	Method	Returns the sin value of a numeric value supplied as an argument.
slice (Array)	Method	Returns a portion of an array. You supply the starting and ending indexes.
slice (String)	Method	Returns a portion of a string. You supply the starting and ending indexes.
small	Method	Surrounds the text of a String object with <small> tags.
sort	Method	Returns a sorted array.
source	Property	Returns the text of a regular expression pattern.
split	Method	Splits the text of a String object into an array of strings separated at the delimiter value you supply.

Continued on next page

TABLE 10.1 CONTINUED: JScript Keywords

Keyword	Type	Description
sqrt	Method	Returns the square root of a numeric argument.
SQRT1_2	Property	Returns the square root of 0.5, or one divided by the square root of 2.
SQRT2	Property	Returns the square root of 2.
strike	Method	Surrounds the text of a String object with `<strike>` strikethrough tags.
String	Object	Object that contains text and exposes methods and properties to manipulate that text.
sub	Method	Surrounds the text of a String object with `<sub>` subscript tags.
substr	Method	Returns a sub-string from the text of a String object beginning from a specified offset with a specified length.
substring	Method	Returns a sub-string from the text of a String object beginning from a specified **start** offset and extending to a specified **end** offset.
Subtraction (-)	Operator	Subtracts numeric values.
sup	Method	Surrounds the text of a String object with `<sup>` superscript tags.
switch	Statement	A code block that conditionally executes one of a group of statements depending on the value of the condition.
tan	Method	Returns the tangent of a numeric value or expression.
test	Method	Returns **True** if a specified pattern exists in a string, otherwise returns **False**.
this	Statement	Contains a reference to the current object.
throw	Statement	Raises an error.
toArray	Method	Converts a VBArray to a JScript array.
toGMTString	Method	Obsolete. Use the **toUTCString** method instead.
toLocaleString	Method	Returns a string representation of a date. Uses the local computer's locale settings.
toLowerCase	Method	Returns a string with all the characters converted to lowercase.
toString	Method	Returns a string representation of an object.
toUpperCase	Method	Returns a string with all the characters converted to uppercase.
toUTCString	Method	Returns a string representation of a date in Universal Coordinated Time (UTC).
try...catch	Statement	Sets up error-handling. Requires two code blocks; a **try** block and a **catch** block. If an error occurs in the **try** block, execution resumes at the start of the **catch** block. You can handle the error locally or raise it to the next level using the **throw** statement.
typeof	Operator	Returns the type of an object or expression as a string. The return value is **number**, **string**, **boolean**, **object**, **function**, or **undefined**.
ubound	Method	Returns the upper-bound of a VBArray.
Unary Negation (-)	Operator	Negates a value or expression.

Continued on next page

TABLE 10.1 CONTINUED: JScript Keywords

Keyword	Type	Description
unescape	Method	Accepts an escaped (HTTP-encoded) string. Returns the string converted to normal text.
Unsigned Right Shift (>>>)	Operator	Shifts bit patterns to the right. Zero-fills the bits on the left.
UTC	Method	Returns the number of milliseconds between the constant January 1, 1970 and the supplied date. Uses UTC time to make the calculation.
valueOf	Method	Returns the primitive value of the object argument. The method returns Arrays as comma-separated strings; Boolean values as strings; dates and times as milliseconds (see UTC method); Functions as the text of the function; Numbers as a numeric value; Objects as themselves; and Strings as text.
var	Statement	Used to declare a variable.
VBArray	Object	Used to contain and manipulate COM safe-array arrays, known as VBArrays.
void	Operator	Used to evaluate an expression. The void operator returns the value undefined.
while	Statement	Begins a conditional code block. The block executes if the condition following the while statements evaluates to True.
with	Statement	Sets the default object for the following statement or group of statements. Equivalent to the With statement in VBScript.

Variables and Syntax

JScript, like VBScript, does not use typed variables, everything is a Variant; however, like VBScript, you can declare variables using the var statement. Unlike VBScript, you can declare a variable and initialize its value in the same statement. For example:

```
var myVar = 3;
var myString = new String("This is a string");
```

Note that each line in the script requires a semicolon. Also, remember that JScript is case-sensitive. The following code will not work correctly:

```
var myVar = 3
Response.Write(MyVar);
```

You can assign expressions in JScript during variable declaration:

```
var myVar = (3 * 6);
```

You can also declare several variables on one line. Separate the individual variable declarations with commas. For example:

```
var myVar = 3, myString = new String("Test"), i, j
```

The keyword var is optional. JScript, like VBScript, tries to interpret unrecognized keywords as variables. Unlike VBScript, there's no equivalent to the Option Explicit statement, which forces variable declaration. When you mix automatic variable creation with case sensitivity, you have a recipe for trouble. In longer scripts, such problems may be very difficult to find and debug.

In JScript, you can create both single and compound statements. A compound statement is a group of statements surrounded by braces. For example, an if conditional structure is a single statement if it has only one executable code line. For example:

```
if (true)
    x = 1;
```

If the preceding statement had two lines, you would write it as a compound statement, because you want to execute both of the code lines following the if condition when the condition evaluates to true. For example:

```
if (true) {
    x = 1;
    y = 1;
}
```

NOTE   In VBScript, the constant for a Boolean True value is True, with a capital T. In JScript, the constant is true with a lowercase t. In both languages, the value of True is −1, and the value of False is 0.

The equals sign is an overloaded operator in VB and many other languages because you use it for both assignment and equality tests. In Jscript, however, like C, you use a single equals sign for assignment and a double equals sign (==) for an equality test. This is hard to remember, mostly because using the single equals sign doesn't normally cause an error. JScript happily assigns the value you think you're testing to the variable on the left side of the equals sign.

To test object variables for equality in JScript, use a triple equals sign (===), and an exclamation point (often called a bang) with a double equals sign (!==) to test objects for inequality.

Using the ASP Objects with JScript

The ASP objects have exactly the same properties and methods using JScript as they do with VBScript, but the syntax is slightly different. For example, you must remember to add the semicolons at the end of each line, and you must remember to enclose the arguments to the built-in methods in parentheses. For example, in VBScript, you could write:

```
Dim myVar
myVar = 2
Response.Write myVar & "<br>"
```

In JScript, you could code the same functionality as:

```
var myVar = 2;
Response.write(myVar + "<br>");
```

Use the same syntax alterations for Request object methods. For example, to enumerate the keys and values in the `Request.ServerVariables` collection, use a for loop and an `Enumerator` object:

```
var en = new Enumerator(Request.ServerVariables);
for (;!en.atEnd(); en.moveNext())
    Response.Write(en.item() + "="
        + Request.ServerVariables(en.item())
        + "<br>");
```

The `for` loop shown above is equivalent to the following VBScript code:

```
For Each V in Request.ServerVariables
    Response.Write V & "=" & Request.ServerVariables(V) & "<BR>"
Next
```

Interestingly, although JScript itself is a case-sensitive language (for example, you can't write `For` when you mean `for`) JScript ignores case for the ASP-intrinsic object methods and properties, but not for the objects themselves. In other words, this code works:

```
Response.Write("Hello");
```

and this code works too:

```
Response.write("Hello");
```

but this code does not:

```
response.write("Hello");
```

Apparently, after you create the variable reference, non case-sensitive code running internally in the ASP engine itself must interpret all method and property references; otherwise, JScript would force you to write the references with proper case.

The lesson in this section is that you must constantly remain aware that case and syntax are more important in JScript than in VBScript.

Using JScript Arrays

Although most variable types are roughly equivalent in JScript and VBScript, arrays are not. In JScript, arrays are objects; in VBScript, arrays are not objects. In JScript, the lowest array index is always 0; in VBScript, you can create arrays where the lowest index is any integer value. But they do have similarities. Both VBScript and JScript arrays are dynamic—you can extend or truncate them at runtime. Both VBScript and JScript arrays can hold any kind of value—in other words, the elements of the array do not have to have the same data type; you can freely mix objects and scalar values.

You can create a JScript array both explicitly, by declaring the array, and implicitly, using the split function. For example:

```
// create an array with 4 elements
var arrWords1 = new Array(3);

// implict array creation
var sWords = "one,two,three,four";
var arrWords2 = sWords.split(",");
```

You can also create an array using a list of constants:

```
var arrWords3 = new Array("one", "two", "three", "four");
```

After creating an array, you access individual elements using an index:

```
var arrWords3 = new Array("one", "two", "three", "four");
Response.Write(arrWords3[0]);
// writes "one"
```

The length property of a JScript array returns the number of elements in the array:

```
var days = new Array("Sun", "Mon", "Tue", "Wed", "Thu", "Fri", "Sat");
Response.Write(days.length);
// writes 7
```

You can also extend or truncate the number of elements in a JScript array using the length property:

```
var arr = new Array();
arr.length=10;
Response.write(arr.length);
```

Note that the number of elements of an array is not necessarily the same as the number of assigned values in the array. Array elements with unassigned values have the initial value undefined.

Built-In Methods

You've seen all these methods in the JScript keywords table in this chapter, but some of them require a little more explanation. JScript uses both primitives and objects to manipulate values. For example, an integer constant is perfectly viable—so is a Number object containing an integer value:

```
var myInt = 2;
var myIntObject = new Number(2);
Response.Write(myInt + "<br>");
Response.Write(myIntObject.toString() + "<br>");
```

JScript contains a large number of built-in date and time methods. You access these through a Date object. For example:

```
var myDate = new Date('2/1/99 4:54:23 pm');
Response.write(myDate.toString() + "<br>");
// writes " Mon Feb 1 16:54:23 CST 1999"
Response.write(myDate.getMonth() + "<br>");
// writes 1 (month numbers are 0-based)
Response.write(myDate.getSeconds() + "<br>");
// writes 23
Response.write(myDate.getUTCSeconds() + "<br>");
// writes 23
```

Logical Structures

JScript has two main logical structures: the if...else structure and the switch statement. In JScript terminology these are logical statements. You've already seen both of these in action in the previous section. In this section, you'll take a closer look at the syntax and requirements.

The *if...else* Statement

In JScript, a single statement may cover several lines, but each statement must end with a semicolon (;), the statement terminator. JScript if...else statements are no exception, but they look like an exception because most people write the statement on two lines, as follows:

```
if (condition)
    do something;
```

Note that the else portion of the statement is optional. Most people break the statement into two lines for clarity, but it's perfectly legal to write:

```
if (condition) do something;
```

Even most of the spaces are optional. For example:

```
var s="1234" // the space between var and s is required
// The following line works even without spaces
if(s="1234")Response.Write("1234"); // writes 1234
```

Note that JScript requires spaces only where no other separator divides the text into recognizable parts. In the variable declaration line of the previous fragment, if you omit the space between var and s, JScript creates a variable called vars. No error occurs until the following line, where JScript attempts to compare the value 1234 to the now undefined variable s as shown in the following example:

```
//This code causes an error
vars="1234" // no error
Response.Write(s + "<br>");
//
```

The previous line causes the error because s is undefined. At any rate, one of the most common syntax errors in JScript with the if...else structure is that beginners often forget to create a compound statement for multi-line conditional code. In other words, if you need to execute more than one conditional statement for an if or else, add braces around the statements. For example:

```
//This code does not work properly
var i = 3;
if (i < 3)
    Response.write("Hello ");
    Response.write("World<br>");
else
    Response.write("i is not less than three<br>");


//This code works properly
var i = 3;
if (i < 3) {
    Response.write("Hello ");
    Response.write("World<br>");
}
else
    Response.write("i is not less than three<br>");
```

The first version causes a hard-to-understand error—a syntax error on the line containing the first else. The cause of the problem though isn't the else, it's that the if statement is a compound statement, and thus requires braces. The second version works properly.

JScript, unlike VBScript, has no elseif and there is no equivalent construction. Instead, you must chain if statements. For example:

```
' VBScript version
Dim i
i = 3
If i = 1 Then
    Response.Write "1<br>"
Elseif i = 2 then
    Response.Write "2<br>"
Elseif i = 3 then
    Response.Write "3<br>"
Else
    Response.Write "i is not 1, 2, or 3.<br>"
End If


//JScript version
var i = 3;
if (i == 1)
    Response.Write("1<br>");
if (i == 2)
    Response.Write("2<br>");
if (i == 3)
    Response.Write("3<br>");
else
    Response.Write("i is not 1, 2, or 3.<br>");
```

The *switch* Statement

When you want to test a single condition that may have multiple values, it's much easier to use the switch statement than the if statement. The switch statement conditionally executes code based on the value of a condition. The syntax is:

```
switch (condition) {
    case 1:
        code when condition is 1:
        break;
    case 2:
        code when condition is 2,
        break;
    default:
        code when condition is neither 1 or 2;
}
```

The `switch` statement acts in several ways. First, Microsoft's JScript documentation states that the `switch` statement causes execution to jump to a label based on the value of condition. The documentation defines a label as a text string followed by a colon. In the `switch` statement, the labels follow the keyword `case`. That's confusing because the label, in this case, can be a numeric value. Listing 10.1 shows an example of a `switch` statement that executes code based on a numeric value. If you run the code, you may get a surprise!

LISTING 10.1   `switch` **Statement Example (ch10i1.asp).**

```
var i = 1;

Response.Write("The variable i has a value of " + i + "<br><br>");
switch (i) {
   case 1:
      Response.Write("This statement prints when i=1<br>");
   case 2:
      Response.Write("This statement prints when i=2<br>");
   case 3:
      Response.Write("This statement prints when i=3<br>");
   default:
      Response.Write("This statement prints when i does not " +
         "equal 1, 2, or 3<br>");
}
```

I've added a form to the file in ch10i1.asp that lets you change the value of i interactively. If you view the file in your browser, it looks like Figure 10.1. Note that the figure represents the file on the CD, not the previous listing. The default value for the variable i is 1.

When you view the file in the browser, you'll see that initially, when i is 1, all the statements print. That doesn't make sense because only one of the statements should print. The example points out the most important difference between the `switch` statement and VBScript's `Select Case` structure—the `switch` statement requires a `break` command after each `case`. In JScript, if you neglect to insert the `break` statements, JScript executes all the statements following the first `case` statement that meet the condition. In contrast, the `Select Case` structure doesn't fall through to the next statement.

If you're still confused, try changing the value of the variable i to 3. When i=3 only the statement at `case 3` and the default statement will print. Listing 10.2 contains a fixed version of the `switch` statement. After adding the `break` statements to each condition, the statement works properly—only one message prints for any value of i.

FIGURE 10.1:

Switch statement example
(ch10i1.asp)

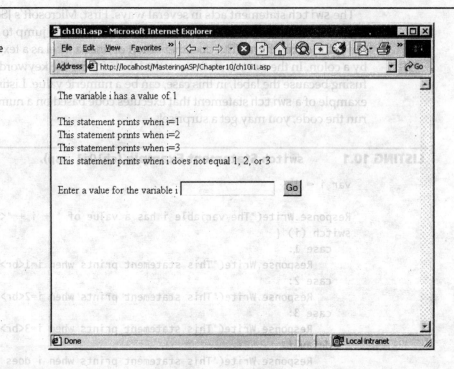

LISTING 10.2   Fixed switch example (ch10i2.asp)

```
switch (i) {
    case 1:
        Response.Write("This statement prints when i=1<br>");
        break;
    case 2:
        Response.Write("This statement prints when i=2<br>");
        break;
    case 3:
        Response.Write("This statement prints when i=3<br>");
        break;
    default:
        Response.Write("This statement prints when i does not equal 1, 2,
        or 3<br>");
}
```

The Trinary (?:) Operator

JScript has one special operator that behaves like an `if...else` statement. The
syntax is:

```
condition ? execute if true : execute if false
```

It's called the trinary operator because it has three parts—the condition, the statement to execute when the condition is true, and the statement to execute when the condition is false. For example:

```
var i = 1; y = 0;
(i==0) ? y = 1: y = 2;
Response.Write(y);
// writes 2
```

The operator evaluates the condition, then executes the statement following the question mark when the condition evaluates to true or the statement following the colon if the condition evaluates to false. VBScript has a similar (but less efficient) function—the Iif function. The logic for the trinary operator is exactly the same as the following if statement:

```
if (condition)
    execute if true;
else
    execute if false;
```

The code statements for the trinary operator may be compound statements.

Looping

JScript has fewer looping constructs than VBScript, but the ones it has are more flexible. Use a for loop when you know how many times you want the loop to execute. The syntax of the for statement is:

```
for(start counter; end condition; statements) {
    loop code
}
```

For example, the following code builds an array, then displays the value of each item in the array:

```
var i;
var arr = new Array(10);
for (i = 0; i < 10; i++) {
    arr[i] = "Item " + i.toString();
}
for (i = 0; i < 10; i++) {
    Response.write(arr[i] + "<br>");
}
```

A more generic example tests the `length` property of the array as the loop end condition:

```
for (i = 0; i < arr.length; i++) {
    Response.write(arr[i] + "<br>");
}
```

You can iterate through an array using the `for...in` syntax. Interestingly, the item retrieved for each element in an array is the index, not the value. For example:

```
var aList = new Array("1","2","3","4","5");
for (i in aList)
    Response.write(i + ", ");
Response.Write("<br>");
// writes the index numbers: 0, 1, 2, 3, 4,
```

More typically, you want to retrieve the values. To do that, use code like this:

```
var aList = new Array("1","2","3","4","5");
for (i in aList)
Response.write(aList[i] + ", ");
Response.Write("<br>");
// writes the list of values:
1
2
3
4
5
```

```
JScript treats objects and arrays essentially the same. For example,
JScript indexes property values. You can retrieve a value with either
the name or the index. Therefore, JScript's for...in structure can also
iterate through the properties of an object. The following example
shows a function to create an object and a for...in loop to iterate
through its properties:
// function to create an object
function myObj() {
    var name;
    var type;
    return this;
}
var obj = new myObj();
obj.name="A. Russell Jones"
obj.type="Person"
for (i in obj) {
    Response.write(obj[i] + "<br>");
}
// writes:
// A. Russell Jones
// Person
```

> **NOTE**
>
> You cannot use JScript's `for...in` syntax to loop through the properties of a VBScript array. To use `for...in` on a VBScript array you must first convert it to a JScript array using the **toArray** method. Similarly, you cannot use `for...in` to loop through the items in any of the ASP object collections.

String-Handling

JScript treats strings as objects. You can declare a variable as a String object explicitly, or you can let JScript create a String object implicitly by assigning a string value to a variable. For example:

```
var s = new String();
var s1 = new String("This is a string");
var s2;
s2 = "This is another string";
Response.Write(typeof[s] + "<br>"); // writes "object"
Response.Write(typeof[s1] + "<br>"); // writes "object"
Response.Write(typeof[s2] + "<br>"); // writes "object"
```

Note that you can use either the single-quote (') or the double-quote (") character as the string delimiter:

```
var s = new String("This is a string");
var s = new String('This is a string');
```

You can't use some characters directly in JScript because it treats them as special characters. To print or use the special characters in code, you use a combination of the backslash character (called the escape character) plus another character. These two-character combinations substitute for the special characters shown in Table 10.2.

TABLE 10.2: JScript Special Characters

Escape Sequence	ASCII Character Value	Description
\r	13.	Carriage return
\n	10	New line (line feed)
\f	12	Formfeed
\t	9	Tab
\'	39	Single-quote
\"	34	Double-quote
\b	8	Backspace

For example, to embed a tab in a string, use the \t special character:

```
var s="Fruit\tPrice\n\rApple\t$0.20\n\rBanana\t$0.22";
Response.Write("<pre>" + s + "</pre>");
```

Note that the Response.Write method uses the <pre> tag to display the contents of the variable s; otherwise the browser will ignore the tabs and carriage return/linefeed characters. Here's a complete example:

```
<%@ Language=JScript %>
<html>
<head><title>JScript Special Characters Example</title>
</head>
<body>
<h2 align="center">JScript Special Characters Example</h2>
<%
var s="Fruit\tPrice\n\rApple\t$0.20\n\rBanana\t$0.22";
Response.write("<b>With &lt;pre&gt; tag in
    effect</b>:<p>");
Response.Write("<pre>" + s + "</pre>");
Response.write("<hr><p>");
Response.write("<p><b>Without &lt;pre&gt; tag in
    effect</b>:<p>");
Response.Write(s);
%>
</body>
</html>
```

Figure 10.2 shows how the previous listing displays in a browser, both with and without the <pre> tag.

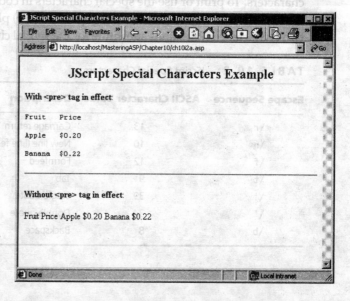

FIGURE 10.2:

JScript special characters example (ch10i2a.asp)

NOTE

To embed the escape character (\) itself in a string, use two consecutive escape characters. For example, to display the string `c:\somePath\someFile.txt`, use the syntax `Response.Write("c:\\somepath\\someFile.txt");`

To concatenate two strings in JScript you can use either the `concat` method or the concatenation (+) operator. For example:

```
var s1 = new String("Happy ");
var s2 = new String("Birthday");
Response.Write(s1 + s2 + "<br>");
// writes "Happy Birthday"

s1 = s1.concat(s2);
Response.Write(s1 + "<br>");
// writes "Happy Birthday"

Response.write("Happy ".concat(s2));
// writes "Happy Birthday"
```

JScript contains several functions to wrap HTML tags around text. For example:

```
s = new String("This is bookmarked text.<br>");
Response.Write((s.anchor("bookmark1")) + "<br>");
// creates the HTML string
//<A NAME="bookmark1">This is bookmarked text.<br></A><br>s = new
String("Link to ch10i1.asp<br>");
Response.Write((s.link("ch10i1.asp")) + "<br>");
// creates the HTML string
// <A HREF="ch10i1.asp">Link to ch10i1.asp<br></A>
```

Of course, after the browser renders the response you can't see the HTML unless you right-click and select View Source. Listing 10.3 shows the other JScript functions that create HTML.

LISTING 10.3   JScript String Object HTML-Producing Methods (ch10i3.asp)

```
s = new String("This is bold text.");
Response.Write(s.bold());
Response.Write ("<br>");

s = new String("This is big text.");
Response.Write(s.big());
Response.Write ("<br>");

s = new String("This is blinking text (Netscape Browsers Only).");
Response.Write(s.blink());
Response.Write ("<br>");
```

```
s = new String("This is blue text.");
Response.Write(s.fontcolor("0000FF"));
Response.Write ("<br>");

s = new String("This is size 5 text.");
Response.Write(s.fontsize(5));
Response.Write ("<br>");

s = new String("This is italicized text.");
Response.Write(s.italics());
Response.Write ("<br>");

s = new String("This is small text.");
Response.Write(s.small());
Response.Write ("<br>");

Response.Write("Normal Text");
s = new String("Superscript");
Response.Write(s.sup());
Response.Write ("<br>");

Response.Write("Normal Text");
s = new String("Subscript");
Response.Write(s.sub());
Response.Write ("<br>");
```

Figure 10.3 shows how the previous listing displays in a browser.

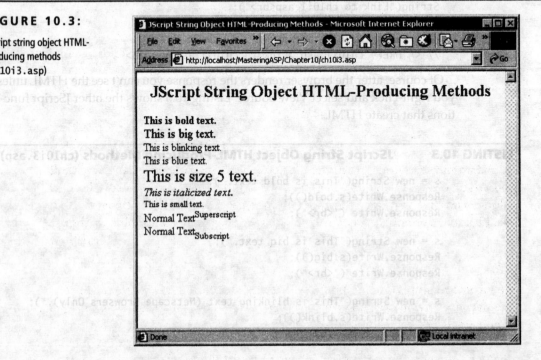

Many of the String object methods become even more useful when you wrap them in function code as shown in the next section.

Functions

The body of a function is a compound statement. Therefore, you must surround the function body with braces. The syntax for a function in JScript is:

```
function name(argument1, argument2, ... argument n) {
    function body code here
}
```

Arguments are optional. It's perfectly acceptable to create a function that accepts no arguments. The placement of the braces surrounding the function body (or any compound statement, for that matter) is unimportant other than for style or clarity. Because JScript ignores white space, you can place all of your code on a single line if you wish.

As a simple but useful function example, you can duplicate some of the methods available in VBScript. Listing 10.4 contains three functions that are JScript equivalents to the VBScript LTrim, Rtrim, and Trim methods, which remove white space from the front, back, and both front and back of strings, respectively.

LISTING 10.4 **JScript ltrim, rtrim, and trim Functions (ch10i4.asp).**

```
function ltrim(s) {
    var count=0;
    var i = 0;
    var space = " ";
    var newLine="\n";
    var cr = "\r";
    var tab = "\t";
    var sRet;
    while (
        (s.charAt(i) == space) |
        (s.charAt(i) == newLine) |
        (s.charAt(i) == cr) |
        (s.charAt(i) == tab)){
        count++;
        i++
    }
    if (count > 0)
        sRet = s.substring(count, s.length);
```

```
        return(sRet);
    }
function rtrim(s) {
    var count=0;
    var i = s.length - 1;
    var space = " ";
    var newLine="\n";
    var cr = "\r";
    var tab = "\t";
    var sRet;
    while (
        (s.charAt(i) == space) |
        (s.charAt(i) == newLine) |
        (s.charAt(i) == cr) |
        (s.charAt(i) == tab)) {
        count++;
        i--
    }
    if (count > 0)
        sRet = s.substring(0, s.length - count);

    return(sRet);
}

function trim(s) {
    return(ltrim(rtrim(s)));
}
```

The ltrim and rtrim functions do the real work—the trim function simply calls both of the other functions. Each function accepts a string argument. Because string concatenation is a relatively expensive operation, the function counts the number of white-space characters, then performs a single string copy in both the ltrim and rtrim functions. Note that the return value from each function is a String object—the functions don't alter the original string. In addition, because the return value is a String object, you can treat the function exactly as you would treat any other String object.

Having defined the functions, you may subsequently use them just like any other function call. For example:

```
var s = "   This is a string containing "
    + "leading and trailing spaces.   ";
Response.Write("<pre>'" + s + "'</pre>");
Response.Write("<hr>");
Response.Write("<b>ltrim(s)</b>:<pre>'" + ltrim(s) +
    "'</pre><br>");
Response.Write("<hr>");
```

```
Response.Write("<b>rtrim(s)</b>:<pre>'" + rtrim(s) +
    "'</pre><br>");
Response.Write("<hr>");
Response.Write("<b>trim(s)</b>:<pre>'" + trim(s) +
    "'</pre><br>");
```

Figure 10.4 shows the results of the previous code in a browser.

FIGURE 10.4:

ltrim, rtrim, and trim
function examples
(ch10i4.asp)

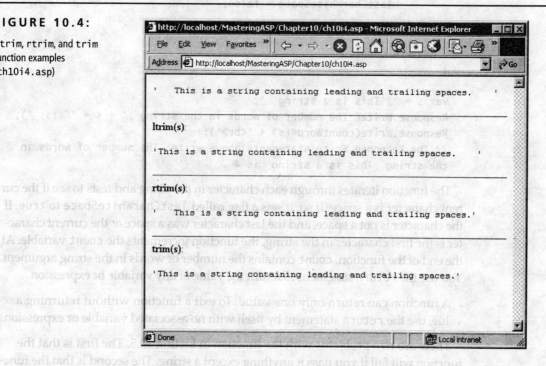

Listing 10.5 shows a slightly more complex function to count the number of words in a string argument passed to the function.

LISTING 10.5   CountWords Function Example 1 (ch10i5.asp)

```
function countWords(s) {
    var count = 0;
    var i;
    var lastCharWhiteSpace = 0;
    // loop through the string
    for (i = 0; i < s.length; i++) {
        // get the character at position i
        if (s.charAt(i) == " ") {
            // if it's a space
```

```
            lastCharWhiteSpace = true;
        }
        else {

            // it's not a space
            if (lastCharWhiteSpace == true | i == 0 )
                count++;
            lastCharWhiteSpace = false;

        }
    }
    return count;
}

var s = "  This is a string  ";
Response.Write("The number of words in the string '" + s + "' is: ");
Response.Write(countWords(s) + "<br>");
// The Response.Write statements above write: The number of words in
the string 'This is a string' is 4
```

The function iterates through each character in the string and tests to see if the current character is a space. If so, it sets a flag called lastCharWhiteSpace to true. If the character is not a space, and the last character was a space *or* the current character is the first character in the string, the function increments the count variable. At the end of the function, count contains the number of words in the string argument. You use the return statement to return the value of any variable or expression.

A function can return only one value. To exit a function without returning a value, use the return statement by itself with no associated variable or expression.

There are two problems with the function in Listing 10.5. The first is that the function will fail if you pass it anything except a string. The second is that the function only looks for spaces, but spaces aren't the only word separators. Carriage returns, tabs, and in some cases, punctuation can separate words as well. For example, in JScript, you can embed a carriage return using the syntax \n, called a newline character. As written, the countWords() function would not count the words separated by the newline character as separate words. The following code shows the JScript version:

```
var s = "  This is\n\na string  ";
Response.Write("The number of words in the string '" + s + "' is: ");
Response.Write(countWords(s) + "<br>");
// writes 3
```

Listing 10.6 contains an improved version of the function. The countWords2() function iterates through the characters in the string using the switch statement to determine the character code of each character. If the character is a space, a tab, or a newline character, the function treats it as white space.

LISTING 10.6   Improved CountWords Function Example 1 (ch10i6.asp)

```
function countWords2(s) {
    var count = 0, i, charCode, lastCharWhiteSpace = false;
    if (!(typeof(s) == "string")) {
        Response.Write("The countWords2 function expects a String
        argument.");
        return;
    }
    for (i = 0; i < s.length; i++) {
        switch (s.charCodeAt(i)) {
        case 32:
            lastCharWhiteSpace = true;
            break;
        case 10:
            lastCharWhiteSpace = true;
            break;
        case 13:
            lastCharWhiteSpace = true;
            break;
        case 9:
            lastCharWhiteSpace = true;
            break;
        default :
            if (lastCharWhiteSpace == true | i == 0 ) {
                count++;
                lastCharWhiteSpace = false;
            }
        }
    }
    return count;
}
```

The countWords2 function improves on the original in three ways: First, the function checks the argument type using the typeof function. If the argument is not a string, the function writes a message and exits. Second, the function tests for white space consisting of characters other than spaces by checking the character code for each character in the string argument. It obtains the character code using the charCodeAt() function, which returns the character code for a character at a specific offset in a string. Finally, the function trims the string by calling the trim() function shown earlier in this chapter before counting the words in the string.

Creating Objects in JScript

As I stated at the beginning of this chapter, JScript is more object-oriented than VBScript, although VBScript version 5 has narrowed the gap. You've already seen how to use the built-in objects. Since version 3, JScript has had the ability to create objects. To create an object in JScript, you create a constructor function. The constructor function creates and initializes the object's properties, then returns the object. For example, to create an audio CD object you might want a `title` property, an `artist` property, a `trackCount` property, a variable to hold an array of track titles, and the name of the record company:

```
function CD() {
    var title;
    var artist;
    var trackCount;
    var trackTitles;
    var recordCompany;
    return(this);
}
```

To create the new CD object, you call the constructor function preceded by the new keyword:

```
var myCD = new CD();
```

After creating the object variable, you can now set its properties as shown in the following fragment:

```
myCD.title="Fraser and DeBolt Together Again";
myCD.artist = "Alan Fraser and Daisy DeBolt";
myCD.trackCount = 12;
myCD.trackTitles = new Array(myCD.trackCount - 1);
for (i=0; i < myCD.trackCount; i++)
    myCD.trackTitles[i] = "Track " + i.toString();
myCD.recordCompany="Columbia Records";
```

There are some quirks to JScript object creation. Note that you must set the `trackTitles` property to an Array object from outside the constructor function. If you create the Array object inside the constructor function, but try to change its size from outside the constructor function as shown below, the code causes a run-time error. However, you can call an initialization function to make the constructor function assign default values to the properties. You can even pass default values to the constructor function. For example:

```
function CD() {
    var title;
    var artist;
```

```
        var trackCount;
        var trackTitles = new Array();
        var recordCompany;
        return(this);
}
myCD.title="Fraser and DeBolt Together Again";
myCD.artist = "Alan Fraser and Daisy DeBolt";
myCD.trackCount = 12;
myCD.trackTitles.length = myCD.trackCount - 1
//the previous line causes an error.
```

Regular Expressions

JScript has powerful regular expression matching abilities. A regular expression consists of text you want to search for combined with special characters or commands that describe how you want to search.

Microsoft's MSDN documentation is somewhat confused on this topic. It documents two separate objects, stating that the Regular Expression object holds search criteria, and the RegExp object holds the results of a search or match operation, but you can create only one object—the RegExp object.

You can create a RegExp object either implicitly, by surrounding the search criteria with forward slashes, or explicitly, by creating a new Regular Expression object and providing the search criteria as a String argument:

```
// implicit RegExp creation
rgxp = /boy/;
```

```
// explicit RegExp creation
rgxp = new RegExp("boy");
```

You can perform global (find all matches) and case-insensitive searches using an optional argument in both the implicit and explicit forms. The possible flag values are:

i   Perform a case-insensitive search.

g   Perform a global search.

You can combine the flags in any order. For example:

```
// case-insensitive search
rgxp = /boy/i
```

```
// global search
rgxp = /x/g

// case-insensitive global search
rgxp = new RegExp("boy", "ig");
```

You can approach using a RegExp object from two directions: by passing a Reg-Exp object as an argument to the String object's `search` and `match` methods, or by passing a String argument to the RegExp object's `exec` method. The String object's `search` method returns the zero-based character offset of the first matching character in the string, or −1 if no match is found.

For example, the following code uses the `String` `search` method to search for the word boy in the string `Every good boy does fine`.

```
var s1 = new String("Every good boy does fine.")
var s2 = /boy/i
Response.write(s1.search(s2));
// writes 11
```

The difference between searches and matches is that a search returns the index of the first match for the regular expression in a string, whereas the return value of a match is an array.

The String object `match` method and the RegExp object's `exec` method are functionally identical. It doesn't matter whether you perform the `match` method on a RegExp object or `exec` a String, both methods return an array. You can use the `compile` method of the RegExp object to improve the speed of matches run multiple times, for example, in a loop.

The power of regular expression-searching lies in its ability to match patterns using special characters and character sequences. Table 10.3 lists the special characters and sequences you may use in a regular expression.

TABLE 10.3: JScript Regular Expression Special Characters and Sequences

Character/ Sequence	Description
\	Escape character. Use this to embed newline, tab, or other special characters into the regular expression string.
^	Limits matches to the beginning of a line or string.
$	Limits matches to the end of a line or string.
*	Matches the character preceding the asterisk zero or more times. For example, /bo*/ matches both bed and book.
+	Matches the character preceding the plus sign one or more times. /bo+/ matches book, but not bed.

Continued on next page

TABLE 10.3 CONTINUED: JScript Regular Expression Special Characters and Sequences

Character/ Sequence	Description
?	Matches the character preceding the question mark zero or one time. /be?/I matches **best** and **bit**, but not **been**.
.	The period is a wildcard character. It matches any single character other than a newline.
(pattern)	Enclose a pattern in parentheses to find matched patterns. You can retrieve the matched patterns using the RegExp object's $1...$9 properties. Use \(and \) to match parentheses.
a|b	Matches either **a** or **b**.
{n}	Matches exactly n times, where n is an integer greater than or equal to 1. For example, /m{2}/ matches **immediate**, but not **magic**.
{n,}	Matches at least n times, where n is an integer greater than or equal to 1. Non-negative integer. For example, /e{2}/ matches **seer**, but not **her**.
{nMin, nMax}	Matches between **nMin** and **nMax** times, inclusive, where both **nMin** and **nMax** are integers greater than or equal to 1.
[abc]	Matches any of the characters enclosed in the brackets. /[mno]/ matches the **n** in **bin** or the **m** in **Mom**.
[^abc]	Matches any character not enclosed in the brackets. /[^mno]/ matches the **b** in **bin** and the **M** in **Mom**.
\b	Matches a word boundary, such as a space, tab, or punctuation. For example, /p\b/ matches the **p** in the word **help** in the phrase **please help me** and in the phrase **please help**. Place the /b before the pattern to find matches at the beginning of words or at the end of the pattern to find matches at the end of words.
\B	Matches text not on a word boundary. For example, /\Bp/ matches the **p** in the word **help** in the phrase **please help me**, but not the **p** in the word **please** in that same phrase. That's because the **p** in **please** lies at the start of a word.
\d	Matches any digit character. Equivalent to [0-9].
\D	Matches any non-digit character. Equivalent to [^0-9].
\f	Matches a formfeed character.
\n	Matches a linefeed character.
\r	Matches a carriage return character.
\s	Matches any white space including space, tab, formfeed, and so on. Equivalent to [\f\n\r\t\v].
\S	Matches any non-white space character. Equivalent to [^ \f\n\r\t\v].
\t	Matches a tab character.
\v	Matches a vertical tab character.
\w	Matches any word character including underscore. Equivalent to [A-Za-z0-9_].
\W	Matches any non-word character. Equivalent to [^A-Za-z0-9_].
\num	Matches **num**, where num is a positive integer. \1 matches what is stored in RegExp.$1.
/n/	Matches n, where n is an octal, hexadecimal, or decimal escape value. Allows embedding of ASCII codes into regular expressions.

The array returned by the `match` or `exec` functions contains items at several positions.

Position 0   The string that was searched.

Position 1   The index of the first match, if any.

Position 2   The index of the first character after the last match. In other words, this holds the match index in position 1 to the length of the matched portion of the string. Start at this position to search for the next match.

Position 3   The portion of the searched string that was matched.

Position 4 to n   Holds matched items (duplicate of $1...$9 properties).

The number of items in the array increases as the match list grows longer. For example, Listing 10.7 searches the word `immediate` for the regular expression `/(med)\S/`. The expression will match any occurrence of the string med followed by any character.

LISTING 10.7   **Match Example (ch10i7.asp)**

```
function matchExample(re, str)
{
 var s = "";
 var arr = re.exec(str);
 for (i in arr)
  s += "\'" + arr[i] + "\'<br>";
return(s);
}
Response.Write (matchExample(/(med\S)/ig, "immediately") + "<br>");
// OUTPUT
// 'immediately' (string searched)
// '2' (first match index)
// '6' (index of first character after first match)
// 'medi' (matched string)
// 'medi' ($1 property)
```

In addition to the information in the array shown above, when you use the pattern syntax shown in Table 10.3, the built-in properties $1 through $9 hold the results of a match operation. Listing 10.8 shows the same search as Listing 10.7, but the code displays the RegExp properties $1 through $4.

LISTING 10.8:   Extended Match Example (ch10i8.asp)

```
function matchExample(re, str)
{
    var s = "";
    var arr = re.exec(str);
    for (i in arr)
        s += "\'" + arr[i] + "\'<br>";
    s += "$1 contains: " + RegExp.$1 + "<BR>";
    s += "$2 contains: " + RegExp.$2 + "<BR>";
    s += "$3 contains: " + RegExp.$3 + "<BR>";
    s += "$4 contains: " + RegExp.$4 + "<BR>";
    s += "$5 contains: " + RegExp.$5 + "<BR>";
    s += "$6 contains: " + RegExp.$6 + "<BR>";
    return(s);
}
Response.Write (matchExample(/i(m{2})(e.)(i\S)(tel)(y)/ig,
    "immediately") + "<br>");
```

Figure 10.5 shows the output from Listing 10.8.

FIGURE 10.5:

Extended match example
(ch10i8.asp)

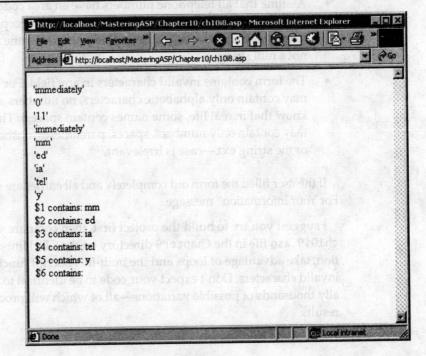

Project: Use JScript to Control Responses

In this project, you'll write an ASP page that submits information to itself with a form. This project is identical to the project in Chapter 9, *Introduction to VBScript*, so if you've already completed that project, this one presents a translation problem.

The problem is to respond with a message, the content of which depends on whether the person submitting the form filled it out completely and correctly.

Build a form that requests a person's last name, first name, address, and telephone number. Add a button to submit the form. On the server, when the user submits the form, return a message if:

- The user submitted an incomplete form. For example, if the user omitted a Last Name, you might reply with the message "Your Last Name is required. Please enter a last name."

- If the length of either the Last Name or the First Name field is less than 2 characters or longer than 20 characters.

- Assume that all telephone numbers have an area code and a seven-digit number, with or without an extension. You may accept any format for the telephone number. You may accept any length for the address as long as it is not a null string.

- The form contains invalid characters in any field. For example, name fields may contain only alphabetic characters, no numbers and no spaces (yes, I know that in real life, some names contain spaces). The telephone number may contain only numbers, spaces, parentheses, dashes, and the character x or the string ext—case is irrelevant.

If the user filled the form out completely and all entries are valid, return a "Thanks For Your Information" message.

I suggest you try to build the project first, then compare your results with the ch10i9.asp file in the Chapter9 directory on the CD. Hints: See the length function, take advantage of loops and the built-in VBScript function instr to look for invalid characters. Don't expect your code to be identical to mine; there are literally thousands of possible variations—all of which will produce roughly the same results.

Project: Build a URL-Parsing Object

JScript contains several methods that can help you parse strings efficiently. Sometimes you need to know where your application is running. Applications often move between servers and directory names change, so you should avoid hardcoding this information in your application. In this project, you'll write a function that runs on the server that will let you know both the virtual and physical directories for the current page.

The problem is to find the protocol, IP address, server name, virtual path, script name, and physical path of the current page. You should package it all up into a server-side object that you can query to retrieve any single item with one call. For example, to retrieve the current page name, you should be able to write code similar to this:

```
var page;
var p = new PageInfo();
Response.Write(p.pageName + "<br>");
// should write the current page name
Response.Write(p.server + "<br>");
// should write the name of the server.
```

I suggest you try to build the project first, and then compare your results with the ch10i10.asp file in the Chapter9 directory on the CD. Don't expect your code to be identical to mine; there are literally thousands of possible variations—all of which will produce roughly the same results.

CHAPTER
ELEVEN

The Scripting Dictionary Object

- **Introduction to Complex Data Objects**

- **Dictionary Object Methods/Properties**

- **Project: Exploring the Dictionary Object**

In addition to the ASP intrinsic objects, ASP ships with and installs a number of other objects that you will find useful—in some cases, indispensable. One of the indispensable objects is the Dictionary object.

The Dictionary object is part of the Microsoft Scripting Runtime, which also contains objects for file access, as you'll see in Chapter 12, *File Access With ASP*. The Dictionary object lets you store key-value pairs in a manner similar to the way ASP presents data through its intrinsic object collections. The difference is that a Dictionary object contains only what you put into it.

Introduction to Complex Data Objects

So far, the ASP objects you've seen have had a relatively simple interface. The Dictionary object has a much more complex interface, primarily because you need to populate it yourself. Creating the Dictionary object is easy; use the `Server.CreateObject` method with the project ID string for a Dictionary:

```
Set d = Server.CreateObject("Scripting.Dictionary")
```

Note the use of the `Set` keyword. You must use `Set` to create an object reference in VBScript.

Internally, a Dictionary consists of two arrays: a `Variant` array for the keys and a `Variant` array for the values, called *items*. A Dictionary key can be any type of variable except an array, even an object variable, but you should usually use `String` values for the keys. An item can hold any type of value, including an array. The advantage of a Dictionary (and the reason it's called a Dictionary) is that you can look up a value very quickly by providing the key, much the same way you retrieve word definitions from a printed dictionary. Similarly, the Dictionary object stores an index to its keys in alphabetical order, which is the reason it can retrieve an individual value quickly.

The Dictionary object, like all the other objects (except the JScript objects) that you'll see in this book, is a COM object. That means two things: First, it has methods to expose its interface—its public properties and methods—to other COM-aware code, and second, the fact that its a COM object implies that the interface will not change. There's a significant speed advantage to using compiled code rather than interpreted script, especially for loops and code that executes frequently. Sure, you could create your own Dictionary-like functions in VBScript using arrays, but your site's performance would suffer.

At the same time, there are specific ways in which you should not use COM objects. One of those has to do with the way Microsoft chose to implement threading in certain COM objects (including the Scripting Dictionary object).

There are three threading models for COM objects: single-threaded, apartment-threaded, and free-threaded. You won't—and shouldn't—run into many single-threaded objects on the Web, because Web applications are inherently multiuser applications. Apartment-threaded code can handle many threads, but each object exposed by an apartment-threaded DLL can exist on one, and only one thread. The internal COM code handles new thread creation when needed. Each apartment-threaded object gets its own copy of any global variables. Free-threaded objects handle their own threading issues, and the programmer must create the code with critical sections and semaphores that notify other processes when the critical code has completed.

You'll find that most ActiveX objects used on the Web are apartment-threaded. There are several reasons for that; they're highly efficient, easy to build with popular development tools such as Visual Basic, and they scale reasonably well because the IIS server processes responses on a single thread, when possible.

The problem is that the thread used to process a given request may be different for each request. Consider this example. Suppose you create and store a Dictionary object in a `Session` variable for each user. When only one user is active in the site, there's no problem. Regardless of which thread IIS initially selects to process the request, all other threads are free, so IIS can transfer the request to the thread containing the Dictionary object without interference. However, as more users become active in the site, the problem soon begins to affect response time. For example, suppose IIS stored user #1's Dictionary object on thread 243. Now user #2 requests a page and you store her Dictionary on thread 248. User #1 requests a second page. IIS selects thread 248 to handle the response. Because user #1 has a Dictionary object on a different thread, IIS must activate that thread to process the request. In the meantime, user #2 has requested a page and IIS has selected thread 243 to handle that request. Now IIS needs both threads, and neither user can retrieve the Dictionary object from the other thread, leading to a lock situation.

Normally, you won't see this happen with just two users, but as you add users to a site, it will happen. At that point, the site will become extremely slow for all users until the requests forcing the lock time out. The locked-out users will see error messages (assuming they've waited that long).

You can avoid this situation by following a single rule: Never store an apartment-threaded ActiveX object in a `Session` variable. Fortunately, ASP doesn't let you store apartment-threaded objects in an `Application` variable, because the problem there would be even worse.

WARNING   Never store an apartment-threaded ActiveX object in a `Session` variable because it causes thread contention and can lock up your site.

The only COM objects specific to ASP that you'll see in this book are the intrinsic objects—the Request, Response, Server, Session, Application, and ObjectContext objects. The rest are general-purpose objects available to any COM-compliant language. You can use them with VB, VBA, J++, Delphi, C++, or many other languages. Almost all of these are objects exposed by apartment-threaded COM DLLs. The rule about not storing them in Session variables applies to all these objects, not just to the Dictionary object.

NOTE   The version of the Dictionary object installed with VBScript 2 incorrectly marked the Dictionary object in the registry as **both-threaded**. If you're running an early version of VBScript, you should either change the registry setting to **Apartment** (look in the registry for the ThreadingModel value at HKEY_LOCAL_MACHINE\ SOFTWARE\Classes\CLSID\{EE09B103-97E0-11CF-978F-00A02463E06F}\ InprocServer32), or obtain an updated version of VBScript (a free download from Microsoft).

One final note on Dictionaries and threading models: Microsoft has recently made available a read-only, Dictionary-like object called the LookupTable object. LookupTable objects are both-threaded and highly scalable. You can store LookupTable objects in **Application** variables without a significant performance penalty. You can download the LookupTable object from: http://msdn.microsoft.com/ workshop/server/downloads/lkuptbl.asp.

WARNING   Microsoft does not officially support the LookupTable object; however, the MSN site uses the object in production, and the download includes source code (as of this writing) that may enable you to solve any problems.

Dictionary Object Methods/Properties

You can add a new value to a Dictionary object in two ways: explicitly, by using the Add method, and implicitly, by assigning a value to a new key. For example, the following code adds two values to the Dictionary:

```
Dim d
Set d = Server.CreateObject("Scripting.Dictionary")
d.Add "Kidney Beans", "CG598880103"
d("Black-Eyed Peas") = "CG59763209"
```

The first method is explicit; another programmer can easily tell that you wanted to add a new value. The second, implicit method is dangerous. Without knowing the purpose of the code, you can't tell whether it adds a new value or changes an existing value. I recommend you avoid the implicit method for adding new values like the plague. One reason is that you can add items without meaning to. For example, the following code causes an error:

```
Dim d
Set d = Server.CreateObject("Scripting.Dictionary")
if d("name") = "" then
        Response.Write d.Count & "<BR>"
end if
d.Add "name", "Bill"
' The previous line causes the error:
' "This key is already associated with
' an element of this collection."
```

The third line in the previous example implicitly adds the key "name" to the Dictionary. You can prove that by looking at the output from line 4, which prints 1. The fifth line causes the error because the key "name" already exists.

Another reason to avoid the implicit syntax is that shortly after writing complex code, you may not remember whether you're adding a new value or changing an existing value. Unfortunately, the Dictionary object does not contain a setting to disable this implicit Add behavior.

Now that you know how to add values, how do you retrieve them? Fortunately, the syntax is exactly the same as the ASP object collections:

```
Dim KidneyBeansID
Dim BlackEyedPeaID
KidneyBeansID = d("Kidney Beans")
BlackEyedPeaID = d.Item("Black-Eyed Peas")
```

You cannot retrieve items by index number because the Dictionary object tries to interpret the index as a key. However, you can retrieve a key using an index number, then use that value to retrieve the item value. For example, the lines below return the same values as using the keys:

```
dim arr
arr = d.Keys()
Response.Write d(arr(0))
' writes "CG598880103"
Response.Write d(arr(1))
' writes "CG59763209"
```

One quirk of the Dictionary object is that, by default, its keys are case-sensitive. For example, the code below does not work properly because the line assigning the variable `BlackEyedPeaID` contains a Null value due to the difference in case between the `"Black-Eyed Pea"` and `"Black-eyed Pea"` keys:

```
Dim d
Dim KidneyBeansID
Dim BlackEyedPeaID
Set d = Server.CreateObject("Scripting.Dictionary")
d.Add "Kidney Beans", "CG598880103"
d("Black-Eyed Peas") = "CG59763209"
KidneyBeansID = d("Kidney Beans")
BlackEyedPeaID = d("Black-eyed Peas")
```

I spent several hours debugging the difference between `d("EMail")` and `d("Email")` before I realized what the problem was. Having case-sensitive keys is unlike the VBScript syntax for other objects; however, you can defeat this behavior by setting the `CompareMode` property. The flag can take either of two values.

Value	Constant	Result
0	vbBinaryCompare (default)	Case sensitive keys
1	vbTextCompare	Case insensitive keys

Microsoft's MSDN documentation states that there is a third possible value for the `CompareMode` constant, the `vbDatabaseCompare` (value, 2), but that value is invalid. After discovering the `CompareMode` flag, I immediately created a function to create a case-insensitive Dictionary. I've been using it ever since. The function turned out to be so useful that I created versions for other objects as well, primarily because it's irritating to have to write the long `Server.CreateObject` command for something as common as creating an object. Listing 11.1 shows the `newDictionary` function.

LISTING 11.1   **The `newDictionary` Function**

```
Function newDictionary()
    Dim d
    Set d = Server.CreateObject _
        ("Scripting.Dictionary")
    d.CompareMode = TextCompare
    set newDictionary = d
End Function
```

Unfortunately, that doesn't work, because the `TextCompare` constant, while part of the Microsoft Scripting Runtime library, doesn't define the constant. Use the `vbTextCompare` (or for case-sensitive Dictionaries, `vbBinaryCompare (0)`) constants instead, because VBScript contains those definitions, and they have the same values as the `TextCompare` and `BinaryCompare` constants.

The `newDictionary` function returns a case-insensitive Dictionary object. Like an array or an ASP collection object, you can iterate through the collection using the `For Each...Next` syntax. With a Dictionary though, you must explicitly state which items you want to iterate through—the keys or the values. For example:

```
Dim d ' Dictionary variable
dim V ' Variant
Dim KidneyBeansID
Dim BlackEyedPeaID
Set d = Server.CreateObject("Scripting.Dictionary")
d.Add "Kidney Beans", "CG598880103"
d.Add "Black-Eyed Peas" , "CG59763209"
For each V in d.Keys
    Response.Write V & "=" & d(V) & "<br>"
Next
```

The `For Each...Next` loop in the previous example prints the contents of a Dictionary object; but because the value array of the Dictionary consists of `Variant` values, the loop isn't sufficiently robust to print any Dictionary. For example, consider the following code:

```
Dim dMain
Dim d ' Dictionary variable
Dim i
Dim j
dim V ' Variant
set dMain = newDictionary()
' see newDictionary function
' earlier in this chapter
For i = 1 to 50
    Set d = newDictionary()
    For j = 1 to 10
        d.Add cstr(j), j
    Next
    dMain.Add cstr(i), d
Next
```

The code creates a Dictionary object containing a list of 50 Dictionaries, each containing 10 items. If you were to try to print the dMain dictionary using the following loop, you would immediately receive an error:

```
For Each V in dMain.Keys
    Response.Write V & "=" & dMain(V) & "<br>"
Next
' Causes error: " Wrong number of arguments
' or invalid property assignment
```

Instead, you need to improve the print code by checking for various types of values. Listing 11.2 contains a printDictionary function that prints Dictionaries that contain both other Dictionaries and arrays.

LISTING 11.2   The printDictionary Function Example (ch11i2.asp)

```vbscript
<%@ Language=VBScript %>
<% option explicit %>
<%
Function newDictionary()
    dim d
    set d = Server.CreateObject("Scripting.Dictionary")
    d.CompareMode=vbTextCompare
    Set newDictionary=d
End Function
Function printArray(arr)
    Dim V
    For Each V in arr
        If isArray(V) Then
            call printArray(V)
        Elseif isObject(V) Then
            If Typename(V) = "Dictionary" then
                Call printDictionary(V)
            Else
                Response.Write "{Object: " & _
                    Typename(V) & "}<br>"
            End If
        Else
            Response.Write V & "<br>"
        End If
    Next
End Function
Function printDictionary(d)
    For Each V in d.Keys()
        If isObject(d(V)) Then
            If Typename(d(V)) = "Dictionary" Then
                Call printDictionary(d(V))
            End If
        Elseif isArray(d(V)) Then
            Call printArray(d(V))
        Else
            Response.Write V & "=" & d(V) & "<br>"
        End If
    Next
End Function
```

```
Dim dMain
Dim d ' Dictionary variable
Dim i
Dim j
Dim arr
Dim V ' Variant
set dMain = newDictionary()
' see newDictionary function
' earlier in this chapter
For i = 1 to 50
    Set d = newDictionary()
    For j = 1 to 10
        d.Add cstr(j), j
    Next
    dMain.Add cstr(i), d
Next
arr = Array("This", "is", "an", "array", "of", "strings")
dMain.Add "Array", arr
call printDictionary(dMain)
%>
```

The printDictionary function in Listing 11.2 checks specifically to see if an item is a Dictionary, then recursively calls itself to print the contents of that Dictionary as well. It also checks for items that are arrays and calls the printArray function if it finds them. The point of this discussion is that a Dictionary is not a scalar variable; it isn't limited solely to string or numeric values. Because it can contain Object variables, you must be careful to test the value before assigning it to a variable and use the Set keyword when necessary:

```
If varType(d("someKey")) = vbObject then
    Set myValue = d("someKey")
Else
    myValue = d("someKey")
End If
```

The Dictionary object exposes several other properties that you will find useful; the most useful of these are the Count and Exists properties. The Count property tells you how many items are in the Dictionary and the Exists property tells you whether an item at a specific key or index exists:

```
Dim d
Set d = Server.CreateObject("Scripting.Dictionary")
d.Add "Name", "Bill"
Response.Write d.Exists("Name") & "<br>"
' writes True
Response.Write d.Count
' writes 1
```

Table 11.1 lists all the `Scripting.Dictionary` object's properties and methods.

TABLE 11.1: Scripting.Dictionary Object Methods and Properties

Method/Property	Description
Add (key, value)	Adds a new string key to the Dictionary associated with the specified value. If the key already exists, an error occurs.
CompareMode (CompareMethod)	Controls the way the Dictionary object compares keys. Sets or returns one of the `CompareMethod` enumeration constants. Use the predefined VBScript constants vbBinaryCompare and vbTextCompare rather than the `CompareMethod` constants listed below:
	BinaryCompare (0) (case-sensitive)
	TextCompare (1) (case-insensitive) DatabaseCompare (2) (NA).
Count (read-only)	Returns the count of the number of associations in the Dictionary object.
Exists(key) Property	Returns a Boolean value that shows whether the specified key exists.
Item(key or index)	Returns or sets a value associated with the specified string key or integer index.
Items	Returns a variant array of all the values currently stored in the Dictionary.
Key (key)Property (write-only)	Changes a string key from one string to another.
Keys	Returns a variant array of all the keys currently stored in the Dictionary.
Remove(key)	Removes the specified key, if it exists.
RemoveAll	Removes all keys.

NOTE   The documentation doesn't list the `DatabaseCompare` as a valid `CompareMode` value for a Dictionary object. Although it doesn't raise an error if you use it, it acts exactly like the `TextCompare` constant.

Project: Exploring the Dictionary Object

One use for a Dictionary object is to pass values to a function when you don't know the exact number of values you might pass. For example, suppose you get a set of strings from a form where users input their address into a `<textarea>` tag. You know that at least one of the strings must contain a number, and at least one must contain a zip code. The problem is, you don't know how many lines are in the address, so you must write a function that accepts a variable number of arguments.

In this project, you should create a Dictionary object that holds each string from the `<textarea>` tag in the form and pass the Dictionary as the function argument. Inside the function, use the properties of the Dictionary object to extract the strings. Check each string to see if it contains a numeric value or a zip code, then return a new Dictionary object that contains only the street number and the zip code.

For example, suppose a user entered this address:

```
1594 St. John St.
Charters, IL 85002
```

You should return a Dictionary object with two keys and two items as shown in Table 11.2.

TABLE 11.2: Contents of Dictionary Object After Analyzing Address

Key	Item
"StreetNumber"	1594
"ZipCode"	85002

Because addresses may contain more than one line, you may assume (for the purposes of this exercise) that any number contained in the first line is the street number. You may also assume that the last number contained in the last line is the zip code. You should return both five- and nine-digit zip codes properly.

For example, suppose a user entered this address:

```
1220 N. 5th Ave.
Building 342 #1500
Dubai, SD 23929-9201
```

Regardless of how many lines of text the user enters, you should return a Dictionary object with two keys and two items—the street number from the first line containing text and the zip code from the last line containing text. Be sure to remove any white space from the text entered by the user before analyzing the address. If you print the Dictionary, you should get two lines of output as shown in Table 11.3.

TABLE 11.3: Contents of Dictionary Object With 9-Digit Zip Code

Key	Item
"StreetNumber"	1220
"ZipCode"	23929-9201

The `ch11i4.asp` file on the CD contains the main code for this project. Note that the file uses the `#Include` directive to include the `general.inc` file, which contains the `newDictionary`, `printDictionary`, and `printArray` functions you saw earlier in this chapter.

I suggest you try to build the project first, then compare your results with the `ch11i4.asp` file in the `Chapter11` directory on the CD. Don't expect your code to be identical to mine; there are literally thousands of possible variations—all of which will produce roughly the same results.

C H A P T E R

T W E L V E

File Access with ASP

In addition to the Dictionary object, the Microsoft Scripting Runtime also contains a group of objects that provide access to the file system of the host computer. The name for a group of objects dedicated to a common purpose is an object model. In its first implementation, the File System Object (FSO) object model was extremely simple and provided only limited functionality. With the latest release (version 5.1), the model has grown considerably more complex, but now provides nearly complete access to the Windows file system.

The Scripting FSO Object Model

The objects in the Scripting FSO object model function much like the intrinsic ASP objects you've already seen, with the minor exception that you cannot create some of these objects directly. For example, you can obtain a reference to a TextStream object only by using the methods of the FSO object model. Table 12.1 lists the objects and collections in the FSO object model.

TABLE 12.1:   Objects and Collections in the FSO Object Model

Object/Collection	Description
FileSystemObject Object	This is the base object of the FSO model. You must create a FileSystemObject object to gain access to some of the other objects in the FSO model. The FileSystemObject has many methods that duplicate those in other FSO objects. This duplicate functionality helps flatten the model and helps minimize the need to create multiple objects to accomplish a task.
Drive Object	Lets you access drive information from all attached drive devices, including network drives.
Drives Collection	Provides a list of all drives attached to the system regardless of type, and regardless of whether the drive has media. For example, a CD-ROM drive attached to your system appears in the Drives collection even if no CD is currently in the drive.
File Object	Provides system-level file access. You can create, delete, and move files, or query the system for information about a file, such as its name, path, and other properties.
Files Collection	Contains a list of all files within a folder.
Folder Object	Provides system-level folder access. You can create, delete, and move folders, or query the system for information about a folder, such as its name, path, and other properties.
Folders Collection	Contains a list of all folders (directories) within a Folder.
TextStream Object	Allows you to read and write text files.

Accessing Files

In ASP applications, most file access happens automatically. When you reference a file, the server opens the file, reads its contents, or executes it; but even in Web applications, you sometimes need to read information from or write information to a file.

TIP   Because direct file access isn't part of the Web model, it doesn't (currently) work with virtual filenames; you must provide a physical path to read or write data to files.

You can use the `Request.ServerVariables` collection to determine the physical path for the current file of your application, and you can use the `Server.MapPath` method to map a virtual path to a physical path. Therefore, the requirement for physical paths shouldn't keep you from accessing files easily—in fact, these methods make it easy for you to use relative paths throughout your application. I heartily recommend that you force yourself to use virtual paths and perform the translation. I also recommend that you store all external resource names and paths in `global.asa` or in an external file that you can load when your application starts. If you follow this advice, your application will be more portable and have fewer problems than if you hard-code external resource names and paths.

Checking Whether a File Exists

Before you open a file, you often need to know whether it exists or not; you don't want to overwrite critical file contents. To check for the existence of a file, create a FileSystemObject object and use its `FileExists` method. To create a FileSystemObject object, use the `Server.CreateObject` method. The `FileExists` method returns True if the file exists, and False otherwise. You must provide the absolute or relative path to the file, but you can often take advantage of the `SpecialFolders` method, which returns the physical path for named folders in the Windows operating system. For example, Listing 12.1 shows how to check for the `NotePad.exe` file in the Windows folder.

LISTING 12.1   Checking if a File Exists

```
Dim s
Dim fs
Set fs = Server.CreateObject("Scripting.FileSystemObject")
s = "The file 'NotePad.exe' exists "
s = s & "in the directory " & fs.GetSpecialFolder(WindowsFolder)
```

```
s = s & ": <b>" & fs.FileExists _
   (fs.GetSpecialFolder(WindowsFolder) & "\notepad.exe") _
   & "</b>"
Response.Write s
' writes "The file 'NotePad.exe' exists in the directory
' C:\WINNT: True" (on my system)
```

Because you should repeat code as rarely as possible, you can wrap this functionality up nicely in an easy-to-use function. Listing 12.2 shows how to avoid writing all the code in the previous listing every time you want to check for the existence of a file.

LISTING 12.2   **Wrap FileSystemObject Functionality (fileOps.inc)**

```
Function newFileSystemObject()
   set newFileSystemObject = _
      Server.CreateObject("Scripting.FileSystemObject")
End Function
Function fileExists(aFileSpec)
   fileExists = newFileSystemObject.FileExists(aFileSpec)
End Function
Function getSpecialFolder(whichFolder)
   getSpecialFolder = _
      newFileSystemObject.getSpecialFolder(whichFolder)
End Function
Function getWindowsFolder()
   getWindowsFolder = getSpecialFolder(WindowsFolder)
End Function
Function getSystemFolder()
   getSystemFolder = getSpecialFolder(SystemFolder)
End Function
Function getTempFolder()
   getTempFolder = getTempFolder(TemporaryFolder)
End Function
```

The functions shown in Listing 12.2 wrap object creation, file existence, and special folder retrieval in a way that makes these operations easy and intuitive to use. For example:

```
Response.Write fileExists(getWindowsFolder & "\notepad.exe")
' writes True
Response.Write fileExists(getSystemFolder & "\x7893025q.txt")
' writes False (on my system)
```

For folders other than the three special folders, WindowsFolder, SystemFolder, and TemporaryFolder, you must provide the physical path string yourself. For example, to find out if the file explorer.exe exists in the path C:\Program Files\

Internet Explorer, you can call the `fileExists` function with the concatenated path and filename as an argument:

```
Dim s
s = "C:\Program Files\Internet Explorer\iexplore.exe"
Response.Write fileExists(s)
' writes True (on my system)
```

Similarly, to discover if the subdirectory of the current directory called `Sub1` contains a file called `myFile.txt`, you can retrieve the current directory using the `Server.MapPath` method, then check for the file:

```
s = Server.MapPath("sub1/myFile.txt")
Response.Write fileExists(s) & "<br>"
' writes False (on my system)
```

Opening Files

To open a file, use the `FileSystemObject` method to create a TextStream object. The TextStream object provides sequential access to files. Unfortunately, as its name implies, it only reads and writes text files. If you want to read and write binary files you need to create your own object or obtain a suitable commercial or shareware object.

You may use either of two `FileSystemObject` methods to create a TextStream object. The older version, called `OpenTextFile`, accepts more arguments than the newer `OpenAsTextStream` method. Both methods return a TextStream object.

The `OpenTextFile` method accepts up to four arguments:

```
TextStream = FileSystemObject.OpenTextFile _
    (filename, <iomode>, <create>, <format>)
```

The last three arguments are optional, but—as with all optional arguments— you should get in the habit of supplying them whenever you use a function.

The `iomode` argument can be one of three `IOMode` constants. I've listed the numeric value of each constant in parentheses after the constant name.

ForReading (1)   Opens a file in read-only mode. If you try to write to a file opened in this mode, an error occurs.

ForWriting (2)   Opens a file for write operations. If the file already exists, opening the file in this mode destroys the contents of the file.

ForAppending (8)   Opens a file such that write operations append new content to the end of the file.

The `create` argument tells the `FileSystemObject` method whether to create a new file if the file doesn't already exist. Note that this does not keep the `FileSystemObject` method from overwriting an existing file when you open the file using the `IOMode` `ForWriting` constant. Pass `True` when you want the `FileSystemObject` method to create a new file, and `False` if you do not want to create a new file. The default value is `False`. If you try to open a file that doesn't exist and the `create` argument is `False`, an error occurs.

The `format` argument tells the `FileSystemObject` method whether the file contains ASCII or Unicode. You use one of the `TriState` constants (called `TriState` because the argument takes one of three values) to specify the file format. I've listed the numeric value of each constant after the constant name.

TriStateTrue (-1)   Opens the file as Unicode.

TriStateFalse (0)   Opens the file as ASCII.

TriStateUseDefault (-2)   Opens the file using the system default setting.

In some development environments, such as Visual InterDev, you can add a project reference to the Microsoft Scripting Runtime, which defines the `IOMode` and `TriState` constants. In other environments, you may need to define the constants.

WARNING   I've defined the constants in the `fileOps.inc` file. If you are using Visual InterDev and you have set a reference to the Microsoft Scripting Runtime you must either remove the project reference, or delete or comment out the constants in the `fileOps.inc` file.

Listing 12.3 shows how to use the TextStream object. The code uses the `#include` directive to include the functions from the `fileOps.inc` include file you saw in the previous section.

LISTING 12.3   **Example of the TextStream Object**

```
<%@ Language=VBScript %>
<% Option Explicit %>
<!- #INCLUDE FILE="fileOps.inc" ->
<html>
<head>
</head>
<body>
<%
dim fs
dim ts
```

```
set fs = newFileSystemObject()
set ts = fs.OpenTextFile("ch12test1.txt", _
    ForAppending, True, TristateUseDefault)
ts.WriteLine "Got here<br>"
ts.close
set ts = nothing
set ts = fs.OpenTextfile("ch12test1.txt", _
    ForReading, False, TristateUseDefault)
Response.Write ts.ReadAll
ts.Close
set ts = nothing
set fs = nothing
%>
</body>
</html>
```

There are several methods in the previous listing that you haven't seen before. First, the code creates a FileSystemObject method, then uses its OpenTextFile method to create a TextStream object suitable for appending text to a file. The listing writes the text "Got here
" to the file using the writeLine method. The writeLine method writes text plus a carriage return/linefeed (vbCRLF) combination to the file. Next, the code closes the file using the Close method, and then reopens the file in read-only mode. The readAll method reads the entire contents of a TextStream object into a variable.

The TextStream Object

Having obtained a TextStream object, you use its methods and properties to read and write data to the TextStream object's associated file. When you're done, you close the TextStream object, just as you would a regular file. Table 12.2 lists the methods and properties of the TextStream object.

TABLE 12.2: TextStream Object Methods and Properties

Method/Property	Description
AtEndOfLine Property	True if the file pointer is at the end of a line (if the next character is a new-line (vbLF) character).
AtEndOfStream Property	True if the file pointer is at the end of the file.
Close Method	Closes the file associated with the TextStream object.
Column Property	Returns the current column number (the character position within a line) of the file pointer. The column number for the first character in any line is 1. This is a read-only property.

Continued on next page

TABLE 12.2:   TextStream Object Methods and Properties

Method/Property	Description
Lines Property	Returns the line number of the current line. The first line number is 1. This is a read-only property.
Read Method	Reads a specified number of characters from the file and returns the text.
ReadAll Method	Reads the entire contents of the file.
ReadLine Method	Reads the next line from the file, up to a newline (vbLF) character. The method returns the text of the line read, but does not return the newline character.
Skip Method	Skips a specified number of characters forward in the file. Attempting to skip backward in the file by providing a negative offset causes an error.
SkipLine Method	Only applies when reading a file. Moves the file pointer to the beginning of the next line.
Write Method	Writes a specified string to the file beginning at the current file pointer.
WriteLine Method	Writes a specified string to the file and appends a newline character (vbLF) at the end of the line.
WriteBlankLines Method	Writes a blank line to the file. A blank line contains only a newline character (vbLF).

Writing Text to Files

The TextStream object only deals with sequential files. That means to insert text anywhere except at the end of the file, the computer must rewrite the entire file. It's a slow operation, even for a disk Input/Output (I/O) operation. Keep this in mind as you work with text files. In contrast, appending text to a file is a relatively fast operation.

Typically, you read and write text files one line at a time. One common use for a text file is to log operations. For example, suppose you want to keep track of the SessionID and IP address of each person who enters and leaves your Web site. Pretend at this point that you don't care about duplicate records—you just want to log entry and exit. For example:

```
Function logEntryOrExit(anAction)
    Dim fs
    Dim ts
    Dim anIP ' user's IP address
    Dim aLogFile
    Dim aPath

    ' get the physical path
    aPath = Request.ServerVariables("PATH_TRANSLATED")
```

```
' strip the file name from the path
aPath = Left(aPath, instrRev(aPath, "\"))

' add the log file name
aLogFile = aPath & "ch11log.txt"

' create a FileSystemObject and open the file
Set fs = Server.CreateObject _
    ("Scripting.FileSystemObject")
Set ts = fs.OpenTextFile(aLogFile, 8, True, 0)

' get the reqesting IP address
anIP = Request.ServerVariables("REMOTE_ADDR")

' append the information to the file
ts.WriteLine anAction & ": " & FormatDateTime(now(), _
    vbGeneralDate) & ", " & anIP & ", " & _
    Session.SessionID

' clean up
ts.Close
Set ts = Nothing
Set fs = Nothing
End Function
```

Note that the line that creates the TextStream object (the one starting with Set ts =) uses the constant values rather than the constant names. That's because you can't write an #INCLUDE directive in global.asa. You could, of course, define the constant names within the function to make it easier to read.

In the Session_OnStart event, call the logEntryOrExit function with an "Entry" argument. In the Session_OnEnd event in global.asa, call the function with an "Exit" argument:

```
Sub Session_OnStart
    Call logEntryOrExit("Entry")
End Sub
Sub Session_OnEnd
    Call logEntryOrExit("Exit")
End Sub
```

If you save the code in your global.asa file, you'll find that it logs session entry but not session exit. That's because the global.asa file has some restrictions—rather severe ones on session exit. You can't use #INCLUDE directives, you can't use the Server.MapPath method, and you can't use the Response.Write method to write text or HTML to the browser, which can cause problems—especially during the Session_OnEnd event. In addition, buggy code in or called from the Session_OnEnd event doesn't raise a visible error at runtime (although it does at compile time). Therefore, unless you log a result to a database or a disk file, you have no way of knowing whether your Session_OnEnd code is working properly. I recommend that you debug code you plan to run in global.asa in some other file first. After you have debugged the code, move it to the global.asa file and make minimal modifications.

You can work around the global.asa file restrictions during Session startup by using the Response.Redirect method to redirect the user to another file. Perform any necessary processing in that file. Unfortunately, you can't do this during Session_OnEnd processing, so the Response.Redirect command isn't available at that point—because you can't respond. The Request object isn't available either, because the Session_OnEnd happens via code when you issue the Session.Abandon command or when the session has been idle for the number of minutes specified by the Session.Timeout setting.

To fix the problem and log exit from the site, you should make some alterations. Listing 12.4 shows the fixed code, which properly logs both session entry and session exit.

LISTING 12.4   Logging Session Entry and Exit (global.asa – ch11)

```
Sub logEntryOrExit(anAction)
    Dim fs
    Dim ts
    Dim anIP ' user's IP address
    Dim aLogFile
    Dim aPath
    aPath = Request.ServerVariables("PATH_TRANSLATED")
    ' strip the file name from the path
    aPath = Left(aPath, instrRev(aPath, "\"))
    ' add the log file name
    aLogFile = aPath & "ch12log.txt"
    Session("Logfile") = aLogFile
    Set fs = Server.CreateObject _
        ("Scripting.FileSystemObject")
    Set ts = fs.OpenTextFile(aLogFile, 8, True, 0)
    anIP = Request.ServerVariables("REMOTE_ADDR")
    Session("IP") = anIP
    ts.WriteLine anAction & ": " & FormatDateTime(now(), _
        vbGeneralDate) & ", " & anIP & ", " & _
        Session.SessionID
    ts.Close
    Set ts = Nothing
    Set fs = Nothing
End Sub
```

```
Sub Session_OnStart
    call logEntryOrExit("Entry")
    Session.Timeout=1
End Sub
Sub Session_OnEnd
    Dim fs
    Dim ts
    Dim anIP ' user's IP address
    Dim aLogFile
    aLogFile = Session("LogFile")
    Set fs = Server.CreateObject _
        ("Scripting.FileSystemObject")
    Set ts = fs.OpenTextFile(aLogFile, 8, True, 0)
    ts.WriteLine "Exit" & ":  " & FormatDateTime(now(), vbGeneralDate) _
    & ", " & Session("IP") & ", " & Session.SessionID
    ts.Close
    Set ts = Nothing
    Set fs = Nothing
End Sub
```

Reading Text from Files

To read text from a file, you follow almost the same procedure as when writing to a file. You can read a specific number of characters, one line at a time, or the entire file all at once. For example, to read the file you created in the previous section, you create a `Scripting.FileSystemObject` method, use it to open the file, which returns a TextStream object, and then use one of the TextStream object's methods. Listing 12.5 reads the ch12log.txt file you created in the previous section one line at a time and displays it in the browser.

LISTING 12.5   Reading the ch11log.txt File

```
<%@ Language=VBScript %>
<% option explicit %>
<!- #INCLUDE FILE="fileOps.inc"->
<%
dim fs
dim ts
Dim aPath
Dim aLogFile

aPath = Request.ServerVariables("PATH_TRANSLATED")
' strip the file name from the path
```

```
aPath = Left(aPath, instrRev(aPath, "\"))
' add the log file name
aLogFile = aPath & "ch12log.txt"
set fs = newFileSystemObject()
Set ts = fs.OpenTextFile(aLogFile, ForReading, False,
    TriStateUseDefault)
while not ts.AtEndOfStream
    Response.Write ts.ReadLine & "<br>"
wend
ts.Close
set ts = nothing
set fs = nothing
%>
```

Listing 12.5 uses the AtEndOfStream property to test whether the stream has reached the end of the file. As long as the AtEndOfStream property returns false, the code reads the next line from the file and writes it to the browser, along with a <br> tag. (Remember that the ReadLine method doesn't return the newline character, and that browsers treat newline characters as white space.)

Project: Read and Write Form Content

In Chapter 6, *The Request Object*, in the section *Working with Forms*, I promised to discuss data validation after you learned more about VBScript and JScript. To fulfill that promise, unlike the previous projects in this book, I'm going to walk you through part of this project.

In this project, you will read the contents of a form filled out by a user and write the contents of that form to a file in such a way that you can retrieve it later. The form contains text fields for a user-selectable login and password, the person's name, and the person's color preference.

You will store the user's preferences in a file, then restore those preferences when the user subsequently logs in without selecting a color preference or entering a name. You should store the preferences in a single file. To retrieve a preference, read the file one line at a time until you find the user's login and matching password. Note that you must not allow more than one row in the file with the same login and password.

I've listed parts of the code in the rest of this section. You can find the complete code for the project in the Chapter12\ch12i5.asp file on the CD. Hints: Use the ReadAll function and the Split function to separate the lines. Your code doesn't have to be identical to mine; there are innumerable variations—all of which could produce roughly the same results.

I have included this project to give you some hands-on practice in validating user input and manipulating files. It is not meant to be a lesson in login/password security, and you should not consider this a viable means for storing logins and passwords on the server, because it's insecure. Similarly, this is not a very scalable method for retrieving stored logins and passwords. I have deliberately left out all the important aspects of security. You'll see a much more effective way of handling such information after you've learned about database access using ASP.

In the browser, the form looks like Figure 12.1.

FIGURE 12.1:

Read and write form content (ch12i5.asp)

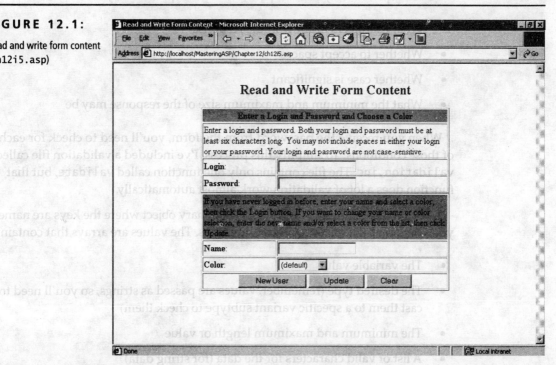

The first time you use the form, follow the directions to enter a login and password, and to enter your name and select a color preference. On subsequent entries, you only need to enter your name and password. The code will retrieve your name and color preference and change the colored rows in the table to match your preference.

The code stores user information in the `Chapter12\ch12Project1.txt` file. Internally, the code uses the `fileOps.inc` and `general.inc` files you saw in this chapter and in Chapter 11, *The Scripting Dictionary Object*, to read and write to the user information file. All the logic to find and update user information is in the main file.

Whenever you have a form into which users enter information, the first thing you should consider is how to validate the information. Unless your form lets the user enter free-form text, you should try very hard to make sure the information you're about to process meets the data specifications for the code. Not only does form data validation improve your programs, it also saves you from writing extensive error-checking code within your functions. By the time the data reaches any data-processing code, you should already know that the data meets your minimum specification for that code.

For example, when you ask a person to enter a password, you must decide:

- What characters to allow in the response
- Whether to accept spaces
- Whether case is significant
- What the minimum and maximum size of the response may be

When you receive the password from the form, you'll need to check for each of those conditions. To simplify this process, I've included a validation file called `validation.inc`. The file contains only one function called `validate`, but that function does a lot of validation work almost automatically.

The `validate()` function accepts a Dictionary object where the keys are names you want to use in validation error messages. The values are arrays that contain:

- The variable value
- The desired type (remember, values are passed as strings, so you'll need to cast them to a specific variant subtype to check them)
- The minimum and maximum length or value
- A list of valid characters for the data (for string data)
- An `allowNull` flag controlling whether or not the variable must contain a value

The function returns a string containing a default error message if any value fails any validation test. In this project, for example, the user can enter three pieces of information: a login, a password, and optionally, a name. Users can select a color name, but because they don't enter any text, you only need to determine whether they actually selected an item. The following code validates the form values:

```
' store user-entered values in local variables for speed and
    convenience
Login = Trim(Request("Login"))
Password = Trim(Request("Password"))
```

```
Name = Trim(Request("Name"))
ColorPref = Request("ColorPref") ' user's color choice

' create a Dictionary to pass to the validate function
Set d = newDictionary() ' see function in general.inc

' create an array of values for each item you want to validate
d.Add "Login", Array(Login, vbString, 6, 10, AlphaNumeric, False)
d.Add "Password", Array(Password, vbString, 6, 10, AlphaNumeric, False)
If Len(name) > 0 Then
   d.Add "Name", Array(name, vbString, 2, 40, AlphaNumeric & " ",
False)
End If

' validate the response values
msg = validate(d)

' if validation fails, the variable msg contains a default error
     message.
If len(msg) <> 0 Then
   ' Validation failed
End If
```

The `validate()` function does the real work. It loops through the set of keys in the Dictionary, using the information in the array to check for null strings and cast each value to an appropriate type. The function treats each variable type slightly differently. For each type, it checks the minimum and maximum length or value, and finds invalid characters. If the function encounters an error or finds an inappropriate value, it returns an error string.

```
Function validate(d)
Dim name
Dim conditions
Dim value
Dim subtype
Dim minVal
Dim maxVal
Dim allowNull
Dim i
Dim typeString
Dim validChars
validate = vbNullString
For Each name In d
   conditions = d(name)
   subtype = conditions(1)
   minVal = conditions(2)
   maxVal = conditions(3)
```

```
validChars = conditions(4)
allowNull = conditions(5)
If Not allowNull Then
    If conditions(0) = vbNullString Then
        validate = "<font color='#ff0000'>You must " _
            & "enter a name. </font><BR>"
        Exit Function
    End If
End If
On Error Resume Next
Select Case subtype
Case vbInteger
    typeString = "Integer"
    value = CInt(conditions(0))
    If IsNumeric(minVal) Then
        If value < minVal Then
            validate = "<font color='#ff0000'>" & name _
                & " must be at least " & minVal & _
                ".</font><BR>"
            Exit Function
        End If
    End If
    If IsNumeric(maxVal) Then
        If value > maxVal Then
            validate = "<font color='#ff0000'>" & name & _
                " may be at most " & minVal & ".</font><BR>"
            Exit Function
        End If
    End If
    d.Item(name) = value
Case vbLong
    typeString = "Long"
    value = CLng(conditions(0))
    If IsNumeric(minVal) Then
        If value < minVal Then
            validate = "<font color='#ff0000'>" & name & _
                " must be at least " & minVal & ".</font><BR>"
            Exit Function
        End If
    End If
    If IsNumeric(maxVal) Then
        If value > maxVal Then
            validate = "<font color='#ff0000'>" & name & _
                " may be at most " & minVal & ".</font><BR>"
            Exit Function
        End If
    End If
```

```
                    d.Item(name) = value
            Case vbString
                typeString = "String"
                value = CStr(conditions(0))
                If Len(value) < minVal Then
                    validate = "<font color='#ff0000'>" & name & _
                    " must be at least " & minVal & _
                    " characters long.</font><BR>"
                    Exit Function
                ElseIf Len(value) > maxVal Then
                    validate = "<font color='#ff0000'>" & name & _
                    " may only be " & maxVal & _
                    " characters long.</font><BR>"
                    Exit Function
                End If
                ' check characters
                If Len(validChars) > 0 Then
                    For i = 1 To Len(value)
                        If InStr(validChars, Mid(value, i, 1)) = 0 Then
                            validate = "<font color='#ff0000'>" & name _
                            & " contains invalid characters.</font><BR>"
                            Exit Function
                        End If
                    Next
                End If
                d.Item(name) = value
            Case vbDate
                typeString = "Date"
                If Not IsDate(conditions(0)) Then
                    validate = "<font color='#ff0000'>" & name & _
                    " is not a valid date.</font><BR>"
                    Exit Function
                End If
                value = CDate(conditions(0))
                If IsDate(minVal) Then
                    If value < minVal Then
                        validate = "<font color='#ff0000'>" & name & _
                        " must be at least " & minVal & ".</font><BR>"
                        Exit Function
                    End If
                End If
                If IsDate(maxVal) Then
                    If value > maxVal Then
                        validate = "<font color='#ff0000'>" & name & _
                        " may be at most " & minVal & ".</font><BR>"
                        Exit Function
                    End If
```

```
            End If
            d.Item(name) = value
        Case Else
            Err.Raise 50000, "validate", _
            "Unhandled variable type in validate function."
            ' add more types as needed
        End Select
        If Err.Number <> 0 Or VarType(value) <> subtype Then
            validate = "<font color='#ff0000'>Invalid value-" _
            & name & ". Expected a " & typeString & _
            " value.<BR></font>"
            Exit Function
        ElseIf typeString = "String" And Len(value) _
            < minVal Then
            validate = "<font color='#ff0000'>" & name & _
            " must be at least " & minVal & _
            " characters long.</font><BR>"
            Exit Function
        ElseIf typeString = "String" And Len(value) _
            > maxVal Then
            validate = "<font color='#ff0000'>" & name & _
            " may only be " & maxVal & _
            " characters long.</font><BR>"
            Exit Function
        End If
    Next
End Function
```

A user can enter the page either by entering a new login and password, then pressing the New User button, or by entering an existing login and password. In either case, the user may optionally enter a name and select a color. Regardless of which button the user clicks, the form submits the data to the server. If the user selects the Clear button, the server ignores any submitted values and re-displays the form without any values. If the user selects New User, or Update, the code validates the input, then opens the ch12Project1.txt file and searches it for a matching login/password combination. If no match exists, the code either adds a new record (user selected New User) or returns an error message (user selected Update).

If you were using a full programming language, you would probably define a structure to hold each user's information, then write those structures as records to a binary-formatted file. Unfortunately, scripting languages only let you work with serial text files as streams. As long as you're adding (appending) information to a text file, that works fine; however, when you're trying to update information anywhere else in the file, you must rewrite the entire file.

The project uses four functions to read user information, find, update, and add users: `getUsers`, `findUser`, `updateUser`, and `addUser`. Because the project always needs the file contents, the program reads the file contents into a local variable each time it's run:

```
' read the contents of the user file
arrUsers = getUsers()
```

The `getUsers` function returns an array of lines from the file:

```
Function getUsers()
    Dim s
    s = readTextFile(aFilename)
    getUsers = Split(s, vbCrLf)
End Function
```

The arguments to the `findUser` function are the array of comma-delimited file lines, each containing the information for a single user, and the login and password of the user to search for. The function loops through the array, splitting each line into four pieces of information: the login, password, name, and color preference for that user. To improve the code's readability, I defined constants for those four index values:

```
Const USER_LOGIN = 0
Const USER_PASSWORD = 1
Const USER_NAME = 2
Const USER_COLORPREF = 3
```

The `findUser` function uses the `StrComp` method to compare the first two values in the line with the login and password entered by the user and passed as arguments:

```
Function findUser(users, aLogin, aPassword)
    Dim i
    Dim aLine
    Dim arrLineVals
    For i = 0 To UBound(users)
        ' retrieve the individual values in
        ' the line as a string
        aLine = users(i)
        aLine = Trim(aLine)
        If Len(aLine) > 0 Then
            ' retrieve the individual values in the line
            'as an array
            arrLineVals = Split(aLine, ",")
            ' compare the first value with the login
            If StrComp(arrLineVals(USER_LOGIN), _
                aLogin, vbTextCompare) = 0 Then
```

```
            If StrComp(arrLineVals(USER_PASSWORD), _
                aPassword, vbTextCompare) = 0 Then
                    findUser = i + 1
                Exit Function
            End If
        End If
      End If
  Next
End Function
```

If the findUser function finds a matching line, it returns the index value of that line, plus 1. There are several reasons why I return the index value offset by 1. First, you'll find that it's common practice for collections, file systems, and other counted values to start with 1 rather than 0. Second, if you allow 0 as a valid return—meaning you found a matching value in the first array position—your function is harder to read. As coded, you can call the function like this:

```
If not findUser(arrUsers, Login, Password) Then
    ' do something
End If
```

If the function doesn't find a matching user, it returns 0. Not (0) evaluates to True, therefore the statement works.

The opposite check is equally intuitive:

```
If findUser(arrUsers, Login, Password) Then
    ' do something
End If
```

Any user found will have an index + 1 value greater than 0; therefore the If condition evaluates to True and the conditional code executes properly.

In contrast, if you allow the 0 return you must write:

```
If findUser >= 0 Then
    ' do something
End If
```

Finally, it's convenient to have a 1-based count for the array or collection. It's not intuitive to say that the array has three positions—it's much easier to say it has four positions, because people think in 1-based terms.

If you find a matching user in the file, and the user selects the Update button on the form, you can replace that array item with a new line, then rewrite the file to update the record. Note that this function subtracts 1 from the index passed to the function because the caller doesn't know that it's working with a 0-based array. It retrieves that array item, splits it into the four values, updates the name and color preference, joins the items back into a single, updated text line, replaces the original line in the user array, then rewrites the file:

```
Function updateUser(arrUsers, anIndex, aName, aColor)
    Dim aLine
    Dim arrLineVals
    Dim s
    anIndex = anIndex - 1
    If anIndex >= 0 And anIndex <= UBound(arrUsers) Then
        aLine = arrUsers(anIndex)
        arrLineVals = Split(aLine, ",")
        arrLineVals(USER_NAME) = aName
        arrLineVals(USER_COLORPREF) = aColor
        aLine = Join(arrLineVals, ",")
        arrUsers(anIndex) = aLine
        s = Join(arrUsers, vbCrLf)
        Call writeTextFile(aFilename, s, True)
    End If
End Function
```

Adding a user is simply a matter of creating the new line for the file and appending it:

```
Function addUser(aLogin, aPassword, aName, aColor)
    Dim aLine
    aLine = aLine = aLogin & "," & aPassword & "," & _
        aName & "," & aColor
    Call AppendToTextFile(aFilename, aLine, True)
End Function
```

The File Transfer Protocol

The File Transfer Protocol (FTP) provides a method for transferring files between a client and server. Unfortunately, ASP doesn't have any built-in support for FTP or for any method of moving files between the client and server. Fortunately, both Microsoft and numerous third-party vendors supply file transfer solutions for ASP. Microsoft's version is the Posting Acceptor (supplied with the NT 4.0 Option Pack and Site Server, or available for download from Microsoft). Some third-party solutions are ASPUpload and SA-FileUp. You can find these third-party components at http://www.15seconds.com, a good resource for all ASP-related issues.

A bigger question is whether you truly want to use the FTP protocol at all. To post a file to your server, a user must either have an account on the server or you must allow anyone to post files via anonymous FTP. Creating and managing multiple accounts on your NT server is painful and time-consuming. Anonymous

FTP is inherently insecure. For Web applications, HTTP is often a better protocol for managing file transfers because:

- You can authenticate a user via your application rather than through user accounts management

- Firewalls usually allow HTTP uploads, but often deny FTP transfers

- You can take advantage of HTTPS to encrypt transfers

I don't recommend using the Posting Acceptor because it has numerous problems, but it is free.

Sending and Receiving Files

Sending a file to a browser is relatively easy. All you need to do is write an ftp link. When users click the link, the browser brings up a dialog box asking where they want to put the file. The following example would let users download the `sample.exe` file. (This is just an example; the file does not exist on the CD.)

```
<a href="ftp://localhost/MasteringASP/Chapter12/sample.exe">Download
Sample</a>
```

However, there are some problems. File types transfer differently. HTM and TXT files transfer directly and load into the browser. Other file types, such as EXE and ZIP files, ask the user whether to open the file or save it (see Figure 12.2).

FIGURE 12.2:

Internet Explorer File Download dialog

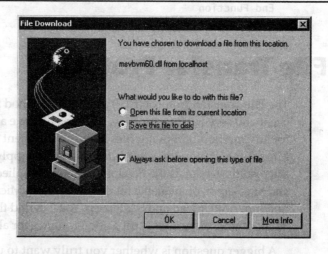

When the user clicks the OK button, the browser opens a file dialog box and lets the user select the location of the file. In other words, you don't have any control over where the user will put the file. Consequently, some sites wrap the download functionality inside an EXE file. First, users elect to run the EXE file, which then copies other files automatically to the correct locations on the user's computer. Even more commonly, the site designer compresses all the files into a self-expanding executable file. Users download that file and place it anywhere on the computer. When they run the file, it expands all the files, then automatically runs an install program that moves the dependent files to the correct locations.

If you want to save an HTM or TXT file on a user's computer, the self-expanding executable is the simplest method; otherwise, the browser downloads the file to its cache and displays the file without displaying the download dialog.

Uploading files to the server is another matter. HTML and ASP provide little assistance. There are three problems to solve before you can successfully transfer files from a client to a server. First, you have to encode the file data in some known manner on the client to package it into HTTP packets. Second, on the server, you need to recognize the encoding scheme and be able to write binary data to a file. Third, you need some method to allow transfers via anonymous access to IIS, yet still be able to authenticate users before allowing them to write files on your server.

Typically, HTTP requires URL-encoded data. The encoding scheme recognizes some characters directly, such as letters and numeric characters, but encodes all other characters using a three-character code consisting of a percent sign and the hexadecimal representation of the byte value to be transferred. For example, a space (ASCII 32) URL-encodes to %20. Because most binary file data consists of characters that HTTP doesn't recognize, URL-encoding a binary file often expands the data by two or three times the original size of the file.

To avoid the inefficiencies of sending a file much larger than the original, there are three alternatives for sending file data via HTTP. HTTP 1.1 introduced the PUT method. You obtain the file data on the client and post it using a form containing the attribute `method="put"`. When you post form data using the PUT method, IIS authenticates the user and writes the file data directly to the Web server. You can't intercept the data with ASP code, because IIS processes the request before it reaches your ASP page. Therefore, you can write forms with ASP that use the PUT method, but you won't know if any problems occur. Don't use the PUT method.

RFC1867, which became standard with HTML 3.2, uses the MIME type `multipart/form-data`. Browsers that recognize this MIME type can send and receive binary file data without URL-encoding every byte. To upload a file, use an `<input type="file">` tag, then include the attribute `enctype="multipart/form-data"` in your form tag:

```
<form name="frmSendFile" method="post" enctype="multipart/form-data">
```

RFC1867 is probably the best choice for now. Unfortunately, ASP doesn't understand the `multipart/form-data` MIME type. To take full advantage of RFC1867, you need to install an ISAPI extension on your server. The Microsoft Posting Acceptor, SA-FileUp, and ASPUpload all work by intercepting the upload, then either sending messages to your application or redirecting to a specific ASP page after the upload has completed.

Most recently, Microsoft has proposed the Web Distributed Authoring and Versioning (WebDAV) extensions that allow client applications, like Word or FrontPage, to read and write files directly from Web servers. Like the PUT method, WebDAV interacts with the Web server directly—you can't (currently) intercept the requests with ASP code. I suspect that will change in the future.

The Posting Acceptor Object

The Posting Acceptor object (CPSHost.dll) is an ISAPI filter that runs on IIS. Microsoft installs the Posting Acceptor with later versions of the NT 4.0 Option Pack (when you select the Site Server Express option). You also get the DLL with Visual Studio 6, Visual InterDev 6, or Visual Basic 6. Finally, you can download it directly from Microsoft at http://www.microsoft.com/Windows/software/webpost/post_accept.htm.

The Posting Acceptor object uses the multipart/form-data MIME type. It works by accepting a posted file, then redirecting to an ASP script after completing the upload. It posts the uploaded filename, which allows you to confirm the upload operation. Note that you can't deny the upload based on the file type because you don't regain control in ASP until after the upload is complete.

Third-Party Options

In addition to the Microsoft Posting Acceptor, there are numerous shareware components that let you manage file uploads and downloads. Two of these that I've already mentioned are ASPUpload and SA-FileUp. These third-party components provide many more features than the Microsoft Posting Acceptor.

Build Specialized Page Counters

In this project, you'll use a file to count the number of times a person visits your pages—with a twist. You want to count the first visit to your page during any session, but ignore subsequent visits during that session. To do that, you'll create a file that contains two entries per line: the page name and the total count for that page. Finally, because the solution must be automatic, if you add new pages to the site, you want those pages added and counted automatically.

Save the page names and counts in the `MasteringASP/Chapter12/Ch12Project2.log` file.

Here's a sample file:

`Ch12i7.asp,22`

`Ch12i8.asp,18`

`Ch12i9.asp,5`

And so on.

Hints: Don't read the file for every request and don't store the data in a Dictionary object. On the CD, the main project code is in the `counter.inc` file. The three files, `ch12i7.asp`, `ch12i8.asp`, and `ch12i9.asp`, are for test purposes only. They show the current user count for each page. Each ASP file includes the `counter.inc` file. Don't expect your code to be identical to mine; there are literally thousands of possible variations—all of which could produce roughly the same results.

In the next chapter, you'll see standard debugging and error-handling techniques that will improve the quality of your code and speed up ASP development.

CHAPTER

THIRTEEN

Debugging ASP and Error-Handling

- **Defensive Coding—How to Avoid Errors**

- **How to Approach Error-Handling**

- **Err Object Properties and Methods**

- **Raising Errors**

- **Logging Errors**

- **Debugging ASP Scripts**

If you're a VB programmer, you'll soon find that trapping errors and debugging in ASP is relatively primitive when compared to Visual Basic. If you're not a VB programmer, you are in for a treat if you ever get to use the VB debugging facilities. In this chapter, you'll see how to trap for errors and debug ASP pages by writing debug statements to the browser.

Defensive Coding—How to Avoid Errors

The best approach to handling errors is to eliminate them. Unfortunately, as long as I've been coding, I still haven't learned how to do that in all cases. In some cases, errors are beyond your control. Hardware breaks down, networks are sometimes unreliable, files get lost or moved, resource names change—the list of possibilities is endless. Even if such errors aren't your responsibility, it's your job to handle them insofar as it's possible for you to do that at the application level. Therefore, the first, and truly the only, rule you really need to learn to write solid code is that the closest your program will ever come to a perfect environment is the one on your development machine. Once your code leaves that home it has to stand on its own two feet. As soon as it leaves, everything will break unless you practice defensive coding.

Defensive coding is not the mark of a paranoid programmer—it's the mark of an intelligent programmer. The lack of good error-handling examples is one of the worst things about magazine articles and books about programming. There's often not enough room or time to add the error-handling code. In addition, the volume of error-handling code sometimes visually overshadows the code that does the real work.

If you built the project "Read and Write Form Content" at the end of the previous chapter, you saw a small example of defensive coding in the `validate` routine. Sure, I could have shown you the project without input validation, but that would be unrealistic. In the real world, people enter numbers where they're supposed to write letters, they mistype dates, they leave out required information, they unwittingly add spaces, carriage returns, and control characters to their input. For example, the password "123456" and "123456 " are not the same—the second password has a space at the end.

Validating input is just one point where you need to code defensively. Any external resources used by your program comprise another potentially large source of errors. External resources are files, directories, databases, COM DLLs, or any other source of information or code required by your program that doesn't reside within your program—in other words, anything you didn't code yourself. While you may think these resources are static, they aren't. People move and rename files and directories—even executable files. A database location may change, newer (or sometimes older) installations may overwrite critical DLLs, and servers may change names.

Even date formats may become obsolete—witness the enormous amount of money spent recently to upgrade systems that used two-digit years. You may not be able to control all of these changes, but that doesn't matter. Coding defensively is an attitude you use to force yourself to think about the possibilities for things to go wrong. Control those things you can; write good error messages for those you can't.

Until recently, scripting languages have had extremely weak error-handling capabilities. JScript had no error-handling until version 5, but now has try...catch block error-handling. VBScript has only one method to handle errors—ignore them. Fortunately, the ASP engine itself traps errors; otherwise, your program could crash the server and potentially damage other applications. There's no panacea—you'll be struggling with errors for your entire programming career; but in this chapter, I want to provide you with an approach to error-handling that can help minimize the problems you will encounter.

How to Approach Error-Handling

One way to approach the understanding of a large subject is to categorize it into smaller chunks. There are five main categories of errors:

- Syntax errors
- Parameter/input errors
- Logic errors
- Errors in external code
- Resource errors

Your goals in trapping these types of errors should be, in order of importance, to:

1. Keep your application from crashing
2. Provide as much information as possible about the error
3. Propagate errors back to a critical decision point
4. Degrade gracefully

In an ASP application, you can't usually crash the application—the ASP engine won't let that happen, but by default, any error that occurs on a page causes the ASP engine to stop executing the code on that page. To your users, it doesn't matter whether your application crashed or not. If users can't accomplish their goals, then your program is broken, no matter what the reason. For error-handling purposes, each page of your application is a program unto itself. Therefore, the first goal is to make the page run properly. Failing that, the second goal is to write an informative error message to the user, who may then inform you, and to a log file or the Application event log. The more information you provide about the error, the easier it will be for you to find and fix it. You don't want your page to stop processing—even with good error messages—if you can work around the error, so you'll want to categorize errors based on how they affect your application. For example, input errors should never be fatal; you should trap them all and provide reasonable error messages so the user or programmer providing the information can solve the problem.

The third goal—to propagate errors back to a critical decision point—refers to the process of trapping errors in lower-level routines. When an error occurs in a low-level routine, that traps the error and passes upward through the call stack until the error reaches a critical decision point. In an ASP script, the critical decision point is usually the code running on that page. You generally don't have much need to propagate errors in VBScript because you won't normally be very deep in the call stack for any given page.

During development you should focus primarily on the first two goals. In some cases, you won't have enough information to do more than approach the third goal during initial development. Later in the development cycle, after several users have tested your application, you should be able to improve your error-handling to solve common problems. Save the fourth goal until last. It does you no good to spend lots of time degrading gracefully if that causes you to miss fatal errors that crash the application.

The *On Error Resume Next* Statement

Your first and only line of defense in an ASP application is the On Error Resume Next statement. The statement doesn't stop errors from occurring—it just causes VBScript to continue execution on the next line. Take heed that means the next line, not the next logical statement. Listing 13.1 contains an example. Suppose a variable contains an Array, but you accidentally test it as if it were a String.

LISTING 13.1   **On Error Resume Next Example (ch13i2.asp)**

```
Dim aVar
aVar = Array()
On Error Resume Next
If StrComp(aVar, "20005", vbTextCompare) = 0 Then
    Response.Write "aVar is not an array<br>"
    Response.Write TypeName(aVar)
Else
    Response.Write "The variable is: " & aVar
End If
```

When you run the example in Listing 13.1, it prints "aVar is not an array" despite the fact that the value in the variable aVar is clearly a Variant array, as shown by the output of the next line, "Variant()". The point is that the error in the If condition doesn't cause the condition to evaluate to False—the code performs as if the condition were True. This behavior can cause serious errors in your program.

Similarly, the On Error Resume Next statement can hide syntax and logic errors in your programs. For example, the following code will cause an error if you comment out the On Error Resume Next statement:

```
<%@ Language=VBScript %>
<%
    dim anArray
    anArray = array()
    on error resume next
    if anArry(0) = 1 then
        response.write "True"
    end if
%>
```

I believe you should minimize the use of On Error Resume Next in your code. So if that's the only error-trapping statement available to you, and I'm advising you to use it sparingly, when is it appropriate?

Use the On Error Resume Next statement when you anticipate that an error outside your control may occur. For example, when you open a file, you always take a chance that the file may not open properly. The file may be in use by another process, the file may be corrupt, or you may not have permission to open the file. Your ability to trap these types of errors in advance is usually limited. For example, you can check whether the file exists before you open it, but until you actually issue a call to open or write to a file, you won't know whether your permission settings allow you to perform the operation. In this case, using On Error Resume Next is completely appropriate—as long as you immediately check for an error and then turn off error-trapping.

The *On Error Goto 0* Statement

You turn off error-trapping with the On Error GoTo 0 statement. Probably the most common error programmers make with the On Error Resume Next statement is forgetting to turn off error-trapping. Listing 13.2 shows a marginally appropriate error-trapping example.

LISTING 13.2   **Appropriate Use of** `On Error Resume Next` **(ch13i3.asp)**

```
<%@ Language=VBScript %>
<% option explicit %>
<!-- #INCLUDE FILE="../include/fileOps.inc" -->
<%
' open a non-existent file
dim s
dim aFilename
On Error Resume Next
aFilename = "x:\MasteringASP\missing.txt"
s = readTextFile(aFilename)
if err.number <> 0 then
    Response.Write "Error: " & Err.number & "<br>" & "Source: " &
    Err.source & "<br>" & "Description: " & Err.description & "<br>" &
    "Unable to open the file " & aFilename & "."
end if
%>
```

When you turn off error-trapping with the `On Error GoTo 0` statement, you also clear any current error values, so check for errors before your code executes the `On Error GoTo 0` statement. For example, the following variation on Listing 13.2 never displays an error, even though an error occurs:

```
<%@ Language=VBScript %>
<% option explicit %>
<!-- #INCLUDE FILE="../include/fileOps.inc" -->
<%
' open a non-existent file
Dim s
Dim aFilename
On Error Resume Next
aFilename = "x:\MasteringASP\missing.txt"
s = readTextFile(aFilename)
On Error GoTo 0
If Err.Number <> 0 Then
    Response.Write "Error: " & Err.Number & "<br>" & "Source: " & _
    Err.Source & "<br>" & "Description: " & Err.Description & "<br>" & _
    "Unable to open the file " & aFilename & "."
End If
%>
```

I mentioned that the code in Listing 13.2 is only marginally acceptable. That's because if I were to critique this code, I'd say the programmer was just lazy. An error trap was used to catch an error that could have been caught by using the `fileExists` method.

Another appropriate use for the On Error Resume Next statement is when the check code to anticipate an error is slower than simply trapping the error. For example, to check file write permission you would need to instantiate an ActiveX permission-checking component, and read the file Access Control List (ACL) before beginning the write operation. It's much faster to trap that type of error than to write code to avoid the error. The key is that it's an anticipated error.

Your biggest problems will arise when you don't have any parameter- or resource-checking in a routine. Code that works every time in development often fails in production—often due to outside factors.

Err Object Properties and Methods

The VBScript Err object has only a few methods and properties, some of which are not applicable in VBScript. You can still take advantage of them by using them in a slightly different context.

Method/Property	Description
Clear Method	Clears the properties of the Err object.
Description Property	(optional) A String value containing a brief description of the last error that occurred. Despite the fact that this property is optional, you should always set it if you raise your own errors.
HelpContext Property	(optional) In VB, this property can contain a context ID that refers to a specific topic in a Windows help (HLP) file. When you click the Help button on an error dialog, you see the topic associated with that context ID. This property has no meaning in server-side VBScript, but you can use the property to hold a long value for other purposes.
HelpFile Property	(optional) In client-side VBScript, this property can contain the name of a Windows help (HLP) file, which can then display an appropriate explanation. Normally, this property has no meaning in server-side VBScript, but you can use the property to hold the name of an HTM or ASP file containing help, as I'll show you later in this chapter.

Continued on next page

Method/Property	Description
Number Property	(Required) Contains the number of the error that occurred.
Raise Method	Allows you to set the Err object properties and cause an error to occur.
Source Property	A String value containing the source of the error. In ASP scripts, the Source property usually contains the name of the currently executing ASP file.

Error-Handling in VBScript

Consider this scenario. You have a file containing a list of items that you use to fill an HTML select list on the browser. You want to display a list of names associated with UserIDs. The user submits a form containing the UserID associated with the selection back to your application. You want to open the file and search the list of users for a matching entry. What are the possibilities for failure?

- You could fail to open or read from the file.

- The file could be empty.

- Critical data may be missing.

- The user could submit the form without selecting an item.

- The item selected might not match an item in the file.

Generic error-handlers will catch all these errors, but may not provide enough information to solve the problem. You saw how to avoid and handle the last two types of errors through data validation in Chapter 12, *File Access with ASP*. Let's take the first three error possibilities and analyze each of them from the standpoint of each error type and goal.

Failing to Open or Read from the File

This is a call to external code. You can't control whether the FileSystemObject statement will be able to read the file; therefore, you should trap the call with the On Error Resume Next statement. You always test for errors after the call. If the call fails, you can raise an error in your routine. If you follow the guidelines in this section, either your application will decide what to do at that point, or it will propagate the error back to a critical decision point.

The following code illustrates one way to handle external errors:

```
Sub showSelectList
    Dim fs
    Dim ts
    Dim methodName
        methodName = "showSelectList"
    On Error Resume Next
    Set fs = Server.CreateObject("Scripting.FileSystemObject")
        Set ts = fs.ReadAll
        rs.close
    If Err.Number <> 0 then
        Err.Raise Err.Number, Err.Source & ", " & _
        methodName, Err.Description & _
        "Error obtaining data " & _
        "for selection list."
    End If
    ' continue processing
End Sub
```

The methodName variable is necessary because VB and VBScript don't provide run-time access to the call stack. This is an irritating oversight that should have been remedied in VB several versions ago. However, by appending the current method-Name variable to the Err.Source property whenever an error occurs, you can log the state of the call stack without too much effort. You can also maintain a global array or stack object to store the state of the call stack, thus allowing you to log it when errors occur.

For external errors, use the On Error Resume Next statement and test for errors when the call returns. If the external code raises an error you'll catch it in the If Err .Number <> 0 trap. You have two choices whenever you catch an error: you can decide how to handle the error at that point (create a critical error-handler) or you can defer the decision to the calling code. Of course, you can also choose to ignore the error, but that's only advisable under certain specific circumstances, when you're expecting the error to occur and know exactly what you'll do if the error does occur.

The File Could Be Empty

Treat this as a parameter or input error. If the external code successfully opens and reads the file, then it has performed successfully. It's your responsibility to check if the returned data is valid. Normally, your critical error-handler for parameter or input errors is internal to the routine. You don't always want to raise an error for parameter/input validation failure—sometimes you want to return a message. The deciding factor here is usually the type of person using your application. If the person calling your code is an end-user, return an error code and an informative status message. The purpose is to enable the end-user to communicate coherently with technical support so they can help solve the problem. Remember, in many cases you'll be the one supporting the application. If the user is another programmer using your DLL as a data source or functional component, return a detailed error message, like the following:

```
Sub showSelectList
    Dim s
    Dim methodName
    methodName = "showSelectList"
    On Error Resume Next
    S = readTextFile(aFilename)
    If Err.Number <> 0 then
        Err.Raise Err.Number, Err.Source & methodName, _
        Err.Description & "Error obtaining data " & _
        "for selection list."
    End If
    If len(trim(s)) = 0 then
        ' no data, do something, maybe raise an error
    End If
    ' etc
```

Critical Data May Be Missing

At this point, you're reasonably sure that no error occurred while retrieving the file data, and that the file actually contains at least one row of data. Now you need to make sure the file contains the values you need. I call errors like these Resource errors because they stem from missing, unreachable, or invalid resources, which include file and database data, network connections, database connections, etc. Refer to the following code:

```
Sub showSelectList
    Dim s
    Dim methodName
    Dim lines
    Dim lineVals
    Dim aLine
    Dim i
    methodName = "showSelectList"
    On Error Resume Next
    S = readTextFile(aFilename)
    If Err.Number <> 0 then
        Err.Raise Err.Number, Err.Source & methodName, _
        Err.Description & "Error obtaining data " & _
        "for selection list."
    End If
```

```
If len(trim(s)) = 0 then
    ' no data, do something, maybe raise an error
End If
' split the data on the carriage-return / line feed characters
lines = split(s, vbCrLf)
For i = 0 to Ubound(lines)
    aLine = lines(i)
    ' split each line at the commas
    lineVals = split(aLine, ",")
    ' Each line should contain a UserID, a LastName, and a First Name
    ' check the number of items in lineVals
    if Ubound(lineVals) <> 2 then
        Err.Raise 50001, methodName, "A required field " _
        & "is missing in the list of user names."
    End If
    ' continue processing...
Next
End Sub
```

You can now be sure that each line contains the required number of values, but you can't be sure that the individual values are in the correct order. It's often difficult to be completely certain with text data, but you can check the format for known types and you can always check the length to ensure that the data is present. Refer to the following code:

```
Dim aUserID
Dim aLastName
Dim aFirstName
' ...code to retrieve the lines - see previous listing
For i = 0 to Ubound(lines)
    aLine = lines(i)
    ' split each line at the commas
    lineVals = split(aLine, ",")
    ' Each line should contain a UserID, a LastName, and a First Name
    ' check the number of items in lineVals
    if Ubound(lineVals) <> 2 then
        Err.Raise 50001, methodName, "A required field " _
        & "is missing in the list of user names."
    End If
    ' retrieve the values
    aUserID = lineVals(0)
    aLastName = lineVals(1)
    aFirstName = lineVals(2)
    ' Check the UserID - in this case, UserIDs are 6 numbers
    ' like 123456, stored in string form. All IDs are > 0
    if val(aUserID) = 0 then
        Err.Raise 50001, methodName, "Line" & cstr(i) & _
```

```
            & " contains an invalid User ID value."
        end if
        ' last names are > 1 and <= 20 characters
        if len(aLastName) < 1 or len(aLastName) > 20 Then
            Err.Raise 50001, methodName, "Line" & cstr(i) & _
            & " contains an invalid Last Name."
        end if
        if len(aFirstName) < 1 or len(aFirstName) > 20 Then
            Err.Raise 50001, methodName, "Line" & cstr(i) & _
            & " contains an invalid First Name."
        end if
    Next
```

As you may remember from Chapter 12, *File Access with ASP*, there are other data validity checks you might make here, but because the file contains data your program presumably wrote, you could conceivably ignore these checks altogether. In other words, if your program only writes good data to the file, do you need to check that data again when you read the file? The answer depends on how trusting (or paranoid) you are. For example, in the future, another programmer might also access the file, the file might be corrupt, a person might manually open and change the file. In this scenario, because you (I hope) validated the data before you wrote the file, a cursory check of format and length is probably sufficient to catch unwanted changes.

Raising Errors

In the examples in the previous chapter, I showed you how to raise errors. For example, the following code fragment raises an error if a string is too long or too short:

```
if len(aFirstName) < 1 or len(aFirstName) > 20 Then
    Err.Raise 50001, methodName, "Line" & cstr(i) & _
    & " contains an invalid First Name."
end if
```

There's no point raising errors in an ASP script unless the code that raises the error is inside a function, a subroutine, or inside code in a COM object. The reason is that raising errors in a top-level ASP script causes the script to stop processing. You can raise errors at the top level, and you'll see the standard error display with your error information, but you're probably better off redirecting to an error page. The error page would display only those parts of an error that you want to reveal to your clients. For example, while debugging a page that connects to several different databases, you might want to display the connection string used to connect to that database, so you can easily tell exactly which database call caused the problem. In production, however, you would never want to display the connection string because it's a security risk.

For example, you can set an Application-scope flag to determine whether the page is running in debug or production mode. If the flag value shows that the site is in debug mode, the error-display page displays all the error information; otherwise, it displays only the error number and a generic error message. Listing 13.3 shows a function called showError and a short ASP example. The code for the showError subroutine is in the include file MasteringASP\include\errors.inc on the CD.

LISTING 13.3   **Using a Subroutine to Display Errors (errors.inc, ch13i4.asp)**

```
' ********************************************************
' The following code is in the errors.inc file
' ********************************************************
Sub showError(ErrNumber, ErrTitle, ErrSource, _
    ErrDescription, ErrHelpFile, appendError)
    On Error GoTo 0
    Dim s
    dim debugFlag
    debugFlag = cbool(Application("DebugFlag"))
    Select Case debugFlag
    Case True
    With Response
        If Not CBool(appendError) Then
            .Clear
            .Write "<html><head><title>" & ErrTitle & _
            "</title></head><body>"
        End If
        .Write "<table align='center' width='85%' " & _
        "border='1' cols='2'>"
        .Write "<tr><td colspan='2'>An error has " & _
        "occurred in this application. The error was " & _
        "not caused by anything that you did.</td></tr>"
        If VarType(ErrHelpFile) = vbString Then
            If ErrHelpFile <> vbNullString Then
                .Write "Click <a href='" & ErrHelpFile & _
                "'>Help</a>for more information about " & _
                "this error."
            End If
        End If
        .Write "</tr><td width='30%'>Error Number:" & _
        "</td><td width='*'><b>" & ErrNumber & _
        "</b></td></tr>"
        .Write "</tr><td width='30%'>Error Source:" & _
```

```
          "</td><td width='*'><b>" & ErrSource & _
          "</b></td></tr>"
          .Write "</tr><td width='30%'>Error Description:" & _
          "</td><td width='*'><b>" & ErrDescription & _
          "</b></td></tr>" &
          .Write "</table>"
          If Not CBool(appendError) Then
              .Write "</body></html>"
          End If
      End With
      Case False
      With Response
          If Not CBool(appendError) Then
              .Clear
              .Write "<html><head><title>" & ErrTitle & _
              "</title></head><body>"
          End If
          .Write "<hr>"
          .Write "<table align='center' width='85%' " &_
          "border='1' cols='2'>"
          .Write "<tr><td colspan='2'>An error has " & _
          "occurred in this application. The error was " &_
          "not caused by anything that you did.</td></tr>"
          If VarType(ErrHelpFile) = vbString Then
              If ErrHelpFile <> vbNullString Then
                  .Write "<tr><td colspan='2'>Click <a href='" & _
                      ErrHelpFile & "'>Help</a> for more " & _
                      "information about " & _
                      "this error.</td></tr>"
              End If
          End If
          .Write "</tr><td width='30%'>Error Number:" & _
          "</td><td width='*'><b>" & ErrNumber & _
          "</b></td></tr>"
          .Write "</tr><td width='30%'>What To Do:" & _
          "</td><td width='*'><b>" & "Print this screen, " & _
          "then call the Help Desk at 7-4500 to report " &_
          "this error." & "</b></td></tr>"
          .Write "</table>"
          If Not CBool(appendError) Then
              .Write "</body></html>"
          End If
      End With
   End Select
End Sub
```

```
' ******************************************************
' The following code is in the ch13i4.asp file
' ******************************************************
<%@ Language=VBScript %>
<% option explicit %>
<!--
    #INCLUDE VIRTUAL="/MasteringASP/include/fileOps.inc"
-->
<!--
    #INCLUDE VIRTUAL="/MasteringASP/include/errors.inc"
-->
<%
Dim s
Dim arr
Dim item
Function getSelectList()
Dim s
Dim aFilename
On Error Resume Next
aFilename = getScriptPath() & "aNonExistentFile.txt"
s = readTextFile(aFilename)
Response.Write "ErrNumber=" & Err.Number & "<BR>"
If Err.Number <> 0 Then
    Call showError(Err.Number, "Title", Err.Source, _
    Err.Description & "<br>" & _
    "Error obtaining data for selection list.", _
    "fileErrorHelp.htm#" & Err.Number, False)
    Response.End
End If
On Error GoTo 0
getSelectList = s
End Function
%>
<html><head><title>Error Processing Example</title></head>
<body>
<form name="frmErrTest" method="post">
    <%
    s = getSelectList()
    s = Split(s, vbCrLf)
    %>
    <select name="aList">
    <%
    For Each item In s
        Response.Write "<option value='" & item & "'>" & _
        V & "</option>"
    Next
```

```
       %>
     </select>
  </form>
  </body>
  </html>
```

As I mentioned earlier, although you can't use the Err object's `HelpFile` property as it was intended on the server, you can use the property to hold the name of a help file. The code in Listing 13.3 shows how you can use the error number to provide a link to a help file containing more information about the error. The help file itself, `ErrorHelp.htm` (not shown in Listing 13.3) contains a set of named anchor tags that correspond to the error numbers. You could easily extend this scheme. For example, you might want to redirect to the help file rather than display any specific error.

You should also notice that the `getSelectList` subroutine in Listing 13.3 uses the `On Error Resume Next` statement before calling the `readTextFile` function to read the non-existent file. By anticipating the error, you can check the `Err.Number` property in the next statement. In this case, the `getSelectList` subroutine functions as a critical error-handler because it displays the error message and stops processing. To see how you can move the critical error-handler, Listing 13.4 shows the same page with alterations. The altered code transfers error-handling responsibility up to the top level by re-raising the error rather than handling it inside the `getSelectList` subroutine.

LISTING 13.4   **Moving the Critical Error-Handler (ch13i5.asp)**

```
<%@ Language=VBScript %>
<% option explicit %>
<!--
    #INCLUDE VIRTUAL="/MasteringASP/include/fileOps.inc"
-->
<!--
    #INCLUDE VIRTUAL="/MasteringASP/include/errors.inc"
-->
<%
Dim s
Dim arr
Dim item
Function getSelectList()
    Dim s
    Dim aFilename
    aFilename = getScriptPath() & "aNonExistentFile.txt"
    s = readTextFile(aFilename)
    Response.Write "ErrNumber=" & Err.Number & "<BR>"
    On Error Resume Next
    If Err.Number <> 0 Then
```

```
            Err.Raise Err.number, Err.source & _
            "; getSelectList()", _
            Err.Description & "<br>" & _
            "Error obtaining data for selection list."
        End If
        On Error Goto 0
        getSelectList = s
End Function
%>
<HTML><HEAD><title>Error Processing Example</title></HEAD>
<BODY>
<form name="frmErrTest" method="post">
    <%
        On Error Resume Next
        ' Change this variable to False in production
        Application("DebugFlag") = True
        s = getSelectList()
        If Err.number <> 0 Then
            Call showError(Err.Number, _
            "Error Retrieving Select List", Err.Source, _
            Err.Description & "<br>" & _
            "Error obtaining data for selection list.", _
            "ErrorHelp.htm#" & Err.number, False)
            Response.End
        End if
        s = Split(s, vbCrLf)
    %>
    <select name="aList">
    <%
        For Each item In s
            Response.Write "<option value='" & item & "'>" & V &
"</option>"
        Next
    %>
    </select>
</form>
</BODY>
</HTML>
```

There's one other change you may have already noticed if you ran the code in the previous listing. I set the Application("DebugFlag") variable to True, so you can see the difference in the output between development mode error display and production mode error display. Normally, of course, you would set the Application("DebugFlag") mode in your application's global.asa file. Figure 13.1 shows how the error appears in a browser with the Application("DebugFlag") variable set to False (production mode).

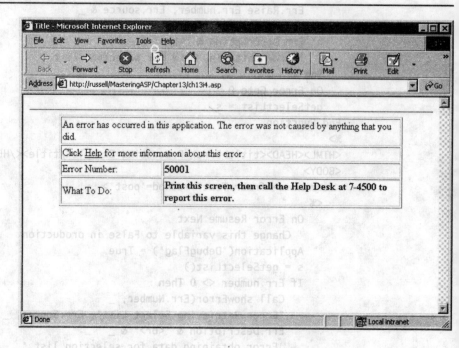

Figure 13.2 shows the same error in a browser with the `Application("Debug-Flag")` variable set to `True` (development mode).

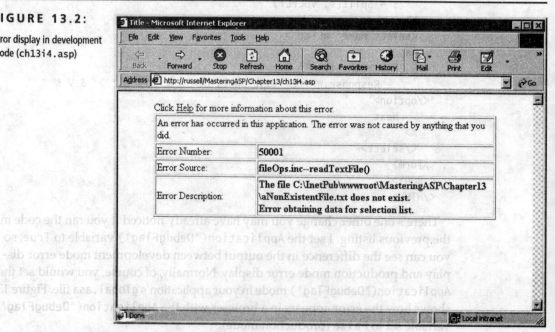

Logging Errors

When you're developing an application, you typically work on a local server—or at least on a server where your development activity won't cause much disruption. When errors occur, you can usually see them in your browser. However, after you deliver an application, your ability to track code defects in that manner disappears; you're now dependent on your users to give you information about what they were doing when the error occurred. As you probably know, you don't always get that information, and even when you do get verbal reports, the quality of the information is often suspect.

You can partially solve this problem through the use of the IIS log and by logging errors for your application. If you are lucky enough to have `write` permission for a directory on the server, you can log errors to your own error files. If you're not, you can still log errors to the Windows NT Application event log.

Logging Errors to a File

To log errors to a file, you'll need to build a subroutine that you can call whenever an error occurs. For example, the following routine logs errors to a named file:

```
Sub logError(aFilename, ErrNumber, ErrSource, _
    ErrDescription)
    Dim s
    s = FormatDateTime(Now, vbGeneralDate) & ", "
    s = s & ErrNumber & ", "
    s = s & Chr(34) & ErrSource & Chr(34) & ", "
    s = s & Chr(34) & ErrDescription & Chr(34)
    Call appendToTextFile(aFilename, True, s)
End Sub
```

To test the logging capability, you must allow `write` access for the `MasteringASP` `Chapter13` directory for the anonymous Internet account (`IUSR_MACHINENAME`). Listing 13.5 contains a short file to log an error.

LISTING 13.5   **Error Logging Example (ch13i5.asp)**

```
<%@ Language=VBScript %>
<% option explicit %>
<!--
    #INCLUDE VIRTUAL="/MasteringASP/include/fileOps.inc" -->
<!--
    #INCLUDE VIRTUAL="/MasteringASP/include/errors.inc" -->
<%
```

```
Call logError(getScriptPath() & "ch12Error.log", _
    50000, "ch13i6.asp", _
    "This is a test error description.")
%>
```

This example performs minimal error logging. It writes the current date and time, the error number, source, and description. You may also want to log the name of the page and (if applicable) the routine that was executing at the time the error occurred. If you follow my recommendation and append the current script name to the Err .Source property whenever you raise an error again, you'll be able to log not only the current script, but also the entire call stack, which can be critical when you're trying to debug your application.

Logging Errors to the IIS Log

If you don't have write permission to any directory on the server, the good news is that you can still log errors. The bad news is that you need access to the Windows IIS log to see them.

To log an error to the IIS log, use the Response.AppendToLog method. You pass the method a string to append to the event log.

NOTE   The string you pass to the Response.AppendToLog method must not contain commas because the log uses the comma character as a field separator.

For this method to work, you'll need to check your IIS logging options. Follow this procedure:

1. Open the MMC and right-click on the Default Web Site (or on the site where your MasteringASP Web resides). Click the Properties button to open the Default Web Site Properties dialog (see Figure 13.3).

2. Select the Web Site tab and make sure the Enable Logging checkbox is checked.

3. Make sure the Active log format selection is set to W3C Extended Log File Format.

4. Click the Properties button next to the Active log format selection box to view the Extended Logging Properties dialog (see Figure 13.4).

5. Note the location of the log file. The IIS log normally resides in your %SystemRoot%\System32\LogFiles directory, but because that's also a customizable property, the location may be different on your server.

FIGURE 13.3:

Default Web Site Properties
dialog

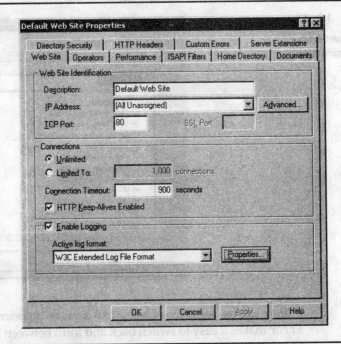

FIGURE 13.4:

Extended Logging Properties
dialog

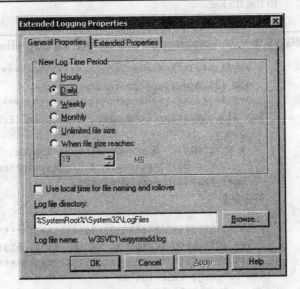

6. Click on the Extended Properties tab (see Figure 13.5) and make sure the URI Stem checkbox is checked. The URI Stem checkbox must be checked for the `Response.AppendToLog` method to work.

7. Close all the dialogs by clicking the OK buttons.

FIGURE 13.5:

Extended Properties tab –
Extended Logging Properties
dialog

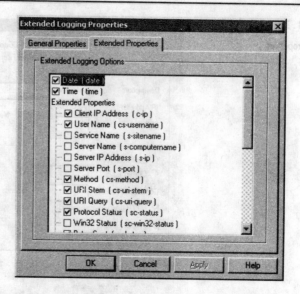

Now you can log errors. Listing 13.6 contains an example. The subroutine IISLog-Error makes it easy to switch back and forth between logging to a file and logging to the IIS log.

LISTING 13.6   **Logging Errors to the IIS Log File (ch13i7.asp. errors.inc)**

```
' ******************************************************
' Sub IISLogMessage is in errors.inc
' ******************************************************
Sub IISLogMessage(ErrNumber, ErrSource, ErrDescription)
  dim s
  s = "Error: " & ErrNumber & "; Source: " & ErrSource & _
        "; Description: " & ErrDescription
  Call Response.AppendToLog(s)
End Sub


' ******************************************************
' The following script is in the file ch13i7.asp
' ******************************************************
<%@ Language=VBScript %>
<% option explicit %>
<!--
#INCLUDE VIRTUAL="/MasteringASP/include/errors.inc" -->
<%
Call IISLogMessage(50000, "ch13i7.asp", "This is a test error descrip-
tion.")
%>
```

In the log, the text appears on a single line. When you run the script, IIS appends a line to the IIS log that is similar to the following:

```
1999-11-22 02:30:06 169.254.25.129 - GET /MasteringASP/Chapter13/ch13i7
.asp Error:+50000;+Source:+ch13i7.asp;+Description:+This+is+a+test+error+
description. 200 0 Mozilla/4.0+(compatible;+MSIE+5.01;+Windows+NT+5.0)
ASCLIENTDEBUG=1;+SITESERVER=ID=79eb3d5438d3eb10cf23d6f3cff266e2;
+ASPSESSIONIDGQGGQUDQ=OAELMJJCCKKPMKHLDBEOLJDD -
```

You can see the text of the message—with the spaces encoded to + signs—in the text of the Application log by using the Event Viewer application.

Debugging ASP Scripts

Despite your best efforts, errors occur during development and you must track them down. Debugging ASP is still awkward, even at the best of times. There are several different environments for writing ASP scripts, but to my knowledge, only Microsoft's Visual InterDev environment has debugging facilities. The Visual Inter-Dev debugger isn't nearly as good as Visual Basic's debugger, but it can be of great help in finding errors in your scripts. However, in this book I'm going to show you how to use the older but equally effective approach of writing debug output to the screen. Writing debug output isn't dependent on any particular environment—you can use it effectively even with a plain text editor.

Unless you're using Visual InterDev with its built-in debugging capabilities, the principal tool you can use to debug ASP scripts is the Response.Write statement. Unfortunately, expertise in debugging isn't a skill that you can teach in a clear manner, because effective debugging depends in large part on prior knowledge and experience. However, you can follow a specific process to help you find and fix errors. For example, Listing 13.7 has an error in it.

LISTING 13.7   Debugging ASP Scripts (ch13i8.asp)

```
<%@ Language=VBScript %>
<%
dim d
dim V
Set d = Server.CreateObject("Scripting.Dictionary")
d.Add "LastName", "Parsons"
d.Add "FirstName", "Bill"
d.Add "Telephone", "509-267-5830"
d.Add "Address", "2534 N. 14th St., Barstow, NY 89082"
d.Add "Email", "bParsons@aol.com"
```

```
%>
<html>
<head>
<title>Debugging ASP</title>
</head>
<body>
<table align="center" width="75%" border="1" cols=2>
    <tr>
        <td width="30%" align="left">
            <b>Last Name</b>:
        </td>
        <td width="*" align="left">
            <%=d("LastName")%>
        </td>
    </tr>
    <tr>
        <td width="30%" align="left">
            <b>First Name</b>:
        </td>
        <td width="*" align="left">
            <%=d("FirstName")%>
        </td>
    </tr>
        <tr>
            <td width="30%" align="left">
                <b>Telephone</b>:
        </td>
        <td width="*" align="left">
            <%=d("Telephone")%>
        </td>
    </tr>
        <tr>
            <td width="30%" align="left">
                <b>Address</b>:
        </td>
        <td width="*" align="left">
            <%=d("Address")%>
        </td>
    </tr>
        <tr>
            <td width="30%" align="left">
                <b>Email</b>:
        </td>
        <td width="*" align="left">
            <%=d("EMail")%>
```

```
          </td>
        </tr>
      </table>
    </body>
  </html>
```

When you look at listing 13.7 in a browser, you see a table containing the Dictionary properties (see Figure 13.6).

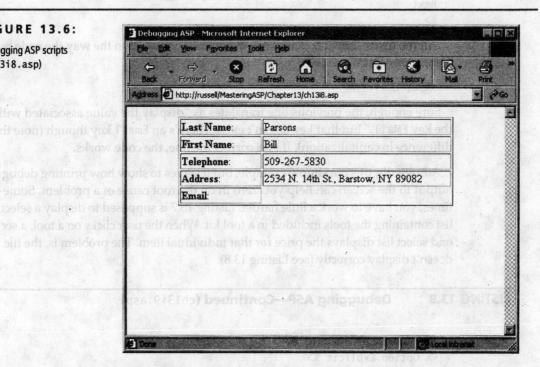

The problem is that one of the table columns is blank. The Email field doesn't appear. How can you find out what the problem is? First, look at what you know:

1. The code creates the Dictionary object properly, otherwise the first assignment would raise an error.

2. The values are apparently assigned properly because no error occurred— but because of the way Dictionary objects work, you can't be absolutely sure of that.

3. The HTML code is well formatted—all the rows and columns appear in the table.

Next, look at what you don't know. You don't know if the Dictionary contains the Email value, or whether it just isn't showing up properly. One test is to write a loop that displays all the keys and values in the Dictionary. Insert the following code after the `<body>` tag, but before the `<table>` tag:

```
<%
for each V in d
    Response.Write V & "=" & d(V) & "<br>"
next
%>
```

All the fields show up. Therefore, the problem must lie in the way the code references the Email value.

```
<%=d("EMail")%>
```

Sure enough, the previous line translates as "display the value associated with the key EMail," but that key doesn't exist. There's an Email key though (note the difference in capitalization). If you correct the line, the code works.

Admittedly, this is a simple example, but it serves to show how printing debug output to the screen can help you zero in on the root cause of a problem. Sometimes, you have to work a little harder. Listing 13.7 is supposed to display a select list containing the tools included in a tool kit. When the user clicks on a tool, a second select list displays the price for that individual item. The problem is, the file doesn't display correctly (see Listing 13.8).

LISTING 13.8   **Debugging ASP—Continued** (ch13i9.asp)

```
<%@ Language=VBScript %>
<% Option Explicit %>
<!-- #INCLUDE VIRTUAL="/MasteringASP/include/fileOps.inc" -->
<!-- #INCLUDE VIRTUAL="/MasteringASP/include/errors.inc" -->
<!-- #INCLUDE VIRTUAL="/MasteringASP/include/general.inc" -->
<%
' read the ProductList.txt file
dim s
dim d
dim arrItems
dim anItem
dim arrTmp
dim aName
dim aPrice
dim toolKitPrice
dim separatePriceTotal
s = readTextFile(getScriptPath() & "ProductList.txt")
```

```
            arrItems = split(s, vbcrlf)
            Set d = newDictionary()
            For Each anItem in arrItems
                arrTmp = split(anItem, "=")
                aName = arrTmp(0)
                aPrice = arrTmp(1)
                d.add aName, aPrice
                separatePriceTotal=separatePriceTotal + aPrice
            next
            toolKitPrice=(separatePriceTotal * .8)
            %>
<HTML>
<HEAD>
<title>Debugging ASP--Continued</title>
<script language="JavaScript">
    function syncLists(List1, List2) {
        var i = List1.selectedIndex;
        List2.selectedIndex=i;
    }
</script>
</HEAD>
<BODY bgcolor="#b0e0e6">
<h2 align="center">Savings!!!</h2>
<P align="center">If you buy the toolkit, you save
<%=formatCurrency(separatePriceTotal -  toolKitPrice,2)%></P>
<table align="center" width="300" cols="2">
<tr>
    <td colspan="2">
        This list contains all the items in the toolkit. Click on any
item to see how much it costs individually.
    </td>
</tr>
<tr>
    <td width="50%" align="center" valign="top">
        <select name="lstItems" size=12
        onchange="syncLists(this, document.all.lstPrices);">
        <%
        For Each anItem in d.Keys
            Response.Write "<option>" & anItem & "</option"
        Next
        %>
        </select>
    </td>
    <td width="50%" align="center" valign="top">
        <select name="lstPrices"
        onchange="syncLists(this, document.all.lstItems);">
```

```
<%
For each anItem in d.items
    Response.Write "<option>" & ccur(anItem) & "</option>"
Next
%>
</select>
</td>
</tr>
</body>
</html>
```

The script reads a file called `ProductList.txt`, splits the file into individual lines, then splits each line at the equals (=) sign to obtain an item name and a price. The `ProductList.txt` file contains the following data:

```
Socket Wrench Driver=12.95
Assorted sockets=34.65
Large flat-bladed screwdriver=7.99
Small flat-bladed screwdriver=6.25
Large Phillips-head screwdriver=9.11
Small Phillips-head screwdriver=6.95
Hex key set=8.59
Short socket extension=6.99
Long socket extension=8.99
Large vice-grip pliars=15.77
Small vice-grip pliars=12.79
```

When you run this script, the following error occurs:

```
Error Type:
Microsoft VBScript runtime (0x800A0009)
Subscript out of range: '[number: 0]'
/MasteringASP/Chapter13/ch13i9.asp, line 22
```

Line 22 contains the code:

```
aName = arrTmp(0)
```

The error appears to be saying that the `arrTmp` variable doesn't contain an item at index 0. Let's write some debug code to ensure the data is correct. Add the following line before line 22:

```
Response.Write Ubound(arrTmp) & "<br>"
```

Run the file again—doesn't help, does it? That's because the pre-processor redirects to the error file before the ASP engine actually writes the data. You can solve that problem. Insert an `On Error Resume Next` statement on the line just above the `Response.Write` statement you just added. Run the file again. This time, you should see a screen similar to Figure 13.7.

FIGURE 13.7:

Debugging ASP—continued
(ch13i9.asp)

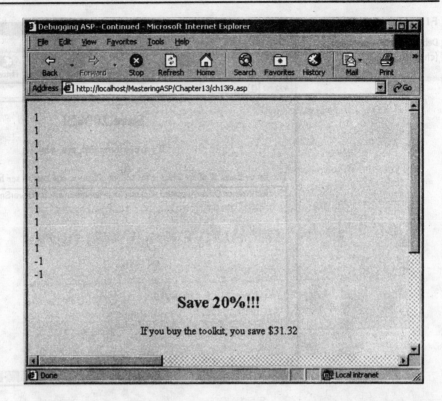

Because each line in the data file contains two items, you should see a list of 1's. But the last two items are negative 1's. Variant arrays have an upper bound of −1 when they contain no items. Therefore, there must be blank lines in the data file. Sure enough, if you open the ProductList.txt file, you'll see that there's a blank line at the end. Delete the line, save the file, then run the script in Listing 13.8 again. If you still see a −1 in the list, delete the final carriage return from the data file, then save the file. When the browser contains only 1's, you can remove or comment out the Response.Write line that you added from the code. Now the output in the browser should look like Figure 13.8.

Obviously, that still isn't correct. There must be another error in the file. Comment out the On Error Resume Next statement and run the file again. You'll see the following error:

```
Error Type:
Microsoft VBScript runtime (0x800A000D)
Type mismatch: '[string: "12.9534.657.996.259."]'
/MasteringASP/Chapter13/ch13i9.asp, line 27
```

FIGURE 13.8:

Debugging ASP—continued
(ch13i9.asp)

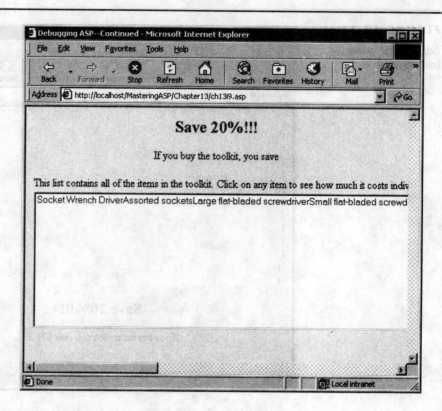

Line 27 is:

```
toolKitPrice=(separatePriceTotal * .8)
```

The error seems to be saying that VBScript can't perform either the multiplication or the assignment. The `separatePriceTotal` variable is simply the sum of the individual prices from the data file:

```
For Each anItem in arrItems
    arrTmp = split(anItem, "=")
    aName = arrTmp(0)
    aPrice = arrTmp(1)
    d.add aName, aPrice
    separatePriceTotal=separatePriceTotal + aPrice
next
```

Let's see what the real values are. Add a `Response.Write` statement before line 27 to show the value of the `separatePriceTotal` variable (you'll need to add the `On Error Resume Next` statement again to see any output), as follows:

```
Response.Write "separatePriceTotal=" & separatePriceTotal & "<br>"
```

This time, you should see a line at the top of your browser that shows:

```
separatePriceTotal=12.9534.657.996.259.116.958.596.998.9915.7712.79
```

If you look at the data file carefully, you'll see that the prices look familiar. VBScript, rather than adding each value as a number, has concatenated them together as a string! That's a problem with Variant values—they aren't always what you might think they are. You can solve this problem by casting each value to a number—in this case, currency—before you add it to the separatePriceTotal variable. Inside the loop, change the calculation as follows:

```
For Each anItem in arrItems
    ...
    separatePriceTotal=separatePriceTotal + cCur(aPrice)
next
```

Comment out the added On Error Resume Next and Response.Write statements, save your changes, then run the file again.

This time, the file runs without an error, but the display is incorrect; instead of two select lists, you see only one list, and it's too wide to fit on the screen. The items in the list appear as if they were one long string rather than a list. Take a closer look at the loop that creates the first select list:

```
<%
For Each anItem in d.Keys
    Response.Write "<option>" & anItem & "</option"
Next
%>
```

The end option </option> tag is missing the final bracket. If you fix this error, the file should run correctly. You can see how writing debug output to the screen can help solve problems. Sometimes, you can't find HTML problems easily by looking at the code. In such cases, it's often much more helpful to right-click on the browser and select the View Source option to see the HTML itself after it has been sent to the client page. If you have a color-coded HTML editor, it's even easier to find errors. Select the HTML, paste it into the editor and look for anomalies. In Visual InterDev, for example, the <option> tags following the invalid end option tags turn pink to show that an HTML error occurred.

In this chapter, you've seen how to approach error-trapping and debugging. You'll need these techniques to catch and find errors both with your own code and with external components. Microsoft installs several external components with ASP. In Chapter 14, *The Browser Capabilities Component*, you'll see a detailed explanation showing how to use one of these components. Then, in Chapter 15, *Other ASP Components*, I'll explain how to use the other components delivered with ASP.

PART IV

Using Components

CHAPTER
FOURTEEN

The Browser Capabilities Component

- Differences between Browsers

- How the Browser Capabilities Component Works

- Browser Capabilities Component Properties/Methods

- Using the Browser Capabilities Component

Microsoft installs several other components with ASP in addition to the Microsoft Scripting Runtime. One of these is the MSWC Browser Capabilities component or BrowseCap for short (`browscap.dll`). You may also see the component referred to as the BrowserType object, because BrowserType is the public class name exposed by the component. The BrowseCap component is most useful when you're delivering content to different types of browsers; for example, both Netscape and IE. It's even more useful when you want to change your display based on features available in some browsers, but not in others.

Differences between Browsers

All modern browsers (from Netscape 2x on) support HTML 3.2; however, they differ in the way they support some features. For example, some browsers—like IE—are extremely tolerant of badly written HTML. IE will display tables correctly even if you don't close the `<td>` tags, whereas other browsers, like Netscape, refuse to display a table at all if you forget the closing `</table>` tag. Similarly, some browsers support Java, some don't. Some support client-side script, some don't. IE supports VBScript, but no other browser does. Early browsers (yes, there are a few die-hards using NCSA's Mosaic) and some shareware browsers lack frame support. Only version 3 and higher browsers support CSS stylesheets, and only version 4 and higher browsers support Dynamic HTML (DHTML)—and the major browsers differ radically in their implementation.

To complicate matters, different browsers have different plug-ins and helper applications, all of which are external DLLs or executables. Browser installation programs install some plug-ins automatically; users must download others. IE is the only browser that supports ActiveX controls. If your application uses any special client-side features—script, Java applets, ActiveX controls, audio, video, animation, DHTML—you'll need to make sure that the target browsers support those features.

Finally, most browsers let users selectively disable certain features. For example, users can turn off graphics, and disable cookies, Java, and script support. To cope with this cornucopia of capabilities, you need to know which features the client's browser supports. After you know, you can make decisions in your application about how best to deliver content to that feature set.

Netscape vs. Internet Explorer

Netscape and Internet Explorer (IE) browsers together own well over 95% of the total browser market. Netscape began marketing browsers before Microsoft and soon captured a large market share, because its product was considerably better than the existing alternatives. Netscape dominated the market to the point that Netscape was able to influence the development of the HTML language itself, by implementing features such as frames, then proposing those extensions to the W3C as a *fait accompli*. Microsoft's first browser wasn't nearly as good as Netscape's, but in true Microsoft fashion, by version 2, they had achieved feature set parity, and by version 3, had surpassed Netscape's offering in everything but speed.

Microsoft didn't stop there. Version 4 introduced the first browser compliant with the W3C Document Object Model (DOM) recommendation. The DOM gives HTML authors and programmers access to the individual elements on the browser screen. Until then, once a browser had rendered a page, the content on that page was completely static (except for content inside form controls). The DOM, together with CSS technology, lets you alter the contents of the browser screen without erasing the page. For example, you can hide and show objects, place objects precisely on the page, draw graphics primitives—in short, you can manipulate every element on the screen. By the time Microsoft released the browser, it supported most of the W3C DOM recommendation. In contrast, Netscape's version 4 release had extremely limited DOM support.

IE version 4 also introduced the world to XML, in the form of channels. Channels are a simple form of XML that never caught on with users. Nevertheless, even the limited XML support in IE 4 opened the way for corporate developers to see how XML could improve many aspects of development.

Naturally, Microsoft's browser began to gain market share. Currently IE has about a 70% market share among corporate users, due primarily to its ActiveX and DOM support, but its share is somewhat lower among general Internet users.

IE version 5 extends XML support to the point that IE 5 can natively display XML files. By installing a validating parser with the browser, Microsoft has ensured that IE will continue to gain corporate market share.

In the meantime, Netscape collapsed trying to sell browsers with a primitive feature set into a market where Microsoft gave IE away for free. Netscape was finally acquired by Sun. Netscape continues to make and sell browsers, but their latest version (version 5) lacks XML support, does not support ActiveX controls, and still lacks full DOM compliance.

While the various browser makers battle for control, developers are left to grapple with the problems of supporting a large and varied set of browsers. The Browser Capabilities component makes that task slightly easier.

How the Browser Capabilities Component Works

The idea behind the BrowseCap component is simple. As you saw in Chapter 6, *The Request Object,* browsers send a great deal of information to the server to accompany each request. One piece of information is the HTTP_USER_AGENT header, which holds a string listing the type and version of the browser requesting the page. You can retrieve the HTTP_USER_AGENT header with the Request.ServerVariables collection:

```
Request.ServerVariables("HTTP_USER_AGENT")
```

The BrowseCap component uses a Windows Application Initialization (INI) file called browscap.ini that contains information about most common browser types. An INI file consists of sections (originally called Applications in Windows 3.1), each of which may contain one or more key-value pairs.

NOTE   An INI file is a text file. It contains strings in brackets called sections. Each section contains zero or more entries. Each entry consists of a key and a value. Comment lines begin with a semicolon. In Windows 3.x, INI files held application initialization and settings, hence the name INI. Microsoft abandoned INI files (mostly) starting with Windows 95. Windows now stores most application settings in the registry. Nonetheless, Windows still contains the Application Programming Interface (API) functions to read and write data to INI files.

Each major version of a given browser has a base section, followed by additional sections, one for each platform version, or updated version of the browser. For example, the base entry for the Netscape 4 beta release looks like this:

```
[Netscape 4.00]
browser=Netscape
version=4.00
majorver=4
minorver=00
frames=TRUE
tables=TRUE
cookies=TRUE
backgroundsounds=FALSE
vbscript=FALSE
javascript=TRUE
javaapplets=TRUE
ActiveXControls=FALSE
beta=True
```

In contrast, the base entry for the IE 5 production release looks like this:

```
[IE 5.0]
browser=IE
Version=5.0
majorver=5
minorver=0
frames=True
tables=True
cookies=True
backgroundsounds=True
vbscript=True
javaapplets=True
javascript=True
ActiveXControls=True
Win16=False
beta=True
AK=False
SK=False
AOL=False
Update=False
```

Both browsers support frames, tables, cookies, Java applets, and JavaScript. IE additionally supports VBScript and ActiveX Controls. Browsers change as companies release minor version upgrades and bug fixes. Netscape released several 4.0 versions. I've shown the b1 and b2 releases for Windows 95 and NT below:

```
[Mozilla/4.0b1 (Win95; I)]
parent=Netscape 4.00
platform=Win95

[Mozilla/4.0b1 (WinNT; I)]
parent=Netscape 4.00
platform=WinNT

[Mozilla/4.0b2 (Win95; I)]
parent=Netscape 4.00
platform=Win95

[Mozilla/4.0b2 (WinNT; I)]
parent=Netscape 4.00
platform=WinNT
```

For example, if a user running on Windows 95 is using Netscape 4, release b2, the HTTP_USER_AGENT string will contain Mozilla/4.0b2 (Win95; I). The section entries in the browscap.ini file (the lines in square brackets) correspond to the HTTP_USER_AGENT string. When the BrowserType object finds a matching string, it reads the parent section, if one exists—in this case, Netscape 4.00. It then combines the keys and values in the parent section with the keys and values in the section matching the HTTP_USER_AGENT string. If the BrowserType object can't find an exact match, it searches for a partial match using wildcards. For example, the following listing contains the wildcard entry for Navigator 4 in the browscap.ini file. You can then read the property values from the BrowseCap object.

```
;;;;; Navigator 4.x WILDCARD (IF ALL ABOVE FAIL)
[Mozilla/4.0*]
parent=Netscape 4.00
```

If the BrowseCap component can't find a match even with wildcards, it sets all property values to the string Unknown.

Until IE and IIS version 5, the BrowseCap component had some serious limitations. For example, as vendors released new browser versions, you had to update the browscap.ini file on each server; otherwise, the capability list for that browser might be incorrect or unavailable. In addition, even if the INI file listed the browser, the information only told you which features were available, not which features were enabled. IIS 5 and IE 5 have solved that problem by adding:

- The ability for the BrowseCap component to read browser capabilities from a cookie generated by the browser.

- A special status code, generated by a header, that instructs the browser to run a specific file that generates the cookie values.

You can include this header in an ASP file. If the browser request doesn't contain the BrowsCap cookie, the server returns the 449 special status code. The code instructs the browser to load the sendcook.htm file, which then generates the cookie. The following header instructs IIS to check for a BrowsCap cookie:

```
<!-- METADATA TYPE="Cookie" NAME="BrowsCap" SRC="sendcook.htm" -->
```

The sendcook.htm file contains a client-side script that creates the cookie values. The browser then re-requests the original file and sends the new BrowsCap cookie with the request. Because the cookie now exists, the server automatically sets the properties of the BrowserType object, and sends the contents of the ASP file.

Browser Capabilities Component Properties/Methods

The Browser Capabilities component exposes one public object, the BrowserType object. The only property in the BrowserType object is `Value`, which is a key. Because this is the default (and only) public property of the BrowserType object, you do not need to use the keyword `Value`. For example, if you have a Browser-Type object reference in the variable bc, you can retrieve the value with the syntax `bc.Value("Browser")` or `bc("Browser")`, or even `bc.Browser`. All versions return the same value string.

Using the Browser Capabilities Component

To create an instance of the Browser Capabilities component, create a Browser-Type object, as follows:

```
<%
dim bc
set bc = Server.CreateObject("MSWC.BrowserType")
%>
```

The object automatically searches the `browscap.ini` file to find the matching browser information, or (if you're using the IIS 5/IE 5 cookie method explained earlier in this chapter) reads the `BrowsCap` cookie and sets the `Value` properties. Listing 14.1 is an example of the Browser Capabilities component.

LISTING 14.1   Using the Browser Capabilities Component (ch14i1.asp)

```
<%@ Language=VBScript %>
<HTML>
<HEAD>
</HEAD>
<BODY>
<%
dim bc
set bc = Server.CreateObject("MSWC.BrowserType")
```

```
With Response
    .Write "The HTTP_USER_AGENT String is: " & _
        Request.ServerVariables("HTTP_USER_AGENT") & "<br>"
    .Write "<html><head></head><body>"
    .Write "Browser=" & bc.Browser    & "<br>"
    .Write "Version=" & bc.Version & "<br>"
    .Write "Cookies=" & bc.Cookies & "<br>"
    .Write "VBScript=" & bc.VBScript & "<br>"
    .Write "JavaScript=" & bc.JavaScript & "<br>"
End With
%>
</BODY>
</HTML>
```

Figure 14.1 shows how Listing 14.1 looks in the browser using IE 5 to request the file. Depending on which browser version you're using, you'll see different information.

FIGURE 14.1:

Browser Capabilities component example (ch14i1.asp)

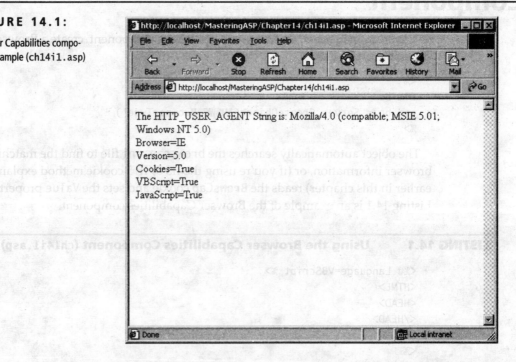

In this chapter, you've seen how to use one of the components Microsoft installs for use with ASP—the MSWC Browser Capabilities component. The MSWC project contains several other components. In the next chapter, I'll briefly explain how to use each component.

CHAPTER

FIFTEEN

Other ASP Components

- The AdRotator Component

- The Content Linking Component

- The Content Rotator Component

- The Counters Component

- The Logging Utility

- The MyInfo Component

- The Page Counter Component

- The Permission Checker Component

- The Tools Component

In addition to the Browser Capabilities component that you've already seen, Microsoft also installs several other components with ASP that you may find useful. In this chapter, I'll visit each of these briefly and explain what they do and how to use them. Several of these objects help solve specific problems that you have seen earlier in this book.

TABLE 15.1:   Components Installed with ASP

Component	Description
Ad Rotator	Creates an AdRotator object that loops through a series of advertisement graphics, displaying each one for a configurable length of time.
Content Linking	Creates a NextLink object that provides automatic **Next** links for a series of pages.
Content Rotator	Creates a ContentRotator object that automates the display of a series of content strings, displaying a different string each time the page loads.
Counters	Creates a Counters object that can create, store, increment, and retrieve any number of individual counters.
Logging Utility	Allows you to read the HTTP activity log files that IIS generates.
MyInfo	Creates a MyInfo object that keeps track of personal information, such as the site administrator's name, address, and display choices.
Page Counter	Keeps track of the number of visits to a Web page.
Permission Checker	Uses the password authentication protocols provided in Microsoft Internet Information Services (IIS) to determine whether a Web user has permission to read a file.
Tools	The Tools object provides utilities that enable you to easily add sophisticated functionality to your Web pages.

The rest of this chapter describes each component in a separate section, followed by a section containing a project using several of the components.

The AdRotator Component

You've probably seen sites that have banner ads at the top of the page. The ad changes every 10 or 15 seconds. The AdRotator component makes such sites easy to set up (which is probably why they're so common). You need a list of ad graphics, each of which should be the same size. I've provided a set of very simple graphics to show you the idea.

To use the AdRotator component, you must first create an AdRotator Schedule text file. The AdRotator Schedule file contains two parts:

- A general section containing the name of an ASP file to which the browser redirects when a user clicks on a graphic, and the image and border size for the ad images.

- A detail section containing a list of advertising images, associated URLs to browse when the user clicks that image, alternate text (for image-disabled browsers), and a number that specifies the weight of that particular ad.

The weight is an integer value that controls how often (relative to the other ads in the file) any specific ad will appear. The AdRotator component adds all the weights in the AdRotator Schedule file, then divides each weight by the total weight to obtain a percentage. That percentage is the average number of times the AdRotator component will select a specific image file out of every 100 page requests. An asterisk separates the general section from the detail section.

Listing 15.1 shows the contents of an AdRotator Schedule file called ch15AdRedir.txt.

LISTING 15.1   AdRotator Schedule File Example (ch15AdRedir.txt)

```
REDIRECT ch15AdRedir.asp
WIDTH 468
HEIGHT 60
BORDER 1
*
../images/f1501a.gif
ch1501a.asp
Jump to ch1501a
5
../images/f1501b.gif
ch1501b.asp
Jump to ch1501b
2
../images/f1501c.gif
ch1501c.asp
Jump to ch1501c
3
```

When a user clicks one of the ad graphics, the browser requests the ASP file specified in the REDIRECT line of the text file. Inside that ASP file you can do whatever you like, such as increment a counter that keeps track of the number of users who click on a particular ad, redirect to an alternate page, or any other appropriate action. The browser passes the URL associated with that graphic in the Request .QueryString("URL") variable. After performing actions appropriate for your application, you can redirect to the associated URL.

For example, in Listing 15.1, the REDIRECT line tells the AdRotator component to redirect to the ch15AdRedir.asp file when a user clicks any ad. Listing 15.2 shows a sample redirection ASP file.

LISTING 15.2   **Sample Redirection File (ch1501.asp)**

```
<%
Dim newURL
newURL = Request.QueryString("URL")
If newURL <> "" Then
    Select case newURL
    Case "ch1501a.asp"
        Response.Write "Redirecting to ch1501a.asp"
        Response.Redirect "ch1501a.asp"
    Case "ch1501b.asp"
        Response.Write "Redirecting to ch1501b.asp"
        Response.Redirect "ch1501b.asp"
    Case "ch1501c.asp"
        Response.Write "Redirecting to ch1501c.asp"
        Response.Redirect "ch1501c.asp"
    End Select
End If
%>
```

I've shown one of the files referenced by the preceding listing below (ch1501a.asp), all of the referenced files are similar.

```
<%@ Language=VBScript %>
<!- #INCLUDE FILE="../include/fileOps.inc" ->
<html>
<head>
</head>
<body>
<%
dim counter
dim scriptFile
scriptFile = getCurrentFile()
Response.Write scriptFile & "<br>"

Application.Lock
counter = Application(scriptFile)
Application.UnLock
if counter <> "" then
    Response.Write "This page has been visited " & _
    counter & " times.<br>"
end if
%>
<table align="center" border=1>
<tr>
    <td>
        You have reached the page ch1501a.asp by clicking
```

```
        the ad image shown below. Click <A HREF="ch1501.asp">
        back</a> to return to the page that rotates the ads.
    </td>
</tr>
<tr>
    <td align="center" valign="center">
        <IMG SRC="../images/f1501a.gif" ALT="Ad graphic
        for page ch1501a" WIDTH="200" HEIGHT="40" BORDER="0">
    </td>
</tr>
</table>
</body>
</html>
```

Run the ch1501.asp file in your browser to see the program in action. Each time you refresh the file, it creates an AdRotator component, reads the contents of the ch15AdRedir.txt file, selects an ad to display, then displays that ad.

NOTE   You may need to refresh the browser several times because half the time (due to the weight number assigned to the ads) it will display the ch1501a.gif ad image.

Figures 15.1 and 15.2 show an ad display in the main ASP file and the result of clicking that ad, respectively.

FIGURE 15.1:

AdRotator example
(ch1501.asp)

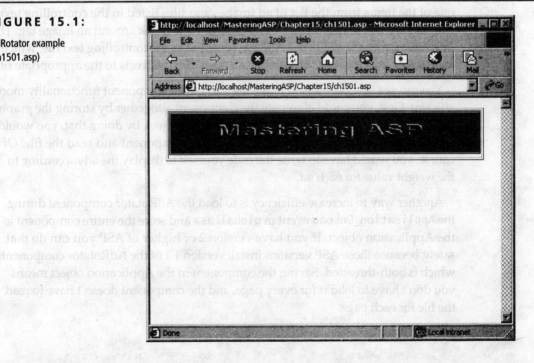

FIGURE 15.2:

AdRotator example
after clicking an ad
(ch1501a.asp)

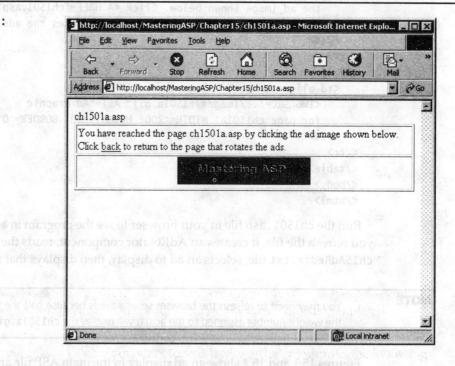

If you right-click on the browser and select View Source after loading the main
ASP file (ch1501.asp), you can see that all the AdRotator component does is select
one of the items from the list of ad images and files listed in the controlling text
file, and use the Response.Write method to write a link around an image tag. The
link redirects to the REDIRECT ASP file specified in the controlling text file, which
increments an Application variable counter, then redirects to the appropriate file.

You can see several ways to make the AdRotator component functionality more
efficient. First, you could eliminate the component altogether by storing the graphic
filenames and redirection data in the Application object. By doing that, you would
save the time required to create the AdRotator component and read the file. Of
course, you would have to write the code yourself to display the ads according to
the weight value for each ad.

Another way to increase efficiency is to load the AdRotator component during
the Application_OnLoad event in global.asa and store the entire component in
the Application object. If you have version 2 or higher of ASP you can do that
safely, because those ASP versions install version 1.1 of the AdRotator component,
which is both-threaded. Saving the component in the Application object means
you don't have to load it for every page, and the component doesn't have to read
the file for each page.

The method you select, loading the AdRotator component on each page at Application scope, or replacing it with custom code, depends on the needs of your specific application.

The Content Linking Component

The Content Linking component reads a list of files stored in a text file on the server called the Content Linking List file, and treats those files as if they were pages in a book. It can help you create a table of contents to manage the user's navigation forward and backward through the file list.

The Content Linking component, like the Browser Capabilities component and the AdRotator component, is part of the MSWC project installed with ASP. It has one public object, called NextLink. To create an instance of the NextLink object, you write:

```
Dim CLC
Set CLC = Server.CreateObject("MSWC.NextLink")
```

The NextLink object has no methods. Table 15.2 lists the NextLink object properties.

TABLE 15.2: NextLink Object Properties

Property	Description
GetListCount	Counts the number of items linked in the Content Linking List file.
GetListIndex	Gets the index of the current page in the Content Linking List file.
GetNextDescription	Gets the description of the next page listed in the Content Linking List file.
GetNextURL	Gets the URL of the next page listed in the Content Linking List file.
GetNthDescription	Gets the description of the Nth page listed in the Content Linking List file.
GetNthURL	Gets the URL of the Nth page listed in the Content Linking List file.
GetPreviousDescription	Gets the description line of the previous page listed in the Content Linking List file.
GetPreviousURL	Gets the URL of the previous pages listed in the Content Linking List file.

After you create the NextLink object, for each property you want to retrieve, you must pass the name of a Content Linking List file. The Content Linking List file contains the list of links (URLs). After each URL, you write a space and a text description for that URL. Listing 15.3 shows a sample Content Linking List file.

LISTING 15.3   Sample Content Linking List File (ch1502.txt)

```
Ch1502a.htm First File in Content Linking Sequence
Ch1502b.htm Second File in Content Linking Sequence
Ch1502c.htm Third File in Content Linking Sequence
Ch1502d.htm Return to the table of contents
```

The Content Linking component is both-threaded, so you can create it at Application scope using the <object> syntax. For example:

```
<OBJECT RUNAT=Server SCOPE=Application ID=NextLink PROGID="MSWC
.NextLink">
</OBJECT>
```

You can then use the NextLink object on any page to write an anchor tag using the return value for either or both of the getNextURL or getPreviousURL methods. For example:

```
<a href="<%= NextLink.getPreviousURL("ch1502.txt")%>">Previous _
    Page</a>nbsp;
<a href="<%= NextLink.getNextURL("ch1502.txt")%>">Next Page</a>
```

Internally, the NextLink object reads the text file, finds the current page by comparing the page name to the list of files available, then selects links and descriptions based on the current page index.

So that you can see how simple this object is, I've created a pure ASP version showing how you can supplant the Content Linking component with ASP code. Create your own version, as follows:

- Create two arrays and store them in the Session or Application object. These arrays hold the list of URLs and descriptions. Store both of the arrays in a single Variant array variable.

- Create an index pointer variable to the arrays and store that in the Session object (because each user may be on a different page).

- For each request, retrieve the arrays, find the current page, then increment the index pointer in the appropriate direction (add 1 to go forward, -1 to go backward).

- To create a table of contents, loop through the arrays. Use the first array (array of URLs) as the HREF parameter for the links and the second array (array of descriptions) as the link text.

The main file is ch1502.asp. Most of the code, including function calls that match the properties of the Content Linking component, resides in the ContentLinker.inc file in the Chapter15 directory. When you run the ch1502.asp file in a browser, it constructs a table of contents (see Figure 15.3).

FIGURE 15.3:

Content Linking example— ASP version

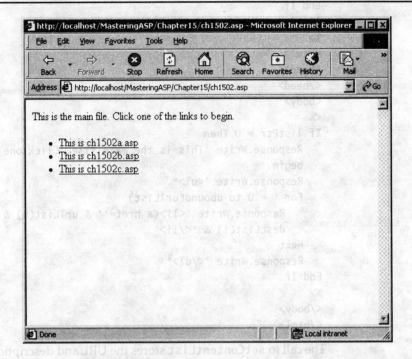

The ch1502.asp file initializes the Application-level URL and description arrays (if necessary), retrieves those arrays, then loops through the arrays to format the links for the table of contents. Listing 15.4 shows the contents of the ch1502.asp file.

LISTING 15.4   Content Linking Example—ASP Version (ch1502.asp)

```
<%@ Language=VBScript %>
<!- #INCLUDE FILE="ContentLinker.inc" ->
<%
Dim urlList
Dim descList
Dim listPtr
Dim i
Call clearContentList("ch15")
urlList = getURLList("ch15")
descList = getDescriptionList("ch15")
If urlList = "" Then
   urlList = Array("ch1502a.asp", "ch1502b.asp", "ch1502c.asp")
   descList= Array("This is ch1502a.asp", "This is ch1502b.asp", _
   "This is ch1502c.asp")
   Call setContentList("ch15", urlList, descList)
```

```
      End If
      listPtr = getListIndex("ch15")
%>
<html>
<head>
</head>
<body>
<%
If listPtr = 0 Then
   Response.Write "This is the main file. Click one of the links to
   begin."
   Response.Write "<ul>"
   For i = 0 to ubound(urlList)
      Response.Write "<li><a href='" & urlList(i) & "'>" & _
      descList(i) & "</li>"
   Next
   Response.Write "</ul>"
End If
%>
</body>
</html>
```

The call to `setContentList` stores the URL and description arrays at Application scope. The aName argument contains a unique string value used as a key to store the arrays in the Application object. The `urlList` argument contains an array of URLs, and the `descriptionList` argument contains a parallel array of descriptions. For example:

```
Sub setContentList(aName, urlList, descriptionList)
   Dim aList
   aList = Array(urlList, descriptionList)
   Application.Lock
   Application(aName) = aList
   Application.Unlock
End Sub
```

For simplicity, the function places both the URL and description arrays in a single variant array variable, which it then stores in the Application object using the aName argument value. The purpose of this is that you can subsequently retrieve both arrays from the Application object using a single assignment. For example:

```
Function getContentList(aName)
   Application.Lock
   getContentList = Application(aName)
   Application.Unlock
End Function
```

All subsequent calls to functions in the ContentLinker.inc file must specify the name of the array to use. That requirement means you have to write a little more code for each call, but also means you can set up multiple instances of URL/description arrays in your application, provided you give each one a unique name.

In the example, when you select a link in the table of contents, you'll jump to one of three almost identical files. Listing 15.5 shows the contents of one of the files (ch1502a.asp).

LISTING 15.5   Content Linking Example—ASP Version (ch1502a.asp)

```
<% @Language=VBScript %>
<!- #INCLUDE FILE="ContentLinker.inc" ->
<HTML>
<HEAD>
<META NAME="GENERATOR" Content="Microsoft Visual Studio 6.0">
<TITLE></TITLE>
</HEAD>
<BODY>
<%
dim curIndex
dim nextURL
dim prevURL
curIndex = getListIndex("ch15")
prevURL=getPreviousURL("ch15", curIndex)
nextURL = getNextURL("ch15", curIndex)
%>
<form method="post" id=form1 name=form1>
<table align="center" border="1" width="70%" cols="2">
<tr>
   <td colspan="2" align="left">
      This is ch1501a.asp. Click the Next or Back button to move
      forward or backward.
   </td>
</tr>
<tr>
   <td align="center" width="50%"  valign="bottom">
      <%
      if getPreviousURL("ch15", curIndex) <> "" then
         Response.Write "<input type='button' name='back' value='Back'
" & _
         onClick=window.location='" & prevURL &  "';>"
      else
         Response.Write " "
      end if
      %>
```

```
        </td>
        <td align="center" width="50%" valign="bottom">
            <%
            if getNextURL("ch15", curIndex) <> "" then
                Response.Write "<input type='button' name='next' value='Next'
        " & _
                    onClick=window.location='" & nextURL & "';>"
            else
                Response.Write " "
            end if
            %>
        </td>
    </tr>
    </table>
    </form>
</BODY>
</HTML>
```

Each file contains three calls:

> **getList**—Index retrieves the index pointer for the current page. Note that internally, the ContentLinker.inc files work with zero-based arrays, but return one-based values.

> **getPreviousURL**—retrieves the URL preceding the current URL in the URL array.

> **getNextURL**—retrieves the URL after the current URL in the URL array.

The getPreviousURL and getNextURL functions return null strings if the current URL is first or last in the URL array.

The Content Rotator Component

NOTE By default, the IIS 4 installation program does not install the Content Rotator component. You can install it from the CD included with the IIS Resource Kit. The component installs with IIS 5 by default.

The Content Rotator component is very similar to the AdRotator component, except that it manages the rotation of HTML text strings instead of images. It works from a text file called the Content Schedule file, which contains the list of strings and the relative weight for each string. Remember that the weight value controls how often the Content Rotator selects a specific item.

The Content Schedule file can contain any number of string entries. Each entry has two parts: a line that begins with double percentage signs (%%) and contains both the relative weight value preceded by a pound (#) sign and any comments, and a second part (starting on a new line) that contains the HTML content string itself. The file may also contain comments. Listing 15.6 shows a sample Content Schedule file.

LISTING 15.6   Sample Content Schedule File (ch15ContentScheduleFile.txt)

```
%% // This is a sample Content Schedule file
%% // Note that you can place comments in the file using
%% // the double forward slash syntax and also that
%% // HTML may consist of more than one line.
%% #3 // Comment for line 1
<h2 align="center">
    <font color="#0000FF">
        Sample Content Schedule HTML String 1
    </font>
</h2>
%% #2
<h2 align="center">
    <font color="#FF0000">
        Sample Content Schedule HTML String 2
    </font>
</h2>
%% #1
<h2 align="center">
    <font color="#00FF00">
        Sample Content Schedule HTML String 3
    </font>
</h2>
```

The Content Rotator component exposes one public object, the MSWC.Content-Rotator object. The ContentRotator object has only two methods: ChooseContent and GetAllContent. Both methods accept the name of a Content Schedule file as an argument. You can only use virtual filenames, but those can be relative filenames. The ChooseContent method returns a single string that is selected from among all the available strings based on the weight value. The GetAllContent method returns all the strings. To use the Content Rotator component, create an instance of a MSWC.ContentRotator object and write the results of the ChooseContent method to the browser. For example:

```
<%@ Language=VBScript %>
<html>
```

```
<head>
</head>
<body>
<%
Dim oCR
Set oCR = Server.CreateObject("MSWC.ContentRotator")
Response.Write oCR.ChooseContent("ch15ContentScheduleFile.txt")
Set oCR = Nothing
%>
</body>
</html>
```

The Counters Component

The Counters component is a simple counter you can add to your applications. The component writes persistent integer values to disk in the counters.txt file—located in the same directory as the counters.dll file (typically, c:\winnt\system32\inetsrv\data). You create one Counters component in global.asa for your entire site. That component then supports any number of individual counter values. Create the counter at Application scope using the <object> tag. For example:

```
<OBJECT RUNAT=Server SCOPE=Application ID=Counter PROGID="MSWC.Counters">
</OBJECT>
```

The Counters component has four methods. Each method accepts a single string argument containing the name of a counter value. Table 15.3 lists the Counters component methods.

TABLE 15.3: Counters Component Methods

Method/Property	Description
Get(counterName)	Returns the value of the counter.
Increment(counterName)	Increases the counter by 1.
Remove(counterName)	Removes the counter from the counters.txt file.
Set(counterName)	Sets the value of the counter to a specific integer.

To create a new counter value, you provide a unique name. For example, you can use the Counters component to count page hits for your entire site. On each page, you increment the counter for that page. I've included two example pages on the CD, the files ch15i5a.asp and ch15i5b.asp. Listing 15.7 shows the contents of ch15i5a.asp.

LISTING 15.7 **Counters Component Example (ch15i5a.asp)**

```
' On each page
<%@ Language=VBScript %>
<html>
<head>
</head>
<body>
<%
Dim aPage
Dim count
aPage = "ch15i5a"
Response.write ("You are visitor number " & CLng(Counter
.Increment(aPage)) & ".<Br>")
%>
<a href="ch15i5b.asp">Next Page</a>
</body>
</html>
```

The Logging Utility

The Logging Utility lets you read IIS log files. This capability is useful for reports of many types; in fact, it's so important that an entire industry, called clickstream analysis, is growing up around the idea that Web server log files contain invaluable business data. For example, by closely analyzing users' paths through a Web site, you might be able to tell which products or techniques are most attractive to customers. When you make changes to a site, before-and-after log file analysis can help you determine whether those changes provide an expected return on investment. The Logging Utility, by itself, doesn't provide any analytical capabilities, but it does give you automated access to the log file format. You can create your own analysis code.

To use the Logging Utility, you must be an authenticated Administrator or Operator on the NT or Windows 2000 system hosting IIS. In other words, you will never be able to use the Logging Utility component unless you disable Anonymous Access to the ASP pages that instantiate the component. I'll repeat that, slightly louder.

WARNING You may only use the Logging Utility if you are an authenticated Administrator or Operator on the NT or Windows 2000 system hosting IIS. You will never be able to use the Logging Utility component unless you disable Anonymous Access to the ASP pages that instantiate the component.

To force a user to authenticate for one or more pages, check the `Request.Server-Variables("LOGON_USER")` variable. If the value is a null string, set the `Response.Status` to `401 Unauthorized` and stop processing the page. For example:

```
<%@ Language=VBScript %>
<% Response.Buffer = True %>
<%
dim logonUser
logonUser = Request.ServerVariables("LOGON_USER")
if logonUser = "" then
Response.Status = "401 Unauthorized"
   Response.Clear
   Response.AddHeader "WWW-Authenticate","NTLM"
   Response.End
end if
%>
<html>
<head>
</head>
<body>

<p>You have been authenticated as: <%=logonUser%></p>

</body>
</html>
```

When your ASP page responds to an anonymous request with a `401 Unauthorized` status, IIS checks the virtual directory settings and sends a header listing the types of authentication it will accept, either Basic Authentication, NT Challenge/Response, or both.

What happens next depends on which browser you're using.

- If you check both Basic Authentication and NT Challenge/Response, IE versions 3 and higher select NT Challenge/Response, which transparently and securely authenticates the user, if possible. The process is transparent because the user doesn't have to manually enter a username and password; and it's secure because the process is encrypted.

- If you check only Basic Authentication, IE Base64 encodes the username and password and returns that information to the server, which then attempts to log the user on as a local user. Base64-encoded information is insecure; anyone that can intercept the TCP/IP packets using a network sniffer can discover the username and password.

- Netscape always selects Basic Authentication. That means the user must manually enter a username and password. The browser Base64 encodes the user's information and returns it to the server, which then logs the user on as a local user. Again, Base64-encoded information is insecure; anyone that can intercept the TCP/IP packets can discover the username and password.

Ignoring the irritation of entering a username and password and the security risk of sending unencrypted passwords over the network, there are some fundamental differences between Basic Authentication and NT Challenge/Response. A user authenticated with NT Challenge/Response has rights only on the server computer itself—the user still has no permission to access resources elsewhere on the network. That's because IE never sends an actual username and password to the server—it sends a hashed value instead. IIS forwards the hash value to a domain controller, which tries to authenticate the user. Assuming that authentication succeeds, the computer on which IIS is running can be sure that the user has appropriate permissions. At this point, IIS is impersonating the authenticated user. IIS can access all resources on the server computer, but it doesn't have the user's name and password, it only has the hash value. Therefore, it will not be able to access any resources on any other networked computer. That's because IIS cannot respond with a valid username and password when the other computer asks for security information.

This leads to many problems. For example, if you try to access a file on a remote computer, the file access will fail. In fact, if you try to access even a local file using a UNC naming convention, the file access fails. That's because NT treats all file accesses that use UNC names as network accesses. Network access of any kind requires authentication. Similarly, you may not launch executables or use components registered on remote computers when you authenticate via NT Challenge/Response because IIS cannot authenticate with the remote machine.

In contrast, when you use Basic Authentication, IIS *does* have your username and password. In essence, the Web server can now act just as if you had logged in to the server; therefore, you have normal access to network resources. Given these advantages, in an intranet situation with no access from outside, you may wish to consider Basic Authentication as a viable alternative to NT Challenge/Response. Of course, if you have Netscape clients, that's your only choice.

Regardless of which authentication method you select, users who can authenticate as Administrators or Operators can use the Logging Utility component freely. The Logging Utility is part of the project called MSWC. The Logging Utility has one public object, called SCRIPTLib.LogScripting. You create a LogScripting object in the same manner as you create other objects in ASP. For example:

```
Set objLog = Server.CreateObject("MSWC.IISLog")
```

The LogScripting object has a large number of methods, divided into two groups. The first group lets you select, read, and write log files programmatically. The second group of methods lets you read individual log values. Table 15.4 lists the LogScripting object methods.

> **NOTE**
>
> This documentation applies to IIS 5. The LogScripting object delivered with IIS 4 has similar methods but with different names. Check your documentation for the appropriate IIS 4 method calls.

TABLE 15.4: LogScripting Object Methods

Method	Description
Methods to read and write log files	
AtEndOfLog	Indicates whether all records have been read from the log file.
CloseLogFiles	Closes all open log files.
OpenLogFile	Opens a log file for reading or writing.
ReadFilter	Filters records from the log file by date and time.
ReadLogRecord	Reads the next available log record from the current log file.
WriteLogRecord	Writes a log record to the current log file.
Methods to retrieve individual values	
BytesRecieved	Retrieves the bytes received.
BytesSent	Retrieves the bytes sent.
ClientIP	Retrieves the client's IP address.
Cookie	Retrieves the client's cookie, if any.
CustomFields	Returns an array of custom headers.
DateTime	Retrieves the date and time, in GMT.
Method	Retrieves the HTTP operation type.
ProtocolStatus	Retrieves the protocol status.
ProtocolVersion	Retrieves the IISLog object's version string.
GetProtocolStatus	Retrieves the HTTP protocol status.
Referer	Indicates the referrer page.
ServerIP	Retrieves the server's IP address.
ServerName	Retrieves the server name.
ServerPort	Retrieves the port number of the server.
ServiceName	Retrieves the service name.
TimeTaken	Retrieves the total time required to process this request.
URIQuery	Retrieves any QueryString parameters passed with the request.
URIStem	Retrieves the target URL, without any appended QueryString values.
UserAgent	Retrieves the user agent string.
Win32Status	Retrieves the server status.

For example, to read the current log file (assuming you have the default log settings), open the %SystemRoot%\System32\LogFiles\W3SVC1exyymmdd.log file. Substitute your server's system directory for the %SystemRoot% portion of the path and substitute the current date values for the yymmdd portion of the file-name. The following script shows how to use the LogScripting object:

You will need to change the log file path and filename to the location and name of a log file on your server for the following script to work properly.

```
<%@ Language=VBScript %>
<% response.buffer = true %>
<%
Dim logonUser
Dim objLog
Dim aLogFile
Dim counter
logonUser = Request.ServerVariables("LOGON_USER")
If logonUser = "" Then
    Response.Clear
    Response.Buffer = True
    Response.Status = "401 Unauthorized"
    Response.AddHeader "WWW-Authenticate", "NTLM"
    Response.write "<h3 align='center'>You must enter your username"_
    & "and password to view the IIS log.</h3>"
    Response.End
End If
Set objLog = Server.CreateObject("MSWC.IISLog")
aLogFile = "c:\winnt\system32\logfiles\w3svc1\ex991203.log"
Call objLog.OpenLogFile(aLogFile, 1, "russell", 1, "")
%>
<HTML>
<HEAD>

</HEAD>
<BODY>
<table align="center" border="1" width="100%">
<%
Do While Not objLog.AtEndOfLog
    counter = counter + 1
    objLog.ReadLogRecord
    With Response
        .write "<tr>"
        .write "<td>" & counter & " " & "</td>"
        .write "<td>" & Trim(objLog.BytesReceived) & " " & "</td>"
        .write "<td>" & Trim(objLog.BytesSent) & " " & "</td>"
        .write "<td>" & Trim(objLog.ClientIP) & " " & "</td>"
        .write "<td>" & Trim(objLog.Cookie) & " " & "</td>"
        .write "<td>" & Trim(objLog.CustomFields) & " " & "</td>"
        .write "<td>" & Trim(objLog.DateTime) & " " & "</td>"
```

```
            .write "<td>" & Trim(objLog.Method) & " " & "</td>"
            .write "<td>" & Trim(objLog.ProtocolStatus) & " " & "</td>"
            .write "<td>" & Trim(objLog.ProtocolVersion) & " " & "</td>"
            .write "<td>" & Trim(objLog.Referer) & " " & "</td>"
            .write "<td>" & Trim(objLog.ServerIP) & " " & "</td>"
            .write "<td>" & Trim(objLog.ServerName) & " " & "</td>"
            .write "<td>" & Trim(objLog.ServerPort) & " " & "</td>"
            .write "<td>" & Trim(objLog.ServiceName) & " " & "</td>"
            .write "<td>" & Trim(objLog.URIQuery) & " " & "</td>"
            .write "<td>" & Trim(objLog.URIStem) & " " & "</td>"
            .write "<td>" & Trim(objLog.UserAgent) & " " & "</td>"
            .write "<td>" & Trim(objLog.UserName) & " " & "</td>"
            .write "<td>" & Trim(objLog.Win32Status) & " " & "</td>"
            .write "<tr>"
            'if counter > 2500 then
            '    exit do
            'end if
        End With
    Loop
%>
</table>
</BODY>
</HTML>
```

When you run this script, it writes a table to the browser containing the log file you specified. Because you can loop through the log, you can use it to count accesses, do clickstream analysis, or help improve your application. For example, you might check to see which pages people click most often from the main page of your application, or analyze how people navigate through your site—knowledge you can't glean from simple page counting components.

You can also use the component to help monitor security violation attempts (or successes). For example, your company or clientele may have a specific block of IP addresses. By analyzing the log, you can tell whether foreign IP addresses have been visiting your site. As an aside—you can be sure that your company and the sites you visit perform this kind of analysis on *your* movement through *their* applications.

The MyInfo Component

The MyInfo component keeps track of personal and site information. If you're using the Microsoft Personal Web Server (PWS) on Windows 95/98, you don't need to create an instance of the MyInfo object, because the server automatically creates one for you. If you're using IIS on Windows NT or Windows 2000, you should create one instance of the MyInfo object at application scope in your `global.asa` file. For example:

```
<object runat="Server" scope="Session" id="MyInfo"
    progid="MSWC.MyInfo">
</object>
```

Alternatively, you can create the component using `Server.CreateObject`. For example:

```
Set myInfo = Server.CreateObject("MSWC.MyInfo")
Application.Lock
Set Application("myInfo") = myInfo
Application.Unlock
```

Regardless of which method you elect to instantiate the component, you only need to create one instance for your entire site.

The MyInfo component is newer than most of the components you've seen so far. Like many of the previous components, it uses a file to store data; but there's a major difference—the MyInfo component stores data in XML form in a file called `MyInfo.xml`. I'll discuss XML last in this book because it's outside the scope of Mastering ASP—XML is a generic technology that can be used in any programming environment. However, you should start learning about XML as soon as possible. An XML file is a universal, self-describing file format. All that means is that just as HTML has become a standard for displaying information, XML is rapidly becoming the standard for encapsulating information and moving that information from place to place.

XML looks like HTML, but you can specify your own tags. You read XML files using an XML parser. An XML parser is a component that understands how to read and write XML-formatted documents. Microsoft provides an XML parser with IE 5, so if you've installed IE 5 on your server, you already have the XML parser. Alternatively, you can download the component and use it with IE 4 and ASP.

At any rate, most new components are likely to use XML to store and export data, and the MyInfo component is just the first one you may see. After you write the `<object>` tag in your `global.asa` file, you can use the component on any page.

In Windows 95/98, the MyInfo component has a large list of built-in properties. In Windows NT or 2000, the component has no built-in properties. The advantage (the only advantage) the MyInfo component has over using variables stored in the Application object directly is that the MyInfo component persists data between application instances. For example, if you stop your Web server, you lose any values in the Application object. The MyInfo component saves the values to a disk file; therefore, you have more protection against accidental or malicious server failure.

Listing 15.8 shows a sample script.

LISTING 15.8   Using the MyInfo Component (ch15i8.asp)

```
<%@ Language=VBScript %>
<html>
<head>
</head>
<body>
<%
Dim myInfo
Application.Lock
Set Application("MyInfo") = Server.CreateObject("MSWC.MyInfo")
Set myInfo = Application("MyInfo")
Application.Unlock

myInfo.FirstName = "Russell"
myInfo.LastName = "Jones"
myInfo.MusicalInstrument = "Piano"
Response.write myInfo.LastName & ", " & myInfo.FirstName & _
    " Musical Instrument: " & myInfo.MusicalInstrument & "<br>"
%>
<p> </p>

</body>
</html>
```

The example stores three new values—Firstname, LastName, and Musical-Instrument in the MyInfo component, which subsequently stores the information on disk. Note that you do not have to save the information explicitly—the component saves it for you automatically.

If you run the example, then search your hard drive for the file myinfo.xml. You should find it in the directory c:\WINNT\system32\inetsrv\Data. If you open the file with NotePad, it should contain the following information:

```
<XML>
<FirstName>Russell</>
<LastName>Jones</>
<MusicalInstrument>Piano</>
</XML>
```

That's all very well, but not very impressive. For example, how would you store information about multiple users using this component? It's easy. You can extend the dot notation to any level you desire to create new levels of information. For example, add this line to the script in Listing 15.8:

```
myInfo.MusicalInstrument.years = 24
```

That line causes the MyInfo component to create a hierarchical structure where the property named `years` is a child item of the property `MusicalInstrument`. If you run that script, then look at the `myinfo.xml` file again. It looks like this:

```
<XML>
<FirstName>Russell</>
<LastName>Jones</>
<MusicalInstrument>Piano
    <years>24</>
</>
</XML>
```

The ability to create hierarchical information means that you can store multiple sets of information for individuals or any other hierarchy you like in the component. In addition to the documented syntax, the component supports the same key syntax as a Dictionary or any intrinsic ASP collection. For example:

```
Response.Write myInfo("MusicalInstrument").years
' writes 24
```

Don't count on the component to store information for many thousands of people, because it has some serious problems. First, it reads the entire XML file into memory, taking up valuable space. Second, it gets slower as you add more information—probably because it has to read and write a larger and larger file each time. Finally, Microsoft developed the component specifically to save personal information for the owner of the PWS Web server. PWS administrators enter that information through an HTML form, so the component only needs to be able to save key names and values—it doesn't provide any method for removing names and values. You can set a value to a null string, but you can't remove it unless you stop the Web server, edit the XML directly, then restart the Web server. In addition, the MyInfo component doesn't conform to the XML file specification; therefore, you cannot use Microsoft's XML parser to read and modify the information it contains.

Despite the fact that the control is crippled, the idea behind it—storing information in an XML file—is a good idea. Keep it in mind because you'll revisit storing XML in files later.

The Page Counter Component

You've already seen several ways to count page visits in this book. Here's yet another method. The Page Counter component tracks the number of visits to a page. I'll be brief. To use the component, create an instance on a page. For example:

```
set pgCounter = Server.CreateObject("MSWC.PageCounter")
```

Like the other components in the MSWC project, the Page Counter component keeps page count information in a text file called `hitcnt.txt` (typically in the `$system$\inetsrv\data` directory). Each entry in the file consumes a single line and contains a count, a space, and a path and filename. For example:

```
18    /MasteringASP/Chapter15/ch15i9.asp
```

Because it's both-threaded, you can instantiate the component at application scope in `global.asa` or create an instance of the component on a page, then store it in the Application object.

The Permission Checker Component

The Permission Checker component lets you check whether a person has permission to open a file. For example, if your application needs to read a file on another server, the IUSR_MACHINENAME account may not have sufficient permission to open the file. You can create a PermissionChecker object and use the `HasAccess` method to determine whether the user can read the file.

WARNING   To test this object, you'll need administrator permissions on the computer hosting your Web server.

Create a text file called `NoAccess.txt` in your `MasteringASP\Chapter15` directory. Enter some text in the file and save it. Navigate to the file with Windows Explorer, right-click on the filename and select Properties from the pop-up menu. Click the Security tab and give Administrators full permission for the file. Remove any access for all other users. Click OK to save your changes. Close the Properties dialog.

Now you can check the file permissions. Listing 15.9 shows a script with a function to check file permissions.

LISTING 15.9   **Using the PermissionChecker object (ch15i10.asp)**

```
<%@ Language=VBScript %>
<% option explicit %>
<%
Function hasPermission(aFile)
    Dim pChecker
    Set pChecker = Server.CreateObject("MSWC.PermissionChecker")
    hasPermission = pChecker.HasAccess(aFile)
    set pChecker = nothing
```

```
End Function
Response.Write hasPermission("NoAccess.txt")
%>
```

When you run this script, it writes False in the browser window—verifying that you do not have access to the NoAccess.txt file. In the ch15i10.asp file I've also provided the script you used to force the browser to authenticate users from *The Logging Utility* section in this chapter. Initially, that portion of the script is commented out. Uncomment the script, or add the script fragment below to the top of the file:

```
<% Response.Buffer = True %>
<%
dim logonUser
logonUser = Request.ServerVariables("LOGON_USER")
if logonUser = "" then
Response.Status = "401 Unauthorized"
    Response.Clear
    Response.AddHeader "WWW-Authenticate","NTLM"
    Response.End
end if
%>
```

Run the script again. This time your browser will present you with a login dialog (if you're using Netscape) or will authenticate you transparently via NT Challenge/Response (if you're using IE). In either case, you should now see True in the browser window when you run the script.

The Permission Checker component is most useful when your site contains pages anyone can see, as well as restricted-access pages for which you must authenticate users.

The Tools Component

The Tools component contains a hodge-podge of methods with which you can:

- Retrieve a random number (Random method)

- Check if a file exists (FileExists method)

- Process the contents of a form (ProcessForm method)

- (PWS only) check if the current user is the site owner (Owner method)

- (Macintosh only) check if a plug-in exists on the server (PluginExists method)

I suspect that this component is obsolete because you can now perform these tasks with script and other components. For example, you can retrieve a random number with the Rnd function in VBScript or the random method in JScript. You can check whether a file exists with the FileExists method of the FileSystemObject object. However, the object is both-threaded, so if you need to perform any of these tasks many times in your application, you can instantiate it at application scope, which will improve the performance slightly.

Using the Components

In this section, you'll create a project that uses several of the components. Create an ASP page called ch15MyProject.asp in the Chapter15 directory of your MasteringASP site, and secure it using the Security tab of the Properties dialog from Windows Explorer so that only administrators have access. Count the number of accesses for the page. Create a special page counter that differentiates between attempted accesses for the secured page and authenticated accesses. For users who don't have access to the secured page, you should return a message stating that only authenticated users may view the page.

Authenticated users should see a listing of the number of authenticated and denied accesses to the page, followed by a random number of log entries (between 10 and 20) for the current server log. Select the entries from the end of the log, not the beginning. If you implement the project correctly, you will always see the file you requested immediately prior to the current request as the last entry in the log. There should be no empty rows in the table.

I suggest you try to build the project first, then compare your results with the ch15Project.asp file in the Chapter15 directory on the CD. Don't expect your code to be identical to mine; there are literally thousands of possible variations—all of which could produce roughly the same results.

Now that you're comfortable with using external components in ASP, you should be glad to know that in addition to the components shown in this chapter, there are a huge number of objects available that work with ASP. In the next chapter, you'll see how to use one of these components to send and receive email.

CHAPTER

SIXTEEN

16

Sending and Receiving Email
with ASP

■ Introduction to CDO for NTS (CDONTS)

■ Using the CDONTS NewMail Object

■ Sending Messages with CDONTS

■ Receiving Messages with CDO

■ Third-Party Mail Components

In this chapter, you'll see how to use Microsoft's Collaboration Data Objects for NT Server (CDONTS) to send mail with ASP scripts. To run the code, you need access to a Simple Mail Transfer Protocol (SMTP) server. Microsoft Exchange server works best, but the SMTP server shipped with IIS 4 or 5 will also work. There are several advantages to using Exchange though—primarily easy access to address books and calendars.

Introduction to CDO for NTS (CDONTS)

As you've probably grown to expect by now, Microsoft provides you with the ability to program CDONTS through a Component Object Model (COM). Microsoft first provided this model in Object Linking and Embedding (OLE) Messaging, later renamed it ActiveX Messaging, and finally Collaboration Data Objects (version 1.2) when Exchange Server 5.5 was released. CDONTS is a subset of CDO 1.2, which has a larger (but also more difficult) object model, with access to calendaring, address resolution (where you type part of an address and the server maps the address to an SMTP email address), and other Exchange features. If your application needs these features, you should explore the CDO 1.2 object model, but if you just want to send mail, CDONTS is considerably easier to use.

CDONTS has a simple feature set that enables you to send single or bulk emails with minimal code. Figure 16.1 shows the CDONTS object model.

FIGURE 16.1:

CDONTS object model

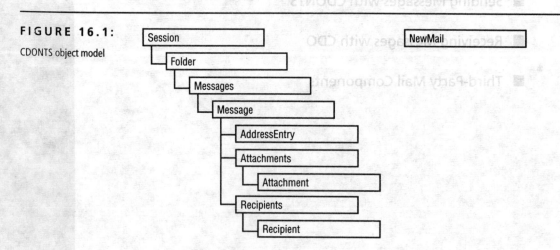

As you can see from Figure 16.1, the CDONTS object model consists of a neat hierarchy headed by the Session object. All other objects in the model are subordinate to the Session object except for the NewMail object. The NewMail object lets you send mail very easily, while the Session object hierarchy gives you more control. The NewMail object has some severe limitations for sending multiple messages; nevertheless, it's the easiest way to get started using CDONTS, and may be all you'll ever need.

Using the CDONTS NewMail Object

To send mail using the NewMail object requires just a few lines of code; you instantiate the object, then use the Send method:

```
<%
Dim mail
Set mail = Server.CreateObject("CDONTS.Newmail")
Call mail.Send("me@mymail.com", "you@yourmail.com", _
    "Mastering ASP", "This mail was sent using CDONTS")
Set mail = Nothing
%>
```

The Send method shown above takes four optional arguments: From, To, Subject, and Body. The listing sends an email message from me@mymail.com to you@yourmail.com with the subject MasteringASP and the content This mail was sent using CDONTS. You can't get much simpler than that. You can also set the NewMail object's properties individually. For example:

```
<%
Dim mail
Set mail = Server.CreateObject("CDONTS.Newmail")
mail.From = "me@mymail.com"
mail.To = "you@yourmail.com"
mail.Subject = "Mastering ASP"
mail.Body = "This mail was sent using CDONTS"
mail.Send
%>
```

The NewMail object lets you send attachments as well, using either the Attach-File or AttachURL method. No surprises here; the methods do exactly what you'd expect—AttachFile attaches a file and AttachURL includes a URL that the rendering object on the receiving end can use to obtain the attached data. Here's the code to send a message with an attached file:

```
<%
Dim mail
Set mail = Server.CreateObject("CDONTS.Newmail")
mail.From = "me@mymail.com"
```

```
mail.To = "you@yourmail.com"
mail.Subject = "Mastering ASP"
mail.Body = "This mail was sent using CDONTS"
mail.AttachFile "c:\test.txt"
mail.Send
%>
```

You must specify a full drive and pathname for the file—the CDONTS object won't work with relative filenames. The `AttachURL` method works exactly the same way as `AttachFile`, but you use a URL string rather than a file pathname. The Microsoft documentation states that you can use an IStream object in place of the filename argument—but you can't do that in VBScript, or even in VB, only with C++ and Java.

Both methods take an optional second argument called `EncodingMethod`. The `EncodingMethod` argument must be one of two constant values, either `CdoEn-codingUUEncode` (0) or `CdoEncodingBase64` (1). The default is `CdoEncodin-gUUEncode`.

Setting the properties individually should let you easily send a single message to a large number of people. For example, if I wanted to send a message to every address in an array of email addresses, I could write code similar to the following:

```
<%
Dim mail
Dim addressList
dim address
AddressList = array("you@yourmail.com", "bob@hisMail.com", _
    "jennifer@hermail.com", "sally@hermail.com")
for each address in addressList
    Set mail = Server.CreateObject("CDONTS.Newmail")
    mail.From = "me@mymail.com"
    mail.Subject = "Mastering ASP"
    mail.Body = "This mail was sent using CDONTS"
    mail.To = address
    mail.Send
    set mail = nothing
next
%>
```

Now the questions is, why did I create a new `mail` object for each iteration in the loop? Highly inefficient isn't it? The answer is that, unfortunately, you can't reuse a NewMail object after you've used it to send a message—you must create a new NewMail object each time. Similarly, the NewMail object has only one readable property called `Version`, which returns a CDONTS version string (currently `1.2.1`). The `Version` property is common to all CDONTS objects. Therefore, if you want to send multiple messages you should use the other objects in the CDONTS object model.

Table 16.1 contains the properties and methods of the CDONTS.NewMail object.

TABLE 16.1: Properties and Methods of the CDONTS.NewMail Object

Method/Property	Description
AttachFile Method	Attaches a file to the message. Refer to the previous section in this chapter for a full explanation of this method.
AttachURL Method	Attaches a file specified by a URL to the message. Refer to the previous section in this chapter for a full explanation of this method.
Bcc Property	The Bcc property specifies the blind carbon copy recipient(s). The property accepts a single email address or list of email addresses separated by semi-colons. People on the blind carbon copy list receive mail, but the people on the to list and the cc list do not know that the people on the bcc list have received a copy.
Body Property	The message body.
BodyFormat Property	The format used for the body of the message. The property takes one of two values, either CdoBodyFormatHTML (0), which informs the control to send the body as HTML-formatted text or CdoBodyFormatText (1), which sends the body as plain text. CdoBodyFormatText is the default.
Cc Property	The Cc property specifies the carbon copy recipient(s). The property accepts a single email address or list of email addresses separated by semi-colons.
ContentBase Property	The ContentBase property controls the base URL for the entire message body, letting you send messages that contain relative URLs. You should set this property if you send messages in HTML format.
ContentLocation Property	Although confusing, the ContentLocation property does exactly the same thing as the ContentBase property—unless you set them both, in which case the NewMail object combines them. For example, you can use the ContentBase property to set the base URL: `ObjNewMail.ContentBase="http://aSite.com/"` and the ContentLocation property to add a subdirectory: `ObjNewMail.ContentLocation="contenthome/"`. The result is that relative URLs, such as filenames for `<img>` and `<a>` tags are relative to the URL: http://aSite.com/contenthome/.
From Property	Sets the email address of the sender.
Importance Property	Sets a value that specifies the importance of the message. You may use any of these values: CdoLow (0), CdoNormal (1), or CdoHigh (2).
MailFormat Property	The encoding scheme used to send the message, either CdoMailFormat-Mime (0) or CdoMailFormatText (1). The latter is the default. You should be aware that changing the value of the EncodingMethod argument to the AttachFile or AttachURL method may change the value of the MailFormat property.
Send Method	Sends the message.

Continued on next page

TABLE 16.1 CONTINUED: Properties and Methods of the CDONTS.NewMail Object

Method/Property	Description
SetLocaleIDs Method	Sets the default code page identifier for the message. The code page ID controls the language, format of times and dates, and other location-specific formatting.
Subject Property	A string specifying the message subject.
To Property	Specifies the message recipient(s). The To property accepts a single email address or a list of email addresses separated by semicolons.
Value Property	Use the Value property to add one or more headers in addition to the To, From, Subject, and Date headers. For example, you might add a File or Reply-To header.
	You must know in advance what additional headers the recipients can use. The header strings must match exactly or the recipient will not be able to view the header value.
Version Property	Returns a string containing the CDONTS version number (currently 1.2.1).

Sending Messages with CDONTS

Although using the Session object hierarchy is more complicated than using the NewMail object, it's also more powerful. To create a new Session object, use:

```
Dim objSession
Set objSession = Server.CreateObject("CDONTS.Session")
```

You normally call the LogonSMTP method as the first action after creating a Session object; otherwise, no other methods or properties will work properly. For example:

```
objSession.LogonSMTP "Your Name", "you@yourmail.com"
```

> **TIP**
> Always use the LogonSMTP method first unless you want to change the user's code page ID. To do that, call the SetLocaleIDs method before setting the LogonSMTP property.

After setting the LogonSMTP property, you can use the CDONTS.Session object and its subordinate objects normally. All CDONTS objects except the NewMail object have some common properties and methods. Table 16.2 shows the CDONTS common object properties and methods.

TABLE 16.2: Methods and Properties Common to all CDONTS Objects

Method/Property	Description
Application	Always returns the string `Collaboration Data Objects for NTS version 1.2.1`.
Class Property (read-only)	Each CDONTS object has a Long class value. The `Class` property accepts a CDONTS object argument and returns the class value for the object. The CDO type library defines constants for the values. The possible values are: AddressEntry—`CdoAddressEntry (8)` Attachment—`CdoAttachment (5)` Attachments collection—`CdoAttachments (18)` Folder—`CdoFolder (2)` Message—`CdoMsg (3)` Messages collection—`CdoMessages (16)` Recipient—`CdoRecipient (4)` Recipients collection—`CdoRecipients (17)` Session—`CdoSession(0)`
Session Property	Returns the Session object associated with the current object. For example, calling the `Folder.Session` property would return the Session object for that Folder. If you use this property with a Session object, it returns itself.
Parent property	Returns the immediate parent of an object. For example, a Folder object's immediate parent is a `Folders` collection object. If you use this method with the `CDONTS.Session` object, it returns `Nothing`—Sessions have no parent.

In addition to the common object properties, each object has its own set of properties and methods. Table 16.3 shows the `CDONTS.Session` object properties and methods.

TABLE 16.3: Properties and Methods of the `CDONTS.Session` Object

Method/Property	Description
Inbox Property	Returns a Folder object representing the current user's incoming mail folder.
GetDefaultFolder Method	Returns a Folder object representing the default folder of a specified `type` argument. The `type` argument must be either `CdoDefaultFolderInbox (1)`, or `CdoDefaultFolderOutbox (2)`.
Logoff Method	Logs the current user off of the Session and invalidates all other objects subordinate to that Session.
LogonSMTP Method	Logs a user onto the Session. You must supply a display name and a full SMTP email address as arguments.
MessageFormat Property	Returns the default message encoding type. The value returned is either `CdoMime (0)` or `CdoText (1)`.
Name Property	Returns the display name used to log onto the Session (see the `LogonSMTP` method).

Continued on next page

TABLE 16.3 CONTINUED: Properties and Methods of the CDONTS.Session Object

Method/Property	Description
Outbox Property	Returns a Folder object representing the current user's outgoing mail folder.
SetLocaleIDs Method	Sets the default code page identifier for the current user. The code page ID controls the language, format of times and dates, and other location-specific formatting. If you use this method, you must call it before using any other method or property of the Session object, including the **LogonSMTP** method.
Version Property	Returns the string 1.2.1.

After creating and initializing a Session object with the **LogonSMTP** method, you can use the methods and properties of the subordinate objects to send mail. The process to send mail is:

1. Create a Session object.

2. Initialize the Session object using the **LogonSMTP** method.

3. Retrieve the outbox for the user with the getDefaultFolder(cdoDefault-FolderOutbox) method.

4. Retrieve the **Messages** collection from the folder.

5. Use the Add method of the **Messages** collection to add a new message.

6. Set the Message object's properties.

7. Use the Message object's **Send** method to send the message.

For example, the following code creates and sends a new message from the user bob@mySite.com to janedoe@anothersite.com:

```
Dim sess As CDONTS.Session
Dim fldr As CDONTS.Folder
Dim msgs As CDONTS.Messages
Dim msg As CDONTS.Message
Set sess = New CDONTS.Session
sess.LogonSMTP "Bob Arnold", "bobarnold@mySite.com"
sess.MessageFormat = CdoText
Set fldr = sess.GetDefaultFolder(CdoDefaultFolderOutbox)
Set msgs = fldr.Messages
msg.Recipients = "janedoe@anothersite.com"
msg.Sender = "bobarnold@mySite.com"
msg.Subject = "Test"
msg.Text = "Test"
msg.Send
msgs.Add "test", "test"
```

The CDONTS collection objects, `Recipients`, `Attachments`, and `Messages` are fairly standard collection objects. They support common collection object methods such as `Add`, `Delete`, `Count`, and `Item`. The `Messages` collection also supports iteration over the collection through the `GetFirst`, `GetLast`, `GetNext`, and `GetPrevious` methods. To use the `GetNext` or `GetPrevious` methods, you should first use either the `GetFirst` or `GetLast` method to initialize the position pointer for the collection.

I'm not going to list all of the properties and methods for all the CDONTS objects—they're available in your MSDN documentation or online at the Microsoft site; however, I will list the properties and methods of the Message object; the AddressEntry object, which represents a user; the Attachment object; and the Recipient object.

NOTE   For simplicity, I have omitted the common object properties listed in Table 16.2 from the property and method lists in the remainder of this section.

Table 16.4 lists the properties and methods of the CDONTS.`Message` object.

TABLE 16.4: Properties and Methods of the CDONTS.`Message` Object

Property/Method	Description
`Attachments` Property	Attachment object or `Attachments` collection.
`ContentBase` Property	Set this property if you send messages in HTML format. It controls the base URL for the entire message body, letting you send messages that contain relative URLs.
`ContentID` Property	Retrieves the automatically generated unique ID associated with every message.
`ContentLocation` Property	Although confusing, the `ContentLocation` property does exactly the same thing as the `ContentBase` property—unless you set them both, in which case the NewMail object combines them. For example, you can use the `ContentBase` property to set the base URL: `ObjNewMail.ContentBase="http://aSite.com/"` and the `ContentLocation` property to add a subdirectory: `ObjNewMail .ContentLocation="contenthome/"`. The result is that relative URLs, such as filenames for `<img>` and `<a>` tags are relative to the URL: `http://aSite.com/contenthome/`.
`Delete` Method	Removes the current message from the `Messages` collection. You must have sufficient permission to delete messages.
`HTMLText` Property	Sets or returns the HTML text associated with the message.
`Importance` Property	Sets a value that specifies the importance of the message. You may use any of these values: `CdoLow` (0), `CdoNormal` (1), or `CdoHigh` (2).
`MessageFormat` Property	Returns the default message encoding type. The value returned is either `CdoMime` (0) or `CdoText` (1).

Continued on next page

TABLE 16.4 CONTINUED: Properties and Methods of the CDONTS.Message Object

Property/Method	Description
Recipients Property	Returns a single Recipient or a **Recipients** collection.
Sender Property	Returns an AddressEntry object representing the user who sent the message.
Size Property	Returns the approximate number of bytes in the message, including all attachments.
Subject Property	Sets or returns the message subject.
Text Property	Returns or sets the text of the message body.
TimeReceived Property	Returns the date and time the message was received (valid for inbox messages only).
TimeSent Property	Returns the date and time the message was sent (valid for inbox messages only).
Send Method	Sends the current message.

Table 16.5 lists the properties and methods of the CDONTS.Attachment object.

TABLE 16.5: Properties and Methods of the CDONTS.Attachment Object

Property/Method	Description
ContentBase Property	Returns the base URL for the attachment (valid for inbox attachments only).
ContentID Property	Retrieves the Content-ID header associated with an attachment (valid for inbox attachments only).
ContentLocation Property	Returns the Content-Location header of the attachment (valid for inbox attachments only).
Delete Method	Deletes the attachment from the **Attachments** collection.
Name Property	Sets or returns the display name of the attachment.
ReadFromFile Method	Loads an attachment from a file. You must specify the full drive and path-name for the file. To use this method, the value of the **Type** property must be **CdoFileData** (1). CDONTS does not support the **ReadFromFile** method for embedded messages.
Source Property	Sets or returns the location of the data for the attachment. The return value depends on the **Type** property (which you must set before setting the **Source** property). When the **Type** property is **CdoFileData**, the **Source** property returns an empty string. When the **Type** property is **CdoEmbeddedMessage**, the **Source** property sets or returns the Message object to be embedded in the attachment.
Type Property	Sets or returns the attachment type. The possible values are **CdoFileData** (1) and **CdoEmbeddedMessage** (4).
WriteToFile Method	Writes the data of an attachment to disk. You must specify the full drive and pathname for the output file. To use this method, the value of the **Type** property must be **CdoFileData** (1). CDONTS does not support the **WriteToFile** method for embedded messages.

To add an attachment, set a reference to the Message object's `Attachments` collection, then use the `Add` method. The following code fragment assumes that the `myMsg` variable refers to a valid Message object:

```
<%
Dim mAttachments
Dim mAttachment
Set mAttachments = myMsg.Attachments
Set mAttachment = mAttachments.Add
mAttachment.Name = "Read Me"
mAttachment.Type = cdoFileData
mAttachment.ReadFromFile "c:\somefile.txt"
%>
```

You can add a new attachment with a single statement using the `Add` method of the `Attachments` collection. The `Add` method accepts up to five optional arguments: `Name`, `Type`, `Source`, `ContentLocation`, and `ContentBase`. For example, the following code is functionally equivalent to the previous listing:

```
<%
Dim mAttachments
Dim mAttachment
Set mAttachments = myMsg.Attachments
Set mAttachment = mAttachments.Add("Read Me", _
    CdoFileData, "c:\somefile.txt"
%>
```

The AddressEntry object represents a person. CDONTS has no knowledge of any real people; a user consists of a display name and a unique string specifying the person's address. You can't create an AddressEntry object directly, you must use the Message object's `Sender` property to obtain an AddressEntry object. Because the message must have been sent to have a `Sender` property, all AddressEntry properties are read-only. Table 16.6 lists the properties of the `CDONTS.AddressEntry` object (the object has no methods).

TABLE 16.5: Properties of the `CDONTS.AddressEntry` Object

Property/Method	Description
Address Property	Returns the unique string address associated with the AddressEntry object. The string format is mail-system specific.
Name Property	Returns the display name for the AddressEntry object.
Type Property	Specifies the address type. Currently the only supported type is **SMTP**.

When you obtain a Message object from the user's inbox, the Recipient object properties are read-only. You may only modify the Recipient object's properties when it is associated with a Message object from the user's outbox, before the message has been sent. You obtain an individual Recipient object from a Message object's `Recipients` collection. For example:

```
<%
Dim mRecipients
Dim mRecipient
Set mRecipients = myMsg.Recipients
Set mRecipient= mRecipients.Add
mRecipient.Address = "bobarnold@mySite.com"
mRecipient.Name = "Bob Arnold"
%>
```

You can add a new Recipient to the collection using the `Add` method of the `Recipients` collection. As with the `Attachments` collection, you can either use the `Add` method with no arguments, or up to three optional arguments called `Name`, `Address`, and `Type`. In both cases, the `Add` method returns the new Recipient object.

Table 16.6 lists the methods and properties of the `CDONTS.Recipient` object.

TABLE 16.6: Properties and Methods of the `CDONTS.Recipient` Object

Property/Method	Description
Address Property	Returns the unique messaging address associated with the Recipient object.
Delete Method	Deletes the Recipient object from the `Recipients` collection.
Name Property	Returns the display name for the Recipient object.
Type Property	Returns or sets the type of recipient (To, Cc, or Bcc). The possible values are CdoTo (1), CdoCC (2), and CdoBcc (3).

Receiving Messages with CDO

To receive messages with CDO, you follow much the same procedure as to send a message. The process to receive mail is:

1. Create a Session object.

2. Initialize the Session object using the `LogonSMTP` method.

3. Retrieve the inbox for the user with the `getDefaultFolder(cdoDefault-FolderInbox)` method.

4. Retrieve the `Messages` collection from the folder.

5. Check the `Count` property of the `Messages` collection. You should not use any of the `Get...` methods if there are no messages.

6. Use the `GetFirst` method of the `Messages` collection to retrieve the first message.

7. To iterate through the inbox messages, use the `GetNext` method of the `Messages` collection to retrieve the next message until the method returns `Nothing`.

Third-Party Mail Components

You aren't limited to CDO—in fact, a large number of people find third-party mail programs easier and more flexible, especially if they're not using Exchange. Among the more popular components are ASPMail, ASPMailer, ASPFreeMail, ASPEMail, JMail, SA-SmptMail, and several others. You can find many of these components at the ASP site `http://www.15Seconds.com`.

PART V

Accessing Databases with ASP and ADO

PART V

Accessing Databases with ASP and ADO

CHAPTER
SEVENTEEN

17

Introduction to Relational Databases and SQL

- ■ Databases vs. Files

- ■ Tables, Indexes, Primary Keys, and Foreign Keys

- ■ Set-based Data Retrieval

- ■ Introduction to SQL

At this point you should be comfortable with both scripting and component use in ASP files. This chapter contains an introduction to relational database technology. All the database access code and discussion in this book centers around Open Database Connectivity (ODBC) databases—primarily SQL Server, since that's the database with which I'm most familiar—but you can apply the information to Oracle, Sybase, or any relational SQL database just as effectively.

Databases vs. Files

You've seen how to use sequential files to save data. You probably also realize that sequential files aren't always the most efficient way to store data—especially large data sets. Whenever someone begins to discuss efficiency you should immediately become skeptical. Why aren't files efficient? Wait—I didn't say files in general, I said sequential files. Also, I didn't say sequential files in general are inefficient; I said data sets (especially large ones) stored in sequential files are inefficient.

If you're streaming data to a browser, like Web servers stream HTML files, sequential files are the most efficient method for storing data long-term. But if you only need a single item of information, sequential files are inefficient. One reason they're inefficient is that you can't jump directly to a single item within the file. You must either read the file sequentially up to the point where the requested data resides for each request, or read the entire file at application or session startup and store the information at application scope, which wastes memory. Another reason sequential files are inefficient is that you can't write data to the middle of the file without rewriting the entire file.

With a sequential file, fixed field lengths or delimiters define the separation between individual items, called fields. The most common type of delimited file is the comma-delimited file, which uses the comma character to separate fields. You don't have to use a comma—although commas are the most common separator character, they're not always the most efficient. Commas appear in most text. Therefore, text fields containing commas always present a problem: how can the computer tell the difference between a comma that acts as a field delimiter and delimits a field, and a comma that's part of the data?

Delimiters provide separation between fields, but they don't specify the length for any particular field. Delimiters separate variable-length fields. But for many field types, you know exactly how long the field needs to be to contain the data. A date/time field, for example, formatted in mm/dd/yyyy hh:mm:ss am/pm form, is always exactly 22 characters long. A name field, on the other hand, may vary between 2 and 20 characters in length. Comma-delimited files work extremely well when you're working with streaming data, but don't work nearly as well when you need to access or alter individual items in the middle of the file.

For example, suppose I have a sequential file containing names and addresses. I want to change the address for the first person in the file. If the new address is longer than the existing address, I can't overwrite the information without also potentially overwriting critical information that follows the address. For example:

```
' Original File contents
Doe,John,15440 St. Paul Ave,Minneapolis,MN,99820

' New Address
98029 Livonia Ave #205,Minneapolis,MN,99820
```

The new address is longer than the old address. If I simply start at the current beginning-of-address position and write the new data, the file will look like this:

```
' Overwritten File contents
Doe,John,98029 Livonia Ave #205,neapolis,MN,99820
```

As you can see, the new address line overwrites part of the city field. Similarly, if the new address were shorter than the old address, overwriting the data would leave extraneous characters from the previous address, and I would need to pad the new data with blanks to completely erase the old data. Therefore, I need to rewrite the file to replace the address. Rewriting the entire file to change a value is not a problem when a sequential file contains a small number of items, but as the file grows to hundreds, thousands, or millions of items, it takes longer and longer to write the data. To avoid such problems, programmers invented the concept of random access files. With a random access file you aren't concerned with separator characters; instead, your primary concern becomes field length.

With a random access file, you store data in records. Each record consists of fields, and each field is a pre-selected size. For example, you can store a date in six bytes—as six text characters, e.g., 041299 (which is the root cause of the Y2K problem); as a number that's an offset from a single known date; or as two one-byte values for the month and day combined with a two-byte value for the year. All these date-storing schemes rely on the fact that the program storing the data and the program reading the data both understand and agree on the format in which dates are stored.

Similarly, you could arbitrarily assume that last names are never longer than 30 characters; therefore, you could create a 30-character field to store last names. Unfortunately, the size you select is critical. Having decided that last names are 30 characters, you may not be able to change that length easily. When you find a last name longer than 30 characters, you won't be able to accommodate it. In other words: random access files waste storage space.

The advantage of the random access file is that you can replace data in the middle of the file without rewriting the entire file. As long as the new data conforms to the field type and size of the existing data, you can overwrite the old data without a problem.

Because all the fields in each record are the same length, all the records are also the same length. You can also think of the data as a set of records, or a record set. Each record set consists of an arbitrary number of records, each of which contains the same number and type of fields. That conveniently lets you think of random access files in terms of tables. A table is a set of records in which the data in a given column is always the same type and size. Therefore, a record set and a table are essentially the same thing.

With a random access file, you can do much more than replace records; you can sort records as well. For example, suppose I have a list of grammar school children. Each child belongs in a specific grade and several teachers teach each grade. I want to divide the children into classes such that each teacher gets roughly the same number of children. I want a final listing by grade, teacher, and child.

To obtain my final list, I'm going to need to sort the data. I need to separate the children into classes and group the class records together. Assume that the records are originally on disk as shown in Table 17.1.

TABLE 17.1: Sample Class Records—Students

ID	Grade	Teacher	LastName	FirstName
1	1	NA	Jones	Barry
2	2	NA	Templeton	Bill
3	2	NA	Jones	Meredith
4	1	NA	McArthur	Isabel
5	3	NA	Said	Mohammed
6	3	NA	Chen	Xiulian
7	2	NA	Barker	Charles

To determine how many teachers I need for each grade, I first need to count the number of students in each grade. To do that, I need to loop through the file, reading each record and keeping a separate counter for each grade. At the end of the loop, I will know the number of students in each grade.

Next, I can assign teachers by desired class size. For example, if I have 160 first-grade students, I will need 8 teachers if the average class size is 20, but only 6 teachers if the average class size is 25. I could now loop back through the file and assign a teacher to each student.

The data is complete, but I still have a problem: how am I going to display the data? On disk, the records are still in their original sequence. To display the data in order, I'll need to sort it. I could rewrite the file in the correct sequence, moving each record to its sorted position, but that's inefficient. If I add a student, I'll have to rewrite the data again, and if I have to rewrite all the data to add a record, a random access file provides very little advantage over a sequential file!

Suppose that instead of rewriting the data in the proper sequence, I keep a separate list of the IDs as a file on disk. Each ID in the separate file is associated with the record number of the complete file. I can now say that the list of IDs is an index into the data file—let's call it the Grade-Teacher-Name (GTN) index. If I can find an ID in the index file, I can obtain the record number of the data in the main file.

Using the index, I can retrieve the list in GTN sequence without altering the physical position of the data. Similarly, if I add a new student record to the end of the main file, I can loop through my GTN index to find out where the new student belongs, then insert the new student ID number at that location. The index file is a sequential file, but it's relatively small compared to the data file. It's much faster to rewrite the index file than to rewrite the data file.

I still have some problems though. Suppose a teacher gets married during the school year. I now need to update each student's record with the teacher's new name. Not only that, I probably need to go back to the data from prior years and replace that teacher's name throughout my data set. It would be much simpler if I could keep the teacher names in one file and the student names in another and join them together when I needed a report.

For example, suppose that instead of using up valuable space to put a teacher name in each row, I changed the data design so each row contains a `TeacherID` column as shown in Table 17.2.

TABLE 17.2: Sample Class Records—Students

ID	Grade	TeacherID	LastName	FirstName
1	1	32	Jones	Barry
2	2	86	Templeton	Bill
3	2	87	Jones	Meredith
4	1	21	McArthur	Isabel
5	3	45	Said	Mohammed
6	3	45	Chen	Xiulian
7	2	86	Barker	Charles

Now, rather than changing each row associated with that teacher, I can change a single row in another, related table called Teachers, as shown in Table 17.3.

TABLE 17.3: Sample Class Records—Teachers

TeacherID	LastName	FirstName
32	Franklin	Marsha
86	Barstow	Emily
21	Bannister	Henry
87	McAllister	Ian
45	Pinker	Dorothy

Now, no matter how many teacher changes I make, I can either update a single row in the Teachers table or the TeacherID column in the Students table. A data design like this consists of relationships. The TeacherID column in the Teachers table is a primary key, meaning one and only one row may be associated with a single value. The related TeacherID column in the Students table is a foreign key because it contains data that originates from outside the table—in other words, from a foreign table. Because one teacher may teach many students, there is a one-to-many relationship between the tables.

Extend this idea a little bit. Imagine that in this school, each student takes many classes during the day, and further, that those classes aren't all the same each day. In other words, each student may have many teachers and classes, which changes the relationship between teachers and students from one-to-many into a many-to-many relationship. If you can imagine that, then you can also imagine that managing the key relationships and indexes isn't an easy task. You probably wouldn't want to write that code yourself. Well, fortunately, you don't have to. Managing relationships like this is exactly what relational databases were meant to do.

Part of managing data relationships involves ensuring that the data you're putting into the database is the right data. With a file, you must write the data validation code yourself. Databases simplify that process by refusing to store data that doesn't meet the requirements (field types and sizes) specified when you created the database. But modern databases go far beyond simple data type validation. You can define complex data types, such as combinations of numeric and string values, as well as rules about how the data in columns must relate. For example, you could create a data type called ORDER_ID. An ORDER_ID consists of two characters identifying the product, a dash, a four-character product subtype number, a dash, and the order date in MMDDYYYY format. For example:

FB-8382-12041999

When you assign the ORDER_ID data type to a column, the database enforces validity on that column. If your company subsequently changes the rules, you can theoretically revise the ORDER_ID data type and change the data in the database to fit the new rules without having to change the code in all the applications that access the data.

Databases can also enforce data-relationship rules. The simplest example involves a one-to-many primary-foreign key relationship between two tables. Each row in the table on the many side of the relationship must have a matching row in the table on the one side of the relationship. The database rejects data that doesn't fit those requirements. Similarly, the database would not let you delete a row from the one side that had matching rows on the many side.

Indexes, primary keys, and foreign key relationships are all part of a larger concept called constraints. A constraint is a limitation, a way to prevent error conditions from occurring. For example, a primary key has unique value for each row in a table. Primary keys may not be null. The database enforces five types of constraints:

Not null   the field may not contain a null value.

Unique   the field must be unique within its column.

Primary key   a combination of unique and not null. A table may have only one primary key.

Foreign key   defines a relationship between two tables, either one-to-one, (1:), one-to-many (1:M), or many to many (M:N).

Check   enforces rules concerning data values; for example, an Employee_Age column must be between 18 and 70.

Databases have one more huge advantage over files—they can run queries. A query is a request to retrieve, alter, or add data to a database. You write queries in a special language called Structured Query Language (SQL, pronounced sequel). Because most databases store the database objects themselves in standard tables, you can use SQL to modify the database itself.

Transactions and Logging

A transaction is a unit of work that must either complete successfully or fail completely. For example, when deleting a row of data, you don't want the database to delete only part of that row; you want it to delete the whole row. Therefore, if any error occurs during the delete operation, you want the database to abandon any deletions it may have already made. You control this by telling the database to start a transaction. Then, if any errors occur you can roll back the transaction—putting the database back into the state it was before the transaction began.

Modern relational databases such as SQL Server handle all internal operations as transactions. Before a transaction begins, the database logs the current value of all affected data. After the operation completes, the database logs the operation itself. By logging all data and structure modification to the database, the Database Management System (DBMS) ensures that you can recover from disasters. For example, if the power should suddenly fail in the middle of an operation, you would be able to recover, or roll back the state of the database to exactly what it was before the power outage. To do that, you would combine the most recent backup with the transaction log. Essentially, the database would replay the transactions in the exact sequence they occurred until it reached the last operation that was logged.

The log file used by databases to maintain the list of transactions is called the transaction log. You cannot disable the transaction log, even though disabling it would speed up operations that alter data, because the database would be unable to recover from disasters. Most databases allow some unlogged operations. For example, truncating (deleting all the data from) a table is an unlogged operation. In contrast, using a DELETE statement to delete the data is a logged operation. Some databases let you load data from a backup as an unlogged operation.

Although Microsoft Access and most other file-based databases support transactions, they do not maintain a transaction log for each operation. Therefore, their disaster recovery is limited to restoring the database from the latest backup. You cannot recover data changes that occurred since the last backup, a prime reason why they are unsuitable for transactional applications and for applications containing critical data.

Tables, Indexes, Primary Keys, and Foreign Keys

You've already seen a small example of tables, primary keys, and foreign keys in the first section of this chapter. To recap: A table is a collection of rows. Rows consist of fields (or columns), which for any given row, are exactly the same size and data type as in any other row. An index is a sorted column that lets a database management system find a row very quickly—much more quickly in most cases than scrolling through the data. A primary key is a number, string value, or combination of field values that uniquely identifies a specific row, and a foreign key is a value inserted in another table to form a relationship with the same value in a different table.

The easiest way to create and maintain tables is with some sort of front-end management system. For example, Visual Studio contains some rudimentary but highly functional tools to help you create tables, indexes, and relationships. I strongly recommend that you obtain and learn to use such a tool. SQL Server treats tables, indexes, and certain types of relationships as objects. They have properties and methods, and you can create them in code. With most DBMSs you can also create them with the flavor of SQL supported by that DBMS.

Your aim in designing a database is two-fold: First, you want to define the tables so you store a specific item in only one place. For example, if I stored the teacher names in both the Teachers table and repeated it in the Students table (both shown in the previous section) I would have violated that rule. The process of partitioning information among tables such that the information appropriate to any given row appears only in that row is called normalization. Normalization is important because it lets you change information in only one place. Second, you want to be able to retrieve data from the database quickly.

These two goals are often in direct opposition. For example, to show a report of students by teachers, it is obviously more work to obtain a set of student records and then insert the corresponding teacher names, than it is to read the student records with the teacher names already present in the Student table rows. Sometimes (but not often) for speed reasons, you may need to denormalize a table. Consider denormalization to be a process of optimization—a process that occurs only after a normalized design has proven to be a bottleneck.

Every table should have a primary key. That sounds deceptively simple, but it's not always easy to find a meaningful value that is unique to every row. For example, you can't use a LastName field as a primary key because too many people have the same last name. You can't use a combination of LastName and FirstName values for the same reason. You can't even use a telephone number—what if you have a husband and wife both teaching in the same school? A much better choice would be a Social Security number, which the government guarantees to be unique for each individual.

When no meaningful data field presents itself as a good primary key candidate, you can use an artificial value. This condition is so common that most databases support an automatically incrementing field. The database increments a value—usually a long integer—whenever you add a row. The incremented value ensures that you have a column containing a unique value for each row of the table. In SQL Server, this type of field is an identity field. Identity fields are perfect for differentiating rows in a single database, but they're not perfect if you have several databases and need to merge the data.

For example, suppose my Web application supports a distributed sales force. Each salesperson enters orders into a program running on a laptop during the day, and then uploads the new or edited rows to a central database whenever they can connect via a dial-up connection. If the database on the laptops uses an identity field, it's highly likely that the central server will eventually receive two rows from separate salespeople that both have the same number. Consider the first row that any salesperson sends. With a fresh database on a laptop, the first row will have an identity value of 1, so each salesperson would tend to send rows with the same numbers. Of course, you could elect to ignore the identity value on the local database and create a new one in the central database when you add the row, but that defeats the purpose of having a unique value because it's no longer unique; the salesperson's row has a different identifier than the central row.

In such cases, you can take advantage of a Windows concept called a Globally Unique ID (GUID). A GUID is a string of numbers and letters guaranteed to be unique—no other computer will generate that ID. Unfortunately, you can't create a GUID with script because it requires an API call, but SQL Server can create one for you. SQL Server versions 7 and higher support GUIDs as a native data type. Because GUIDs are globally unique, you can merge remote data into a central store without worrying about whether the row IDs might collide, and without the central row ID being different from the local row ID.

A primary key is an index, but not all indexes are primary. Primary keys must be unique indexes. A unique index consists of column values in which each value in the entire column is unique; each row contains a single unique value in that column. Not all indexes are unique—that is, they index columns in which values are repeated from row to row. Often, you need to index a field that is not unique, for example, a list of names. Similarly, you may want to create a unique index on a field that is not a primary key. For example, a Social Security number is unique, but doesn't necessarily make a good primary key, because it's long. A shorter unique value, such as an identity field, would be faster.

Indexes don't have to consist of values from a single column. You can use a combination of columns, called a composite index. For example, an application to schedule rooms in a public facility could use a composite index consisting of both the room number and the date it was scheduled as a primary key. The room number isn't unique, a given room may be booked every day, and the date isn't unique, many rooms may be booked on the same date, but the combination is unique. A given room may be booked only once on any given date.

You should normally index all fields:

- Used to sort data
- Used as foreign keys
- Ones that appear as conditional values in queries

If you think about how the database must apply the index to find and sort data, these rules are nothing more than common sense. If you join two tables on a common field—a foreign key relationship—it's obvious that the DBMS can find matching rows in the tables much faster if you index the columns in both tables. Similarly, sorting an index is considerably faster than sorting an entire table.

An important index type in SQL Server is a clustered index. A clustered index controls the physical order of records in the database. A database keeps data in pages. Each page consists of a fixed number of bytes. Typically, databases don't completely fill up a page before beginning to place data into another page. That way, when you add a record, there's a larger chance that it will fit into an existing page. A clustered index forces the database to maintain the data in a specific order, making it much faster to request data sorted in that order—because the data is already sorted. All the DBMS has to do is retrieve the records in their physical order.

You should create a clustered index on a column that controls the order in which you most often wish to retrieve the data. Some types of values aren't suited for clustered indexes. For example, bit fields, which can take only two values, 1 or 0, are unsuitable for clustered indexes. Similarly, columns containing sequential values, such as identity fields, are not good candidates for a clustered index.

As with many database issues, when you discuss indexes, there are invariably design trade-offs between ease-of-use, speed, and maintainability. For example, a GUID is a long string. It will be slower and use more storage and memory space than a simple identity value; however, you may elect to use a GUID because you need to merge data from many locations. There are no hard and fast rules. You must decide which issues are most important for your application. With that said, there are several considerations that are common to all database applications.

In general, you should try to keep primary keys (and all indexes) as short as possible. Wide values (those that take up many bytes) are slower than narrow values. Numeric values are generally faster than string values.

Index all foreign key columns and columns used to sort data. You need to be able to differentiate between when you should and should not follow this rule, because slavishly following the rule leads to slow databases. Indexes improve data selection operations, but slow down data alteration operations. That's because the DBMS must alter table indexes, deleting, inserting, or resorting as needed when you alter data in that table. Therefore, if most of your application's interaction with a table consists of inserting data, such as an application to handle online order processing, you want to minimize the number of indexes on that table. In contrast, if most of your data operations involve selecting data, you want to index every column that might improve the response time. The point is that you should look at the foreign key columns, columns with selection constraints, and columns that control sort order and make a decision as to whether you should or should not index the column based on your application's needs.

Set-based Data Retrieval

When you access data from a file, you often scroll through data line-by-line, processing values when you find specific values in the line or processing each line. Relational databases, although you may think about them as individual lines, don't work that way. Instead, they work on sets of data. A data set is a combination of one or more rows and columns—in other words, a set of records, called a record set. Note that the columns in the record set do not have to come from a single table. In fact, with relational databases, most of your queries will not come from a single table—if they do, you're making poor use of the relational capabilities of modern databases.

> **NOTE**
> When I say relational databases, I'm specifically not discussing Microsoft Access or any other file-based database. Although you can use Access for practice, it's not suitable for a full-scale Web application with more than a small number of users. It's not suitable for any users if the data is critical. If you were considering using Access for your Web application—don't. In fact, I recommend that you not use it at all, even for practice. Consider using the newer MSDE (Microsoft Data Engine) instead. It supports the same syntax as SQL Server, which means you won't have to change your application when you deploy it for use. MSDE is no more suited for a large-scale or critical Web application than Access, but it is considerably easier to upgrade.

For all discussion of databases throughout the rest of this book, you can assume that I mean both MSDE and SQL Server, even though, for brevity, I will omit the term MSDE. I'm not trying to ignore Oracle, Sybase, Informix, DB2, or any other relational database management system—all the general database information, (but not the Transact-SQL code itself), applies equally well to those DBMSs as to SQL Server. This is, after all, a book about Microsoft technology, so it is Microsoft-centric.

Working with sets requires a different mindset than working with rows of data. It forces you to think in terms of relationships rather than in terms of rows. You also begin thinking about data as collections of records rather than as individual data items. Typically, you join a column from one table with a matching column in another table to retrieve a set of records. A join finds matching values in the columns, then selects a specified set of columns from the intersection of the two sets.

For example, consider a teacher-student relationship. One teacher has many students. Conversely, one student may have several teachers. This is an example of a many-to-many relationship. For your application, you want to be able to select the set of students taught by any given teacher, as well as the set of teachers for any given student. To create this relationship in a database, you must model that many-to-many relationship in table relationships. If the `Teachers` table contains a unique or primary key index on a `TeacherID` field and the `Students` table contains a unique or primary key index on a `StudentID` field, you can create a separate table called `TeacherStudent` that contains nothing but rows that contain the two IDs.

Using the `TeacherStudent` table, it's easy to determine which students have which teachers and obtain the set of students taught by any teacher. For example, the teacher Marsha Franklin (TeacherID=32) teaches Barry Jones, Meredith Jones, and Mohammed Said. If you query a database for this information, you need to find the intersection of the three tables as shown in Figure 17.1.

FIGURE 17.1:

Teachers-to-Students relationship query

TeacherID	StudentID
32	1
86	5
87	3
21	7
45	2
45	7
86	4
32	3
86	4
32	5
45	1

TeacherID	LastName	FirstName
32	Franklin	Marsha
86	Barstow	Emily
21	Bannister	Henry
87	McAllister	Ian
45	Pinker	Dorothy

StudentID	Grade	LastName	FirstName
1	1	Jones	Barry
2	2	Templeton	Bill
3	2	Jones	Meredith
4	1	McArthur	Isabel
5	3	Said	Mohammed
6	3	Chen	Xiulian
7	2	Barker	Charles

The result of this query is another table—a record set, shown in Table 17.4.

TABLE 17.4: Teachers-to-Students Relationship Query Result

Teacher ID	Teacher LastName	Teacher FirstName	Student ID	Student LastName	Student FirstName
32	Franklin	Marsha	1	Jones	Barry
32	Franklin	Marsha	3	Jones	Meredith
32	Franklin	Marsha	5	Said	Mohammed

To obtain the information from the database, you must frame the question in SQL. In the next section, I'll show you how to do that, but first, you'll need a database with which you can test your SQL statements.

In the remainder of this chapter, you'll work with a database called `ClassRecords`. You've already seen a few examples from the database in previous sections in the chapter. The ClassRecords database contains information from an imaginary school in which teachers teach classes to different grades. All the students in the school move from class to class and from teacher to teacher.

The SQL statements to create and populate the database in SQL Server or MSDE are on the CD. For learning purposes, the data is in a Microsoft Access database as well. You need Access, MSDE, or SQL Server to work through the examples and code in the remainder of this book.

Creating the *ClassRecords* Database

To create the database in SQL Server 6.5, open the ISQL application and paste the code from the CD into the code window. In SQL Server 7, ISQL has changed names; it's now called the Query Analyzer. Open the Query Analyzer applet and paste the code from the CD into the code window.

If you're using the Access version, create a Database subdirectory in your MasteringASP directory. Copy the ClassRecords.MDB database file to that directory, then use Windows Explorer to set the file security so the IUSR_MACHINENAME account has Change (RWXD) permission for the file.

NOTE   You will not be able to query an Access database unless it is on the same computer as your server because IIS will be unable to authenticate across the network. Don't store the Access database on a network drive.

SQL Code Conventions

By convention, I will show SQL keywords in uppercase in the book, even though SQL is not case-sensitive. As with VBScript code, I have not been as careful to adhere to any case conventions in the code itself.

SQL doesn't have line termination characters or line continuation characters, so I've broken the lines to fit the layout of this book. You don't have to do that. SQL lets you format the code however you like—including one long line (but don't do that). Indent SQL code like you would indent your VBScript code—make it readable.

SQL has two types of comments: inline comments, which begin with a double-dash (--) and continue to the end of the line, and block comments, which, like Java or C, begin with a slash-star (/*) and end with the reverse—a star-slash (*/). For example:

```
-- This is an inline comment.
/*
This is a block comment.
*/
```

You can freely nest inline comments within block comments. For example:

```
/* The following SELECT statement has been commented out
-- SELECT * FROM SomeTable
*/
```

You may not continue a code line after a comment. For example, the following statement is invalid:

```
SELECT - This is a select statement -- * FROM ...
```

SQL Server ignores all but the first double-dash on any line.

Introduction to SQL

Structured Query Language (SQL) is a straightforward subject, partly because it doesn't do much, and partly because the language is standardized. Most modern databases use a variant of SQL that, for the most part, conforms to the American National Standards Institute (ANSI) 92 standard. That standard means you can use similar, although not quite identical, SQL code to access many different databases. Fortunately, for basic operations, there's no difference between most common databases.

SQL lets you perform four basic operations:

SELECT – Retrieve data

INSERT – Add data

UPDATE – Change data

DELETE – Remove data

The *SELECT* Statement

The SELECT statement retrieves data from the database. To retrieve the data, you specify a field list, a table list, a list of fields to sort by, and the sort order. The parts of a SQL statement are called clauses. A basic SELECT statement has up to four clauses. For example:

```
SELECT (field1, field2, etc.) FROM (table list) WHERE (condition)
ORDER BY (field1 [ASC|DESC], field2 [ASC|DESC], etc.)
```

The WHERE and ORDER BY clauses are optional. If you omit the WHERE clause, the query returns all rows from the specified tables. If you omit the ORDER BY clause, SQL retrieves rows in the sequence in which they're stored in a table. By default, when you retrieve data from multiple tables, SQL uses the row order from the first specified field.

At the most basic level, you can obtain all the information from a table using an asterisk (*) as a shorthand way of specifying all fields. For example:

```
SELECT * FROM Teachers
```

The previous query returns all the columns in all rows of the Teachers table:

TeacherID	LastName	FirstName
32	Franklin	Marsha
86	Barstow	Emily
21	Bannister	Henry
87	McAllister	Ian
45	Pinker	Dorothy

Of course, you don't have to select all fields; you can specify the exact fields and field order that you wish. For example:

```
SELECT LastName, TeacherID FROM Teachers
```

This query returns a different result:

LastName	TeacherID
Franklin	32
Barstow	86
Bannister	21
McAllister	87
Pinker	45

Programmers moving from file-based databases to relational databases often make the mistake of thinking that the simple SELECT statement is all they need. They are accustomed to scrolling (moving sequentially from field to field) through a set of records to find the ones they need. That's absolutely the wrong way to approach relational databases. Don't search for records yourself—let the database do the work. That's what the WHERE clause does—it limits the returned records to exactly the ones you need. For example, to find only the teachers with last names starting with M, you add a WHERE clause to the SELECT statement:

```
SELECT * FROM Teachers WHERE LastName LIKE 'M%'
```

This query returns one row:

TeacherID	LastName	FirstName
87	McAllister	Ian

The ORDER BY clause of the SELECT statement controls the order of the records returned by the query. For example, to select all students by grade, you could use the following SELECT statement:

```
SELECT * FROM Students ORDER BY Grade, LastName, FirstName
```

The fields in the ORDER BY clause do not have to appear in the selected field list. The default sort order is ascending (ASC), but you can retrieve fields in reverse order by specifying the DESC keyword after the appropriate field name. You don't have to select all the fields, and you may select them in any order you desire. The following SELECT statement includes all the basic SELECT clauses:

```
SELECT StudentID, LastName, FirstName FROM Students ORDER BY Grade DESC
```

If you run the query and compare the results to the Grade column in the Students table, you can see that the query does indeed return the data sorted in reverse Grade order.

INNER and OUTER JOIN Statements

You can use the SELECT statement to retrieve data from more than one table at a time. SQL statements referencing more than one table typically (but not necessarily) use a JOIN statement to connect the tables on a common field or value.

For example, suppose you want a list of all students taught by Marsha Franklin. To obtain the list, you need to join the Teachers table to the Students table on the common TeacherID field. In the Teachers table, the TeacherID field is a primary key; in the Students table the TeacherID field is a foreign key. Because the primary key in a table is always unique and not null, you know that the TeacherID exists in each row of the Teachers table. For this example, assume you know that every student has been assigned a teacher.

There's a many-to-many relationship between teachers and students. That's because one teacher teaches many students, and each student has several teachers. That relationship appears in the TeacherStudent table. Therefore, you need to join the Teachers table with the TeacherStudent table to find the students assigned to a particular teacher. For example:

```
SELECT StudentID
FROM TeacherStudent INNER JOIN Teachers
```

```
ON TeacherStudent.TeacherID=Teachers.TeacherID
WHERE Teachers.LastName='Franklin' AND Teachers.FirstName='Marsha'
```

When you run the query, the result is a single column of StudentIDs:

StudentID
1
3
5

Although accurate, a list of StudentID values is not a satisfactory solution because you still don't know the names of the students assigned to the teacher. The TeacherStudent table contains the StudentIDs, but not the students' names. To get the names of the students, you need to include the Students table in the query. You can create multiple joins in a single SELECT statement.

To retrieve the names, you need two INNER JOIN statements, because there's no direct relationship between teachers and students. For example:

```
SELECT Students.*
FROM Students INNER JOIN
(TeacherStudent INNER JOIN Teachers ON Teachers.TeacherID=
TeacherStudent.TeacherID)
ON Students.StudentID=TeacherStudent.StudentID
WHERE Teachers.LastName='Franklin'
ORDER BY Students.LastName
```

The previous statement has several interesting features. First, when you use two tables, you can't use the asterisk shorthand to retrieve all the fields from only one of the tables (although you can use it to retrieve all the fields in both tables). In such cases, the Tablename.* syntax selects all the fields from the named table. Second, the INNER JOIN statement requires that you specify which tables and fields the database should join to produce the query. Finally, when you work with more than one table you must specify the table name as well as the column name for each field where the field name appears in more than one table. The LastName and TeacherID fields appear in both the Teachers and TeacherStudent tables. In other words, if the column name is not unique among all fields in all tables in the FROM clause, the server will raise an error, because it can't distinguish the table from which to extract the data.

Now suppose some students haven't been assigned a teacher. In this case, the INNER JOIN clause still works, but the resulting record set will omit the rows in the Students table for which the TeacherID column value is Null. For example:

```
SELECT Teachers.*, Students.*
```

```
FROM Students INNER JOIN
(TeacherStudent INNER JOIN Teachers ON Teachers.TeacherID=
TeacherStudent.TeacherID)
ON Students.StudentID=TeacherStudent.StudentID
ORDER BY Students.LastName
```

When you know that a foreign key may not exist, or may not match a key value in the joined table, you can perform a LEFT (OUTER) JOIN or a RIGHT (OUTER) JOIN. The OUTER keyword is optional. Outer joins return all the values from one of the tables even if there's no matching key. For example, if you run the following statement, you'll find that it displays more rows than the previous SELECT example:

```
SELECT Teachers.*, Students.*
FROM Students LEFT JOIN
(TeacherStudent INNER JOIN Teachers ON Teachers.TeacherID=TeacherStudent
.TeacherID)
ON Students.StudentID=TeacherStudent.StudentID
ORDER BY Students.LastName
```

That's because the LEFT JOIN selects all the students, regardless of whether they have been assigned a teacher. Similarly, you could list all the teachers even if no students had been assigned to them. RIGHT JOIN works the same way, but returns all the rows from the right-hand side of the join. One other variation supported by some databases (including SQL Server), the FULL (OUTER) JOIN, retrieves unmatched rows from tables on both sides of the join.

Calculated Values and the *GROUP BY* Clause

Transact-SQL (T-SQL) contains a number of functions to calculate values. A calculated value is a result of an operation on one or more columns in multiple rows; for example, a sum, average, or total. In T-SQL, calculated values are called aggregates, and the functions are aggregate functions because they aggregate, or collect a number of values into a single value using a calculation. For example, you can retrieve the total number of rows in any table with the following SELECT statement, substituting an appropriate table name in the FROM clause:

```
SELECT count(*) FROM <tablename>
```

A count of the Students table returns 7. Counting is even more useful when you group results by another column. For example, if you want to know the total number of students taught by each teacher, you could obtain a count of students and group the results by teacher. The results look like Table 17.5.

TABLE 17.5: Count of Students by Teacher

TeacherID	LastName	FirstName	TotalStudents
21	Bannister	Henry	1
86	Barsow	Emily	1
32	Franklin	Marsha	3
87	McAllister	Ian	1
45	Pinker	Dorothy	1

The SELECT statement to obtain the results in Table 17.5 includes a new clause, the GROUP BY clause. The syntax is:

```
SELECT (field1, field2, etc.) FROM (table list) WHERE (condition)
GROUP BY (field1, field2, etc.) HAVING (condition) ORDER BY (field1
[ASC|DESC], field2 [ASC|DESC], etc.)
```

Here's the statement to select the data in Table 17.5.

```
SELECT Teachers.TeacherID, Teachers.LastName, Teachers.FirstName,
    COUNT(TeacherStudent.StudentID) AS TotalStudents

FROM Students INNER JOIN (TeacherStudent INNER JOIN Teachers
    ON Teachers.TeacherID=TeacherStudent.TeacherID) ON
    Students.StudentID=TeacherStudent.StudentID

GROUP BY Teachers.TeacherID, Teachers.LastName, Teachers.FirstName

HAVING count(TeacherStudent.StudentID) > 0

ORDER BY Teachers.LastName
```

That's an intimidating statement at first, but take each clause separately and it's quite straightforward. The first clause—the column list—simply lists the names of the columns you want the query to return. Note that you can provide a name for the calculated column using the AS keyword followed by the name to use. Actually, the AS keyword lets you rename any column or table in SQL statements. The FROM clause lists the table names and the relationships between them, using joins to tell the database how to combine the tables. The GROUP BY clause controls the groupings. You must include all referenced columns in the GROUP BY clause except the calculated columns. Put the columns in the sequence you want the database to group them by. In this case, I put the TeacherID column first because I want to obtain the count of students for each teacher. The order of the rest of the fields in the GROUP BY statement is immaterial, but they must appear.

The HAVING statement lets you add conditions—just like the WHERE clause. The difference is that the WHERE clause selects records before the grouping occurs, whereas the HAVING clause selects records after the grouping. If you don't include a WHERE clause, the HAVING clause acts the same as a WHERE clause.

T-SQL can also perform other, more familiar functions. For example, you can add or concatenate values using the + operator. If you want to retrieve the list of teachers as a single first-last formatted string, you could write a query like this:

```
SELECT Teachers.FirstName + ' ' + Teachers.LastName AS Name
ORDER BY Teachers.LastName
```

Running the query produces a list of teacher names in first-last format:

Name

Henry Bannister

Emily Barstow

Marsha Franklin

Ian McAllister

Dorothy Pinker

You've seen the rudiments of how to select data. Selecting data doesn't change it, so selecting is a safe operation. All the other statements change data in some way. You'll be happy to know that the other statements are considerably less complex than the SELECT statement. I suggest you make a backup copy of your database before you continue.

The *INSERT* Statement

SQL INSERT statements add one or more new rows to a table. The INSERT statement has two variations. The first variation adds one row by assigning values to a specified list of columns in a specified table. The values you want to insert follow a VALUES statement. You put parentheses around both the `field list` and the `values list`. For example:

```
INSERT INTO table name (field list) VALUES (values list)
```

You must provide a value for all fields that cannot accept a null value and do not have a default value. You do not have to provide values for identity columns. For example, to insert a row into the Teachers table, you must provide a last name and a first name:

```
INSERT INTO Teachers (LastName, FirstName)
VALUES('Swarthmore', 'John')
```

The second variation lets you add multiple rows using a SELECT query in place of the VALUES list, as follows:

```
INSERT INTO table name (field list) SELECT query
```

For example, suppose you had a list of students waiting to be enrolled. You could add all the students simultaneously to the Students table. There's a StudentWaitingList table you can use to test this query. For example:

```
INSERT INTO Students (Grade, LastName, FirstName) SELECT Grade, Last-
Name, FirstName FROM StudentWaitingList
```

If you're inserting data into all the columns in the target table, you can omit the field list. The SELECT statement you use to obtain the data you want to insert can include any clause or condition discussed in the previous section, including calculated fields and a GROUP BY clause.

The *UPDATE* Statement

UPDATE statements change data in one or more columns and in one or more rows. The UPDATE statement is dangerous, because if you forget to specify conditions, your database will happily update all the rows in the table. You should always specify a WHERE condition when updating data. The UPDATE statement has the following syntax:

```
UPDATE (table name) SET field1 = (value/expression), field2 = (value/
expression), ... FROM (table/query source) WHERE (condition)
```

The UPDATE statement has four clauses. In the UPDATE clause, you must specify a table name containing the fields to update. You may not update multiple tables simultaneously.

The SET clause contains the list of fields you wish to update. You separate the list with commas. Each item in the list consists of a field name, an equals sign, and a new value. You can use a constant, a variable, a field from another table, or an expression for the value on the right-hand side of the equals sign.

The FROM clause is optional. If you're updating a single row with constant values, you can omit the FROM clause. You need the FROM clause when you're updating data in one table from values stored in a different table (or in another place in the same table). Fortunately, the FROM clause is identical to the FROM clause you saw earlier in this chapter in *The SELECT Statement* section. You may update from multiple tables using JOIN statements as appropriate.

The WHERE clause (don't forget the WHERE clause!), again, is a condition that identifies the rows in the target table you wish to update. For example, suppose the student Isabel McArthur announces that she is changing her name to Serena McArthur. You can update her student record with the following SQL statement:

```
UPDATE Students SET FirstName = 'Serena' WHERE Students
.LastName='McArthur' AND Students.FirstName='Isabel'
```

The *DELETE* Statement

The DELETE statement is the simplest of all, but quite powerful. You can use the DELETE statement to delete one or more rows in one or more tables. For example, after inserting all the records from the StudentsWaitingList table, you can delete all the records in the table using the following statement:

```
DELETE FROM StudentsWaitingList
```

The DELETE statement is just as dangerous as the UPDATE statement, as you can see, because it cheerfully deletes data without prompting. If you accidentally run a DELETE statement it's difficult to recover your data. You should rarely use a DELETE statement without a WHERE clause. If you want to delete all the data from a table it's much more efficient to use a different type of statement, one of a group of statements that alters the database itself—the TRUNCATE TABLE statement. Truncating a table removes all the data and resets the identity column value to its default—usually 1. For example, to delete all the data in the StudentsWaitingList table, you can write:

```
TRUNCATE TABLE StudentsWaitingList
```

I said you should rarely use DELETE without a WHERE clause. There is one reason to do so. The TRUNCATE statement is not logged—that means you can't recover if you use it automatically, whereas the DELETE statement is a logged operation. That's the reason TRUNCATE is so much more efficient—it avoids the log operations, but it also means the data is unrecoverable from the transaction log.

The DELETE statement becomes slightly more complex when you want to delete data based on values from another table. For example, suppose you decide to delete all the students who have no assigned teachers. You need to join the Teacher-Student table to the Students table, find the rows where the TeacherID columns contain Null values in the TeacherStudent table, and then delete those rows in the Teachers table. This may sound like a two-step operation, but you can accomplish it in SQL in a single step, as follows:

```
DELETE FROM Students
WHERE StudentID NOT IN
    (SELECT DISTINCT StudentID FROM TeacherStudent)
```

The previous statement uses the NOT IN keywords to test for the existence of a StudentID in a subquery (the portion of the previous query contained in parentheses). A subquery is a separate query that returns data. In this case, the subquery returns the list of all StudentIDs that appear in the TeacherStudent table. Any StudentIDs that do not appear in that table have no assigned teachers, and can be deleted.

When you want to delete data from one table in a join, you must specify the name of the table after the DELETE keyword. For example, suppose you add all the rows in the StudentWaitingList table to the Students table, then decide to remove them:

```
DELETE Students
FROM Students INNER JOIN StudentWaitingList
  ON Students.LastName=StudentWaitingList.LastName AND
  Students.FirstName=StudentWaitingList.FirstName
```

Without the DELETE Students clause, the database cannot decide which table to delete the data from.

Generate Unique IDs

I've discussed identity fields, but there are other ways to uniquely distinguish one row from another. Identity fields work wonderfully within a table, but have serious weaknesses when you're working between tables, or worse, between databases, because the database only guarantees the uniqueness of an identity value for new rows.

For example, suppose your company has a mobile sales force using laptops. Each salesperson generates a few dozen orders per day. The salespeople enter these orders into a local Access database on their laptops. Periodically, the salespeople connect to the central office to upload the orders.

Further, suppose you were given the task of writing both the local order-entry application and an ASP page to accept the orders via a secured connection. You must contrive a means to create a table that can accept the rows from many remote databases—and you're not allowed to change the data from the laptops.

This is a tough problem because you must avoid identical OrderID values from any two machines. To solve it, you can use Globally Unique IDs (GUIDs). A GUID is a string consisting of a sequence of numbers and letters guaranteed to be unique among all computers everywhere. As you can imagine, these numbers are long. Microsoft Windows uses GUIDs to identify COM objects. If you look in the Windows Registry, you'll find that the HKEY_CLASSES_ROOT\CLSID key contains a large number of GUIDs, which look like this:

```
{098f2370-bac0-11ce-b579-08012b30bfeb}
```

GUIDs are globally unique because they depend on the local machine's network card MAC address, the local date and time, and for all I know, the internal ID of your microprocessor and the phase of the moon. It doesn't matter—believe me, the chances of another computer being able to generate a GUID that matches any GUID produced on any other computer in the world is vanishingly small.

SQL Server 7 and higher support GUIDs natively, but earlier versions do not. You can create a custom VB or C++ DLL to generate GUIDs. I'll show you how to do that in Chapter 26, *Build Your Own Components*.

There's a great deal more to know about SQL and SQL Server, but the information in this chapter should give you a good start. You may see some SQL constructions and functions in the remainder of this book that you haven't seen so far. I'll try to briefly explain those as they appear.

I strongly suggest you spend some more time exploring SQL's capabilities. The Transact-SQL help files and the SQL Server Books Online contain an enormous amount of information. In addition, there are many excellent reference and tutorial works on SQL.

CHAPTER

EIGHTEEN

Introduction to ADO

- ■ The Connection Object

- ■ The Recordset Object

- ■ The Field Object

- ■ ADO Data Types

- ■ The Web Approach to Data Access

ASP's primary interface to relational databases is through Microsoft's ActiveX Data Objects (ADO). ADO can access other types of data as well, such as Excel spreadsheets, delimited text files, Exchange data, or any other type of data store for which someone has written an Object Linking and Embedding Database (OLEDB) driver. Regardless of which type of data store your application accesses, the ADO objects and methods are remarkably similar. This ability to access multiple types of data stores, along with a relatively simple and flat object model, make ADO the simplest method yet devised for retrieving data. In this book, I'm going to limit the discussion to using ADO with relational databases, specifically, SQL Server. You can use the same techniques to retrieve data from Access, Oracle, Excel, or Exchange.

In this chapter, I'll show you the three main objects in the ADO object model and their most useful and common methods. In ADO, there are often several ways to accomplish a task. I'll explain when and why you should prefer one object or method instead of another.

The Connection Object

Before you can retrieve any data from a database, you have to create and initialize a connection to that database. In ADO, you use a Connection object to make and break database connections. A Connection object is a high-level object that works through a provider (think driver) that actually makes the data requests.

Opening a Database Connection

A single project called ActiveX Data Objects Database (ADODB) contains all the ADO objects. You create a Connection object in the same way as any other ASP object—with the `Server.CreateObject` method. For example:

```
Dim conn
Set conn = Server.CreateObject("ADODB.Connection")
```

By default, connections are read-only, but you can create a read-write or write-only connection by setting the Connection object's Mode property. There are several Mode constants—in fact, ADO is rife with constants. If you're using Visual InterDev 6, it automatically understands the ADO object references and constants. Earlier versions of InterDev and other environments do not automatically load the constants, so you have to include the adovbs.inc file (installed with ASP in the directory `C:\Program Files\Common Files\System\ADO`). To use the constants, include the following line in each file where you use ADO, substituting the appropriate drive and path for your server:

```
<!-- #INCLUDE FILE="<drive:\path>\adovbs.inc" -->
```

Alternatively, you can set a reference to the ADODB project in your `global.asa` file using the following syntax:

```
<!--METADATA TYPE="TypeLib" NAME="Microsoft ActiveX Data Objects 2.1
Library" UUID="{00000201-0000-0010-8000-00AA006D2EA4}" VERSION="2.1"-->
```

> **NOTE**   The version shown is correct for ADODB version 2.1; you will need to alter the line for earlier or later versions.

If you open the `adovbs.inc` file with NotePad or another text editor, you'll see groups of constants. The `ConnectModeEnum` constants are:

```
'-- ConnectModeEnum Constants --
Const adModeUnknown = 0
Const adModeRead = 1
Const adModeWrite = 2
Const adModeReadWrite = 3
Const adModeShareDenyRead = 4
Const adModeShareDenyWrite = 8
Const adModeShareExclusive = &Hc
Const adModeShareDenyNone = &H10
Const adModeRecursive = &H400000
```

Typically, you only need to select one of the first three values. If you only need to read information from the database (the most common action), use the `adMode-Read` constant. If you only need to write data, use the `adModeWrite` constant. If you need to read and write data within a single page, use the `adModeReadWrite` constant. Some people always use the `adModeReadWrite` constant, but that slows down data access when you only need to read or write, but not both.

The last five constants are of less use in a Web application where you may not know how many people are simultaneously connected. The `adModeShareDeny-Read` constant prevents other connections from reading the database. Similarly, the `adModeShareDenyWrite` constant lets other connections read from but not write to the database. The misnamed `adModeShareExclusive` constant (which would have been more consistent if it were called `adModeShareDenyAll`) prevents all other connections from opening the database. To thoroughly confuse the issue, the `adMode-ShareDenyNone` constant allows all other connections to attach to the database with any type of permission. The `adModeRecursive` constant works in concert with all of the Share-type constants except `adModeShareDenyNone` to propagate the setting to sub-records of the current record. For example, you can use `adShareDenyRead + adModeRecursive` to deny read permissions to sub-records. I've never had a need to use any of these constants in a Web application.

Even if you're using the default `adModeRead` constant, it's a good idea to acquire the habit of setting all the properties for each ADO object and supplying all the parameters accepted by each method call, even if they're optional. If you don't set the values manually, the internal ADO code has to set them for you. While this may be convenient, it's also dangerous because you lose control, as well as a little speed.

I've seen numerous examples of code where lazy programmers use the constants themselves rather than their names. If you memorize the constants, you can avoid including the ADODB project reference or including the `adovbs.inc` file, but it's a bad idea. First, consider the poor programmers who have to maintain your code—do you really want to force them to memorize the constants as well? Second, Microsoft may change the meaning of the constants in future versions of ADO, which will then break your code.

After setting the mode, you must set the Connection object's `ConnectionString` property. Although you must set this property each time you open a new Connection object, you should define the connection string (or strings) in your application's `global.asa` file as an application-level or session-level variable. There are at least three reasons to define the connection string in the `global.asa` file: it means you only have one place to check for connection string problems, you can change the connection from one database to another with minimal code changes during development, and you can copy or move your application from one server to another very quickly.

The `ConnectionString` property is both simple and complicated. It has several parts, all of which are optional, depending on which type of connection string you're using, but typically, you specify the following:

- Provider name
- Name of the database server
- Name of the database you want to use
- User ID (UID) with which to connect
- Password (PWD) for that user ID

You separate the parts of the connection string with semicolons. For example, at the simplest level, you can use an Open Database Connectivity (ODBC) Data Source Name (DSN), a user ID, and password to connect to your database. A DSN already contains the provider, the database server, and the database name, so you don't have to specify those again. For example:

```
Dim conn
Set conn = Server.CreateObject("ADODB.Connection")
conn.Mode = adModeReadWrite
conn.ConnectionString = "DSN=myDSN;UID=sa;PWD="
```

Unfortunately, that's not the best method for connecting to SQL Server. By default, ODBC DSNs use the MDASQL (SQL Server's ODBC driver) provider, but the SQLOLEDB provider is faster and provides more functionality. Use this type of connection string instead:

```
Dim conn
Dim aConnectionString
aConnectionString ="Provider=SQLOLEDB;Data " _
    & "Source=(local);Database=ClassRecords;" _
    & UID=sa;PWD=;"
Set conn = Server.CreateObject("ADODB.Connection")
conn.Mode = adModeReadWrite
conn.ConnectionString = aConnectionString
```

The connection string contains the provider name, the name of the server (in this case, (local)), the database name, and the user ID and password. As is usual with ADO, there's more than one way to accomplish a goal; you can set some of these properties individually, as well as with the ConnectionString property. For example:

```
Dim conn
Dim aConnectionString
aConnectionString = "Source=(local)"
Set conn = Server.CreateObject("ADODB.Connection")
conn.mode=adModeReadWrite
conn.Provider="SQLOLEDB"
conn.DefaultDatabase="ClassRecords"
conn.UserID="sa"
conn.Password=""
```

If you're using Access instead of SQL Server or MSDE, use the Microsoft Access driver instead of SQLOLEDB. For example:

```
Dim aConnectionString
aConnectionString="Provider=Microsoft.Jet.OLEDB.4.0;" _
    & "Data Source=" _
    & C:\Inetpub\WWWRoot\MasteringASP\ClassRecords.mdb"
```

You must set most of the Connection object's properties before opening the connection. If you later want to change a property, close the connection, change the property value, and then reopen the connection.

To open a connection, use the Open method of the Connection object. For example:

```
Conn.Open
```

If the Open method executes without errors, you have a working connection to the database. Now that you've seen how to open a Connection object, I'll show you an alternate syntax. The Open method accepts up to four optional arguments: a connection string, a user ID, a password, and the ubiquitous `Options` argument consisting of a `ConnectOptionEnum` constant, which, at this time, you never need to use, because there's only one value, `adAsyncConnect`. For example:

```
Conn.Open aConnectionString, "sa", "", adAsyncConnect
```

You'll find that several of the ADO methods include an `Options` argument. All the `Options` arguments consist of one or more values from a set of enumerated constants. You can specify more than one value by adding the constants together.

Selecting a Cursor Location

After opening a Connection object, you can use it to execute queries, manage transactions, and control the location of cursors, the code that lets you scroll through query result sets. You can create cursors on the server or the client. Server-side cursors (the default) keep most of the data from a query result on the server. Cursors manage movement between records. Typically, server-side cursors send only a small part of a large result set to the client at one time. As you scroll through the data on the client, the client requests more data as needed.

The advantage of server-side cursors is that your application can begin accessing the data almost immediately, because the server initially needs to transfer only a small part of the data. The disadvantage of a server cursor is that SQLOLEDB only supports one server-side cursor at a time. Also, when you use server-side cursors, you must keep the database connection open as long as you need to work with the result set. In contrast, client-side cursors initialize more slowly because the server must transfer all the data, but you may have multiple client-side cursors open simultaneously, and you may disconnect a Recordset object with a client-side cursor from its Connection object. That's important in a Web application because connections are expensive resources. When you free a connection, another client can use it.

You can control the location of cursors with the Connection object's `Cursor-Location` property. (You can also control the cursor location with the Recordset object's `CursorLocation` property, as you'll see in the next section.)

The *Connection.Execute* Method

There are three ways to obtain data from a database using ADO. All of them require a connection. The simplest way is to use the `Execute` method of the Connection object. The `Execute` method accepts three arguments: an SQL statement or query, table, view, or stored procedure name called the `CommandText` argument; a variable called `RecordsAffected` that will contain the number of records affected by the statement or query after the `Execute` method completes; and a `CommandTypeEnum` constant called `Options` that tells the database what type of statement or query you want to run, and whether to return a Recordset object.

Connection objects can open tables and views (which are virtual tables you create with SQL statements) directly, and can execute SQL in either pre-compiled form (called stored procedures—roughly the equivalent of Microsoft Access queries on steroids) or dynamically by interpreting and executing the SQL statement at runtime. All these types of requests return records. The returned records are called result sets, and ADO wraps the resulting rows in a Recordset object.

The return value of the Execute method, by default, is a Recordset object that contains the result of the statement or query. You can control whether the Execute method returns a Recordset object by adding the adExecuteNoRecords constant to the Options constant. If you're running a SELECT statement, you generally need the resulting Recordset object; but when you're running an INSERT or UPDATE query, you usually don't need any records returned.

For example, the following script obtains a list of all students in the Class-Records database:

```
Dim conn
Dim SQL
Dim R
Dim RecsAffected
Dim aConnectionString
aConnectionString ="Provider=SQLOLEDB;Data " _
    & "Source=(local);Database=ClassRecords;" _
    & " UID=sa;PWD=;"
Set conn = Server.CreateObject("ADODB.Connection")
conn.Mode = adModeReadWrite
conn.ConnectionString = aConnectionString
conn.CursorLocation=adUseClient
conn.open
SQL = "SELECT * FROM Students"
Set R = conn.execute(SQL, RecsAffected, adCmdText)
```

The Connection object submits the query to the database and returns all the student records. Despite the fact that the script specifies a read-write connection to the database, the Execute method always returns a Recordset object with a read-only, forward-only cursor. That type of cursor is often called a firehose cursor, because it can spray records quickly—it's the fastest type of cursor and the one you should try to use most often.

As I mentioned, the last two arguments to the Execute method are optional—you can omit them entirely and the method works just fine. In fact, there's no point in providing the RecordsAffected argument for firehose cursor Recordset objects, because the Connection object never sets the value. You can leave it out and write:

```
Set R = conn.execute(SQL, , adCmdText)
```

Although you don't have to specify the RecordsAffected argument, you should never leave out the Options argument. If you don't specify the type of query you want to run, the data provider must search through the list of object types looking for a match. In essence, the provider looks to see if the SQL statement is equal to the name of a table, view, or stored procedure. If none of these match the contents of the CommandText argument, the SQL parsing engine attempts to execute the Command-Text argument as a dynamic SQL statement. When you specify the type of query or statement, you can avoid the time required for the search. Admittedly, we're talking about a typical search time of microseconds, but when you have hundreds of users accessing your Web site, microseconds add up quickly.

If you're running an UPDATE, INSERT, or DELETE query, you can simply ignore the Recordset object return value. For example:

```
SQL = "UPDATE Students SET FirstName='Isobel' "
SQL = SQL & "WHERE StudentID=4"
conn.Execute SQL,,adCmdText
```

The SQL statement changes Isabel McArthur's name to Isobel McArthur. Because it's an UPDATE statement, the query won't return records, so you won't need the Execute statement to return a Recordset object. You can improve the response time slightly by specifying the adExecuteNoRecords option. For example:

```
conn.Execute SQL, , adCmdText + adExecuteNoRecords
```

Managing Transactions with a Connection Object

When you submit a command that changes data to SQL Server, such as an UPDATE, INSERT, or DELETE query, it always treats the statement as a transaction. If the statement fails, all operations in the statement fail. However, you often need to execute one or more statements as a transaction. To do that, you must wrap the statements in a high-level transaction yourself. You manage transactions with the Connection object's BeginTrans, CommitTrans, and RollbackTrans methods. For example, suppose you had an Orders database. When a customer places an order, you want to save the order and decrement the number of items available for the ordered items. In other words, you want to manage orders and inventory as a single transaction. You could write:

```
conn.BeginTrans
SQL="INSERT INTO Orders"
SQL = SQL & "(CustomerID, ItemID, Quantity, "
SQL = SQL & "DateOrdered, Amount)"
SQL = SQL & "VALUES(387198, 'A37B3298', 4, 352.98)"
conn.Execute SQL,,adCmdText + adExecuteNoRecords
SQL = "UPDATE Inventory SET Quantity=Quantity - 4 "
SQL = SQL & "WHERE ItemID = 'A37B3298'"
conn.Execute SQL,,adCmdText + adExecuteNoRecords
```

```
If conn.Errors.Count = 0 Then
    conn.CommitTrans
Else
    conn.RollbackTrans
End If
```

The previous script begins a transaction, inserts the order record, and decrements the inventory record for that item. If any errors occur, the script rolls back the transaction. If the order record insert fails, the script will not update the inventory, and if the inventory adjustment fails, the order will fail as well. If both actions complete successfully, the script commits the transaction.

You can think of the Connection object as the root object in ADO. To recap, use the Connection object to:

- Establish and terminate sessions with data sources
- Execute queries to obtain forward-only, read-only (firehose cursor) Recordset objects, and execute statements to alter data
- Manage transactions

After you open a Connection object, you can use it with two other types of ADO objects—Recordset and Command. In the next section, you'll see how to use the Recordset object.

The Recordset Object

You've already seen one way to obtain a firehose cursor Recordset—by using the Execute method of the Connection object. Recordset objects provide more functionality than simply a method for holding and scrolling through data. A Recordset object is a table of values. It has rows and columns like a database table; but a Recordset object is not a table—it's more like a virtual table or view. First, the values of the Recordset object's columns may come from several different tables via a JOIN operation. Second, the column values may be calculated values—they may not match any value in the database. Finally, you can search and sort Recordset objects, turn them into strings or arrays, and even persist them to and retrieve them from disk storage as objects or as XML data.

Using the *Recordset.Open* Method

If you need a Recordset object with any type of cursor other than a forward-only, read-only cursor, you need to open it directly rather than calling the Execute method of a Connection object. Recordset objects also have an Open method, which takes several arguments. The syntax is:

```
Recordset.Open CommandText, Connection/ConnectionString, _
    CursorType, LockType, Options
```

The CommandText argument contains the SQL query. The Connection/ConnectionString argument contains either a reference to an open Connection object or a valid ConnectionString argument. If you use a ConnectionString argument, the Open method creates a Connection object for you. If you're going to make only one call to the database in a page, letting ADO create a Connection object is a viable option. However, if you're going to make more than one call, you should create and open your own Connection object. The reason is that you have more control over the type and duration of the Connection object if you open and close it yourself.

The CursorType argument is a value derived from one or more adCursorTypeEnum values. The following list shows the valid values and a description of each:

adOpenForwardOnly   Returns a forward-only cursor. This is the default cursor type. If you don't specify a cursor type, ADO always returns a forward-only cursor. As the name implies, you can only move forward, not backward, through the Recordset object. You should use this whenever you need to make only one pass through a Recordset object because it's the fastest type of cursor.

adOpenKeyset   Returns a keyset cursor. You can move in any direction with this cursor type: first, last, forward, backward, skip, or move to bookmark (if the provider supports bookmarks). You can see changes that others make to the records in the Recordset object, but you can't see records added since you opened the Recordset object. You cannot access or change records that other users delete. Use a keyset cursor for large record sets where you need to be able to scroll backward or you need to change. The server creates a unique bookmark for each row when you first run the query. Those bookmarks don't change during the life of the Recordset object, which is why you can't see new records.

adOpenDynamic   Returns a dynamic cursor. This type is exactly like a keyset cursor except that you can see new records that others add. A dynamic cursor checks constantly for updates and additions to the result set. It does not build a set of bookmarks for the result set, so a dynamic cursor often opens more quickly than a keyset cursor. Dynamic cursors require the most resources of all cursor types, so you should not use them unless you need to see additions to the result set while the Recordset object is open.

adOpenStatic   Returns a static cursor, which is a fixed copy of a set of records. You cannot see any changes or inserts by others without querying the database again. Recordset objects with static cursors can be updated.

Depending on the provider, you may be able to see changes your application makes to data with a static cursor.

The `LockType` argument tells ADO how to treat database locks. In general, you want to avoid locking data for updates or inserts because locks created by one user can cause problems for other users in your application. Read-only locks do not cause such problems. The valid `LockType` arguments are:

adLockReadOnly   Read-only—you cannot alter the data.

adLockPessimistic   Pessimistic locking is the strongest type of lock. Records with pessimistic locking are unavailable to other users of your application. Pessimistic locks occur when the server delivers the record. The record remains locked until you close the Recordset object. You should avoid pessimistic locking in Web applications whenever possible.

adLockOptimistic   Optimistic locking locks records just before an update occurs, and unlocks them immediately afterward. Other users can access data during the time you're updating the record, which means they may potentially be viewing outdated data. Similarly, with optimistic locking, multiple users may simultaneously try to update the same data, leading to problems. You should avoid optimistic locking in Web applications whenever possible.

adLockBatchOptimistic   Optimistic batch locks act like optimistic locks, except they work for batch updates—deferring immediate updates in favor of updating many records at one time rather than updating each record immediately as with `adLockOptimistic` locking. It's your call whether batch updates or immediate updates are better for your application. In part, it depends on the level of interactivity your application demands and how people expect to use the application. For example, an Internet-based airline reservations system would probably work best with optimistic locking, because people typically use it to make one reservation at a time. In contrast, a human resources application where an administrator typically makes many changes during each session might work better with batch optimistic locking. In either case, you should try to avoid locking records whenever possible.

The final `Recordset.Open` argument is the `Options` flag. The `Options` flag takes exactly the same values as the `Connection.Execute Options` argument. Again, the `Options` argument is not required, but you should always include it. It tells ADO whether the query is a table, view, stored procedure, or dynamic SQL statement.

Before you use the `Recordset.Open` method, you should know that one of the most common mistakes beginning ADO programmers make is opening a read-only Connection object (forgetting to set the Mode property to adModeRead-Write), retrieving a Recordset object, and trying to update a record. The Update method fails because even though the Recordset object may have an updatable cursor type, the underlying connection is read-only. To open an updatable Recordset object you must set the Connection.Mode property to adModeReadWrite.

The second most common mistake made by beginning ADO programmers is to use the Execute method to open the Recordset object containing the data they want to update. The Execute method returns the default Recordset type, which has a forward-only, read-only cursor type. Even when you set the underlying Connection.Mode property to adModeReadWrite, you must use the Recordset.Open method rather than the Execute method to open the Recordset object. The following script opens a Recordset object with a static, updatable cursor:

```
Dim conn
Dim SQL
Dim R
Dim RecsAffected
Dim aConnectionString
aConnectionString ="Provider=SQLOLEDB;Data " _
    & "Source=(local);Database=ClassRecords;" _
    & UID=sa;PWD=;"
Set conn = Server.CreateObject("ADODB.Connection")
conn.Mode = adModeReadWrite
conn.ConnectionString = aConnectionString
conn.CursorLocation=adUseClient
conn.open
SQL = "SELECT * FROM Students WHERE LastName='Frederick'"
Set R = Server.CreateObject("ADODB.Recordset")
R.Open SQL, conn, adOpenStatic, adLockOptimistic, adCmdText
' you can update this Recordset
R.LastName = "Fredericks"
R.Update
R.Close
```

Batch Updating

When you open a Recordset object with a lock type of adLockOptimistic or adLockPessimistic, change data values and call the Update method, the Recordset object immediately sends those changes to the database. Therefore, Recordset objects opened in this manner make one call to the database every time you update a record. Sometimes, you need to make many modifications to a set of records. In such cases you should open the Recordset object for batch update.

Batch updates let you make the changes within the Recordset object's copy of the data, but defer the update to the database until you call the BatchUpdate method. Batch updating improves performance considerably because it reduces all updates to a single database call. When you know you're going to make many changes to a Recordset object, you should make those changes in batch update mode.

Here's an example. Suppose you wanted to change all class times forward by half-an-hour. You could retrieve the Classes table in a Recordset object opened in batch update mode and loop through it adding 30 minutes to each start time, updating each record as you go. When you finish updating all the records, call the Update-Batch method to write the changes to the database. Listing 18.1 shows the code.

LISTING 18.1   Batch Update Example (ch18i1.asp)

```vbscript
<%@ Language=VBScript %>
<% Option Explicit %>
<html>
<head>
</head>
<body>
<%
Dim conn
Dim SQL
Dim R
Dim aConnectionString
Dim aTime

aConnectionString = "Provider=SQLOLEDB;Data " _
    & "Source=(local);Database=ClassRecords;" _
    & "UID=sa;PWD=;"
Set conn = Server.CreateObject("ADODB.Connection")
conn.Mode = adModeRead
conn.ConnectionString = aConnectionString
conn.CursorLocation = adUseClient
conn.Open
Set R = Server.CreateObject("ADODB.Recordset")
SQL = "SELECT ClassID, Time FROM Classes " & _
    "ORDER BY ClassID"
R.Open, SQL, conn, adOpenStatic, adLockBatchOptimistic, _
    adCmdText
If Not (R.EOF And R.BOF) Then
    Do While Not R.EOF
        aTime = R("Time")
        ' add 30 minutes
        aTime = DateAdd("n", 30, aTime)
        R("Time") = aTime
        R.Update
        R.Movenext
    Loop
    R.UpdateBatch
End If
```

```
        R.Close
Set R = Nothing
conn.Close
Set conn = Nothing
%>
</body>
</html>
```

You can update disconnected Recordset objects as well as those that have an active Connection object but, of course, you must first reconnect to a Connection object before calling the UpdateBatch method.

Positioning a Recordset Object—the *Move* Methods

After opening a Recordset object, you can use the Move methods to move forward and (depending on the cursor) backward through the data rows. Recordset objects provide a RecordCount property, which tells you the number of records in the Recordset object. For example, Listing 18.2 creates a Recordset object that can move in any direction.

NOTE

From this point forward, you can assume (for clarity and brevity) that all references to a conn variable refer to an opened Connection object. Where you need to see how the Connection object was opened, I'll show you the full code; otherwise I'll omit it. Where the code exists on the CD (in other words, a listing references a filename) you'll find the full code in that file on the CD, even if the listing doesn't contain the full code.

LISTING 18.2   **Recordset Move Methods Example (ch18i2.asp)**

```
<%@ Language=VBScript %>
<% option explicit %>
<%
Dim conn
Dim SQL
Dim R
Dim F
Dim RecsAffected
Dim aConnectionString
aConnectionString = "Provider=SQLOLEDB;Data " _
    & "Source=(local);Database=ClassRecords;" _
    & "UID=sa;PWD=;"
Set conn = Server.CreateObject("ADODB.Connection")
conn.Mode = adModeRead
conn.ConnectionString = aConnectionString
conn.CursorLocation = adUseClient
conn.Open
```

```
SQL = "SELECT * FROM Students ORDER BY LastName, FirstName"
Set R = Server.CreateObject("ADODB.Recordset")
R.Open SQL, conn, adOpenStatic, adLockReadOnly, adCmdText
Response.Write "<b>By default, when you first open a " _
    & "Recordset object, it's positioned at the first " _
    & "record.</b><br>"
Response.Write "First Record: " & R("LastName") & ", " _
    & R("FirstName") & "<br>"
Response.Write "<b>Moved to the last record.</b><br>"
R.moveLast
Response.Write "Last Record: " & R("LastName") _
    & ", " & R("FirstName") & "<br>"
Response.Write "<b>Moved to the previous record.</b><br>"
R.MovePrevious
Response.Write "Next-To-Last Record: " & R("LastName") _
    & ", " & R("FirstName") & "<br>"
R.MoveFirst
Response.Write "<b>Moved to the first record.</b><br>"
R.MoveNext
Response.Write "<b>Moved to the next record.</b><br>"
Response.Write "Second Record: " & R("LastName") _
    & ", " & R("FirstName") & "<br>"
Response.Write "<br>"
Response.Write "<h3>All Records</h3>"
R.MoveFirst
Response.Write "<table align='left' border='1'>"
Response.Write "<tr>"
For Each F In R.Fields
    Response.Write "<td>" & F.Name & "</td>"
Next
Response.Write "</tr>"

While Not R.EOF
    Response.Write "<tr>"
    For Each F In R.Fields
        Response.Write "<td>" & F.Value & "</td>"
    Next
    Response.Write "</tr>"
    R.MoveNext
Wend
Response.Write "</table>"
R.Close
Set R = Nothing
conn.Close
Set conn = Nothing
%>
```

Figure 18.1 shows how the previous listing appears in the browser.

FIGURE 18.1:

Recordset Move methods
example (ch18i1.asp)

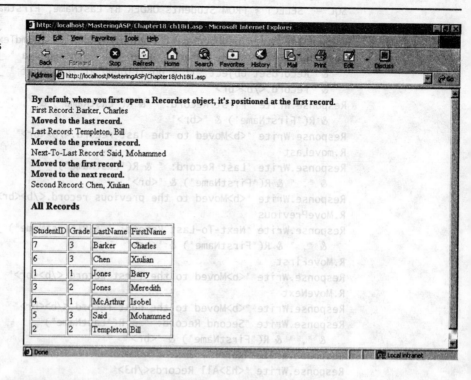

Think of a Recordset object as a table with an empty row at the top and bottom, and a current-record pointer. The record pointer points to only one record at a time. When you use one of the Move methods, you don't scroll the record set—you move the record pointer. Recordset objects have EOF (end-of-file) and BOF (beginning-of-file) methods to let you know when the record pointer has moved past the last record or prior to the first record. EOF and BOF are Boolean properties. If you look at the loop that creates the table in Listing 18.2, you'll see an example of how to use the EOF property:

```
While Not R.EOF
    ' Do something
    R.MoveNext
Wend
```

It's important to check whether a Recordset object is at the BOF or EOF position before requesting data, because Recordset objects raise an error if you request data when the Recordset object is at either of these two positions.

Recordset Sorting and Searching Methods

You can search and sort data with Recordset methods, although it's much more efficient to obtain only the data you need from the server and retrieve it already sorted. Because of the inefficiency, I'll be brief. To sort a record set, assign its sort property

the names of the field(s) you want to sort by. For example, to sort the Recordset
`SELECT * FROM Students` by `LastName`, you would write:

```
R.Sort = "LastName"
```

To sort by more than one field, separate the field names with commas, as follows:

```
R.Sort = "LastName, FirstName"
```

The default sort order is always ascending, so you don't need to write an explicit
direction (although you can). To sort in a specific order, append either ASC or DESC
to the end of the sort string. For example:

```
R.Sort = "LastName, FirstName DESC"
```

Figure 18.2 shows the difference between a sorted and an unsorted record set.

FIGURE 18.2:

Recordset Sort example
(ch18i2.asp)

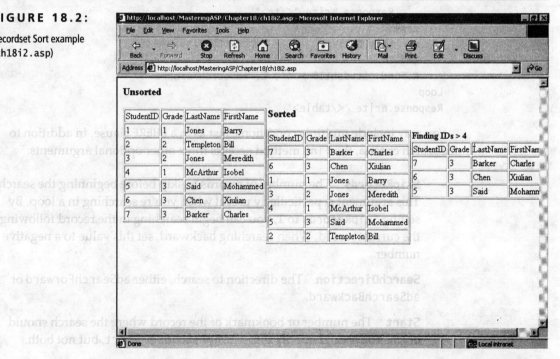

You can also search for specific records in a record set. To perform the search,
use the `Recordset.Find` method. You specify the search conditions with the
equivalent of a SQL WHERE clause, without the word WHERE. After performing a
find, the Recordset object is positioned at the first record found, or if no records
are found, at the end of the Recordset (EOF). For example, assuming you have a
Recordset object containing all the student records, to find all records where the
`StudentID` is greater than 4, you could write:

```
R.movefirst
Response.Write "<b>Finding IDs > 4</b>"
```

```
Response.Write "<table align='left' border='1'>"
Response.Write "<tr>"
For Each F In R.Fields
    Response.Write "<td>" & F.Name & "</td>"
Next
Response.Write "</tr>"
R.movefirst
R.Find "StudentID > 4", , adSearchForward

Do
    If Not R.EOF Then
        Response.Write "<tr>"
        For Each F In R.Fields
            Response.Write "<td>" & F.Value & "</td>"
        Next
        Response.Write "</tr>"
    Else
        Exit Do
    End If
    R.Find "StudentID > 4", 1, adSearchForward
Loop
Response.Write "</table>"
```

You may include multiple conditions, just as in a WHERE clause. In addition to the search criteria, the Find method accepts three other optional arguments:

SkipRecords   The number of records to skip before beginning the search. This argument is particularly useful when you're searching in a loop. By setting SkipRecords to 1, you can begin searching in the record following the current record. When searching backward, set this value to a negative number.

SearchDirection   The direction to search, either adSearchForward or adSearchBackward.

Start   The number or bookmark of the record where the search should begin. You should specify either SkipRecords or Start, but not both.

The Field Object

Although I've been telling you to think of Recordset objects as tables, that's just a convenient mental model; Recordset objects actually consist of a two-dimensional array of Field objects. In the ADO object model, Field objects contain the data. Therefore, each Field object has a type, a size, and a value. A Field object also has properties for the numeric scale of its value, the original value, the underlying value (in the database), the defined size, the actual size, and the precision, as well as a list of other attributes. Most of the time you will not need to deal with the Field object properties and methods, but its useful to study them in case you do need them.

The properties you are likely to use most are the `Name`, `Type`, `ActualSize`, `Value`, and `UnderlyingValue` properties. For example, one common method for displaying Recordset object data is in a table. In the first row you typically need to show the column names. You can take advantage of standard COM collection methods to do that. Assume the variable R contains an open record set. For example:

```
Dim F ' variable to use as a Field object
Response.Write "<table border='1' align='center'><tr>"
For Each F in R.Fields
    Response.Write "<td align='center'><b>" & F.Name _
    & "</b></td>"
Next
Response.Write "</tr></table>"
```

The preceding code fragment writes a single table row containing the `Field` names in the Recordset object in bold type. You can then fill in the table values with a similar loop that displays the values:

```
Do While Not R.EOF
    Response.Write "<tr>"
    For Each F in R.Fields
        Response.Write "<td>" & F.Value & "</td>"
    Next
    Response.Write "</tr>"
    R.MoveNext
Loop
```

The loop writes a series of column values for each row in the Recordset object. The preceding loop is generic—the logic will work for all Recordset objects, but the code will not. First, the code doesn't test for null values. Although a null database value doesn't cause an error in ASP, because variants accept `Null` as a valid value, it does display incorrectly. The Response object, seeing that the variable contains `Null`, casts the value to a null string and sends that to the browser. Empty string data, or string data consisting only of spaces, displays incorrectly in tables in HTML—the browser ignores the field altogether and doesn't even display the border. You can solve this problem with a simple test. For example:

```
For Each F In R.Fields
    If IsNull(F.Value) Then
        Response.Write "<td> </td>"
    ElseIf F.Value = "" then
```

```
            Response.Write "<td> </td>"
        Else
            Response.Write "<td>" & F.Value & "</td>"
        End If
    Next
```

The escaped text   tells the browser to write a non-breaking space. That's acceptable column content, so the column displays the border properly.

The second problem occurs when you have SQL Server Text fields or Microsoft Access Memo fields. You need to determine if a field contains one of the long data types (Text or Binary) before attempting to retrieve the value. To do so, check the Attributes property of the Field object. Use a Boolean AND operation to see if the Field attribute contains the value adFldLong. For example:

```
If (F.Attributes AND adFldLong) = adFldLong Then
    ' the field contains a long data type
Else
    ' the field does not contain a long data type
End If
```

To obtain the value of such fields, you need to use the GetChunk method of the Field object. The GetChunk method retrieves characters in chunks of a specified size. You can specify how many characters to get in each chunk as a variable or constant, or you can retrieve all the characters by using the Field object's Actual-Size property. Here's the fixed loop:

```
For Each F In R.Fields
    If IsNull(F.Value) Then
        Response.Write "<td> </td>"
    ElseIf (F.Attributes AND adFldLong) = adFldLong then
        Response.Write F.GetChunk(F.ActualSize)
    ElseIf F.Value = "" then
        Response.Write "<td> </td>"
    Else
        Response.Write "<td>" & F.Value & "</td>"
    End If
Next
```

For non-text data types, the Response object casts the value to a string before writing it to the browser, so you don't have to explicitly cast the values yourself. However, you do need to consider field types, especially when updating data. Therefore, you need to know what the various field types are and how to map each type to a VBScript or JavaScript variable or the data types for your database server.

ADO Data Types

ADO has a large number of field types that accommodate all the various database servers. I'm only going to cover the most common types in this section. They include:

adBigInt   An 8-byte integer.

adBinary   A fixed-length field that accepts binary data.

adBoolean   A Boolean type. Unlike VBScript Boolean values, a True value is not −1; the database accepts 1 and 0 for True and False, respectively.

adChapter   A field type containing a child record set. ADO 2 and higher support child record sets.

adChar   A character field that stores fixed-length strings. Character fields can contain up to 255 characters. Databases pad the field with spaces when the data is shorter than the defined field size.

adCurrency   A currency field (8 bytes). The field holds four decimal places.

adDate   A date field (8 bytes). SQL Server stores dates as doubles where the integer portion is the number of days since December 30, 1899, and the fractional portion is a fraction of a day.

adDBDate   Identical to adDate but stores only the date (integer portion) in yyyymmdd form even though the field is still 8 bytes long.

adDBTime   A time field that stores time in hhmmss form.

adDBTimeStamp   A date/time field that stores a full date and time in yyyymmddhhmmss form, plus a fraction in billionths. You should use this value to store date/time values in ASP.

adDecimal   A field that stores a numeric value with a fixed precision and scale.

adDouble   Stores double-precision (8-byte), floating-point values.

adGUID   Stores GUIDs (SQL Server 7 and higher).

adInteger   Stores 4-byte integer values.

adSingle   Stores single-precision, floating-point values.

adSmallInt   Stores 2-byte integers.

adTinyInt   Stores 1-byte integers.

adVarChar   Stores variable-length string data up to 255 characters in length.

The Web Approach to Data Access

In Web applications, you are attempting to make a central Web server act as an application server, providing data to tens or hundreds of simultaneous users. Therefore, you should be acutely aware of several issues. First, you want the response time to be as fast as possible for each user. People won't wait forever for your page to load. Second, you need to consider the resources available on your server. For example, you must pay for database connections. If your application opens a connection for a session and holds it in a Session variable, that connection becomes unavailable for other users. Finally, although memory is less expensive now than it was a few years ago, it's still a limited resource. If you store large amounts of data for each user of your application, you're likely to run out of memory sooner or later.

In addition, you often don't know when stored resources or connections opened for a single user are no longer needed. A person who views one or more pages in your application may be just about to request yet another page—or may have packed up the computer and moved to Beirut; you just don't know. Any Session variables left over from that person's session tie up resources until the session times out.

For these reasons, you need to approach database access in a Web application with specific goals in mind. Those goals are:

1. Open Connection objects as late as possible and close them as soon as possible. Never store a Connection object in an Application or Session variable.

2. Open Connection objects read-only whenever possible, and read-write only when you need to update data.

3. Request only the data you need. Sure, it's convenient to write SELECT * FROM <tablename> but it's highly inefficient—even if you need all the columns. Specify the field names.

4. Don't update data with Recordset objects—use dynamic SQL, or better, stored procedures to update data. You'll see how to use stored procedures in Chapter 19, *Accessing Data with ADO*.

5. Use disconnected Recordset objects to free connections earlier.

6. Don't store Recordset objects in Application or Session variables.

In the next chapter, I'll explain the reasoning behind these rules and show you how to use the ADO Command object and SQL Server stored procedures.

C H A P T E R

N I N E T E E N

Accessing Data with ADO

- **Opening and Closing Connections**

- **Retrieve Only What You Need**

- **Use Disconnected Recordsets**

- **Introduction to Stored Procedures**

- **The Command Object**

You've already seen a few examples of how to retrieve data with ADO. Because database access is such an important part of many (if not most) ASP applications, in this chapter, I want to expand on the topic of data access and show you why some methods are more efficient than others.

Opening and Closing Connections

I've mentioned several times that connections are scarce resources and you need to conserve them by opening a database connection only when necessary, and then close them as soon as possible thereafter. In addition, opening a connection is normally a time-consuming process (it's not for pooled connections). To understand why, you need to take into consideration how ADO and IIS work with database connections.

To ADO, a database connection is a set of properties—the settings in the string you use for the `ConnectionString` property of the Connection object. In some applications, you may open all database connections with the same connection string. For example, you may use a single database with a User ID of **sa** and a blank password for every connection. Other applications may specify a different User ID and password for each user.

IIS pools connections, which means it maintains a collection of reusable connections. When your application requests a connection via the `Connection.Open` method, IIS checks to see if it has a free connection with the same connection string in the pool. If so, it uses that connection; otherwise, it creates a new connection using the connection string properties from your application. Therefore, if your connection request matches an available connection, IIS doesn't really have to open a connection—it already has an open connection. Instead, it returns a reference to that connection. That's why pooled connections open very quickly, because in many instances, the connection is already open.

This is counter-intuitive to many client-server programmers. You might think that opening and keeping a Connection object alive by storing it in a `Session` variable would be the most efficient method for any specific user; but because of the problems associated with apartment-threaded objects and the efficiency of the pool, that's not the right way to approach database connections in Web applications. Open connections only when necessary and close them as soon as possible.

In addition to the total number of free connections, the efficiency of the connection pool depends on the fact that many connections use the same connection string. For example, if every Connection object in your application uses the same connection string, any connection in the pool is available for any `Open` request. In contrast, if your application uses a different `ConnectionString` property for each user, the pool will be highly inefficient because each user will consume one connection, and no user will be able to use any other user's connection—in other words, the pool is almost useless in this situation.

The pool recycles connections only after they're closed. A connection closes:

- When you explicitly call the `Close` method
- When you set a Connection object reference to `Nothing`
- When a page in which you create a Connection object completes
- When a Session containing an open Connection object stored in a `Session` variable times out
- When an application containing an open Connection object ends

Therefore, the pool works most efficiently when you explicitly call the `Close` method or set a Connection object to `Nothing`, because all the other ways to close a Connection object take longer. Rather obviously, the more Connection objects you have in the pool, the more users you can potentially handle. Closing your Connection objects as soon as possible returns them to the pool, where they can be reused during another request.

You should open connections in read-only mode whenever possible. It's very easy to cut and paste code between ASP pages. I've seen numerous examples where people simply open all connections in read/write mode because it's easier to copy the code they already have than to change the code to open the connection in read-only mode. You can consider this a warning—don't do that. Whenever you open a Connection object, think ahead. What do you want to accomplish with the connection? Are you planning to update data or just select data? If only the latter, open the Connection in read-only mode. Read-only mode is considerably faster than read/write mode because the database doesn't have to apply any locks to the data.

Retrieve Only What You Need

Whenever you make a database call, the database server looks up the information requested and transfers it either from disk or cache to another memory location. Each lookup and memory transfer takes time and resources. You don't normally notice the time during development because the database and the Web server aren't usually under a heavy load. We're talking about microseconds, after all. But all these microseconds add up when you add many users to a production application.

You can minimize the resources and time required for each call by specifying exactly the fields you need in exactly the order you want to retrieve them. Doing so adds time to development. For example, it's much harder to type a query specifying the field names than it is to use the SELECT * syntax. For example:

```
SELECT Students.StudentID, Students.Grade,
   Students.LastName, Students.FirstName FROM Students
```

Contrast the statement above with this easy-to-type version:

```
SELECT * FROM Students
```

Both queries return exactly the same data. The database server has to look up the field names whether you explicitly list them or whether you use the SELECT * syntax. So, even though you save a few keystrokes, you still lose time by selecting fields you don't need. But there are more benefits to selecting exactly the fields you need than just server time and resources. First, suppose you use the * syntax and someone changes the database by adding a new column. If your code expects four fields but receives more than that, what happens? Your display or loop code may break, depending on how you've written it. If, instead, you specify the field names, it won't matter if someone adds a column—you'll still get the four requested fields.

In addition, you'll retrieve the fields in the same order—something you can't guarantee using the * syntax. While I'm on the subject, you should avoid using index numbers to reference fields in your Recordset objects unless you also specify the field names. For example, I've seen numerous examples of code similar to the following:

```
'...
SQL = "SELECT * FROM Teachers"
Set R = conn.Execute(SQL,,adCmdText)
Response.Write R.Fields(1).Value & ", " & R.Fields(2).Value
'... etc.
```

The code will work fine. It is probably slightly faster than the equivalent syntax that references the field names. For example:

```
'...
SQL = "SELECT TeacherID, LastName, FirstName FROM Teachers"
Set R = conn.Execute(SQL,,adCmdText)
Response.Write R.Fields("LastName").Value & ", " _
   & R.Fields("FirstName").Value
'... etc.
```

The problem is that the first example will break if someone changes the order of the columns in the database or inserts a column, because the column positions will no longer be the same as they were when the code was written. In addition, using index values to reference fields in a Recordset object is much more difficult to read.

Use Disconnected Recordsets

Recordset objects opened with the `Execute` method are dependent on an open Connection object. They're child objects. Closing the Connection object also closes and destroys any dependent children. Unfortunately, this ties up the Connection object as long as you need the Recordset object.

Starting with ADO version 1.5, Microsoft introduced a concept called disconnected Recordsets. A disconnected Recordset relies on a Connection object only to obtain the data. After the Recordset object has been filled with rows, you can close the Connection object without affecting the Recordset object. This was a major improvement because it drastically reduces the time you need to tie up a pooled connection, resulting in an immediate increase in scalability.

To disconnect a Recordset object, open it, then set the `Recordset.ActiveConnection` property to `Nothing`. The Recordset object must have a client cursor. In other words, set the `Connection.CursorLocation` to `adUseClient` (Recordset objects inherit the `CursorLocation` of their active Connection object) or set the `Recordset.CursorLocation` property to `adUseClient`. For example, the following script creates a Recordset object, then disconnects it:

```
Dim conn
Dim SQL
Dim R
Dim aConnectionString
aConnectionString = "Provider=SQLOLEDB;Data " _
    & "Source=(local);Database=ClassRecords;" _
    & "UID=sa;PWD=;"
Set conn = Server.CreateObject("ADODB.Connection")
conn.Mode = adModeRead
conn.ConnectionString = aConnectionString
conn.CursorLocation = adUseClient
conn.open
Set R = conn.Execute("SELECT * FROM Students", , adCmdTexT)
' disconnect the Recordset
Set R.activeConnection = Nothing
' the following line causes an error if the Recordset is closed--
' which it will be if it is not disconnected.
Response.Write R("LastName")
```

The previous example opens a read-only Recordset object, but you can open updatable disconnected Recordsets as well. Set the `LockType` property to `adLockBatchOptimistic`. Now you can open the Recordset object, disconnect it, update values, re-connect to a Connection object, and call the `UpdateBatch` method of the Recordset object.

Introduction to Stored Procedures

In the previous chapter, I showed you how to use the `Execute` method of the Connection object and dynamic SQL to retrieve data into a Recordset object. Now I want to discuss why you should avoid using dynamic SQL in production applications.

First, dynamic SQL is relatively slow. You will not notice this in development when only a few people use the server, but in production, dynamic SQL is noticeably slower than pre-compiled SQL, called stored procedures. Fortunately, you can use the `Execute` method to execute stored procedures as well as dynamic SQL. The rule is, never use dynamic SQL unless you have to—and you only have to if the SQL changes completely each time. By completely, I mean the statement itself changes, not just a constant value.

For example, look at the following two queries:

```
SELECT LastName, FirstName FROM Students WHERE StudentID=12
SELECT LastName, FirstName FROM Students WHERE StudentID=14
```

The queries differ only in the value specified for the `StudentID`. In other words, you can think of queries such as this as a function call. You provide the `StudentID` as an argument and the function returns the `LastName` and `FirstName` values associated with that ID. To do this with SQL Server, you write a stored procedure that accepts one parameter—the `StudentID`.

The reason dynamic SQL is slower is because SQL Server must not only parse the SQL statement or query, but also create a query plan. The query plan looks at the query itself, and at the table structure and indexes to determine the most efficient method to obtain the data. When you create a stored procedure, SQL Server stores the query plan. I'll discuss ideas and methods which demonstrate from that point forward, the plan is reusable.

NOTE
If you change the table structure or indexes, you should recompile all the stored procedures that depend on that table. In SQL Server, objects that depend on other objects are dependent objects. You can find the list of dependencies for any object through the SQL Enterprise Manager or by running the **sp_depends** system stored procedure.

Therefore, while you can use the `Execute` method for both dynamic SQL and stored procedures, you should preferentially use stored procedures whenever possible if you need your application to scale well.

When to Use Stored Procedures

During development you can use dynamic SQL initially, but you should move the SQL into stored procedures before moving the application into production. Using stored procedures lets you change and update queries without changing application code, improves the response time for your application, and separates database (SQL) code from ASP (display) code. I'll discuss the idea and methods for improving that separation even more later in this book.

You should create stored procedures whenever:

- Your application runs the same query multiple times (by that I mean across users as well as multiple times for any individual user)

- You need to run multiple queries one after the other

- More than one application needs to run the same query

- You need to run a query in a loop

- The query requires temporary tables

If you study the preceding guidelines, you'll see that there are very few cases in a Web application where dynamic SQL is more appropriate than a stored procedure; however, there are two instances when dynamic SQL is more appropriate, as follows:

- User input is crucial to the construction of the SQL statement. For example, consider an application where a user builds a report by selecting field names and sort orders by selecting checkboxes and option buttons. Your code accepts the user's input and constructs a query based on that input. The number of possibilities soon grows so large that creating stored procedures for every possibility becomes impossible.

- Every connection is different because each connection contains a specific User ID and password. SQL Server caches stored procedures on a connection-specific basis. In a case where each connection is different, SQL Server's caching mechanism may become overloaded because it will cache a different instance of the stored procedure for each user. The cache will fill up quickly with duplicate copies of the stored procedure. The time lost in clearing and caching the stored procedures will more than outweigh the time it takes SQL Server to process dynamic SQL.

In every other case I can think of, stored procedures are more efficient than dynamic SQL.

You create a stored procedure using Data Definition Language (DDL) commands, which are nothing but an extension of SQL. For example, consider the query shown in the previous section:

```
SELECT LastName, FirstName FROM Students WHERE StudentID=12
```

The query returns a Recordset object containing the LastName and FirstName fields from the row containing the StudentID 12. If you were to write this query as a stored procedure, thus making it reusable, you would need to give it a name (like getStudentName) and you would need to pass it a StudentID value. There are many tools for writing stored procedures, including those that ship with Visual InterDev and with SQL Server itself. Which tool you use is up to you. The end result should be the same. The syntax to create a stored procedure is:

```
CREATE PROCEDURE <procedure name>
<parameter1 name type [=value], parameter2 name type [=value]>
AS
<SQL statement(s)>
```

Most tools precede the procedure definition with a DROP PROCEDURE or ALTER PROCEDURE statement to drop or alter any existing procedure with the same name. For example, Listing 19.1 contains the full definition for the getStudentName stored procedure.

LISTING 19.1   **GetStudentName Stored Procedure Definition (ch19i1.sql)**

```
CREATE PROCEDURE getStudentName @StudentID int
AS
SELECT LastName, FirstName FROM Students WHERE StudentID=@StudentID
```

The @StudentID in the first line of the procedure definition is the parameter. Note that it's an integer value, which is the same as the data type for the StudentID column definition in the Students table. After creating the stored procedure, you use the Execute method of the Command object to run it. I'll show you that in the next section, but first, I want to introduce the idea of retrieving data via output parameters.

Using *Output* Parameters

The last operation in the getStudentName procedure is a SELECT statement; therefore, the procedure returns a Recordset object containing the data. But for small amounts of data, such as field values from a single row, it's overkill to invoke the overhead of creating and populating a Recordset object. Instead, you can use output parameters to return the values. An input parameter transfers values into a stored procedure; an output parameter transfers results back to the calling code.

For example, you could define two output parameters and return the Last-Name and FirstName values in those parameter variables rather than returning the values in a Recordset object. You would pass in some empty variables of a type suitable for storing the returned values—in this case, text defined as variable-length string data up to 20 characters in length (VarChar(20)). Listing 19.2 contains the altered CREATE PROCEDURE statement; I've called it getStudentName2 to differentiate it from the original version.

LISTING 19.2   getStudentName2 **Stored Procedure Definition (ch19i2.sql)**

```
CREATE PROCEDURE getStudentName2
    @StudentID int,
    @LastName varChar(20) output,
    @FirstName varChar(20) output
AS
SELECT @LastName=LastName, @FirstName=FirstName FROM Students WHERE
StudentID=@StudentID
```

To execute the stored procedure you need to know a little about the last major ADO object, the Command object.

The Command Object

While you can run stored procedures that return data with the Execute method of the Connection object, you cannot directly run stored procedures that require input or output parameters because the Connection.Execute method doesn't accept parameters. ADO has a special object called the Command object designed to run stored procedures that accept or return data via input or output parameters. Such procedures are parameterized, stored procedures.

You create a Command object using the Server.CreateObject method. For example:

```
Set cm = Server.CreateObject("ADODB.Command")
```

NOTE   I'll use the variable called cm throughout this section to mean a Command object.

A Command object, like the Recordset object, requires a Connection object before you can access a database. You use the ActiveConnection property to attach the Command object to a Connection object. Although the ActiveConnection property is a reference to an object variable, you do not have to use the Set keyword. That's because the property accepts either a Connection object or a valid connection string.

If you don't supply a Connection object, ADO uses the connection string to create one, then destroys it when you destroy the Command object. For example:

```
Set conn = Server.CreateObject("ADODB.Connection")
aConnectionString ="Provider=SQLOLEDB;Data " _
    & "Source=(local);Database=ClassRecords;" _
    & UID=sa;PWD=;"
Set conn = Server.CreateObject("ADODB.Connection")
conn.Mode = adModeReadWrite
conn.ConnectionString = aConnectionString
conn.open
Set cm = Server.CreateObject("ADODB.Command")
Set cm.ActiveConnection = conn
```

The Command object also has an `Execute` method. You can use a Command object to execute dynamic SQL or stored procedures, just like a Connection object. The `Command.Execute` method returns a Recordset object by default, again, just like the Connection object, but you can append parameters (both `input` and `output` parameters) to the Command object's `Parameters` collection before calling the `Execute` method. For example, to call the original `getStudentName` procedure from the previous section, you need to create a parameter to hold the `StudentID` value. To create a parameter, use the `CreateParameter` method of the Command object. For example:

```
Dim param
set param = cm.CreateParameter _
    ("StudentID",adInteger,adParamInput, 4,7)
cm.Parameters.Append param
```

The `CreateParameter` method accepts up to five arguments, all of which are optional. The syntax is:

```
CommandObject.CreateParameter(Name, Type, Direction, Size, Value)
```

As I've suggested before, don't rely on ADO to supply default values for the arguments to the method call, provide them yourself. In the example, the `Name` of the parameter is `StudentID`. The `Type` is the `ADO.DataTypeEnum` constant `adInteger`, which matches the type definition for the `StudentID` column. The third argument, `Direction`, is one of five constants. Table 19.1 lists the five `ADO Parameter Direction Enum` constants

TABLE 19.1: ADO Parameter Direction Enum Constants

Constant	Description
adParamUnknown	Indicates that the parameter direction is unknown. You should never use this value.
adParamInput	Input parameter. This is the default if you don't supply a value.

Continued on next page

TABLE 19.1 CONTINUED: ADO Parameter Direction Enum Constants

Constant	Description
adParamOutput	Output parameter. This means that SQL Server will supply the value and you can obtain it after the stored procedure has completed.
adParamInputOutput	Input-output parameter. You can use a parameter to both supply and receive a value from a stored procedure. For example, you might provide a seed value to a stored procedure that returns a unique ID. As long as both the input and output value are the same type (or two different types that SQL Server can automatically convert, such as char and varChar) you can use a parameter for both input and output.
adParamReturnValue	Return value parameter. Stored procedures can return an integer value. You can obtain the value via a return value parameter.

An input parameter is a value you supply for use within the stored procedure. Output and return value parameters are variable placeholders that the stored procedure fills with values. In the example, the Direction argument is adParamInput—you're supplying the StudentID value to the getStudentName procedure.

The final two arguments are the Size (in this case, a four-byte integer) and the Value, which is the value you want to supply to the stored procedure.

Before executing the procedure, you need to tell SQL Server what type of command you want to run with a CommandType constant. The possible values are the same as those you've seen for the Connection.Execute and Recordset.Open methods, so I won't repeat them here. In this case, you want to run a stored procedure, so you set the Command.CommandType property to adCmdStoredProc:

```
cm.CommandType = adCmdStoredProc
```

You also need to specify the name of the stored procedure you want to run by setting the CommandText property:

```
cm.CommandText = "getStudentName"
```

Finally, you're ready to execute the stored procedure. The Command.Execute method, like the Connection.Execute method, returns a Recordset object:

```
Set R = cm.Execute
```

Because the SELECT statement in the stored procedure selects two fields, you can obtain the values from the returned Recordset object. If the procedure fails to select data; for example, if the supplied StudentID property doesn't exist in the database, the Execute method returns an empty Recordset object. Therefore, you should always check before accessing any of the Recordset object's values. For example:

```
If Not R.EOF then
    Response.Write R("LastName") & ", " & R("FirstName")
```

Listing 19.3 contains the full code to execute the getStudentName stored procedure.

LISTING 19.3   **Executing the `getStudentName` Stored Procedure (`ch19i3.asp`)**

```
<%@ Language=VBScript %>
<% Option Explicit %>
<html>
<head>
</head>
<body>
<%
Dim conn
Dim SQL
Dim R
Dim F
Dim RecsAffected
Dim aConnectionString
Dim cm
Dim param
aConnectionString = "Provider=SQLOLEDB;Data " _
    & "Source=(local);Database=ClassRecords;" _
    & "UID=sa;PWD=;"
Set conn = Server.CreateObject("ADODB.Connection")
conn.Mode = adModeRead
conn.ConnectionString = aConnectionString
conn.CursorLocation = adUseClient
Set cm = Server.CreateObject("ADODB.Command")
cm.ActiveConnection = conn
Set param = cm.CreateParameter("StudentID", adInteger, _
    adParamInput, 4, 7)
cm.Parameters.Append param
Response.Write cm.Parameters.Count
cm.CommandText = "getStudentName"
cm.CommandType = adCmdStoredProc
conn.open
Set R = cm.Execute '(RecsAffected, 7, adCmdStoredProc)
If Not R.EOF Then
    For Each F In R.fields
        Response.Write F.Name & "=" & F.Value & "<br>"
    Next
End If
R.Close
Set R = Nothing
conn.Close
Set conn = Nothing
%>
</body>
</html>
```

If this seems like a lot of work at first, bear with me. I believe the method you've just seen is the most efficient method for calling parameterized, stored procedures, but there are a few shortcuts. You can both create and append Parameter objects to the `Parameters` collection in a single line. For example:

```
cm.Parameters.Append cm.CreateParameter("StudentID", _
    adInteger, adParamInput, 4, 7)
```

Calling stored procedures also becomes easier when you begin to see it as a process:

1. Open a Connection object.

2. Create a Command object.

3. Set the `CommandType`, `CommandText`, and `ActiveConnection` properties.

4. Create and append any parameters.

5. Execute the Command object.

By default, the `Command.Execute` method returns a Recordset object with a read-only, forward-only cursor. If you need a Recordset object with a keyset or static cursor, you must use the `Recordset.Open` method instead. Set the `ActiveCommand` property of the Recordset object to the Command object you want to run before calling the `Open` method. You don't need to set both the `ActiveConnection` and `ActiveCommand` properties. You can keep the Command object from returning an empty Recordset object for queries that don't return data by adding the `adExecuteNoRecords` constant to the `Options` argument.

There's an even shorter way of using parameters with the `Command.Execute` method. I purposely showed you the longer version first because it's more efficient and easier to debug and maintain. The `Command.Execute` method accepts a list of items containing the parameter values. When the procedure executes, ADO attempts to map the values in the array to the parameter list declared in the stored procedure, casting the array items to the correct types, if possible. You must pass the parameters in the exact order they are defined in the procedure. For example, to execute the `getStudentName` procedure, you can write:

```
Set R = cm.Execute("getStudentName", 7, adCmdStoredProc)
```

This line is equivalent to the process of creating and appending Parameter objects to the `Parameters` collection. If you need to pass multiple parameters, you can put them in an array. For example:

```
Set R = cm.Execute("someProcedure", Array(param1, _
    param2, param3), adCmdStoredProc)
```

Retrieving *Output* Parameter Values

At the end of the section of this chapter entitled *Introduction to Stored Procedures*, you saw a variation of the getStudentName procedure called getStudentName2 that used output parameters to return the data. The reason this is important is that it saves the time required to create and populate a Recordset object. You create output parameters in the same way you create input parameters—using the Command object's CreateParameter method. To execute the getStudentName2 procedure, you must create three parameters: the StudentID parameter to determine which record to retrieve, and two output parameters, LastName and FirstName, to hold the returned data. You retrieve the output parameter values after the procedure executes. Listing 19.4 shows how to execute the procedure.

LISTING 19.4   Retrieving Output Parameter Values (ch19i5.asp)

```
<%@ Language=VBScript %>
<% Option Explicit %>
<html>
<head>
</head>
<body>
<%
Dim conn
Dim SQL
Dim R
Dim F
Dim RecsAffected
Dim aConnectionString
Dim cm
Dim param
aConnectionString = "Provider=SQLOLEDB;Data " _
    & "Source=(local);Database=ClassRecords;" _
    & "UID=sa;PWD=;"
Set conn = Server.CreateObject("ADODB.Connection")
conn.Mode = adModeRead
conn.ConnectionString = aConnectionString
conn.CursorLocation = adUseClient
conn.open
Set cm = Server.CreateObject("ADODB.Command")
cm.ActiveConnection = conn
cm.Parameters.Append cm.CreateParameter("StudentID", _
    adInteger, adParamInput, 4, 7)
cm.Parameters.Append cm.CreateParameter("LastName", _
    adVarChar, adParamOutput, 20, "")
```

```
cm.Parameters.Append cm.CreateParameter("FirstName", _
    adVarChar, adParamOutput, 20, "")
cm.CommandText = "getStudentName2"
cm.CommandType = adCmdStoredProc
Call cm.Execute(RecsAffected, , adCmdStoredProc + _
    adExecuteNoRecords)
Response.Write cm.Parameters("LastName").Value & ", " _
    & cm.Parameters("FirstName").Value & "<Br>"
Set cm = Nothing
conn.Close
Set conn = Nothing
%>
</body>
</html>
```

The important points in this script are toward the end. First, note that the script defines the two output parameters with the adParamOutput constant. Second, the call to the Execute method specifies that you don't need a Recordset object return value through the adExecuteNoRecords option. Finally, after the Command object executes the stored procedure, you obtain the returned parameter values with the syntax:

```
MyVar = cm.Parameters("<parameter name>").Value
```

Using parameterized queries takes a little longer than writing an equivalent statement in dynamic SQL, but has payoffs in speed and scalability. In the next section, you'll see how to create a set of routines to display data automatically from a Recordset object.

Build a Recordset Data-Display Engine

One common ASP task is displaying Recordset object data in a table. Displaying data has common elements, but you may need specific requirements for a specific table. For example, you may want to align a table differently from one page to another, specify width by percentage or in pixels, and control whether the table displays borders, among other preferences. Because this is a common task, you should immediately think, include file. Placing your common code into include files provides a single place to debug and extend your procedures. It also considerably simplifies maintenance.

Your task is to write a routine called RecordsetToTable that you can place in an include file that will display any Recordset object—even record sets containing long text fields—in a table in the browser. You should be able to specify the alignment, the width (by percentage or in pixels), control whether the table displays borders, and how wide those borders should be. The routine should display column headers in bold text.

Create the routine so you can pass it a single value or arrays of values to set the background and text colors for all columns or for individual columns. The routine should return a string containing the HTML table, including all the values from the rows of the Recordset object. Try to limit the routine to three arguments.

By altering only the arguments to the routine, not the code itself, you should be able to make the returned string display in ways as different as the two tables shown in Figure 19.1.

FIGURE 19.1:

Sample output from Record-setToTable routine

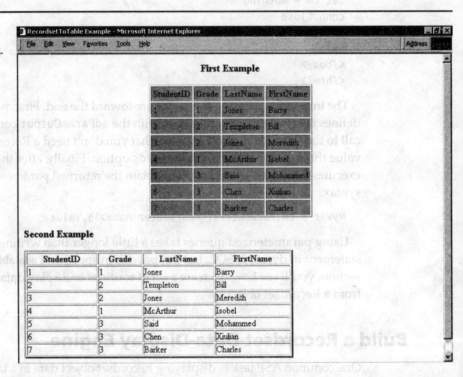

You'll find the sample code for this section in the ch19i5.asp and Recordset-ToTable.inc files, which contain the database calls to create the Recordset object and the RecordsetToTable routine, respectively. You should try to create the routine before viewing the sample code. Because there are innumerable ways to write this routine, your code may not look the same as mine, but it should provide the same functionality.

In the next chapter, you'll see how to use SQL Server and ASP's built-in connection to Microsoft Transaction Server (MTS, now part of COM+ applications in Windows 2000) to manage transactions.

CHAPTER
TWENTY

Controlling Transactions
in ASP

- ■ **Introduction to MTS/COM+ Applications**

- ■ **ASP and Transactions**

- ■ **Components and MTS Transactions**

A transaction is a unit of work that must either succeed completely or fail completely. A transaction is a failure if any of the actions taken during the transaction fail. In other words, all actions in a transaction must succeed for the transaction to be successful, but only one action must fail for the entire transaction to fail. I've discussed transactions as they relate to SQL Server, but that's not the only way to manage transactions in ASP. An ASP page itself can manage transactions where the work for the transaction occurs in external components and in SQL Server. All of this happens through Microsoft Transaction Server (MTS), which is part of the COM+ services in Windows 2000.

> **NOTE**
>
> For brevity, I'm going to use the term MTS/COM+ in this book. Those of you running Windows NT 4 should think MTS and ignore the COM+ terminology. Those of you running Windows 2000 should think COM+ Application whenever you see the term MTS.

Introduction to MTS/COM+ Applications

MTS/COM+ serves two purposes. First, as its name implies, it manages transactions. Second, it provides a memory space in which to run and manage component instances. MTS doesn't appear as a separate item in Windows 2000; you access it through the Component Services administrative application under the name COM+ Applications. Nevertheless, the functionality and much of the administrative interface and procedures are similar between the two server versions.

You've already seen some components that you instantiated with ASP, but you may not know that those components are already running in MTS/COM+. Yes, that's right, all IIS applications, including the root Web, pooled IIS applications, and IIS applications that run in their own memory space, run in MTS/COM+.

MTS/COM+ manages components by intercepting the `Server.CreateObject` call. When you create an object, MTS/COM+ intercepts the call, creates the object within MTS/COM+, and passes back an object reference that points to the MTS/COM+ instance of that object. Your code uses the object normally. When the page ends or you destroy the object explicitly, MTS/COM+ doesn't actually destroy the object. The object remains instantiated and ready for another call to one of its methods or properties.

The end result is that MTS/COM+ lets you avoid much of the overhead of object creation and destruction by maintaining a pool of live objects in memory. Because IIS applications run inside MTS/COM+, your Web sites can take advantage of MTS/COM+ transactions with a few simple commands.

MTS/COM+ is completely integrated with SQL Server. When you create transactional ASP pages, you don't need to test the transaction results yourself; instead, MTS/COM+ raises events that let you know whether the transaction succeeded or failed. MTS/COM+ considers all calls to transactionally aware components and database calls that occur within the transactional page to be part of the transaction.

MTS/COM+ raises events through the ObjectContext object, which as you may remember from the previous section is ASP's connection to MTS/COM+.

The ObjectContext Object

The ObjectContext object appeared with IIS 4 and does not work with IIS 3.0. I haven't introduced it before now because you don't need it until you're either writing transactional pages or writing components for use with ASP.

The ObjectContext object has two purposes. It gives other components access to the same transactional context as your ASP page, which means those other components use the ObjectContext object to gain references to the other ASP intrinsic objects, such as the Request and Response objects. You'll see this in more detail in Chapter 26, *Build Your Own Components*.

The second purpose for the ObjectContext object is to manage transactions. Like the other ASP intrinsic objects, your pages have access to the ObjectContext object automatically—you don't have to create one with the `Server.Create-Object` method. The object has two methods, as shown in Table 20.1.

TABLE 20.1: ObjectContext Object Methods

Method	Description
SetComplete	Completes a portion of a transaction. Each component involved in the transaction must also call the `SetComplete` method. When all components in the transaction have called `SetComplete`, the transaction will complete.
SetAbort	Rolls back a transaction. The `SetAbort` method prevents the components involved in the transaction from updating any resources, leaving the resources in the same state they were in prior to the beginning of the transaction.

The ObjectContext object also raises two events, as shown in Table 20.2.

TABLE 20.2: ObjectContext Object Events

Event	Description
OnTransactionCommit	This event fires when the transactional script and all the components involved in the transaction have called the SetComplete method.
OnTransactionAbort	This event fires if any of the components involved in the transaction call the SetAbort method.

Before you can use these methods and events in an ASP script, you must declare your script as a transactional script. In the next section, you'll see how to do that.

ASP and Transactions

The first step in an ASP transaction is to create a transactional script. To do that, place the @TRANSACTION=<transactionMode> directive at the top of the page. The transactionMode constant may take one of the values shown in Table 20.3.

TABLE 20.3: ASP transactionMode Constants

Value	Description
REQUIRES NEW	Starts a new transaction.
REQUIRED	Starts a new transaction.
SUPPORTED	Does not start a transaction.
NOT_SUPPORTED	Does not start a transaction.

Although you can use any of the four values in an ASP script, only the first two begin a transaction. There are four values so that you can have components during a transaction that are not part of the transaction. You must place the @Transaction directive on the first line in the script, otherwise ASP raises an error. You can combine directives on the same line, but you cannot enter both the @LANGUAGE and @TRANSACTION directives on separate lines. For example:

```
<%@ Language=VBScript @TRANSACTION=REQUIRED %>
```

The directive begins a transaction. When the transaction succeeds or fails, the ObjectContext object raises either the OnTransactionCommit or OnTransaction-Abort event. You can define subroutines to handle these events by naming the subroutines with the name of the event. For example:

```
<%
Sub onTransactionCommit()
    Response.Write "<br>Transaction Committed<Br>"
```

```
End Sub
Sub onTransactionAbort()
    Response.Write "<br>Transaction Aborted<br>"
End Sub
%>
```

If the transaction succeeds, the onTransactionCommit subroutine executes. If the transaction fails, the onTransactionAbort subroutine executes. In neither case can you reverse the outcome of the transaction. For example, you can't successfully use the onTransactionCommit routine to call the ObjectContext.SetAbort method because the transaction has already committed by the time the onTransactionCommit routine begins executing.

Listing 20.1 contains all the necessary parts for a transaction. It begins a transaction, uses a SQL statement to update a table row, then explicitly calls the SetAbort method to roll back the result. Note that the script does not use SQL Server's BEGIN TRAN or ROLLBACK TRAN methods to create or control a transaction. MTS/COM+ automatically begins and rolls back the SQL Server transaction for you.

LISTING 20.1   Sample Transactional Script (ch20i1.asp)

```
<%@ Language=VBScript @TRANSACTION=REQUIRED %>
<%
Sub onTransactionCommit()
    Response.Write "<br>Transaction Committed<Br>"
End Sub
Sub onTransactionAbort()
    Response.Write "<br>Transaction Aborted<br>"
End Sub
%>

<HTML>
<HEAD>
</HEAD>
<BODY>
<%
Dim conn
Dim SQL
Dim aConnectionString
aConnectionString = "Provider=SQLOLEDB;Data " _
    & "Source=(local);Database=ClassRecords;" _
    & "UID=sa;PWD=;"
Set conn = Server.CreateObject("ADODB.Connection")
conn.Mode = adModeRead
```

```
conn.ConnectionString = aConnectionString
conn.CursorLocation = adUseClient
conn.open
SQL = "Update Students SET Grade = 4 WHERE LastName='Chen'"
conn.Execute SQL
ObjectContext.SetAbort
%>
</BODY>
</HTML>
```

To prove to yourself that the SQL statement actually executed properly, you can add two SELECT statements surrounding the UPDATE statement. Listing 20.2 shows the script.

LISTING 20.2   SetAbort Method Rolls Back SQL Server Transaction

```
<%@ Language=VBScript @TRANSACTION=REQUIRED %>
<%
Sub onTransactionCommit()
    Dim conn
    Dim SQL
    Dim aConnectionString
    aConnectionString = "Provider=SQLOLEDB;Data " _
        & "Source=(local);Database=ClassRecords;" _
        & "UID=sa;PWD=;"
    Set conn = Server.CreateObject("ADODB.Connection")
    conn.Mode = adModeRead
    conn.ConnectionString = aConnectionString
    conn.CursorLocation = adUseClient
    conn.open
    SQL = "SELECT Grade FROM Students WHERE LastName='Chen'"
    Set R = conn.execute(SQL, , adCmdText)
    Response.Write "After commit, grade = " & R("Grade").Value & "<br>"
    R.Close
    Response.Write "<br>Transaction Committed<Br>"
End Sub
Sub onTransactionAbort()
    Dim conn
    Dim SQL
    Dim aConnectionString
    aConnectionString = "Provider=SQLOLEDB;Data " _
        & "Source=(local);Database=ClassRecords;" _
        & "UID=sa;PWD=;"
    Set conn = Server.CreateObject("ADODB.Connection")
    conn.Mode = adModeRead
```

```
            conn.ConnectionString = aConnectionString
            conn.CursorLocation = adUseClient
            conn.open
            SQL = "SELECT Grade FROM Students WHERE LastName='Chen'"
            Set R = conn.execute(SQL, , adCmdText)
            Response.Write "After abort, grade = " & R("Grade").Value & "<br>"
            R.Close
            Response.Write "<br>Transaction Aborted<br>"
        End Sub
        %>
        <html>
        <head>
        </head>
        <body>
        <%
        Dim conn
        Dim SQL
        Dim aConnectionString
        aConnectionString = "Provider=SQLOLEDB;Data " _
            & "Source=(local);Database=ClassRecords;" _
            & "UID=sa;PWD=;"
        Set conn = Server.CreateObject("ADODB.Connection")
        conn.Mode = adModeRead
        conn.ConnectionString = aConnectionString
        conn.CursorLocation = adUseClient
        conn.open
        SQL = "SELECT Grade FROM Students WHERE LastName='Chen'"
        Set R = conn.execute(SQL, , adCmdText)
        Response.Write "Before update, grade = " & R("Grade").Value & "<br>"
        R.Close
        SQL = "Update Students SET Grade = 4 WHERE LastName='Chen'"
        conn.execute SQL, , adCmdText
        SQL = "SELECT Grade FROM Students WHERE LastName='Chen'"
        Set R = conn.execute(SQL, , adCmdText)
        Response.Write "After update, Grade = " & R("Grade").Value & "<br>"
        R.Close
        ObjectContext.SetAbort
        Set conn = Nothing
        %>
        </body>
        </html>
```

When you run this script, it looks like Figure 20.1.

FIGURE 20.1:

Transactional script
(ch20i2.asp)

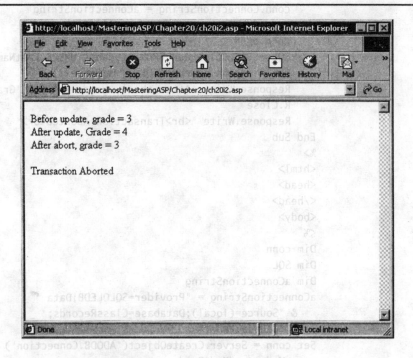

Components and MTS/COM+ Transactions

The examples in the previous section were simplistic. You can control more than SQL Server with MTS/COM+ transactions; you can control components as well. You haven't seen how to create components yet, but to illustrate the point I've included a small component on the CD as a VB-generated DLL called UpdateStudent.dll. This DLL changes a student's last name, first name, or grade.

The component works in concert with two HTML forms. You alter the information in the form. First, select a student from the list and click the Details button (see Figure 20.2).

When you click the Details button, the application displays the details for that student. You may change the contents of any field or fields and click Save to save your changes. You've seen forms similar to this already; the difference is that this form submits its information to a page that requires a transaction. When you submit this form, it creates a ClassRecords.CStudent component to update the Students table. The component participates in the update by checking each submitted value to see if it meets certain requirements. If so, the component updates the row, then calls the SetComplete method; otherwise, it calls SetAbort, which cancels the transaction. Figure 20.3 shows the student detail form.

FIGURE 20.2:

Student selection form
(ch20i3.asp)

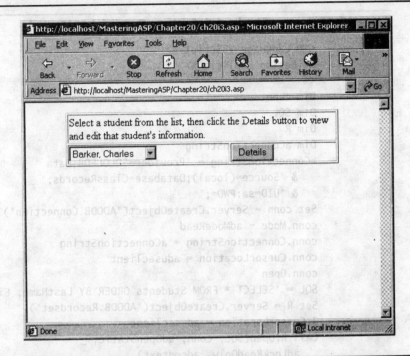

Listing 20.3 contains the code for the student selection form.

LISTING 20.3   **Student Selection Form (ch20i3.asp)**

```asp
<%@ Language=VBScript %>
<% Option Explicit %>
<%
Dim conn
Dim SQL
Dim R
Dim aConnectionString
aConnectionString = "Provider=SQLOLEDB;Data " _
    & "Source=(local);Database=ClassRecords;" _
    & "UID=sa;PWD=;"
Set conn = Server.CreateObject("ADODB.Connection")
conn.Mode = adModeRead
conn.ConnectionString = aConnectionString
conn.CursorLocation = aduseclient
conn.Open
SQL = "SELECT * FROM Students ORDER BY LastName, FirstName"
Set R = Server.CreateObject("ADODB.Recordset")
R.CursorLocation = aduseclient
Call R.Open(SQL, conn, adOpenStatic, _
    adLockReadOnly, adcmdtext)
Set R.ActiveConnection = Nothing
conn.Close
Set conn = Nothing
%>
<html>
<head>
</head>
<body>
<form name="frmSelectStudent" method="post" _
    action="ch20i4.asp">
<table align="center" width="80%" border="1">
    <tr>
        <td colspan="2">
            Select a student from the list, then click
            the Details button to view and edit that
            student's information.
        </td>
    </tr>
        <td valign="top" width="60%">
            <select name="StudentID">
                <%
                While Not R.EOF
                    Response.Write "<option value='" & _
```

```
                              R("StudentID").Value & "'>" & _
                              R("LastName").Value & ", " & _
                              R("Firstname").Value & "</option>"
                          R.movenext
                      Wend
                      R.Close
                      Set R = Nothing
                      %>
                  </select>
              </td>
              <td valign="top">
                  <input type="Submit" value="Details"
                    name="Details">
              </td>
          </tr>
      </table>
  </form>
  </body>
  </html>
```

Listing 20.4 contains the ASP script for the detail form.

LISTING 20.4   Student Detail Form (ch20i4.asp)

```
<%@ Language=VBScript %>
<% Option Explicit %>
<% Response.Buffer=True %>
<%
Dim oStudent
Dim StudentID
Dim LastName
Dim FirstName
Dim Grade
Dim conn
Dim SQL
Dim R
Dim aConnectionString
StudentID = Request("StudentID")
If StudentID = "" Then
    Response.redirect "ch20i3.asp"
End If
aConnectionString = "Provider=SQLOLEDB;Data " _
    & "Source=(local);Database=ClassRecords;" _
    & "UID=sa;PWD=;"
Set conn = Server.CreateObject("ADODB.Connection")
conn.Mode = adModeRead
```

```
conn.ConnectionString = aConnectionString
conn.CursorLocation = adUseClient
conn.open
SQL = "SELECT * FROM Students WHERE StudentID=" & StudentID
Set R = conn.execute(SQL, , adcmdtext)
LastName = R("LastName").Value
FirstName = R("FirstName").Value
Grade = R("Grade").Value
conn.Close
Set conn = Nothing
%>
<html>
<head>
</head>
<body>
<form name="frmSelectStudent" method="post" action="ch20i5.asp">
<input type="hidden" name="StudentID" value="<%=StudentID%>">
<table align=center width="60%">
    <tr>
        <td width="30%">
            <b>Last Name</b>:
        </td>
        <td width="*">
            <input type="text" name="LastName"
            value="<%=LastName%>">
        </td>
    </tr>
    <tr>
        <td width="30%">
            <b>First Name</b>:
        </td>
        <td width="*">
            <input type="text" name="FirstName"
            value="<%=FirstName%>">
        </td>
    </tr>
    <tr>
        <td width="30%">
            <b>Grade</b>:
        </td>
        <td width="*">
            <input type="text" name="Grade"
            value="<%=Grade%>">
        </td>
    </tr>
```

```html
<tr>
  <td colspan="2">
    <input type="Submit" name="Submit" value="Submit">
  </td>
</tr>
</table>
</form>
</body>
</html>
```

Listing 20.5 contains the transactional ASP script to update the row.

LISTING 20.5   Transactional Script to Update Student Information (ch20i5.asp)

```asp
<%@ Language=VBScript @TRANSACTION=REQUIRED%>
<%
Dim oStudent
Dim StudentID
Dim LastName
Dim FirstName
Dim Grade
Sub onTransactionCommit()
    Response.Write "The record has been updated.<br>"
    Response.Write "Click <a href='ch20i3.asp'>here</a> to return to the
    list."
    Response.end
End Sub
Sub onTransactionAbort()
    Response.Write "Some of the information you "
        & "entered is not valid.<br>"
    Response.Write "Error Description: " & _
        Err.Description & "<br>"
    Response.Write "Click <a href='ch20i4.asp?StudentID=" _
        & StudentID & "'>here</a> to update the information."
    Response.end
End Sub
Set oStudent = server.CreateObject("ClassRecords.CStudent")
StudentID = Request("StudentID")
LastName = Request("LastName")
FirstName = Request("FirstName")
Grade = Request("Grade")
On Error Resume Next
Call oStudent.UpdateStudent(StudentID, LastName, _
    FirstName, Grade)
If Err.Number <> 0 Then
    objectContext.setAbort
```

```
        Else
            objectContext.SetComplete
        End If
    %>
```

Finally, Listing 20.6 contains the code for the ClassRecords.Cstudent class that updates the row.

LISTING 20.6   **ClassRecords.CStudent Class** – UpdateStudent **Method (CStudent.cls)**

```
Option Explicit
Implements ObjectControl
Private Const Classname = "ADCTResponses"
Private oc As ObjectContext
Public Enum CStudentErrorEnum
    ERR_BAD_STUDENTID = vbObjectError + 1500
    ERR_BAD_LASTNAME
    ERR_BAD_FIRSTNAME
    ERR_BAD_GRADE
End Enum

Public Sub UpdateStudent(StudentID As Variant, LastName As Variant,
FirstName As Variant, Grade As Variant)
    On Error GoTo ErrUpdateStudent
    If Val(StudentID) <= 0 Then
        Err.Raise ERR_BAD_STUDENTID, "UpdateStudent", "Invalid StudentID"
    End If
    If VarType(LastName) <> vbString Then
        Err.Raise ERR_BAD_LASTNAME, "UpdateStudent", "Last name must be
a string."
    End If
    If Len(LastName) < 2 Or Len(LastName) > 20 Then
        Err.Raise ERR_BAD_LASTNAME, "UpdateStudent", "The last name
must be between 2 and 20 characters in length."
    End If
    If containsNumbers(CStr(LastName)) Then
        Err.Raise ERR_BAD_LASTNAME, "UpdateStudent", "The last name may
not contain numbers."
    End If
    If VarType(FirstName) <> vbString Then
        Err.Raise ERR_BAD_FIRSTNAME, "UpdateStudent", "Last name must
be a string."
    End If
```

```
        If Len(FirstName) < 2 Or Len(FirstName) > 20 Then
            Err.Raise ERR_BAD_FIRSTNAME, "UpdateStudent", "The last name
must be between 2 and 20 characters in length."
        End If
        If containsNumbers(CStr(FirstName)) Then
            Err.Raise ERR_BAD_FIRSTNAME, "UpdateStudent", "The last name
may not contain numbers."
        End If
        If Not containsNumbers(CStr(Grade)) Then
            Err.Raise ERR_BAD_GRADE, "UpdateStudent", "Invalid grade."
        End If
        If Grade <= 0 Or Grade >= 9 Then
            Err.Raise ERR_BAD_GRADE, "UpdateStudent", "The grade must be
between 1 and 8."
        End If
        Dim conn
        Dim SQL
        Dim aConnectionString
        aConnectionString = "Provider=SQLOLEDB;Data " _
            & "Source=(local);Database=ClassRecords;" _
            & "UID=sa;PWD=;"
        Set conn = CreateObject("ADODB.Connection")
        conn.Mode = adModeReadWrite
        conn.ConnectionString = aConnectionString
        conn.CursorLocation = adUseClient
        conn.Open
        SQL = "UPDATE Students SET LastName='" & LastName & "', FirstName='"
& FirstName & "',Grade=" & Grade & " WHERE StudentID=" & StudentID
        conn.Execute SQL, , adCmdText
        conn.Close
        Set conn = Nothing
ExitUpdateStudent:
        Exit Sub
ErrUpdateStudent:
        Call setAbort
        Err.Raise Err.Number, Err.Source, Err.Description
        Resume ExitUpdateStudent
End Sub
Private Sub setComplete()
    If Not oc Is Nothing Then
        oc.setComplete
    End If
End Sub
Private Sub setAbort()
    If Not oc Is Nothing Then
```

```
            oc.setAbort
        End If
    End Sub
    Private Function containsNumbers(s As String)
        Dim i As Integer
        Const numbers = "0123456789"
        For i = 1 To Len(s)
            If InStr(numbers, Mid$(s, i, 1)) > 0 Then
                containsNumbers = True
                Exit Function
            End If
        Next
    End Function
    Private Sub ObjectControl_Activate()
        On Error GoTo ErrObjectControl_Activate
        Dim methodname As String
        methodname = Classname & ".ObjectControl_Activate"
        Set oc = GetObjectContext
    ExitObjectControl_Activate:
        Exit Sub
    ErrObjectControl_Activate:
        Err.Raise Err.Number, methodname, Err.Description & vbCrLf &
    "Unable to acquire a reference to the ObjectContext object."
        Resume ExitObjectControl_Activate
    End Sub

    Private Function ObjectControl_CanBePooled() As Boolean
        ObjectControl_CanBePooled = False
    End Function

    Private Sub ObjectControl_Deactivate()
        On Error GoTo ErrObjectControl_Deactivate
        Dim methodname As String
        methodname = Classname & ".ObjectControl_Deactivate"
        Set oc = Nothing
    ExitObjectControl_Deactivate:
        Exit Sub
    ErrObjectControl_Deactivate:
        Err.Raise Err.Number, methodname, Err.Description & vbCrLf &
    "Unable to release the reference to the ObjectContext object."
        Resume ExitObjectControl_Deactivate
    End Sub
```

You don't need to worry about the code in this listing at the moment—I've included it for informational purposes only so the curious can see how it works internally. The component participates in a transaction by implementing the `ObjectControl` interface, using the command:

```
Implements ObjectControl
```

The `ObjectControl` interface provides access to the ObjectContext object, defined in the class as the oc variable. When MTS/COM+ receives the `CreateObject` call, it fires an event called `ObjectControl_Activate`. The component sets the oc variable to the object context for the calling code. When the client releases the CStudent object (in this case, when the calling ASP page ends) MTS/COM+ fires the `Object-Control_Deactivate` event, which releases the ObjectContext object.

The only public method in the class is `UpdateStudent`, which accepts `StudentID`, `LastName`, `FirstName`, and `Grade` as arguments, checks the arguments, opens a connection, and updates the row values. The component raises a specific error from the list of public `CStudentErrorEnum` values, as well as raising any other error back to the calling code.

I've written this component so it can run both inside and outside MTS/COM+. If the component runs outside of MTS/COM+, the `ObjectControl_Activate` event code never executes; therefore, the oc ObjectContext variable has the default value of `Nothing`. The calls in the `setAbort` and `setComplete` subroutines first check to see if the oc variable is `Nothing`. If so, the code doesn't try to set any properties, thus avoiding errors if the object is not running in MTS/COM+.

Creating the component is relatively simple, but setting it up to run in MTS/COM+ involves a slightly more complicated set of steps—and the steps are different for NT 4 and Windows 2000. I've included both procedures below. Follow the procedure for your server to register the component with MTS/COM+.

NT 4 MTS Package Creation and Component Registration

This procedure must be performed on your server, either physically or remotely using the Microsoft Management Console (MMC) application.

1. **Install the Component**: The `ClassRecords.DLL` resides in the `MasteringASP\VBCode\Chapter20` directory. There's a `Setup.exe` file in that directory. Run the installation program to install the component. If you already have the Visual Basic 6 runtime files installed on your computer, you can ignore the setup program and just register the component by clicking Start, Run, and

typing the following line into the Run field (ignore any line breaks that appear in the text of this book; enter the information on a single line):

```
c:\winnt\system32\regsvr32.exe "c:\inetpub\wwwroot\MasteringASP\
VBCode\Chapter20\ClassRecords.dll"
```

2. **Create a MasteringASP Package in MTS**: Open the Microsoft Transaction Server Explorer applet. Click Start, Programs, Windows NT 4.0 Option Pack, Microsoft Transaction Server, Transaction Server Explorer. Expand the items in the left-hand pane under Computers by clicking the + signs until you see the Packages Installed item. Right-click on that item and select New, then click Package. From the dialog that appears, click the Create an Empty Package button. Enter MasteringASP as the title of the package, then click Next. You'll see the Set Package Identity screen. Accept the default, which is Interactive User..., then click the Finish button. MTS creates your new package.

3. **Set Package Properties**: Find your new package by clicking the + sign next to the Packages Installed item. Right-click on the MasteringASP package and select Properties. Click the Security tab and check the Enable Authorization Checking checkbox. Click the OK button to save your changes.

4. **Add Roles**: Click the + sign next to the MasteringASP package. Select and then right-click on the Roles item and select New, then Role, from the context menu. Enter MasteringASPUser into the name field, then click the OK button. MTS creates the new Role. Click the + sign until you see the new entry in the list.

5. **Add Users to Role**: Click the + sign next to the MasteringASPUser entry. Right-click on the Users entry and select New, then User, from the context menu. You'll see a standard NT user/group dialog. Click the Show Users button to list the users. Select the IUSR_MACHINENAME account. Remember, the MACHINENAME corresponds to your server's machine name so you won't actually see MACHINENAME. IIS impersonates this account for anonymous requests. You want this account to have permission to launch your component. Click OK to add the account to the list of Users for this role.

6. **Add Components**: Scroll the list until you can see the MasteringASP\Components entry. Right-click on the Components entry and select New, then Component, from the context menu. Click the Install New Component(s) button. From the Install Components dialog, click the Add Files button and navigate to the directory that contains the ClassRecords.dll file you registered in

Step 1. Double-click on that file. MTS adds the filename and the list of public components contained in the class to the Install Components dialog. Click Finish to close the dialog. MTS adds the new component to the Components item.

7. **Assign Role**: You want the CStudent component to run in the MasteringASP role you created in Steps 4 and 5. To assign that role, click the + sign next to the ClassRecords.CStudent item, then right-click on the Role Membership item. Select New, then Role, from the context menu. Select the MasteringASP-User role from the list, then click the OK button to add the role. An icon for the new role appears in the right-hand pane of the Transaction Explorer.

Windows 2000 MTS Package Creation and Component Registration

NOTE

This procedure must be performed on your server, either physically or remotely using the Component Services application.

1. **Install the Component**: The ClassRecords.DLL resides in the MasteringASP\ VBCode\Chapter20 directory. There's a Setup.exe file in that directory. Run the installation program to install the component. If you already have the Visual Basic 6 runtime files installed on your computer, you can ignore the setup program and just register the component by clicking Start, Run, and typing the following line into the Run field (ignore any line breaks that appear in the text of this book; enter the information on a single line):

NOTE

The paths below work on my server, but you may need to adjust the paths for your server.

```
c:\winnt\system32\regsvr32.exe "c:\inetpub\wwwroot\MasteringASP\
VBCode\Chapter20\ClassRecords.dll"
```

2. **Create a MasteringASP COM+ Application**: Open the Component Services application. Click Start, Programs, Administrative Tools, Component Services. Expand the items under the Component Services item by clicking the + signs until you see the COM+ Applications item. Select the COM+ Applications item, then right-click on it and select New, then click Application. You'll see the COM Application Install Wizard. Click Next once, then click the Create an Empty Application button. Enter MasteringASP as the name of the application and select the Server Application radio button, then click Next. You'll see the Set Application Identity screen. Accept the default, which is Interactive User…, click the Next button, then the Finish button to create the application.

3. **Set Application Properties**: Find your new application in the list of applications under the COM+ Applications item. Select the MasteringASP application, then right-click on it and select Properties. Click the Security tab and check the Enforce access checks for this application checkbox. Leave all other options set to the defaults. Click the OK button to save your changes.

4. **Add Roles**: Click the + sign next to the MasteringASP package. Select and then right-click on the Roles item and select New, then Role, from the context menu. Enter `MasteringASPUser` into the name field, then click the OK button. Click the + sign next to Roles to see the new entry in the list.

5. **Add Users to Role**: Click the + sign next to the MasteringASPUser role item. Select the Users entry, then right-click on it and select New, then User, from the context menu. Select the IUSR_MACHINENAME account. Remember, the MACHINENAME corresponds to your server's machine name so you won't actually see MACHINENAME. IIS impersonates this account for anonymous requests. You want this account to have permission to launch your component. Click OK to add the account to the list of Users for this role.

6. **Add Components**: Scroll the list until you can see the MasteringASP\Components entry. Select the Components entry, then right-click on it and select New, then Component, from the context menu. You'll see the COM Component Install Wizard. Click Next, then click the Install New Component(s) button. From the Select Files to Install dialog, navigate to the directory that contains the `ClassRecords.dll` file you registered in Step 1. Double-click on that file. The COM Component Install Wizard adds the filename and the list of public components contained in the class. Click Next, then Finish, to close the dialog. Component Services adds the new component to the Components item.

7. **Assign Role**: You want the CStudent component to run in the MasteringASP role you created in Steps 4 and 5. To assign that role, select the ClassRecords .CStudent item, then right-click on it and select Properties from the context menu. Click the Security Tab, then select the MasteringASPUser role from the list. Click the OK button to add the role.

The steps in the previous procedure (although not the individual names and selections) are generic; you can create a new package and assign roles using these steps. Registering and updating components in MTS/COM+ can be a painful process; follow the procedure exactly or you may need to reboot your server to get things working again.

The point of this exercise is to create a component that can participate in transactions. Unless the component runs inside MTS/COM+, it cannot either initiate a transaction or inherit the context of its instantiator, hence it will not be able to participate in a transaction. You can use the component outside of MTS/COM+, so you can run the code even if you don't have access to a server with MTS/COM+ installed, although it will not run correctly.

You won't see anything except the messages in the browser, so it's enlightening to watch the transactions in the Microsoft Transaction Explorer (Windows NT 4) applet or Component Services (Windows 2000) application. Resize your browser so you can see both the browser window and the appropriate application/applet for your server.

Select, then right-click on the Components entry under the MasteringASP package or application title (see Figure 20.4), then select View, Status View from the context menu. Now select a student and submit the Details form (you don't have to change any data to watch the transaction occur). You will see numbers (zeroes) appear in the Status View pane (NT 4 only). You may even briefly see one of the zeroes change to a one, signifying that the object was active. Depending on your server, this may happen too fast to see with a single client.

FIGURE 20.4:

MTE status view

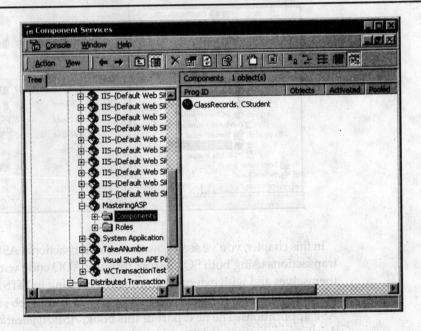

What you're seeing is a display showing the count of objects instantiated, activated, or actually performing work at the point in time the display was last refreshed. You can repeat the transaction many times by pressing F5 from the informational screen that appears after you click the Submit button from the Student Details screen (you will get a dialog that asks if you want to resubmit the information; that's OK, click the Retry button to resubmit the form). If you do this many times in rapid succession, you'll see the ball icon next to the CStudent component item begin to spin, showing you that the component is currently in use.

NOTE The ball icon doesn't spin in Windows 2000 in this view.

You can also view transaction statistics showing how many transactions are in progress, have completed, aborted, or are still in doubt, as well as transaction totals since MS DTC was last started on the server. In NT 4, the Transaction Statistics item is the last entry under the My Computer item in the left-hand pane. Click on it to change to the Transaction Statistics view. In Windows 2000, scroll to the bottom of the COM+ Applications list and select the Transaction Statistics item under the Distributed Transaction Coordinator entry (see Figure 20.5).

FIGURE 20.5:

MTE Transaction Statistics view in Windows 2000

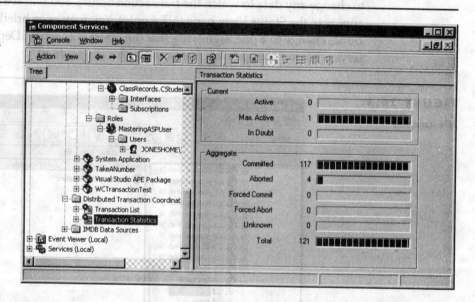

In this chapter, you've seen how to create transactional ASP pages that control transactions using both SQL Server through ADO code within the ASP pages themselves and with external components running in MTS/COM+. At this level of complexity, you're beginning to move away from Web sites into the realm of ASP applications. The next part of this book, *ASP Applications*, provides an in-depth investigation of ASP applications that will provide you with options for approaching the design of your own applications.

PART VI

ASP Applications

PART VI

ASP Applications

CHAPTER
TWENTY-ONE

Introduction to
ASP Applications

■ Applications vs. Web Sites

■ The *global.asa* File

■ How do *global.asa* Files Interact in Subdirectories?

■ What to Put in *global.asa* Files

■ What Not to Put in *global.asa* Files

■ Useful Directory Structures

What is an ASP application? You can argue that any Web site that uses ASP to provide dynamic content is an ASP application. But for the purposes of this book, I'm going to define an ASP application as a set of pages that uses HTML forms and user input to store or alter persisted data on the server. In that sense, you've already seen a number of applications (albeit short ones) in this book. You should recognize that my definition doesn't cover all possible ASP applications, but it probably covers the ones you're most likely to write.

Applications vs. Web Sites

A Web site provides information. An ASP application not only provides information, it lets users interact with that information, often adding to or altering the information, thus changing the future display of that information, either for themselves (user-specific changes) or for everyone using the application. For example, an online contact information program is user-specific; when a user enters or changes information, the display of that information changes for only that user. In contrast, when a user adds an item to a discussion group application, the display changes for everyone using the application.

In both cases, the critical factor is that the information isn't static. Users feel more involved in a Web application than in a Web site because they have to interact with (and therefore think about) the content. Because the content changes significantly over time, there are some fundamental differences between creating a Web site and creating a Web application that you should recognize. Ask these questions when you begin planning the application:

- How does the application obtain information—where's the data?

- Where should the application store information? Do you need global (application-level) information? Do you need to store data in Session variables?

- Must the application be moveable? Will it run on one server or on many servers? In one location or many locations?

- How many simultaneous users must the application support?

- How responsive must the application be?

- Is the application critical; will a failure cause critical business functions to be lost?

- Must the application be secure? Is the information sensitive or private? Do you require a secured site?

The answers to questions like these play a large role in determining how you should set up the application. For example, an e-commerce application may use a database to store product and order information, but use cookies to store user information during the shopping and ordering process. Only when the order is complete does the application need to update the database. On the other hand, a note-taking application needs to store user-entered information immediately, and has little need for cookies.

As the starting point for your application and for each session, you need to pay particular attention to the global.asa file.

The *global.asa* File

You've already seen several examples of global.asa files and the events that fire during Application and Session initialization and termination. Now I want to discuss the global.asa file in relation to an application.

To create an ASP application (like the MasteringASP application you created at the start of this book) you need to create a virtual directory in IIS 4 and higher, and mark it as an application using the IIS administration program. You place your global.asa file in the root application directory. If you don't mark the virtual directory as an application, IIS will not process the global.asa file at all. This is different from IIS version 3. In that version, the presence of a global.asa file in a virtual directory automatically made that virtual directory an application, which led to confusion when multiple directories within an application contained global.asa files. The new version is simpler. The rule is: IIS processes only global.asa files contained in a virtual directory marked as an application, and then only when the request references the virtual root directory as the root of the request. I know, that's not as simple as I had hoped, but here are some examples that may help.

Create two physical directories. The top-level directory is AppRoot. The AppRoot directory has one sub directory, called App1. Each directory contains two files, a global.asa file and a default.asp file (see Listing 21.1).

NOTE   On the CD, the files are in the MasteringASP\Chapter21\AppRoot directory. To use the files, create the AppRoot directory and the App1 subdirectory and copy the files to the new directories. Next, create two virtual directories pointing to the new directories and mark each one as an application so the rest of the code in this section will work properly.

LISTING 21.1 **Sample global.asa and default.asp Files**

```
' ****************************************************
' Global.asa file in AppRoot
' ****************************************************
<SCRIPT LANGUAGE=VBScript RUNAT=Server>
Sub Application_OnStart
   Application("AppName") = "AppRoot"
End Sub
</SCRIPT>


' ****************************************************
' Default.asp file in AppRoot
' ****************************************************
<html><head><title>AppRoot Default File</title></head>
<body>
<%
Response.write "Application Appname variable=" & _
Application("AppName")  & "<br>"
Response.write "Got to AppRoot Default File"
%>

' ****************************************************
' Global.asa file in App1
' ****************************************************
<SCRIPT LANGUAGE=VBScript RUNAT=Server>
Sub Application_OnStart
   Application("AppName") = "App1"
End Sub
</SCRIPT>

' ****************************************************
' Default.asp file in App1
' ****************************************************
<html><head><title>App1 Default File</title></head>
<body>
<%
Response.write "Application Appname variable=" & _
Application("AppName")  & "<br>"
Response.write "Got to App1 Default File"
%>
</body>
</html>
```

Each `global.asa` file creates an `Application` variable containing the name of the corresponding directory. The `default.asp` files display the value of that `Application` variable, as well as the location and name of the file. Create an App-Root virtual directory with the physical directory pointed to the physical `AppRoot` directory. Create an `App1` virtual directory with the physical directory pointed to the physical `App1` directory. Now try running the default files. Table 21.1 shows the URL and result for each of three requests.

TABLE 21.1: Result of URL in Browser

URL	Result in Browser
`http://localhost/AppRoot/default.asp`	Application Appname variable=AppRoot
	Got to AppRoot Default File
`http://localhost/AppRoot/App1/default.asp`	Application Appname variable=AppRoot
	Got to App1 Default File
`http://localhost/App1/default.asp`	Application Appname variable=App1
	Got to App1 Default File

The first and third URLs act just as you would expect; they display the value.

The `global.asa` file is different from other ASP files. When ASP receives a request, it checks to see if an Application object has been instantiated for that virtual directory. If not, it searches upward through the directory hierarchy for a `global.asa` file. ASP uses the highest-level `global.asa` file it finds in a directory marked as a virtual Web site in the IIS administration program and processes the contents.

As the starting point for your application, the location of the `global.asa` file is critical; it must reside in the root directory of the application. IIS assumes that the `global.asa` file is always at the highest directory level for your application.

How Do *global.asa* Files Interact in Subdirectories?

You can mark any directory as a virtual directory. From another point of view, every virtual directory is a pointer to a physical directory. If the directory is marked as an application and contains a `global.asa` file, IIS assumes any files you run in that directory are part of that application. Therefore, if you mark a subdirectory of an existing application as another application, and you place a `global.asa` file in that subdirectory, IIS will treat it as the start of a new application. A user requesting files first in one, and then the other of those two directories, will switch applications as well as `Session` and `Application` variables each time they move between applications.

Here's a scenario. Suppose you have a directory-structure for your company's intranet such that people normally enter at the top-level application. Beneath that top-level directory, you have another application directory. Each application directory contains a `global.asa` file. For example:

```
MyCompany
    App1
```

When a user requests a file in the MyCompany application, IIS processes the `global.asa` file in that directory (if there is one). If a user subsequently requests a file in the App1 application, IIS will execute the `global.asa` file in the App1 directory. Thus, from your point of view as the programmer, the user has changed applications.

Most people prefer to have a single, top-level application directory and place only subordinate content in the subdirectories because managing resources is much easier that way, but IIS lets you arrange applications in hierarchies as well.

What to Put in *global.asa* Files

The `global.asa` file should contain resource information, global application and session-scope `<object>` tags, and initialization and shutdown code. For example, you should create Application-level variables for connection information, file resources needed throughout the application like error log or user-specific file references, and any other values used globally for the entire application, or session-wide for a specific session.

You should try to limit declarations and assignments in `global.asa` to string resources for application startup, but you often must include database operations during the `Session_OnEnd` and `Application_OnEnd` events, because that's the only sure way to perform clean-up. Unfortunately, it's also difficult to debug Session and Application shutdown code in `global.asa` because the browser is no longer available during those events. So you can't use `global.asa` to write debug information and you won't receive any error messages from ASP because, again, the browser isn't available.

There are a few things you can do to ease this problem. First, you can develop the shutdown code in another page. Developing `global.asa` code in another page lets you use the Response object to track errors. If you develop in Visual InterDev, you can use the debugger to step through the code. You can also develop VBScript code in Visual Basic, which gives you better debugging capabilities, as long as you're careful to stick to the capabilities of VBScript and avoid features that are specific to VB. After you have the code thoroughly debugged, you can place it into the `global.asa` file. Second, you can log shutdown operations (and shutdown errors) to a file, or if you have access to the server, to the event log. I recommend you always log `global.asa` shutdown code, as there is no other way you can track errors during production.

What Not to Put in *global.asa* Files

I've said this before, but I'll repeat it here because it's important. *Do not create any apartment-threaded objects at Application or Session scope*. For example, it's tempting to create one Connection object for each Session and store it in a `Session` variable rather than creating a new Connection on each page. Avoid that temptation. Don't store Dictionary objects at Application or Session scope either.

Other than that, the only restrictions to keep in mind are that you don't have access to the Session object during the `Application_OnStart` or `Application_OnEnd` events, and you don't have access to the `Session` values during the `Session_OnEnd` event.

Useful Directory Structures

Because of the way IIS treats virtual directories, you can have applications that share data as long as you place them in a subordinate position to a virtual directory marked as an application. For example, if you own a chain of hotels, you might want an individual site for each hotel, but you would want to gather data about individuals who visit any of the sites in one location. To do that, you could set up a virtual directory as the application `root`, but place each of the hotel sites below that directory, without a `global.asa` file. When people visit one of the subordinate sites, IIS will run the `global.asa` file at the root level. Now people can move between the hotel sites and their `Session` variables will remain constant.

You can use this capability to gather statistical information about all hotel guests in one place. For example, by giving each browser a cookie, you would be able to count the number of repeat visits even if the guest chose a different hotel during the next visit to the site. You wouldn't need to have any content in the `root` directory other than a list of links to the lower-level sites.

CHAPTER
TWENTY-TWO

State Maintenance in ASP Applications

- ■ Don't Cache Data

- ■ Sessionless Applications – Advantages/Disadvantages

- ■ State Maintenance Options

- ■ Maintaining State with Cookies

- ■ Maintaining State with *QueryString* Variables

- ■ Maintaining State with *Hidden Form* Variables

- ■ Maintaining State with *Session* Variables

- ■ Summing Up State Maintenance Options

State maintenance is the process of keeping track of the state of your application as it applies to a specific individual or to the application as a whole. One example is a shopping cart at an e-commerce site. As a potential customer moves from page to page placing items into the cart, you need to maintain the list of items selected. If the customer purchases one or more items from the cart, you must remove those, but maintain the remaining items. You may also need to know other information about that person: whether they've ever visited the site before, what they bought or selected during previous visits, what promotions or discounts apply to that person, etc.

You definitely need to keep track of this information during any specific visit, but you probably have longer-term storage needs as well. What if the customer leaves, but returns in half an hour? Do you make the customer re-select each item? If not, how long should you maintain the information? One day? One month?

In this chapter, you'll see the various options for state maintenance and the advantages and disadvantages of each.

Don't Cache Data

"The best Web application doesn't need to cache data, it's a stateless application." I've seen this statement over and over in the press and have come to believe that stateless applications aren't really applications, they're Web sites. If you don't need to maintain the state of your application, then your application doesn't do anything other than allow the user to click links. If your application involves security or user input, you must maintain state. What the term *stateless* application really means is that you persist information between pages either on the client or the server in such a way that you can retrieve the applicable state during each request. In other words, the application doesn't use `Session` variables, `Application` variables, or (in some cases) cookies.

These applications are called stateless because you don't maintain the state in memory, you retrieve state as needed. You then use that state information to service the request, alter the information if necessary, and store it again at the end of the request. In the rest of this book, each time you see *stateless application*, think of it as meaning applications that retrieve persisted-state information for each request.

You maintain state in a typical client-server application with variables. You know when the session started and you know before it ends, so you can persist the information stored in variables to disk. You have control over when and how individuals move from screen to screen. You know which screen the individuals are on now, and which page they're requesting. In short, you have a large body of knowledge about any specific individual, their history, and what they can do next. You don't have to do anything special to maintain the data—put information in a variable and it's available until the person closes the application (barring machine crashes).

In a Web application, much of this information is difficult to obtain and even more difficult to store. You have a thin client—the browser—where your data-storage options are limited, in most cases, to cookies (approximately 4 KB or 4096 bytes). You have a limited amount of resources on the server—you often can't simply move the data you would normally store on the client to the server because it's too large. Even if you have sufficient memory on the server to hold the information, the length of time to service requests rises as the volume of information required for that request rises. Therefore, storing all the data in server memory soon begins to limit scalability—the number of simultaneous users that can access your application.

So if you can't cache much data on the client and you can't cache much data on the server, where should you cache the data? The answer is, don't cache data. Design your application so you minimize the data necessary for any particular request. This takes planning; you can't simply have an idea and begin coding like you can with many standalone applications.

The idea of building stateless applications is probably the single most difficult skill to master for programmers moving from standalone and client-server applications. The task gets much easier if you immediately begin thinking of each page as a tiny program. For each request, you're going to accept input from the browser, process the request, provide the requested information, and end the program. That means that tasks you would normally think of as a single operation may in fact be several linked operations.

The key to this kind of processing is to force the browser to provide sufficient information so you don't have to maintain the entire application state on the server. You do this by sending pointers to information from the browser rather than the information itself. For example, when a person selects an item from the shopping cart, you store an `ItemID` cookie on the browser rather than the item title or description. Using the `ItemID` cookie value, you can display the associated information on the browser screen, and you can use the `ItemID` to look up related information on the server for each request. You haven't reduced the need to display the associated information, but you have reduced the volume of that information. Of course, you've also complicated your programming because now you must look up the information for each request.

You should spend a considerable fraction of your application-planning time deciding how and where to store information , and how much information you must maintain from one request to the next. Web application design is a process of compromise between ease of development and scalability. It's easiest to store all the information once, then retrieve it from memory. The most scalable applications look up everything from a minimum number of cached information pointers, but they take longer to develop. As you develop more applications, you'll begin to plan these lookups more carefully. The interface between the browser and the page is similar to the interface between a function and the calling code, and you can think of them in the same way. The items of information the browser sends are the input arguments. The HTML returned by the page is the return value.

Advantages and Disadvantages of Sessionless Applications

A stateless application must either be designed as a series of small, independent transactions, or at minimum, must be able to identify a browser from one request to another. You'll see two kinds of stateless applications—those that use cookies and those that don't.

IIS uses cookies to associate a browser with a specific SessionID, and subsequently, to associate information stored for that SessionID with a request. There are two problems with this scheme. First, not every browser accepts cookies. For example, with IE 5, you can refuse cookies by clicking the Tools menu and selecting Internet Options, then the Security tab and clicking the Custom Level button. You'll see the Security Settings dialog (see Figure 22.1).

FIGURE 22.1:

Internet Explorer 5 Security
Settings dialog

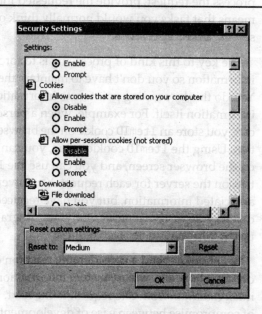

The Security Settings dialog lists two types of cookies: per-session cookies and cookies stored on your computer. The difference is that when you write a cookie, if you give it a valid future expiration date, the browser writes the cookie to the user's browser cache folder (the cookie is stored on the computer). If you omit the expiration date, the browser maintains the cookie in memory only as long as the browser is open. When the user closes the browser, the cookie disappears (the per-session cookie). Note that the term *per-session* as used by Microsoft has nothing to do with ASP sessions. A person using a browser may move through many ASP sites during the course of a browser session.

You cannot only enable and disable cookies, you can also set the browser to warn you with a message box whenever a server tries to write a cookie value. Many people use the warning setting—don't ignore it!

ASP tries to write the `SessionID` cookie to the browser during the response to the first request by a browser to that server, regardless of the application. For subsequent applications the browser accesses on the same server during the same browser session, IIS uses the `SessionID` cookie already written to the browser. For requests after the browser has accepted the `SessionID` cookie, ASP doesn't fire the `Session_OnStart` event. In other words, for each application, ASP uses the presence of the `SessionID` cookie value to determine whether to fire the `Session_OnStart` event or not.

This logic leads to a problem when a browser doesn't accept cookies. Because the `SessionID` cookie never exists, ASP runs the `Session_OnStart` event code for each request. In IIS 3 that meant that people who had the cookie warning setting enabled avoided ASP sites altogether because they received two cookie warnings for each request (unless they accepted the cookie). This was an unfortunate, but also unavoidable, consequence of using ASP. With IIS 4, Microsoft added a setting that lets you disable all use of Sessions for an ASP application. When you turn Sessions off, IIS doesn't check for a `SessionID` value, doesn't try to write a `SessionID` cookie, and you have no access to Sessions (no Session object, `Session` variables, and `Session_OnStart` or `Session_OnEnd` events).

At first, this may seem like a foolhardy act—after all, isn't one of the major advantages of ASP the ability to associate data with a specific request? That's true, but like most advantages, there are tradeoffs. When you use `Session` variables, you're tied to a specific server. This problem won't affect most ASP sites, but if your application must scale beyond the number of users a single server can support, it becomes a major problem. In return for disabling Session use, you gain the ability to process requests on any server. Because you no longer depend on the `SessionID` cookie to associate the browser with a specific set of data, you can process the request on any server that has access to the user's information. For example, a Web farm is a set of Web servers that can handle requests. You also gain speed if you disable Sessions. It's often (but not always) faster to make an association between data sent by the browser and server-side data yourself than it is to rely on ASP Sessions to do it for you.

If you don't use Sessions, you must store the information required to connect a browser with a specific set of data yourself. You can use cookies just like ASP does, if the browser has cookies enabled. If the browser doesn't have cookies enabled, you'll need to use embedded `form` variables or `QueryString` variables to maintain state pointers on the browser.

Why would this be faster? As I stated, it isn't always faster. If you can store all the information required in cookies, embedded `form` variables, or `QueryString` variables, you eliminate the time required to create a Session object and look up any associated data between the `SessionID` cookie and the data stored for that Session. You can eliminate some processing overhead by limiting your dependence on `Variant` variables and out-of-process object instantiations.

I started this section with the cookie discussion because Sessions and cookies are two separate considerations, but they influence each other. The primary decision of whether to use Sessions depends on two factors:

- whether you need multiple servers to service the application, and

- how much planning and programming you're willing to do to improve the response time of your application.

The primary decision of whether to support browsers that don't accept cookies depends on how friendly you want to be to the clients. In an intranet situation, the company might decide that all browsers must accept cookies. In a commercial Internet application, you probably have to plan for browsers that don't accept cookies or risk losing business.

State Maintenance Options

In an ASP application you can maintain user state with the following:

- `Session` variables

- Cookies

- `QueryString` variables

- `Hidden form` variables

- Database tables or files

I'll discuss all these options and show you when each might be appropriate. For each method I'll use this example. You have a database table containing demographic information about registered users; UserIDs, signons, names, etc. When a user signs on, you use the `signon` value the user entered to look up the user's information in the database.

Now assume your application needs access to the user's demographic data for each page in the application. To be able to retrieve the user's information, you need to somehow make, and keep, an association between the user's browser and the information related to that browser. Remember that you may decide to disable Sessions, in which case you cannot rely on ASP to make the association for you.

For purposes of this discussion, I'm going to assume you have decided to support only browsers with cookies enabled, and that you have access to `Session` variables. At the end of the discussion, I'll show you what you need to do if you disable Sessions, and how to write applications that support browsers with cookies disabled.

Basically, there are only two places to store state information—on the client or on the server. I don't necessarily mean on the Web server itself, but on the server side of the browser-server relationship.

Maintaining State with Cookies

Cookies are highly efficient from the server point of view because they push the burden of maintaining data onto the browser. You can write persistent or temporary (per-session) cookies, depending on your needs. However, if you rely on cookies you have six considerations:

1. **Cookies increase network traffic**. Each time you store a cookie on a browser, the browser subsequently sends the cookie name and value(s) back to the server for each request. Assume you store the maximum amount of information (approximately 4 KB) of information in your cookies set. If you have 20 users on your site, it won't make a significant impact on network traffic; but if you have 2000 users, each making requests 4 times per minute, you've increased network traffic to 32 MB per minute. While that may not bring your network and server to its knees, you should consider that your application may not be the only one on the server, and is most certainly not the only traffic on the network.

2. **Cookies increase the time required to service a request**. The server must parse the cookie string and create the `Request.Cookie` collection for each

request. Therefore, the more values you store in the cookie string, the longer it takes the server to parse the string, thus increasing your response time and reducing scalability. Again, this is a minor consideration for a small user base, but all those milliseconds add up.

3. **Cookies are machine-dependent**. When you write a persistent cookie to a computer, the browser will return that cookie value the next time a user visits your application. But if the person uses a different computer to access your application, the cookie value won't be there. You may not think this is a serious problem, but it is. Consider an individual who accesses a travel reservations site from work, makes a reservation, then accesses the same site from home. That person has every right to expect that the application will remember the prior access. If the site relies on cookies to maintain state, the user's reservation information will be on the work computer, but not on the home computer.

4. **Cookies are browser-dependent**. The problem is actually worse than described in the previous paragraph. Cookies belong to a specific browser. Suppose a user has two browsers. After accessing the travel application with IE, the user later (that same day) returns to the site with Netscape. The two browsers maintain cookies independently. That means that any cookie you write with IE isn't sent with Netscape, and vice versa. Therefore, the application won't have access to the information stored in cookies for visits by other browsers, even if the machine and user are the same.

5. **Cookies may disappear**. Perhaps worst of all, because browsers store persistent cookies in directories accessible to the users, those users can delete the files, or the machine can crash, or the user can rebuild the machine. In other words, you can't store critical data in cookies because you can't rely on the information to be present in the future.

6. **Users control cookies**. Even with per-session cookies, there's a small chance that a person may start your application with cookies enabled, but turn cookies off during the session. That means your application may lose cookie values in the middle of the application—not an attractive scenario for critical applications. Therefore, to be absolutely safe, you must check constantly to ensure that the expected cookie values exist, and plan for application flow if the cookies suddenly disappear—or at least trap any errors that result.

The point of this discussion isn't to tell you not to use cookies; it's that cookies aren't necessarily the best place to store data. They're limited in size, aren't guaranteed to be present between sessions (or even during a session), and not all browsers accept them. Nevertheless, cookies are the method that Microsoft chose to associate a browser with server-side data, because they work most of the time. I agree with that decision—it's the best of a bad bargain.

Cookies do have some advantages. You can create and read cookies easily with both client- and server-side code, they work in all modern browsers, and you can create secure (encrypted) cookies so people watching the network can't read the values.

In your hypothetical application, you could use cookies to store all the demographic user information, or you could store just the UserID in a cookie, then look up the user information on the server each time you need it. In other words, you can use cookies the same way the ASP engine uses them to identify users. The browser associates the cookie with a given site and sends the cookie information along with each request.

From the ASP server-side scripting point of view, a cookie is a collection of keyed values, much like a Dictionary object. You use the Request object to retrieve cookie values and the Response object to create or alter them. Therefore, in the example, you would store the UserID in a cookie after you have authenticated the user during sign-on:

```
Response.Cookies("UserID") = rs("UserID").Value
```

To retrieve the value in subsequent requests, use:

```
aUserID = Request.Cookies("UserID")
```

Even better, a cookie can have multiple keyed values, called sub-keys. You can group the user information in a single cookie. For example:

```
Response.Cookies("User")("UserID") = rs("UserID").Value
Response.Cookies("User")("Signon") = rs("UserSignon").Value
Response.Cookies("User")("LastName") = _
    rs("UserLastName").Value
Response.Cookies("User")("FirstName") = _
    rs("UserFirstName").Value
Response.Cookies("User")("UserEMail") = _
    rs("UserEmail").Value
' etc.
```

To retrieve a sub-key value from a cookie, use this syntax:

```
aUserID = Request.Cookies("User")("UserID")
```

If you're not sure whether a cookie has sub-keys, you can check by using the HasKeys property. The HasKeys property returns True when the cookie contains sub-keys. For example:

```
If Request.Cookies("myCookie").HasKeys then
    ' do something
End If
```

When the server receives a request, it parses the cookies into a Collection object, which understands the For...Next syntax. To process all the cookies in a request, you can use a loop like this:

```
With Request
    For Each aKey In .Cookies
        If .cookies(aKey).HasKeys Then
            For Each subKey In .Cookies(aKey)
                response.write subKey & "=" _
                    & .cookies(aKey)(subkey) & "<BR>"
            Next
        End If
    Next
End With
```

If you don't need to store much information between requests and you aren't much concerned about losing the information, cookies are an excellent way to maintain state because they don't take up any memory on the server. You can even write permanent cookies that store data on the client's hard drive. Permanent cookies make it possible to store state between sessions.

To make a cookie permanent, use the Expires property. When you set the Expires property to a date later than the current date, the browser will store the cookie on the user's hard drive. For example, to create a cookie that expires in one week:

```
Dim nextWeek As Date
NextWeek = dateAdd("d", 7, now())
Response.Cookies("User").Expires = NextWeek
```

By default, the browser sends all cookies set by an application back to that application. If your application has more than one directory, you can specify which cookies the browser should send to each directory in your application by adding a path to the cookie. The browser compares the path of the request to each cookie and sends the cookie only if it matches the path. To add the path, use the Path property:

```
Response.Cookies("myCookie").Path = "/myPath"
Response.Cookies("myCookie") = "someCookie"
```

In the example above, the browser would send the "myCookie" cookie only to requests for pages in the /myPath virtual directory.

For cookies that have an expiration date, you can set the domain as well as the path, which lets you create a cookie in one application that the browser will send to a different application in another domain.

In the background, transparent to developers, the Response object writes an HTTP header to tell the browser to save the cookie. You can use the Response object AddHeader method to bypass the automatic cookie-management and storage functions. To add a cookie, use this syntax:

```
Response.AddHeader "Set-Cookie", "<name>=<value> " _
     & [; <name>=<value>]...[; expires=<date>][; " _
     & domain=<domain_name>][; path=<some_path>][; secure]
```

Here's an example:

```
Response.AddHeader "Set-Cookie", "myCookie=someCookie"
```

The result is the same as if you had used the Response.Cookies collection—the browser stores the cookie.

The browser stores cookies in a Cookies subdirectory of your Profile directory. On Windows NT, your profile is in the Profiles subdirectory of the $systemRoot$ path—usually called WinNT. On Windows 95/98, your profile in is a subdirectory of the $systemRoot$ path—usually called Windows. On Windows 2000, your profile is under the Documents and Settings directory under your username. When you add a cookie using the Response.Cookies collection, you can set the Expires parameter using any valid date format. When you use the HTTP method, you need to specify the date in the format ddd, dd-mmm-yyy hh:mm:ss GMT.

You can look in the appropriate Cookies directory to check that your application sent the cookie in the correct format—if it did, the browser will create a file like username@domain.txt that stores the cookie information.

The browser stores and transmits cookies as text files, so you need to encrypt the cookie if the information is sensitive, such as sign-on and password information. You can manually encrypt the information or tell the browser to encrypt the data automatically. Cookies have a Secure attribute that tells the browser to store cookies in encrypted form, and send them only to sites that support Secure Sockets Layer (SSL) encryption.

Maintaining State with *QueryString* Variables

There's been a great deal of press coverage (mostly negative) about how unscrupulous Web sites are stealing your privacy by storing unwanted information on your computer in cookies. Therefore, some of the more paranoid individuals have improved their privacy by turning cookies off. For clients that won't accept cookies, you can't store anything in the Session object because the ASP engine won't find the SessionID cookie, and (if Sessions are enabled for the application) will try to create a new Session cookie for each request. Of course, you can't use cookies to maintain state either. Instead, you can pass information through the QueryString collection.

Remember that QueryString data is text appended to the URL. On the server, you receive the data in the Request object as the Request.QueryString collection. As is typical with Web communications, the raw data is in key=value form like cookies, form variables, etc. Ampersands separate the key-value pairs. A question mark separates the entire query string from the URL. The following URL example contains two QueryString values—LastName (1) and FirstName (2):

```
http://myServer/mySite.com?LastName=Doe&FirstName=John
```

Most browsers support up to about 1024 characters in QueryString data. The server parses the QueryString data into a collection, so you can retrieve it using keys or indexes (1-based, not 0-based). The QueryString collection supports standard For Each...Next syntax. Using the QueryString values from the previous example:

```
Response.Write Request.QueryString("LastName") ' prints Doe
Response.Write Request.QueryString.Count ' prints 2
Response.Write Request.QueryString(2) ' Prints John
```

That makes it extremely easy to retrieve the data sent by the browser. You can add QueryString parameters to HTML you send to the browser by concatenating strings together to produce a valid URL.

Concatenating strings together is a straightforward process, you just need to remember to separate the first key-value pair with a question mark and all subsequent pairs with ampersands. For example, suppose you had a record set of usernames. You want to display the names as a list of links. When an administrator clicks on one of the names, you want to display a form to edit the user's information. For each link, you'll want to return the user's ID, as follows:

```
While Not R.EOF
   With Response
      .Write "<a href=somepage.asp?ID=" & _
      R("UserID").Value & ">" & R("Name").Value & _
      "</a><br>"
   End With
   R.MoveNext
Wend
```

Now, when the administrator clicks on the link, you'll be able to pull the UserID from the QueryString collection to display the form to edit the user's information. For example:

```
Dim anID
anID = Request.QueryString("ID")
' display form based on anID
```

When you show the form, you'll need to keep track of the ID in the form page too, and possibly in several subsequent pages—that's the application user's state—editing the user with the ID anID. All that concatenation can become painful when you're trying to keep track of multiple variables. Imagine trying to append enough information to keep track of 20 or 30 critical variables in an application!

There are some undesirable characteristics of using QueryString data to maintain state. First, the user (and other observers) can see the data because it appears in the address bar. Therefore, you should never use this method to send any private information unless you also apply your own encryption scheme to the data. Second, if you use QueryString data and your data contains spaces or other non-alphanumeric characters, you must apply the Server.URLEncode method to the query string before appending it to a URL.

NOTE   The Server.URLEncode method replaces characters with a percent sign followed by the hex value of the character. For example, a space (ASCII 32) is "%20".

Finally, because the information in the QueryString on the browser appears in the address field, users can change the QueryString data, which can lead to errors in your application. Therefore, you can't always depend on the validity of the information in the QueryString variables.

Maintaining State with *Hidden Form* Variables

Yet another way of maintaining state on the client is to use hidden form variables. If you do this, you need to create a <form> tag and insert the hidden form variable for each page for which you need to pass state back to the server. You also need to ensure that the client submits the form using the POST method so the browser returns the values to the server. That means you will either have to have a Submit button for each page, or you need to write client-side script to submit the form when a navigation event—such as a click on a link or button—occurs.

For example, to pass a variable called "ID" with a value of 2817 from one page to another, the first page could contain:

```
<form name="frmHidden" method="post">
    <input type="hidden" name="ID" value="2817">
    <input type="submit" value="Submit">
</form>
```

When the user clicks the Submit button, the form will send the value ID=2817 to the server. You can retrieve the value using the `Request.Form` collection, then use the value in a form on the next page.

To submit the form from a link, use client-side script such as this:

```
<script language="javascript">
    function doSubmit() {
        document.frmHidden.submit();
    }
</script>
<form action="mypage.asp" name="frmHidden" method="post">
    <input type="hidden" name="ID" value="2817">
    <input type="submit" value="Submit">
</form>
```

Somewhere on the page you would put a link to the ASP page to which you want the user to navigate. For example:

```
<a href='mypage.asp' onClick='doSubmit();'>Click Here</a>
```

If you wanted to continue the sequence, you would retrieve the ID value in `mypage.asp` script, using `Request.Form("ID")` and send the ID forward to the next page. The process of setting and retrieving the ID variable would continue as long as you needed the variable value on the server to maintain state.

`Hidden` form variables are in some ways better than cookies or `QueryString` variables. There's no size restriction on `hidden form` variables, they're not visible in the browser's address field, and users can't change them; but they are visible to users savvy enough to use the View Source feature of the browser. You should not use them for values you don't want the user to see (e.g., answers to test questions) unless you encrypt them.

Maintaining State with *Session* Variables

`Session` variables are the easiest way to maintain state. You can store any data type in a `Session` variable. You'll recall that the Session object is an associative array much like a Scripting Dictionary object. A Session can hold practically an unlimited number of name-value pairs. Each `Session` variable name must be unique. The value associated with that name is a `Variant`; therefore, you can store both primitive data types, such as strings or numeric values, and COM objects, like Dictionary or custom ActiveX objects.

So you could store the UserID in a `Session` variable. Now, whenever the user makes a request, you can use the value of the `Session("UserID")` variable to look up the user's information in the database, as seen in the example.

```
Set R = conn.execute("SELECT * FROM Users " & _
    "WHERE UserID=" & Session("UserID"), , _
    adCmdText)
```

But wait! Retrieving database data is an expensive operation in terms of both time and server resources. You may not want to perform a database lookup for each user request. You retrieved the data once during the signon request—you could store the entire row in Session variables during the signon operation. That way, you wouldn't need to go back to the database for each subsequent request. Instead, you can create a Session variable for each field in the table row for that user. For example:

```
Session("UserID") = rs("UserID").Value
Session("UserSignon") = rs("UserSignon").Value
Session("UserLastName") = rs("UserLastName").Value
Session("UserFirstName") = rs("UserFirstName").Value
Session("UserEMail") = rs("UserEmail").Value
' etc…
```

Now you have access to the user data from anywhere in the application without returning to the database. In essence, you've cached the demographic data for this user in the Session object.

This is absolutely the easiest way to cache data for an individual user of your application, and probably the one you'll use most often. There's only a couple of problems with it (you knew this was coming, didn't you?). First, think about what the ASP engine must be doing while it retrieves the variable values for each user. Imagine that the Session object is a Dictionary where each key is a SessionID and each value is itself a Dictionary. The keys of this sub-dictionary are the names you give your Session variables, and the values are your Session variable values. I don't know exactly how the Session object stores data, but it must be with a method similar to what you see in Figure 22.2.

The point is that using Session variables at all forces the server to access a single object for each request. Therefore, the use of Session variables must force the server to serialize requests, at least during retrieval of the sub-dictionary containing the Session variables associated with that user's SessionID.

So why use sessions at all? You can disable them, either for your entire server or for a specific site, using the IIS administration program. Sessions can be enabled or disabled at either the Web level or at the virtual directory level, so you'll need to decide how you want to set up your server. To disable Sessions for the entire server, start the IIS administration program. The checkbox to enable/disable sessions is in the Application Configuration dialog. Right-click on the Default Web Site entry in the left-hand pane, select Properties, then click the Home Directory tab. Click the Configuration button, then the App Options tab (see Figure 22.3).

Ser R = conn.execute(SELECT [* FROM USers * a

WHERE Uxers iSession ID = iD).

FIGURE 22.2:

Hypothetical Session Object structure

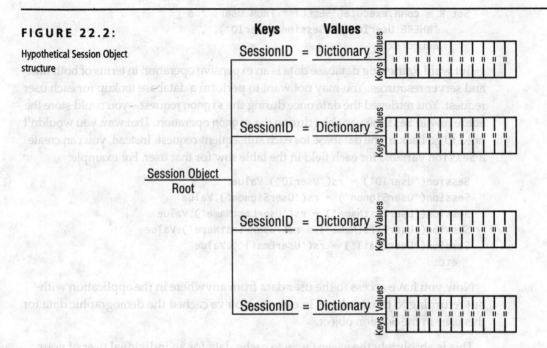

Now you have easy access to the user's data from anywhere in the application with-

This is absolutely the easiest way to cache data for an individual user of your application, and probably the one you'll use most often. There's only a couple of problems with it you knew this was coming, didn't you). First, think about what

FIGURE 22.3:

IIS Application Configuration dialog

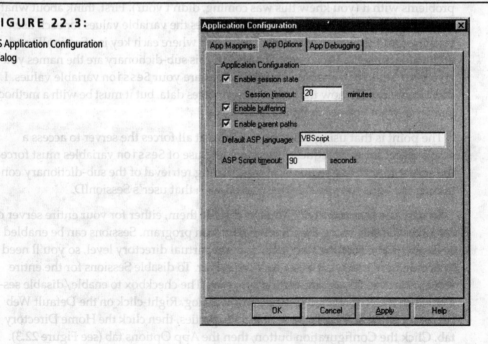

Uncheck the Enable Session State checkbox. When you do that, IIS will ask if you want all the other child applications to inherit that setting (assuming there are other applications on that server). You can select the specific applications for which you want to disable sessions. You can disable sessions for a specific application by first right-clicking on that application, then following the same process you just saw with the Default Web Site.

Sessions are a mixed blessing. They make development extremely easy, but Microsoft itself recommends you should use another method besides Sessions to maintain state if you want to build Web sites that will scale to large numbers of users.

Consider a Web farm where you use more than one server to service requests. If you use `Session` variables, you need some method to route requests from one browser to the same server for each request. If you don't have such a method (and the ASP engine doesn't currently provide one), the Session information either won't be available or will be different on each server.

Commercial routers are available that let you use Sessions on sites with multiple servers; you can consider one of these as an alternative to disabling Sessions if you build a site with heavy use. For smaller sites, it's relatively easy to write your own multi-server router. Suppose you have a single, publicly-available address for your site; e.g., `http://www.mySite.com`. You have four servers, only one of which has a public IP address corresponding to the `mySite.com` IP address. The other three servers' IP addresses are not mapped to the `mySite.com` address. Together, all four servers constitute a Web farm. The public server receives all initial requests for your site.

The first time a new request arrives, the public server uses a script to route the request to one of the three Web farm servers. That server then provides a SessionID. Subsequent requests by the same browser bypass the public server and go directly to the Web farm server. The script on the public server uses a round-robin method to ensure that each of the servers in the Web farm receives an equal number of requests. You need to use relative paths to ensure that graphics and other resources are available on all the servers. Because you need to balance the load, you may want to ensure that people can't bookmark pages on a specific server by redirecting any users without SessionIDs (new sessions) back to the public server for routing.

Note that this scheme doesn't truly balance the load between servers—it only balances the number of browsers assigned to each server. Load balancing itself is beyond the scope of this book, but you can easily write a simple round-robin scheme. Depending on your setup and application requirements, that may be sufficient, but typically you'll want to at least poll the servers to find out if they're running, which one currently has the smallest load, etc. You will probably need fail-over protection and may even want to bring additional servers online, as needed.

Finally, although it may not always be an issue, you need to be aware of the memory requirements when you use Session variables. Storing a few small strings and numbers for each user won't use much memory, but storing entire record sets, even as arrays, will use up large amounts of memory in a hurry. If the server runs out of RAM, it will begin spooling the data out to virtual memory, and that will definitely adversely affect your application's response time and scalability.

Maintaining State with Files

Although reading a file for each request may sound like a totally inefficient method for maintaining state, it's not as bad as it sounds. IIS caches files—in fact, you can set the number of files it caches to suit the resources available on your server. Because requests tend to come in clusters—a single user will use your application, then quit—you can rely on IIS's file caching services to improve the speed of file reads and writes.

You still need to rely on one of the previous forms of data-caching to make the association between the browser and the file, but you may use any of them. For example, you may save a UserID as a cookie, place it in the QueryString, save it as a Session variable, or submit it as a hidden form variable; the method you select doesn't matter. The result is that you obtain the UserID value and use that value to open a file. For example, Listing 22.1 shows a file to obtain a user's first and last name. When the user requests the file it does the following:

1. Checks to see if the browser sent a cookie called Filename; if so, it redirects to the ch22i2.asp file.

2. Checks to see if the user submitted the form; if so, it checks and processes the form contents, then writes a file containing the user's first and last name, writes a cookie to the browser, and redirects to ch22i2.asp.

3. If neither condition 1 nor condition 2 are true, the file displays a form into which users enter their names.

LISTING 22.1   User Name Form (ch22i1.asp)

```
<%@ Language=VBScript %>
<% option explicit %>
<%
If Request.Cookies("FileName") <> "" Then
    Response.Redirect "ch22i2.asp"
End If
```

```
If Request("Submit") = "Submit" Then
    Dim fs
    Dim ts
    Dim aFilename
    Dim LastName
    Dim FirstName
    Dim ForWriting
    Dim TriStateUseDefault
    Dim aPath
    Dim pathLen
    aPath = Request.ServerVariables("PATH_TRANSLATED")
    pathLen = Len(aPath)
    Do While (pathLen > 0) And (Mid(aPath, pathLen, 1) <> "\")
        pathLen = pathLen - 1
    Loop
    aPath = Left(aPath, pathLen)
    ForWriting = 2
    TriStateUseDefault = -2
    FirstName = Request("FirstName")
    LastName = Request("LastName")
    If LastName <> "" And FirstName <> "" Then
        ' write the user's name into a file
        ' create a file name
        aFilename = LastName&FirstName & "_" & year(now) & _
            "_" & month(now) & "_" & day(now)
        Set fs = server.CreateObject("Scripting.FileSystemObject")
        Set ts = fs.OpenTextFile(aPath & aFilename & ".txt", _
            ForWriting, True, TriStateUseDefault)
        ts.write "LastName=" & LastName & vbCrLf
        ts.write "FirstName=" & FirstName
        ts.Close
        Set ts = Nothing
        Set fs = Nothing
        ' write a cookie to the browser so you'll know that the
        ' file was created in future pages
        Response.Cookies("FileName") = aFilename
        Response.Cookies("FileName").Expires = DateAdd("d", 2, Now())
        Response.Redirect "ch22i2.asp"
    End If
End If
%>
<html>
<head>
<title>Maintaining State With Files</title>
</head>
<body>
```

```
<form name="frmUserName" method="post" cols="2">
<table align="center" border="1">
<tr>
    <td colspan=2>
        Enter your first and last names.
    </td>
</tr>
<tr>
    <td width="40%">
        <b>First Name</b>:
    </td>
    <td width="*">
        <input type="text" name="FirstName" value="<%=FirstName%>">
    </td>
</tr>
<tr>
    <td width="40%">
        <b>Last Name</b>:
    </td>
    <td width="*">
        <input type="text" name="LastName" value="<%=LastName%>">
    </td>
</tr>
<tr>
    <td colspan=2 align="center">
        <input type="submit" name="Submit" value="Submit">
    </td>
</tr>
</table>
</form>
</body>
</html>
```

The Filename cookie has an expiration date of two days from today, making it a persistent cookie. Therefore, when users return to the application within two days, they won't have to re-enter their names. Instead, the browser will redirect to the ch22i2.asp file, which displays the name (see Listing 22.2), as follows:

1. Reads the cookie to construct the filename.

2. Reads the file and extracts the first and last names.

3. Displays Hello <name>.

LISTING 22.2   Using a Persistent Cookie as a File Pointer

```asp
<%@ Language=VBScript %>
<% option explicit %>
<html>
<head>
</head>
<body>
<%
' read the file
Dim fs
Dim ts
Dim aFilename
Dim s
Dim FirstName
Dim LastName
Dim aPos
Dim ForReading
Dim TriStateUseDefault
Dim aPath
Dim pathLen
aPath = Request.ServerVariables("PATH_TRANSLATED")
pathLen = Len(aPath)
Do While (pathLen > 0) And (Mid(aPath, pathLen, 1) <> "\")
    pathLen = pathLen - 1
Loop
aPath = Left(aPath, pathLen)
ForReading = 1
TriStateUseDefault = -2
aFilename = Request.Cookies("Filename")
If aFilename = "" Then
    Response.Redirect "ch22i1.asp"
End If
Set fs = server.CreateObject("Scripting.FileSystemObject")
Set ts = fs.OpenTextFile(aPath & aFilename & ".txt", _
    ForReading, False, TriStateUseDefault)
Do While Not ts.AtEndOfStream
    s = ts.readLine()
    aPos = InStr(1, s, "=", vbBinaryCompare)
    If aPos > 0 Then
        Select Case LCase(Left(s, aPos - 1))
        Case "firstname"
            FirstName = Mid(s, aPos + 1)
        Case "lastname"
            LastName = Mid(s, aPos + 1)
```

```
        End Select
      End If
Loop
ts.Close
Set ts = Nothing
Set fs = Nothing
Response.write "Hello " & FirstName & " " & LastName & "."
%>
</body>
</html>
```

NOTE   The `IUSR_MACHINENAME` account must have read/write-access to the `Chapter22` directory for the code to run properly.

You should be able to extrapolate from this example to see how you could asso-ciate a reasonably large amount of data with a single pointer item stored on the client—in this case, the filename. This method works well, but is not without prob-lems. For example, the files become hard to manage when you have 10,000 or 1,000,000 users. You also have the problem of managing obsolete files and dupli-cates. If a user visits the site once, how long should you maintain the data? For some sites, you'll need to maintain the data forever. For others, you can delete it when the session ends. But how would you associate the file with a SessionID so you can find it to delete it at the end of the Session? You can't rely on the browser to find the filename during the `Session_OnEnd` event because, by definition, the browser isn't visiting the application at that point—otherwise, the Session wouldn't have timed out.

In this particular example, you could delete any user files older than two days—the expiration date for the cookie; however, if users re-visit the site within the two-day period, you would need to update the file date by writing data to the file so it didn't get deleted. As you can see, it would be nice to have a more robust way to associate data with a pointer stored on the client. And you do have access to that method—with a database.

Maintaining State in a Database

Databases are probably the most scalable way to maintain state. Storing state in a database is definitely slower when your application has only a few users, but as the number of users and the size of the data increases, using a database to store state quickly outstrips using `Session` variables. It's also easier to script than using

QueryString or Form variables, especially when you have a large application where you must store many more state variables.

Another major advantage of storing state in a database is that you can maintain state not only during a session, but also between sessions. The only other way to maintain state between sessions is to use persistent cookies or files. Cookies maintain state on the client, whereas state stored in a database resides on the server. Maintaining cross-session state on the server is better. People frequently change computers, delete cookie files, or sign on to their computers using other sign-ons, so client-side state is less certain.

To store state in a database table, you must set up the table properly. By that, I don't mean you must have a column for every variable, but you must be able to identify the data row or rows that belong to an individual or session. You do this by setting a single identifying cookie that acts as a primary key to the table, then retrieving the data using that cookie value when each request starts. You can create and set your own cookie value—for secured sites, you will probably want to use the user's unique ID or signon. For cross-session state maintenance, you'll need to have each user sign on with a login and password. For single-session state maintenance, you can use the SessionID cookie as long as you don't care about storing state for an individual user, just an individual session.

Here's how to store state in a database on a single-session basis:

1. In the Session_OnStart event in the global.asa file, create a new row(s) for the new SessionID or signon.

2. At the start of each page in your application, read the cookie, then retrieve the appropriate row(s) from the database.

3. During page processing, add or remove state information as appropriate.

4. At the end of each page, update the database with any changed state information.

5. In the Session_OnEnd event in global.asa, delete the row(s) from the database.

To store state between sessions, you defer Step 1 until after the user has signed on, and create a new row only if the user doesn't already have data. You would eliminate Step 5 unless an administrator deletes the signon.

You'll need a scheme to delete or archive obsolete state data (data you've stored for individuals that never return to your site). For many public sites, this is the bulk of the data collected, for internal sites, it may occur only when an employee leaves the company. If you use persistent cookies to connect people to their data, you will probably also want a way for a user whose cookie has been lost to reconnect to his or her data. That's why many sites ask you to provide special personal information so they can ask you about it if you lose or delete the site cookie.

Summing Up State Maintenance Options

If you only need to store small amounts of data (less than 4 KB), and especially if you don't need cross-session data, use cookies. Cookies work well and you'll be able to develop the application quickly.

If you don't expect to ever have to scale the site beyond a single server, use `Session` variables. If you need to keep data across sessions, or if the data you need to maintain is large, you can use a file or database to persist the data.

If your client doesn't have cookies enabled, use `hidden form` or `QueryString` variables to store a pointer value on the client. Use the pointer value to retrieve associated information from files or database tables on the server. You can also use these methods if your server doesn't have sessions enabled.

If you need high scalability, use database tables in combination with any other method that can store a pointer to the data. Remember that the less data you must retrieve for any request, the faster and more scalable your application becomes.

Finally, you can use more than one method at the same time—database tables, files, and cookies to store information between sessions, as well as `Session` variables, `QueryString` variables, `hidden form` variables and cookies to store information during a session. I usually work to get the best of both worlds—the persistence of databases and the in-memory access to `Session` variables except in sites that can't use Sessions. In the next chapter, you'll use the methods you've seen here to build a secured application where people need to register and log in before being allowed access to the application.

CHAPTER

TWENTY-THREE

23

Controlling Access and Monitoring

- ■ More IIS Security

- ■ Using UserID/Password Security

- ■ Building a Secured Site

- ■ Monitoring Your Site—Beyond Page-Counting

- ■ Disabling an Application for Maintenance

One of the problems with Web applications is that they're public. By default, anyone who knows the URL can access the site. Another problem is that, by default, you don't know who's accessing the site. For many applications that's not a problem; you want users to access the information. But for others, such as banking and financial transactions, human resources information, insurance, and corporate information systems, you need to know who's using the site and, in many cases, you want to limit access to a specified group of individuals. You probably want to set up applications that are otherwise open so there are certain areas—for example, usage reports, database alteration operations, content change operations—that application administrators can access, but other users cannot.

You can approach the topic of controlling access and monitoring in several different ways. For example, in Chapter 15, *Other ASP Components*, you saw how to authenticate users through NT permissions. In this chapter, I'll approach security from both the NT perspective, which is most useful in an intranet situation with IE browsers, and from the UserID/Password perspective, which works in all cases. You can decide which method works best for you.

More IIS Security

In IIS 4, there were three security options:

- Anonymous access, in which case IIS impersonates the IUSR_MACHINE-NAME account, which belongs to the Guests group, and thus has, by default, limited access to machine resources. You would normally use this type of access for unsecured applications, and for applications where you manage security yourself using UserID/Password security. If you allow anonymous access, all other types of authentication take effect only if the server denies access to a resource, such as a secured file. To force security across the entire application, you must turn off Anonymous Access.

- Basic Authentication works with all browsers. When a user requests a page in a site with Basic Authentication turned on, the server denies the request, which forces the browser to display a UserID/Password dialog. The browser sends the entered UserID and password across the network in plain text, which means the information is insecure. This is the only integrated security option that works with Netscape and other browsers in IIS 4. The server checks to see if the information represents a valid account and whether that account has access to the resource. If so, it allows access; otherwise, it returns another Access Denied message.

- NT Challenge/Response works only with IE browsers. When a user requests a page from an application with NT Challenge/Response turned on, the server denies the request, just as with Basic Authentication, but the server also returns a challenge. IE recognizes that the server is an NT server and answers the challenge with a hashed value. The server recognizes that the hashed value represents a specific account and checks to see if that account has access to the resource. If so, it allows access, otherwise it returns another Access Denied message. Because the server only has access to the hash value, not to the actual UserID and password, NT Challenge/Response doesn't allow access to resources on other servers in the network, because the Web server can't provide the UserID and password when challenged by other servers that have secured resources. NT Challenge/Response also does not work across firewalls.

Windows 2000 has added more security features and a new method called Digest Authentication. Digest Authentication uses a hash feature like NT Challenge/Response, but because the server has a copy of the UserID and password, the method works across firewalls and proxy servers and also throughout the network. All machines involved in the initial exchange (the Web server and the browser computer) must be running some version of Windows 2000 for this method to work.

Windows 2000 also adds Fortezza encryption services (a government-approved encryption standard), which strongly encrypts values passing over the network.

In both NT 4 and Windows 2000, you can allow or deny access to an application based on IP addresses or network accounts. A full discussion of the security features in IIS is beyond the scope of this book; however, the entire process is well documented through the online help that installs with IIS. I urge you to read and explore the security options thoroughly if your application has security needs beyond simple UserID/Password security.

Using UserID/Password Security

The idea behind UserID/Password security is to limit access to all or specific parts of an application. For example, you may have a human resources application where people can change their personal information related to paycheck deposits, insurance or 401K benefits, or apply online for internal company positions. For all these types of applications, you want to ensure that only the person to whom the information belongs can view the information. To do that, you must identify the user.

Just as with other network applications, you need a token of information to identify the user. Typically, you manage access to network resources through a combination of a UserID and password. To acquire the UserID and password, you can build your own form, or you can use the UserID/Password dialog built into the browser. In either case, when you acquire the information, you'll need to look up the UserID in a database table and verify the password. You'll need to decide in advance what kind of information to accept. For example, you may allow people to select their own UserID and password, or you might provide them. You may decide to set a minimum length, or to require mixed numbers, letters, and symbols, and you can force a case-sensitive match or disregard case.

Most sites require at least six characters in the UserID and password, because the chances of two different people selecting the same combination is higher than you might think as the length of tokens decreases. Because people tend to select the same UserID and password many times for many different sites, and because they tend to select easy-to-remember (and easy-to-guess) passwords, some applications don't let individuals select their own password. That way they can format the passwords so they're difficult to guess using programs that run through a dictionary trying each password combination through brute force.

After matching a combination, you store a cookie or create a `Session` variable showing that the user is authenticated and has access to the site. The advantage of the cookie is that people can enter and leave your application many times during a single session without having to re-authenticate. Using this method, you still need to check if any other `Session` variables you use in the application are still valid; otherwise, you need to route the user to the place where those variables are initialized. The advantage of the `Session` variable is that people can't delete it, and it times out when the Session ends, which manages the authentication information in the same way as any other `Session` variable.

In the next section, you'll build a secured site using the integrated browser UserID/Password dialog and a database to hold the UserIDs and passwords.

Building a Secured Site

Because the method you use to authenticate users is identical for both SQL Server and Access, I've used an Access database for this section. The application is a sample U.S. survey form that asks users to enter their sex, the number of children they have, and their state of residence. The application consists of four pages: an entry page, a registration page, a form for the user to place the requested personal information, which they can subsequently see and change only after authenticating, and a report page accessible only to administrators. Behind the scenes there's an Access 2000 database containing two tables: one to hold UserIDs and passwords, and another to hold the associated user information, as well as an `include` file that manages connections and database queries and checks authentication.

You need to set up a virtual directory and a Data Source Name (DSN) to build the application. On the CD, the Chapter23 directory contains all the files. Copy the directory to your hard drive, then create a virtual directory through the IIS Management application that points to that directory. Use the Open Database Connectivity (ODBC) Data Source Administrator program to set up a System DSN for the Access database SecuredSite.mdb file in the Chapter23 directory. Call the DSN SecuredSite. If you change the DSN name, you will need to edit the Connection-String entry in the global.asa file. You must allow read/write access for the IUSR_MACHINENAME account to the directory that contains the database (you can do this through the IIS Management application or through the NTFS security dialogs) for the program to work.

The administrator UserID is Admin and the password is Chapter23. If you forget, you can open the database and view it—the passwords are not encrypted in the database itself. For maximum security, you should place the database in a directory that is not a virtual directory; otherwise, people can download the file (assuming they can guess its name) by requesting it from a browser. For simplicity in setting up the application, I haven't done that in this case.

When users request the entry page (see Figure 23.1), they can elect to either enter the site, which displays the UserID/Password dialog, or to register, which lets them select a UserID and password (see Figure 23.2).

FIGURE 23.1:

Survey entry page
(ch23i1.asp)

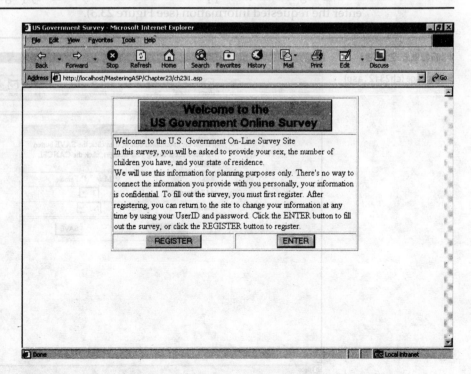

FIGURE 23.2:

Survey registration page
(ch23i3.asp)

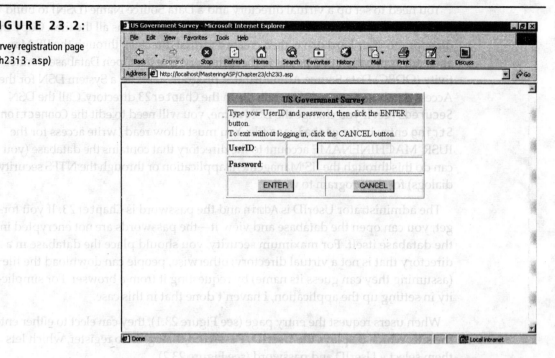

After registration, the application takes users to a survey page where they can enter the requested information (see Figure 23.3).

FIGURE 23.3:

Survey page (ch23i2.asp)

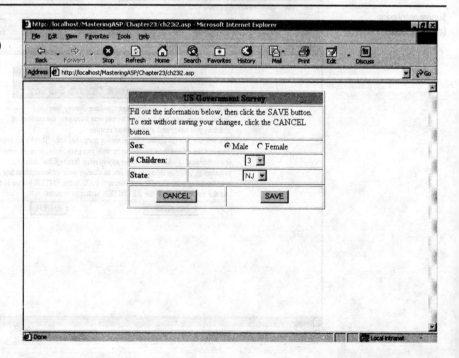

Users can revisit the site at any time to update their information by selecting the ENTER button from the site entry page and entering their UserID and password. If users re-enter the site this way, the application looks up the previously saved information (if any) and displays the survey page with the previous information filled in so they can change the information.

After completing the survey form, the application displays an acknowledgement page and issues a `Session.Abandon` command. Therefore, people have to log in again if they want to change the information. While this may not be entirely friendly, it does solve the problem of people leaving the acknowledgment page open and unattended on their computers, where anyone with access to the computer could click the Back button and alter the information. Obviously, that wouldn't matter in this case, but you do need to consider the security ramifications.

If you log in to the site as an administrator, you'll see a graphical summary report bar chart that displays the average number of children reported by males and by females from each state (see Figure 23.4).

FIGURE 23.4:

Reported children by state by sex

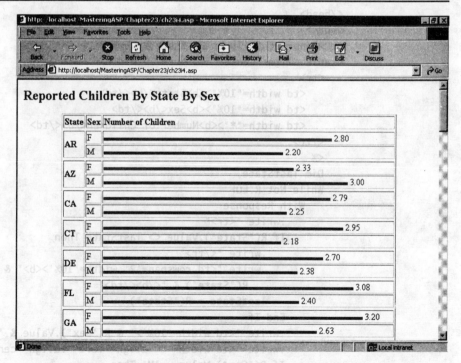

The last file uses two images that are only 1-pixel wide to draw the bars of the chart. The code stretches the image using the `width` attributes of the `<img>` tag (see Listing 23.1).

LISTING 23.1 **Survey Administrator Report Code** (ch23i4.asp)

```
<%@ Language=VBScript %>
<!- #INCLUDE FILE="SecuredSite.asp" ->
<%
If Session("UserID") <> "Admin" Or _
Session("Password") <> "Chapter23" Then
    Response.write "You are not authorized to view this page."
    Response.write Session("UserID") & ", " & Session("Password")
    Response.end
End If
Dim conn
Dim R
Set conn = openConnection(adModeRead)
Set R = conn.execute("ChildrenByStateBySex", , adCmdStoreProc)
%>
<html>
<head>
</head>
<body>
<h2>Reported Children By State By Sex</h2>
<table align="center" border="1" width = "75%">
    <tr>
        <td width="10%"><b>State</b></td>
        <td width="10%"><b>Sex</b></td>
        <td width="*"><b>Number of Children</b></td>
    </tr>
    <%
    Dim lastState
    While Not R.EOF
        With Response
            .write "<tr>"
            If R("State").Value <> lastState Then
                .write "</tr>"
                .write "<td rowspan='2' width='10%'><b>" & _
                    R("State") & "</b></td>"
                lastState = R("State")
            End If
            .write "<td width='10%'>" & R("Sex").Value & "</td>"
            .write "<td width='*' align='left' valign='center'>"
            If R("Sex").Value = "M" Then
                .write "<img src='F23Red.gif' "
            Else
                .write "<img src='F23Blue.gif' "
```

```
                End If
              .write "width='" & 150 * R("TotalChildren").Value & _
                  "' height='5'>" & " " & R("TotalChildren").Value
              .write "</td>"
          End With
          R.movenext
      Wend
      Response.write "</tr>"
      %>
  </table>
  </body>
  </html>
```

Both of the secured pages in this site use functions from an include file called SecuredSite.asp. You may notice that the name of the include file doesn't have the INC extension shown in previous include file examples. That's because, by default, users can download files with the INC extension if they know or can guess the filename, which is a security hazard because such files might contain sensitive information, or allow a hacker to gain insight into ways to attack the site. The ASP extension forces the server to execute the file, which (if all the code is inside functions and subroutines) will return an empty page if a user requests the file.

The SecuredSite.asp file contains wrapper functions for database access. I'll only show you one here because they're all similar. The findUser function accepts a UserID and password, opens a connection, creates a Command object and sets its properties, creates the parameters required by the stored procedure, and then executes the command. If the command returns data, the function sets some Session variables with the returned information. The function returns True if it found the requested user, and False otherwise (see Listing 23.2).

LISTING 23.2   **FindUser Function (SecuredSite.asp)**

```
Function findUser(UserID, Password)
    Dim conn
    Dim cm
    Dim R
    Set conn = openConnection(adOpenReadOnly)
    Set cm = server.CreateObject("ADODB.Command")
    Set cm.ActiveConnection = conn
    cm.CommandText = "FindUser"
    cm.commandType = adCmdStoredProc
    cm.Parameters.append cm.createParameter("UserID", _
        adVarChar, adParamInput, 10, CStr(UserID))
```

```
cm.Parameters.append cm.createParameter("Password", _
    adVarChar, adParamInput, 10, CStr(Password))
Set R = cm.execute
If Not R.EOF Then
    Session("InternalID") = R("InternalID")
    Session("UserID") = R("UserID")
    Session("Password") = R("Password")
    findUser = True
Else
    findUser = False
End If
R.Close
Set R = Nothing
Set cm = Nothing
Set conn = Nothing
End Function
```

Monitoring Your Site—Beyond Page-Counting

In addition to counting pages or total uses of the application, you might want to know other meta-information about your site, such as who's currently accessing the site, how many requests were denied, where specific users go, or how users navigate to specific pages. Application meta-information provides you with ammunition to justify the cost of the application. An application that costs thousands of dollars to develop might pay for itself in just a few weeks if you can show that it saves money by providing timely information or by reducing the time necessary to accomplish a task.

Tracking Application Variables

There are several ways to track site usage. Which one you select depends entirely on the accessibility of your server and your personal preferences—all of them work well. If you're in an intranet situation and you have Allow Anonymous Access turned off, the simplest method for tracking site usage is to analyze the server log files. With any other type of authentication, IIS logs the UserID of the account that requested the page.

Back in Chapter 15, *Other ASP Components*, in the section entitled *The Logging Utility*, there's a file that forces the browser to authenticate (ch15i6.asp). Browse to that file, then open your Web server's log file. The last entry in that file (assuming you're the only person using the server) will show you the authenticated account. For example, on my computer the log entry shows:

```
ASPCLIENTDEBUG=1;+SITESERVER=ID=79eb3d5438d3eb10cf23d6f3cff266e2;+ASPSE
SSIONIDGGQQGZFK=IGLFJPODBLBPLPDFLNBFLKKL -
2000-01-15 03:11:30 129.254.25.109 JONESHOME\Russell GET /MasteringASP/
Chapter15/ch15i6.asp - 200 0 Mozilla/4.0+(compatible;+MSIE+5.01;+Win-
dows+NT+5.0)
```

Although it's impossible to show the individual fields on the page of a book, I've highlighted the relevant portion of the log file line in the preceding listing, showing the domain and UserID of the person accessing the page—in this case, me.

If you don't have access to the IIS log, perhaps because your application resides on a commercial server, or perhaps because you work in a location where you don't have physical or administrator rights to the server—you must find another way to track who's accessing your site. You can do that with a file, then implement your own reporting mechanism. For example, you can write the date and time and the UserID to the file, then write a secured ASP page to display a report for you. IIS begins a new log file each day. Depending on the traffic, you might want to do the same thing. In that case, you would want to write your report so you can access any of the files.

Another method is to test the size of the file. When it reaches or exceeds a pre-determined size, you read the file, then write only the last X number of entries, thus shortening the file.

While file methods work well, storing site access information in a database table is both easier to maintain and simplifies reporting. For example, you can write a time-stamped entry in the table when a person successfully authenticates, and another when that person exits or the Session times out. If you have the resources, you can log a record for every page entry, thus tracking the user through the site.

Knowing Who's On

If you don't care about long-term reporting, but just about who's currently active in the site—for example, to allow individuals to chat privately with one another—you can keep the information in an array in the Application variable. When a user authenticates, add the UserID and the current time to the array. Remember to lock the Application object, copy the array into a local variable, perform your updates, then reassign the array to the Application variable and unlock the Application object. Also, remember to make sure the Application variable contains an array—it won't when the application initializes (see Listing 23.3).

LISTING 23.3   **Maintaining an Active User List (in `SecuredSite.asp`)**

```
' assume the user has authenticated successfully
' and the UserID is in a Session("UserID") variable
' the array "arr" is a two-dimensional array where the
' first dimension is 1 (holds UserID and Date/Time information
' and the second dimension equals the total number of users.
Sub addAppUser(UserID)
   ' the user has authenticated successfully
   ' the array "arr" is a two-dimensional array where the
   ' first dimension is 1 (holds UserID and Date/Time information
   ' and the second dimension equals the total number of users.
   Dim arr
   Dim foundIndex
   Dim i
   Dim newArray
   foundIndex = 0
   newArray = False
   Application.Lock
   arr = Application("Users")

   ' check for valid array
   If Not IsArray(arr) Then
      newArray = True
      arr = Array()
      ReDim arr(1, 0)
   End If
   Response.write UBound(arr, 1) & "<br>"
   Response.write UBound(arr, 2) & "<br>"
   ' get local copy of UserID
   UserID = Session("UserID")
   For i = 0 To UBound(arr, 2)
      If arr(0, i) = UserID Then
         ' already have this user
         foundIndex = i
         Exit For
      End If
   Next
   If foundIndex = 0 Then
      ' add the UserID and time to the array
      If Not newArray Then
         ReDim Preserve arr(1, UBound(arr, 2) + 1)
```

```
         End If
         arr(0, UBound(arr, 2)) = UserID
         arr(1, UBound(arr, 2)) = Now()
     Else
         ' already have this user - signing on again before
         ' Session timeout-just update the Date/Time information
         arr(1, foundIndex) = Now()
     End If
     Application("Users") = arr
     Application.Unlock
 End Sub
```

If you have several hundred users on your site, this method works fine, but it it is a brute force method for finding the UserID. You could improve this method significantly by adding a method to add the records in sorted order and perform lookups using a binary search on the UserID field. However, it's probably easier to add the records to a database table and have the database perform an optimized search.

Restricting Access to Individuals

You can restrict access to your site to specific individuals—not only the entire site, but also individual pages. You saw an example in the Survey project in this chapter; the administrator report (ch23i4.asp) is restricted to users who have logged in with the administrator sign-on. You can use IIS to restrict access to a range of IP addresses or individually-specified IP addresses. You can also use NT security to restrict access to individual files by setting New Technology File System (NTFS) permissions on the files. When you restrict a file with NTFS permissions, the sequence of events is identical to those that occur when you return a header with a value of 401 Unauthorized—the user must authenticate with a valid UserID and password. With IE, when IIS authorization is set to NT Challenge/Response, this process can happen transparently. Alternatively, if all machines involved in the request are running Windows 2000, the client machine is running IE, and the IIS authorization setting is Digest Authentication, the process can also happen transparently.

To set NTFS permissions on a file, right-click on the file from Windows Explorer, select Properties from the context menu, then click the Security tab. You can assign access rights for any combination of groups or individual accounts. Figure 23.5 shows the NTFS Properties Security tab settings for the IIS log file ex000114.log.

File properties, Security tab

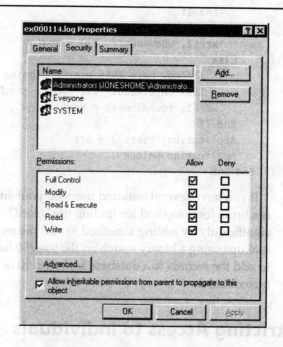

To restrict access to a site through IIS, right-click on the virtual directory name in the Internet Information Services applet, click Properties, then the Directory Security tab (see Figure 23.6).

FIGURE 23.6:

Virtual directory Properties dialog, Directory Security tab

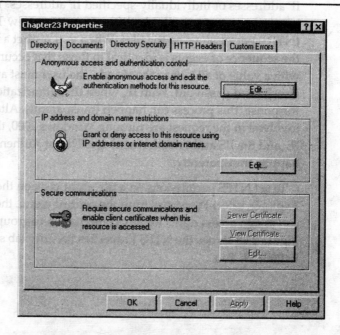

Click the Edit button in the section of the dialog titled IP Address and Domain Name Restrictions (see Figure 23.7).

FIGURE 23.7:

IP Address and Domain Name Restrictions dialog

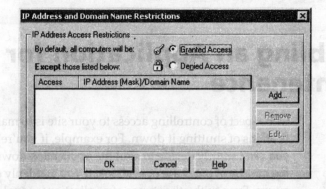

From the IP Address and Domain Name Restrictions dialog, you can set domain and IP restrictions to either allow or deny access to the site. To deny access, click the Granted Access radio button, then add the domain and IP addresses that should not have access. To restrict access to a specified set, click the Denied Access radio button, then enter the domain and IP addresses that should be granted access. To add domains and IP addresses, click the Add button. Depending on which radio button you clicked, you'll see either the Deny Access On dialog or the Grant Access On dialog, which are identical except for the title. Figure 23.8 shows the Deny Access On dialog.

FIGURE 23.8:

Deny Access On dialog

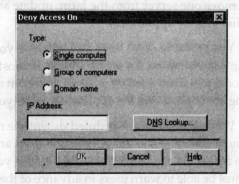

Just to make sure you understand the difference: restricting access with NTFS file permissions allows only those individuals who have permission to access the file. In contrast, restricting site access with IIS IP Address and Domain Name restrictions denies the restricted accounts from any access to the site, regardless of any other access rights they might otherwise have to the computer. NTFS restrictions require users to authenticate through a UserID and password to gain access to the resource. IIS virtual directory restrictions don't allow the user to authenticate, they simply deny access.

Disabling an Application for Maintenance

One aspect of controlling access to your site is to make sure you consider the ramifications of shutting it down. For example, if you're running an e-commerce site, you can't simply decide to shut the application down—you may have customers in the middle of purchase operations. If you suddenly close the site, they may never return. Even with other types of applications, people are justifiably irritated if they try to reach the application and it isn't available or if it disappears in the middle of a task. You are likely to have enough network and Internet infrastructure problems to turn some users off without exacerbating the problem by stopping your own program while users are accessing it.

In some cases, you can schedule application downtime at periods of low activity. For example, you can probably schedule maintenance on a business application that primarily serves a Mon-Fri, 9-5 audience during the weekend with little or no impact on active users. In contrast, a large public Internet application may never have periods of low activity. These very large sites typically switch servers to perform maintenance. They run on a server farm in stateless mode, so they can remove one server from the farm, update and replace it, without significantly affecting the application.

You probably don't have that option in your applications—and this discussion isn't about taking the server offline. In most intranet and small Internet applications, you share a server with an unknown number of other applications. I'm talking about disabling the application while you add functionality or fix a problem.

While publicizing scheduled downtime may work, you don't automatically know that no one is using the application, and you don't know that no one will try to access the application during the time you are working on it. Therefore, you must be able to warn users in advance of the shutdown. Ideally, you should be able to detect any current users and provide them with sufficient advance warning so they can exit the application normally before it shuts down. Additionally, it would be nice if you could then warn anyone who tried to start the application that it is temporarily out-of-service and to try again at a specified time.

If you don't perform these tasks according to a schedule or by using messaging, it's likely that the Help desk in your organization will receive unwanted and unnecessary calls, and your application will gain a reputation for being unreliable.

So you have three considerations:

- Schedule maintenance at periods of low activity.

- Warn current users that the application will shut down at a specified time.

- Inform users trying to access the application that it is down for maintenance, not broken, and they can access it later.

By this time you should be able to analyze your application's log files or database tables to determine the best time for maintenance, so I'll concentrate on the last two bullet points.

Sending Internal Application Messages

To send messages, you need to hook requests and re-route them through a messaging module in your application. In ASP you can do this with `include` files, which give you the ability to run specific code at the beginning and/or end of each request. For example, you've already seen how to use an `include` file to automatically check if a user has authenticated. To add messaging capability, you add an `include` file that checks to see if a message is required. Here's the logic:

1. User makes a request.

2. `Include` file checks an Application-level variable to see if messaging is enabled.

3. `Include` file checks the `Request.Cookies` collection, a `Session` variable, or a database table to find out if the user has already seen the message.

4. If the user has not seen the message, the application redirects to a message file, or inserts a message into the HTML for the current request.

5. The application sets a cookie, a `Session` variable, or makes an entry in a database table stating that the user has seen the message.

So you can see this in action, you'll build messaging capability into the Survey application you saw earlier in this chapter. Open the `global.asa` file in the `MasteringASP\Chapter23` directory and add an `Application` variable called `MessagingStatus` to the `Application_OnStart` event code. Initially set the variable value to `False`. For example:

```
Sub Application_OnStart
    Application("ConnectionString") = "DSN=SecuredSite;UID=sa;PWD="
    Application("MessagingStatus") = False
End Sub
```

Next, create a new `include` file called `messages.asp`. To activate the `include` file, add this line to all the other ASP files in the application:

```
<!- #INCLUDE FILE="messages.asp" ->
```

The `messages.asp` file contains only a few lines of code. For each request, the `messages.asp` file checks the `Application("MessagingStatus")` variable. If the variable value is `False`, the code doesn't do anything, which means you can add messaging capability with very low overhead. If the variable value is `True`, the code redirects to a message file. I've written the code using the `Server.Execute` syntax, which works only with IIS 5; but by absorbing the overhead of placing the code directly into the `messages.asp` file as a subroutine, you can obtain exactly the same functionality with IIS 4.

Listing 23.4 shows the content of the `messages.asp` file.

LISTING 23.4   **Content of `messages.asp` Include File**

```
<%
Dim messageStatus
messageStatus = Application("MessageStatus")
If messageStatus Then
    If Not Session("SeenMessage") = True Then
        Server.execute "showMessage.asp"
    End If
End If
%>
```

For each request, the code checks the value of the `Application("Message-Status")` flag variable, which controls messaging at the application level. If the flag is `True`, the code checks the value of a `Session("SeenMessage")` flag variable to see if this user has already seen the message. If not, the code executes the `showMessage.asp` file. For any other condition, the code does nothing.

The `showMessage.asp` file uses Dynamic HTML (DHTML) to superimpose a message over the top of any content that might already be on the page (see Listing 23.5).

LISTING 23.5   **Code to Display a Message (`showMessage.asp`)**

```
<%
Dim closeTime
Dim sCloseTime
Session("messageCounter") = Session("messageCounter") + 1
If Session("messageCounter") > 4 Then
    Session("SeenMessage") = True
End If
closeTime = #11:00:00 PM#
If DateDiff("n", Time(), closeTime) > 60 Then
```

```
        sCloseTime = "at " & closeTime
    Else
        sCloseTime = "in " & CStr(DateDiff("n", Time(), closeTime)) _
        & " minutes"
    End If
%>
<div id="message_div" style="position: relative; top: 20 zorder"
    align="center">
    <h1><font color="red">This application will close
    <%=sCloseTime%>.</font></h1>
</div>
<script language="JavaScript">
    document.all("message_div").zorder = "front";
    document.all("message_div").style.visibility = "visible";
    window.setTimeout("hideMessage()", 3000)
    function hideMessage() {
        document.all("message_div").style.visibility = "hidden";
    }
</script>
```

The first part of the code increments a Session("MessageCounter") variable.
Any given user will see the message up to five times. After that, the code sets the
Session("SeenMessage") flag to True, turning off the message. Next, it calculates
the time difference, in minutes, between the current time and the time the administrator wants to turn off the application. If the time difference is more than one
hour, the message displays the time when the application will become unavailable
(see Figure 23.9).

FIGURE 23.9:

Application shutdown mes-
sage—time of shutdown

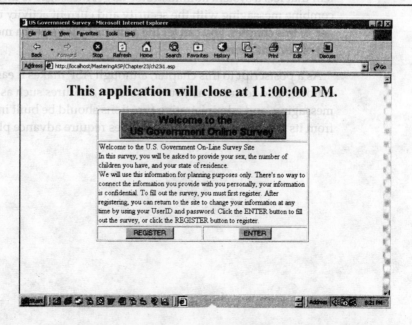

If the time difference is less than one hour, the application displays the number of minutes remaining until the application will be shut down (see Figure 23.10).

FIGURE 23.10:

Application shutdown message—time until shutdown

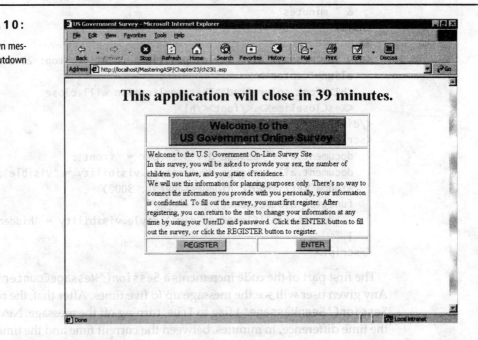

I've written this code to show you a few of the possibilities involved, but there are many more possibilities. For example, you could create a messaging subsystem that lets a system administrator target messages to an individual. When you combine messaging with the security and current activity techniques shown earlier in this chapter, you can let the administrator select a message target from a list of current users.

As a postscript to this chapter, although ASP makes it easy to modify an application to add features, as you've just seen, features such as security, monitoring, messaging, and administrative functions should be built into your application from its inception. All these capabilities require advance planning.

CHAPTER

TWENTY-FOUR

24

Planning Applications

- Define the Audience

- Determine Application Requirements

- Create a Vision

- Plan the Interface

- Plan Database Requirements

- Plan Object Responsibilities

- Create Data-Access Components

- Create Business Components

- Test the Application

- Create a Deployment Plan

- Create an Application Support Plan

Every application is different, so this chapter is not a procedure. At the same time, every application has common elements, so you should use this chapter as a way to jog your memory when planning a new application. You may not need all the features, but you are sure to need some of them. You should at least consider them in relation to your application. This chapter covers the requirements for a large application, but it applies equally well to smaller applications.

Define the Audience

Before you begin any application you should consider the audience. You may or may not have a well-defined target audience. By well-defined, I mean you may or may not know who the users are, what their average reading level is, how much experience they have with computers or with the subject of the application, and what equipment they have to run your application.

For example, if you're building a browser-based, front-end application to a mainframe application, you probably know, or can find out, exactly who the end-users are. You probably know which browser and which version they'll be using. You can find out the speed of the local machines. You can visit and talk with them to find out which features they would like, which features they absolutely have to have, and you can use them during development to try out your application, allowing you to make changes before deployment. However, if you're building an Internet application, you may have no control over the end-users. You'll need to plan for multiple browsers; unknown versions; slow computers; people who turn off graphics, change fonts, and have varying screen resolutions and color depth.

You may need to plan training into your application. While you may completely understand all the features, not everyone will. Find out how and when people want to use the application. A data-entry program that people use every day, all day, has different requirements than a data-entry application that people use once or twice a year. Consider colors carefully—a significant percentage of people are color-blind, so writing your informative messages in red over a yellow background is self-defeating.

What's the average age of the audience? You would probably write a different application for children than for adults—and you'd write a different application for teenagers than for senior citizens. Use language at an appropriate level and with appropriate content for the age of your audience.

Some people read extremely well while others are much better at absorbing information through spoken language and pictures. No one likes to use a computer to read page after page of text, regardless of how well the text is written. Consider the font size. After age 45, people generally have trouble reading small fonts. Take computer experience into account. People who are familiar with computers generally understand file systems, are unafraid to try new features, and can use a browser effectively; others refuse to take any action unless prompted when confronted with a new program.

Begin thinking about the help system at the beginning of the planning process. Do you need a help system? What should it contain? How will people access help? Consider language requirements. Does your application need to support multiple languages? If so, you'll want to write the application so it draws all text from resource files written in different languages.

No application, no matter how well written, can be successful unless it meets the needs of the people who use it. For that to happen, you must determine what those needs are before you write the application.

Determine Application Requirements

ASP applications require resources: network resources, server resources, browser resources, memory, database, security, and support and maintenance resources. All of these topics fall into the category of application requirements. For small test applications where you control the server, you can mostly ignore these requirements, but for larger applications, and those where you do not control the server, you'll need to do some advance planning.

How big is your application? How many programmer hours will it require? What about other support like subject-matter experts, system analysts, graphic artists, quality control personnel, technical writers, network and server support personnel, and database administrators? Human resources are the single greatest expense in building an application—and in most cases, people underestimate the costs involved in creating them. Coordinating human resources to deliver an application can be a difficult task, especially when rollout deadlines are imposed externally.

Human resources are only one aspect of application requirements. ASP applications also require machine resources. For example, you may be able to run your application on a single server, but which server? What are the disk space requirements? What are the memory requirements? Does the application require a database server? If so, which server? What's the size of the database initially? Eventually? Do you have a maintenance and backup plan in place? How will the application affect the network? Can the intended audience reach the server? Can they authenticate on that server? Does your application require resources on other servers? Does the IUSR_MACHINENAME account on the server have access rights to those resources?

If any of these questions affect your application, you need to write a plan detailing which resources you will require, then follow the plan to ensure that everyone involved in the application rollout understands their role and tasks and can schedule for them appropriately. It won't do you any good to create an application that requires SQL Server if your company only has licenses for Oracle. The security requirements for applications that need authentication or need to access resources on other computers can be prohibitive. You need to ensure in advance that you have permission to set the server parameters and create the network accounts your application needs.

Create a Vision

You'll find that as you determine the audience and application requirements, you build a vision of the application that you can communicate to the various people involved. Use that vision to let others understand why you need the application and what it will do. The goal is to create a vision that others can share; if they can share your vision, they can help you make the application a reality. Without a shared vision, you'll be hard-pressed to co-opt others into working with you effectively.

Not everyone needs the same vision, and not everyone needs or wants to know about the application in its entirety. You probably want to communicate the vision differently to different individuals depending on their interests. For example, describing to a senior manager how the network architecture of your application will reduce resource contention doesn't constitute a shared vision, but the same language may be of great interest to a Network Administrator. Discussions of database relationships with a Database Administrator may win you friends, but the same vision, when shared with a data-entry clerk, may only tag you as a consummate bore.

With each group, you should share the portion of your application's vision that will gain a champion for the application. Unless you have total control of the human resources, the network, the server, and can tell the end-users what to do, you'll need some help. Champions are people in each area that can influence others. Pick the people that can help your application, then communicate your vision so they'll want the application. They will only want it if it solves a problem. Perhaps the application saves money, or time. Perhaps it simplifies a task through automation. Perhaps it does none of these things, but provides integration with other applications they already have, or grafts an aesthetic face onto an unappealing application. The point is that each group has different interests and it's your task to create a vision that appeals to each group.

Plan the Interface

The interface is the public persona of your application. Some applications have no interface requirements—in fact parts of your ASP applications, as you begin writing data-access and business components, won't need an interface. However, those portions that do require an interface are the ones that people see. You need to groom and plan them artistically and aesthetically because if people don't like the interface, they're unlikely to use the application.

By the terms artistically and aesthetically, I don't mean you should add graphics or try to disguise the purpose of the application in favor of making it beautiful, I mean you should pay attention to the way you lay out controls, images, and text on the page. Take the time to align and size controls properly. Don't select a gray background color for text input fields—people think they're disabled or locked and won't try to type in them. Don't create a text field 200 characters wide if people are only going to enter 10 characters into the field. Similarly, leave enough room between controls. I've seen numerous applications—especially data-entry applications—where the designer has packed so many controls onto the screen that it's impossible to pick out the important features.

Think about how people will use the application. Try to make the application time-sensitive—by that I mean make the most common actions both easy to perform and as responsive as possible. Spend your efforts on the 30% of the application that people use every day. Minimize difficult input. Sure, it's hard to gather the information for pick lists and program intelligence into the application, but a program that responds rapidly and in consistent ways is much more pleasant to learn and use. Remember that many people don't like computers. Try to make the computer adjust to humans. If people want to see spreadsheet-like applications and reports, provide them. If you want to provide an alternate interface for those who would rather fill out forms, do that. Have the application remember its state from one session to another. There's little that's more irritating than having to reset your preferences because a program designer forgot to save them.

In addition to human interfaces, your application has programmatic interfaces. These are the points through which one module in your application communicates with the other modules. For example, passing information from page to page through `hidden form` variables is an interface. If, later on, you decide to modify the code or add functionality, you'll need to interact with your application at those points. Similarly, the names of functions, subroutines, methods, properties, and the arguments to those routines are an interface. Think about how the application will look to you or a maintenance programmer six months later.

As you move toward programming components, the programmatic interfaces gain importance. As you build more applications, you'll see that the programmatic interfaces often have lifetimes far beyond the front-end interfaces seen by the users.

Plan Database Requirements

ASP and Access have made it nearly painless to get a database application up and running, but for any substantive application, that's neither complete nor sufficient. When you build a database, you probably plan to gather information. Unless your application is so completely isolated that no one else wants to interact with the information you gather, it's highly likely that others will eventually need to interact with the database as well.

The database is the backbone of your application; therefore, it should be bullet-proof. That means it should not accept information that doesn't meet requirements. It's easy to write code that tests for information validity, but you can't be sure everyone will write bulletproof code. While *you* would never allow an invalid value in a field, you can be sure that eventually one will slip through someone else's code.

Databases on the Web must service all the application's users, and because of the stateless nature of the Web, they are called upon to provide more information much more often than would normally be required in a standard client-server situation. Because database operations are inherently machine- and network-intensive, it's your job to minimize the volume of data that must traverse the network for any given request. That means your task is to learn to take advantage of the power of SQL to select only the required data. But that's only the beginning.

The relationships you build into your database during the planning stages will grow deep roots. For example, the way you plan to store something as simple as a phone number has major ramifications. Not all phone numbers are alike. Some phone numbers require area codes. Many people would prefer to dial numbers using their phone card PIN number to transfer charges. Some phone numbers have extensions. Foreign phone numbers are completely different than U.S. phone numbers. Consider the total phone numbers a person has. You might put the phone numbers in a Contacts table using fields like HomePhone, WorkPhone, FaxPhone, and CellPhone. But how many fields are sufficient? Those four may meet your application's needs today, but it's almost certain that however many fields you predefine, someone will have a need for more. You can circumvent this problem by normalizing the database. Put the telephone numbers in a separate table with the UserID as a foreign key and use JOIN operations. Add a field to that table called TelephoneType. Index the UserID field and the TelephoneType field, because those are the fields you'll use to look up values. After a database enters production, and especially after other programs begin using the database, it becomes much more difficult, if not impossible, to change the structure of the database.

Plan the interface to your database as carefully as you plan the names and arguments of your routines or the methods and properties of your objects. You can control access to the database through security, but your primary methods for controlling content are through stored procedures, triggers, and views. For example, you can (and often should) deny direct access to any database table. Instead, you provide SELECT access through views and stored procedures, and INSERT and UPDATE operations though stored procedures, defaults, and triggers. For example, if you have a CreatedOn field, you don't have to trust programmers to update the field. Write a default value or a trigger to insert the value. Create a rule or constraint that protects the field from invalid or out-of-range values. Don't expose the field for update.

You need to consider database administration. The rule of thumb is that you need to create at least four ASP pages for each top-level database table for administration purposes. These are: a page from which the administrator can select records to modify, a form for adding new records, a form for editing existing records, and a script to delete records. If you have password fields in your database, the administrator will need to be able to clear the passwords. You'll need a form where administrators can select an individual and a clearPassword script. If there are database processes that must be run on a schedule, such as archiving or deleting obsolete records, you need to create a mechanism that will launch the processes. You'll also need a way to let the appropriate people know if the process did or did not complete successfully.

Plan your data size requirements. Databases tend to grow over time. A SELECT query on an unindexed field may perform adequately when the database has a few hundred records. But when the database grows to hundreds of thousands of records, that same query will bog down the application. You need to plan for the future. Does the data expire or become obsolete? How will you remove obsolete data from the database? Manually? Automatically? What will you do with the records you remove? Discard them? Archive them?

The size of the data at any given time may also affect the application code. You should cringe whenever you see a query like SELECT * FROM <Tablename>. Unless you know the table contains a fixed number of rows, such queries are an invitation to disaster. The first few hundred rows won't matter, but when the code needs to display or winnow through thousands of records, it will make a huge difference in the responsiveness of your code.

How many servers will it take to service the total anticipated number of users? If it takes more than one, how will you split up or replicate the data? Test the queries using the database server's analysis tools. If the database doesn't have such tools built in, obtain them. These tools can help you find and anticipate problems. For example, the SQL Server Query Analyzer tool can show you the query plan for any query. You should particularly look for table scan operations, because they mean the database was unable to find a suitable index to use, and therefore must read the entire column. For an enterprise application, spending a few hundred dollars to determine query efficiency can mean the difference between success and failure.

How do you plan to back up the database? What happens if the drive fails? If you don't have a backup plan, ask yourself how much data you can afford to lose? If the answer is none, then you must implement a fail-over plan and a back-up plan. If you're willing to lose transactions in progress, you only need the backup plan. Sometimes, Server and Database Administrators have already solved the problem because your application shares space with a critical application—but don't be complacent—find out. If your application needs access to archived information, you'll need to build that into your plan. How do you obtain the archive? How do you load it? How long does that take?

You should be able to answer all these questions—or at least have asked them—before you begin building your application. If you think most of this doesn't apply to you as a program designer/developer, that such questions are the Database Administrators' (DBAs) job, then you should get ready for a long antagonistic relationship with the DBAs. Don't be surprised if some of these issues surface only after the application becomes successful, but try to anticipate your reaction. It's often difficult or impossible to spend time and money to implement all these features for applications that may not need them initially, and your application may not ever need them all. The point is, you need to understand and plan for database expansion, backup, data validity, security, and efficiency throughout the lifetime of the application.

Plan Object Responsibilities

If databases are the backbone of a modern Web application, objects are the legs. Objects in a Web application are often transient—created, used, and destroyed as quickly as possible. Consider the ASP intrinsic objects. Only the Application object is permanent; IIS creates and destroys all the others for each request. That's a lot of objects. Does the ASP engine really create all the intrinsic objects for each request or does it create them only when you write a reference in your code? Quite truthfully, I don't know, except for the Request.ServerVariables collection. The Microsoft documentation states that ASP creates the Request.Server-Variables collection only if you reference it, because the overhead involved in creating the collection is relatively high. In any case, the ASP object model has stood the test of time—it has remained relatively static ever since version 1. IIS 4 introduced transactional capabilities and added the ObjectContext object. IIS 5 introduced the Server.Transfer and Server.Execute methods, as well as the Session and Application Contents collections; but most methods and properties remain unchanged.

That's the type of stability you should strive for with your own objects. You want to plan an interface that will not need to change. Object modeling is beyond the scope of this book, but a little common sense can take you a long way. First, try to separate objects using the same type of logic you used to create normalized databases. That's not to say that an object's properties should always match the structure of a single table, but if your objects begin to span many tables, you might want to take a long hard look at the object's responsibilities. Try to create reusable objects. The more features you build into an object, the less generic it becomes. For example, you should never tie an object to a single database location by hard-coding a DSN or `ConnectionString` property into the object itself.

Try to capture the methods and properties that objects exhibit in the real world. For example, think of a Person object. Not all people are alike, but all have common elements. Build the common elements into a Person object, then create child objects that both inherit and extend the capabilities of their common ancestor.

Create Data-Access Components

The most scalable Web applications use data-access objects to request data from and update database tables. That's not the most efficient way to develop your application—it's much easier and faster to write dynamic SQL queries directly into your ASP code than to plan and develop COM database components. Nevertheless, dynamic SQL queries can be used only by your application, whereas COM components may be used by many different applications. Data-access components become much more important when your application isn't the only application using the database.

The purpose of a data-access component is to mediate data transfer to and from the database. These components often run inside of Microsoft Transaction Server (MTS), which instantiates objects on demand, rather than on request. That means any given object may be shared between many different clients. Therefore, you should write (and use) the components with a strong bias toward efficiency over ease-of-use. For example, don't create large numbers of individual properties that must be set before calling a method that acts on those properties. Instead, pass the properties to the method. That way, MTS can provide a reference to the component, perform the work, and transfer ownership of the component to another process with only one call.

Similarly, try to write the components so they use database connections efficiently. If you know you need two forward-only record sets, retrieve them both in a single call using a stored procedure or chained SQL statements. By doing so, you minimize both the time and number of connections needed to retrieve the data.

Build the components so they meet the requirements of both program users and program administrators. Provide `select`, `update`, `insert`, and `delete` methods for every exposed column. It's often very difficult to gain permission to put data-access components on a production server, so try to anticipate future needs and build and test them during development.

Create Business Components

Business components contain the business rules that act on the data provided by data-access components. You often want to isolate these rules in a separate layer because they change more often than the front-end interface requirements. Consider an application that arranges route patterns for salespeople. The route data—the customer list and locations, resides in a database. Although the data changes constantly, the format of the data does not. You might build a data-access component to retrieve and update the data. On the other hand, the rules for calculating the route change constantly, depending on pricing, availability, the potential size of orders from different customers, and many other business factors.

The application must be able to adapt to the changing route rules. You do that by adding or changing business components. For example, one rule might be that salespeople must visit each customer a minimum of once each month unless the customer has been inactive for three or more months. Another might be that customers with total orders exceeding $1,000,000 per year receive a discount of 15% on all orders over $10,000, whereas customers with total orders between $500,000 and $999,999 receive a 10% discount. Customers with yearly orders totaling less than $500,000 get discounts that depend on the size of each individual order.

If (or rather, when) these rules change—perhaps the business focus changes to acquiring new customers, so discounts to smaller customers increase—the business logic must also change. Therefore, the main purpose of a business component is to isolate business rules so you can replace the logic inside the component without disturbing any other parts of the application.

Although this sounds simple, it's not. If the interface to the component changes, you must also change other parts of the application. The challenge is to design the components so you can change the logic inside the components without changing the external programmatic interface. Consider building an external interface that can adapt to changing needs. For example, a method that accepts an array of `Variant` parameters and returns a `Variant` data array is adaptable for many different purposes, albeit at the cost of efficiency. For example, you could pass it an ad-hoc SQL statement and it would return the data. Don't design all of your data-access calls in this manner, but think about including one with each component.

Test the Application

Development is often a tradeoff between efficiency and stability. While you may win praise for delivering an application on time, such praise will rapidly turn to censure if the application fails to work as anticipated. Therefore, don't forget to plan for testing. In my experience, there are, at minimum, three testing phases for an application. Each testing phase should answer one or more questions. The phases are:

Programmatic testing   Does the application work according to specifications? This phase begins when code development begins and continues throughout the development of the application. As the program moves from development into maintenance, you must repeat this phase for every change to the application.

User testing   Can the members of the target audience use the application to accomplish the task for which the application was designed? Do they use it? You can and should discover the answer to the first question before you deploy the application. You cannot answer the second question until after you deploy the application. Unfortunately, the answer to the second question is much more important than the first.

Goal testing   Does the application meet the goals for which it was created? Depending on the application, the goals might involve an increase in productivity, or accuracy, or cost reduction. Such questions are rarely answered for several reasons. First, the application designers are usually satisfied when the application is complete—regardless of whether it is ever used. The end-users are usually more interested in completing tasks than in using your application—they're certainly not interested in measuring how well the application meets its goals; many of them may not be aware of the goals. Finally, measuring application success requires baseline measurements before application deployment. The people who envision, design, and create applications are rarely the ones who could accomplish the measurement; therefore, goal testing rarely occurs.

Think back to your targeted audience. What kinds of computers do they have? What network connection speeds? Which browsers and what operating systems? You must create a testing plan that takes these factors into account. Just because it works on your development system doesn't mean it will work on the target systems—it won't. I wish I had a quarter for each time a programmer has said "but it works on *my* system...." If you can't set up a laboratory environment that matches the target audience's hardware, set up a test server the users can reach, then schedule times where they can help you test the application. Don't just turn them loose with the application. Provide a script they can follow. Be sure they understand that it's a test. You can gain other benefits from testing in this manner. Interview the users afterward. Find out what they liked and didn't like. Find out which features are missing, which ones they didn't need, and which, if any, features they'd like to have added.

For solid development you need three servers: a development server, a staging server, and a production server.

NOTE   I've used the term server in the singular, but you should understand that applications requiring a server farm need to be tested in that environment.

You need these three servers even if you're the only developer. During the initial application development, programmers use the development server to write and test the code. For user and beta testing, place the entire application on the staging server. The staging server should be, as much as possible, an exact duplicate of the production server. Never make any changes to the staging server—make the changes on the development server, then migrate them to the staging server for testing. When you roll out the application, copy the application from staging to production. Changes must always flow in a single direction, from development, to staging, to production.

At this point, you might think you're done with the staging server, but you need to keep it. If the application needs any modification, you'll need to make the changes, test them, and then migrate the affected portions of the application to production. The development-staging-production cycle works only if you manage it carefully. There's a tremendous temptation to make changes on the staging and production servers, but you should resist that temptation, because if you make changes on the production server, they'll be overwritten if you ever move future changes into production from the staging server. Similarly, changes made on the staging server often disappear as programmers move code from development onto the staging server.

The development-staging-production cycle works for code, but doesn't work nearly as well for databases. After an application that collects user data is in production, you can't overwrite it with a staging copy of the database. Therefore, the cycle for databases works initially, before production, just like the code cycle; but after deployment to production, you must replicate the database from production to staging for testing. As you make changes and solve problems, you still can't copy the staging database into production unless you're absolutely certain the staging copy contains all of the data from the production copy—and it's difficult to be certain unless you can shut the production application down. Because many applications must run 24 x 7 in production, that may not be an option.

Fortunately, most database changes involve database objects—stored procedures, table definitions, view, indexes, etc.—not data. Therefore, your deployment task for databases is to build a process through which you can move a copy of the structure of a staging database into production without affecting the data. You'll need to be able to practice the operation on the staging database. Set up a process for changing the database in use from one copy on the staging database to another copy. I've found that the best way to do this is to have only one place in your application that defines database connection strings—for ASP applications, the `global.asa` file is a good place to put it. Remember that changing `global.asa` shuts down the application; if that's a problem for you, find another method to define the connection strings. Where you acquire the connection strings isn't nearly as important as acquiring them from only one place.

Create a Deployment Plan

Designing, building, testing, and debugging applications are the fun parts of program development. Deployment is rarely as satisfying because deployed machines are rarely completely under your control. You'll have the best chance of success, and deployment will be less painful if you follow these guidelines.

Prepare for Deployment

Deploying an ASP application isn't much different from deploying a standard Windows application, but there are three critical differences:

1. Anonymous Web applications run under different permissions than standard applications. Web applications using NT Challenge/Response run under the user's account on the server, but cannot authenticate across the network.

2. Web applications run on multiple threads. Resource contention that you may not see during development can become an issue after deployment.

3. The production server will not be your development server, won't have the same directory permissions that your server does, may not be the same service pack version, and will have different security settings. If you're lucky, you'll have administrator access to the production server. In both cases, you can help either yourself or the Server Administrators by following the guidelines in this chapter.

You need a minimum of two servers to test an installation—the staging server and a test server. They can't be the same server—in other words, you can't just publish the application to another virtual directory, because all paths, files, DSNs, graphics, virtual directories, permissions, DLLs, and other resources and settings presumably already exist and work on the development server. The point of testing the installation is that the target environment is usually unknown, and often uncontrollable. In other words, you may be delivering your application to a server that is radically different from your staging server.

Clean Up the Code

Now's a good time to go through the code and eliminate unneeded methods and variables. It's too early to remove any debugging code, although you should be able to easily turn the debug output on and off for testing.

- Check all component references and remove any unnecessary references. Installation programs often include external DLLs based on the project references list rather than the references the program actually uses.

- Delete unused files—you'll need a clean list to create your installation.

- Back up the project. As a developer, you're sure (or you should be) that the application runs perfectly right now. You should save that known state in case you make changes during the deployment process and want to undo them later, if you need the information to set path or file references.

- Make sure all file references within the project use relative URLs. Never include the server name or IP address in any code. The server name will always change. If your root directory name clashes with an existing name, or if, for whatever reason, the clients want to change the root to another name, your program will still work. You can obtain the server name and program root at runtime, with the `Server.MapPath` method.

- Search your program for references to external resources like log filenames, database DSNs, etc. As you find them, move them to the `global.asa` file and store them as Application-level variables. Change the code so it references the `Application` variables. That way you can change DSN names, signons, passwords, and external file references easily, no matter where those resources are or what their names are. If security is an issue, put the references in an external file and encrypt the file. The point here is that those filenames, paths, machine resources, and database resources can and will change names and locations. In many cases, these changes are outside your control and will break your application. You want to get the references from a location that you can change easily, preferably without recompiling and reinstalling your application.

- Try to rename files specific to the application in a consistent manner. That makes it much easier to find and remember files later. It also decreases the risk that a file you're installing will conflict with the name of a file already on the system.

- Make a version number for your program and provide a method to retrieve it. For example, the About box found on the Help menu in most Windows programs provides that information. Although your browser-based application may not have an About box, you can provide a way to display it.

Generate Likely Errors

Generate errors for the things most likely to happen. By likely errors, I mean things your application depends on that tend to change over time. For example, if your application opens a connection to a database, shut the database down, then see how your application traps the error. Where do the errors appear? On the browser screen? In the NT Application Event log? In the Event Security Log? You need to know this so you can debug the application remotely on an unfamiliar server.

If your application needs write access to a directory, shut off that access. Delete log files and change Distributed Common Object Model (DCOM) permissions. All of these things are out of your control once the application leaves the development stage, but they all happen. Neither you nor anyone else on the development team will remember the information after a few weeks, so write down the exact error messages and the solutions.

If you follow this advice, you'll probably want to go through at least one more testing and revision cycle to beef up the error reporting. I can assure you this is time well spent if you're deploying to a remote server—one you can't physically reach or on which you don't have administrator permissions.

I often write hidden features into a program that can aid in debugging deployed applications. It's best to isolate these features as far as possible from other program requirements. ASP programs are excellent candidates for these programs because they're small, and they work as long as the server is working. Some examples are an ASP file that tests database connections; one that lists the contents of the global .asa file, one that checks resources; one that lets you run SQL code against a database, like the SQL Server Query Analyzer (iSQL) program. If you have FTP or FrontPage access to the target server, you can even write and deploy such applets after a problem occurs.

Put the error messages and solutions in an HTM file that accompanies your application and keep a copy for yourself. When you get a support call, you'll be able to tell the caller where to look and what to do to solve the problem.

Deploy to a Test Server

If possible, install and test the application on a local server—one where you can physically access the machine, start, stop, and even reboot it. While event logs can be helpful, other Server Administrators may not want to help you debug your application. Do not install any other code on the server unless you can also install the same code on all of the target servers.

Debugging an application in production is a skill that's different from debugging a program in development. Practice on your own server, not your production server; and practice on a test server, not the staging server.

Beta Test the Application

Many applications run perfectly when tested by the author, but fail miserably when tested by real users. By real users I mean members of the target audience. Real users don't know what input the application expects, so they do unexpected things.

As early as possible, and on an ongoing basis during development, try to get several members of your target audience to use or at least critique the application. A decent sample is 5-10 people. You'll find that you can catch most of the bugs, misconceptions, and missing features if you let just a few people use the application.

A real beta test though, occurs as a next-to-final step. Install the application on a server and let several people use it. They should treat the application as though it were the production version. Fix any problems that arise.

When the application has passed muster in beta form, you can remove the debugging code—it's ready for production. Be sure to test again without the debugging code—sometimes removing the code creates problems.

Determine the Production Server's Configuration

When you're delivering to a known production server, you may be able to call ahead to find out the configuration of that server. The earlier you can do this in the development process, the better. For example, it will do you no good to develop with the latest and greatest version of ADO if the target server is still running version 1.5. Similarly, taking advantage of the many convenient features of SQL Server version 7, such as 8000-character varChar fields, won't work if the production database server is still running version 6.5. Server Administrators are notoriously difficult when you tell them they must upgrade their equipment or software to accommodate your application.

If you're developing commercial applications, you will need to create more than one version of the application, design for the lowest common denominator, or be willing to give up possible sales to use the latest technology.

In all cases you'll want to design the application to isolate version-dependent issues, so you can change component versions and databases easily to meet the technical requirements of the customers. For example, if all of your database accesses happen via stored procedures, your application will work on any database where you can re-create the set of stored procedures. Moving the application from SQL Server to Oracle may be as simple as creating the tables and the stored procedures and copying the data. In contrast, the more database functionality you place in your code, the harder it will be to change the database.

I've sometimes found it useful to begin applications by having the program itself check resource availability and versions. While that may slow down application initialization, it's better than end-user error messages. Alternatively, you can write these checks so they are performed on demand—perhaps via Administrator options, or via an unreferenced backdoor URL that runs a hidden page in your ASP application. Using these techniques, you can at least help determine problems after deployment.

When all else fails, you'll want to keep people from accessing your application while you work on it. Use the techniques in Chapter 23, *Controlling Access and Monitoring*, in the section titled *Disabling an Application for Maintenance*, to temporarily disable the application.

Create an Installation Program

ASP programs, by themselves, don't need an installation package. If the target server already has ASP installed, you can simply copy the directory containing your application files and mark the directory as the source of a virtual directory on the target server. However, any components you have created or acquired that are not installed with ASP do need an installation program. That's because components require registration on the target server—you can't simply copy the DLL files to the target and expect them to work.

Configure the Target Server

Almost all ASP applications require a change to the server's configuration. At minimum you need to create a virtual directory. If your application requires write access to files, you will need to set NTFS file-access permissions as well. If you have a database, you must create and configure a DSN. For more complex applications, you may need to create special accounts or groups, set permissions, alter the registry, and install packages into MTS.

Capture the Server Configuration Settings

As soon as you create and test the installation package, capture the current settings for IIS and MTS from your test server. Screen captures work best, but you can write down all of the settings as well. Be sure to capture them all.

If you're using an installer other than the Packaging and Deployment Wizard (PDW), one that can create virtual web directories and perform MTS installations, you'll need to know the server settings to create your package. Otherwise, you or the Server Administrator will need to know them to configure the target server. There are too many settings to remember and you won't remember them long-term, so write them down. Put the settings, graphics and all, in the HTM file that accompanies the application, and keep a copy for yourself.

Practice the Installation

To configure the server you'll need to perform some of these steps, but probably not all of them. Consider this list as a resource only, not as a procedure—I don't know what your applications require, what the server situation is, or whether you're delivering in-house or commercial applications. In general, unless you own the server, try to be polite—don't break existing applications just to get your application running. I've assumed that you're performing the installation yourself, or at least you are present during the installation. If not, you need to assemble all of the documentation and provide it to the person doing the installation. If you can't be present, have someone else practice the installation using your documentation on the test server before delivering the application.

- Consult with the Server Administrator before beginning your installation. If you plan to install any system DLLs, make sure the Administrator knows the files and versions in advance. Installing such files often (usually) requires a reboot; therefore, you should schedule the installation in advance. Most production server reboots can be performed only during low usage hours. Remember that it's much harder to remove most upgrades than to install them. Many upgrades aren't perfectly compatible with previous versions. Most servers run multiple applications. You don't want to be responsible for breaking someone else's program.

- Set up your virtual directory first, using the Internet Service Manager application. Set the directory and applications' permissions the same as those from the tested staging version. If you captured those settings as screen shots, this step will be straightforward.

- Run the installation packages to install any components.

- Create any other required directories—for example, log directories—and set the necessary directory and/or file permissions.

- Edit the `global.asa` and any other external reference files and change the entries so they match the requirements of the server. Such entries include DSNs, file paths, global variables, company names, etc.

- If your application uses a database, make sure the database has been properly set up. In some cases that may be as simple as using a wizard to move the database to a production database server. In others, it's an involved process fully as complex as setting up and creating your IIS application. Database setup is beyond the scope of this book. Just be aware that the database needs to be online and ready, with appropriate permissions set, by this stage of deployment.

- Check the database connection(s), signon(s), and password(s). Many IIS installations break down at this stage because the IUSR_MACHINENAME account doesn't have permission to access the database server. Test several representative procedures, including procedures with updates, inserts, and deletes to ensure your application has sufficient permissions. I usually create special ASP files to do these kinds of checks because you can alter them quickly based on the immediate needs, conditions, and problems involved. The test ASP files run inside your virtual directory, but more importantly, they run with exactly the same permissions as your application, which can help debug problems.

- Set up the appropriate packages and import components into MTS. You can perform this step manually if you have access to the server and you're performing the installation, otherwise you'll need to write a detailed procedure, or use MTS on your staging server to create an MTS package (PAK) file. The PAK file stores all component names, IDs, and settings. MTS also exports the DLLs themselves. Keep the PAK file and the DLLs together. Don't substitute a later version of a DLL for the version exported by the PAK file or your installation may not work. To re-create the package on another system, right-click on the Packages Installed item and select New Package to import the PAK file. Click the Install Pre-Built Packages button and browse to the PAK file for your package.

- When you create an MTS PAK file, you have the option to include role names and the NT UserIDs associated with those roles. If you're delivering internal applications that can be useful, but you should not include that information if you're delivering to another company or to a location that is not part of your NT network. Make sure you set up any required roles and users. Bear in mind that you may need to re-create these roles exactly as they appeared on the test server if any program code checks a user's role assignment.

- Check the DCOM default access and launch permissions. Make sure they include the IUSR_MACHINENAME account if you're delivering an application that uses anonymous access security.

- If you call remote objects, you'll need to repeat the permissions setting checks on the remote machines as well. You may need to set up a trust relationship between your server and the remote computer and add the IUSR_MACHINENAME account to the remote computer's account list. Alternatively, (and this is preferable) you can switch the Web server's anonymous account to a network account with sufficient permissions to run the application on both computers.

Dealing with Permissions Issues

It's been my experience that security issues arise for almost every ASP application deployment. Some of these problems you can solve in advance—the rest of them you'll need to solve during deployment. There's little chance that everything will run perfectly. If you trap the errors properly, practice the installation and document the settings from your staging server, you may only have a few problems. If you haven't done those things, I hope you're a lucky person.

Most security-related errors won't appear on the browser screen or in any log files generated by your application even if you trap them properly. The on-screen or in-log errors typically say something like Access Denied, which is not helpful. A better description of most security-related errors appears in the Event log. You need to check both the System log and the Application log if your application isn't running properly.

Most ASP application security errors occur when the IUSR_MACHINENAME account requests access or launch permission to a class, component, or file. In some cases these errors appear in the System or Application logs, in other cases they don't. When your own error-trapping and the system error-trapping don't provide enough information, you can use NT's auditing feature to help find the problem.

You need to be an Administrator to enable auditing for a computer. Document what you do—you'll want to turn it off later, and there's no easy way to turn off auditing without disabling all auditing. To enable auditing, start User Manager for Domains and click the Policies menu, then select the Audit entry. You can audit many things, but usually you need to audit only File and Object access to debug ASP applications. Work with your Server Administrator to enable auditing on the files, components, and other resources used by your application.

Despite all of these warnings and error-trapping resources, your application may still have problems. Microsoft's MSDN site and the newsgroups can sometimes provide expert advice.

Create an Application Support Plan

After deployment you should be prepared to receive problem calls from end-users. Sometimes such calls are questions about how to activate or use the application, but sometimes they're problem reports. Unless you plan to take the calls yourself, you need to provide program documentation to the Help desk or to the people who work with the end-users to solve the problem. The work you did to document error messages and program requirements during the deployment phase should form the basis of your application support plan.

The people taking the calls will need to know the error messages that appear on the user's browsers and how those error messages relate to the application, otherwise they'll refer the errors to you. In many cases, errors that appear after deployment are infrastructure-related: the server's down, the network's down, the proxy or firewall won't allow access. Sometimes the errors are resource-related: a database server name changed, someone reset file permissions on the server, someone upgraded a DLL that's not backwardly compatible with your program code. Finally, some problems are code-related. Even with your best efforts, code-related bugs will occur. You need to plan how to resolve these problems, document them for the support personnel, and test any changes.

If all of this seems like overkill for your ASP application, it probably is. Not every application needs such an elaborate infrastructure, but at the same time, from a business standpoint, an application must not be dependent on a single individual. If you leave the company for another job, someone else will need to take over maintenance and support. Try to document the tasks you would want someone else to document for you if you were taking over the application.

PART VII

Advanced ASP

PART VII

Advanced ASP

C H A P T E R

TWENTY-FIVE

Client-Side Scripting

- ■ VBScript vs. Jscript/JavaScript/ECMAScript

- ■ Sending Script to the Browser

- ■ The Document Object Model

- ■ Accessing the DOM from Script

- ■ Client-Side Form Validation

- ■ Using ActiveX Controls

- ■ Client-Side Data Access

- ■ Sending Java Applets to the Client

At this point, you've completed the task of learning about ASP itself. The rest of this book is devoted to raising your awareness level of peripheral technologies that can affect the depth and quality of your applications. The first, and probably most important of these, is client-side scripting. Through your server-side ASP scripts you have the ability to write code that executes within the client browser—in other words, you can use code to write code. The code you write can be dynamic— you can write browser-specific code. That's a difficult concept for beginning ASP programmers to master—that client-side code can consist of text generated from server-side code. Nevertheless, in this chapter you'll see how client-side code can improve the effectiveness and efficiency of your ASP applications.

VBScript vs. JScript/JavaScript/ECMAScript

Unfortunately, different browsers support different types of script. IE is the only browser (that I'm aware of) that supports VBScript, but almost all browsers support JavaScript. Therefore, if you're developing an Internet application, you probably need to write your client-side script in JavaScript. If you're deploying an application to an intranet where all the target users have IE, you can use VBScript.

The browser requirements make the VBScript vs. JavaScript decision for you— if you're going to use client-side script at all, it must be able to run in the target browsers, but again unfortunately, it's not quite that simple. Not all browsers support all versions of JavaScript, the various versions of JavaScript differ in functionality, and the browsers themselves have different object models. That's equally true for all IE shops. Even if everyone has the same browser version, not everyone may have the same version of the scripting runtime. Therefore, code that runs perfectly well in one browser may not execute in another. You should plan to test extensively if you decide to use client-side script.

On a brighter note, the syntax for client- and server-side script is identical, with the exception that the ASP intrinsic objects aren't available through client-side script. However, you can obtain access to the values of the ASP object variables and properties on the client. I'll show you how to do that in the next section.

In this chapter, I'm going to provide some examples of both JavaScript (JScript) and VBScript, but I'll concentrate more heavily on the VBScript examples. If you're running Netscape, you can run the JavaScript examples without modification, except for those that demonstrate ActiveX functionality, but you'll need to translate the VBScript examples before they'll work. If you're using IE, both types of examples should work properly. I'm personally using IE 5, but all the examples in this chapter will work with IE 4 as well, and all but the DHTML examples will work with IE 3.

Sending Script to the Browser

From an ASP page, you send script to the browser just as if it were HTML. You place client-side script between `<script>` tags. For example:

```
<script language="VBScript">
</script>
```

Between the `<script>` tags you place functions, subroutines, and global code and definitions. The difference is, just as with server-side script, that code within subroutines and functions executes only when called, whereas global code—script not placed within functions and subroutines—executes immediately after the script engine on the browser compiles it. Listing 25.1 shows an ASP file that writes a client-side script to display two Alert message boxes.

LISTING 25.1   Client-Side Script to Display Alerts (ch25i1.asp)

```
<%@ Language=VBScript %>
<html>
<head>
</head>
<body>
This script creates two "alert" boxes that execute on the client
using JavaScript.
<script language="JavaScript">
    function showAlert() {
        alert("Hello from showAlert function!");
    }
    alert("Hello world");
    showAlert();
</script>
</body>
</html>
```

Note that there's a difference between `<script>` tags intended for server-side script, such as you've seen in the `global.asa` file, and `<script>` tags for client-side script. The ASP engine assumes you want the script to execute on the client unless you specifically mark it as server-side script using the `runat=server` attribute. You can include both server- and client-side `<script>` tags in the same ASP file, but there's a trick. Listing 25.2 shows an example.

LISTING 25.2   Combining Server and Client `<script>` Tags (ch25i2.asp)

```
<%@ Language=VBScript %>
<html>
<head>
```

```
<script language="VBScript" runat="server">
Sub writeShowAlertScript()
   With Response
      .Write "<scr" & "ipt language='JavaScript'>" & vbCrLf
      .Write "function showAlert() {" & vbCrLf
      .Write "alert('Hello from showAlert function!');" _
         & vbCrLf
      .Write "}" & vbCrLf
      .Write "alert('Hello world');" & vbCrLf
      .Write "showAlert();" & vbCrLf
      .Write "</scr" & "ipt>"
   End With
End Sub
</script>
</head>
<body>
The script that shows the alert boxes on the client were written dynam-
ically with ASP.
<% call writeShowAlertScript()%>
</body>
</html>
```

Notice that the server script writes the client script. However, it breaks the
client-side <script> tag itself into separate parts. If you don't do this, the ASP
engine tries to compile the <script> tag meant for the client and generates a
Nested Script Block error. To see this in action, change the first and last lines after
the With Response statement to recombine the word script into a single word:

```
With Response
   .Write "<script language='JavaScript'>" & vbCrLf
   .Write "function showAlert() {" & vbCrLf
   .Write "alert('Hello from showAlert function!');" _
      & vbCrLf
   .Write "}" & vbCrLf
   .Write "alert('Hello world');" & vbCrLf
   .Write "showAlert();" & vbCrLf
   .Write "</script>" & vbCrLf
End With
```

Execute the file by requesting it from the browser. You should see the Nested
Script Block error.

After each line of the client-side script, the server script writes a carriage return/
linefeed character combination (the constant vbCrLf, also called the end-of-line
character, although it's two characters in length—ASCII characters 13 and 10).
End-of-line characters are optional with JavaScript, which uses the semicolon to
delimit the ends of code lines, but they're required for VBScript, which relies on

the end-of-line character to delimit the code lines. I usually write them for both languages because in the browser, the end-of-line character makes the code easier to read for debugging purposes.

You can use script to pass information from the server to the client. One of the most common ASP questions is how a client-side page can gain access to the value of Session and Application variables. You do this by dynamically writing script to the browser. For example, Listing 25.3 shows how to assign the Session .SessionID variable to client-side script.

LISTING 25.3	Transferring Server-Side Variables to Client-Side Scripts (ch25i3.asp)

```
<%@ Language=VBScript %>
<html>
<head>
<script language="VBScript">
    Dim SessionID
    MsgBox "Your SessionID is: <%=Session.SessionID%>", _
    vbOK,"SessionID"
</script>
</head>
<body>
How to transfer ASP variable values to a client script.
</body>
</html>
```

On the server, the ASP engine writes the string value of the code <%=Session .SessionID%> as part of the client-side script, which it sends to the client. The scripting engine running on the browser parses and compiles the script, then displays the message box. VBScript message boxes are more flexible than JavaScript alerts because you can control the number and content of buttons and display a title, whereas JavaScript alerts have no programmable title or button control capabilities. In addition, VBScript's MsgBox function returns which button the user clicked, which can be extremely useful.

You can use client-side script to force the browser to request other pages or to submit forms. For example, the Browser Capabilities component gives you the ability to determine which browser a client is using, and which scripting engine the browser supports, but doesn't provide the screen resolution. You can use a client-side script to obtain and send the screen resolution to your ASP program. Listing 25.4 uses the VBScript Screen object to determine the screen resolution width and height, then directs the browser back to the originating ASP page with the information stored in the QueryString.

LISTING 25.4   **Obtaining the Screen Resolution of the Client Computer (ch225i4.asp)**

```
<%@ Language=VBScript %>
<% option explicit %>
<%
Dim screenWidth
Dim screenHeight
If Request.QueryString("ScreenWidth") = "" Then
    %>
    <script language="VBScript">
        Dim screenWidth
        Dim screenHeight
        screenWidth = Screen.Width
        screenHeight = Screen.Height
        document.location.href = "ch25i4.asp?ScreenWidth=" _
        & screenWidth & "&ScreenHeight=" & screenHeight
    </script>
    <%
Else
    screenWidth = Request.QueryString("ScreenWidth")
    screenHeight = Request.QueryString("ScreenHeight")
    %>
<html>
<head>
</head>
<body>
Your screen resolution is <%=ScreenWidth%> x <%=ScreenHeight%>
</body>
</html>
    <%
End If
%>
```

The script first tests to see if the `Request.QueryString("ScreenWidth")` variable has a value. If not, it writes a client-side script to obtain the screen dimensions. The last line in the script sets the `document.location.href` property. The `document` is the current browser document. The `location` is a collection of properties containing information about the browser's location. The `href` property, like the equivalent HTML `href` attribute for `<a>` anchor tags, directs the browser to request a page. For example:

```
document.location.href = "ch25i4.asp?ScreenWidth=" _
& screenWidth & "&ScreenHeight=" & screenHeight
```

The rest of the line concatenates the page request with the screen width and height that the script obtained from the Screen object to create a URL. After concatenation, the URL looks like this:

```
ch25i4.asp?ScreenWidth=800&ScreenHeight=600
```

When the browser submits the request to the server, the ASP engine fills the QueryString collection with the parameters appended to the URL—in this case, the ScreenWidth=800 and ScreenHeight=600 parameters. Because the variables now have a value, the Else portion of the ASP script executes, displaying the resolution in the browser window.

At this point, it should become obvious to you that there's another object model you need to learn if you want to work effectively with the objects exposed by the browser. The W3C Document Object Model (DOM) specification describes how browsers should expose the objects they contain. While no current browser completely meets the W3C DOM specifications, IE is far closer than Netscape and other browsers. IE's implementation of the DOM, and most recently its ability to use XML, have made it the most popular browser for development. I'll show you more about the DOM throughout this chapter.

You should begin thinking of all HTML as describing objects that have properties and methods rather than as tags with attributes, because the DOM describes all HTML tags as objects. For example, a <p> paragraph tag has properties describing its position, width, and height. It has border and background properties, and contains both HTML (all the markup between the <p> and </p> tags) and text (all the text between the <p> and </p> tags not inside angle brackets).

The Document Object Model

The Document Object Model (DOM) contains two central rules: all the tags in an HTML document must be accessible as objects and it must be possible to retrieve the HTML source from which those objects originate. As you can see, that means you should be able to use the DOM to obtain a reference to any object on an HTML page, change its properties, and call its methods (assuming it has any). You should also be able to delete DOM objects and create new DOM objects, thus dynamically changing the collection of objects on the page. These capabilities are at the heart of Dynamic HTML (DHTML). If you can change the properties of objects on the page, delete objects, and add new objects, then you can change the look and action of the page dynamically, with script.

As the browser HTML-parsing engine reads the incoming page, it creates objects and collections of objects. The top-level objects in this model are the navigator object (browser), the window object, the `frames` collection, and the document object. A window contains a document. Even if the browser hasn't fulfilled an HTML request, the window still contains a document—albeit one with no contents. A window may contain several child windows, each of which corresponds to a frame. The window object bundles the child windows together in a `frames` collection. Each frame is itself a window, with its own `frames` collection and its own document.

In this chapter, you'll work primarily with the document object, which contains the HTML on the page. You may remember from Chapter 4, *HTML Basics*, that some tags are `block` elements, which can contain other tags. For example, a `<div>` tag may contain font, paragraph, and other formatting tags, as well as other `<div>` tags. These tags contained inside a `<block>` tag translate to collections in object parlance. Therefore, `block` elements all have an `all` property and a `children` property. The difference is that `all` refers to all contained tags, even tags where the end tag overlaps the containing tag's end tag. For example:

```
<p><b>This is bold text</p></b>
```

The `all` collection would include the first `<b>` tag. The `children` collection contains only tags entirely contained between the start and end tag of the `block` element. The `children` collection, in the preceding example, would not contain the `<b>` tag because it's an overlapped tag (and bad HTML practice, I should add).

Each tag has attributes, which translate to properties, although not always directly. For example the `<p align="center">` tag has one attribute. The difference between the attributes of an HTML element and the properties of a DOM object are that the DOM object always has all its properties, even if they aren't explicitly set. Attributes that set visible characteristics, such as `align`, `color`, `size`, `visibility`, etc. are subsumed under the `style` property for each object. The `style` property itself is a character string containing the `style` attribute. An example that translates directly is the `bgcolor` attribute of a `<body>` tag. The body DOM object has a `bgColor` property whose value is the same type of value—a hex color string or named color—as the `<body>` tag itself.

As you work with the DOM, you'll begin to memorize the properties and capabilities of each object. Because they're generally similar, you'll find that your HTML experience translates easily into the DOM objects and properties.

Accessing the DOM from Script

To manipulate the DOM, you need to be able to reference the various element types. Because there may be many tags of the same type on a page, you need a way to identify the specific tag you want to reference. You can reference a tag by name, which is a translation from the name attribute in HTML 3.2, or you can reference it by ID. All DOM objects have an ID. You can create a specific ID by writing it into the HTML, but if an element doesn't contain an explicit ID, you may not be able to differentiate it from similar elements.

You obtain a reference to the document object automatically when you refer to the document object. For example, the following script changes the background color of the page using the VBScript InputBox function. The InputBox function displays a dialog at a specified location containing a prompt, a title, and a text field, and returns a user's input. The last two arguments to the InputBox function below contain the x and y positions for the upper-left corner of the dialog. Notice that you specify the location in *twips* (a twip equals 1/1440 in.), not pixels. The script assigns the user's input to the document.bgColor property. In this example, the default value for the InputBox is the current background color of the document. Listing 25.5 contains the code.

LISTING 25.5   Using the document Object (ch25i5.asp)

```
<%@ Language=VBScript %>
<html>
<head>
</head>
<body bgcolor="lightblue">
</body>
</html>
<script language="VBScript">
    dim s
    s = Inputbox("Enter the background color for the " & _
        "document.","Background Color", _
        document.bgColor,3000,2000)
    document.bgColor = s
</script>
```

When you run this script you may enter either a hex-formatted color number, like #ffffff, or a named color, such as red. You'll see the background color of the document change instantly.

NOTE   It's important to understand that changes you make to the document's contents with script are not reflected in the background HTML for the document.

After changing the background color, if you right-click and select View Source from the context menu, you won't see the color value you entered in the <body> tag of the HTML, you'll see the original color value.

You can obtain references to child elements of the document using the docu-
ment.all("ID/name") or you can omit the parentheses and quotes and use
document.all.ID, where ID is the value of the ID attribute for the element you
want to reference. For example, Listing 25.6 shows how to change the text of a
paragraph.

LISTING 25.6   Changing Paragraph Contents with Script (ch25i6.asp)

```
<%@ Language=VBScript %>
<html>
<head>
</head>
<body bgcolor="lightblue">
<p id="p1">This is a paragraph tag.</p>
</body>
</html>
<script language="VBScript">
   Dim el
   Set el = document.all("p1")
   el.innertext = "The text of this paragraph was " & _
      "changed via script"
</script>
```

The paragraph tag has an ID of p1. The code inside the <script> tag sets a reference to the paragraph element using the following code:

```
Set el = document.all("p1")
```

Now, the el variable refers to the paragraph. Next it changes the innerText
property of the paragraph. When the property changes, IE instantly updates the
text on-screen so it reflects the new property value. Until IE 4, such client-side
content changes were limited to the contents of input controls, but with DHTML,
you can control the content and appearance of every element on the screen.

You can scroll the text across the screen by using absolute positioning. For
example, Listing 25.7 extends the previous script by changing the left position
attribute of the paragraph element's style property. To control the speed, the script
uses a window method called setTimeOut. The setTimeout method accepts three
arguments: the name of a function or subroutine, a time interval specified in milliseconds (one-thousandths of a second), and an optional language argument. You
can use the language argument to call a JScript function from a window.SetTime-
out method called from VBScript, or vice versa. When the specified interval has
elapsed, the scripting engine calls the routine specified in the first argument.

LISTING 25.7   **Moving Objects On-Screen (ch25i7.asp)**

```
<%@ Language=VBScript %>
<html>
<head>
</head>
<body bgcolor="lightblue">
<p id="p1" style="position: absolute; left: 640">This text will move
from right to left across the screen.</p>
</body>
</html>
<script language="VBScript">
Call window.setTimeout("moveText()", 50)
Function moveText()
    Dim pos
    Set el = document.All("p1")
    pos = el.Style.Left
    If Right(pos, 2) = "px" Then
        pos = Left(pos, Len(pos) - 2)
    End If
    el.Style.Left = pos - 10
    If CLng(pos) >= -300 Then
        Call window.setTimeout("moveText()", 50)
    End If
End Function
</script>
```

A proposed W3C specification called HTML+TIME, and an existing specification called SMIL, both address the problems of coordinating multiple simultaneous actions for on-screen elements. For example, if you wanted to coordinate the movement of a cartoon character's mouth with an audio clip, and at the same time coordinate the wind moving through computer-generated trees, you would have a difficult time doing it with timed scripts. Both the SMIL and HTML+TIME specifications provide a syntax to perform complex positioning and coordination actions.

If all you could do with client-side script were to change colors and text in the browser, it wouldn't be a subject for this book, but client-side script can do much more than that from an application perspective. You can use script to pre-validate user input, thus saving a round trip to the server; and you can use script to move server-side processing to the client, effectively partitioning your application. I'll show you how to validate user input and process data on the client in this chapter; and you'll see an example of partitioning in Chapter 30, *Using XML/XSL with ASP*.

Client-Side Form Validation

One of the most useful tasks for client-side script is form validation. When a person fills out a form on the browser, there's little point in submitting all the information over the network if the data is incomplete or invalid. You can save server and network resources by validating the data on the client before sending the form data to the server for processing.

You use the DOM to gain script access to the contents of form input controls using the same syntax as for HTML elements. For example:

```
set myVar = document.all("controlName")
```

Suppose a user must enter a date. You provide an input text control and some directions, but you can't rely on the user to enter either a properly formatted date, a valid date, or for that matter, any date at all before submitting the form. Therefore, you need to check the data. You've already seen how to validate data on the server, but you can save the round trip, improve your user interface, and make your users happier all at the same time by validating the data on the client. Listing 25.8 illustrates this example.

LISTING 25.8	Client-Side Validation Example (ch25i8.asp)

```
<%@ Language=VBScript %>
<%
If request.Form("txtDate") <> "" Then
    response.write "You entered the valid date " & request.Form("txt-
Date") & "."
    response.end
End If
%>

<html>
<head>
<script language="VBScript">
    Dim errMsg
    Dim submitVal
    Function frmDate_onSubmit()
        frmDate_onSubmit = doSubmit()
    End Function
    Function setErrorMsg(s)
        errMsg = s
        Call window.setTimeout("showErrorMsg", 100)
    End Function
```

```
Function clearErrorMsg()
    errMsg = ""
    document.All("errMsg").innerText = _
    "Please re-enter the date in the form 'mm/dd/yyyy'."
End Function
Function showErrorMsg()
    document.All("errMsg").innerText = errMsg
    Call window.setTimeout("clearErrorMsg", 2000)
End Function
Function doSubmit()
    Dim dateVal
    Dim aDate
    Dim el
    Dim parts
    dateVal = document.All("txtDate").Value
    On Error Resume Next
    aDate = CDate(dateVal)
    If Err.Number <> 0 Then
        Call setErrorMsg(Err.Description)
        Call setErrorMsg("That doesn't appear to be " & _
        "a valid date.")
        doSubmit = False
        Exit Function
    ElseIf InStr(1, dateVal, "/", vbBinaryCompare) = 0 Then
        Call setErrorMsg("You entered a date in the " & _
        "incorrect format. Use the format 'mm/dd/yyyy'.")
        doSubmit = False
        Exit Function
    End If
    parts = Split(dateVal, "/")
    If UBound(parts) < 2 Then
        Call setErrorMessage("You must enter a month, a " & _
        "day, and a year.")
        doSubmit = False
        Exit Function
    ElseIf (CLng(parts(0)) <> CLng(Month(dateVal))) _
        Or CLng(parts(1)) <> CLng(Day(dateVal)) _
        Or CLng(parts(2)) <> CLng(Year(dateVal)) Then
        Call setErrorMsg("You entered an invalid date. " & _
        "Use the format 'mm/dd/yyyy'.")
        doSubmit = False
        Exit Function
    End If
    document.frmDate.submit
```

```
                doSubmit = True
        End Function
</script>
</head>
<body>
<form name="frmDate" method="post">
<div id="errMsg" style="color: red"></div><br>
Enter a date in the form "mm/dd/yyyy" <input id="txtDate" type="text"
name="txtDate" maxLength="10"></input> 
<input type="button" value="Submit" onClick="doSubmit()">
</form>
</body>
</html>
```

The data validation code aside, the script contains a few interesting points I haven't discussed yet. First, there are three ways to trap events in IE. The first way is to place the name of a script routine inside a tag as the value of an attribute whose name is the name of the event. For example:

```
<input type="button" name="btnSave" value="Save"
onClick="doClick()">
```

When the named event occurs—following the example, when the user clicks the Save button—IE calls the named routine.

The second method works like Visual Basic event procedures. You write a procedure named using the syntax controlName_eventName. For example:

```
<script language="VBScript">
Sub btnSave_onClick()
    ' code for event
End Sub
</script>
```

Using this method, IE automatically executes the routine when the user clicks the button.

The third method also works automatically. You provide the scripting language, the name of the object, and the event for which you want to write code. For example:

```
<script language="VBScript" for="btnSave" event="onclick">
    ' your code here
</script>
```

The first and third methods are generic because they work with any scripting language. All methods for executing a script when an event occurs are called binding script to events, or (usually) just binding events. In this page, to validate the input before the browser sends the data, you need to bind two events—the form submission event and the button click event.

You may notice that the script has two routines that deal with form submission—the automatically bound script frmDate_onSubmit and the doSubmit function called by the button, which validates the date. Interestingly, the frmDate_onSubmit also calls the doSubmit function. When I wrote this script, I originally bound just the button click event, reasoning that I would then submit the form through code. That worked fine as long as the user clicked the button. But if the user pressed Enter on the keyboard, the doSubmit event never fired—but the form still submitted its data to the server! It turns out that in IE, a form with a single input control submits automatically if you press the Enter key on the keyboard. The only solution to this feature is to bind the onSubmit event. Since the button and automatic form submission using the Enter key both call the doSubmit function, you can intercept the form submission, validate the data, and either submit the form or cancel submission and display an error message.

The only reason you can bind form submission at all is that form submission is a function; therefore the form object expects a return value. By returning the value False you can prevent the form from submitting. If you omit the return value or return any other value, the form submits normally.

Using ActiveX Controls

Sometimes, even with DHTML, the capabilities available through HTML and a browser just aren't enough. For example, suppose you want to use a slider control to let a user control audio volume. You could create your own slider using lines or images and a great deal of code, but in doing so you would have recreated functionality that's already available on every Windows computer in the form of ActiveX controls. Recognizing this problem, Microsoft did two things to IE that made it the premier browser for development. First, IE is an ActiveX host. That means you can *site* (place) ActiveX controls within the browser and control them via script. Second, Microsoft made IE itself an ActiveX control. That means you can site IE within a window and instantly gain access to a custom browser for your own programs. In this section, you'll see how to use ActiveX controls inside IE.

WARNING   The examples in this section work only in Internet Explorer!

You've already seen how to instantiate ActiveX components on the server. The client-side analogues of ActiveX components are ActiveX objects or ActiveX controls. All three—ActiveX components, objects, and controls—are COM objects.

The only difference is that ActiveX controls are usually visible so people can interact with them directly, whereas components and objects are usually invisible. To instantiate ActiveX controls within the browser, you use an <object> syntax that's similar to the syntax you've already used to create Application- and Session-scope components in the global.asa file. For example:

```
<object
    classid="clsid:25bdf09d-ec8b-11cf-bd97-00aa00575603"
    codebase="/Controls/MyContrl.cab#version=1,0,0,0"
    id=myControl left: 40px; top: 10px; width: 385px;
    height: 42px; >
    <param name="property1">
    <param name="property1">
    <param name="property1">
</object>
```

The <object> tag tells the browser to:

1. Look up the classid in the registry.

2. Find the registry child key called InProcServer32, which contains the name of the OCX or DLL file that contains the code for the control.

3. If the control is not registered on the local computer, or if the version installed on the local computer is lower than the version specified in the optional code-base attribute, the browser can download and install the control from the URL specified in the codebase attribute.

4. The browser instantiates the control, sites it, resizes it, and finally displays the control.

5. The browser doesn't use the optional <param> tags—the control itself obtains the property values specified in the <param> tags and uses them to initialize its own properties.

The advantages of using ActiveX controls are:

- You gain instant access to a wide range of pre-built and tested code.

- You can perform tasks with ActiveX controls that are difficult or impossible through any other technology.

The disadvantages are:

- Only IE browsers can use ActiveX technology natively. Netscape users can obtain a third-party plug-in that extends Netscape so it can use ActiveX controls, with mixed results.

- ActiveX controls and objects have full access to the local machine, therefore they are a security risk. To help alleviate this problem, Microsoft introduced code signing, which lets you know the code producer. Code signing uses a third-party to provide a code authentication certificate stating that the code actually comes from the code producer. When the browser downloads an unknown ActiveX control, the browser warns you that the page is trying to download new code. If the code is signed, you can follow a URL to the authentication site to read about and verify the code. You can then choose to continue or to ignore the download.

Sending ActiveX Objects to the Client

To instantiate an ActiveX control on the client, you simply include the `<object>` tag in the response. For example, the following ASP script creates a client-side slider control:

```
<%@ Language=VBScript %>
<html>
<head>
</head>
<body bgColor=#c0c0c0>
<object align=right
   classid="clsid:373FF7F0-EB8B-11CD-8820-08002B2F4F5A"
   height=42 id=Slider style="COLOR: #c1c1cd;
   height: 42px; left: 40px; top: 10px; width: 385px;
   position: absolute;"
   width=385 valign="top">
   <param name="Enabled" value="1">
   <param name="Orientation" value="0">
   <param name="LargeChange" value="10">
   <param name="SmallChange" value="1">
   <param name="Min" value="0">
   <param name="Max" value="100">
   <param name="TickStyle" value="0">
   <param name="TickFrequency" value="10">
   <param name="Value" value="50">
</object>
</body>
</html>
```

The browser uses the `classid` attribute of the `<object>` tag to find and instantiate the slider object (part of the Windows Common Controls contained in the `mscomctl.ocx` file) on the client. You should note that the previous example does not include the optional `codebase` attribute. Because the browser won't know where to obtain the control, if it's not already registered on the client, the browser won't be able to create the control and errors will occur.

Accessing ActiveX Objects from Client-Side VBScript

Sending ActiveX controls to the browser would be of little use if you couldn't access their properties and respond to their events, but you can bind script to ActiveX control events in the same way you bind code to HTML elements. For example, Listing 25.9 instantiates the same slider control as the preceding example, but then binds two events to display the value of the control on-screen using DHTML.

LISTING 25.9 **Communicating with Client-Side ActiveX Controls** (ch25i9.asp)

```
<%@ Language=VBScript %>
<html>
<head>
</head>
<body bgColor=#c0c0c0>
<div id="sliderValue" style="position: absolute; top:
    10; left: 10"></div>
<object align=right
    classid="clsid:373FF7F0-EB8B-11CD-8820-08002B2F4F5A"
    height=42 id=Slider style="COLOR: #c1c1cd;
    height: 42px; left: 40px; top: 10px; width: 385px;
    position: absolute;"
    width=385 valign="top">
    <param name="Enabled" value="1">
    <param name="Orientation" value="0">
    <param name="LargeChange" value="10">
    <param name="SmallChange" value="1">
    <param name="Min" value="0">
    <param name="Max" value="100">
    <param name="TickStyle" value="0">
    <param name="TickFrequency" value="10">
    <param name="Value" value="50">
</object>
<SCRIPT LANGUAGE=VBScript>
<!-
    dim slider
    sub document_onReadyStateChange()
        if document.readyState = "complete" then
            set slider = document.all("slider")
            document.all("sliderValue").innerText = slider.value
        end if
    end sub
    sub slider_Change()
        document.all("sliderValue").innerText = slider.Value
    end sub
```

```
        sub slider_Scroll()
            document.all("sliderValue").innerText = slider.Value
        end sub
//-->
</script>
</body>
</html>
```

The script creates a global `slider` variable. The salient points in this script are that it binds to the document object and uses the `onReadyStateChange` event to test whether the document is complete. When the document is complete, the `onReadyStateChange` event code sets a reference to the slider object. The point is that if you try to set the reference without testing whether the document is complete, the slider object may not yet have been instantiated, thus causing an error.

The other two routines in the script are bound to the slider `Change` and `Scroll` events. Both of these scripts do exactly the same thing—they change the contents of a `<div>` tag based on the slider's `Value` property. These changes appear immediately, giving the user instant numeric feedback about the exact position of the slider control.

So far, you've seen how to use the `<object>` tag to create controls from the ASP page, but you can also use client-side VBScript directly to create non-visual ActiveX objects.

NOTE   You can create ActiveX controls as well as ActiveX objects without errors, but you can't site them with client-side VBScript code, so unless you need an invisible control for some reason, it won't do you much good.

For example, Listing 25.10 creates a Dictionary object, stores a few hundred items, then displays the dictionary contents in a `<div>` tag. You do, of course, need to ensure that the Microsoft Scripting Runtime (`scrrun32.dll`) is installed and registered on the client computer before trying to create a Dictionary object.

LISTING 25.10   Creating Client-Side ActiveX Objects with Script (ch25i10.asp)

```
<%@ Language=VBScript %>
<html>
<head>
</head>
<body>
<script language="VBScript">
    Dim d
    Dim i
    Dim V
```

```
Dim aDiv
Dim s
Call window.setTimeout("docComplete", 100)
Sub docComplete()
    Do While document.readyState <> "complete"
        Call window.setTimeout("docComplete", 100)
    Loop
    Call showDictionary
End Sub
Sub showDictionary()
    Set d = Createobject("Scripting.Dictionary")
    For i = 1 To 500
        d.Add "Item" & CStr(i), i
    Next
    Set aDiv = document.All("dictionaryDiv")
    For Each V In d.Keys
        s = s & V & "=" & d(V) & "<br>"
    Next
    Set d = Nothing
    aDiv.innerHTML = s
End Sub
</script>
<div id="dictionaryDiv"></div>
</body>
</html>
```

In this script, because the code references a `<div>` tag that appears *after* the script, you must wait until the document has created the `<div>`. This time, the code uses the `window.setTimeout` method to repeatedly test the document `readyState` property rather than binding a routine to the `onReadyStateChange` event. Which do you think is more efficient?

To end this section, here's a short observation on the relative merits of using the `<object>` tag syntax vs. using the `createObject` function in client-side script. The `<object>` syntax, while awkward and time-consuming, lets you specify the code-base from which the client can download the control if it's not already installed. You can use `createObject` only if you're delivering to clients when you know the ActiveX controls and objects have already been installed and registered on the client workstations.

Accessing ActiveX Objects from Client-Side JScript

You don't have to use VBScript to access ActiveX controls and objects—you can use JScript as well. To reference a client-side ActiveX control loaded with an `<object>` tag, you use an almost identical syntax as you do with VBScript. Listing 25.11 shows the slider control example from the previous section rewritten in JScript.

LISTING 25.11   Communicating with Client-Side ActiveX Controls—
JScript Version (ch25i11.asp)

```
<%@ Language=VBScript %>
<html>
<head>
</head>
<body bgColor=#c0c0c0>
<div id="sliderValue" style="position: absolute; top: 10; left:
10"></div>
<object align=right
    classid="clsid:373FF7F0-EB8B-11CD-8820-08002B2F4F5A"
    height=42 id=Slider style="COLOR: #c1c1cd;
    height: 42px; left: 40px; top: 10px; width: 385px;
    position: absolute;"
    width=385 valign="top">
    <param name="Enabled" value="1">
    <param name="Orientation" value="0">
    <param name="LargeChange" value="10">
    <param name="SmallChange" value="1">
    <param name="Min" value="0">
    <param name="Max" value="100">
    <param name="TickStyle" value="0">
    <param name="TickFrequency" value="10">
    <param name="Value" value="50">
</object>
<script language="JScript" for="document"
    event="onreadystatechange">
    if (document.readyState == "complete")
        document.all("sliderValue").innerText = Slider.value;
</script>
<SCRIPT LANGUAGE=JScript FOR="Slider" defer EVENT="Change">
    document.all("sliderValue").innerText = Slider.value;
</script>
<SCRIPT LANGUAGE=JScript FOR="Slider" defer EVENT="Scroll">
    document.all("sliderValue").innerText = Slider.value;
</script>
</BODY>
</HTML>
```

Other than the scripting language used for the client-side script, there's no functional difference between Listing 25.11 and Listing 25.9—both show the value of the
slider whether you change it by clicking or dragging the thumb.

JScript access to client-side ActiveX objects, like the `Scripting.Dictionary`, is
slightly different. You don't have a `createObject` method as in VBScript; instead,

you use the JScript `ActiveXObject` object to instantiate and create references to COM objects. Listing 25.12 shows the JScript equivalent of Listing 25.10—both create a Dictionary object, add 500 items, then display the key and item values in a `<div>` tag.

LISTING 25.12   Accessing ActiveX Objects with JScript (ch25i12.asp)

```
<%@ Language=VBScript %>
<html>
<head>
</head>
<body>
<script language="JScript">
   var d, i, V, aDiv, s="";
   window.setTimeout("docComplete();",100);
   function docComplete() {
      while (document.readyState != "complete") {
         window.setTimeout("docComplete",100);
      }
      showDictionary();
   }
   function showDictionary() {
      var keys;
      var items;
      d = new ActiveXObject("Scripting.Dictionary");
      for (i=1; i <= 500; i++) {
         d.Add("Item" + i, i);
      }
      aDiv = document.all("dictionaryDiv");
      keys = new VBArray(d.Keys());
      keys = keys.toArray();
      for (i=0; i < keys.length; i++) {
         s = s + keys[i] + "=" + d.item(keys[i]) + "<br>";
      }
      aDiv.innerHTML = s;
      return("");
   }
</script>
<div id="dictionaryDiv"></div>
</body>
</html>
```

I've written this script specifically to show you a few differences. Microsoft has extended its version of JScript to be able to access ActiveX objects—the script will not work in any browser other than IE because the scripting language is IE-specific, even if it does look like JavaScript.

The script creates the variable d to hold the Dictionary reference. In JScript, you create the reference as follows:

```
d = new ActiveXObject("Scripting.Dictionary");
```

You add objects to the Dictionary in a manner similar to VBScript (but don't forget the parentheses—they're required in JScript). For example:

```
d.Add("Item" + i, i);
```

The major difference is how you gain access to the Dictionary's collections. JScript doesn't have a direct way of accessing ActiveX arrays or collections, such as the keys collection. Instead, you must create a VBArray object and assign it to a variable. For example:

```
keys = new VBArray(d.Keys());
```

After you have a reference to the VBArray object, you can convert it into a JScript array using the toArray function. For example:

```
keys = keys.toArray();
```

After conversion, you use the array normally. The remainder of the script concatenates a string (the variable s) and sets the innerHTML property of the <div> to the contents of the string variable, thus displaying all the keys and values contained in the Dictionary object.

Client-Side Data Access

You can use client-side script to handle data processing, thus effectively partitioning your application. The simplest solution is to use the Remote Data Service (RDS) Data Control, because it's almost exactly like a Connection object; it can use a Data Source Name (DSN) or a connection string as the connection source. Using the control is straightforward; you embed it into the response with an <object> tag. For example:

```
<OBJECT CLASSID="clsid:BD96C556-65A3-11D0-983A-00C04FC29E33"
   ID="RDSDC1">
   <PARAM NAME="SQL"
     VALUE="{an SQL Statement"}>
   <PARAM NAME="CONNECT"
     VALUE="{your connectionstring}">
   <PARAM NAME="SERVER" VALUE=http://{yourServer}/>
</OBJECT>
```

NOTE	Replace the values between braces in the preceding example with the appropriate SQL statement, connection string, and server name for your needs.

The `<param>` tags set the initial properties of the control and include a SQL statement, a connection string, and the name of the `http` server that can supply the data. When the browser creates the object, it contacts the server, which automatically creates an instance of the `RDS.DataFactory` object. The `RDS.DataFactory` object retrieves the data and proxies the resulting record set over `http` (which means it transfers the data to the client). The mechanism by which this happens is beyond the scope of this book, but for those of you who are interested, there are several excellent documents at the MSDN site that explain the process. Search for the phrase `RDS.DataFactory` to find the documents.

The next two listings reference the `(local)` database server, which is SQL Server's default name for a database running locally, and the `http://localhost/` domain, which is the Web server's default local name. These may work for you if you're running a Web server and SQL Server on the same machine; otherwise, you should substitute your server and Web domain name when you run the code. Listing 25.13 contains a complete RDS Data Control example.

LISTING 25.13   **Client-Side Data Access with the RDS Data Control (ch25i13.asp)**

```
<%@ Language=VBScript %>
<html>
<head>
<title>Retrieving Data With the RDS.DataFactory Object</title>
</head>
<body>
<div id="students"></div>
<object classid="clsid:bd96c556-65a3-11d0-983a-00c04fc29e33"
    id="RDSDC1">
    <param name="SQL" VALUE="SELECT StudentID, Grade,
        LastName, FirstName FROM Students ORDER BY Grade, LastName">
    <param name="CONNECT" value="Provider=SQLOLEDB.1;
        Persist Security Info=False;User ID=sa;
        Initial Catalog=ClassRecords;Data Source=(local)">
    <param name="SERVER" value=http://localhost/>
</object>
<script language="VBScript" for="RDSDC1"
    event="onDataSetComplete">
    Dim s
    Dim R
    Dim F
```

```
                Set R = RDSDC1.Recordset
                s = "<h2 align='center'>Students List</h2>"
                s = s & "<table border='1' align='center' width='100%'>"
                s = s & "<tr>"
                For Each F In R.fields
                    s = s & "<td><b>" & F.Name & "</b></td>"
                Next
                s = s & "</tr>"
                While Not R.EOF
                    s = s & "<tr>"
                    For Each F In R.fields
                        s = s & "<td>" & F.Value & "</td>"
                    Next
                    s = s & "</tr>"
                    R.movenext
                Wend
                s = s & "</table>"
                R.Close
                document.All("students").innerHTML = s
            </script>
        </body>
    </html>
```

If you found this example exciting (and I do), then you should be even more
excited by the fact that you can bind some DOM objects to the RDS Data Control.
For example, you can bind a table by using a `datasrc` attribute in the `<table>` tag
or by setting the property from script. You can then bind the table columns by setting a `datafld` attribute in the `<td>` tags (or by setting the property from script).
Listing 25.14 shows an example.

LISTING 25.14	Data-Binding Example (ch25i14.asp)

```
<%@ Language=VBScript %>
<html>
<head>
<title>Binding Data With the RDS.DataFactory Object</title>
</head>
<body>
<table id=Students DataSrc=#RDSDC1 width=100% border=1>
<thead align=left>
    <tr>
        <th>StudentID</th>
        <th>Grade</th>
        <th>Last Name</th>
        <th>First Name</th>
```

```
        </tr>
      </thead>
        <tr>
            <td><div datafld=StudentID></div></td>
            <td><div datafld=Grade></div></td>
            <td><div datafld=LastName></div></td>
            <td><div datafld=FirstName></div></td>
        </tr>
      </table>
<object classid="clsid:BD96C556-65A3-11D0-983A-00C04FC29E33"
    id="RDSDC1">
    <param name="SQL" value="select studentid, grade, lastname,
        firstname from students order by grade, lastname">
    <param name="CONNECT" value="provider=sqloledb.1;
        persist security info=false;user id=sa;
        initial catalog=classrecords;data source=(local)">
    <param name="SERVER" value=http://localhost/
        style="display: none">
</object>
</body>
</html>
```

By binding the table to the RDS Data Control object, you can automatically fill the table with the data. If you want to display one record at a time, you can place the Recordset object exposed by the RDS Data Control under script control and place buttons on the page connected to scripts that use the Move methods of the Recordset object. As the Recordset object moves from one record to another, the values of bound controls will update automatically.

There are some security risks associated with using the RDS Data Control with the server-side RDS.DataFactory. Because the client control must connect to a database, you expose the connection string, username, and password to the client machine. That can make the control unsuitable for use in secure applications because anyone can view the page source in the browser and acquire the username and password. You can improve the security somewhat by using a custom server-side business or data-access object—or an ASP page. The RDS Data Control sends an http request and the RDS.Data connects to the specified object or page to obtain data rather than connecting directly to a database. That way you can limit the functionality of the connection rather than allowing the client free access to the database. Of course, you can also limit the actions a client can take via the database's internal security.

Table 25.1 shows the elements you can bind to data.

TABLE 25.1: Data-Bindable HTML Elements

Element	Updatable	Renders HTML	Bound Property
a	False	False	href
applet	True	False	property value via PARAM
button	False	True	innerText, innerHTML
div	False	True	innerText, innerHTML
frame	False	False	src
iframe	False	False	src
img	False	False	src
input type=checkbox	True	False	checked
input type=hidden	True	False	value
input type=label	True	False	value
input type=password	True	False	value
input type=radio	True	False	checked
input type=text	True	False	value
label	False	True	innerText, innerHTML
marquee	False	True	innerText, innerHTML
select	True	False	obj.options (obj.selectedIndex).text
span	False	True	innerText, innerHTML
textarea	True	False	value

Sending Java Applets to the Client

Java applets—from the client-side scripting viewpoint—are much like ActiveX controls. Both are executable code and both are downloadable. You embed a reference to the code into an HTML response. ActiveX controls use the `<object>` syntax that you've already seen. Java applets use the `<applet>` syntax that you'll see in this chapter. Both tags have similar syntax. The big differences between the two happen invisibly. Internally, Java applets differ from ActiveX controls in several ways:

- Java applets are language-specific and operating-system neutral—they're written in the Java programming language and run on numerous operating systems, including Unix, Linux, Mac, and Windows systems. ActiveX controls are operating-system specific (for now) and language neutral. They run on Windows, but can be created with C, C++, VB, Delphi, and Java (J++).

- Java applets are relatively safe to download and run. They run in a sandbox, which means they have limited access to the local machine. ActiveX controls have complete access to the local machine, which is both good from a functional point of view, and bad from a security standpoint.

- Java applets require a virtual machine that translates the Java byte code to executable machine instructions as the program runs. ActiveX controls consist of (more or less) standalone code, although you usually need several supporting DLLs to run ActiveX controls created in any one language.

So why would you use one over the other? There isn't any hard-and-fast reason. ActiveX controls are usually faster than Java applets, primarily because they exist in executable form, while applets must be interpreted via the virtual machine. After you've downloaded an ActiveX control once, the control remains on your computer, ready to run almost instantly thereafter. Even after you've downloaded an applet, the virtual machine must load and translate the byte code each time the applet executes, which increases the startup time and is a major contributor to the difference in speed between applets and ActiveX controls.

If you're worried about security, Java applets can help solve your problems. Because they're unable to access most local machine resources, there are very few malicious applets; it's difficult to damage the computer if you can't write data to the disk or alter system files. In contrast, any novice can write an ActiveX control to reformat your hard drive or corrupt your registry files.

Using Java Applets

To download a Java applet to a browser, use an `<applet>` tag. Like the `<object>` tag, the `<applet>` tag specifies an embedded program that may or may not have a visual interface. If it does have a visible interface, the applet will commandeer part of the browser client window for its own display. You can include `width`, `height`, and `alignment` parameters to specify the physical screen space the applet requires.

The `<applet>` tag requires a `code` parameter specifying a Java `class` file. The optional `codebase` parameter specifies a URL from which the browser can obtain the code if it's not already resident on the client computer. For example:

```
<applet code="someApplet.class" codebase= _
    "http://mySite.com/applets/someApplet/"
width="400" height="300" align="bottom"></applet>
```

Like the `<object>` tag, applets can read initialization values from `<param>` tags included within the `<applet>` tag. For example, to initialize user-specific colors for an applet that accepts color names, you might write:

```
<applet code="someApplet.class" codebase="http://mySite.com/
applets/someApplet/"
width="400" height="300" align="bottom">
<param name=backgroundcolor value="blue"></param>
<param name="textcolor" value="white"></param>
</applet>
```

Both the code and codebase parameters accept either absolute or relative URLs. For example, Microsoft includes a sample applet called CoolHeadLines with IIS and the example ExAir site. I've included the applet's class file on the CD. The CoolHeadLines applet displays a list of headlines by scrolling them up the screen at a specified time interval. Listing 25.15 shows an HTML page that loads the applet with data.

WARNING   The code in Listing 25.15 and 25.16 was adapted from the Microsoft Internet Information Server 4.0 online sample ExAir installed with IIS. If you don't have the ExAir sample application, you will receive an error when you click on the scrolling items in the CoolHeadLines applet, but you will still be able to see the headlines scroll.

LISTING 25.15   Sample ExAir CoolHeadLines Applet (ch25i15.asp)

```
<html>
<head>
<title>CoolHeadLines</title>
</head>
<body>
<table border=1>
<tr><td>
<applet code="CoolHeadLines.class"
name="CoolHeadLines"
codeBase="applets"
width=170
height=76>
<PARAM NAME="BackColor" VALUE="255 255 255">
<PARAM NAME="TextColor" VALUE="0 0 0">
<PARAM NAME="HiliteTextColor" VALUE="60 179 113">
<PARAM NAME="ScrollDelay" VALUE="2">
<PARAM NAME="MessageDelay" VALUE="4">
<PARAM NAME="URLPrefix" VALUE="http://localhost/iissamples/exair">
<PARAM NAME="Text0" VALUE="EA Named Airline of the Year">
<PARAM NAME="URL0" VALUE="pr/970129a.asp">
<PARAM NAME="Text1" VALUE="We Match Blue Yonder!!!">
<PARAM NAME="URL1" VALUE="pr/970122a.asp">
<PARAM NAME="Text2" VALUE="Great Deals for the Holidays">
<PARAM NAME="URL2" VALUE="pr/961212a.asp">
<PARAM NAME="Text3" VALUE="Free Flights to Eugene">
<PARAM NAME="URL3" VALUE="pr/970312a.asp">
<PARAM NAME="Text4" VALUE="EA Donates $2 Million">
<PARAM NAME="URL4" VALUE="pr/970212a.asp">
<PARAM NAME="Text5" VALUE="New Domestic Routes">
```

```
<PARAM NAME="URL5" VALUE="pr/970222a.asp">
<PARAM NAME="Text6" VALUE="Free Flights to Chicago">
<PARAM NAME="URL6" VALUE="pr/970301a.asp">
<PARAM NAME="NumItems" VALUE="7">
</applet>
</td></tr>
</table>
</body>
</html>
```

Accessing Java Applets from Script

You might think that Java applets must be controlled programmatically from JavaScript, but that's not true. When you load a Java applet into IE, Microsoft wraps a COM interface around the applet. The public methods and properties of the applet are then available to VBScript or any other Scripting Host-compatible scripting language. For example, the CoolHeadLines applet exposes a MessageDelay property. In Listing 25.15, the property was initialized (via a <param> tag) to 4. The script in Listing 25.16 resizes the applet using a timer, creating an accordion effect.

LISTING 25.16   Controlling Applets from VBScript (ch26i16.asp)

```
<%@ Language=VBScript %>
<html>
<head>
</head>
<body>
<table border=1>
<tr><td>
<applet code="CoolHeadLines.class"
name="CoolHeadLines"
codeBase="applets"
width=170
height=76>
<PARAM NAME="BackColor" VALUE="255 255 255">
<PARAM NAME="TextColor" VALUE="0 0 0">
<PARAM NAME="HiliteTextColor" VALUE="60 179 113">
<PARAM NAME="ScrollDelay" VALUE="0">
<PARAM NAME="MessageDelay" VALUE="1">
<PARAM NAME="URLPrefix" VALUE="http://localhost/iissamples/exair">
<PARAM NAME="Text0" VALUE="EA Named Airline of the Year">
<PARAM NAME="URL0" VALUE="pr/970129a.asp">
<PARAM NAME="Text1" VALUE="We Match Blue Yonder!!!">
<PARAM NAME="URL1" VALUE="pr/970122a.asp">
<PARAM NAME="Text2" VALUE="Great Deals for the Holidays">
```

```
<PARAM NAME="URL2" VALUE="pr/961212a.asp">
<PARAM NAME="Text3" VALUE="Free Flights to Eugene">
<PARAM NAME="URL3" VALUE="pr/970312a.asp">
<PARAM NAME="Text4" VALUE="EA Donates $2 Million">
<PARAM NAME="URL4" VALUE="pr/970212a.asp">
<PARAM NAME="Text5" VALUE="New Domestic Routes">
<PARAM NAME="URL5" VALUE="pr/970222a.asp">
<PARAM NAME="Text6" VALUE="Free Flights to Chicago">
<PARAM NAME="URL6" VALUE="pr/970301a.asp">
<PARAM NAME="NumItems" VALUE="7">
</applet>
</td></tr>
</table>
<script language="VBScript">
    Dim direction
    direction = 0
    Call window.setTimeout("accordion", 1000)
    Sub accordion()
        Call window.setTimeout("accordion", 1000)
        Dim applet
        Set applet = document.All.Coolheadlines
        If Not direction Then
            applet.Width = applet.Width + 50
        Else
            applet.Width = applet.Width - 50
        End If
        direction = Not direction
    End Sub
</script></body>
</html>
```

You can see from the code that you access applets just as you would any other
COM object. You've seen how to leverage your scripting language knowledge by
partitioning your application—putting some of the logic on the client. As you
grow your DHTML knowledge and improve your client-side scripting abilities,
you'll begin to appreciate the power of a browser-based application model.

There are more opportunities to leverage your knowledge. In the next chapter,
you'll see how to build your own COM components using Visual Basic.

```
        <PARAM NAME="URL2"  VALUE="pr/961212a.asp">
        <PARAM NAME="Text3" VALUE="Free Flights to Eugene">
        <PARAM NAME="URL3"  VALUE="pr/970112a.asp">
        <PARAM NAME="Text4" VALUE="EA Donates $2 Million">
        <PARAM NAME="URL4"  VALUE="pr/970212a.asp">
        <PARAM NAME="Text5" VALUE="New Domestic Routes">
        <PARAM NAME="URL5"  VALUE="pr/970222a.asp">
        <PARAM NAME="Text6" VALUE="Free Flights to Chicago">
        <PARAM NAME="URL6"  VALUE="pr/970301a.asp">
        <PARAM NAME="NumItems" VALUE="7">
      </applet>
    </td></tr>
  </table>
  <script language=VBScript>
    Dim direction
    direction = 0
    Call window.setTimeout("accordion", 10000)
    Sub accordion()
      Call window.setTimeout("accordion", 10000)
      Dim applet
      Set applet = document.All().CoolHeadlines
      If Not direction Then
        applet.Width = applet.Width + 50
      Else
        applet.Width = applet.Width - 50
      End If
      direction = Not direction
    End Sub
  </script></body>
</html>
```

You can see from the code that you access applets just as you would any other COM object. You've seen how to leverage your scripting language knowledge by partitioning your application—putting some of the logic on the client. As you grow your DHTML knowledge and improve your client-side scripting abilities, you'll begin to appreciate the power of a browser-based application model.

There are more opportunities to leverage your knowledge. In the next chapter, you'll see how to build your own COM components using Visual Basic.

CHAPTER

TWENTY-SIX

Build Your Own Components

- ■ Interacting with ASP Objects

- ■ Referencing ASP Objects

- ■ Variants vs. Typed Variables

- ■ Communication between ASP Pages and Components

- ■ Build the `HTMLCalendar` Component

In this chapter, you'll see how to build a server-side ActiveX component called `HTMLCalendar`. You'll code and compile the component into a DLL, then use it on a Web page. You will gain some insight into the process by reading the chapter and using the compiled version of the component on the CD, but for the full benefit, you need to create and run the component yourself. Therefore, you'll need Visual Basic version 6 (or version 5 with the latest service pack).

Interacting with ASP Objects

You can write standalone components that interact with different languages and environments. For example, you can use the Dictionary object from ASP, VB, C, C++, Delphi, FoxPro, Access, Office, or any other language, program, or environment that supports COM components. The reason the Dictionary object is so accessible is that it doesn't offer any special functionality. For example, it doesn't write HTML, doesn't return pointers to functions, doesn't access databases or use any database objects, and doesn't use the file system.

You can also write components that work very closely with a particular language or environment. The `HTMLCalendar` component belongs to this group. The component interacts with the ASP objects to output HTML and set `Session` values. To use ASP objects within your programs, you need to acquire references to the ASP intrinsic objects.

Referencing ASP Objects

ASP exposes two objects that you can use to obtain references to ASP objects from other COM-aware languages. The first is the ScriptingContext object and the second is the ObjectContext object. The ScriptingContext object is obsolete (although it still works) and you should not use it.

TIP I'm mentioning the ScriptingContext object only because it is still included in the ASP object model. Microsoft recommends you use the ObjectContext object instead.

You can also gain access to ASP objects by passing them to other components as arguments—exactly as you might pass any other object as an argument.

Using the ScriptingContext Object

ASP raises two events for every page, the OnStartPage and OnEndPage events. ASP itself does not trap these events—it won't fire an OnStartPage or OnEndPage event routine in an ASP page (too bad), but you can trap them in an external ActiveX object. To use the ScriptingContext object from VB you must first set a reference to the Microsoft Active Server Pages Object Library, and create the OnStartPage and OnEndPage event routines. Write the OnStartPage routine to accept a ScriptingContext object as its only argument. For example:

```
Sub OnStartPage(SC as ScriptingContext)
    ' your code here
End Sub
```

You use the ScriptingContext object to gain access to the other intrinsic ASP objects. For example:

```
Dim ASPResponse
Sub OnStartPage(SC as ScriptingContext)
    Set ASPResponse = SC.Response
    ASPResponse.Write "Hello from VB"
End Sub
```

As usual, if you create a variable that references an object, you should set it to Nothing when you no longer need the object reference. That's the purpose of the OnEndPage event:

```
Sub OnEndPage()
    Set ASPResponse = Nothing
End Sub
```

Despite the ease with which you can implement this method, you should no longer use it. When your ASP pages use transactions, this method does not let your components access the ASP object context and participate in the transaction. Use the ObjectContext object or pass references to the ASP objects explicitly, as arguments.

Using the ObjectContext Object

The ObjectContext object is more difficult to use, but works with all ASP pages, including those that are transactional. You must run your components in MTS (or as COM+ applications in Windows 2000) to gain access to the ASP ObjectContext object. You've already seen how to set up a COM+ application or add components to an MTS package in Chapter 20, *Controlling Transactions in ASP*, so you might want to review that procedure after you create the calendar component.

To acquire references to the ASP objects using the ObjectContext object, you add project references to the Microsoft Transaction Server Library (in Windows 2000, the COM+ Services Library), the Microsoft Active Server Pages Object Library, and the Microsoft Active Server Pages ObjectContext object. Next, register your component in a package (or COM+ application), and set the appropriate security and role(s) for the package or application.

After completing that process, you can reference any other ASP object by using the `getObjectContext` function, and using the resulting reference to create references to the ASP objects. That sounds more complicated than it is; here's an example:

```
Dim oc as ObjectContext
Dim ASPResponse as Response
Set oc = getObjectContext()
Set ASPResponse = oc("Response")
```

Again, when you're done with the objects, release the references by setting the variables to `Nothing`. For example:

```
Set oc = Nothing
Set ASPResponse = Nothing
```

The simplest way to acquire the references is to implement the `ObjectControl` interface and add the code to set the references in the `ObjectControl_Activate` event procedure. The following example shows how to acquire a reference to the Response object each time MTS activates the component. The variables named oc and `Response` are module-level variables:

```
' code in component
Private oc as ObjectContext
Private Response as Response

Private Sub ObjectControl_Activate()
    On Error GoTo ErrObjectControl_Activate
    Dim methodname As String
    methodname = Classname & ".ObjectControl_Activate"
    Set oc = GetObjectContext()
    If Not oc Is Nothing Then
        Set Response = oc("Response")
    Else
        Err.Raise 50000, methodname, "Unable to set a " & _
        "reference to the Response object."
    End If
ExitObjectControl_Activate:
    Exit Sub
ErrObjectControl_Activate:
    Err.Raise Err.Number, methodname, Err.Description
    Resume ExitObjectControl_Activate
End Sub
```

Passing ASP Objects as Arguments

Perhaps the simplest method for gaining references to ASP objects is to have ASP pass the references as arguments. When you pass ASP object references in this manner, your component can use the objects, but cannot participate in transactions. For example:

```
' code in ASP page
Dim myObj
Set myObj = Server.CreateObject("SomeProject.SomeClass")
' the following method passes references to the ASP objects
myObj.setASPReferences(Request, Response, Server, _
    Application, Session)


' code in the myObj component
Private mRequest as Request
Private mResponse as Response
Private mServer as Server
Private mApplication as Application
Private mSession as Session
Public Sub setASPReferences(Request as Variant, _
    Response as Variant, Server as Variant, _
    Application as Variant, Session as Variant)
    Set mRequest = Request
    Set mResponse = Response
    Set mServer = Server
    Set mApplication = Application
    Set mSession = Session
End Sub
```

Having acquired the ASP object references, you may now use them within the component just as you use them from ASP. For example:

```
mResponse.Write "Hello from myObj!"
```

Remember to release the references before IIS destroys the component when the end of the ASP page completes. In VB, write the release code inside a procedure when you create the reference in the procedure, or in the `Terminate` event when you create the references as module-level variables.

Variants vs. Typed Variables

In the preceding section, you may have noticed that the code in the `setASP-References` routine defined all the arguments as Variants even though they were objects. When you're writing components for use with ASP, it's a good idea to accept `Variant` arguments because ASP has no typed variables—every variable in ASP is a Variant. If you write your routines to accept typed arguments, the ASP programmer must cast the variable to the correct type in the call, which is awkward. For example, here's a VB function that splits a name into its component parts. The function accepts only typed arguments:

```
' in component
Public Function SplitNames(aName as String) as Variant
    SplitNames = split(aName, " ")
End Function
```

To call the SplitNames function, an ASP programmer must use the CStr function to cast the Name variable to a String inside the calling code. For example:

```
Dim objSplitter
Dim aName
Dim arrNames
aName = "Ayn Rand"
set objSplitter = Server.CreateObject("NameSplitter.CNameSplitter")
arrNames = objSplitter.SplitNames(CStr(aName))
```

That might be acceptable if you're the only person using the component, but it's unacceptable or at least unfriendly if you're creating components for others to use.

Unfortunately, the corollary to accepting Variant arguments is that you need to test carefully in your component code to ensure that the arguments can be cast to the types you expect. For example, if you're expecting a string, test the subtype of the Variant argument using the VarType function:

```
' in component
Public Function SplitNames(aName as Variant) as Variant
    If varType(aName) <> vbString Then
        Err.Raise 50000, "NameSplitter.CNameSplitter", _
        "Invalid Argument Type—Expected String "
    Else
        SplitNames = split(aName, " ")
    End If
End Function
```

When you write your code this way, an ASP programmer can use your component easily. For example:

```
Dim objSplitter
Dim aName
Dim arrNames
aName = "Ayn Rand"
set objSplitter = Server.CreateObject("NameSplitter.CNameSplitter")
arrNames = objSplitter.SplitNames(aName)
```

If by accident the programmer sends an invalid Variant type, your function will catch the error and raise an error specifying exactly what the problem is.

Communication between ASP Pages and Components

When you create a component in Visual Basic for use with standard Windows programs, you typically create Let and Get properties, and for objects, Set methods. People using your component can then set or retrieve these properties individually. That type of interface isn't as useful in an ASP environment for two reasons. First, each method you invoke on a component from ASP takes longer than making the same method call from within Visual Basic because VBScript objects are always late-bound, meaning VBScript uses the IDispatch interface rather than the more efficient COM (Vtable) interface. But more importantly, each property access takes time—and the one thing you don't have in Web applications is time. Because your goal is to service requests as fast as possible, you don't want to waste precious milliseconds setting properties. Therefore, you should write the components so that each method call accepts the arguments it needs to complete the method.

That's a rather abstract idea, so maybe a little code can help explain it better. Suppose you have an Order object, which has several properties: CustomerID, ProductID, OrderDate, Price, Quantity, ShipToAddress, BillToAddress, ShipDate, DeliveryDate, and Returned. You might normally create the object, then set its properties. For example:

```
Dim oOrder
Set oOrder = Server.CreateObject("MyCompany.Order")
With oOrder
    .CustomerID=458392
    .ProductID='T158G32'
    .OrderDate=now()
    .Price=14.99
    .Quantity=5
    .ShipToAddress="John Tucker, 1414 Mebrun Cr., Kansas 01436"
    .BillToAddress="John Tucker, 1414 Mebrun Cr., Kansas 01436"
    .DeliveryDate=DateAdd("d", 42, now())
    .Returned=0
    .SaveOrder
End With
```

When your program and the oOrder object are on the same machine, running in VB and executing on the same thread, that method is fine—the code executes extremely fast. However, when your VBScript and the oOrder object are on separate machines running in different threads, and all object accesses occur over the network, you will see severe performance degradation. The solution is to code the oOrder object so you only need to make a single call. For example:

```
Dim oOrder
Set oOrder = Server.CreateObject("MyCompany.Order")
oOrder.SaveOrder(458392, 'T158G32', now(), 14.99, 5, _
    "John Tucker, 1414 Mebrun Cr., Kansas 01436", _
    "John Tucker, 1414 Mebrun Cr., Kansas 01436", _
    DateAdd("d", 42, now()), 0)
```

You might easily see a 100% improvement by using the concepts in the second example.

Let's take this idea one step further. Suppose you now want to keep track of the number of orders by this customer by storing them in memory for future reference, and that both the oOrder object and your page need to know that the customer has made a previous request. You can't store the data in the oOrder object because it has page-scope; it will be destroyed when the current page ends. You can't store the oOrder object itself in a Session variable because that would lock the Session down to a single thread. The answer is to store the properties of the oOrder object in Session variables, but not the object itself. Among several other choices, you could write a getProperties method for the oOrder object that returned the values as a Variant array, which you can store in a Session variable without the threading penalties imposed by storing the object itself.

The point of this discussion is that you can use Application and Session variables to communicate between one ASP page and another, between ASP pages and COM objects, and between COM objects and other COM objects.

Build the *HTMLCalendar* Component

The component you'll create displays a calendar in HTML. The calendar highlights the current date, lets people move forward or backward one month at a time, and provides a way for ASP or HTML pages to take a specific action when a user double-clicks any date.

The HTMLCalendar component contains only one public method—showCalendar. The showCalendar method requires a date argument, which it uses to determine which month and year to show. It accepts several other optional arguments controlling the width, height, and colors used for displaying and highlighting the calendar.

To create the component, start Visual Basic. From the New Project dialog, select the ActiveX DLL project type (see Figure 26.1).

FIGURE 26.1:

VB New Project dialog

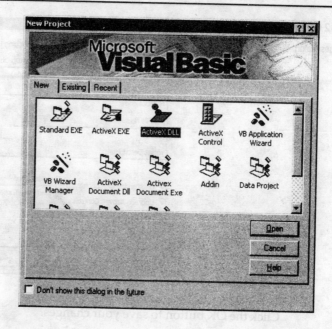

VB creates a new project with one public class. Figure 26.2 shows the Project Explorer window after creating the new ActiveX DLL project.

FIGURE 26.2:

VB Project Explorer—New
ActiveX DLL project

Right-click on the project title (Project1) and select Project1 Properties from the context menu. You'll see the Project Properties dialog. Make sure you select the General tab, then change the name of the project to HTMLCalendar and check the Unattended Execution and Retained In Memory options (see Figure 26.3).

FIGURE 26.3:

Project Properties dialog

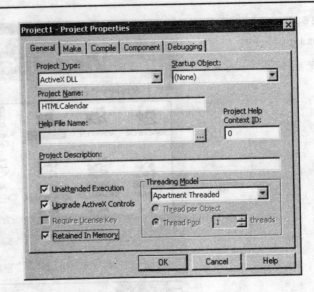

Click the OK button to save your changes.

Right-click on the Class1 class entry in the Project Explorer window and select Properties from the context menu. The class properties appear in the Properties window. Change the name of the class to CHTMLCalendar, change the MTSTransactionMode property to No Transactions, and accept the defaults for the other class properties as shown in Figure 26.4.

FIGURE 26.4:

CHTMLCalendar Class Properties window

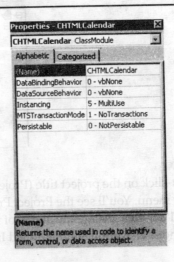

Because this object will run in MTS and needs to access the ASP intrinsic objects, you'll need to set some project references. Click the Project menu and .

select References. VB responds (eventually) by displaying the References dialog. The References dialog contains a list of all registered type libraries on your system, arranged so that selected items appear at the top of the list and other items appear in alphabetical order. If you're running Windows 2000, scroll through the list and select the COM+ Services Type Library entry. If you're running Windows NT 4, select the Microsoft Transaction Server Type Library entry. For both operating systems, select Microsoft Active Server Pages Object Library and Microsoft Active Server Pages ObjectContext Object Library. Click OK to save and close the dialog. If you re-open the dialog, your selections will appear at the top of the list (see Figure 26.5).

FIGURE 26.5:

HTMLCalendar Project References dialog

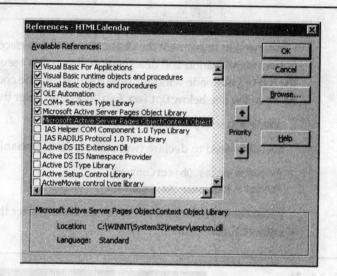

Save your changes by clicking the File menu, then selecting Save Project1. You'll need to select a directory in which VB will save the project files. After saving the project the first time, the Save Project1 entry changes to the name of the current project followed by a Visual Basic Project (VBP) extension. For example, `Save HTMLCalendar.vbp`.

Double-click on the `CHTMLCalendar` class to open a code window for the `CHTMLCalendar` class module. If you don't see the keywords `Option Explicit` in the first line, enter them at the top of the code window. At this point your code should look like Figure 26.6.

In VB, a class is a specific type of code module. There are other types of modules, but because there's only one module in this project, the terms *module* and *class* or *class module* are interchangeable. You're in the Declarations section of the module. In this section, you declare external functions and create module-level variables.

FIGURE 26.6:

CHTMLCalendar code module

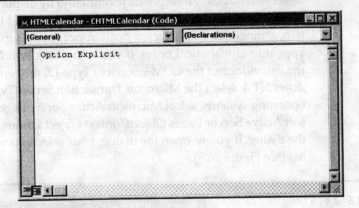

You need to implement the `ObjectControl` interface so MTS will notify your component on activation and deactivation. If you don't see the line `Option Explicit` at the top of your code window, type the line into the code window and press Enter. Move to the line below `Option Explicit` and enter the following line:

```
Implements ObjectControl
```

You also need to declare two module-level variables, as follows:

```
Private oc As ObjectContext
Private Response As Response
```

Enter the preceding two lines immediately after the `Implements` statement, as shown in Figure 26.7.

FIGURE 26.7:

CHTMLCalendar Declarations section

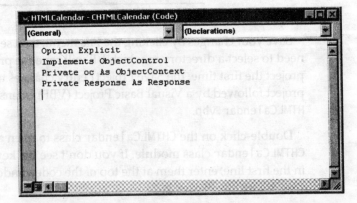

It's usually a good idea to create a `Classname` property that you can use internally for error reporting. Begin on a new line and enter the following code:

```
Public Property Get Classname() As String
    Classname = "CHTMLCalendar"
End Property
```

In each method, create a `methodname` variable and concatenate the `Classname` property with the name of the method. For example:

```
Dim methodname As String
methodname = Classname & ".ShowCalendar"
```

If any error occurs within your method, you can set the `Err.Source` property to the value of the `methodname` variable to get the complete class and method name where the error occurred.

The `ObjectControl` interface exposes three events. These show up in the drop-down list at the top left of the code module. MTS raises an `ObjectControl_Activate` event whenever it activates your object. During the event, you can set the `oc` `ObjectContext` reference and obtain references to any intrinsic ASP objects your method needs. For example:

```
Private Sub ObjectControl_Activate()
    On Error GoTo ErrObjectControl_Activate
    Dim methodname As String
    methodname = Classname & ".ObjectControl_Activate"
    Set oc = GetObjectContext()
    If Not oc Is Nothing Then
        Set Response = oc("Response")
    Else
        Err.Raise 50000, , _
        "Unable to set a reference to the Response object."
    End If
ExitObjectControl_Activate:
    Exit Sub
ErrObjectControl_Activate:
    Err.Raise Err.Number, methodname, Err.Description
    Resume ExitObjectControl_Activate
End Sub
```

Similarly, MTS raises an `ObjectControl_Deactivate` event before deactivating your object. During this event, you should release any object references. For example:

```
Private Sub ObjectControl_Deactivate()
    On Error GoTo ErrObjectControl_Deactivate
    Dim methodname As String
    methodname = Classname & ".ObjectControl_Deactivate"
    Set Response = Nothing
    Set oc = Nothing
ExitObjectControl_Deactivate:
    Exit Sub
ErrObjectControl_Deactivate:
```

```
        Err.Raise Err.Number, methodname, Err.Description
        Resume ExitObjectControl_Deactivate
    End Sub
```

MTS may also call a function asking if your object can be pooled. Visual Basic apartment-threaded objects may not be pooled, so you should respond with a `False` value. For example:

```
    Private Function ObjectControl_CanBePooled() As Boolean
        ObjectControl_CanBePooled = False
    End Function
```

Paste or copy all three `ObjectControl` methods into the module. The order in which you enter the methods doesn't matter, but don't try to place them before the Declarations section.

The series of actions you've just gone through are (except for the `Response` references in the `Activate` and `Deactivate` events) completely generic—you can cut and paste the code into any class you plan to run in MTS/COM+.

The `CHTMLCalendar` component has only one public method—`showCalendar`. Listing 26.1 contains the entire method.

LISTING 26.1   **CHTMLCalendar Component—ShowCalendar Method**
                    (CHTMLCalendar.cls)

```
    Sub ShowCalendar(aDate As Variant, _
        Optional align As Variant = "center", _
        Optional width As Variant = "300", _
        Optional height As Variant = "300", _
        Optional bgcolor As Variant = "lightcyan", _
        Optional cellcolor As Variant = "lightcyan", _
        Optional cellhighlightColor As Variant = "lightgreen", _
        Optional textcolor As Variant = "black", _
        Optional textHighlightColor As Variant = "red")
        On Error Goto ErrShowCalendar
        Dim startDate As Date
        Dim endDate As Date
        Dim dt As Date
        Dim col As Integer
        Dim cellStyle As String
        Dim tableStyle As String
        Dim cellhighlightstyle As String
        Dim methodname As String
        methodname = Classname & ".ShowCalendar"
        If IsDate(aDate) Then
            aDate = CDate(aDate)
```

```
Else
    Err.Raise 50000, , "Invalid Date argument"
End If
tableStyle = " style='background-color: " & bgcolor & _
";'
cellStyle = " style='background-color: " & _
    cellcolor & "; color: " & textcolor & ";' "
cellhighlightstyle = " style='background-color: " & _
cellhighlightColor & "; color: " & textcolor & ";' "
startDate = CDate(CStr(Month(aDate)) & "/1/" & _
CStr(Year(aDate)))
endDate = DateAdd("m", 1, startDate) - 1
With Response
    .Write "<form name='frmCalendar' method='post'>"
    .Write "<input type='hidden' name='calDate' " & _
    "value='" & FormatDateTime(aDate, vbShortDate) & _
    "'></input>"
    .Write "<input type='hidden' name='selDate' " & _
    "value='" & FormatDateTime(aDate, vbShortDate) & _
    "'></input>"
    .Write "<input type='hidden' name='startDate' " & _
    "value='" & FormatDateTime(startDate, vbShortDate) _
    & "'></input>"
    .Write "<input type='hidden' name='Action' value=''>"
    .Write "<table align='" & align & "' width='" & _
    width & "' height='" & height & "' border='1' " & _
    "cols='7'" & tableStyle & ">"
    .Write "<tr style='height: 45px;'><td " & _
    "id='cal_prevmonth' align='center' " & _
    "valign='center'>" & "<img src='larr.gif'></td>" & _
    "<td colspan='5' " & "align='center'><strong><em>" _
    & MonthName(Month(aDate)) & ", " & Year(aDate) & _
    "</em></strong></td><td " & "id='cal_nextmonth' " & _
    "align='center' valign='center'>" & _
    "<img src='rarr.gif'></td></tr>"
    .Write "<tr>"
    For col = 1 To 7
        .Write "<td" & cellStyle & "align='center' " & _
        "valign='center' bgcolor='" & cellcolor & _
        "'><b>" & Left(UCase(WeekdayName(col)), 1) & _
        "</b></tr>"
    Next
    .Write "</tr><tr>"
    For col = 1 To Weekday(startDate) - 1
        .Write "<td" & cellStyle & "> </td>"
    Next
```

```
              For dt = startDate To endDate
                 col = Weekday(dt)
                 If Int(dt) = Int(aDate) Then
                    .Write "<td id='cal_td'" & cellhighlightstyle _
                    & " align='center' valign='center'>" & _
                    Day(dt) & "</td>"
                 Else
                    .Write "<td id='cal_td'" & cellStyle & _
                    " align='center' valign='center'>" & Day(dt) _
                    & "</td>"
                 End If
                 If col = 7 Then
                    .Write "</tr><tr>"
                 End If
              Next
              dt = endDate
              Do While col < 7
                 dt = DateAdd("d", 1, dt)
                 col = Weekday(dt)
                 .Write "<td" & cellStyle & "> </td>"
              Loop
              .Write "</tr></table>" & vbCrLf
              .Write "</form>"
              .Write vbCrLf
              .Write "<scr" & "ipt language='VBScript' " & _
              "for=cal_td event=onmouseover>" & vbCrLf
              .Write Chr(9) & "window.event.srcElement." & _
              "style.color=" & Chr(34) & textHighlightColor _
              & Chr(34) & vbCrLf
              .Write "</script>" & vbCrLf
              .Write "<scr" & "ipt language='VBScript' " & _
              "for=cal_td event=onmouseout>" & vbCrLf
              .Write Chr(9) & "window.event.srcElement." & _
              "style.color=" & Chr(34) & textcolor & Chr(34) _
              & vbCrLf
              .Write "</script>" & vbCrLf
              .Write "<scr" & "ipt language='VBScript' " & _
              "for=cal_td event=onclick>" & vbCrLf
              .Write "dim el" & vbCrLf
              .Write "dim daynum" & vbCrLf
              .Write Chr(9) & "if " & _
              "window.event.srcElement.style.backgroundcolor=" & _
              Chr(34) & cellcolor & Chr(34) & " then " & vbCrLf
              .Write Chr(9) & Chr(9) & "dayNum = " & _
              "window.event.srcElement.innerText" & vbCrLf
              .Write Chr(9) & Chr(9) & "document.all(" & Chr(34) _
```

```
                    & "selDate" & Chr(34) & ").value=" & _
                    "dateAdd(" & Chr(34) & "d" & Chr(34) & ", dayNum-1, _
                    & "cDate(document.all(" & Chr(34) & "startDate" & _
                    Chr(34) & ").value))" & vbCrLf
                    .Write Chr(9) & Chr(9) & "for each el " & _
                    "in document.all(" & Chr(34) & "cal_td" & Chr(34) _
                    & ")" & vbCrLf
                    .Write Chr(9) & Chr(9) & Chr(9) & "if " & _
                    "el.style.backgroundColor=" & Chr(34) & _
                    cellhighlightColor & Chr(34) & " then " & vbCrLf
                    .Write Chr(9) & Chr(9) & Chr(9) & Chr(9) & _
                    "el.style.backgroundColor=" & Chr(34) & cellcolor & _
                    Chr(34) & vbCrLf
                    .Write Chr(9) & Chr(9) & Chr(9) & "end if" & vbCrLf
                    .Write Chr(9) & Chr(9) & "next" & vbCrLf
                    .Write Chr(9) & Chr(9) & _
                    "window.event.srcElement.style.backgroundcolor=" & _
                    Chr (34) & cellhighlightColor & Chr(34) & vbCrLf
                    .Write Chr(9) & "end if" & vbCrLf
                    .Write "</script>" & vbCrLf

                    .Write "<scr" & "ipt language='VBScript' " & _
                    "for=cal_td event=ondblclick>" & vbCrLf
                    .Write "dim el" & vbCrLf
                    .Write "dim daynum" & vbCrLf
                    .Write Chr(9) & "if " & _
                    "window.event.srcElement.style.backgroundcolor=" & _
                    Chr(34) & cellcolor & Chr(34) & " then " & vbCrLf
                    .Write Chr(9) & Chr(9) & "dayNum = " & _
                    "window.event.srcElement.innerText" & vbCrLf
                    .Write Chr(9) & Chr(9) & "document.all(" & Chr(34) _
                    & "selDate" & Chr(34) & ").value=" & _
                    "dateAdd(" & Chr(34) & "d" & Chr(34) & ", dayNum-1, _
                    & cDate(document.all(" & Chr(34) & "startDate" & _
                    Chr(34) & ").value))" & vbCrLf
                    .Write Chr(9) & Chr(9) & "document.all(" & Chr(34) _
                    & "Action" & Chr(34) & ").value=" & _
                    Chr(34) & "SelectDate" & Chr(34) & vbCrLf
                    .Write Chr(9) & Chr(9) & "for each el " & _
                    "in document.all(" & Chr(34) & "cal_td" & Chr(34) _
                    & ")" & vbCrLf
                    .Write Chr(9) & Chr(9) & Chr(9) & "if " & _
                    "el.style.backgroundColor=" & Chr(34) & _
                    cellhighlightColor _
                    & Chr(34) & " then " & vbCrLf
                    .Write Chr(9) & Chr(9) & Chr(9) & Chr(9) & _
```

```
                            "el.style.backgroundColor=" & Chr(34) & cellcolor & _
                          Chr(34) & vbCrLf
                          .Write Chr(9) & Chr(9) & Chr(9) & "end if" & vbCrLf
                          .Write Chr(9) & Chr(9) & "next" & vbCrLf
                          .Write Chr(9) & Chr(9) & _
                          "window.event.srcElement.style.backgroundcolor=" & _
                          Chr(34) & cellhighlightColor & Chr(34) & vbCrLf
                          .Write Chr(9) & "end if" & vbCrLf
                          .Write Chr(9) & "document.frmCalendar.submit" _
                          & vbCrLf
                          .Write "</script>" & vbCrLf
                          .Write "<scr" & "ipt language='VBScript' " & _
                          "for=cal_prevmonth event=onclick>" & vbCrLf
                          .Write Chr(9) & "document.all(" & Chr(34) & _
                          "selDate" & Chr(34) & ").value=dateAdd(" & Chr(34) _
                          & "m" & Chr(34) & ", -1, document.all(" & Chr(34) _
                          & "selDate" & Chr(34) & ").value)" & vbCrLf
                          .Write Chr(9) & Chr(9) & "document.all(" & Chr(34) _
                          & "Action" & Chr(34) & ").value=" & _
                          Chr(34) & "PrevMonth" & Chr(34) & vbCrLf
                          .Write Chr(9) & "document.frmCalendar.submit" _
                          & vbCrLf
                          .Write "</script>" & vbCrLf
                          .Write "<scr" & "ipt language='VBScript' " & _
                          "for=cal_nextmonth event=onclick>" & vbCrLf
                          .Write Chr(9) & "document.all(" & Chr(34) & _
                          "selDate" & Chr(34) & ").value=dateAdd(" & Chr(34) _
                          & "m" & Chr(34) & ", 1, document.all(" & Chr(34) _
                          & "selDate" & Chr(34) & ").value)" & vbCrLf
                          .Write Chr(9) & Chr(9) & "document.all(" & Chr(34) _
                          & "Action" & Chr(34) & ").value=" & Chr(34) & _
                          "NextMonth" & Chr(34) & vbCrLf
                          .Write Chr(9) & "document.frmCalendar.submit" & _
                          vbCrLf
                          .Write "</script>" & vbCrLf
                      End With
              ExitShowCalendar:
                  Exit Sub
              ErrShowCalendar:
                  Err.Raise Err.Number, methodname, Err.Description
                  Resume ExitShowCalendar
              End Sub
```

Basically, the showCalendar routine consists of a few variables, a form, and a single loop to write a table containing the calendar. The entire bottom half of the routine writes client-side script to control the actions a user can make with the calendar.

Note that all the arguments are defined as variants and most of them are optional. VB has the ability to define optional arguments that function exactly like the optional arguments you use with ADO methods—you can supply a value for the argument or not. If you don't supply a value, the code assigns a default value.

The method first sets up error-handling. Again, this is slightly different than VBScript. The `On Error Goto ErrShowCalendar` statement tells VB to resume processing at the `ErrShowCalendar:` label at the end of the method in the event of an error. VBScript, as you may remember, does not have an `On Error Goto` statement, just the `On Error Resume Next` statement.

The method defines variables, then checks to see if the `date` argument is a valid date. If not, it raises an error, which forces VB to resume processing at the error-handler beginning after the `ErrShowCalendar:` label. The code in the error-handler again raises the error to the calling code—in this case, the ASP page that instantiated the component. Why didn't I define error-handlers for the rest of the arguments? I should have, but because the other arguments define attributes for the HTML tags, it isn't critical—an improper value won't normally cause an error—the calendar just won't display correctly.

The calendar code itself calculates the starting and ending date for the month specified in the `aDate` argument. For example:

```
startDate = CDate(CStr(Month(aDate)) & "/1/" & _
CStr(Year(aDate)))
endDate = DateAdd("m", 1, startDate) - 1
```

The other variable assignments are style settings. I included them for convenience to make the `Response.Write` statements easier to read and write. The calendar code itself writes a header row containing arrows so the user can change months. Next it writes the empty cells (if any) before the first day of the month; a cell containing a day number for each day in the month; and finally, the empty cells (if any) at the end of the month to fill out the calendar page. For the month 02/2000, using a width of 500 pixels and a height of 400 pixels, but using the default values for all other arguments, the calendar looks like Figure 26.8.

The last third of the `showCalendar` method writes client script to the browser. The code binds to several events for each cell: `click`, `mouseover`, `mouseout`, and `dblclick`. When you move the mouse over a numbered cell, the number changes color. When you click a numbered cell, the event code sets a `hidden` input control value, then highlights the cell by changing its background color. Note that any previously highlighted cells must first revert to the original background color. When you double-click on a numbered cell, the code highlights the cell, sets a hidden `Action` input control, and then submits the form.

FIGURE 26.8:

CHTMLCalendar for
February 2000

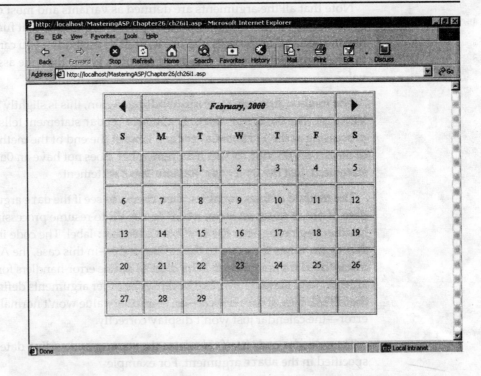

Clicking on the month arrows also submits the form. The calling ASP page can determine the user's action by the value of the `Request.Form("Action")` variable. When the value is empty (which it will be when the user first requests the page) the user hasn't taken any action. Otherwise the variable will contain one of the following values:

`SelectDate`   the user double-clicked on a cell containing a day number.

`PrevMonth`   the user clicked on the left arrow.

`NextMonth`   the user clicked on the right arrow.

You need to compile the `HTMLCalendar` component before you can run it in MTS. Click the File menu, then select Make HTMLCalendar.DLL. You'll see a file dialog. Select a location for your DLL. I suggest the Windows or WinNT system directory, but you may specify any local drive on your server. Click OK and VB will compile your component. If there are any syntax errors, the compiler will catch them. Fix the problem, then repeat the compile process until the component compiles without errors.

Packaging the *HTMLCalendar* Component

For components you create with Visual Basic, you can create an installation program using the Visual Studio Package and Deployment Wizard (PDW). If your Web server is on the same computer you used to create the component in VB, you can skip the package and installation process; but if you plan to install the component on a different server, you need to create an installation program.

To launch the Wizard, click Start, Programs, Microsoft Visual Studio 6.0, Microsoft Visual Studio 6.0 Tools, and select the Package and Deployment Wizard. Enter the path to the project's VBP file in the project field or select the VBP file from the browse dialog (see Figure 26.9).

FIGURE 26.9:

Visual Studio Package and Deployment Wizard

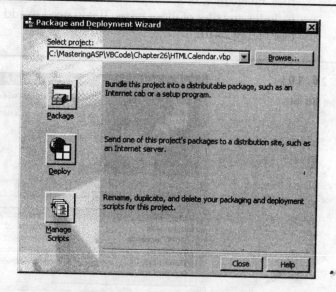

Click the Package button to create a new package. The Wizard will list several types of packages. Select the Standard Setup Package item, not the Internet Package item. Click the Next button and select the location for the setup files. Make sure you do not select the same directory as your project. Click the Next button to continue.

The Wizard will check the project files for dependencies. If it is unable to find the dependency information for one or more files, it will show you a list of those files. At that point, you can mark files that have no dependencies. Your DLLs may appear in this list, but other DLLs also appear. For example, you should see the `asptxn.dll` file. If you're using NT 4, you should see the `mtsax.dll` file because of the reference to the Microsoft Transaction Server Type Library. If you're using Windows 2000, you should see the `comsvcs.dll` file because the project references the COM+ Services Library. It's difficult to know exactly what to do with this information—I've never found it useful. If the Wizard can't find the dependency information, I can't either. I'm sure it's useful to someone and there's probably a wealth of PDW information available that may help you if you need it. You can probably ignore the dependency dialog without adverse consequences. An obvious exception is if you know that a component makes calls to an external DLL that *isn't* listed in the PDW process. Click the Next button to continue. The PDW shows you the list of files it will include with your component.

In this case, you have no special files to include with the installation, but you should check the list of files carefully. Make sure that all the required components and files appear. If your project requires external resource files, such as HTML files, image files, or text files, you must add them manually—the Wizard never includes any files of those types. If you need to add a file, click the Add button (see Figure 26.10).

FIGURE 26.10:

PDW—Included Files list

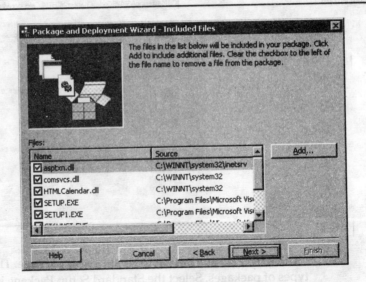

Click the Next button to continue. The Wizard typically marks DLLs for installation in the system folder. It also asks you which DLLs to mark as shared. Place shared DLLs in the system folder, and application-specific DLLs in the application folder. Click the Next button to continue. From the CAB options dialog, select Single Cab.

Follow the Wizard's instructions to complete the package process. Although they should not affect you for this project, be aware that there are many wizard and installation issues you may need to solve for other projects. The MSDN documentation includes information about many of these problems. Microsoft's Web site contains the most up-to-date version. The Microsoft newsgroups and information on the many VB Web sites can also help you solve installation problems. I urge you to take advantage of these resources by reading them before you undertake a complex installation.

The PDW is neither the most robust nor the most flexible installation program available. Third-party vendors supply much more powerful and configurable programs. The best of these can install essentially anything. As the programs gain in features, they also gain in difficulty. Each vendor has a set of Wizards. Some have customized scripting languages. The more involved your application installation is, the more difficult it will be to create the installation. Don't let the application installation languish while you tinker with background colors. You'll need a dedicated programmer and a substantial amount of time—two to three days for a simple application, possibly several weeks for a complex application—to create and test a robust installation program. The more you're willing and able to install manually, the simpler your installation will be. Unfortunately, the corollary to that approach is that the more you're willing to install manually, the more difficult it will be for anyone else to perform the installation.

Install the *HTMLCalendar* Component in MTS/COM+

Follow the procedure in Chapter 20, *Controlling Transactions in ASP*, to install the `HTMLCalendar` component into MTS/COM+. You can install the component into the `MasteringASP` MTS package or COM+ application you created in that chapter. Remember to set the `MasteringASPUser` role for the component so IIS will have sufficient permission to launch it.

Using the *HTMLCalendar* Component

After installing the component into MTS/COM+, you can use the `HTMLCalendar` component just like any other component. Listing 26.2 shows an ASP script that displays the calendar.

LISTING 26.2   ASP Script for `HTMLCalendar` Component (ch26i1.asp)

```
<%@ Language=VBScript %>
<%Response.Expires = -1%>
<html>
<head>
</head>
<body>
<%
```

```
Dim cal
Set cal = server.CreateObject("HTMLCalendar.CHTMLCalendar")
If Request.Form("selDate") = "" Then
    Call cal.showCalendar(Now, "center", 500, 400, _
    "lightcyan", "lightcyan", "lightgreen", "black", "red")
Else
    Select Case Request.Form("Action")
    Case "SelectDate"
        Response.write "You selected the date " & _
        Request.Form("selDate") & ".<br>"
    Case "PrevMonth", "NextMonth"
        ' OK, just show the calendar
    End Select
    Call cal.showCalendar(Request.Form("seldate"), "center", _
    500, 400, "lightcyan", "lightcyan", "lightgreen", _
    "black", "red")
End If
%>
</body>
</html>
```

Using *CHTMLCalendar* with Frames

Because the calendar itself is pure HTML, it can adjust quite easily to differing sizes. For example, you can put the calendar in a small frame, then display information in another frame when the user clicks the calendar. To do this you need a frameset page—a page containing no <body> tag that defines the frame sizes, names, and initial page sources. Listing 26.3 shows the frameset definition.

LISTING 26.3   CHTMLCalendar frameset **Definition (ch26i2.asp)**

```
<%@ Language=VBScript %>
<html>
<head>
<title>Using the HTMLCalendar with Frames</title>
</head>
<frameset cols="250,*">
    <frameset rows="250,*">
        <frame name="frameCalendar" src="ch26i3.asp">
        <frame name="frameBlank" src="blank.htm">
    </frameset>
    <frame name="frameMain" src="main.htm">
</frameset>
</html>
```

The frameset defines three frames: a 250 x 250 pixel frame in the top-left corner named frameCalendar, and a large frame on the right called frameMain. The portion of the screen under the calendar contains a frame named frameBlank that isn't used in this example. Listing 26.4 shows the ASP file for the frameCalendar frame.

LISTING 26.4   ASP Source File for the frameCalendar Frame (ch26i3.asp)

```
<%@ Language=VBScript %>
<%Response.Expires = -1%>
<html>
<head>
</head>
<body>
<%
Dim cal
Dim calWidth
Dim calHeight
Dim calBackColor
Dim selDate
calWidth = 200
calHeight = 200
calBackColor = "#c0c0c0"
Set cal = server.CreateObject("HTMLCalendar.CHTMLCalendar")
If Request.Form("selDate") = "" Then
   Call cal.showCalendar(Now, "center", calWidth, calHeight, _
   calBackColor, calBackColor, "yellow", "blue", "red")
Else
   Select Case Request.Form("Action")
   Case "SelectDate"
      selDate = Request.Form("selDate")
   Case "PrevMonth", "NextMonth"
      ' OK, just show the calendar
   End Select
   Call cal.showCalendar(Request.Form("seldate"), "center", _
   calWidth, calHeight, calBackColor, calBackColor, _
   "yellow", "blue", "red")
%>
<script language="VBScript">
   Dim doc
   Set doc = window.Parent.frames(2).document
   doc.All("calInfo").innerHTML = _
   "You selected the date <%=selDate%>."
   Set doc = Nothing
```

```
                </script>
                <%
            End If
            %>
            </body>
            </html>
```

The script in Listing 26.4 is almost identical to the script in Listing 26.2—both check the form variables selDate and Action to see if the user selected a date, and if so, write the selected date. However, this script writes the selected date into the mainFrame. For example, if I double-click on the date 2/25/2000, the main frame contents changes to reflect the selected date (see Figure 26.11).

FIGURE 26.11:

Using the HTMLCalendar component with frames

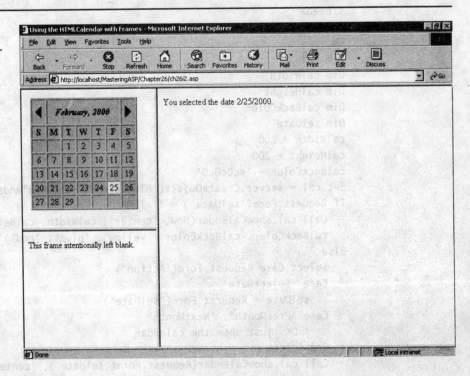

In this chapter, you've seen how to create a compiled component running in MTS/COM+ within a specified role, and then use it in conjunction with client-side scripts to create interactive browser frames that communicate with one another. That's quite an accomplishment.

In the next chapter, you'll see ways to run ASP scripts automatically at specified times.

CHAPTER

TWENTY-SEVEN

Automating Active Server Pages

- ■ Why Automate?

- ■ Setting up a Startup Shortcut

- ■ Using System Agent (Windows 95/98)

- ■ Using NT/2000 Task Scheduler

- ■ Using a VB Program

- ■ Using a Service

- ■ Other Options

Because ASP files are often programs that process data, it's highly likely that at some point you'll find it useful to run ASP scripts automatically. In this section, you'll see several options for running scripts automatically.

Why Automate?

There are many reasons why you might want to automate ASP pages. Any process that doesn't require user input is a candidate for automation. For example, suppose you populate your database every 24 hours with data from a mainframe system that is the master repository for orders. You need to create several reports from this data, but since the data isn't live, that is, it changes only when you reload the next day's data, any report you create is valid for the entire 24-hour period. Therefore, it would be a total waste of resources to re-query the database and re-create the reports each time a user requested the information. Ideally, you would create a set of ASP pages that would run the queries after loading the database and create HTML pages that would serve to fulfill the requests for the rest of the day.

You could assign a person the task of running the ASP pages to create the HTML-based reports each morning, but it might not happen—the person might forget, might call in sick, or might quit. It would be more efficient if you could run the ASP pages automatically at a scheduled time. The problem is: How do you start the browser and query the pages automatically?

As usual, there are several answers. I'll start with the simplest solutions and progress to the more complex versions.

The simplest possible solution is to create a shortcut and put it in your Startup folder. Your computer will then run the program each time you reboot or log on. This method has the advantage of being easy to create, but has the same disadvantages as assigning the task to someone else—you can't guarantee it will run. Nevertheless, it's a useful technique for non-critical tasks and it works on any computer with no extra software.

Setting up a Startup Shortcut

In DOS, there were two types of executable files: EXE (executable) files and BAT (batch) files. Windows adds two more types—the LNK file and (in NT/2000) the CMD file. A link file contains the path and name of an executable or batch file program as well as—and this is the salient point for this topic—startup parameters for the program. To set up a shortcut that runs automatically each time you reboot or sign on, right-click on your Start button and select Explore. Find the Programs folder and expand it by clicking the plus (+) sign. Double-click on the Startup folder in the expanded Programs list. Move your mouse into the right-hand pane and right-click, then select New, ShortCut from the context menu. You'll see the Create Shortcut dialog (see Figure 27.1).

FIGURE 27.1:

Create Shortcut dialog

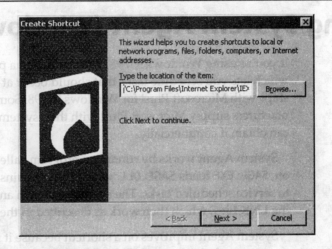

Don't worry if your dialog box looks slightly different than the figure—different Windows versions have slightly different dialogs, but they all create identical short-cuts. Use the Browse button to select the Internet Explorer (IEXPLORE.EXE) file on your system. By default, IE installs to the C:\Program Files\Internet Explorer directory, but the location may be different on your system. When you click OK, the Create Shortcut dialog displays the full drive:\path\filename you selected, in double-quotes. Enter a space after the final double-quote, then the full URL of the file you want to run. The following example is on two lines for layout reasons, but you should enter the URL on the same line as the executable program:

```
"C:\Program Files\Internet Explorer\IEXPLORE.EXE" http://localhost/Mas-
teringASP/Chapter26/ch26i2.asp
```

Click the Next button to continue with the Wizard. Enter a name for your shortcut, then click the Finish button to save the shortcut. If you double-click on the shortcut, it will open IE and navigate immediately to the URL you entered as the parameter. If you reboot or log off, then log on again; IE will also run because the shortcut is in your startup folder.

This simple system works well if the ASP process is non-critical, if you're the person responsible for the process, and the process isn't tied to a tight schedule. It also works well if you don't have access to the server, because you can force the ASP page to run from any computer that can launch a browser.

A CMD file launches a new instance of the Win32 command line interpreter (cmd.exe), and then executes the statements in the CMD file. Essentially, a CMD file is a more powerful version of a BAT file. For more information, see the NT/2000 documentation under the topic cmd.

Using System Agent (Windows 95/98)

If you're using Windows 95/98, you can obtain a program called System Agent, which lets you schedule tasks that should occur at specific times. System Agent ships with Microsoft Plus! for Windows 95/98. Some computer resellers and manufacturers supply Microsoft Plus! with their systems, but if you don't have it you can obtain it commercially.

System Agent works by running a program called SAGE.EXE whenever you log on. SAGE.EXE loads SAGE.DLL, which then remains resident in memory, waiting to service scheduled tasks. The agent can launch any executable program—including LNK files, which then work as described in the previous section.

System Agent improves on a shortcut because it isn't a manual process—it can run unattended, it runs at a scheduled time, and can run on low-end hardware.

Using NT/2000 Task Scheduler

If you're using Windows NT/2000, you can use the Task Scheduler service to accomplish the same tasks as System Agent. Task Scheduler runs as a service that, by default, starts automatically. To open Task Scheduler, click the Start button, select Settings, Control Panel, and then double-click the Scheduled Tasks icon. In Windows 2000, you'll see an Add Scheduled Task item. Double-click on it. You'll see the Scheduled Task Wizard (see Figure 27.2).

Click the Next button to continue. You'll see a list of programs that can be scheduled. If you don't see Internet Explorer in this list, click the Browse button and select the Internet Explorer executable (IEXPLORE.EXE) file on your system. By default, IE installs to the C:\Program Files\Internet Explorer directory, but the location may be different on your system. After you select the file, the filename appears in the next Wizard screen (see Figure 27.3).

Click the Daily radio button if you want to run the report every day, then click the Next button to continue. Select the time at which you want the task to begin, how often you want the task to run (the Every Day option should already be selected), and the starting date (see Figure 27.4).

FIGURE 27.2:

Scheduled Task Wizard

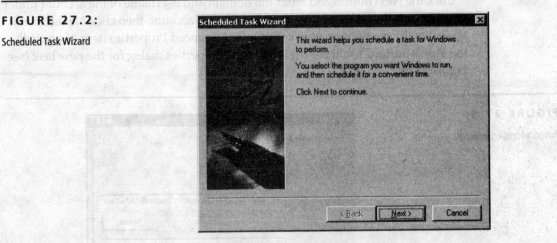

FIGURE 27.3:

Scheduled Task Wizard after selecting IEPLORE.EXE

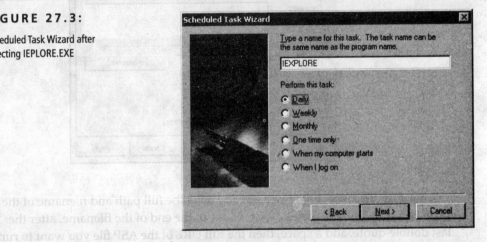

FIGURE 27.4:

Scheduled Task Wizard—time/date selection screen

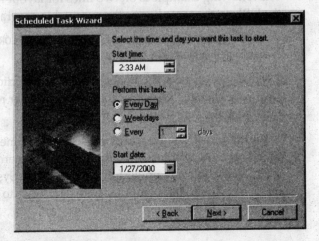

Click the Next button and enter the domain and username of the account under which to run the task and the password for that account, then click Next to continue. On the next screen, check the Open Advanced Properties item, then click the Finish button. You'll see the Advanced Properties dialog for the new task (see Figure 27.5).

FIGURE 27.5:

Advanced properties dialog

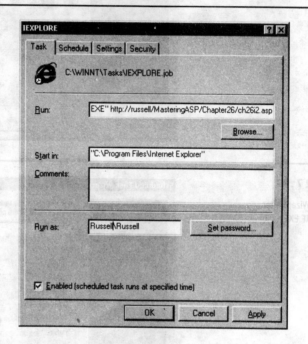

In the Run field, the dialog will already have the full path and filename of the IEXPLORE.EXE file in double-quotes. Move to the end of the filename, after the last double-quote, add a space, then the full URL of the ASP file you want to run. The following example is on two lines for layout reasons, but you should enter the URL on the same line as the executable program:

```
"C:\Program Files\Internet Explorer\IEXPLORE.EXE" http://localhost/Mas-
teringASP/Chapter26/ch26i2.asp
```

Make sure to check the Enabled option, then click OK to close the dialog and save your changes. Note that the Task Scheduler relies on your system date and time, so make sure they're accurate.

Your new task should run at the scheduled time. I suggest you initially set the time to execute within a few minutes, in case there are problems. Task Scheduler is a more flexible and powerful scheduler than System Agent, but it requires an NT or Windows 2000 computer with a browser to run.

Using a VB Program

All the previous solutions depend on your browser performing an `http` request, but do you really need a browser to run what is, after all, essentially an executable program? The answer is, of course, no—you don't. The server doesn't care whether there's a browser on the other end of the `http` request—it just services the request. Therefore, you can force the ASP page to execute using any program that can make `http` requests.

Visual Basic includes such a control—the Internet Transfer Control. To use the control, start a new VB project and select Standard EXE from the New Project dialog. In the Project Explorer, double-click the Form1 item to open the default form. Click the Project menu and select Components, then scroll down to the Microsoft Internet Transfer Control 6.0 item and select it. Click the Apply button, then the Close button to close the Components dialog. Adding the component adds a new item to your toolbox. If you can't see the toolbox, click the View menu, then select Toolbox. The Internet Transfer Control icon should be the last icon on the Toolbox (see Figure 27.6).

FIGURE 27.6:

Visual Basic toolbox with
Internet Transfer Control icon

InternetTransfer
Control icon

Double-click on the icon and the control will appear on the form. Although the control looks like a button at design time, it's invisible at runtime (see Figure 27.7).

FIGURE 27.7:

Visual Basic form after adding Internet Transfer Control

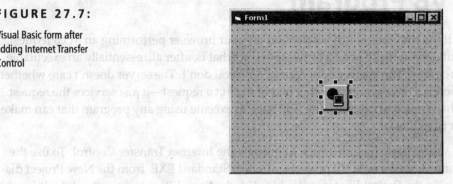

Double-click on the form and enter this code into the **Form_Load** routine:

```
Private Sub Form_Load()
    Dim data
    Dim tmp
    Dim fs As FileSystemObject
    Dim ts As TextStream
    Dim aFilename
    Me.Inet1.URL = _
        "http://localhost/MasteringASP/Chapter26/ch26i4.asp"
    Me.Inet1.Execute
    While Me.Inet1.StillExecuting
        DoEvents
    Wend
    Do
        tmp = Me.Inet1.GetChunk(1000)
        If Len(tmp) > 0 Then
            data = data & tmp
        End If
    Loop While Len(tmp) > 0
    Set fs = New FileSystemObject
    ' Note change the following path to match your system
    aFilename = fs.BuildPath _
        ("c:\inetpub\wwwroot\MasteringASP\Chapter26", "students.htm")
    Set ts = fs.OpenTextFile(aFilename, ForWriting, True, _
        TristateUseDefault)
    ts.Write data
    ts.Close
    Set ts = Nothing
    Set fs = Nothing
End Sub
```

You may need to alter the paths in the preceding code to match the paths on your server.

In a VB form, the keyword Me refers to the form containing the executing code. VB gives the Internet Transfer Control a default name of Inet1. Therefore, Me.Inet1 refers to the Internet Transfer Control you placed on the form.

The code sets a reference to the Internet Transfer Control on the form and tells it to request the contents of the URL http://localhost/MasteringASP/Chapter26/ch26i4.asp. That ASP file connects to the StudentRecords database, obtains the contents of the Students table, and returns the results formatted as an HTML table.

Because the response might take some time, the code loops while the value of the Internet Transfer Control's StillExecuting property is True. When the response is complete, the StillExecuting property changes to False. At that point, the code exits the loop and concatenates the Web server's response 1000 characters at a time into the data variable.

Finally, the code writes the contents of the data variable to disk in the file c:\inetpub\wwwroot\MasteringASP\Chapter26\students.htm.

Press F5 to run the project. What happens? You can't see anything happen, but (unless you received an error) your ASP page just ran. Browse to the URL http://localhost/MasteringASP/Chapter26/students.htm. You should see the contents of the Students table.

You can compile your VB program and automate it with System Agent or Task Scheduler in the same way you can automate the LNK files in the previous sections of this chapter. This type of automation is much more suitable for a server because it doesn't require any visible desktop components. In other words, because it doesn't start IE and use up unnecessary resources, you could safely place this program on your server. However, this solution requires that you install VB code on the server, a process that may be discouraged by Server Administrators.

Using a Service

You can create an NT service to automatically run the page. Although the procedures for writing native services are beyond the scope of this book, you can use a tool that ships with the Windows NT Resource kit called srvany.exe to run any executable file as a quasi-service. Srvany.exe is a service, but it launches other executable files rather than performing a specific task itself.

The advantage of a service over an executable launched from a client computer with System Agent or on the server with Task Scheduler is that you can configure a service so that if it fails, the server will automatically restart the service after a defined interval. Unfortunately, srvany.exe doesn't restart the associated programs, so unless you write a true service, you won't be able to take advantage of the restart capability. The disadvantage of a service is that it doesn't have access to network resources—so it must run on the server.

Other Options

In addition to the options described above, you could conceivably eliminate the ASP page altogether by creating an executable file in any language and using it to perform the tasks of the ASP page. For example, you might move your code to a Windows Scripting Host (WSH) file.

Windows can run DOS BAT files in a virtual DOS machine, but until recently there was no native Windows counterpart to BAT files. In other words, there was no native Windows scripting language. To rectify this oversight (after only 10 years) Microsoft created the WSH. WSH—like ASP, can run code in any WSH-compatible scripting language, such as VBScript or JScript. And the best part is: you already know the scripting language and how to use most of the external COM objects you need to write extremely powerful automation scripts.

By using VBScript in a WHS file you can access databases with ADO, perform file operations with the FileSystemObject and its derivative objects, send email, and even perform registry and account operations. If the page you want to automate is on a remote server, you can use VB and the Internet Transfer Control to obtain the data from the remote page, process it, and write an HTML or ASP file that uses the data.

Automating ASP pages can be a useful tool when you have a tested page that you need to run on a schedule; however, automated ASP pages are not usually the most efficient way to accomplish scheduled tasks. Bear in mind that you may not want to run long tasks on your server, and consider alternatives before you implement ASP automation. As with all your solutions, you need to keep two themes in mind—efficiency and scalability, because they affect your application's current performance and its future viability.

CHAPTER
TWENTY-EIGHT

28

Efficiency and Scalability

- ■ Definition of Terms

- ■ Response Time vs. Development Cost

- ■ Hardware vs. Software

- ■ Move Processing into MTS Components

- ■ Avoid Large Pages

- ■ Remove Dead Code

- ■ Avoid Extra Trips to the Server

- ■ Avoid Sessions

- ■ Use *Server.Transfer* and *Server.Execute* Methods

You've already heard a great deal about scalability in this book, but there's a great deal to think about. Some of you won't ever need scalability—but don't skip this chapter—I want to discuss efficiency as well, which is something developers building even the smallest sites should consider. Efficiency and scalability are separate but interdependent topics. It's possible (but expensive) to create a scalable site built on an inefficient program design. It's also possible to build a highly efficient application that doesn't scale well at all. Ideally, you want to create applications that are both efficient and scalable.

In using the technologies that were introduced throughout this book, you've practiced using them mostly in isolation. This chapter is an attempt to provide a framework for thinking about applications by combining hardware with a design approach that considers efficiency and scalability at every turn.

Definition of Terms

First of all, let me define the terms for this chapter. People usually discuss scalability in terms of *simultaneous* users, but another aspect is scalability for *total* users. For example, you could build a site with a high capacity for total users by storing user information in individual files; but such a site might have a low tolerance for many simultaneous users, because the overhead involved in reading and writing the files would be a bottleneck. Similarly, you could build a site that would handle many simultaneous users by processing data into HTML files during low-usage periods, but the site might begin to falter as the data store grows larger, because the time required to process the data would increase.

Similarly, people discuss efficiency from several different viewpoints. From a management point of view, the most efficient application is often the one that costs the least to develop. From a programmer's point of view, an efficient application is one that executes fast and uses the fewest resources. From a database developer's viewpoint, an efficient application is one in which programmers don't rely on Recordset objects to update, insert, or delete data. From a network administrator's perspective, an efficient application is one that minimizes bandwidth requirements.

In this chapter I've defined *Efficiency* as the process of thinking clearly and concisely, then capturing that thought process in code so you minimize wasted effort. Efficient code is also elegant code. *Scalability* is the process of making an application available to more people, either simultaneously or sequentially.

Response Time vs. Development Cost

Efficiency wears several hats. Creating an application using a point-and-click development tool is one kind of efficiency—it doesn't cost much to get the site up and running. In this case, you're usually trading development time and capability for application speed. You could also do the exact opposite—build an entire site coded in hand-tuned assembly language. The application would probably be extremely fast and highly efficient, but would require many person-years to complete and the costs would probably be prohibitive (that's why you don't see many assembly language sites).

You need to keep efficiency in mind both when you're designing an application and when you're writing the code. For example, a systems designer can specify that an application requires a database lookup for login. Unless the designer also specifies how that lookup occurs, the application can be inefficient. The programmer might retrieve the list of users and scroll through it looking for a match. While this method would work well in testing with a few user records, it wouldn't be efficient with a few hundred thousand records.

There's often tremendous pressure on developers to get something working. Therefore, the developers take shortcuts. It's easy to write loops, and more time-consuming to write binary search routines. Shortcuts in efficiency often show up as problems with scalability—which is where the two are related. An application that works well with 20 users might fall apart with 100 users. Is that a scalability problem or an efficiency problem? The answer depends on the individual application.

At design time, you should concentrate on the most-used features of the application. Suppose you were to use the HTMLCalendar component in an application. Consider what happens when a user clicks on the calendar. The page sends a message back to the server, which instantiates an instance of the component. The HTMLCalendar component calculates the calendar, concatenates the HTML string, and writes it to the client.

Is that an efficient use of resources? How could you improve the efficiency of the calendar? Could you move the calendar-drawing and click-processing code to the client? What if you used a commercial ActiveX calendar component or Java applet? Would the increased cost and delivery requirements be worth the increased efficiency and loss of control over the look-and-feel of the calendar? You have to realize that I don't have the answers to these questions either. Each case is separate and the benefits are debatable. For example, you could replace the HTMLCalendar component with a client-side ActiveX control—if you had only IE clients. You could replace it with a Java applet, which would run in most browsers, but you're now dependent on the client browser security settings—some people and companies won't allow

Java applets to run in their browsers. Perhaps the best alternative would be to write the calendar from the server, but move the highlighting to the client using DHTML. Most modern browsers can change background colors and fonts dynamically. For those that don't, you could still make round trips to the server—of course, that solution requires you to differentiate between browsers and introduces two different code bases for the calendar. By attempting to make one area more efficient, you introduce problems (or at least potential problems) in another area.

Efficiency comes into play in a Web application most often with regard to state maintenance. What data must you save? Where should you save it? How should you save it? The stateless nature of Web connections means you must either persist the data on the server, or send it back and forth with each request. Persistence on the server is more secure, but requires cookies or hidden form fields to match a client with the persisted information, and also requires server resources. Moving the data back and forth for each request is more difficult to code, but pays dividends in scalability. Sometimes a hybrid approach is best, where you cache resources common to all users on the server, but keep user-specific information in cookies. The downside to cookies, as you've seen, is that they're machine-specific. A person who accesses your site from another machine will not have the cookie and, therefore, will have effectively lost the data.

With scripting languages, you must be especially careful how you use objects. Because all objects are late-bound, each property access and method call requires several background tasks. Accessing objects in a loop is particularly inefficient. You'll find that you can improve your page speed considerably by creating local variables to cache object properties. A good rule of thumb is that you should create a local variable whenever you're going to access the property more than once in a page.

You can partially solve this problem by moving such code into compiled COM components. COM components can use early-bound object references, which are an order of magnitude faster than late-bound references from a scripting language. COM components aren't a complete answer though. Concatenating 50,000 characters into a single-string variable isn't much more efficient in a COM component than it is in a scripting language. Assuming the concatenation loop doesn't make object calls, the only difference between the compiled and scripted version is that the scripted version must use Variant variables, where the compiled version can use String variables.

Remember that code efficiency costs money. If you move code into a COM component, you must also factor in the time required to test and install the component. COM components are also more difficult to upgrade, requiring, at best, that you stop the application, and at worst, that you shut down the server.

Hardware vs. Software

Not all scalability problems are software-related. You may write an extremely efficient application, but have scalability problems because the hardware your application runs on is insufficient for the load. There are several hardware-related bottlenecks for ASP applications. The first is memory. Given sufficient memory, IIS can cache compiled ASP pages in memory, but cached information is the first casualty if NT needs memory for other tasks. You may have noticed that ASP pages tend to execute slowly the first time you access them, but rapidly for subsequent accesses. That's because the server has to read the ASP file and compile the page during the first access, but caches the compiled page. Subsequent accesses are much faster because the page is pre-compiled in memory.

Typically, you want to keep your pages compiled in memory and avoid filling the memory with other data; otherwise your cached pages must be recompiled. Once again, this is a point where good design and efficient coding can help. You can help reduce application memory usage by limiting the volume of data you cache for individual users, by writing Sessionless ASP pages, and by writing efficient data-access queries. Retrieve only the data you need. Adding memory to a system is often the only thing you need to do to increase throughput.

Another bottleneck is the processor itself. If you watch your processor usage with the NT Task Manager during an ASP page request, you'll notice that the usage almost always rises to 100% for the initial access of a page, during the compilation process. During that period, the server can't respond to any requests. Even after all pages are compiled and cached, an average single-processor server should be able to process between 20 and 50 requests per second, depending on the complexity of the page.

Multi-processor servers can lift the total number of requests per second significantly. Good multi-processor architecture can result in about an 80% increase in processing power per processor. Unfortunately, that average tends to fall as the number of processors increases because there's some overhead involved in coordination and communication between the processors. Nonetheless, if you have sufficient memory and still have insufficient performance, adding processors is the simplest method for increasing performance.

The database itself can be the third bottleneck; but because modern enterprise-level databases are highly efficient, you should look at several code-related problems before you decide the database is the culprit. The number of connections must be sufficient. If your application is running out of connections in the connection pool, increasing the number of available connections may solve the problem. In the code, ensure that you're opening no more than the required number of connections and closing them as soon as possible.

Use Command objects in conjunction with stored procedures rather than dynamic SQL. Use forward-only, read-only record sets whenever possible, and static record sets if you absolutely need backward scrolling. Moving data from the database to the client entails a cost in time and memory. Use client-side cursors rather than server-side cursors except when you need to scroll through a record set—and then write a stored procedure to handle the scrolling on the database server. If you write INSERT, UPDATE and DELETE stored procedures, you should rarely, if ever, need updatable record sets.

Is your database on the same computer as your Web server? If so, you avoid transferring data over the network, but you can slow down the server because it's pulling double-duty trying to service requests from the Web server and the database server. Moving the database server to a separate computer can help solve problems. Do you place transaction logs and databases on separate physical drives? Enterprise-level databases log each transaction in a separate file. If that file is on the same physical drive as the data, you incur a performance penalty because the drive head must constantly move back and forth between the data and the transaction log to read the data and write the transaction information.

Move Processing into MTS Components

I've already discussed the performance differences between compiled and scripted code, so I won't repeat that here. However, you gain more than execution speed from moving code into components. One advantage is that you can run the compiled components on machines other than your Web server. A COM component can be anywhere on the network—in fact, it can reside on many different computers. If you've isolated the logic and written stateless components, then any component can service a request from any session. In essence, by creating the components, you provide a path for scalability. By placing copies of the components on multiple servers, you can offload the processing from the Web server to the component servers. Because the Web server is performing less work—mostly funneling requests to the component servers and results to the client—the Web server can handle more requests.

To avoid hard-coded dependencies on individual servers, you can use a directory service to inform your program of the components' locations. The entire process now looks like Figure 28.1.

FIGURE 28.1:

Web, Directory, Component, and Database Servers

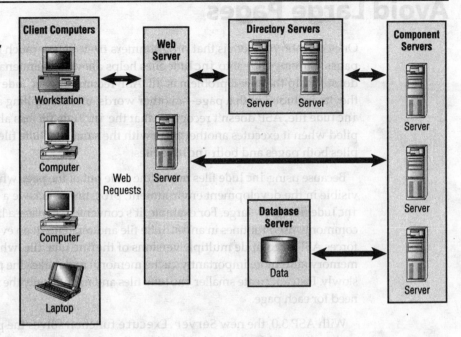

In a configuration like this, Web requests arrive at the Web server, which queries the directory service for the location of free components to service the request. After obtaining the location(s), the Web server creates instances of the components and calls the appropriate methods. The components may, in turn, query the directory service for the locations of other components. They service the request, performing database operations if necessary, and return the data to the Web server, which returns the result to the client.

You could go one step further with this scheme and add load-balancing servers to the mix. Load-balancing servers would allow you to add extra Web servers and could also mediate calls to the component servers, ensuring that the least busy server would get the next request.

The big advantage of the scheme is that you already have all the tools required to implement it in Windows 2000. You know how to create components and move them into MTS/COM+. The Microsoft Active Directory service ships with Windows 2000, letting you query for the location of components—and thus add them to servers other than the Web server itself. That process is beyond the scope of this book, but I can assure you that you make these calls with standard COM objects—and you've seen numerous examples of how to do that with the ASP objects themselves and with external components. You've seen how to set component properties and add roles to handle the security issues. The only thing left is the hardware—you're on your own there!

Avoid Large Pages

One common problem is that programmers try to fit too much into individual pages. Moving code into `include` files helps alleviate maintenance problems, but doesn't help the speed problem at all. ASP recompiles `include` files each time they're included with a page—in other words, after compiling a page with an `include` file, ASP doesn't recognize that the `include` file has already been compiled when it executes another page with the same `include` file. Instead, it compiles both pages and both `include` files.

Because using `include` files moves the code out of the page where it's no longer visible in the development environment, programmers have a tendency to let `include` files grow large. For example, it's convenient to place a large number of commonly used routines in an `include` file and reference it on every page. But that forces ASP to compile multiple versions of the `include` file, which both wastes memory (and more importantly, cache memory) and makes the pages load more slowly. Instead, create smaller `include` files and include only the functionality you need for each page.

With ASP 3.0, the new `Server.Execute` function solves the problem by eliminating the need for `include` files altogether. Instead, use the `Server.Execute` command to execute the functions and routines you need. You can then group commonly used routines together. Because they're in a separate file, the server keeps a single, compiled copy in memory and executes the code as needed, which is considerably more efficient than `include` files.

Remove Dead Code

During development, you often create many routines and code branches that are never used. It's tempting to leave these in the code, both because it saves time and because it's difficult to *know* that the code is dead. I urge you to use a debugger to step through your code often—even when it's working. That process can help you find dead code. If I'm not sure whether I might need the code again, I usually copy it to a text file, so I can reinstate it easily if I made a mistake removing it.

The problem is that the ASP engine must compile dead code right along with active code. Fortunately, ASP doesn't create object references until they're needed, so you're not creating unused objects with the dead code, but it does take up memory and requires compilation time.

Most important, the process of searching for and removing dead code often helps you find other code efficiency improvements. It's good practice to remove the code, and programmers maintaining your applications will appreciate it.

Avoid Extra Trips to the Server

When you're developing an application on your desktop workstation, the round trip time for a `Response.Redirect` command is negligible. When you're sitting in your living room with your 56K dial-up connection, a `Response.Redirect` command issued by a programmer creates a significant delay. The point here is to eliminate extra round trips to the server. You can accomplish this in three ways:

- Use client-side code to validate input, deliver message boxes, and redraw portions of the page. Each time you handle a user action on the client, you eliminate not only the round trip overhead, but also all the processing the request requires. For example, displaying a message box like, "Are you sure you want to delete the record? This action is not undoable." can replace a round trip where you format an HTML page to ask the same question.

- Perform some data processing on the client. As an example, consider a tabular report. You want to set up the report like Windows Explorer, so it sorts a column when you click on the column header. Rather than sending a `hidden` `form` variable or a `QueryString` variable back to the server to obtain the sorted data and re-draw the entire page, sort the data on the client—after all, you already have the data there, why obtain it again?

- Use the `Server.Transfer` command in preference to `Response.Redirect` whenever possible. The `Response.Redirect` command initiates a change of page by sending a redirect header to the client, which then makes a new request to the server, forcing a round trip. In contrast, the `Server.Transfer` command makes the page switch on the server. Because the transfer includes `Form`, `QueryString`, and `cookie` values, it's actually easier to use than the `Response.Redirect` command.

Avoid Sessions

You've already seen how Sessions can cause a performance reduction in your application. I'm reminding you of it here for scalability reasons; Sessions also cause problems when you begin to scale your site to multiple servers. If you use `Session` variables, you must ensure that the same server handles each request for a specific session. With sessionless applications, a load-balancing server can channel each request to any free server.

There are third-party load-balancing applications that manage Sessions across multiple servers in a server farm, but if you use sessionless pages, you are free to choose any load-balancing scheme that meets your needs.

Finally, there are some people who disable cookies in their browsers. You may not have the budget to accommodate these people by using different state maintenance and identification techniques, but you should at least consider them when you're designing your application.

Use *Server.Transfer* and *Server.Execute* Methods

If you have existing ASP code, you may be able to increase efficiency and scalability by replacing older code with newer code. You have the good luck to be using ASP version 3 (I hope), because this version includes two new Server object methods, the Server.Transfer and Server.Execute methods. You've already seen how these methods work, but you may not have thought about them in relation to efficiency and scalability.

The Server.Execute method largely replaces the older include file technology. The purpose of an include file is to place code used in several pages into a single file for easier maintenance and reuse. The server inserts the included file at the specified location into the main file—thus including code from a single file into many files. The server places the contents of include files into the main file before it compiles and executes the script. That means you can write code like the following, but it doesn't work the way you'd expect. The server includes both files regardless of the value of the variable i. The code works properly, but the server must compile both include files.

```
<%
If i = 1 then
    >%
    <!--#INCLUDE FILE="File1.inc" -->
    <%
Else
    %>
    <!--#INCLUDE FILE="File2.inc" -->
    >%
End If
%>
```

Despite this minor problem, including files wouldn't be that bad except that it causes an additional problem—the server compiles large include files whenever they appear. In other words, the server is incapable of using a compiled version of the included page even if the include file appears on every page, and even if it's cached in memory. Instead, the server includes the file and recompiles the included code for each new page.

You can now throw those `include` files away and put your functions in individual files. When you do that, the server compiles the file on the first reference. Because it's a separate file, subsequent references use the pre-compiled, cached version. Not only does this save memory and time, but (after you adjust to it) makes code reuse easier than ever. You no longer have to be reluctant to include a file containing many functions and subroutines when you know you're only going to use one or two of those functions. `Server.Execute` frees you from those restrictions.

The `Server.Execute` method can return values to the calling page. Files executed in this manner can participate in transactions begun in the calling file. By executing rather than including code that resides in external files, you eliminate the duplicate compilation problem and improve both the speed and scalability of your application.

The `Server.Transfer` method replaces and enhances the `Response.Redirect` method in many cases. For example, one common use of the `Response.Redirect` method is after processing form input. You update the database, then redirect to the next logical page in your application. To do that, the server sends a header to the browser telling it to request a specified page. The browser makes the request, and to the user, it causes a (usually) brief delay while the messages make a complete request round trip. With the `Server.Transfer` method, you not only avoid the delay, but you can also transfer the contents of the Request object to another page.

For example, you might need to carry `QueryString` values forward to the next page. Previously, you would have had to either store the values in `Session` variables or forward the values via code. For example:

```
Response.Redirect myPage.asp?Value1=Texas&Value2=Mississipi
```

Now, you can simply call the `Server.Transfer` method, which transfers execution to another ASP page, but maintains the `Request` values from the original page request.

By eliminating the extra round trip and being able to forward `Request` values to another page, you can increase the efficiency of your site. Perhaps equally important, these methods make your code easier to test and maintain.

PART VIII

Beyond ASP

PART VIII

Beyond ASP

CHAPTER

TWENTY-NINE

Other Operating Systems

- **What Are the Alternatives to ASP?**

- **Unix vs. NT/2000**

- **COM on Unix**

- **Extending ASP Beyond IIS**

- **Porting Your Application to Unix**

What Are the Alternatives to ASP?

Windows isn't the only server or operating system on which you can run your ASP applications. There are at least three competitors to ASP and all of them run on multiple platforms.

Chili!Soft ASP, a product from Chili!Soft, is an ASP clone that runs on a truly amazing variety of hardware, operating systems, and Web servers. While there are some differences between Microsoft's ASP and Chili!Soft's version, there's a high level of compatibility—typically in the 90%+ range; meaning that, with a little effort, you can port your ASP applications to other operating systems and Web servers.

JavaServer Pages (JSP) is a technology similar to ASP that uses Java code mixed with HTML (very much like the VBScript/HTML in ASP) to serve dynamic content on any platform that supports Java, which is almost everything.

Finally, the Apache Perl Integration Project provides Apache::ASP, a PerlScript-based ASP port that runs on multiple operating systems, but only with the Apache Web server. If you use ActiveState PerlScript with Microsoft's ASP on IIS, you won't have much trouble porting your applications to Apache::ASP, but VBScript/JScript programmers are, for now, out of luck. Apache::ASP may support VBScript/EcmaScript in the future, if there's ever an open source port of COM to the Unix platform.

Chili!Soft ASP

If you would like to leverage your ASP experience in a company that doesn't run Windows, you should take a long look at Chili!Soft ASP. Similarly, if you already have an application that you need to deploy to non-Windows operating systems, or to a Web server on NT/2000 other than IIS, Chili!Soft ASP may provide a solution for you. Chili!Soft ASP supports (among others) the following Web servers and operating systems:

- Apache on Solaris, AIX, NT, and Linux (in beta)
- HP-UX
- Lotus Domino, Lotus Domino Go (NT, AIX)
- Netscape (NT, Solaris, AIX)
- IIS (NT)
- O'Reilly (NT)
- OS-390 (in beta)

Chili!Soft doesn't support all Web servers on all platforms. Windows NT, Solaris, and AIX have the best support.

Chili!Soft ASP is functionally almost identical to Microsoft's ASP. Chili!Soft supports nearly the entire ASP framework—in other words, they supply the same (or equivalent) objects with the same (or equivalent) methods and properties. All the ASP intrinsic objects with their collections, methods, and properties are present. Chili!Soft ASP can run both JavaScript/JScript and VBScript. Chili!Soft ASP supports `Session` and `Application` variables, ADO, and provides equivalents to the COM components—such as the Browser Type component and the Scripting Dictionary component—that ship with Microsoft's ASP. The level of compatibility is very high.

Nonetheless, there are a few differences, mostly related to the wide variety of Web servers and platforms. Chili!Soft ASP doesn't support ClientCertificates, CodePages and LCIDs (Locale Identifiers), nor can you write COM components using Visual Basic for any system except NT/2000 (which is reasonable, because VB runs only on Windows). On the other hand, Chili!Soft ASP supports Java-based components called Chili!Beans, which consists of Java code contained in a thin COM wrapper so VBScript and JScript can access their methods and properties.

Chili!Soft ASP can run in two ways: as multiple processes (the default), in which each session runs in a separate process and the Chili!Soft ASP engine launches new processes upon demand, or as multiple threads, in which all sessions share a single process, but the Chili!Soft ASP engine assigns threads to requests as required. Chili!Soft states that generally, performance is better with multiple processes, but you should switch to multiple threads if your application makes heavy use of `Application` variables. That's because communicating with the Application object from multiple processes requires a cross-process call, which is slow. Using multiple threads, all sessions run in the same process; therefore, you can access the Application object without making cross-process calls.

The included Chili!Soft ASP versions of VBScript and JScript are compatible with the equivalent versions of Microsoft's VBScript and JScript, but they are several versions behind. Chili!Soft ASP currently supports VBScript/JScript version 3. In contrast, the current versions of VBScript/JScript on NT/2000 are version 5, so you will have problems porting applications if you're using the most recent VBScript features. On NT/2000, Chili!Soft ASP uses the installed version of VBScript and JScript, so you can use the latest version of the scripting languages.

Beyond these few large differences, most variance between Chili!Soft ASP and Microsoft ASP is platform-dependent. For example, Unix operating systems are case-sensitive, where NT/2000 systems are not.

Finally, your pocketbook will quickly discover the major difference between ASP and Chili!ASP. Microsoft can afford to give away ASP with each copy of

Personal Web Server and IIS, but Chili!Soft must make money to stay in business. So—get ready—Chili!Soft ASP costs money. How much money? That depends on your needs. Chili!Soft sells both unlimited and per-seat licenses. You can find more information by visiting the Chili!Soft ASP site at `http://www.chilisoft.com`.

JavaServer Pages

ASP's most recent competitor is a new technology from Sun—with considerable support from IBM—called JavaServer Pages (JSP). Unlike ASP, JSP isn't a scripting host—it uses a special ASP-like syntax. Interestingly, Sun chose to use the same `<%...%>` code delimiters that Microsoft selected. If you use JScript on IIS to write ASP pages, you'll quickly feel at home writing JSP pages. But JSP pages aren't built with JavaScript; they contain dynamically-compiled or precompiled Java code. Just as ASP pages can use COM objects, JSP pages can use JavaBeans and Enterprise JavaBeans to provide data and perform complex operations.

JSPs, being Java, run on almost every operating system and Web server platform. Like the ASP/COM combination, the combination of JSPs and JavaBeans provides a way to cleanly separate the very different developer functions of creating HTML interfaces and creating back-end database functionality and business logic.

JSPs are a much less mature technology than ASP, but Sun and IBM are working hard to change that. One way in which they're attempting to increase awareness of the technology is by giving developers free tools to use. For example, you can download the JavaServer Web Development Kit (JSWDK) for free from `http://java .sun.com/products/jsp/download.html`. The download provides the server components you need to get started, as well as an editor, some online documentation, and examples.

Unix vs. NT/2000

Both Unix and Windows operating systems do much the same thing—they provide file, print, and application services to multiple clients. A Web server is an application, and as such, its feature set should be somewhat independent of the underlying operating system. However, in the quest for speed and scalability, some Web server manufacturers extend their roots deep into the operating system—Microsoft is the perfect example. IIS's integration with MTS/COM+, SQL Server, and the NT/2000 security model has made it (arguably) the fastest Web server available. But it only runs on Windows. Others sacrifice speed and integration for platform independence. For example, the Apache Web server runs on more platforms than any other major server—and it's free on many of them.

NT/2000's main limitation has been scalability. Only recently has it been possible to run NT/2000 on servers with more than four processors. In contrast, Unix servers routinely scale to 24 or more processors. So what's the main difference? Price. For a small- to medium-sized site, you can set up a Windows 2000 Advanced Server to serve ASP applications for the price of the hardware, the NT/2000 server itself (roughly $4000), and the client licenses. Client licenses vary widely depending on whether you want to serve intranet or Internet-only clients.

Unix has traditionally cost considerably more than NT/2000. The Unix vendors justify this by citing increased uptime and scalability statistics. These two features interest large sites and e-commerce sites more than prices, but most individuals are priced out of the market. It's tough to justify spending several thousand dollars for an operating system just to practice your coding skills. Therefore, the development community has gravitated to Microsoft products, where the price for admission is not so high.

The cost factors begin to even out when you realize that Chili!Soft ASP is in a late beta program for providing ASP on the Linux platform. Linux, as you probably know unless you've been living in a box, is an open-source (read free) Unix operating system clone. It has recently enjoyed a surge in popularity, largely because companies such as Red Hat, Caldera, and Corel realized that putting a modern GUI interface on the operating system would attract more users. These companies do charge for their add-ons and additions, but you can buy the latest out-of-the-box Linux operating system version for less than $200. If you're willing to do a lot of work, you can still download and compile the core code for free.

Linux has a great deal of support from the developer community through online newsgroups, community user groups, and many Web sites. Therefore, despite the lack of a central authority such as Microsoft provides for Windows, if you're willing to live without an 800 number—or if you're willing to buy support from companies like Red Hat—you can usually find solutions to almost any problem.

COM on Unix

COM is a Microsoft technology, and—to my knowledge—Microsoft itself has never ported COM to any other platform other than the DEC Alpha—too bad, in my opinion. Similarly, it's shameful that the Unix world hasn't created a compatible solution. The bickering between Microsoft, with COM, and the Unix vendors, with CORBA, has in my opinion, slowed down the rate of progress considerably. At any rate, other vendors have stepped in to the breach with COM ports to Unix.

Chili!Soft uses one of those ports called MainWin, created by MainSoft. If you want to write C++ COM components for Chili!ASP, you need to contact MainSoft to obtain the MainSoft COM development tools. Mainsoft's toolset includes support for the Microsoft Foundation Classes and for registry functions. You can't use Visual Basic to develop COM components on Unix machines because the VB Runtime has never been ported to Unix. If you have to port existing VB COM components to Unix, you may find it easier to translate them to JavaBeans, using Chili!Soft's Chili!Bean technology.

Extending ASP beyond IIS

IIS is a Microsoft-only Web server. That's not surprising, as (other than Internet Explorer) Microsoft has made few efforts to build cross-platform code. The strategy seems to have worked (for the present) because Microsoft's IIS Web server, depending on the information source, currently hosts between 40% and 70% of all of the world's Web sites. Numbers like these aren't conducive to porting code.

Despite IIS's popularity, there are a significant number of companies that use other Web servers, particularly outside the U.S. The Web server market began (like the browser market) in a fragmented fashion, with Microsoft, Netscape, and Apache–still the big three—vying for market share. Fortunately, the servers all implement the Internet Server API (ISAPI) extensions, which is a common API for creating Web server add-ons. Microsoft's ASP is an ISAPI application. Chili!Soft uses ISAPI to hook their version of ASP into most major Web servers. The biggest difference is that Microsoft has integrated ASP tightly with IIS, whereas other servers support ASP only through Chili!ASP, so ASP is more of an add-on than a feature. Therefore, you can't administer ASP settings directly through the server. On Windows NT/2000, Chili!Soft ASP stores most configuration in the registry. On Unix systems, although some information is in the registry, Chili!Soft ASP instead provides configuration files that you can use to manage ASP settings on the server.

Apache::ASP

The Apache Web server is an open-source Web server. You can run ASP scripts on Apache using PerlScript as the scripting language thanks to work by the Apache Perl Integration Project, and especially Joshua Chamas of Chamas Enterprises, Inc. (http://www.nodeworks.com/asp/). The ASP portion of the project is called Apache::ASP, and is a port of the ASP environment to Perl/Apache. Like Chili!ASP, Apache::ASP is a cross-platform solution. Although you can download the technology and run it today, it's not as mature as Chili!ASP, but the price is right. You'll find that Apache::ASP isn't nearly as compatible with ASP as Chili!Soft ASP because they don't support a COM interface on Unix. You can use COM objects on Windows NT/2000 through the Perl `Win32::OLE` interface. Again, if Microsoft would port COM (and VB/VBA) to Unix, you would have a much easier time moving back and forth between the two environments.

Porting Your Application to Unix

If you need to move your IIS ASP application to Unix (or Linux), you'll face a few common barriers no matter which non-Microsoft ASP solution you select. File formats and date formats differ between operating systems. For example, Unix systems use the forward slash to separate the parts of a path, while Windows systems use the backslash. Different systems use different date formats. The bottom line is that you must remove format dependencies from your code to port successfully. What does that mean exactly? Here's an example. Suppose I want to find out whether it's before or after noon. I might write a function that checks a date-time string for the am or pm value. For example:

```
Function isBeforeNoon() As Boolean
    isBeforeNoon = Right$(CStr(Now()), 2) = "AM"
End Function
```

The function returns `True` if the current time is before noon and `False` otherwise. The problem is that it depends on two factors that may not work the same way on other systems. First, it assumes that the time format will be `HH:MM:SS AM/PM`. Second, it assumes that the cast for the return value of the function `Now()` will contain an uppercase `AM` or `PM` string. However, the target system might return times in 24-hour format, in which case the function wouldn't fail—which might help you find the problem during testing—it would always return `False`. The case problem isn't specific to conversion code—it's a common problem. Always cast strings to either uppercase or lowercase before you compare them.

You might be able to fix the problem by throwing some more code at it, but here's a more elegant and cross-platform solution:

```
Function isBeforeNoon() As Boolean
    isBeforeNoon = Hour(Time) < 12
End Function
```

The two functions appear exactly the same to external code, but internally, the second version checks the return value of the hour function, which always returns a number between 0 and 23, inclusive. With Chili!ASP, that's all you would need to port the function successfully. With other solutions, you'd have to *translate* the code from VBScript to the supported language—but that's a much less labor-intensive exercise than redesigning the code.

Before you begin a conversion, make a visual pass through all the project code and try to identify string dependencies. Look for:

- Filenames and paths

- Date and time code

- Data validation code

- Variable naming conventions

I recommend you either enforce case in variable names with a code-checking program or use a rule that all variables must be lowercase. One trick is to paste the page code into a Visual Basic or Visual Basic for Applications (available in Office 97 programs or higher) editor window. The editor will enforce variable case for you. You can then copy the code back out of VB and be sure that the case of declared variables will be the same for that page. Remember that this trick works only on code you paste into a module at one time, so you may need to paste multiple pages into the VB editor to reap the benefits. The editor also can't enforce variable case within quotes, for example `Session("someVar")` or `R("someField")`.

Data validation code presents a problem because it's not always easy to figure out the range of expected data values; therefore, it can be difficult to fix problems. Good error messages included in the code or in resource files can help you pinpoint potential problems. Data validation code is also a problem because the "correct" value can change from platform to platform. This is one of the reasons why I mentioned the absence of CodePage and LCID support in Chili!ASP—these two features make it much less difficult to support code running in multiple languages.

After you port a few programs, you should find that you begin thinking about and writing code differently from the beginning. You'll begin to anticipate where the problems might lie and avoid platform-specific or language-specific code in favor of more generic solutions.

If you look at the long-term trends, you'll see that people are beginning to create and use these more generic solutions in record numbers. HTML, ISAPI, SQL, and most recently XML and XSL are reducing the number of proprietary languages and file formats. We're moving from vendor-specific solutions to worldwide standards at an ever-increasing rate.

CHAPTER

THIRTY

30

Using XML/XSL with ASP

- ■ Beyond HTML

- ■ Introduction to XML

- ■ Using the Microsoft XML Parser from ASP

- ■ Introduction to XSL

- ■ Querying XML with XSL

- ■ Formatting XML with XSL

- ■ Caching Data with XML

In this chapter, you've truly moved beyond the realm of ASP altogether; but because XML is becoming more important every day, I didn't feel a book called *Mastering ASP* would be complete without at least an introduction to this important technology.

XML is a flexible superset of HTML that:

- Is text-based
- Lets you define your own tags
- Is well-suited to complex hierarchical data
- Has the built-in technology to validate its own content
- Is a W3C standard

Using an XML validating parser, you can ensure that an XML file contains the tags you expect, arranged in specified relationships, and the data within the tags meets specified expectations. XML is becoming increasingly important in business-to-business (B2B) Internet commerce.

In this chapter, I'll introduce you to ways you can use XML on the server, within the browser, and within your components to move your applications away from proprietary, program-specific code toward portable, standardized code.

> **NOTE**   To run the examples in this chapter, you'll need IE 5 installed on both the client and server. You must also have the Microsoft XML parser version 2 or higher installed on both machines. You can obtain the latest XML parser from the MSDN site at `http://msdn.microsoft.com/xml/`.

Beyond HTML

HTML provided millions of people with a way to put text and graphics on a computer screen without learning a complex programming language. As a display language, HTML has its limitations, but as the Web became ubiquitous, people began to try to force HTML to act as a data container. For example, programmers moved data to the browser in hidden form fields, hidden list boxes, and hidden frames both to increase interactivity and limit the number of server round trips. Developers often wrapped generic data in huge forms and submitted them to the server for processing, or resorted to automatic email to move data from client to server.

On the server-to-server side, things weren't much better. There's never been a common way to transfer data from one program and one operating system to another. The closest we've ever come has been text files. Text files have been the lowest common denominator since the early DOS days—and text files can contain delimited fields, fixed-width fields, free-form text, and tokenized content. Each has its advantages. For example, to transfer the raw text of a novel from one computer to another, a free-form text file works perfectly well. Unfortunately, if you want to transfer formatted text from one computer to another, both computers must agree on the formatting symbols and what they mean.

In the earliest days of word processors, vendors created their own, proprietary file formats. These formats worked well enough within the application, but it was impossible to open a file generated in one word processor with a different word processing program. Entire companies grew up around the problems involved in translating one format into another, with mixed results. Nevertheless, for most people, the only way to move the files was to save them in plain text—thus losing all the formatting.

These proprietary file formats weren't limited to word processing. Databases, graphics programs, spreadsheets, project management software, page-layout applications, presentation software—each program had a proprietary format.

With the introduction of Windows, Microsoft began to attack the problems. The clipboard was the first easy method to move content from one program to another. The first efforts involved creating a memory buffer shared by all programs that could transfer plain text and bitmapped (BMP) graphics from one program to another. Through the clipboard, for the first time, you could easily take numbers out of your spreadsheet and insert them into your word processor. Of course, they still lost all the formatting, but at least you could move the data.

With Dynamic Data Exchange (DDE), and later, Object Linking and Embedding (OLE), Microsoft made a huge leap. Suddenly, you could not only move data from one program to another, but you could preserve the format of that content, and even (by linking it) automatically update the inserted data when the source data changed. OLE was, and—as ActiveX—still is, a horrendously complex programming task. In addition, it was—and mostly, still is—Windows-specific. But it did provide a vision of multiple applications exchanging data seamlessly.

HTML, because of its ability to display word processor-like data, spreadsheet-like data, and graphics, all in a simple-to-learn and simple-to-understand package, took the major vendors by surprise. To their credit, almost all of the major application vendors embraced the new format eagerly. I guess they were as tired of file incompatibilities as the rest of us. HTML showed how a common file format could extend computing technology far beyond the workplace and make computing ubiquitous. You might say that HTML gave normal people a reason to buy a computer beyond bringing work home from the office.

Unfortunately, these vendors still had to deliver products, and as good as HTML is, a spreadsheet-like display isn't a replacement for a true spreadsheet. HTML is flexible enough to display data, but it has no concept of the content. The problem was, how could you build upon the simplicity and readability of HTML to create a common file format that could accommodate many different types of data and work across many different types of applications. The ideal file format would be text-based, let you define your own tags, be well suited for complex hierarchical data, have the built-in ability to validate its own content, and above all, be a world-wide standard. If these descriptions look familiar, re-read the introduction to this chapter. I've just described XML.

Introduction to XML

Despite all the hype, XML is a very simple idea—the kind of idea that makes you wonder—why didn't I think of that? The easiest way to understand XML is to look at some. Listing 30.1 shows an XML file that describes a person class.

LISTING 30.1   **XML Person Class File (ch30i1.xml)**

```
<?xml version='1.0'?>
<class>
    <name>Person</name>
    <creator>Russell Jones</creator>
    <properties>
        <property type="text" name="lastname" readonly="false"
maxlength="20" allownulls="false" value=""></property>
        <property type="text" name="firstname" readonly="false"
maxlength="20" allownulls="false" value=""></property>
    </properties>
    <methods>
        <method type="function" public="true" name="getname"
        description="Concatenates the Firstname and LastName
        properties into a single &quot;FirstName
        LastName&quot; string.">
        </method>
    </methods>
</class>
```

The code should look quite familiar to you. In fact, except for the tag names themselves, XML looks much like HTML. The file contains tags (markup) like `<class>`, `<name>`, and `<creator>`. Probably the strangest part of the file is the first line. In XML, the first line is required, and you must write it exactly as shown.

The rules for writing XML are simple:

- The first line must be `<?xml version='1.0'?>`.

- Tags are enclosed in angle brackets. Unlike HTML, tags are case-sensitive and each tag must have a matching closing tag.

- Tags may contain attributes in the form `name="value"`. The quotes around attribute values are required. You may use either single- or double-quotes, but the quotes must match. In other words, you can't write an attribute like `somename="somevalue'` because the single-quote at the end of the attribute value doesn't match the double-quote at the start of the value.

- Tags may contain text, other tags, or both. Tag content lies between the starting and closing tag.

There is one exception to the rule that every tag must have a matching closing tag. You can write *empty* tags (those that contain no content) with the closing slash at the end of the tag, before the closing bracket. For example, the following two tags function identically, but the first has an explicit end tag, whereas the second uses the forward-slash shorthand:

```
<property type="text" name="lastname" readonly="false"
    maxlength="20" allownulls="false" value="">
</property>

<property type="text" name="lastname" readonly="false"
    maxlength="20" allownulls="false" value=""/>
```

The content of the file is essentially an outline. The tags delimit content of a particular type. Some tags contain other tags—these tags are called parents, and the contained tags are called children. As you look at the file, you can see that the designation of a tag as a parent or child depends on the context. If you look at the `<class>` tag, it is clearly a parent—it isn't contained within any other tags. However, the `<properties>` tag is both a child and a parent. It's a child of the `<class>` tag, but it contains two `<property>` tags; therefore, it's also a parent.

Internet Explorer 5 natively transforms XML files into outline format. If you look at Listing 30.1 in IE 5, it looks like Figure 30.1.

The file initially appears as an expanded hierarchical outline. IE shows each tag that has children with a small minus sign next to the tag. You can't edit the file directly in IE, but you can open and close the parts of the document by clicking the minus sign (which then changes to a plus sign). Figure 30.2 shows the file with the `<properties>` tag closed.

FIGURE 30.1:

IE 5 native XML file view
(ch30i1.xml)

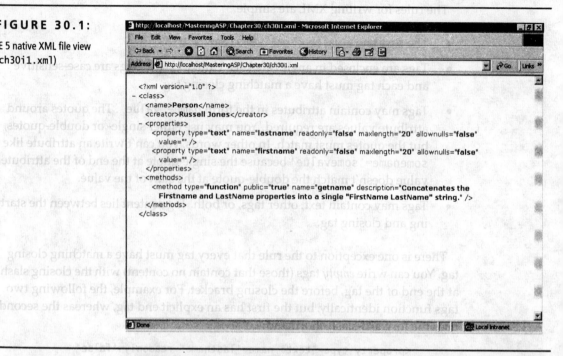

FIGURE 30.2:

XML file with a closed tag
(ch30i1.xml)

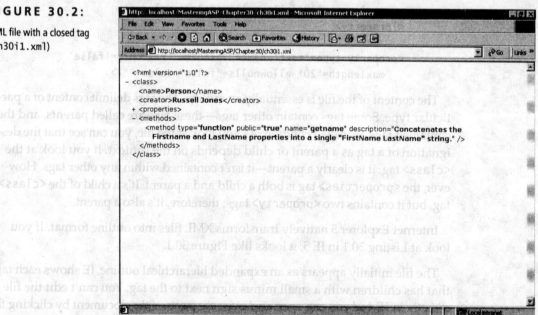

The beauty of this file format is that if the tags are well named, you instantly know the purpose of the data the tag contains. If I were to write this same content into HTML, it might look like Listing 30.2.

LISTING 30.2   One Possible HTML View of the Content In Listing 30.1 (ch30i2.htm)

```html
<html>
<head>
<title>Person Class</title>
</head>
<body>
   <h2>Person Class</h2><br>
   <b>Creator</b>: John Bradford<br>
   <h3>Properties</h3>
   <table cols="6" border="1">
   <thead>
     <th>Type</th>
     <th>Name</th>
     <th>Read-only</th>
     <th>Max Length</th>
     <th>Allow Nulls</th>
     <th>Value</th>
   </thead>
   <tbody>
   <tr>
       <td>text</td>
       <td>LastName</td>
       <td>False</td>
       <td>20</td>
       <td>False</td>
       <td> </td>
   </tr>
   <tr>
       <td>text</td>
       <td>FirstName</td>
       <td>False</td>
       <td>20</td>
       <td>False</td>
       <td> </td>
   </tr>
   </tbody>
   </table>
   <h3>Methods</h3>
   <h4>getName</h4>
   <p>Concatenates the Firstname and LastName properties into a single
   "FirstName LastName" string.</p>
</body>
</html>
```

Figure 30.3 shows the file in a browser.

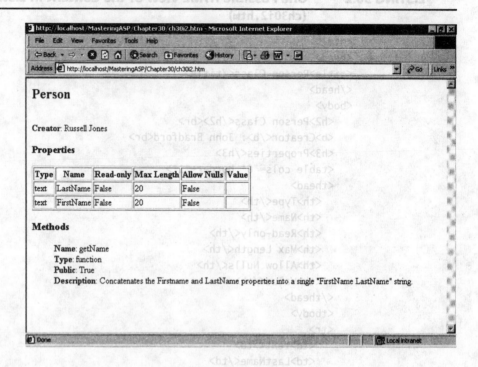

The two technologies are quite similar in content, but quite different in concept. The HTML version is much easier for a human to read, but the format makes it difficult for a computer to extract the content. For example, you might write some code to look for the word Methods, then read a list of methods contained between <h4> and </h4> tags. That code would then work as long as the page designer doesn't change the format of the page. In other words, the code to extract data from an HTML file is too closely tied to the display of the data.

In contrast, the XML file doesn't look as good on-screen and is more difficult for a human to read. However, it's much easier for a computer to extract data from the file.

Ideally, you would be able to place the data in XML, but display the data in HTML. That's the point of XML in a nutshell. XML is a generic data container that you can query and transform via code, applying formatting commands suitable for the display mechanism. The tool for querying and transforming the data in an XML document is called eXtensible Style Language (XSL). In the remainder of this chapter, you'll see how to use XML as a data container and how to use XSL to transform that data into HTML.

Using the Microsoft XML Parser from ASP

You read XML files with a parser. There are several freeware and shareware parsers available, mostly written in Java. Microsoft provides a parser with IE 5 that you can use on the client or the server (assuming IE 5 is installed on the server). You can also download the parser as a redistributable file and install it on computers running IE 4 for use with your applications. The download URL is `http://msdn`
`.microsoft.com/downloads/tools/xmlparser/xmldl.asp`.

The installed Microsoft parser file is `msxml.dll`. It's a COM component you can use with ASP, VB, C++, or any other development tool that understands COM. To use it in Visual InterDev, the easiest way is to create a project reference to the Microsoft XML Version X.X type library. The advantage of setting a reference in InterDev is that its built-in IntelliSense technology shows you the property and method calls available for each object. Of course, you don't have to set a reference—you can simply create the XML objects as with any other COM component. In this book, I'm using XML version 2, but you can run all the code with the version installed with IE 5.

You can create an instance of the XML parser on either the server or the client, letting you perform data and transform operations on either side of the transaction. The advantage of this is that you can store and manipulate data on the server, using transforms to return HTML for non-IE browsers. Without changing much code, you can perform the same operations within IE—essentially offloading the process to the client and partitioning your application.

To create an instance of the XML parser on the server, use the following:

```
<%
Dim domDoc
set domDoc = Server.CreateObject("MSXML.DOMDocument")
%>
```

The previous statement creates an instance of an XML object called an XML DOMDocument object, which is the root object of the Microsoft XML object model. The DOMDocument object can read and write XML from files and streams. You use the `load` method to read a file. For example, to read the XML file in Listing 30.1 (which is in the file `ch30i1.xml`), you can write:

```
<%
Dim domDoc
Dim aFilename
Set domDoc = server.CreateObject("MSXML.DOMDocument")
aFilename = server.MapPath("ch30i1.xml")
If Not domDoc.Load(aFilename) Then
    Response.Write "Could not load the file."
```

```
        Response.end
End If
%>
```

As the DOMDocument object reads an XML file, it parses it into a collection of sub-objects called nodes. The root node is a special node called the document element node. You can retrieve the document element by creating a node object and setting it to the node returned from the DOMDocument's `documentElement` method. For example:

```
<%
Dim domDoc
Dim aFilename
Dim aNode
Set domDoc = server.CreateObject("MSXML.DOMDocument")
aFilename = server.MapPath("ch30i1.xml")
If Not domDoc.Load(aFilename) Then
        Response.Write "Could not load the file " & aFilename _
        & "<br>"
        Response.end
End If
Set aNode = domDoc.documentElement
%>
```

Nodes can be one of several types, but the most important point is that all nodes share some common methods and properties. For example, all nodes expose an xml property. To view the XML loaded in the previous response, you can create an ASP page and send the XML to the browser as HTML (see Listing 30.3).

LISTING 30.3   **Reading/Viewing XML Code From ASP (ch30i3.asp)**

```
<%@ Language=VBScript %>
<% option explicit %>
<%
Dim domDoc
Dim aFilename
Set domDoc = server.CreateObject("MSXML.DOMDocument")
aFilename = server.MapPath("ch30i1.xml")
If Not domDoc.Load(aFilename) Then
        Response.Write "Could not load the file " & aFilename _
        & "<br>"
        Response.end
End If
%>
<html>
<head>
```

```
    </head>
    <body>

    <pre><code>
    <%=server.HTMLEncode("<xml>" & domDoc.documentElement.xml _
        & "</xml>")%>
    </code></pre>

    </body>
    </html>
```

The code in Listing 30.3 loads the XML file ch30i1.xml, and then displays the contents of the xml method for the document element node. You should notice that you must format the XML for viewing using the Server.HTTPEncode method; otherwise, the browser treats most of the XML data as markup and doesn't display anything. You should also notice that the XML doesn't look the same as when you simply loaded the same XML file directly into the browser. That's because the XML parser within IE applies special XSL formatting to XML files that you load directly. In this case, because the file is an ASP file, the MIME type is text/html by default. Therefore, IE has no idea that the file being loaded contains XML and it doesn't use the built-in XSL style sheet.

Introduction to XSL

Reading a tokenized text file is no great feat; neither is reading it into an object hierarchy, but reading it in such a way that you can later query the resulting objects is. You can think of an XML file as a mini-database. The XML parser understands the database structure and can retrieve any set of data items or any specific data item for you. You retrieve data from XML using XSL.

When you use XSL in this way, you're *filtering* the XML. To filter XML, you use *XSL Patterns* to retrieve one or more nodes. There are two methods to retrieve nodes: SelectNodes, which returns a collection of nodes that match the specified pattern, and SelectSingleNode, which returns the first node that matches the specified pattern.

You can use XSL in another way to transform XML into another format. I'll show you how to use XSL to transform XML into HTML a little later in this chapter. For now, just remember that you can use XSL transforms for more than creating HTML—you could just as easily transform XML into a Word document, a spreadsheet, or a text file.

NOTE For brevity, you can assume in the following examples that the code has already created a DOMDocument object called **domDoc** and loaded the **ch30i1.xml** file by executing the **DomDocument.load** method.

Querying XML with XSL

Using XSL queries, you can return one or more nodes from any location in an XML document. For example, to obtain the values of the **<class>** and **<creator>** nodes, you can query the DOMDocument element with an XSL query string. The value of a node is its nodeValue property. The nodeValue property tries to make intelligent decisions about the data type in the node. It returns a number if the node contains a numeric value and a date if it contains a date. If the parser can't determine the data type, it returns a string (the default). You can always obtain the node value as a string using the text property. Listing 30.4 shows the XSL query syntax to retrieve the nodes.

LISTING 30.4 **Retrieving Nodes with XSL Queries (ch30i4.asp)**

```
<%
set aNode = domDoc.SelectSingleNode("class/name")
Response.Write "The class name is: " & aNode.nodeValue & "<br>"

set aNode = domDoc.SelectSingleNode("class/creator")
Response.Write "The class creator is: " & aNode.nodeValue _
    & "<br>"
%>
```

In a browser, the result looks like Figure 30.4.

You can select several nodes at once with a query. When you do that, the query returns a collection of nodes in an IXMLDOMNodeList object. Don't be intimidated by the long name—the IXMLDOMNodeList object acts much like any other COM collection object. Because of its Java heritage, the XML parser uses a length rather than the more common count property to obtain the number of nodes in the collection. For example:

```
dim nodes
set nodes = domDoc.SelectNodes("class/properties/property")
Response.Write nodes.length ' writes 2
```

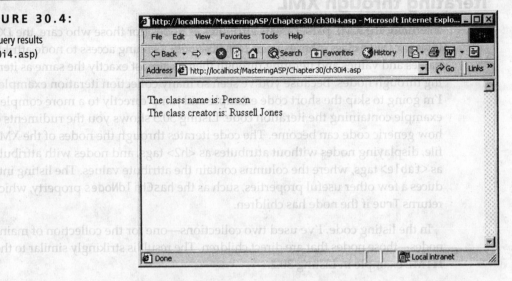

Using `For Each...Next`, you can easily iterate through all of the nodes in a collection. For example:

```
dim nodes
dim node
set nodes = domDoc.SelectNodes("class/properties/property")
For Each node in nodes
   Response.Write node.nodename & "=" & node.nodeValue _
   & "<br>"
Next
```

For nodes that have the same names, you differentiate between them by their attribute values. For example, there are two `<property>` tags, but they have different attribute values. To select a node based on an attribute value, you append a block in square brackets to the XSL query string containing an `@` symbol and the attribute name and value you wish to find. For example:

```
dim node
set node = domDoc.SelectSingleNode _
   ("class/properties/property[@name='lastname']")
Response.Write node.attributes(1).nodeName & "=" & _
   node.attributes(1).nodeValue
' writes name=lastname
```

You can see by the previous code that the attributes of a node:

- Are contained in a collection
- Are themselves nodes (because they have `nodeName` and `nodeValue` properties)

Iterating through XML

Internally, the XML parser treats attributes as nodes (for those who care, the IXML-DOMAttribute class inherits from IXMLDOMNode). Gaining access to node attribute names and values and iterating through them is almost exactly the same as iterating through nodes. Because you've seen so many collection iteration examples, I'm going to skip the short code example and jump directly to a more complex example containing the iteration code. Listing 30.5 shows you the rudiments of how generic code can become. The code iterates through the nodes of the XML file, displaying nodes without attributes as <h2> tags, and nodes with attributes as <table> tags, where the columns contain the attribute values. The listing introduces a few other useful properties, such as the hasChildNodes property, which returns True if the node has children.

In the listing code, I've used two collections—one for the collection of main nodes—those nodes that are direct children. The result is strikingly similar to the HTML example in Listing 30.2.

LISTING 30.5   Iterating Through XML (ch30i5.asp)

```
<%@ Language=VBScript %>
<% option explicit %>
<%
dim domDoc
dim aFilename
Dim node
Dim nodes
dim mainNodes
dim mainNode
dim attr
dim root

Set domDoc = Server.CreateObject("MSXML.DOMDocument")
afilename =server.MapPath("ch30i1.xml")
if not domDoc.load(afilename) then
    Response.Write "Could not load the file " & aFilename _
    & "<br>"
    Response.End
end if
%>
<html>
<head>
</head>
<body>
<%
' display the root node
set root = domDoc.documentElement
```

```
        Response.Write "<h1>" & root.nodename & ": " & _
            root.nodevalue & "</h1>"
    Set mainNodes = root.childNodes
    For Each mainNode In mainNodes
        If mainNode.hasChildNodes = False Then
            Response.Write "<h2>" & mainNode.nodeName & ": " & mainNode
    .text & "</h2><br>"
        Else
            Response.Write "<h3>" & mainNode.nodeName & _
                ": " & mainNode.text & "</h3>"
            Set nodes = mainNode.childNodes
            If nodes.length > 0 Then
                Set node = nodes(0)
                If Not node.Attributes Is Nothing Then
                    If node.Attributes.length > 0 Then
                        Response.Write "<table border='1'>"
                        Response.Write "<thead>"
                        For Each attr In node.Attributes
                            Response.Write "<th>" & _
                            attr.nodeName & "</th>"
                        Next
                        Response.Write "</tr>"

                        For Each node In nodes
                            Response.Write "<tr>"
                            For Each attr In node.Attributes
                                If attr.nodeValue = "" Then
                                    Response.Write "<td>" _
                                    & " " & "</td>"
                                Else
                                    Response.Write "<td>" _
                                    & attr.nodeValue & "</td>"
                                End If
                            Next
                            Response.Write "</tr>"
                        Next
                        Response.Write "</table>"
                    End If
                End If
            End If
        End If
    Next
%>
</body>
</html>
```

Figure 30.5 shows how Listing 30.5 looks in a browser.

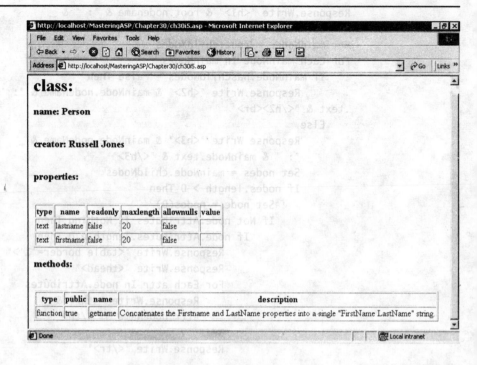

You're probably thinking this isn't any easier than creating the same type of display with record sets. Well, just wait—I'm not through yet. It's important to realize that the code is generic—it can display any XML file. So you can see that in action, I've saved most of the fields in the Employees table from the Microsoft Northwind sample database as an XML file. If you change the filename in the ch30i5.asp file from ch30i1.xml to employees.xml, you can see that the code works equally well with an entirely different record set.

The main points you should have by now are as follows:

- You can find any particular node via an XSL query.

- You can retrieve a collection of nodes with an XSL query.

- You can find one or more nodes that contain a specific attribute and value with an XSL query.

- You can iterate through node collections—whether the collection contains nodes or attributes—using identical syntax (because attributes *are* nodes).

- All nodes have the same properties and methods regardless of their position in the hierarchy.

- Unlike record sets, which represent tables, XML documents represent hierarchies.

The last point is important because you might find it difficult to obtain a single record set from a relational database that contained the same data as the XML file (although you could do it with ADO shaped record sets). Now that you know the basic operations required to transform XML data into HTML, I'll move on to a more automatic method. You should keep in mind that filtering and looping operations like the ones you've just seen are the basis for XSL transforms.

Formatting XML with XSL

An even more generic method for transforming XML into HTML is to create an XSL style sheet template, then reference the style sheet from the XML file.

XSL contains less than 20 element types (tags), each of which consists of XML! For example, the XSL element `<xsl:value-of/>` tells the parser to replace the tag with the value of an XML node.

> **NOTE**
>
> I've made use of the shorthand slash for an empty element. The slash is the equivalent of writing `<xsl:value-of></xsl:value-of>`. XSL is XML, so you *must* close all the tags.

If you don't select a specific XML node, the parser uses the current node. You can select a specific node using a `select` attribute containing an XSL query string. For example, the XSL element `<xsl:value-of select="class/name"/>` replaces the tag with the value `Person`, which is the value of the `<class><name>` tag in the XML file.

You can iterate through nodes using the `<xsl:for-each select="query">` element. For example, the following code iterates through each `<property>` tag in the XML file and selects the value of the name attribute:

```
<xsl:for-each select="class/properties/property">
<xsl:value-of select="@name"/>
</xsl:for-each>
```

Listing 30.6 uses a new copy of the XML file introduced at the beginning of this chapter (ch30i6.xml). The XML content has not changed, but the file contains a reference to an XSL style sheet (ch30i6.xsl). To view the example, point your browser at the file ch30i6.xml.

LISTING 30.6   **XML File with XSL Style Sheet Reference**

```xml
<?xml version='1.0'?>
<?xml-stylesheet type="text/xsl" href="ch30i6.xsl"?>
<class>
  <name>Person</name>
  <creator>Russell Jones</creator>
  <properties>
    <property type="text" name="lastname"
      readonly="false" maxlength="20"
      allownulls="false" value="">
    </property>
    <property type="text" name="firstname"
      readonly="false" maxlength="20" allownulls="false"
      value="">
    </property>
  </properties>
  <methods>
    <method type="function" public="true" name="getname"
      description="Concatenates the Firstname and
      LastName properties into a single &quot;FirstName
      LastName&quot; string.">
    </method>
  </methods>
</class>
```

NOTE   Only IE 5 currently supports viewing XML files directly in the browser. I'll show you how to use the same techniques on the server and output HTML for non-IE browsers.

When IE loads the XML file in Listing 30.6, the XML parser recognizes the style sheet reference, queries the server for the XSL style sheet file, then applies the rules in the template to transform the XML data. The on-screen output is the result of the transformation. Figure 30.6 shows the result.

Interestingly, although the browser is obviously displaying HTML, if you right-click in the browser window and select View Source from the context menu, you won't see any HTML. The source is the XML file itself. The HTML lives only in your browser's memory space.

Transforming data on the browser with XSL is convenient and takes a big load off your server, but only works in IE. If you want to use this technology for down-level browsers, you must perform the XSL transform on the server. To do that, you call the `transformNode` method of the DOMDocument object. Listing 30.7 shows an example.

FIGURE 30.6:

Transforming XML with an XSL style sheet

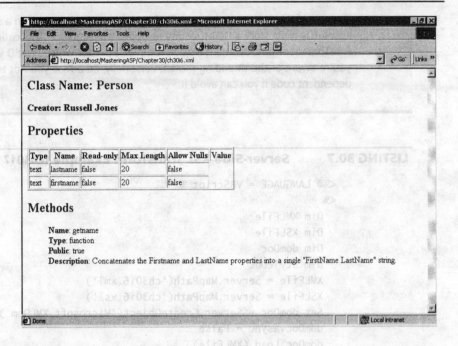

Why So Many ProgIDs?

During this writing, I discovered that the ClassID for the MSXML.DOMDocument object is duplicated under another name—Microsoft.XMLDom. A little research turned up this information:

There are six ProgIDs for creating XMLDOMDocument objects:

- Microsoft.XMLDom is version-independent
- Microsoft XMLDom 1.0 is version-dependent
- MSXML.DomDocument is the class name of the object

With the current release (version 2), all three ProgIDs create the same object—in other words, they all have the same ClassID {2933BF90-7B36-11D2-B20E-00C04F983E60}. The preceding ProgIDs all create apartment-threaded DOMDocument objects.

There are three corresponding ProgIDs that create free-threaded DOMDocument objects:

- Microsoft.FreeThreadedXMLDom
- Microsoft FreeThreadedXMLDom 1.0
- MSXML.DOMFreeThreadedDocument

Continued on next page

Use one of the first set to create DOMDocument objects for use on a single page. If you absolutely must store a DOMDocument object at Session or Application scope, create a FreeThreadedDomDocument object. It doesn't matter which ProgID you use as long as you're aware of the threading model. Personally, I'd advise you not to use any version-dependent code if you can avoid it.

LISTING 30.7   **Server-Side XSL Transform Example (ch30i7.asp)**

```
<%@ LANGUAGE = VBScript %>
<%
  Dim XMLFile
  Dim XSLFile
  Dim domDoc
  Dim styleDoc
  XMLFile = Server.MapPath("ch30i6.xml")
  XSLFile = Server.MapPath("ch30i6.xsl")
  Set domDoc = Server.CreateObject("Microsoft.XMLDom")
  domDoc.async = False
  domDoc.Load (XMLFile)
  If domDoc.parseerror.reason <> "" Then
    Response.Write domDoc.parseerror.reason
    Response.end
  End If
  Set styleDoc = Server.CreateObject("Microsoft.XMLDom")
  styleDoc.async = False
  styleDoc.Load (XSLFile)
  If styleDoc.parseerror.reason <> "" Then
    Response.Write styleDoc.parseerror.reason
    Response.end
  End If
  Response.Write (domDoc.transformNode(styleDoc))
%>
```

The example loads an XML file and the XSL file. It makes no difference if you load an XML file with a style sheet reference or without one. You can prove this by loading either ch30i1.xml, which has no XSL style sheet reference, or ch30i6.xml, as in the example, which does have an XSL style sheet reference. Both versions work identically.

The final line in the listing performs the transform. The transformNode method accepts an XMLDOMNode object (remember that a DOMDocument object is a node) that must contain either a complete XSL style sheet or a style sheet fragment.

Caching Data with XML

You don't have to work with complete XML files to take advantage of XML. Using IE, you can load XML directly inline with HTML or use a URL reference to an XML file on a server, effectively caching the data on the client. To load inline XML into the browser, wrap the XML data with a `<XML ID="someID">` tag. You must provide the ID to be able to access the XML data from a script.

When you place XML inline into the browser it's called a *data island*, perhaps because it's an island of XML data in a sea of HTML.

TIP

You cannot use the processing instruction tag that begins standalone XML files (`<?xml version='1.0'?>`); use a plain `<XML ID="someID">` tag instead. You can place the processing instruction after the `<xml>` tag if you wish.

For example, Listing 30.8 is an HTML file that contains an XML data island.

LISTING 30.8   XML Data Island Example (ch30i8.htm)

```
<html>
<head>
<META NAME="GENERATOR" Content="Microsoft Visual Studio 6.0">
<title></title>
</head>
<body>
<xml id="xmlTest">
<class>
    <name>Person</name>
    <creator>Russell Jones</creator>
    <properties>
      <property type="text" name="lastname"
        readonly="false" maxlength="20"
        allownulls="false" value="">
      </property>
      <property type="text" name="firstname"
        readonly="false" maxlength="20"
        allownulls="false" value="">
      </property>
    </properties>
    <methods>
      <method type="function" public="true" name="getname"
      description="Concatenates the Firstname and
        LastName properties into a single &quot;FirstName
        LastName&quot; string.">
      </method>
```

```
        </methods>
      </class>
    </xml>
  </body>
</html>
<script for="window" event="onload" language="VBScript">
    Call readXML
</script>
<script language="VBScript">
    Sub readXML()
        Dim domDoc
        Dim s
        Dim N
        Set domDoc = xmlTest.XMLDocument
        On Error Resume Next
        s = "Class: " & _
            domDoc.selectSingleNode("class/name").Text _
            & vbCrLf
        s = s & "Creator: " & _
            domDoc.selectSingleNode("class/creator").Text _
            & vbCrLf
        s = s & "PROPERTIES" & vbCrLf
        For Each N In domDoc.SelectNodes _
            ("class/properties/property")
            s = s & "   " & N.Attributes(1).Text & vbCrLf
        Next
        s = s & "METHODS" & vbCrLf
        For Each N In domDoc.SelectNodes _
            ("class/methods/method")
            s = s & "   " & N.Attributes(2).Text & "(" & _
            N.Attributes(3).Text & ")" & vbCrLf
        Next
        MsgBox s
    End Sub
</script>
```

By caching data on the client in XML data islands, you have the complete power of the XML parser and XSL queries available to retrieve the data. But wait! It gets even better! You can create a very generic method to display a table in the browser from a Recordset. You write the data as an XML file, then load the file from the browser along with an XSL style sheet and perform the entire transformation within the browser.

For example, Listing 30.9 shows how to store Recordset data in the browser as XML and transform the XML on the client.

> **NOTE**
>
> You need to provide write and delete access for the `MasteringASP/Chapter30` directory on your server for the `IUSR_MACHINENAME` account before the following script will run properly. It needs write access to persist the Recordset object in XML form and needs delete access to delete the file if it already exists.

LISTING 30.9   Moving Recordset Data to the Browser (ch30i9.asp)

```asp
<%@ Language=VBScript %>
<% option explicit %>
<html><head><title>Transforming XML In the Browser</title></head>
<body>
<%
Dim conn
Dim R
Dim F
Dim fs
Set conn = server.CreateObject("ADODB.Connection")
conn.CursorLocation = adUseClient
conn.Open "DSN=Northwind;UID=sa;PWD="
Set R = server.CreateObject("ADODB.Recordset")
R.CursorLocation = adUseClient
R.Open "SELECT * FROM Products ORDER BY ProductName", conn, adOpenSta-
tic, adLockReadOnly, adcmdtext
Set R.ActiveConnection = Nothing
conn.Close
Set fs = server.CreateObject("Scripting.FileSystemObject")
If fs.FileExists(server.MapPath("products.xml")) Then
    fs.DeleteFile server.MapPath("products.xml")
End If
Call R.Save(server.MapPath("products.xml"), adPersistXML)
%>
<xml id="xmlData" src="products.xml"></xml>
<xml id="xslStyle" src="ch30i9.xsl"></xml>
<div id="xmlResult"></div>
</body>
</html>
<script for="window" event="onload" language="VBScript">
    Call showTable
</script>
<script language="vbScript">
    Sub showTable()
        Dim xml
        Dim xsl
```

```
        On Error Resume Next
        Set xml = xmlData.XMLDocument
        If Err.Number <> 0 Then
            MsgBox Err.Description
        End If
        Set xsl = xslStyle.XMLDocument
        If Err.Number <> 0 Then
            MsgBox Err.Description
        End If
        xmlResult.outerHTML = xml.transformNode(xsl)
        If Err.Number <> 0 Then
            MsgBox Err.Description
        End If
    End Sub
</script>
```

I think what's most interesting about this script is how much it does with so little code.

At this point, you should be fairly comfortable with the rudiments of XML. Don't get complacent though, there's a lot more to learn. For example, you can sort and filter XML using XSL methods. You can update an XML data island, post it to the server, read the data into a Recordset object, then update a database. You can load an ADO.DataControl object with XML data in a data island, then bind controls on the page directly to the DataControl object.

If there's one technology (besides ASP of course) that you concentrate on over the next few months, it should be XML. I urge you to continue exploring XML because it's going to be extremely important in your Web programming career. One excellent source is the Microsoft MSDN Online XML Developer Center at http://msdn .microsoft.com/xml/default.asp. Microsoft has just released XML version 2.5, which extends XML even further throughout the application space.

You've come to the end of this book. I hope you've learned a lot—I certainly have while writing it. A few notes about technologies I didn't cover in the book that you may find worthwhile:

- DHTML behaviors let you store code in a single location on the server that executes on the client. You can apply a behavior to any DOM object. For a good explanation of how to use DHTML behaviors, browse to http://msdn .microsoft.com/workshop/Author/behaviors/howto/using.asp.

- XHTML redefines HTML in a transitional XML format. XHTML recently became a W3C recommendation. A good source of information is http://www.refsnesdata.no/default.asp. You can find the W3C recommendation at http://www.w3.org/TR/xhtml1/.

- XML-based scriptlets are the next version of server scriptlets. These text-based components register themselves as COM objects. You can call them from a browser without changing the page. For example, you might write a validation component as a scriptlet.

- The Simple Object Access Protocol (SOAP) is an XML-based, COM-like protocol that lets you make remote object calls over HTTP. Essentially, you can create an object on a remote server and then access its methods and properties. For more information, browse to `http://www.microsoft.com/mind/0100/soap/soap.asp`.

- Java is a cross-platform language developed by Sun Microsystems. Despite the initial hype, Java has not developed into a super language; nevertheless, in addition to portability, it has three important features that VB does not have (yet). First, you cannot compile a method that calls another method that can raise an error without writing an error-handler. This feature should be standard in every language. I think the greatest weakness of programmers is a lack of attention to error-handling. This leads to weak applications, bad error messages, and frustrated users and support personnel. Second, Java lets you write multi-threaded applications, so you can use it to write components that don't have the threading problems inherent in VB's apartment-only threading model. Third, Java is rapidly becoming the non Microsoft-world's generic language, much as JavaScript/ECMAScript is the preferred scripting language for all browsers except IE. You owe it to yourself to at least become familiar with Java.

APPENDICES

APPENDICES

A P P E N D I X

A

ASP Intrinsic Objects' Methods, Properties, Collections, and Events

Response Object

Response Object Properties

Property	Description
Buffer	Buffers the character stream sent to the browser until page processing completes. You must turn buffering on to issue any commands that write header values, such as `Response.Redirect`. Accepts values of either `True` or `False`.
CacheControl	Controls whether proxy servers can cache the page. Page-caching by browsers and proxies is a problem with ASP, because your server never receives a request if the page is loaded from cache—defeating the purpose of ASP, which is to provide dynamic pages on demand. Accepts values of `"Private"` and `"Public"`. The values are Strings and the quotes are required.
Charset	Controls the character set the browser should use to render the page. The default is `ISO=LATIN-1`. For example, to change the character set to ISO-LATIN-7, use `<% Response.Charset= "ISO-LATIN-7" %>`.
ContentType	Sets a header value that specifies what type of content the page contains. The default value is `text/html`. You may need to change this, particularly if you use the `Response.BinaryWrite` method to send binary data.
Expires	Sets the time interval, in minutes, before the page expires. Until the specified interval elapses, the browser may re-display the page from cache. After the specified period, the browser must return to the server to re-display the page.
ExpiresAbsolute	Sets an exact time when the page expires. Before the specified time, the browser may re-display the page from cache. After the specified time, the browser must return to the server to re-display the page.
IsClientConnected	Before you get excited about this method, it doesn't do what you might think. There's no way to find out whether a specific client is using your application except when a TCP/IP connection is actually in effect. The `IsClientConnected` method is useful only for determining whether you should continue to process a script. For example, if a page takes a long time to respond, you can use this method to check whether the client is still connected. If not, there's no point in continuing to process the script. Note that the `IsClientConnected` method does not tell you *which* client is connected.
Pics	Adds an HTTP header value containing a Platform for Internet Content Selection (PICS) label. The PICS label contains a rating for the page. Using this system, parents can determine the levels of content that their children can see. For more information, see the PICS specification on the W3C Web site: `http://www.w3.org`.
Status	Sets the value of the status line returned by the server. You may have seen this error before—`404 Not Found`. You set the `Status` property to return a specific number and explanation to the browser. The HTTP specification defines the set of valid status values and their meanings.

Response Object Methods

Method	Description
AddHeader	Adds a header with a specified value, for example: `Response.AddHeader "myheader", "myValue"`.
AppendToLog	Appends a custom string to the end of the current IIS log entry. You can use this to write special messages that you may pick up later with a log analysis tool.
BinaryWrite	Used to write non-textual data to the browser. You can use this method to send image, audio, or other binary to the browser. You'll see more about the `BinaryWrite` method in Chapter 6, *The Request Object*.
Clear	Clears the contents of the server response buffer. If you are in the middle of processing a page and some condition causes you to want to restart the page, you can clear the buffer (assuming you're buffering the response) by issuing the `Response.Clear` command.
End	Ends the response. This command takes effect immediately. The server will not process any code or HTML that follows the `Response.End` command.
Flush	Sends any buffered content to the browser. You might want to do this for long pages. Note that the `Response.Flush` method raises an error if you have not set the `Response.Buffer` to `True`.
Redirect	Sends a header to the browser telling it to request a new page. You specify the URL for the page along with any `QueryString` variables and values.
Write	Writes text and HTML content to the browser.

Response Object Collection

Collection	Description
Cookies	Use this collection to write both per-session and persistent cookies to the client browser.

Request Object

Request Object Property

Property	Description
TotalBytes	Returns the total number of bytes in the request, including data from form fields, but not the size of `QueryString` data.

Request Object Method

Method	Description
BinaryRead(count)	Reads posted binary (non-textual) data sent with a request. You must specify the number of bytes you want to read in the count argument. Referring to any other variable in the Request.Form collection before or after using the Binary-Read method causes an error.

Request Object Collections

Collection	Description
ClientCertificate	Contains a collection of certificates sent by the browser with a request to a secured (https) site.
Cookies	Contains a collection of cookie values. The collection includes both per-session and persistent cookies.
Form	Contains a collection of form values. The values include all the `<input>` tag values from the originating page in the browser.
QueryString	Contains a collection of values appended to a URL with a request.
ServerVariables	Contains a collection of generic values sent by the browser with every request. Many of the values are standard—all browsers send the values. Other values are browser-specific. You can retrieve non-standard values by appending the variable name with HTTP_, for example: `Request.ServerVariables _("HTTP_CustomVar")`.

Application Object

Application Object Properties

The Application object has no properties.

Application Object Methods

Method	Description
Contents.Remove(key/index)	Removes the Application variable with the specified key or index from the collection of Application variables.
Contents.RemoveAll	Removes all variables from the collection of Application variables.
Lock	Locks the Application object until you issue an `Application.Unlock` command, until page-processing ends, or until the page times out. You must lock the Application object to add or update variables or values. You do not need to lock the Application object to retrieve variable values.
Unlock	Unlocks the Application object if it is locked. You should always unlock the Application object as soon as possible after locking it.

Application Object Collections

Collection	Description
Contents	Contains the collection of Application variables you have defined in your application.
StaticObjects	Contains the collection of objects defined with `<object>` tags at application scope.

Application Object Events

Event	Description
Application_OnEnd	Occurs after the ASP engine destroys the last session. You should use this event to destroy any objects stored at application scope.
Application_OnStart	Occurs before the ASP engine creates the first Session object. You should use this to create objects and initialize variables with application scope.

Server Object

Server Object Property

Property	Description
ScriptTimeout	Specifies the duration, in minutes, after which a script will timeout if processing is not complete. The default value is 90 seconds, which I consider at least double the optimum value except for very busy sites or extremely large pages.

Server Object Methods

Event	Description
CreateObject(ProgID)	Creates an ActiveX object. You provide a valid `ProgID`, for example: `Server.CreateObject ("Scripting.Dictionary")`.
Execute(filename)	Executes another ASP script. ASP preserves the values of all intrinsic objects during the call. The executed pages may return a value, for example: `ret=Server.Execute ("aPage.asp")`.
GetLastError	Retrieves the last ASP error values. Use this method when creating custom error pages.
HTMLEncode(string)	Encodes the `string` argument by replacing ampersands, angle brackets, and other non-text characters with special tokens that the browser will display as the original character.

Continued on next page

Event	Description
MapPath(path)	Performs virtual path to physical path conversion. The primary use for the MapPath method is to obtain a full physical path to file resources, as required by the FileSystemObject.
Transfer(filename)	Transfers processing to another ASP file. ASP preserves the values of all intrinsic objects. Unlike the Server.Execute method, this method does not return to the caller. Use this to perform server-side redirects and save the round trip to the browser required by Response.Redirect.
URLEncode(string)	Applies Base-64 encoding to the characters in the string argument.

Session Object

Session Object Properties

Property	Description
CodePage	Sets or returns the code page used for mapping characters and symbols. The default is 1252 (American English).
LCID	Sets or returns a Locale Identifier. You can also set the locale with the @LCID directive. Setting the Session.LCID property overrides the @LCID setting. Use this to output dates and currency values in the preferred format for the specified locale.
SessionID	Read-only. Returns the SessionID for the current session. The value returned by the SessionID is unique for the instance of IIS. It is not globally unique; it is only unique to a user during the duration of a single IIS instance. Therefore, if you cycle your server, the value may repeat. Avoid storing user data keyed to a specific SessionID value for data that you need to persist across sessions.
Timeout	Specifies, in minutes, the time until the ASP engine will destroy an inactive session. The default is 20 minutes in IIS 4, 10 minutes in IIS 5.

Session Object Methods

Method	Description
Abandon	Destroys the session and all objects stored at session scope. The ASP engine doesn't actually destroy the session until page-processing completes.
Contents.Remove	Removes an item from the Session.Contents collection. The Session.Contents collection contains all Session variables except those added through an <object> tag with session scope.
Contents.RemoveAll	Removes all items from the Session.Contents collection. You might use this method to clear a session before abandoning it.

Session Object Collections

Collection	Description
Contents	The Session.Contents collection contains all Session variables except those added through an <object> tag with session scope.
StaticObjects	Contains the collection of objects defined with <object> tags at session scope.

Session Object Events

Event	Description
Session_OnEnd	Occurs just before the ASP engine destroys the current Session object. You should use this event to destroy any objects stored at session scope.
Session_OnStart	Occurs just before the ASP engine creates the current Session object. You should use this to create objects and initialize variables with session scope.

ObjectContext Object

ObjectContext Object Properties

The ObjectContext object has no properties.

ObjectContext Object Methods

Methods	Description
SetAbort	Aborts a transaction initiated by an ASP page.
SetComplete	Attests that the page is ready to commit the current transaction. The transaction commits if, and only if, all other components involved in the transaction also call the SetComplete method for the context in which the transaction is running.

ObjectContext Object Events

Event	Description
OnTransactionAbort	Occurs when any component involved in a transaction calls the ObjectContext.SetAbort method. In other words, calling the SetAbort method causes the OnTransactionAbort event to fire. You cannot cancel the abort event—it has already occurred when this event fires.
OnTransactionCommit	Occurs after all components involved in the transaction have called the ObjectContext.SetComplete method.

ASPError Object

ASPError Object Properties

Property	Description
ASPCode	Contains an IIS error code in string form for the most recent error.
Number	Contains a long integer that holds the COM error code generated by the component that raised the error.
Source	Contains a string describing the source of the error—what component or method was running when the error occurred.
Category	Returns a string specifying whether the most recent error was caused by the ASP engine or by a component.
File	Contains the name of the current ASP file. Note that the filename may have little or nothing to do with errors generated by components.
Line	Contains the line number of the line within the current ASP file that was executing when the error occurred.
Column	Contains the column position within the line of the current ASP file that was executing when the error occurred.
Description	Contains a description of the error.
ASPDescription	Contains a detailed description of ASP-generated errors.

ASPError Object Methods

The ASPError object has no methods.

ASPError Object Events

The ASPError object does not raise any events.

A P P E N D I X

B

ASP Components' Methods and Properties

Components Shipped with ASP

ASP 3 and IIS 5 ship with the following components. The IIS standard install does not install all the components—you must manually install some components from the CD.

Component	Description
Ad Rotator	Creates an AdRotator object that loops through a series of advertisement graphics, displaying each one for a configurable length of time.
Browser Capabilities	Creates a BrowserType object you can use to determine the browser type and version making the request to your server.
Content Linking	Creates a NextLink object that provides automatic Next links for a series of pages.
Content Rotator	Creates a ContentRotator object that automates the display of a series of content strings, displaying a different string each time the page loads.
Counters	Creates a Counters object that can create, store, increment, and retrieve any number of individual counters.
Logging Utility	Gives you programmatic access to the HTTP activity log files that IIS generates.
MyInfo	Creates a MyInfo object that keeps track of personal information, such as the site administrator's name, address, and display choices.
Page Counter	Keeps track of the number of visits to a Web page.
Permission Checker	Uses the password authentication protocols provided in Microsoft Internet Information Services (IIS) to determine whether a Web user has permission to read a file.
Tools	The Tools object provides utilities that enable you to add sophisticated functionality to your Web pages easily.

The AdRotator Component (*adrot.dll*)

The AdRotator component manages the timing and display of advertising banners on a site.

AdRotator Component—Required Files

File	Description
Rotator Schedule File	Contains the file and schedule information for advertisements.
Redirection File	Contains a URL and a counter for each ad. When a user clicks on an advertisement, the AdRotator component retrieves the associated URL from the Redirection file and increments the counter.

AdRotator Object Properties

Property	Description
Border	Determines the thickness of the border around advertisements. Set this property to 0 to display ads with no border. The default value resides in the Rotator Schedule file.
Clickable	Determines whether an advertisement is a link.
TargetFrame	Specifies the name of the frame in which to display the advertisement.

AdRotator Object Method

Event	Description
GetAdvertisement	You specify the virtual path and filename to a Rotator Schedule file. The Get-Advertisement method retrieves the next ad from the file. It returns the HTML required to display the ad.

The Browser Capabilities Component

The Browser Capabilities component provides information about the type and version of the browser making a request. It exposes a BrowserType object.

BrowserType Object Property

The BrowserType object has only one property.

Property	Description
Value	Given a string key, the Value property returns an associated value. Because this is the default (and only) public property of the BrowserType object, you do not need to use the keyword Value. For example, if you have a BrowserType object reference in the variable bc, you can retrieve the value with the syntax bc.Value("Browser") or bc("Browser"), or even bc.Browser. All the syntax variations return the same value string.

The Content Linking Component (*nextlink.dll*)

The Content Linking component lets you control a user's path through a Web site. The component exposes the NextLink object.

Content Linking Component—Required File

File	Description
Content Linking List	Contains a list of URLs in the sequence you wish users to traverse the site.

NextLink Object Methods

Method	Description
GetListCount	Counts the number of items linked in the Content Linking List file.
GetListIndex	Gets the index of the current page in the Content Linking List file.
GetNextDescription	Gets the description of the next page listed in the Content Linking List file.
GetNextURL	Gets the URL of the next page listed in the Content Linking List file.
GetNthDescription	Gets the description of the Nth page listed in the Content Linking List file.
GetNthURL	Gets the URL of the Nth page listed in the Content Linking List file.
GetPreviousDescription	Gets the description line of the previous page listed in the Content Linking List file.
GetPreviousURL	Gets the URL of the previous pages listed in the Content Linking List file.

The Content Rotator Component (*controt.dll*)

The Content Rotator component functions much like the AdRotator component, except that it displays a single line of HTML content. That content may consist of any HTML the browser can interpret, meaning you can include sounds, graphics, animations, and links, as well as text. The component rotates the content on a schedule. You can weight the content to force some items to display more often than others.

The Content Rotator component exposes a ContentRotator object.

Content Linking Component—Required File

File	Description
Content Schedule	Contains a list of files, weights, and schedule information.

ContentRotator Object Methods

Method	Description
ChooseContent	Selects the next item for display.
GetAllContent	Retrieves and displays all HTML strings in the Content Schedule file without regard to weighting information.

The Counters Component (*counters.dll*)

The Counters component implements persistent named counters. You need only instantiate one Counters object, which you may then use to maintain many counters. The counters do not increment automatically; you control when the counters increment, making the Counters component highly reusable.

Counters Component Methods

Method/Property	Description
Get (counterName)	Returns the value of the counter.
Increment(counterName)	Increases the counter by 1.
Remove(counterName)	Removes the counter from the counters.txt file.
Set(counterName)	Sets the value of the counter to a specific integer.

The Logging Utility (*logscrpt.dll*)

You use the Logging Utility (also called the IIS Log Component) to programmatically insert and extract information from the IIS log file. The Logging Utility exposes an IISLog object.

Methods to Read and Write Log Files

Method	Description
AtEndOfLog	Indicates whether all records have been read from the log file.
CloseLogFiles	Closes all open log files.
OpenLogFile	Opens a log file for reading or writing.
ReadFilter	Filters records from the log file by date and time.
ReadLogRecord	Reads the next available log record from the current log file.
WriteLogRecord	Writes a log record to the current log file.

Methods to Retrieve Individual Values

Method	Description
BytesReceived	Retrieves the bytes received.
BytesSent	Retrieves the bytes sent.
ClientIP	Retrieves the client's IP address.
Cookie	Retrieves the client's cookie, if any.
CustomFields	Returns an array of custom headers.
DateTime	Retrieves the date and time, in GMT.
Method	Retrieves the HTTP operation type.
ProtocolStatus	Retrieves the protocol status.
ProtocolVersion	Retrieves the IISLog object's version string.
GetProtocolStatus	Retrieves the HTTP protocol status.
Referer	Indicates the referrer page.
ServerIP	Retrieves the server's IP address.
ServerName	Retrieves the server name.
ServerPort	Retrieves the port number of the server.
ServiceName	Retrieves the service name.
TimeTaken	Retrieves the total time required to process this request.
URIQuery	Retrieves any QueryString parameters passed with the request.
URIStem	Retrieves the target URL, without any appended QueryString values.
UserAgent	Retrieves the user agent string.
Win32Status	Retrieves the server status.

The MyInfo Component (*myinfo.dll*)

The MyInfo component maintains personal information in an XML file. You may create only one MyInfo component per site. Create the component at application scope with an <object> tag. For example:

```
<OBJECT RUNAT="SERVER SCOPE=APPLICATION ID=MyInfo
    PROGID="Mswc.Myinfo">
</OBJECT>
```

MyInfo Component—Required File

File	Description
MyInfo.xml	XML file containing personal information. On Windows 95/98, Personal Web Server (PWS) instantiates and uses this file to maintain administrator information. Therefore, the file will contain pre-written values on Windows 95/98.

MyInfo Component—Properties

Under Windows 95/98, the MyInfo component may contain the following properties, depending on how the owner has set up Personal Web Server. Under Windows NT/2000, these properties are not available.

Property	Description
Background	Returns the background for the site.
CommunityLocation	Returns the location of the community.
CommunityName	Returns the name of the community featured on the site.
CommunityPopulation	Returns the population of the community.
CommunityWords	Returns text describing the community.
CompanyAddress	Returns the address of the owner's company.
CompanyName	Returns the name of the owner's company.
CompanyPhone	Returns the phone number of the owner's company.
CompanyDepartment	Returns the owner's department name.
CompanyWords	Returns additional text associated with the owner's company.
Guestbook	Returns −1 if the guest book should be available on the site. Otherwise, returns 0. The default value is "".
HomeOccupation	Returns the owner's occupation.
HomePeople	Returns text listing the people the owner lives with.
HomeWords	Returns additional text associated with the owner.
Messages	Returns −1 if the private message form should be available on the site. Otherwise, returns 0. The default value is "".
OrganizationAddress	Returns the address of the organization.
OrganizationName	Returns the name of the organization featured on the site.
OrganizationPhone	Returns the phone number of the organization.
OrganizationWords	Returns text describing the organization.
PageType	Returns a number corresponding to the value in the "This site is..." pop-up menu in the Personal Web Services control panel. These are the pop-up menu options with their corresponding numerical values:
	1 = About My Company
	2 = About My Life
	3 = About My School
	4 = About My Organization
	5 = About My Community
PersonalAddress	Returns the owner's address.
PersonalMail	Returns the owner's email address.
PersonalName	Returns the owner's name.
PersonalPhone	Returns the owner's phone number.
PersonalWords	Returns additional text associated with the owner.
SchoolAddress	Returns the address of the owner's school.

Continued on next page

Property	Description
SchoolDepartment	Returns the owner's department or class.
SchoolName	Returns the name of the owner's school.
SchoolPhone	Returns the phone number of the owner's school.
SchoolWords	Returns text associated with the owner's school.
Style	Returns the relative URL (starting with "/") of a style sheet.
Title	Returns the user-defined title for the home page.
URL(n)	Returns the nth user-defined URL. Corresponds to the nth link description in `MyInfo.URLWords`.
URLWords(n)	Returns a string containing the nth user-defined description of a link. Corresponds to the nth URL in `MyInfo.URL`.

MyInfo Component—Methods

The MyInfo component has no methods; however, you assign new properties to the component using the syntax:

```
MyInfo.NewName = NewValue
```

APPENDIX

C

Quick HTML Reference

This reference covers the most commonly used tags for HTML 4. Although end tags are not always required for compliance with HTML, you should get in the habit of explicitly ending all tags so that your HTML will be eXtensible Hypertext Markup Language (XHTML) or eXtensible Markup Language (XML) compliant.

HTML is not case-sensitive; but the W3C recommends you use uppercase for tags and lowercase for attributes. XML is case-sensitive. The XHTML specification requires all tags to be lowercase. Therefore, I recommend you use lowercase for all tags, which is the only method that meets the requirements of all three specifications.

Quick Tag Reference

This reference shows the HTML 4 tags in alphabetical order. Some of the tags have been *deprecated*, which means they are no longer recommended (although they still work). To keep your pages from becoming obsolete, use the alternate recommended tag instead.

Tag	Description
`<!--`	Begins a comment section.
`-->`	Ends a comment section.
`!doctype`	Specifies the Document Type Definition (DTD) of the document. For example `<!DOCTYPE HTML PUBLIC "-//W3C//DTD HTML 4.0 Strict//EN">` specifies strict compliance with the W3C HTML 4 specification.
`a`	Defines an anchor tag.
`abbr`	Specifies an abbreviation.
`acronym`	Specifies an acronym.
`address`	Formats text as an address.
`applet`	Embeds a Java applet into the page. This element has been deprecated in HTML 4; use an `<object>` tag instead.
`area`	Defines a clickable shape within a graphic.
`b`	Formats text as bold.
`base`	Sets the base URL for the page.
`basefont`	Sets the base font for the page. Subsequent font settings are relative to the `<basefont>` tag. You should use this tag before any text rendered in the document. This element has been deprecated in HTML 4; use a style sheet instead.
`bdo`	Specifies a different character rendering order for Unicode text. You must include a `dir=` attribute (deprecated) specifying the character rendering direction with the `<bdo>` tag.
`bgsound`	Specifies a background audio file. The file begins loading after the remainder of the page.
`big`	Formats text larger than the surrounding text.
`blockquote`	Indents text.

Continued on next page

Tag	Description
body	Encloses the body of the document.
br	Inserts a carriage return/linefeed.
button	Displays a button.
caption	Specifies a table caption.
center	Centers content. This element has been deprecated in HTML 4; use a style sheet instead.
cite	Indicates a citation.
code	Displays code in a small, fixed-width font.
col	Specifies default settings for a table column.
colgroup	Groups columns with similar formatting needs.
comment	Obsolete—use <-- --> instead.
dd	Used for the definition portion of a definition list.
del	Indicates text that has been deleted from the document.
dfn	Used for the first instance of a term in a document, called the *defining* instance.
dir	Begins a directory listing. The items in the directory listing must begin with an <li> (list item) tag. This element has been deprecated in HTML 4; use a <ul> tag instead.
div	Indicates a document division. In Netscape, these are called layers. Use the <div> tag to separate a document into individually-programmable sections.
dl	Begins a definition list.
dt	Used for the term portion of a definition list.
em	Emphasizes text. Most browsers italicize text with this tag.
embed	Embeds a document into an HTML page. The browser must have the appropriate application or viewer to view the content.
fieldset	Groups fields within a form, placing a border around them with a title—much like the border around related elements on a Windows dialog box.
font	Sets the font size, face, and color. This element has been deprecated in HTML 4; use a style sheet instead.
form	Begins a form.
frame	Defines a frame within a <frameset> tag.
frameset	Defines a frameset—a group of related frames. You define frame sizes within the <frameset> tag.
h1	Heading 1 text (largest).
h2	Heading 2 text.
h3	Heading 3 text.
h4	Heading 4 text.
h5	Heading 5 text.
h6	Heading 6 text (smallest).
head	Denotes the head section of a document. You place header information between the <head></head> tags.
hr	Inserts a horizontal rule (a line).
html	Required start/end tag for an HTML document.
i	Formats text in italics.

Continued on next page

Tag	Description
iframe	Defines an inline frame. The frame appears as an embedded browser window within the document. The embedded browser does not display a frame or toolbars.
img	Places an image into the document.
input	Defines an `<input>` tag. There are several types:
	`text`
	`password`
	`button`
	`submit`
	`reset`
	`radio`
	`checkbox`
	`hidden`
	`image`
	`file`
	These input controls are scriptable even in earlier HTML versions. In some browsers these input controls must appear inside a `<form>` tag. Some browsers don't support the `type=file <input>` tag attribute.
ins	Formats text as having been inserted into a document.
isindex	This element has been deprecated in HTML 4; use an `<input>` tag instead.
kbd	Formats text as if it were input from a keyboard—in a monospaced font.
label	Displays a label and associates the label with an element.
layer	This is a Netscape-specific tag. It is essentially the same as the `<div>` tag.
legend	Adds a legend for a `<fieldset>` tag. The `<legend>` tag must appear immediately after the `<fieldset>` tag.
li	Adds an item to an `<ol>` ordered or `<ul>` unordered list.
link	Used in the `<head>` section of a document to specify a typed link to another document. Most often seen with style sheet references. For example: `<LINK REL="stylesheet" HREF="styles.css" TYPE="text/css">`.
listing	Obsolete. Use `<pre>` instead. Formats text in a fixed-width font for a code listing.
map	Defines a collection of hotspots for a client-side image map. The tag contains a collection of `<area>` tags. You can apply a defined map within an `<img>` tag with the `usemap=` attribute.
marquee	Defines a scrolling text area. The text for the marquee appears between the start and end tags.
menu	Begins a menu list. Place the menu items between `<li></li>` tags. This element has been deprecated in HTML 4; use a `<ul>` tag instead.
meta	Contains meta-information about the document. Place `<meta>` tags in the head section of the document.
nobr	Specifies that you don't want to break text to fit within the boundaries of its container.
noframes	Use this tag with the `<frameset>` tag to provide content to down-level browsers that can't render frames. Place the `<noframes>` tag within the `<frameset></frameset>` tags.
noscript	Defines text that appears for down-level browsers that can't run script.

Continued on next page

Tag	Description
object	Inserts an object—such as an image, ActiveX control, or document—into the HTML document.
ol	Defines an ordered list. The list items appear numbered. Place items in the list between `<li></li>` tags.
option	Defines an item in a `<select>` list.
optgroup	Defines a subgroup of items within a `<select>` list.
p	Defines a paragraph.
param	Defines an initial setting or value for an `<object>` or `<embed>` tag.
plaintext	Obsolete; use `<pre>` instead. Specifies that the browser should render the following text without processing tags. The browser displays the closing `</plaintext>` tag, if present.
pre	Specifies that the browser should render the following text exactly as it appears—the text is "pre" formatted.
q	Formats text as a quotation. Use only with short quotations. Use `<blockquote>` for longer quoted sections.
s	Renders text in strikethrough characters. This element has been deprecated in HTML 4; use a style sheet instead.
samp	Renders text in a small, fixed-width font.
script	Specifies that the following text is script, not HTML. To avoid problems with down-level browsers, place the script within this tag inside a comment. For example: `<script><-script code here -></script>`.
select	Defines a list of selectable items—equivalent to a VB listbox or combobox, depending on the value of the `height=` attribute. Appears as a list when the `height` attribute is greater than 1.
small	Renders text in a smaller font than the surrounding text.
span	Like a `<div>` tag, the `<span>` tag defines a section of a document. You may use it to apply special CSS formatting to individual items on the page.
strike	Renders text in strikethrough font. This element has been deprecated in HTML 4; use a style sheet instead.
strong	Renders text in bold print.
style	Defines a style sheet for a document.
sub	Renders text as a subscript.
sup	Renders text as a superscript.
table	Defines a table.
tbody	Optional tag—serves to separate the body of a table from the head and footer sections.
td	Defines a cell—stands for *table data*.
textarea	Defines a multi-line text input control. Unlike the `<input type="text">` tag, you place the text for the `<textarea>` tag between the start and end tags.
tfoot	Optional tag—defines the footer area of a table.
th	Use this in the `<thead>` section of a table in place of the `<td>` tag.
thead	Defines the header section of a table.
title	Defines the title of the document. The title appears in the browser title bar. Used in the `<head>` section of a document.

Continued on next page

Tag	Description
tr	Defines a table row.
tt	Renders text in a fixed-width font like a teletype terminal.
u	Renders underlined text. This element has been deprecated in HTML 4; use a style sheet instead.
ul	Creates an unordered list. The list items appear as bullets. Place items in the list between `<li></li>` tags.
var	Defines text that specifies a variable name, for example: `<var>filename</var>=c:\someFile`.
wbr	Inserts a soft line break in a line of `<nobr>` text.
xmp	Obsolete, use `<pre>` instead. The `<xmp>` tag renders the text of an example in a small, fixed-width font.

HTML 4 Attribute Reference

This section contains a complete listing of the W3C-approved attributes for HTML 4, including those attributes termed *deprecated* (which means they are no longer recommended and you shouldn't use them). In general, the deprecated attributes assigned style information to their parent element. In HTML 4, you should use style sheets or inline styles to define style information. In addition, all attributes that apply to deprecated tags have been deprecated. I have noted deprecated attributes and deprecated tags with (d).

Unfortunately, no browser currently implements *all* the possible attribute values. Check the browser manufacturer's documentation for specific information about individual browsers.

The HTML 4 specification provides seven main attributes, which are common to nearly all elements and have the same meaning for all elements. These elements are:

- id
- name
- class
- style
- title
- lang
- language

You should avoid setting a tag's `id` and its `name` attribute to the same value if you must deliver content to down-level browsers.

The `name` attribute provides an identifying name for the element. In HTML 4, you should use the `id` attribute in preference to the `name` attribute.

The `id` attribute should identify a single item explicitly and uniquely. In previous versions of HTML, you could link only to anchor tags. In this version, you may create a link to any element with a unique `id`.

The `style` attribute contains a string specifying style settings for that element. Style settings specified in the `<style>` tag are called inline styles, as opposed to style settings an element inherits from a Cascading Style Sheet (CSS). Inline styles always take precedence over CSS styles.

The `class` attribute defines the class name for the tag and determines which CSS class styles apply to the tag element. This is unimportant until you want to begin programming the tag elements from script. It becomes important then because you can easily change the look and feel of the tag by changing its class affiliation.

The `title` attribute defines the tool-tip text that appears when you place your cursor over the element. You may leave this attribute blank.

The `lang` attribute defines the language for the element. The value is any valid language code. You will find the language codes at `http://msdn.microsoft.com/workshop/author/dhtml/reference/language_codes.asp#language_codes`.

The `language` attribute defines the scripting language used to handle element events. The valid values are `VBScript`, `VBS`, `JavaScript`, and `JScript`.

Most elements that reference other documents do so via a Uniform Resource Identifier (URI) as opposed to a Uniform Resource Locator (URL). The change in terminology reflects the reality that not all references refer to a file.

Attribute	Applies To	Value or Description
abbr	td th	Designates an abbreviation for table header cell.
accept-charset	form	Contains a list of supported character sets.
accept	form input	List of MIME types for file upload.
accesskey	a area button input label legend textarea	Specifies a shortcut key.

Continued on next page

Attribute	Applies To	Value or Description
action	form	Specifies the URI to which to submit form data.
align	applet (d)	Specifies alignment. In some cases, the alignment may be relative to a containing parent tag; in others it specifies the alignment of content within the tag.
	caption (d)	
	col	
	colgroup	
	div (d)	
	h1 (d)	
	h2(d)	
	h3 (d)	
	h4 (d)	
	h5 (d)	
	h6 (d)	
	hr (d)	
	iframe (d)	
	img (d)	
	input (d)	
	legend (d)	
	object (d)	
	p (d)	
	tbody	
	td	
	tfoot	
	th	
	thead	
	tr	
alink (d)	body	Color of selected links.
alt	applet (d)	Contains a short text description. This text appears when a user hovers over an element.
	area	
	img	
	input	
archive	applet (d)	Specifies a list of archive locations.
	object	
axis	td	Contains a comma-separated list of related headers.
	th	
background (d)	body	Specifies a background tiled image for the document.
bgcolor (d)	body	Specifies the background color for the element.
	table	
	td	
	th	
	tr	
border (d)	img	Specifies the width of the element's border.
	object	
	table	
cellpadding	table	Specifies the white space between the outer edge of content and the inner edge of a table cell border.
cellspacing	table	Specifies the spacing between table cells.

Continued on next page

Attribute	Applies To	Value or Description
char	col colgroup tbody td tfoot th thead tr	Specifies a character that controls alignment. Used in conjunction with the `align="char"` attribute. For example, if you specify the decimal point as the alignment character, numbers should appear aligned by the decimal point.
charoff	col colgroup tbody td tfoot th thead tr	The offset for the alignment character from the containing element margin.
charset	a link script	Specifies the character-encoding of the content specified in the anchor, link, or script.
checked	input	Controls whether a checkbox or radio button appears selected.
cite	blockquote del ins q	URL for the source of a quote or block quote. For deleted or inserted text, this attribute states the reason for the change.
class	all elements except base basefont (d) head html meta param script style title	Space-separated list of classes to which this element belongs.
classid	object	Specifies the URL for the implementation of a class.
clear (d)	br	Specifies where the line following the ` ` tag should begin. Use style sheets and classes to implement this behavior in HTML 4.
code	applet (d)	Specifies the path to an applet's class file.
codebase	applet (d) object	Determines the base URI for an applet object. After specifying the `codebase`, you may specify all subsequent URIs as relative to the `codebase` URI.
codetype	object	Specifies the content type of an `<object>`.
color (d)	basefont (d) font (d)	Determines the text color. To change the color of other elements, use the `style` attribute.

Continued on next page

Attribute	Applies To	Value or Description
cols	frameset textarea	Specifies the width of a frameset in pixels, or of a textarea in characters.
colspan	td th	Controls the number of columns spanned by a table cell.
compact (d)	dir dl menu ol uldir dl menu ol ul	Reduces the spacing between items.
content	meta	Specifies the content of a `<meta>` tag.
coords	area a	Contains a comma-separated list of coordinates (points) for use with client-side image maps.
data	object	Contains a URI specifying the location of an object's data.
datetime	del, ins	Contains the date and time the content was changed.
defer	script	UA may defer execution of script.
dir	all elements except applet (d) base basefont (d) br frame frameset iframe param script	Specifies the direction for text when the direction information is lacking in Unicode. For the `<bdo>` tag, the `dir=` attribute overrides Unicode directionality.
disabled	button input optgroup option select textarea	Specifies that the input control may not receive focus, does not generate events, and is removed from the control tab order.
enctype	form	Specifies the type of content the form will submit to the server. The default value is `application/x-www-form-urlencoded`. For file uploads (`input type=file`) use the value `multipart/form-data`.
face (d)	basefont (d) font (d)	Specifies a font face name, or optionally, a comma-delimited list of alternate face names.
for	label	Determines the field to which a label belongs.
frame	table	Controls which parts of the table border the browser should render.
frameborder	frame iframe	Specifies whether the browser should render a separator (usually a pixel) between one border and another.

Continued on next page

Attribute	Applies To	Value or Description
headers	td th	Contains a comma-delimited list of column titles. Use this attribute so that non-visual browsers (like speech-enabled browsers for the blind) can deliver information about table contents.
height	applet (d) iframe img object td (d) th (d)	Specifies the height of the element/object in pixels.
href	a area base link	Contains a URL specifying either a content source (base) or a destination (a, area, link).
hreflang	a link	Contains the language code of the language for the destination specified by the href attribute.
hspace (d)	applet (d) img object	Determines the amount of horizontal space added around the element.
http-equiv	meta	HTTP response header name.
id	all elements except base head html meta script style title	Specifies a unique ID for the element.
ismap	img input	Specifies a server-side image map. This attribute does not take a value.
label	option optgroup	Alternate short contents for display.
lang	all elements except applet (d) base basefont (d) br frame frameset iframe param script	Contains the language code for the element.
language (d)	script	Contains a scripting language name. Use a `<meta http-equiv="Content-Script-Type" content="VBScript|VBS|JScript|JavaScript">` tag instead. Despite this attribute having been deprecated, it is still in common use throughout the Web.

Continued on next page

Attribute	Applies To	Value or Description
`link` (d)	`body`	Specifies the initial color of links—the color before they're visited.
`longdesc`	`img`	Specifies a link to a `long` description. Use the `alt` attribute for short descriptions.
`longdesc`	`frame` `iframe`	Link to `long` description (complements title).
`marginheight`	`frame` `iframe`	Determines the top and bottom inside margin height in pixels.
`marginwidth`	`frame` `iframe`	Determines the left and right inside margin width in pixels.
`maxlength`	`input`	Specifies the maximum number of characters allowed in an `input` field.
`media`	`link` `style`	Contains a comma-delimited list of media where the content should be rendered. The possible values are `screen`, `tty`, `tv`, `projection`, `handheld`, `print`, `braille`, `aural`, and `all`. The default value is `screen`.
`method`	`form`	Specifies the HTTP method used to submit a form. Values are `get` and `post`. Unfortunately, `get` is the default, which appends form content to the URL, where it's visible.
`multiple`	`select`	Specifies that the user may select more than one value in a select list. This attribute does not take a value.
`name`	`a` `applet` (d) `button` `form` `frame` `iframe` `img` `input` `map` `meta` `object` `param` `select` `textarea`	Provides a means of identifying elements.
`nohref`	`area`	Specifies that an area on an image map has no target URL.
`noresize`	`frame`	Determines whether the user may resize a frame.
`noshade` (d)	`hr`	Specifies a flat rule rather than a raised rule.
`nowrap` (d)	`td` `th`	Disables automatic text wrapping within the cell.
`object` (d)	`applet` (d)	URI of serialized applet code.
`onblur`	`a` `area` `button` `input` `label` `select` `textarea`	Event raised when an element loses focus.

Continued on next page

Attribute	Applies To	Value or Description
onchange	input select textarea	Event raised when the value of an input element changes.
onclick	all elements except applet (d) base basefont (d) bdo br font (d) frame frameset head html iframe isindex (d) meta param script style title	Event raised when the user clicks a visible element.
ondblclick	all elements except applet (d) base basefont (d) bdo br font (d) frame frameset head html iframe isindex (d) meta param script style title	Event raised when the user double-clicks on a visible element.
onfocus	a area button input label select textarea	Event raised when an element receives the focus.

Continued on next page

Attribute	Applies To	Value or Description
onkeydown	all elements except applet (d) base basefont (d) bdo br font (d) frame frameset head html iframe isindex (d) meta param script style title	Event raised when the user presses a key while an element has the focus.
onkeypress	all elements except applet (d) base basefont (d) bdo br font (d) frame frameset head html iframe isindex (d) meta param script style title	Event raised when the user presses and releases a key while an element has the focus.
onkeyup	all elements except applet (d) base basefont (d) bdo br font (d) frame frameset head html iframe isindex (d) meta param script style title	Event raised when the user releases a pressed key while an element has the focus.

Continued on next page

Attribute	Applies To	Value or Description
onload	frameset body	Event raised when the browser has loaded all frames (for `<frameset>` tag) or the complete document (for `<body>` tag).
onload	body	Event raised when the browser has loaded the document.
onmousedown	all elements except applet (d) base basefont (d) bdo br font (d) frame frameset head html iframe isindex (d) meta param script style title	Event raised when the user presses a mouse button while the mouse pointer is over a visible element.
onmousemove	all elements except applet (d) base basefont (d) bdo br font (d) frame frameset head html iframe isindex (d) meta param script style title	Event raised when the user moves the mouse pointer while over the screen area defined by a visible element.
onmouseout	all elements except applet (d) base basefont (d) bdo br font (d) frame frameset head html	Event raised when the user moves the mouse pointer out of the area defined by a visible element.

Continued on next page

Attribute	Applies To	Value or Description
onmouseout (continued)	iframe isindex (d) meta param script style title	Event raised when the user moves the mouse pointer out of the area defined by a visible element.
onmouseover	all elements except applet (d) base basefont (d) bdo br font (d) frame frameset head html iframe isindex (d) meta param script style title	Event raised when the user moves the mouse pointer into the area defined by a visible element.
onmouseup	all elements except applet (d) base basefont (d) bdo br font (d) frame	Event raised when the user releases a pressed mouse button while the mouse pointer is over a visual element.
onmouseup	frameset head html iframe isindex (d) meta param script style title	Event raised when the user releases a pressed mouse button while the mouse pointer is over a visual element.
onreset	form	Event raised when the user presses a Reset button (input type=reset).
onselect	input textarea	Event raised when the user selects some text.

Continued on next page

Attribute	Applies To	Value or Description
onsubmit	form	Event raised when the user submits a form.
onunload	frameset body	Event raised when the browser has removed all frames (for the `<frameset>` tag) or the document (for a `<body>` tag).
profile	head	Contains a comma-delimited list of URIs that contain meta-information about the document.
prompt (d)	isindex (d)	Contains the input prompt message.
readonly	input textarea	Specifies that the `input` field is not editable.
rel	a link	Specifies the relationship between this document and a forward link.
rev	a link	Specifies the relationship between this document and backward links.
rows	frameset textarea	For a `<frameset>` tag, the attribute value is a comma-delimited list of values that specify the width of frames defined by the `<frameset>` tag. For a `<textarea>` tag, the rows attribute value specifies the width of the `textarea`, in characters.
rowspan	td thtd th	Controls the number of rows spanned by a table cell.
rules	table	Controls whether a table contains inner grid lines (rulings).
scheme	meta	Specifies how to interpret tag content.
scope	td th	Specifies the columns or rows to which a table header applies. The valid values are `row`, `col`, `rowgroup`, and `colgroup`.
scrolling	frame iframe	Determines whether a `frame` or `iframe` displays scroll bars.
selected	option	When present, this attribute controls whether an item in a select list initially appears selected. The attribute has no value.
shape	a area	Specifies the shape of a server- or client-side image map area. The possible values are `rect`, `circle`, `poly`, and `default`.
size	hr (d) font (d) input select basefont (d)	This attribute takes on different meanings depending on the tag. For the `<hr>` (horizontal rule) tag, the `size` attribute controls the width of the rule. For the `<font>` tag, the `size` attribute controls the relative size of text. The default value is 3. Each `<input>` tag specifies this attribute differently. For the `<select>` tag, the `size` attribute controls the number of visible rows in the control. For the `<basefont>` tag, the `size` attribute controls the size of the base font used in the document.
span	col colgroup	For a `<col>` tag, the `span` attribute specifies the number of columns in a `colgroup`. For a `<colgroup>` tag, the `span` attribute determines the default number of columns in the group.

Continued on next page

Attribute	Applies To	Value or Description
src	frame iframe img input script	For a `<script>` tag, the `src` attribute specifies the URI for an external script. For `<input>` and `<img>` tags, the `src` attribute specifies the URI for an associated image. For `<frame>` and `<iframe>` tags, the `src` attribute specifies the URI from which to obtain the document content.
standby	object	Specifies a text message to display while the browser loads the content.
start (d)	ol	Controls the starting number for numbered items.
style	all elements except base basefont (d) head html meta param script style title	Contains style settings for an element.
summary	table	Contains a short description of the table's content for non-visual rendering, such as rendering to audio-enabled browsers or Braille readers.
tabindex	a area button input object select textarea	Controls the position of an element in the document tab order sequence.
target	a area base form link	Specifies the frame in which to render content.
text (d)	body	Controls the default color in which the browser will render a document's text.
title	all elements except base basefont (d) head html meta param script title	For most browsers, this controls the tool-tip text that appears when you hover your mouse over an element. Some browsers render this text while waiting for content (such as an image) to load.

Continued on next page

Attribute	Applies To	Value or Description
type	a button li (d) link object ol (d) param script style input ul (d)	For `<li>`, `<ol>`, and `<ul>` tags, the **type** attribute controls the style of the list item. For `<a>`, `<link>`, `<object>`, `<param>`, `<script>`, and `<style>` tags, the value is the MIME type of the referenced content or item. For `<input>` tags, the value of the **type** attribute controls the type of control, such as **button**, **text**, **password**, etc. For the `<button>` tag, the **type** attribute specifies the type of button: **button**, **submit**, or **reset**.
usemap	img input object	Specifies the named image map associated with the element.
valign	col colgroup tbody td tfoot th thead tr	Determines the vertical alignment of tag content.
value	button input li (d) option param	For all the tags in the Applies To list, except the `<li>` tag, the **value** attribute specifies the value both for initial display and the value sent to the server when the user submits the containing form. For the `<li>` tag in an ordered list, the **value** attribute overrides the default number.
valuetype	param	Specifies how to interpret the **value** parameter of an element.
version (d)	html	Specifies the HTML version number.
vlink (d)	body	Specifies the color of visited links.
vspace (d)	applet (d) img object	Determines the amount of vertical space added around the element.
width	applet (d) col colgroup hr (d) iframe img object pre table td (d) th (d)	Specifies the width of an element.

Attribute	Applies To	Value or Description
type	a button li (d) link object ol (d) param script style input ul (d)	For <li> <ol> and <ul> tag, the type attribute controls the style of the list item. For <a>, <link> <object> <param> <script> and <style> tag, the value is the MIME type of the referenced content or item. For <input> tag, the value of the type attribute controls the type of control, such as button, text, password, etc. For the <button> tag, the type attribute specifies the type of button, button, submit, or reset.
usemap	img input object	Specifies the named image map associated with the element
valign	col colgroup tbody (d) td tfoot th thead tr	Determines the vertical alignment of tag content.
value	button input li (d) option param	For all the tags in the Applies To list, except the <li> tag, the value attribute specifies the value both for initial display and the value sent to the server when the user submits the containing form. For the <li> tag in an ordered list, the value attribute overrides the default number
valuetype	param	Specifies how to interpret the value parameter of an element
version (d)	html	Specifies the HTML version number.
vlink (d)	body	Specifies the color of visited links
vspace (d)	applet (d) img object	Determines the amount of vertical space added around the element
width	applet (d) col colgroup hr (d) iframe img object pre table td (d) th (d)	Specifies the width of an element

APPENDIX
D

D

VBScript Reference

Objects

VBScript itself contains only a few objects, which may surprise you since you've just learned a large number of object models' properties and methods. ASP provides automatic references to many other objects, such as the Dictionary object, the FileSystemObject (part of the Microsoft Scripting Runtime), and the Microsoft ActiveX Data Objects (ADO). These associated objects are defined in separate type libraries and are not part of the VBScript language. I have *not* included the properties and methods for these automatically-referenced objects in this appendix; however, their most common methods and properties are well covered within the chapters.

Object	Description
Class	The object returned when you create a class definition using the Class statement.
Err	Contains error information.
Matches	Collection object returned as the result of a match during a regular expression search.
Match	Object representing a single match in the Matches collection returned from a regular expression search.
RegExp	A regular expression object. Used to perform complex pattern-based searches in a target string.

Properties

VBScript objects have only a few properties, all of which belong to the RegExp, Match, and Err objects.

Property	Description
Description	Returns the description of an error stored in the Err object.
FirstIndex	Returns the character offset of the first character of a Match object returned from a regular expression search. Translated that means the search string was found in the target string and it appears at the index position pointed to by the FirstIndex property. Unlike most other VB collections and the Instr function, the character offset of the first character in the searched string is 0, not 1.
Global	Determines whether a regular expression search should match all occurrences or only the first occurrence.
HelpContext	Sets or returns a HelpContextID value representing the ID of a topic in a help file.
HelpFile	Sets or returns the name of the help file associated with an object.
IgnoreCase	Determines whether or not a regular expression search is case-sensitive.
Length	Returns the length of a Match object found in a regular expression search.

Continued on next page

Property	Description
Number	The error number property of an Err object.
Pattern	Used to set or return the pattern string for a regular expression search.
Source	Returns the source where an error occurred. In server-side VBScript, the source always contains the page name where the error occurred.
Value	Returns the text of a Match object resulting from a successful regular expression search.

Methods

Method	Description
Clear	Clears the Err object.
Execute	Executes a regular expression search for the specified string argument.
Raise	Used to raise an error. The result of raising an error depends on whether On Error Resume Next is in effect and on the current error-processing state.
Replace	Replaces one or more occurrences of a specified sub-string within a string with a different sub-string in a regular expression search. The replacement sub-string need not be the same length as the original sub-string.
Test	Executes a regular expression search.

Functions

Function	Description
Abs	Returns the absolute value of a number.
Array	Creates a Variant array.
Asc	Returns the ASCII value of a character.
Atn	Returns the arctangent of a number.
CBool	Returns a Variant of subtype Boolean (either True or False).
CByte	Returns a Variant of subtype Byte (single-byte integer).
CCur	Returns a Variant of subtype Currency (8 bytes).
CDate	Returns a Variant of subtype Date (8 bytes).
CDbl	Returns a Variant of subtype Double (8 bytes).
Chr	Returns the character representation of an ASCII integer value.
Cint	Returns a Variant of subtype Integer (2 bytes).
CLng	Returns a Variant of subtype Long (4 bytes).
Cos	Returns the cosine of an angle.

Continued on next page

Function	Description
CreateObject	Creates an **object** variable.
CSng	Returns a **Variant** of subtype **Single** (8 bytes).
CStr	Returns a **Variant** of subtype **String**.
Date	Returns a **Variant** of subtype **Date**.
DateAdd	Returns a date or time offset by month, week, day, year, minute, second, or hour.
DateDiff	Returns the difference in months, weeks, days, years, minutes, seconds, or hours between two dates or times.
DatePart	Returns the part of a date or time representing the day, weekday, month, quarter, year, minute, second, or hour.
DateSerial	Returns a date offset by the specified number of days, months, and years.
DateValue	Returns a **Variant** of subtype **Date** corresponding to a string date parameter—turns strings into dates. **CDate** does this as well.
Day	Returns the day of the month.
Eval	Evaluates script passed to the function as an expression. You may evaluate only one expression at a time. Refer to the **Execute** statement for a way to execute multiple lines of code.
Exp	Returns the natural base of logarithms (e) raised to an exponential power.
Filter	Returns a subset of a string array based on conditions passed as a parameter.
Fix	Returns a number truncated to an integer value.
FormatCurrency	Formats currency values according to specific criteria.
FormatDateTime	Formats dates and times according to specific criteria.
FormatNumber	Formats numbers according to a specific format string.
FormatPercent	Formats numbers or numeric expressions as percentages.
GetLocale	Returns the LocaleID of the computer on which the script is running.
GetObject	Returns an object reference for an object loaded from a file. You provide the filename, and optionally, a ProgID. A ProgID consists of a **ProjectName.ClassName** construction like **Excel.Worksheet** or **Word.Application**.
GetRef	Returns a function pointer that you can bind to a DHTML event.
Hex	Returns a numeric value as a hexadecimal string.
Hour	Returns the hour from a specified time expression.
InputBox	Asks a user for input. Doesn't work for server-side script.
InStr	Returns the index of the first character of a matching sub-string within a string.
InStrRev	Returns the index of the last character of a matching sub-string within a string.
Int	Casts a **variable** value to an **Integer** value. Use this to change a string to an Integer or to truncate real values.
IsArray	Returns **True** if the argument is a **Variant** of subtype **Array**. Equivalent to the expression **varType(someVar)** and **vbArray = vbArray)**.
IsDate	Returns **True** if the argument is a **Variant** of subtype **Date** or can be converted to a **Date** subtype.
IsEmpty	Returns **True** if the argument is a **Variant** with the value **Empty**.
IsNull	Returns **True** if the argument is a **Variant** with the value **Null**.
IsNumeric	Returns **True** if the argument is a number or can be converted to a number.

Continued on next page

Function	Description
IsObject	Returns **True** if the argument is a **Variant** of subtype **Object**.
Join	Accepts an array of strings and returns a string separated by the specified delimiter. **Join** is the opposite of **Split**.
LBound	Returns the lower-bound of the array argument.
LCase	Returns a string with all the characters changed to lowercase.
Left	Returns a string consisting of the beginning of a string through the specified index.
Len	Returns the length of the **string** argument.
LoadPicture	Returns a picture object. The command loads an image file from disk. This function works on the server, but doesn't seem to recognize any known properties or methods.
Log	Returns the natural logarithm of a number.
LTrim	Returns a string with all white space (tabs, spaces, carriage returns) trimmed from the left side (front) of the string.
Mid	Returns a sub-string of a string starting with a specified index and a specified number of characters in length.
Minute	Returns the minute of the hour as an integer from 0 to 59.
Month	Returns the month of the year as a number from 1 to 12.
MonthName	Returns the name of the month number passed as an argument.
MsgBox	Displays a Windows message box containing the specified message title and icon or buttons. Returns a constant designating the button the user clicked. This is useful for client-side script. On the server, VBScript writes **MsgBox** messages to the NT Application log.
Now	Returns the current date and time.
Oct	Returns a numeric value as an octal string.
Replace	Replaces one or more occurrences of a specified sub-string within a string with a different sub-string. The replacement sub-string need not be the same length as the original sub-string.
RGB	Changes a set of three individual color values into a single **Long** color value in RGB format.
Right	Returns the specified number of characters from the right side (end) of a string.
Rnd	Returns a random number between 0 and 1.
Round	Rounds floating-point numbers to a specified number of decimal places.
RTrim	Removes white space (tabs, spaces, and carriage returns) from the right side (end) of a string.
ScriptEngine	Returns a string containing the name of the currently executing script engine.
ScriptEngineBuildVersion	Returns the build version number of the currently executing script engine.
ScriptEngineMajorVersion	Returns the major version number of the currently executing script engine.
ScriptEngineMinorVersion	Returns the minor version number of the currently executing script engine.

Continued on next page

Function	Description
Second	Returns the second of the minute of the specified Time value.
SetLocale	Sets the LocaleID for the script context. Use this to output dates, times, and currency values in the format for the assigned LocaleID.
Sgn	Returns the sign of a number.
Sin	Returns the sine of an angle.
Space	Returns a string filled with spaces a specified number of characters in length.
Split	Splits a string into an array of sub-strings according to a defined delimiter. Split is the opposite of Join.
Sqr	Returns the square root of a number.
StrComp	Compares two strings. Returns −1 if the first string is less than the second string, 0 if the strings are equal, and 1 if the first string is greater than the second string. You select whether the comparison is case-sensitive.
String	Returns a string filled with a character repeated a number of times.
StrReverse	Returns a string in which the characters have been reversed.
Tan	Returns the tangent of an angle.
Time	Returns the current time accurate to 1 second.
Timer	Returns the number of seconds since 12:00 midnight.
TimeSerial	Returns a time offset by the specified number of hours, minutes, and seconds.
TimeValue	Returns the time from the argument. If the argument contains both date and time information, the TimeValue function returns the time only.
Trim	Removes white space from both the left- and right-hand sides of a string and returns the string.
TypeName	Returns the VBScript internal type name of a scalar variable or object.
UBound	Returns the upper-bound of an array.
UCase	Returns a string with all the characters changed to uppercase.
VarType	Returns a constant or (for arrays) combination of constants that represent the VBScript internal type of a variable.
Weekday	Accepts a Date argument and returns a number from 1 to 7 representing the day of the week corresponding to the day portion of the argument.
WeekdayName	Accepts a Date argument and returns the string for the day of the week corresponding to the day portion of the argument.
Year	Accepts a date and returns an integer corresponding to the year portion of the argument.

Statements

Statement	Description
Call	Calls a subroutine or function.
Class	Creates a class. You provide the class name, properties, and methods.
Const	Creates a constant.

Continued on next page

Statement	Description
Dim	Declares a variable.
Do...Loop	Surrounds code to be repeated in a loop.
Erase	Clears an array.
Execute	Executes one or more lines of code passed to the statement as a string. You may separate statements with colons or with carriage return/linefeed characters. Script executed in this manner can access global variables, but may only be executed within the context of the currently executing procedure.
ExecuteGlobal	Executes one or more lines of code passed to the statement as a string. You may separate statements with colons or with carriage return/linefeed characters. Script executed in this manner runs in the global context, can access global variables, and may be called from anywhere else in the script.
Exit	Exits a subroutine, function, or repeated code block.
For...Next	Surrounds code to be repeated in a loop a fixed number of times.
For Each...Next	Surrounds code to be repeated for the number of items in a collection object or array.
Function	Defines the beginning of a function.
If...Then...Else	Surrounds code you want to execute only if a specified condition is **true**. If the condition is not **true**, you want to execute the code surrounded by the **Else** condition.
On Error	Used to control what happens after an error occurs at runtime.
Option Explicit	Used to force variable declaration. When **Option Explicit** is in effect, VBScript raises a compile error when it encounters unrecognized symbols. Without **Option Explicit** in effect (the default), VBScript creates a new variable when it encounters an unrecognized symbol.
Private	Used to create a **private** (script-level) variable, subroutine, or function.
PropertyGet	The procedure code to return a property value for a Class object.
PropertyLet	The procedure code to set a property value for a Class object.
PropertySet	The procedure code to set an object property value for a Class object.
Public	Used to create a **public** variable, subroutine, or function.
Randomize	Used to seed the random number generator.
ReDim	Used to change the dimensions of an array. You can use this to change the last dimension of a multi-dimensional array only.
Rem	Used to create a comment. Mostly obsolete. Use a single-quote instead.
Select Case	Block statement that executes code conditionally upon evaluating an expression against several possible cases.
Set	Sets an **object** variable reference.
Sub	Defines the beginning of a subroutine.
While...Wend	Conditional loop block. The loop executes until the condition following **While** evaluates to **True**.
With...End With	Holds a local reference to an object while you perform multiple operations on that object. Using **With...End With** speeds up your code and improves readability.

Operators

Operator	Description
Addition (+)	Used to add values.
And	Used to perform Boolean comparisons and operations.
Assignment (=)	Assigns one value to another. In VBScript, you also use the = operator to test for equivalence.
Concatenation (&)	Concatenates strings. You can also use the Addition (+) operator to add strings, but it's not a good idea to do so.
Division (/)	Divides one number by another.
Eqv	Identical to Boolean And.
Exponentiation (^)	Raises a value to an exponential power.
Imp	Used to perform a logical implication on two numbers. I've never found a good reason to use this operator, although there may be one.
Integer Division (\)	Divides two numbers and casts the result to an Integer (no decimal points).
Is	Tests for object equivalence. Returns True if two object pointers both point to the same object.
Mod	Performs modulo arithmetic.
Multiplication (*)	Multiplies two numbers.
Negation and Subtraction (-)	Returns a number multiplied by –1 or the difference of two numbers, depending on context. When used between two numeric values with a trailing space, VBScript interprets the minus symbol as a minus sign. When used in front of a numeric value with no trailing spaces, VBScript interprets the minus symbol as the negation operator.
Not	Used to negate an expression.
Or	Used to compare two expressions using Boolean Or logic.
Subtraction (-) and Negation	Returns the difference of two numbers or a number multiplied by –1, depending on context. When used between two numeric values with a trailing space, VBScript interprets the minus symbol as a minus sign. When used in front of a numeric value with no trailing spaces, VBScript interprets the minus symbol as the negation operator.
Xor	Performs a Boolean Exclusive Or operation.

Values

Value	Description
Empty	The value of an uninitialized Variant.
False	Boolean logical False value of 0.
Nothing	The value of an uninitialized object variable.
Null	A value meaning no value, not zero, not a null string, not Empty, and not Nothing.
True	Boolean True. In VBScript, True is equal to –1.

Events

Event	Description
Initialize	Occurs when a VBScript class object is instantiated.
Terminate	Occurs just before a VBScript class is destroyed. Use this to clean up by destroying object references and variables.

Collection

Collection	Description
Matches	Collection of Match objects resulting from a successful regular expression search.

Constants

Color Constants

You may use these constants or the equivalent hex value to define the standard colors. For other colors, create a hex value in the same manner you would to define a color in HTML.

Constant	Value	Description
vbBlack	&h00	Black
vbRed	&hFF	Red
vbGreen	&hFF00	Green
vbYellow	&hFFFF	Yellow
vbBlue	&hFF0000	Blue
vbMagenta	&hFF00FF	Magenta
vbCyan	&hFFFF00	Cyan
vbWhite	&hFFFFFF	White

Comparison Constants

Use these constants to define how functions and methods should perform string comparisons.

Constant	Value	Description
VbBinaryCompare	0	Perform a binary comparison.
VbTextCompare	1	Perform a textual comparison.

Date and Time Constants

Use these constants with the date and time functions.

Constant	Value	Description
vbSunday	1	Sunday
vbMonday	2	Monday
vbTuesday	3	Tuesday
vbWednesday	4	Wednesday
vbThursday	5	Thursday
vbFriday	6	Friday
vbSaturday	7	Saturday
vbUseSystem	0	Use the date format contained in the regional settings for your computer.
vbUseSystemDayOfWeek	0	Use the day of the week specified in your system settings for the first day of the week.
vbFirstJan1	1	Use the week in which January 1 occurs (default).
vbFirstFourDays	2	Use the first week that has at least four days in the new year.
vbFirstFullWeek	3	Use the first full week of the year.

Date and Time Format Constants

These constants determine the output format for dates and times.

Constant	Value	Description
vbGeneralDate	0	Display a date and/or time. For real numbers, display a date and time. If there is no fractional part, display only a date. If there is no integer part, display time only. Date and time display is determined by your system settings.
vbLongDate	1	Display a date using the long date format specified in your computer's regional settings.
vbShortDate	2	Display a date using the short date format specified in your computer's regional settings.
vbLongTime	3	Display a time using the long time format specified in your computer's regional settings.
vbShortTime	4	Display a time using the short time format specified in your computer's regional settings.

Locale ID (LCID) Constants

The LCID constants determine the output format of dates , times, and currency values.

Locale id	Value	Description
af	1078	Afrikaans
sq	1052	Albanian
ar-ae	14337	Arabic—U.A.E.
ar-bh	15361	Arabic—Bahrain
ar-dz	5121	Arabic—Algeria
ar-eg	3073	Arabic—Egypt
ar-iq	2049	Arabic—Iraq
ar-jo	11265	Arabic—Jordan
ar-kw	13313	Arabic—Kuwait
ar-lb	12289	Arabic—Lebanon
ar-ly	4097	Arabic—Libya
ar-ma	6145	Arabic—Morocco
ar-om	8193	Arabic—Oman
ar-qa	16385	Arabic—Qatar
ar-sa	1025	Arabic—Saudia Arabia
ar-sy	10241	Arabic—Syria
ar-tn	7169	Arabic—Tunisia
ar-ye	9217	Arabic—Yemen
eu	1069	Basque
be	1059	Belarusian
bg	1026	Bulgarian
ca	1027	Catalan
zh-cn	4	Chinese—PRC
zh-hk	2052	Chinese—Hong Kong
zh-sg	3076	Chinese—Singapore
zh-tw	4100	Chinese—Taiwan
hr	1028	Croatian
cs	1050	Czech
da	1029	Danish
nl	1030	Dutch
nl-be	1043	Dutch—Belgium
en-au	2067	English—Australia
en-bz	3081	English—Belize
en-ca	10249	English—Canada
en-ie	4105	English—Ireland

Continued on next page

Locale id	Value	Description
en-jm	6153	English—Jamaica
en-nz	8201	English—New Zealand
en-za	5129	English—South Africa
en-tt	7177	English—Trinidad
en-gb	11273	English—United Kingdom
en-us	2057	English—United States
et	1033	Estonian
fa	1061	Farsi
fi	1065	Finnish
fo	1035	Faeroese
fr	1080	French—Standard
fr-be	1036	French—Belgium
fr-ca	2060	French—Canada
fr-lu	3084	French—Luxembourg
fr-ch	5132	French—Switzerland
gd	4108	Gaelic—Scotland
de	1084	German—Standard
de-at	1031	German—Austrian
de-li	3079	German—Lichtenstein
de-lu	5127	German—Luxembourg
de-ch	4103	German—Switzerland
el	2055	Greek
he	1037	Hebrew
hi	1081	Hindi
hu	1038	Hungarian
is	1039	Icelandic
in	1057	Indonesian
it	1040	Italian—Standard
it-ch	2064	Italian—Switzerland
ja	1041	Japanese
ko	1042	Korean
lv	1062	Latvian
lt	1063	Lithuanian
mk	1071	Macedonian
ms	1086	Malay—Malaysia
mt	1082	Maltese
no	1044	Norwegian—Bokmål
pl	1045	Polish
pt	2070	Portuguese—Standard
pt-br	1046	Portuguese—Brazil

Continued on next page

Locale id	Value	Description
rm	1047	Raeto-Romance
ro	1048	Romanian
ro-mo	2072	Romanian—Moldova
ru	1049	Russian
ru-mo	2073	Russian—Moldova
sr	3098	Serbian—Cyrillic
tn	1074	Setsuana
sl	1060	Slovenian
sk	1051	Slovak
sb	1070	Sorbian
es	1034	Spanish—Standard
es-ar	11274	Spanish—Argentina
es-bo	16394	Spanish—Bolivia
es-cl	13322	Spanish—Chile
es-co	9226	Spanish—Colombia
es-cr	5130	Spanish—Costa Rica
es-do	7178	Spanish—Dominican Republic
es-ec	12298	Spanish—Ecuador
es-gt	4106	Spanish—Guatemala
es-hn	18442	Spanish—Honduras
es-mx	2058	Spanish—Mexico
es-ni	19466	Spanish—Nicaragua
es-pa	6154	Spanish—Panama
es-pe	10250	Spanish—Peru
es-pr	20490	Spanish—Puerto Rico
es-py	15370	Spanish—Paraguay
es-sv	17418	Spanish—El Salvador
es-uy	14346	Spanish—Uruguay
es-ve	8202	Spanish—Venezuela
sx	1072	Sutu
sv	1053	Swedish
sv-fi	2077	Swedish—Finland
th	1054	Thai
tr	1055	Turkish
ts	1073	Tsonga
uk	1058	Ukranian
ur	1056	Urdu—Pakistan
vi	1066	Vietnamese
xh	1076	Xhosa
ji	1085	Yiddish
zu	1077	Zulu

VBScript User-Defined Error Constant

This error constant defines the lower limit for user-defined error values. You should not create any error values lower than vbObjectError.

Constant	Value	Description
vbObjectError	–2147221504	Don't define error values for your application errors lower than this value.

VBScript *MsgBox* Constants

These constants control the icon and number and caption of buttons shown on the displayed message box.

VBScript *MsgBox* Button and Icon Constants

Add these constants together to define the icon and button set for a message box. For example, the following MsgBox call displays a message box with a Cancel button, an OK button, and the stop sign (critical error) icon.

```
MsgBox "A message."
vbOKCancel + vbCritical
_
    "Message title"
```

NOTE
You may not use the MsgBox function in server-side code. If you do, VBScript writes the message and title to the Event log, but does not display the message box on the server. You may use the MsgBox function in client-side code.

Constant	Value	Description
vbOKOnly	0	Display OK button.
vbOKCancel	1	Display OK and Cancel buttons.
vbAbortRetryIgnore	2	Display Abort, Retry, and Ignore buttons.
vbYesNoCancel	3	Display Yes, No, and Cancel buttons.
vbYesNo	4	Display Yes and No buttons.
vbRetryCancel	5	Display Retry and Cancel buttons.
vbCritical	16	Display Critical Message icon.
vbQuestion	32	Display Warning Query icon.
vbExclamation	48	Display Warning Message icon.
vbInformation	64	Display Information Message icon.
vbDefaultButton1	0	First button is the default.

Continued on next page

Constant	Value	Description
vbDefaultButton2	256	Second button is the default.
vbDefaultButton3	512	Third button is the default.
vbDefaultButton4	768	Fourth button is the default.
vbApplicationModal	0	Application modal. The user must respond to the message box before continuing work in the current application.
vbSystemModal	4096	System modal. On Win16 systems, all applications are suspended until the user responds to the message box. On Win32 systems, this constant provides an application modal message box that always remains on top of any other programs you may have running.

Use the following constants to test the return value of the MsgBox function. The return value identifies which button a user selected.

WARNING

> Unlike the MsgBox button and icon constants, VBScript does not define the MsgBox return value constants; you must explicitly declare them in your code.

VBScript *MsgBox* Function Return Value Constants

Constant	Value	Description
vbOK	1	OK button was clicked.
vbCancel	2	Cancel button was clicked.
vbAbort	3	Abort button was clicked.
vbRetry	4	Retry button was clicked.
vbIgnore	5	Ignore button was clicked.
vbYes	6	Yes button was clicked.
vbNo	7	No button was clicked.

String Constants

VBScript pre-defines some commonly used strings and characters. You should learn and use them because they're faster than the equivalent Chr() or string literals.

Constant	Value	Description
vbCr	Chr(13)	Carriage return.
vbCrLf	Chr(13) & Chr(10)	Carriage return/linefeed combination.
vbFormFeed	Chr(12)	Formfeed; not useful in Microsoft Windows.

Continued on next page

Constant	Value	Description
vbLf	Chr(10)	Linefeed.
vbNewLine	Chr(13) & Chr(10) or Chr(10)	Platform-specific newline character; whatever is appropriate for the platform.
vbNullChar	Chr(0)	Character having the value 0.
vbNullString	String having value 0	Not the same as a zero-length string (" "); used for calling external procedures.
vbTab	Chr(9)	Horizontal tab.
vbVerticalTab	Chr(11)	Vertical tab; not useful in Microsoft Windows.

VBScript *Tristate* Constants

Use these constants with the FileSystemObject to open text files as Unicode or ASCII.

> **WARNING**   These constants are not defined in VBScript itself—you must define them in your code.

Constant	Value	Description
vbUseDefault	-2	Use default from computer's regional settings.
vbTrue	-1	True.
vbFalse	0	False.

VBScript *VarType* Function Constants

These constants are extremely useful in VBScript where all variables are Variants. The only way to determine the subtype of a variant variable is to use the varType function and test for one of these constant values. For arrays of a specific variable type, test for the vbArray constant using a Boolean and condition. For example, to test whether a variant array contains strings, use:

```
<%
dim arr
arr = Array("1", "2", "3", "4")
if ((varType(arr) and vbArray) = vbArray and
      (varType(arr) and vbString) = vbString) then
      Response.Write "the variable arr contains " & _
      a string array"
end if
%>
```

Constant	Value	Description
vbEmpty	0	Uninitialized (default).
vbNull	1	Contains no valid data.
vbInteger	2	Integer subtype.
vbLong	3	Long subtype.
vbSingle	4	Single subtype.
vbSingle	5	Double subtype.
vbCurrency	6	Currency subtype.
vbDate	7	Date subtype.
vbString	8	String subtype.
vbObject	9	Object.
vbError	10	Error subtype.
vbBoolean	11	Boolean subtype.
vbVariant	12	Variant (used only for arrays of variants).
vbDataObject	13	Data access object.
vbDecimal	14	Decimal subtype.
vbByte	17	Byte subtype.
vbArray	8192	Array.

VBScript Runtime Error Constants

Many of the error descriptions are self-explanatory. I've added some comments to help explain those that aren't.

Error Number	Description
5	Invalid procedure call or argument.
6	Overflow—you tried to assign a value that's too large for the variable type. Should not happen because VBScript variables are all variants.
7	Out of memory.
9	Subscript out of range—the array or collection index you're using is too large or too small.
10	This array is fixed or temporarily locked—you're trying to iterate over the same collection in a nested fashion.
11	Division by zero.
13	Type mismatch—the value you're trying to assign isn't a valid value for the variable on the left-hand side of the expression.
14	Out of string space.
17	Can't perform requested operation.
28	Out of stack space.
35	Sub or Function not defined.
48	Error in loading DLL.

Continued on next page

Error Number	Description
51	Internal error.
52	Bad filename or number—the file is closed or the file number is no longer valid.
53	File not found.
54	Bad file mode—you're trying to write from a read-only file, write to a file opened for append, or append to a file opened for write.
55	File already open.
57	Device I/O error.
58	File already exists.
61	Disk full.
62	Input past end of file—you're trying to read past the end of the file. Test the EOF property of the TextStream.
67	Too many files.
68	Device unavailable.
70	Permission denied.
71	Disk not ready.
74	Can't rename with different drive—you must copy or move the file rather than renaming it.
75	Path/File access error.
76	Path not found.
91	`Object` variable not set—you must use the `Set` keyword to create an object reference.
92	`For` loop not initialized—the compiler found a `Next` without a corresponding `For`.
94	Invalid use of `Null`—test for null values with the `isNull` function.
322	Can't create necessary temporary file.
424	Object required—tried to access a property or method of an `object` variable before setting the object reference using the `Set` keyword.
429	ActiveX component can't create object—usually a permission problem.
430	Class doesn't support Automation.
432	Filename or class name not found during Automation operation.
438	Object doesn't support this property or method.
440	Automation error.
445	Object doesn't support this action.
446	Object doesn't support named arguments.
447	Object doesn't support current locale setting.
448	Named argument not found—you passed an argument using a named argument, but the name is invalid.
449	Argument not optional—you must pass a value for this argument.
450	Wrong number of arguments or invalid property assignment—the function requires a different number or order of arguments than you passed to it.
451	Object not a collection—you may only iterate (using `For Each...Next`) over collection objects.
453	Specified DLL function not found.

Continued on next page

Error Number	Description
455	Code resource lock error.
458	Variable uses an Automation type not supported in VBScript.
462	The remote server machine does not exist or is unavailable.
481	Invalid picture.
500	Variable is undefined.
501	Illegal assignment.
502	Object not safe for scripting.
503	Object not safe for initializing.
504	Object not safe for creating.
505	Invalid or unqualified reference.
506	Class not defined.
507	An exception occurred.
5016	Regular Expression object expected.
5017	Syntax error in regular expression.
5018	Unexpected quantifier.
5019	Expected ']' in regular expression.
5020	Expected ')' in regular expression.
5021	Invalid range in character set.
32811	Element not found.

VBScript Syntax Error Constants

Error Number	Description
1001	Out of memory.
1002	Syntax error.
1003	Expected ':'.
1005	Expected '('.
1006	Expected ')'.
1007	Expected ']'.
1010	Expected identifier.
1011	Expected '='.
1012	Expected 'If'.
1013	Expected 'To'.
1014	Expected 'End'.
1015	Expected 'Function'.
1016	Expected 'Sub'.

Continued on next page

Error Number	Description
1017	Expected 'Then'.
1018	Expected 'Wend'.
1019	Expected 'Loop'.
1020	Expected 'Next'.
1021	Expected 'Case'.
1022	Expected 'Select'.
1023	Expected expression.
1024	Expected statement.
1025	Expected end of statement.
1026	Expected integer constant.
1027	Expected 'While' or 'Until'.
1028	Expected 'While', 'Until', or end of statement.
1029	Expected 'With'.
1030	Identifier too long.
1031	Invalid number.
1032	Invalid character.
1033	Unterminated string constant.
1034	Unterminated comment.
1037	Invalid use of 'Me' keyword.
1038	'loop' without 'do'.
1039	Invalid 'exit' statement.
1040	Invalid 'for' loop control variable.
1041	Name redefined.
1042	Must be first statement on the line.
1043	Cannot assign to non-ByVal argument.
1044	Cannot use parentheses when calling a Sub.
1045	Expected literal constant.
1046	Expected 'In'.
1047	Expected 'Class'.
1048	Must be defined inside a Class.
1049	Expected Let or Set or Get in property declaration.
1050	Expected 'Property'.
1051	Number of arguments must be consistent across properties specification.
1052	Cannot have multiple default property/method in a Class.
1053	Class initialize or terminate do not have arguments.
1054	Property Set or Let must have at least one argument.
1055	Unexpected 'Next'.
1056	'Default' can be specified only on 'Property' or 'Function' or 'Sub'.
1057	'Default' specification must also specify 'Public'.
1058	'Default' specification can only be on Get property.

APPENDIX

E

JScript Reference

Like VBScript, you may use JScript on the client or the server. Most ASP programmers use VBScript for server-side script and JScript for client-side script. Most browsers support JScript, while only IE supports VBScript.

JScript Intrinsic Objects

Object	Description
ActiveXObject	Creates and returns references to ActiveX (COM) objects. You provide the class identifier of the object you want to create. For example, `var myOjb = new ActiveXObject ("Scripting.Dictionary")`.
Array	Contains arrays of any data type. JScript can also handle COM (VBScript-type) arrays via special language extensions.
Boolean	Creates a Boolean value.
Date	JScript object for manipulating date and time values.
Dictionary	Object that holds key-value pairs. You can look up a value if you know the key name. The Dictionary object also supports iteration over either the keys or the values.
Enumerator	Object for enumerating or iterating over collections.
Error	Object to hold runtime error information. This object is essentially the equivalent of the VBScript Error object, but has only **number** and **description** properties.
FileSystemObject	Object used to manipulate the file system.
Function	Creates a new function.
Global	A JScript object that holds functions that are globally available.
Math	A JScript intrinsic object used to perform math operations and retrieve constants.
Number	Used to hold numeric values and constants.
Object	Parent object for all **object** variables.
RegExp	Contains the results of a regular expression search.
Regular Expression	Contains the patterns for a regular expression search.
String	Object that contains text and exposes methods and properties to manipulate that text.
VBArray	Used to contain and manipulate COM safe-array arrays, known as **VBArrays**.

JScript Properties

Property	Description
$1 through $9	Contain values from the result of the **RegExp** function.
arguments	Contains an array of the arguments passed to the currently executing function.

Continued on next page

Property	Description
caller	Provides a reference to the function that called the current function. In other words, the caller property gives you access to the item immediately preceding the current item on the call stack.
constructor	The name for a function that constructs an object.
description	Holds a description of a runtime error.
E	Returns Euler's constant, the base of natural logarithms, approximately 2.718.
index	For a RegExp object, returns the index of the first successful search for a regular expression.
Infinity	Number object property that contains an initial value of POSITIVE_INFINITY.
input	For a RegExp object, the input property returns the string that was searched.
lastIndex	Property of a RegExp object that returns the index of the last matching sub-string within a string.
length (Array)	Returns the size of an array or collection.
length (Function)	Contains the number of arguments defined for a function.
length (String)	Returns the length of the text for the String object.
LN2	Returns the natural logarithm of 2.
LN10	Returns the natural logarithm of 10.
LOG2E	Returns the base 2 logarithm of E (Euler's constant).
LOG10E	Returns the base 10 logarithm of E (Euler's constant).
MAX_VALUE	The largest number you can use in JScript, approximately 1.79E+308.
MIN_VALUE	The smallest number you can use in JScript, approximately 2.22E-308.
NaN (Global)	Contains the global initial constant for NaN (Not a Number).
NaN (Number)	NaN is a special value meaning Not a Number.
NEGATIVE_INFINITY	A value that represents negative infinity.
number	Contains a numeric value for a runtime error.
PI	Returns the value of pi (approximately 3.14159).
POSITIVE_INFINITY	Returns a value representing positive infinity.
prototype	Returns a reference to a prototype object. New instances of that object type inherit the behavior of the prototype.
source	Returns the text of a regular expression pattern.
SQRT1_2	Returns the square root of 0.5, or 1 divided by the square root of 2.
SQRT2	Returns the square root of 2.

JScript Methods

Method	Description
abs	Returns the absolute value of a numeric expression.
acos	Returns the arc cosine of a numeric expression.
anchor	Surrounds the text of a String object with an <a> anchor tag.

Continued on next page

Method	Description
asin	Returns the arcsine of a numeric expression.
atan	Returns the arctangent of a numeric expression.
atan2	Returns the angle (in radians) from the x-axis to a specified point (xy).
atEnd	Returns **True** if an Iterator object has reached the end of its associated collection.
big	Surrounds the text of a String object with `<big>` tags.
blink	Surrounds the text of a String object with `<blink>` tags.
bold	Surrounds the text of a String object with `<b>` tags.
ceil	Returns the smallest integer value greater than the value of the argument passed to the method.
charAt	Returns the character at a specified offset within a string.
charCodeAt	Returns the character code for the character at a specified offset within a string.
compile	Compiles a regular expression. Used to improve the speed of loops and repeated code.
concat (Array)	Concatenates two arrays.
concat (String)	Concatenates two strings.
cos	Returns the cosine of a numeric expression.
dimensions	Returns the number of dimensions in a **VBArray** array.
escape	HTTP-encodes strings.
eval	Evaluates JScript code. You use this to execute code strings you build at runtime.
exec	Searches a string for a regular expression.
exp	Returns **e** to the power you supply as an argument to the method.
fixed	Surrounds the text of a String object with `<tt>` teletype tags. The browser renders this text in a fixed-width font such as Courier.
floor	Returns the largest integer value less than the value of the argument passed to the method.
fontcolor	Surrounds the text of a String object with `<font>` tags where the starting tag includes a `color` attribute.
fontsize	Surrounds the text of a String object with `<font>` tags where the starting tag includes a `size` attribute.
fromCharCode	Creates a string from a list of Unicode values.
getDate	Returns the integer (**1–31**) value for the current day of the month stored in a Date object.
getDay	Returns the integer (**0–6**) value for the current day of the week stored in a Date object.
getFullYear	Returns the year as a four-character integer (e.g., **2001**) for the date stored in a Date object.
getHours	Returns the hour of the date stored in a Date object
getItem	Returns the item at a specified position in a VBArray.
getMilliseconds	Returns the milliseconds past the current second for the time stored in a Date object.
getMinutes	Returns the number of minutes past the hour for the time stored in a Date object.

Continued on next page

Method	Description
getMonth	Returns the month as an integer (1-12) for the current month stored in a Date object.
getSeconds	Returns the number of seconds past the minute for the time stored in a Date object.
getTime	Returns the time stored in a Date object.
getTimezoneOffset	Returns the difference (in minutes) between the local time on the computer and Universal Coordinated Time (UTC).
getUTCDate getUTCDay getUTCFullYear getUTCHours getUTCMilliseconds getUTCMinutes getUTCMonth getUTCSeconds	These methods are identical to the getDate, GetDay, etc. methods, except that they perform all calculations using Universal Coordinated Time (UTC) rather than the date and time on the local computer. Note that because the computer must calculate UTC dates and times as an offset of the local computer's date/time, your date/time operations are still only as accurate as the local computer's time.
getVarDate	Returns a JScript date from the date stored in a Date object in COM VT_DATE format. You only need to use this method if you're working with date or time arguments received from a VBScript or ActiveX control function or object.
getYear	Returns the two-digit year from the date stored in a Date object.
indexOf	Returns the starting position of the first matching sub-string within a String object.
isFinite	Returns **True** if the argument supplied is a finite number.
isNaN	Returns **True** if the argument supplied is **NaN** (Not a Number).
italics	Surrounds the text of a String object with <i> italics tags.
item	Property of an Enumerator object. Returns the current item in an enumerated collection.
join	Returns a string consisting of all the elements in a string array joined into a single string with an optional separator character between the values.
lastIndexOf	Returns the starting position of the last matching sub-string within a String object.
lbound	Returns the lower-bound of a VBArray.
link	Surrounds the text of a String object with an <a> anchor tag containing an HREF attribute.
log	Returns the natural logarithm of a numeric value or expression.
match	Performs a search for a sub-string using a RegExp object.
max	Returns the larger of two arguments.
min	Returns the smaller of two arguments.
moveFirst	Resets the current item of an Enumerator object to the first item of its associated collection.
moveNext	Moves the current item of an Enumerator object to the next item of its associated collection.
parse	Parses the text of a String object. Returns the elapsed number of milliseconds between a string or Date and the constant date **January 1, 1970**.
parseFloat	Parses the text of a String object and returns a floating-point value if the String contains a text representation of a number.
parseInt	Parses the text of a String object and returns an **integer** value if the String contains a text representation of a number.

Continued on next page

Method	Description
pow	Returns the value of a numeric expression to the power of an argument you supply to the function.
random	Returns a pseudo-random number between 0 and 1.
replace	Replaces sub-strings found by a regular expression search with other sub-strings.
reverse	Reverses the order of elements in an array.
round	Returns a number rounded to the nearest `integer` value.
search	Searches a string for matches to a regular expression.
setDate	Sets the **date** value of a Date object.
setFullYear	Sets the year of the **date** value of a Date object.
setHours	Sets the current hour of a **time** value contained in a Date object.
setMilliseconds	Sets the number of milliseconds past the second for the **time** value contained in a Date object.
setMinutes	Sets the minutes past the hour for the **time** value contained in a Date object.
setMonth	Sets the current month of the **date** value contained in a Date object.
setSeconds	Sets the number of seconds past the minute for the **time** value contained in a Date object.
setTime	Sets the **time** value of a Date object.
setUTCDate setUTCFullYear setUTCHours setUTCMilliseconds setUTCMinutes setUTCMonth setUTCSeconds	These methods are identical to the `setDate`, `SetFullYear`, etc. methods, except that they perform all calculations using Universal Coordinated Time (UTC) rather than the date and time on the local computer. Note that because the computer must calculate UTC dates and times as an offset of the local computer's date/time, your date/time operations are still only as accurate as the local computer's time.
setYear	Sets the year of the **date** value contained in a Date object.
sin	Returns the `sin` value of a numeric value supplied as an argument.
slice (Array)	Returns a portion of an array. You supply the starting and ending indexes.
slice (String)	Returns a portion of a string. You supply the starting and ending indexes.
small	Surrounds the text of a String object with `<small>` tags.
sort	Returns a sorted array.
split	Splits the text of a String object into an array of strings separated at the delimiter value you supply.
sqrt	Returns the square root of a numeric argument.
strike	Surrounds the text of a String object with `<strike>` strikethrough tags.
sub	Surrounds the text of a String object with `<sub>` subscript tags.
substr	Returns a sub-string from the text of a String object beginning from a specified offset with a specified length.
substring	Returns a sub-string from the text of a String object beginning from a specified **start** offset and extending to a specified **end** offset.
sup	Surrounds the text of a String object with `<sup>` superscript tags.
tan	Returns the tangent of a numeric value or expression.
test	Returns **True** if a specified pattern exists in a string, otherwise returns **False**.

Continued on next page

Method	Description
toArray	Converts a VBArray to a JScript array.
toGMTString	Obsolete. Use the toUTCString method instead.
toLocaleString	Returns a string representation of a date. Uses the local computer's locale settings.
toLowerCase	Returns a string with all the characters converted to lowercase.
toString	Returns a string representation of an object.
toUpperCase	Returns a string with all the characters converted to uppercase.
toUTCString	Returns a string representation of a date in Universal Coordinated Time (UTC).
ubound	Returns the upper-bound of a VBArray.
unescape	Accepts an escaped (HTTP-encoded) string. Returns the string converted to normal text.
UTC	Returns the number of milliseconds between the constant January 1, 1970 and the supplied date. Uses UTC time to make the calculation.
valueOf	Returns the primitive value of the object argument. The method returns Arrays as comma-separated strings; Boolean values as strings; dates and times as milliseconds (see UTC method); Functions as the text of the function; Numbers as a numeric value; Objects as themselves; and Strings as text.

JScript Functions

Function	Description
GetObject	Returns a reference to a COM or OLE object stored in a file.
ScriptEngine	Returns a string containing the name of the scripting language in use.
ScriptEngineBuildVersion	Returns a string containing the build version of the scripting language in use.
ScriptEngineMajorVersion	Returns a string containing the major version number of the scripting language in use.
ScriptEngineMinorVersion	Returns a string containing the minor version number of the scripting language in use.

JScript Statements

Statement	Description
break	Used to end processing in a loop or code block. Processing starts at the code line following the code block.
@cc on	Turns on conditional compilation.
catch	Begins a block containing code to run when a try statement fails.

Continued on next page

Statement	Description
Comment (//) Single-line version	Used to place a comment on a single line. You may place the slashes anywhere in the line. The compiler ignores any text on that line following the slashes. Use the multi-line /*...*/ syntax for multi-line comments.
Comment (/*...*/) Multi-line version	Used to surround comment lines. The compiler ignores all text between the starting /* characters and the */ ending characters.
continue	JScript does not process code following a **continue** statement in a loop. Instead, it begins processing again at the top of the loop.
do...while	Loop structure that always executes at least once.
for	Used at the start of a **for** loop structure. The syntax is **for (value; test; increment) statement or block.** Equivalent to VBScript's **For...Next** statement block.
for...in	Executes a statement or block for each item in a collection or array. Equivalent to VBScript's **For Each...Next** statement block.
function	Declares a new function.
@if	Conditional **if** structure. Used to conditionally compile code where the host-scripting environment may not be able to interpret the code correctly.
if...else	Code block. Performs a Boolean test on an expression and executes the code within the block if the expression evaluates to **True**.
Labeled	A unique identifier that marks a position or label in code. To create a label, append a colon (:) to the end of the label text. For example, **myLabel:**. The code line following the label is called a **labeled** statement. If you include a label after a **continue** statement in a loop, execution continues at the code line following the label.
return	Exits a function and (optionally) returns a value.
@set	Conditional variable creation statement.
switch	A code block that conditionally executes one of a group of statements depending on the value of the condition.
this	Contains a reference to the current object.
throw	Raises an error.
try...catch	Sets up error-handling. Requires two code blocks; a **try** block and a **catch** block. If an error occurs in the **try** block, execution resumes at the start of the **catch** block. You can handle the error locally or raise it to the next level using the **throw** statement.
var	Used to declare a variable.
while	Begins a conditional code block. The block executes if the condition following the **while** statement evaluates to **True**.
with	Sets the default object for the following statement or group of statements. Equivalent to the **With** statement in VBScript.

JScript Operators

Operator	Description
Addition (+)	Adds values. In JScript you use the addition operator for addition and string concatenation.
Assignment (=)	Assigns a value to the variable on the left side of the equals sign.
Bitwise AND (&)	Performs a Boolean **AND** operation on two values.
Bitwise Left Shift (<<)	Shifts the bits of a value one position to the left.
Bitwise NOT (~)	Negates a value by flipping all the bits from 1 to 0 or from 0 to 1.
Bitwise OR (|)	Compares two bit patterns and produces a 1 if either or both bits in a column are 1.
Bitwise Right Shift (>>)	Shifts the bits of a value one position to the right.
Bitwise XOR (^)	Compares two bit patterns and produces a 1 if only one of the bits, but not both, in a column is a 1.
Comma (,)	Causes multiple expressions to be evaluated in sequence as if they were a single expression. It returns the value of the rightmost expression in the list.
Comparison	Less than (<) Greater than (>) Less than or equal to (<=) Greater than or equal to (>=) Equal (==) Not equal (!=) Identity equality—same object (===) Identity inequality (!==).
Compound Assignment	Addition (+=) Bitwise AND (&=) Bitwise OR (|=) Bitwise XOR (^=) Division (/=) Left Shift (<<=) Modulus (%=) Multiplication (*=) Right Shift (>>=) Subtraction (-=) Unsigned Right Shift (>>>=).
Conditional Compilation Variables	These are built-in variables that are either **True** or evaluate to **NaN**. @_win32—**true** if running on a Win32 system. @_win16—**true** if running on a Win16 system. @_mac—**true** if running on an Apple Macintosh system. @_alpha—**true** if running on a DEC Alpha processor. @_x86—**true** if running on an Intel processor. @_mc680x0—**true** if running on a Motorola 680x0 processor. @_PowerPC—**true** if running on a Motorola PowerPC processor. @_jscript—Always **true**. @_jscript_build—Contains the build number of the JScript scripting engine. @_jscript_version—Contains the JScript version number in **major.minor** format.

Continued on next page

Operator	Description
Conditional (trinary) (?:)	Used to execute one of two statements based on an expression. If the expression evaluates to **True**, JScript executes the first statement. If the expression evaluates to **False**, JScript executes the second statement. The syntax is **expression ? statement1 : statement2**.
Decrement (–)	Decrements a value by **1**.
delete	Deletes a property or an **array** element.
Division (/)	Divides two numbers.
Equality (==)	Tests for equality between two values or expressions.
Greater than (>)	Compares the relative size of two numeric values or expressions. Returns **True** if the value of the expression on the left side of the operator is larger than the value of the expression on the right side.
Greater than or equal to (>=)	Compares the relative size of two values or expressions. Returns **True** if the value of the expression on the left side of the operator is larger than or equal to the value of the expression on the right side.
Identity (===)	Compares two **object** variable references and returns **True** if both variables refer to the same object.
Increment (++)	Increments a value by **1**.
Inequality (!=)	Compares two values or expressions. The operation evaluates to **True** if the value on the left side of the operator is not equal to the value on the right side.
InstanceOf	Returns **True** if the object is an instance of the specified **class** argument.
Less than (<)	Compares the relative size of two numeric values or expressions. Returns **True** if the value of the expression on the left side of the operator is smaller than the value of the expression on the right side.
Less than or equal to (<=)	Compares the relative size of two values or expressions. Returns **True** if the value of the expression on the left side of the operator is less than or equal to the value of the expression on the right side.
Logical AND (&&)	Performs a Boolean **AND** operation.
Logical NOT (!)	Performs a Boolean **NOT** operation.
Logical OR (||)	Performs a Boolean **OR** operation.
Modulus (%)	Performs modulo arithmetic.
Multiplication (*)	Multiplies numeric values.
new	Creates a new **object** variable.
Nonidentity (!==)	Returns **True** if the operand on the left side of the operator does not refer to the same object as the operand on the right side.
Subtraction (–)	Subtracts numeric values.
typeof	Returns the type of an object or expression as a string. The return value is **number**, **String**, **Boolean**, **Object**, **Function**, or **undefined**.
Unary Negation (–)	Negates a value or expression.
Unsigned Right Shift (>>>)	Shifts bit patterns to the right. Zero-fills the bits on the left.
void	Used to evaluate an expression. The void operator returns the value **undefined**.

JScript Microsoft-Specific Extensions

Extension Type	Description
Conditional compilation	Use in situations where non-Microsoft browsers or servers may not be able to compile the code. You begin conditional compilation using the `@cc_on` statement or the `@if` or `@set` statements.
`ActiveXObject` object	Creates and returns references to ActiveX (COM) objects. You provide the class identifier of the object you want to create. For example, `var myObj = new ActiveXObject ("Scripting.Dictionary")`.
`VBArray` object	Used to contain and manipulate COM safe-array arrays, known as VBArrays.
`dimensions` method	Returns the number of dimensions in a VBArray object.
`getItem` method	Returns the item at a specified position in a VBArray object.
`getVarDate` method	Returns a JScript date from the date stored in a Date object in COM VT_DATE format. You only need to use this method if you're working with date or time arguments received from a VBScript or ActiveX control function or object.

JScript Constants

JScript Runtime Error Constants

Error Number	Description
5	Invalid procedure call or argument.
6	Overflow.
7	Out of memory.
9	Subscript out of range.
10	This array is fixed or temporarily locked.
11	Division by zero.
13	Type mismatch.
14	Out of string space.
17	Can't perform requested operation.
28	Out of stack space.
35	Sub or Function not defined.
48	Error in loading DLL.
51	Internal error.
52	Bad filename or number.
53	File not found.
54	Bad file mode.
55	File already open.

Continued on next page

Error Number	Description
57	Device I/O error.
58	File already exists.
61	Disk full.
62	Input past end of file.
67	Too many files.
68	Device unavailable.
70	Permission denied.
71	Disk not ready.
74	Can't rename with different drive.
75	Path/File access error.
76	Path not found.
91	`Object` variable or `With` block variable not set.
92	`For` loop not initialized.
94	Invalid use of Null.
322	Can't create necessary temporary file.
424	Object required.
429	Automation server can't create object.
430	Class doesn't support Automation.
432	Filename or class name not found during Automation operation.
438	Object doesn't support this property or method.
440	Automation error.
445	Object doesn't support this action.
446	Object doesn't support named arguments.
447	Object doesn't support current locale setting.
448	Named argument not found.
449	Argument not optional.
450	Wrong number of arguments or invalid property assignment.
451	Object not a collection.
453	Specified DLL function not found.
458	Variable uses an Automation type not supported in JScript.
462	The remote server machine does not exist or is unavailable.
501	Cannot assign to variable.
502	Object not safe for scripting.
503	Object not safe for initializing.
504	Object not safe for creating.
507	An exception occurred.
5000	Cannot assign to `'this'`.
5001	Number expected.

Continued on next page

Error Number	Description
5002	Function expected.
5003	Cannot assign to a function result.
5004	Cannot index object.
5005	String expected.
5006	Date object expected.
5007	Object expected.
5008	Illegal assignment.
5009	Undefined identifier.
5010	Boolean expected.
5011	Can't execute code from a freed script.
5012	Object member expected.
5013	VBArray expected.
5014	JScript object expected.
5015	Enumerator object expected.
5016	Regular Expression object expected.
5017	Syntax error in regular expression.
5018	Unexpected quantifier.
5019	Expected ']' in regular expression.
5020	Expected ')' in regular expression.
5021	Invalid range in character set.
5022	Exception thrown and not caught.
5023	Function does not have a valid prototype object.

JScript Syntax Error Constants

Error Number	Description
1001	Out of memory.
1002	Syntax error.
1003	Expected ':'.
1004	Expected ';'.
1005	Expected '('.
1006	Expected ')'.
1007	Expected ']'.
1008	Expected '{'.
1009	Expected '}'.
1010	Expected identifier.

Continued on next page

Error Number	Description
1011	Expected '='.
1012	Expected '/'.
1013	Invalid number.
1014	Invalid character.
1015	Unterminated string constant.
1016	Unterminated comment.
1018	'return' statement outside of function.
1019	Can't have 'break' outside of loop.
1020	Can't have 'continue' outside of loop.
1023	Expected hexadecimal digit.
1024	Expected 'while'.
1025	Label redefined.
1026	Label not found.
1027	'default' can only appear in a 'switch' statement.
1028	Expected identifier or string.
1029	Expected '@end'.
1030	Conditional compilation turned off.
1031	Expected constant.
1032	Expected '@'.
1033	Expected 'catch'.
1034	Expected 'var'.
1035	'throw' must be followed by an expression on the same source line.

APPENDIX

F

DOM Reference

This reference covers Microsoft's XML Document Object Model (DOM) specification version 2.5. It contains the properties, methods, and events exposed by Microsoft's XML parser (msxml2.dll) that are accessible via scripting languages such as VBScript or JScript. You should be aware that many of the methods and properties in this specification have not been approved by the W3C and are therefore mostly limited to Microsoft's parser. Many of these properties and methods may be (will probably be) approved and other parsers may implement them in the future.

All the DOM objects descend from a single base object. Each object has a type and a value, but each node may also have a parent node, sibling and child nodes, and attribute nodes. There are several types of nodes (see the section *Node Type Constants* for more information).

Object	Description
XMLDOMDocument	This is the imaginary top node of an XML document. The physical top node is the document element.
XMLDOMNode	A single node.
XMLDOMNodeList	A collection of nodes. You can iterate through the collection using For... Each... Next, by using For...Next with an index, or by repeatedly calling the NextNode method
XMLDOMNamedNodeMap	Contains a collection of named attribute nodes. This collection lets you iterate through attributes in the same ways you can iterate through an XMLDOMNodeList node collection
XMLDOMParseError	Contains information about the last error that occurred while parsing an XML document.
XMLHttpRequest	Lets you communicate with a server over HTTP
XTLRuntime	Exposes methods you can call while processing an XSL style sheet

XML Node Type Constants

The DOMNodeType enumeration defines these node type constants. You will find them useful when you need to differentiate between nodes based on their type. The nodeType property returns one of these values.

This reference covers Microsoft's XML Document Object Model (DOM) specification version 2.5. It contains the objects, methods, properties, and events exposed by Microsoft's XML parser (`msxml.dll`) that are accessible via scripting languages such as VBScript or JScript. You should be aware that many of the methods and properties in this specification have not been approved by the W3C and are, therefore, mostly limited to Microsoft's parser. Many of these properties and methods may be (will probably be) approved and other parsers may implement them in the future.

Objects

All the DOM objects are nodes. At the most basic level, a node has a type and a value, but each node may also have a parent node, sibling and child nodes, and attribute nodes. There are several types of nodes (see the section *Node Type Constants* for more information).

Object	Description
XMLDOMDocument	This is the imaginary top node of an XML document. The physical top node is the document element.
XMLDOMNode	A single node.
XMLDOMNodeList	A collection of nodes. You can iterate through the collection using **For Each...Next**, by using **For...Next** with an index, or by repeatedly calling the **NextNode** method.
XMLDOMNamedNodeMap	Contains a collection of named attribute nodes. This collection lets you iterate through attributes in the same ways you can iterate through an XMLDOMNodeList node collection.
XMLDOMParseError	Contains information about the last error that occurred while parsing an XML document.
XMLHttpRequest	Lets you communicate with a server over HTTP.
XTLRuntime	Exposes methods you can call while processing an XSL style sheet.

XML Node Type Constants

The `DOMNodeType` enumeration defines these node type constants. You will find them useful when you need to differentiate between nodes based on their type. The `nodeType` property returns one of these values.

NodeType Constant	Value	Description
NODE_ELEMENT	1	An element node represents a named element that may have attributes and child nodes.
NODE_ATTRIBUTE	2	The attribute node represents an attribute of an element. Attribute nodes, although they belong to an element, are not considered part of the `childNodes` collection of that element.
NODE_TEXT	3	The text node represents the text content of a tag. The text node may not have children and has no attributes.
NODE_CDATA_SECTION	4	The CDATA (character data) node represents a CDATA section in the XML source. You construct a CDATA section using the syntax `![CDATA[... text here...]]`. You wrap text in CDATA sections when it may contain XML reserved characters, such as angle brackets. A CDATA node may not have children and has no attributes.
NODE_ENTITY_REFERENCE	5	The entity reference node represents a reference to an entity in the XML document. An entity is any cohesive part of an XML document.
NODE_ENTITY	6	The entity node represents an expanded node. An entity node may have child nodes.
NODE_PROCESSING_INSTRUCTION	7	A processing instruction is a parser directive. For example, the string `<?xml version="1.0" ?>` that appears at the top of all XML documents is a processing instruction. PI nodes may not have children.
NODE_COMMENT	8	The comment node represents a comment in the XML document. Comment nodes may not have children.
NODE_DOCUMENT	9	The document node represents a document object, which is at the top of the XML object hierarchy.
NODE_DOCUMENT_TYPE	10	The document type node represents the document type declaration (the `<!DOCTYPE >` tag).
NODE_DOCUMENT_FRAGMENT	11	The document fragment node represents a document fragment, which is a single node that may contain child nodes. Use document fragments to append sections of XML to an existing document.
NODE_NOTATION	12	A notation node represents a notation in the document type declaration. The notation node may not have children and is always a child of a document type node.

Interfaces

An interface is a specification for a set of methods. Classes may implement one or more interfaces. The interface itself does not specify how a class may implement a method—only that it must implement the method. Essentially, when a class meets an interface specification, it means that an object instantiated from the class can be considered as a member of the interface class. In other words, if a person object and a chimpanzee object both implement a Bipedal interface, they may be passed to any method that expects a Bipedal object.

Microsoft's XML object hierarchy defines several interfaces, the most important of which is the XMLDOMNode. All other objects in the hierarchy inherit from this interface. Therefore, (conveniently) you may pass any of the XML object types to a method expecting an XMLDOMNode argument.

The names exposed to VB and C++ programmers all begin with an I, which stands for interface. For example, the list of creatable DOM objects in VB includes IXMLDOMNode, IXMLDOMAttribute, etc.

You should notice that the list of interfaces includes several that are not exposed as objects; however, all the interfaces are implemented by one or more of the exposed objects.

Interface	Description
XMLDOMAttribute	Represents an attribute.
XMLDOMCDATASection	Represents a CDATA section, which quotes or escapes blocks of text the XML parser might otherwise attempt to interpret as markup language.
XMLDOMCharacterData	Contains methods to manipulate text.
XMLDOMComment	Represents an XML comment.
XMLDOMDocumentFragment	Represents an object that you can insert into an existing DOM tree.
XMLDOMDocumentType	Contains the information from the document type declaration.
XMLDOMElement	Represents an XML element.
XMLDOMEntity	Represents a parsed or unparsed entity in the XML document.
XMLDOMEntityReference	Represents an entity reference node.
XMLDOMImplementation	Provides methods that may apply to, but are independent of, any DOM object.
XMLDOMNotation	Represents a notation declared in the DTD or schema.
XMLDOMProcessingInstruction	Represents a processing instruction.
XMLDOMText	Represents the text content of a node.

XMLDOMDocument Object

The XMLDOMDocument object appears at the top of the DOM object hierarchy and represents a complete XML document. It has methods to read XML documents from and save XML documents to files and streams. The XMLDOMDocument object can create other nodes, and is the only node type that raises events.

XMLDOMDocument Object Properties

Property	Description
async	Determines whether the parser loads and parses documents synchronously or asynchronously. The default is synchronously, meaning the load method doesn't return until the parsing process completes.
attributes	Returns a collection of attribute nodes.
baseName	Returns the base name for the namespace.
childNodes	Returns a collection of child nodes.
dataType	Returns the data type of the node.
definition	Returns the definition of the node in the DTD or schema.
doctype	Returns the document type node that specifies the DTD for this document.
documentElement	Returns the root element of the document.
firstChild	Returns the first child of this node.
implementation	Returns the XMLDOMImplementation object for this document.
lastChild	Returns the last child node.
namespaceURI	Returns the URI for the namespace.
nextSibling	Returns the next sibling of this node. A sibling node is a node with the same parent at the same hierarchical level within the XML document.
nodeName	For elements, attributes, and entity references, this property returns the name of the element, including the namespace, if present. For other nodes, the property returns a string constant. For example, text nodes return the string #text.
nodeType	Returns one of the XMLDOMNodeType enumeration constants.
nodeTypedValue	Returns the node's value. If the node contains typed data, the property returns the appropriate data type.
nodeTypeString	Returns a constant string associated with the nodeType property value. For example, a node of type NODE_ELEMENT returns the string element.
nodeValue	Returns the text associated with the node. For typed data, use the nodeTypedValue property instead.
ondataavailable	Returns or sets the name of a script event-handler for the ondataavailable event.
onreadystatechange	Returns or sets the name of a script event-handler for the onreadystatechange event.
ontransformnode	Returns or sets the name of the event-handler for the ontransformnode event.
ownerDocument	Returns the root node (the documentElement node) of the document that contains this node.
parentNode	Returns the parent node (if present) of this node.
parsed	Returns True if the XMLDOMDocument has parsed and instantiated this node and all its descendents; otherwise it returns False.
parseError	Returns an XMLDOMParseError object you can use to obtain information about the last error that occurred while parsing the document.
prefix	Returns the namespace prefix. Namespaces serve to keep element names from different domains or with different meanings from colliding. For example, a full namespace declaration might be: xmlns:ap="urn:apparel.org:casualwear". The ap is a shorthand version of the entire namespace. After declaring the prefix, you can use it throughout the document wherever you would otherwise need to include the entire namespace. For example, one tag might be <ap:jeans>. The prefix is the part of the qualified name before the colon (ap).

Continued on next page

Property	Description
preserveWhiteSpace	Returns True if the XMLDOMDocument object will preserve white space; otherwise the property returns False.
previousSibling	Returns the sibling of this node that appears immediately before it in the XML document.
readyState	Returns a value that represents the current state of the XMLDOMDocument object with respect to a physical document. The possible values are: 0 – Uninitialized 1 – Loading 2 – Loaded 3 – Interactive (partially loaded) 4 – Completed
ResolveExternals	Returns or sets a Boolean value that controls whether the XMLDOMDocument object will resolve external definitions—references in other files, such as DTDs and namespaces when parsing a document. The default value is True.
specified	Indicates whether the DTD or schema for this document explicitly specifies that this node must exist or whether the node was derived from a default value in the DTD or schema.
text	Contains the text content of the node and all its children.
url	Returns the URL for the last loaded XML document.
validateOnParse	Returns True if the XML parser should validate this document against a DTD or schema.
xml	Returns the underlying XML for this node and all its descendants.

XMLDOMDocument Object Methods

Method	Description
abort	Stops an asynchronous load.
appendChild	Appends a new child node to the current node. The new child appears after any existing child nodes.
cloneNode	Returns a duplicate of the current node.
createAttribute	Returns a new attribute. You must specify the new attribute's name.
createCDATASection	Returns a CDATA section node. You supply the data for the new node as an argument.
createComment	Returns a new comment node. You supply the data for the new node as an argument.
createDocumentFragment	Returns a new and empty document fragment node.
createElement	Returns a new element node. You supply the node name as an argument.
createEntityReference	Returns a new entity reference node.

Continued on next page

Method	Description
createNode	Returns a new node. You must supply the **DOMNodeType** constant, the name and optionally, the namespace for the new node as arguments.
createProcessingInstruction	Returns a new **XMLDOMProcessingInstruction** node. You supply the target and data as arguments.
createTextNode	Returns a new text node. You supply the text for the new node as an argument.
getElementsByTagName	Returns a collection of elements where the **nodeName** property for each element matches the name you specify.
hasChildNodes	Returns **True** if this node has children.
insertBefore	Inserts a child node as the first child of the current node.
load	Loads an XML document from a specified file or stream.
loadXML	Loads an XML document from a string you supply as the argument to the method.
nodeFromID	Returns the first node where the **ID** attribute matches a specified value.
removeChild	Removes a node from the **childNodes** collection for this element. The method returns the node that was removed.
replaceChild	Replaces an existing child node with a new child node. The method returns the node that was replaced.
save	Saves an XML document to a specified file or stream.
selectNodes	Returns a collection of nodes that match the XSL pattern you supply as an argument.
selectSingleNode	Returns the first node that matches the XSL pattern you supply as an argument.
transformNode	Transforms a node using a specified XSL style sheet. The method returns the result of the transformation.
transformNodeToObject	Transforms a node and its descendents using a specified XSL style sheet. The method returns the result of the transformation.

XMLDOMDocument Object Events

Event	Description
ondataavailable	The XMLDOMDocument raises this event when XML document data becomes available.
onreadystatechange	The XMLDOMDocument raises this event whenever the **readyState** property changes.
ontransformnode	The XMLDOMDocument raises this event before transforming a node in the XML source with a template node from an XSL style sheet.

XMLDOMNode Object

This object contains the base set of properties and methods for all the DOM objects.

XMLDOMNode Object Properties

Property	Description
attributes	Returns a collection of attribute nodes.
baseName	Returns the base name for the namespace.
childNodes	Returns a collection of child nodes.
dataType	Returns the data type of the node.
definition	Returns the definition of the node in the DTD or schema.
firstChild	Returns the first child of this node.
lastChild	Returns the last child node.
namespaceURI	Returns the URI for the namespace.
nextSibling	Returns the next sibling of this node. A sibling node is a node with the same parent at the same hierarchical level within the XML document.
nodeName	For elements, attributes, and entity references, this property returns the name of the element, including the namespace, if present. For other nodes, the property returns a string constant. For example, text nodes return the string #text.
nodeType	Returns one of the XMLDOMNodeType enumeration constants.
nodeTypedValue	Returns the node's value. If the node contains typed data, the property returns the appropriate data type.
nodeTypeString	Returns a constant string associated with the nodeType property value. For example, a node of type NODE_ELEMENT returns the string element.
nodeValue	Returns the text associated with the node. For typed data, use the nodeTypedValue property instead.
ownerDocument	Returns the root node (the documentElement node) of the document that contains this node.
parentNode	Returns the parent node (if present) of this node.
parsed	Returns True if the XMLDOMDocument has parsed and instantiated this node and all its descendents; otherwise it returns False.
prefix	Returns the namespace prefix. Namespaces serve to keep element names from different domains or with different meanings from colliding. For example, a full namespace declaration might be xmlns:ap="urn:apparel.org:casualwear". The ap is a shorthand version of the entire namespace. After declaring the prefix, you can use it throughout the document wherever you would otherwise need to include the entire namespace. For example, one tag might be <ap:jeans>. The prefix is the part of the qualified name before the colon (ap).
previousSibling	Returns the sibling of this node that appears immediately before it in the XML document.
specified	Indicates whether the DTD or schema for this document explicitly specifies that this node must exist or whether the node was derived from a default value in the DTD or schema.
text	Contains the text content of the node and all its children.
xml	Returns the underlying XML for this node and all its descendants.

XMLDOMNode Object Methods

Method	Description
appendChild	Appends a new child node to the current node. The new child appears after any existing child nodes.
cloneNode	Returns a duplicate of the current node.
hasChildNodes	Returns **True** if this node has children.
insertBefore	Inserts a child node as the first child of the current node.
removeChild	Removes a node from the **childNodes** collection for this element. The method returns the node that was removed.
replaceChild	Replaces an existing child node with a new child node. The method returns the node that was replaced.
selectNodes	Returns a collection of nodes that match the XSL pattern you supply as an argument.
selectSingleNode	Returns the first node that matches the XSL pattern you supply as an argument.
transformNode	Transforms a node using a specified XSL style sheet. The method returns the result of the transformation.
transformNodeToObject	Transforms a node and its descendents using a specified XSL style sheet. The method returns the result of the transformation.

XMLDOMNodeList Object

The XMLDOMNodeList object contains a collection of nodes. You obtain a reference to an XMLDOMNodeList from the return value of the selectNodes method. You can iterate through the collection with For Each...Next, with a For...Next loop using an ordinal index, or by repeatedly calling the nextNode method.

XMLDomNodeList Property

Property	Description
length	Returns the number of items in the collection.

XMLDomNodeList Methods

Method	Description
item	Returns a single node from the collection. You provide the index value for the desired node.
nextNode	Returns the next node in the collection. The collection keeps a pointer that initially references the first node in the collection. Each time you call the **nextNode** method, the collection moves the pointer. You can reset the pointer with the **reset** method.
reset	Resets the pointer used with the **nextNode** method so that it points to the first node in the collection.

XMLDOMNamedNodeMap Object

The XMLDOMNamedNodeMap object contains a collection of named nodes. You can retrieve individual named nodes or iterate through the collection with For Each...Next, with a For...Next loop using an ordinal index, or by repeatedly calling the nextNode method.

XMLDOMNamedNodeMap Object Properties

Property	Description
length	Returns the number of items in the collection.
item	Returns a single attribute node from the collection. You provide the index value for the desired node.

XMLDOMNamedNodeMap Object Methods

Method	Description
getNamedItem	Returns the attribute node with the specified attribute name.
getQualifiedItem	Returns an attribute node with the specified namespace and attribute name.
nextNode	Returns the next node in the collection. The collection keeps a pointer that initially references the first node in the collection. Each time you call the **nextNode** method, the collection moves the pointer. You can reset the pointer with the **reset** method.
removeNamedItem	Removes the attribute with the specified attribute name from the collection. Use this method to delete an attribute from an XML document.
removeQualifiedItem	Removes the attribute with the specified namespace and attribute name from the collection. Use this method to delete a qualified attribute from an XML document.
reset	Resets the pointer used with the **nextNode** method so that it points to the first node in the collection.
setNamedItem	Adds a new attribute to the collection of attributes for an element. You supply the new attribute node as an argument. You can create a new attribute node with the **createAttribute** method of the XMLDOMDocument object. Use this method to insert a new attribute into an XML document.

XMLDOMParseError Object

The XMLDOMParseError object contains information about the last error that occurred while parsing an XML document.

XMLDOMParseError Object Properties

Property	Description
errorCode	Returns an error number corresponding to the error code for the last error that occurred while parsing a document.
filepos	Returns the character position in the file where the error occurred.
line	Returns the number of the line that contains the error.
linepos	Returns the number of the character within the line where the error occurred.
reason	Returns a string containing the reason for the error.
srcText	Returns the line containing the error.
url	Returns the URL of the XML document that contains the last error.

XMLDOMParseError Object Methods

The XMLDOMParseError object has no methods.

XMLHttpRequest Object

The XMLHttpRequest object lets you communicate with a server over HTTP. You can send HTTP requests and receive a response from a browser without changing pages. This object makes dynamic interaction with a server extremely easy and solves several common browser problems, such as obtaining the data for a dependent list box. When you combine the XMLHttpRequest object with the ability to directly query a SQL server for XML data over HTTP, you can appreciate how much easier it's going to be to build lightweight, dynamic, database applications.

XMLHttpRequest Object Properties

Property	Description
onreadystatechange	Returns or sets the name of a script event-handler for the onreadystatechange event.
readyState	Returns a value that represents the current state of the XMLHttpRequest object with respect to a physical document. The possible values are: 0 – Uninitialized 1 – Loading 2 – Loaded 3 – Interactive (partially loaded) 4 – Completed

Continued on next page

Property	Description
responseBody	Returns a byte array containing the response from the server. You would normally use the responseBody property to access non-XML data returned from the HTTP request.
responseStream	Contains an IStream object that can stream over the response to the HTTP request. You can use this with the XMLDOMDocument's loadXML method to load and parse the server's response.
responseText	Returns the server's response as a string.
responseXML	Returns the server's response as a parsed XML document.
status	Returns the HTTP status code from the request. You can use this to trap errors.
statusText	Returns the HTTP response line status.

XMLHttpRequest Object Methods

Method	Description
abort	Cancels the current HTTP request.
getAllResponseHeaders	Returns the values of all the HTTP headers.
getResponseHeader	Returns the value of a single named HTTP header from the response.
open	Prepares an XMLHTTP request. You must pass the method (get or post), the URL, and any required authentication information for the request.
send	Sends a prepared HTTP request to the server. You can specify whether to make the request synchronously or asynchronously. If you make a synchronous request, the send method does not return until the response is complete or the request times out. If you make an asynchronous request, you should also write a routine to receive onreadystatechange notifications so you will know when the request completes.
setRequestHeader	Sets an HTTP header value to send with the request. You must specify the header name and value. The header name may not contain any colon characters.

XTLRuntime Object

The XTLRuntime object exposes methods you can call while processing an XSL style sheet. For example, you may need to know the ordinal number of a node. The object can also perform some time, date, number, and outline formatting. Some of the methods should look familiar because they have the same syntax as the equivalent VBScript methods.

In addition to these special methods, because the XTLRuntime object is a node, it inherits all of the properties and methods of an XMLDOMNode. For brevity, I have not re-documented those here. Refer to the *XMLDOMNode Object* section for information on the standard node properties.

XTLRuntime Object Methods

Method	Description
absoluteChildNumber	Returns a number representing the argument node's ordinal position in the set of nodes that are its siblings. The first position is 1.
ancestorChildNumber	Returns the absoluteChildNumber of an ancestor node in the set of nodes that are the ancestor's siblings. You supply a node name for the ancestor node and a node from which to begin the search. For example, you would use this method if you need to know the ordinal position of a node's parent node.
childNumber	Returns a number representing the argument node's ordinal position in the set of nodes that are both siblings and have the same node name. The first position is 1.
depth	Returns a number representing the depth within the document tree at which the specified node appears.
formatDate	Returns a date string formatted with the specified format string. (Refer to the *Date Format String Options* topic in this section.)
formatIndex	Returns a string containing one of a number of optional outline-numbering formats. You supply an integer and a format string. (Refer to the *Index Format String Options* topic in this section.)
formatNumber	Returns a string containing a number formatted with the specified number format string. (Refer to the *Number Format String Options* topic in this section.)
formatTime	Returns a string containing a time formatted with the specified time format string. (Refer to the *Time Format String Options* topic in this section.)
uniqueID	Returns the unique identifier for the argument node.

Date Format String Options

Use these date format string options with the formatDate method of the XTL-Runtime object. You provide a date value, the format string, and an optional LocaleID. The method returns a formatted date. You may combine the date format strings to obtain a custom format.

Date Format String	Result
m	A string between 1 and 12 representing the number of the month.
mm	A string between 01 and 12 representing the number of the month.
mmm	An abbreviated month name from Jan to Dec.
mmmm	A full month name from January to December.
mmmmm	A single character consisting of the first letter of the month. For example, a date in January would return J.
d	A string between 1 and 31 representing the day of the month.
dd	A string between 01 and 31 representing the day of the month.
ddd	An abbreviation for the day of the week. For example, a date falling on Wednesday returns Wed.

Continued on next page

Date Format String	Result
dddd	A full day name for the day of the week. For example, a date falling on Sunday would return Sunday.
yy	A two-character string between 00 and 99 representing the year for the supplied date.
yyyy	A four-character year such as 2000.

Index Format String Options

Use these index format string options with the formatIndex method of the XTL-Runtime object. You specify the index number and the format string, and the function returns a string as shown in the Result column. You may combine the index format strings to obtain a custom format.

Index Format String	Result
1	1, 2, 3, etc.
01	01, 02, 03, etc.
A	An uppercase letter sequence. The sequence begins with A through Z, and then adds an additional letter for items higher in the sequence. For example, calling the formatIndex function with the value 27 returns AA.
a	A lowercase letter sequence. The sequence begins with a through z, and then adds an additional letter for items higher in the sequence. For example, calling the formatIndex function with the value 36 returns jj.
I	I, II, III, IV, etc.
i	i, ii, iii, iv, etc.

Number Format String Options

Use these number format string options with the formatNumber method of the XTLRuntime object. You specify the index number and the format string, and the function returns a formatted string as shown in the Result column. You may combine the format strings to obtain a custom format.

Number Format String	Sample Value	Result/Description
#	003	3 Eliminates insignificant zeros.
0000	003	003

Continued on next page

Number Format String	Sample Value	Result/Description
00	003	03
?	3.25	3.25
	0.325	3.25
	03.250	3.25
		Aligns numbers along a decimal point by eliminating insignificant zeros.
##.#	3.25	3.3
#.##	3.25	3.25
		Determines the placement of the decimal point.
#,###	2000	2,000
		Returns the number with a comma as a thousands separator.
%	65	65%
		Returns the number as a percentage of 100.
E-	2000	2.E3
e-	2000	2.e3
		Returns the number in scientific notation.
E+	-.002	-2.E-3.
e+	-.002	-2.e-3.
		Returns the number in scientific notation with plus or minus signs next to the exponent.

Time Format String Options

Use these time format string options with the formatTime method of the XTL-Runtime object. You provide a time value and the format string. The function returns a formatted string as shown in the Result column. You may combine the format strings to obtain a custom format.

Time Format String	Result
h	A string between 0 and 23 representing the hour of the day.
hh	A two-character string between 00 and 23 representing the hour of the day.
m	A string between 0 and 59 representing the minute of the hour.
mm	A two-character string between 00 and 59 representing the minute of the hour.
s	A string between 0 and 59 representing the second of the minute.
ss	A two-character string between 00 and 59 representing the second of the minute.
AM/PM	Returns the time formatted in 12-hour clock time, with a trailing AM or PM string.
am/pm	Returns the time formatted in 12-hour clock time, with a trailing am or pm string.
A/P	Returns the time formatted in 12-hour clock time, with a trailing A or P string.

Continued on next page

Time Format String	Result
a/p	Returns the time formatted in 12-hour clock time, with a trailing a or p string.
[h]:mm	Returns the elapsed time formatted as a one- or two-character hour with a two-character minute. For example, 1:30 or 12:30.
[mm]:ss	Returns the elapsed time formatted as a one- or two-character minute, with a two-character second value. For example 45:23.
[ss]	Returns the elapsed time in seconds.
ss.00	Returns the elapsed time accurate to 1/1000 of a second.

INDEX

Note to the Reader: Page numbers in **bold** indicate the principal discussion of a topic or the definition of a term. Page numbers in *italic* indicate illustrations.

SYMBOLS

& (ampersand)
    as concatenation operator in VBScript, 163, 804
    in HTML
        double-quote (&quot), 163
        left angle bracket (&lt), 101
        non-breaking space ( ), 101
        right angle bracket (&gt), 101
< > (angle brackets) in HTML
    left angle bracket (&lt), 101
    right angle bracket (&gt), 101
    syntax of, 90–91, 93, 94–95
: (colon) in JScript trinary operator (?:), 336–337, 826
=, = =, = = = (equal signs) in JScript, 329, 826
! (exclamation point) in JScript bang (inequality) operator (!= =), 329, 826
+ (plus sign) as JScript concatenation operator, 341, 825
# (pound sign)
    in HTML hyperlinks, 122
    in Response.ExpiresAbsolute property, 177
? (question mark) in JScript trinary operator (?:), 336–337, 826
" " (quotation marks) in HTML
    in attributes, 96
    double-quote (&quot), 163
' ' (quote marks) in HTML attributes, 96
; (semicolon) in JScript, 328, 332
_ (underscore) as line continuation code in VBScript, 163

A

<a> tag in HTML, 121–128, *122, 127, 128*
Abandon method of Session object, 258, 259, 261, 262, 263, 605
absolute element positioning in HTML, **144–145**, *145*
accepting cookies, 578–580, *578*
Access databases, 486, 490, 492, 509
accessing
    ActiveX objects from client-side JScript, 662–665
    ActiveX objects from client-side VBScript, 660–662
    client-side data access, 665–669
    databases, 17, 19, 84–85
    DOM (Document Object Model) from scripts, 650–653
    files, **19, 371–375**
        determining whether a file exists, 371–373
        opening files, 373–375
    Java applets from script, 672–673
    restricting access to Web sites, 611–614, *612, 613*
Active Server Pages (ASP), **4–32**, 80–87. *See also* automating Active Server Pages
    advantages of, 7–9, 13–14, 80–81
    alternate technologies, **11–14, 726–731**. *See also* ActiveX
        Apache::ASP, 726, 730–731
        Application Servers, 12
        ASP advantages over, 13–14
        C++ language, 13
        Chili!Soft ASP, 726–728, 729–730, 731

H

I

P